Psychoanalysis in Britain, 1893–1913

Psychoanalysis in Britain, 1893–1913

Histories and Historiography

Philip Kuhn

LEXINGTON BOOKS
Lanham • Boulder • New York • London

Published by Lexington Books
An imprint of The Rowman & Littlefield Publishing Group, Inc.
4501 Forbes Boulevard, Suite 200, Lanham, Maryland 20706
www.rowman.com

Unit A, Whitacre Mews, 26-34 Stannary Street, London SE11 4AB

British Library Cataloguing in Publication Information Available

Library of Congress Cataloging-in-Publication Data Available

Name: Kuhn, Philip (Independent Scholar), author.
Title: Psychoanalysis in Britain, 1893–1913 : histories and historiography / Philip Kuhn.
Description: Lanham : Lexington Books, 2017. | Includes bibliographical references and index.
Identifiers: LCCN 2016044360 (print) | LCCN 2016046139 (ebook) | ISBN 9781498505222 (cloth : alk. paper) | ISBN 9781498505239 (Electronic)
Subjects: LCSH: Psychoanalysis—Great Britain—History.
Classification: LCC BF173 .K78 2016 (print) | LCC BF173 (ebook) | DDC 150.19/50941—dc23
LC record available at https://lccn.loc.gov/2016044360

∞™ The paper used in this publication meets the minimum requirements of American National Standard for Information Sciences—Permanence of Paper for Printed Library Materials, ANSI/NISO Z39.48-1992.

Printed in the United States of America

For Frederick

Contents

Acknowledgments

I owe a debt of gratitude to the late John Forrester who, in many ways, was the unwitting catalyst for this book. I first met John in the late 1990s when our paths crossed at a conference and we discovered a shared interest in the early history of psychoanalysis in Britain. After John invited me to Cambridge to talk about my work on Ernest Jones, we would correspond from time to time, our exchanges often prompted by those "surprising presents" we would send each other from the depths of the archives. When I contacted John, in 2013, to ask if he would be interested in publishing one of my papers in *Psychoanalysis and History*, I could have had little idea that his answer would herald the beginnings of an intense two-year exchange of correspondence because, much to my surprise, John published three of my essays in quick succession and to each he attached what I can best describe as an avalanche of e-mails and editorial comments.

> I started off not making comments, then got into the swing. So the density increases alarmingly as I got to the second half. I hope these are useful.

Useful? I may have disagreed, been infuriated or exasperated, and yet his comments were gems and I shall be forever grateful for his detailed, acerbic, insightful, irritating, and wonderful editorial, and dare I say it? Supervisory observations. It remains a great sadness that John died shortly before I finished the first draft of this book so I never had the chance to send him the manuscript let alone receive the astute readings which, I like to believe, he would have offered me.

In February 2014, a commissioning editor from Rowman and Littlefield read the first of those three published essays and invited me to send him a book proposal. So I also thank John for being the unwitting midwife to this book.

My other significant debt of gratitude is to Rosie Musgrave who has endured that thankless lot of a writer's partner, particularly during those all-too-many-times-to-count times when I vanished, physically or metaphysically, drawn into the fascinating and seductive arms of the historical underworlds.

My thanks also to Bushy Benun, Rhys Dafis, and Christopher Hill who took the time and trouble, amid their busy lives, not just to read through the manuscript but also to offer me their valuable and insightful comments and responses. Also to the anonymous reader; thank you!

I have been extremely fortunate in the practical help I have received, over many years, from archivists and librarians: those often unsung heroes whose Herculean labors stand invisibly behind countless publications. I am particularly grateful to Joanne Halford, archivist at the Institute of Psychoanalysis, who has been an incredible source of help and information. Also to the staff of the numerous other archives I have visited and to the staff of the British Library, the Wellcome Library, the Exeter Library and, last but by no means least, my local Ashburton public Library for their invaluable assistance in helping me negotiate the interlibrary loan, that wondrous miracle which has enabled me to consult, often from the comfort of my own home, rare and obscure texts warehoused in some of the remotest depositories in and even out-with the "Kingdom." I acknowledge with thanks all their courteous and silent behind-the-scenes toil.

When I first started researching the early medical career of Ernest Jones the internet was still in its infancy, and so too the digital library. Tracking down obscure and out-of-print publications was time-consuming and, on occasions, fruitless. I still recall my efforts at trying to obtain a copy of T. D. Savill's 1909 *Lectures on Hysteria* which was not to be found in the British Library nor, at the time, in the Wellcome Library even though the catalogue suggested they held the only extant copy in Britain. Eventually I tracked a copy to a bookseller in America; but by the time I had prevaricated over whether or not I could justify their exorbitant price, the book was gone. Now a decade or so later that same book is instantly available through the Internet; and this creation of vast digital libraries has dramatically transformed my world of scholarship. And yet the process of converting the material into the digital and the questions posed as to what then happens to the material raise profound philosophical, ethical, and practical issues which are rarely acknowledged let alone discussed or debated. While this is clearly not the time, or place, to articulate my concerns and fears, I cannot conclude these acknowledgments without also expressing my gratitude to all those organizations who have digitalized their collections *and* also made them freely available to independent scholars, like myself, fortunate enough to have access to the Web. But I would be remiss if I also failed to acknowledge all those anonymous workers who patiently and laboriously dismantled, scanned and checked and hopefully remantled all those books, periodicals, articles, newspapers, and other materials even if they occasionally skipped a page or three or ten or left their ghostly thumbprint imprinted over a critical corner of the text.

Some of the material in Chapters 1, 11, 12, 13, and 14 has previously appeared in *Psychoanalysis and History* (2014–2015) and I am grateful to John Forrester, and to the Edinburgh University Press, for their permission to incorporate it into this book.

I am grateful to The Archives of the British Psychoanalytical Society for kindly permitting me to reproduce Ernest Jones's letter to Anna Freud, April 28, 1945 and James Strachey's letter to Ernest Jones, July 18, 1945.

Buckfastleigh,
August 20, 2016

Introduction

Gathering the Residues

> We know the efficacy of suggestion, and we know it is a good rule of method not unnecessarily to multiply our causes; but we also know that no scientific dictum has been more productive of advance in knowledge than that which tells us to examine our residues. The history of Science affords us many instances in which the neglect of residual phenomena in experimental research has led to the overlooking of important facts, and prevented investigators from making discoveries which, had they paid due attention to their residues, they could hardly have missed. (Mitchell 1911b, pp. 338–39)

Psychoanalysis in Britain, 1893–1913 offers a series of interconnected and disconnected histories differently articulated from that monocular, teleological account of the early history of British psychoanalysis [the early history] first laid down by Ernest Jones over 70 years ago [the Jones Account]. Despite chippings at its edges *the* Jones Account, from which most scholars still instinctively draw, remains legal tender for how we continue to think about the early history not just of British psychoanalysis but also of British experimental and medical psychology. This book argues that the entry of psychoanalysis into British medical culture was far more complex than the Jones Account long since bankrupt by its forger's counterfeit coin.

It was probably terror of subaltern obscurity which impelled Jones to write the early history as a cover story for his absurdly implausible claim to have started practicing psychoanalysis in 1905 or 1906. A detailed reading of the talks which F. W. H. Myers (1843–1901) delivered between 1893 and 1897 to the Society for Psychical Research [SPR] suggests Jones could not possibly have discovered Freud through Myers. Once Myers is removed from the psychoanalytic telescope, we can alter focus away from Jones's carefully manicured psychoanalytic lawn to its outer margins, even to beyond its pale. A new perspective now reveals not that sexually repressed, complacent, quiescent, early-twentieth-century Edwardian Britain of Jones's fertile imagination but medical cultures in profound processes of change. And these changes, already seeded in the early 1890s, were now shaping and reshaping the parameters of medical and experimental psychology in that first long decade of the twentieth century (1900–1913). A few discerning late-nineteenth-century psychologists like Myers, Daniel Hack Tuke, Charles Tuckey or A. T. Schofield sensed those changes and had they discussed them or agreed upon a nomenclature, they would probably have designated them as "Mind Healing." It was this altering focus onto the mind, rather than the brain, which now posed profound challenges to that predominant British neurological order still shackled to its well-worn materialist beliefs that mental diseases, in all their guises, were physiologically or organically determined: a neuropathic heredity, a blot on the brain. All of a sudden a new generation of psychologists—"Mind Healers" and psychotherapists—were questioning the old neurological, physiological, and pathological paradigms. And then they distilled their challenge into one single question: could the mind influence the brain, not just in sickness but also *for* health? Once answered in the affirmative, the psychological, psychical, and metaphysical flood gates opened to a plethora of practitioners, qualified and unqualified, plying, or peddling, their multifidous claims and promises to cure, through the mind, not just mental but also physical diseases. The more cynical materialists no doubt dismissed these new mind healing therapists as bloodless brain surgeons.

And yet once "Mind Healing" was medically articulated, it became medicalized thereby marking the beginnings of what would soon become the psychotherapeutic revolution, which, in turn, legitimized doctors, divines, clergymen, schoolmasters, and other "respectable" lay practitioners, to argue, discuss, debate, and, at times, censor the merits or otherwise of differently competing "mind healing" theories and practices. Freud (1904b, p. 177), for instance, noted: "There are many ways and means of psychotherapy. All methods are good which produce the aim of the therapy." Others, perhaps less emotionally invested in the process, claimed there were at least seven different types of psychotherapy: others quipped, more like 70! Leaving aside the heirs of Charcot, of whom there were still a few, the Nancy school stood at the head with Liébeault (1823–1904) and Bernheim (1840–1919) generally, but by no means universally, considered the founding fathers of this new psychotherapeutic movement. Soon other differently nuanced therapies flowed from their fountain: the re-education or "sentimental dialectic" method of the school of Dubois (1909, p. xiv); the "hypnoidal state" of Sidis; the work of Wetterstrand of Stockholm, or of J.M Bramwell of Goole (Yorkshire), to say nothing of the modifications and amalgamations of some or all of the many different variants of "mind healing" or psychotherapies increasingly peddled by free-lancers employing hypnosis with or without suggestion or with persuasion or through suggestion and persuasion or with persuasion with or without hypnosis. From this babelish confusion there emerged a growing, but by no means universal, consensus that each of these differently organized "mind healing" practices could all be reduced to a single explanation: "suggestion." And so suggestion became the cornerstone of that dominant (hegemonic) medical theory which now claimed to explain how mind healing worked and how mind healers operated: and this despite the fact that, in reality, nobody understood what suggestion meant or how it worked. But this did not prevent the suggestion-explanation theory from taking hold and, by swift degrees, transmuting from a psychological mechanism into a "psychical" mechanism; then to another mechanism called "faith"; then to another called "spirit." And in no time at all there had sprung from "mind healing," "faith healing," "psychic healing," and "spiritual healing." And then before anybody realized it, the suggestion explanation theory was enthusiastically embraced by theologians, spiritualists, theosophists, and, of course "quacks." This sliding and blurring of the secular, medical, psychical, spiritual, and theological lines meant that the suggestion theory not only undercut all the various competing mind healing cures but also defined the debates as to whether the neurotic were best treated through mind-, soul-, spirit-, faith-, psyche- or psychohealing. And it was these debates which shaped and informed the arguments, perceptions, and discussions of most early-twentieth-century British medical and experimental psychologists. One consequence of this babelish confusion was that medically qualified psychotherapists were increasingly forced to define and defend the supremacy of their medical credentials against a growing number of unqualified and, many would say, unscrupulous "mind healers," who by enticing patients were also filching doctors' incomes (Bodie 1905, pp. 156–57). Thus the "mind healing" debates, with their seemingly arcane discussions as to the efficacy of this or that psychotherapeutic procedure (Hill 1901, p. 961), also posed uncomfortable questions as to the nature and status of medicine, the significance and relevance of medical qualifications, the role of the doctor with his [*sic*] privileges, to say nothing of the wider problems concerning the political economies of health. Many of those debates have a familiar, even uncanny contemporaneous feel.

When Freud wrote "The Psychotherapy of Hysteria" for his theoretical contribution to Breuer's and Freud's *Studies in Hysteria* (1895), he was announcing his work as an explicit intervention into these burgeoning psychotherapeutic debates. Although Freud (1904, p. 177) subsequently morphed his psychotherapy into "the analytic method of psychotherapy" and then re-branded it under the *aegis* of psychoanalysis, his new designation should not obscure its primal origins nor should Freud's new technical procedure, known as "free association," conceal how Freud's psychoanalytic methods emerged out of his previous uses of hypnosis and suggestion. Thus when "psychoanalysis" first started arriving in Britain,[1] say around 1908, it was very much seen as another psychotherapy in flux: a practice in process not yet transmuted into a doctrine to be strictly codified (Fromm 1959, pp. 62–67; Makari 2008, pp. 329–37). Thus when medically qualified psychologists and psychotherapists first started studying Freud's work, they tended to assume that psychoanalysis was yet another psychotherapeutic procedure which dove-tailed into the prevailing mind healing climate and, to this end, they set about assessing it not just therapeutically but also according to their own individual medico-socioeconomic position. Even if psychoanalysis appeared therapeutically beneficial at first sight, it was often considered impractical, time-consuming and therefore limiting as to whom it might benefit. In many cases it simply was not feasible for a busy general practitioner [GP] ministering to impoverished patients who could barely afford one visit to the doctor let alone "twice weekly for three months." And yet a surprising number of GPs, as well as medical psychologists working in secured Lunatic Asylums, began studying psychoanalysis so as to test and measure its potential benefits. And because psychoanalysis was still, by and large, doctrinally transitory, it was considered an eclectic and malleable feast, whereby native psychotherapists like Wingfield, Middlemiss, Eder, Shaw, Long, Bryan, and Mitchell, to name just a few, felt the freedom to "mix and match" from a range of other psychotherapeutic practices which, they believed, would fit best. Thus when these early practitioners spoke of psychoanalysis they generally had, in mind, a particular melding of techniques: hypnotism, suggestion, post-hypnotic suggestion, "free talking," Jung's word-association experiments, the original 1895 Breuer-Freud cathartic treatment, free association, and dream interpretation. All of this was just beginning to take shape when Jones, working as a pathologist in a busy children's hospital, was forced to resign his post in late March 1908. This book will argue that despite his autobiographical claims to the contrary Jones had only limited knowledge of Freud's work and no real practical experience of psychoanalysis when he emigrated to Canada in late September 1908. In this he was no different, chronologically speaking, from many of his contemporaries. But when Jones returned to London full-time, in late summer 1913, he was transformed into a committed and, some would say, dogmatic Freudian, set on a mission to protect, at any cost, the unalloyed gold of Freud's psychoanalytic practices. And in the dark shadows cast by the impending break with Jung, this meant attempting to distance, distinguish, and purge native British practices of their heretical, corrupting, metaphysical, and crude psychotherapeutic influences. It is often forgotten that Jones's subsequent account of the early history was deeply infected by his forgetting, or glossing, this process of purgation.[2]

Because the Jones Account has remained so dominant for so long I could see no other way of writing this book other than by meticulously removing Jones's all-pervasive presence from center stage. This has meant, somewhat paradoxically, that I have devoted considerable space to exploring and explaining why Jones's contemporaneous intellectual development was thereby out of kilter with his subsequent autobiographical claims. It was only this clearing of the briars which made it possible to discover and assemble those many residual stories which Jones had cast from his account and thereby offer something of a redress of the historical balance with a very different accounting of the many names, relationships, networkings and events which Jones omitted through forgetting, repressing, suppressing, overlooking, burying or perhaps just plain not knowing. After all Jones was in Toronto during this critical period (1908–1913) when Freud's writings started to enter into the British medico-psychological discourse. But this winding up of the Jones Account also reveals that pre-War British psychoanalysis far from being revolutionary or unique was, in fact, part of a wider medical, theological, spiritual, social, doctrinal, political, and economic movement being played out between competing psychotherapeutists, spiritualists, theologians, magnetists, and magicians as each strove to promote their own differently calibrated visions or versions of "The Psyche," driven, perhaps, by the hope, of enticing, seducing, or converting potential patients into believing that this or that therapeutic offered the best cure not just for mental illness but also for mental health. Psychoanalysis had become just another voice in those babelish British debates.

NOTES

1. Britain is short-hand for the United Kingdom of Great Britain and Ireland, signifying the union of England, Wales, Scotland and Ireland (1801–1922).
2. See also Nandy (1995, p. 102).

Abbreviations

Alienist, a physician engaged in the "scientific" study or treatment of mental disease although commonly used during the nineteenth century the term was already falling into disuse in the early years of the twentieth-century
Amsterdam Congress, First International Congress for Psychiatry, Neurology, Psychology, and the Nursing of the Insane (September 1907)
Annual Meeting, BMA Annual Meeting
APA, American Psychopathological Association
APPB, [London] Association for the Prevention of Premature Burial
Association, The Association of Medical Officers of Asylums and Hospitals for the Insane; subsequently the Royal Medico-Psychological Association (1926–1971) and then the Royal College of Psychiatry (1971–)
Asylum, short hand for those institutions, including specialist hospitals and dedicated establishments catering for patients with functional or organic mental diseases hospitalized either on a voluntary or secured basis; private or pauper patients admitted at the public expense
Bart's, St Bartholomew's Hospital, London
Bethlem, Bethlem Royal Hospital, London
BMA, British Medical Association
BMA Sub-Committee, The Sub-Committee of the BMA Medico-Political Committee
BMA Investigation Committee, The Special Investigation Committee under the auspices of the BMA Sub-Committee
BMA Spiritual Healing, The Report of the BMA Investigation Committee (1911)
Boston Society, Boston Society of Psychiatry and Neurology
BPAS, British Psycho-Analytic Society
BPS, British Psychological Society

Brompton, The Brompton Hospital for Chest Diseases
Browne Committee, The GMC Committee, chaired by Langley Browne, to investigate unqualified medical practices
Burghölzli, Burghölzli Psychiatric Clinic, Zurich
CEPM, Certificate of Efficiency in Psychological Medicine
Charing Cross, Charing Cross Hospital, London
Chichester, The Lady Chichester Hospital for the Treatment of Early Mental Disorders
CMU, Church Medical Union
CSU, [London] Christian Social Union
DPH, Diploma of Public Health
Early History, The early history of British psycho-analysis
Emmanuel Movement, the term used to define the psychotherapeutic practices linked to the Emmanuel Church, Boston
Farringdon, The Farringdon General Dispensary and Lying-in Charity, Holborn
Fitzroy, The Report into unqualified medical and surgical practises (1910)
GMC, General Medical Council
GNRC, Great Northern Railway Company
Golden Age, Order of the Golden Age. One of their aims being "to advocate the Fruitarian System of living"
GP, General [Medical] Practitioner
Guild, The Guild of Health
Guy's, Guy's Hospital, London
ICM, 17th International Congress of Medicine. London, August 1913
IMPA, Incorporated Medical Practitioners' Association
IPA, International Psychoanalytic Association
KCH, Kings College Hospital, London
KCL, Kings College, London University
LCC, London County Council the statutory authority for all London pauper lunatic Asylums
LHS, London Hypnotic Society
LICAS, Leeds Invalid Children's Aid Society
LMI, Liverpool Medical Institution
LMPC, Liverpool Medico-Psychological Clinic
Long Grove, The Long Grove County [Lunatic] Asylum, Horton Lane, Epsom
LPAS, London Psycho-Analytic Society
LSA, London Spiritualist Alliance
LWR Leeds and West Riding Medico-Chirurgical Society
MDU, Medical Defence Union
Medical Corporations, the body for all Medical and Surgical Colleges and Universities teaching Medicine

Metropolitan Branch, The Metropolitan Counties' Branch of the BMA
Ministries of Healing, 1908 report of the Anglican Committee of Enquiry into the subject of Ministries of Healing
Morningside, Royal Morningside Asylum for the Insane, Edinburgh
MOH, Medical Officer of Health
MPC, [London] Medical-Psychological Clinic (1913–)
MSSST, The Medical Society for the Study of Suggestive Therapeutics, subsequently the Psycho-Medical Society [PMS]
NMD Association, Northern and Midland Division of the Association
North Eastern, North-Eastern Children's Hospital, Bethnal Green, London
PMS, Psycho-Medical Society, previously the MSSST
PTS, [London] Psycho-therapeutic Society
Queen's Square, National Hospital for the Paralysed and Epileptic, Queen's Square, London
RSM, Royal Society of Medicine
Ryle Committee, the Clerical and Medical Spiritual Healing Committee set up after the October 1910 Conference on Spiritual Healing
St. Mary's, St. Mary's Hospital, London
Salzburg Congress, 1st International Psycho-Analytic Congress, Salzburg (1908)
Section, the Psychological Section of the BMA Annual Meeting.
Special Medical Part, The 1911 issue of *Proceedings* specially devoted to Psycho-Medical Issues
Special Number, The April 1910 issue of the *American Journal of Psychology* which published translations of the Clark Lectures delivered by Freud and Jung
Special Issue, The June 18, 1910 *BMJ* Special Issue on Mental Healing
Spiritualist Congress, International Spiritualistic and Occult Congress, Paris 1900
SPR, The Society for Psychical Research
SSDC, Society for the Study of Disease in Children
SSI, Society for the Study of Inebriety
UCH, University College Hospital, London
UCL, University College, London University
War, short hand for the 1914-1918 War, aka the Great War
West End, West End Hospital for Diseases of the Nervous System, Paralysis and Epilepsy, Welbeck-Street, London

Part I

FORGING THE EARLY HISTORY OF BRITISH PSYCHOANALYSIS: FOR THE LOVE OF TRUTH

The interest of [psychoanalysis], and of your person in England is identical, now I trust that you will *'schmieden das Eisen solange es warm ist'* (Sigmund Freud to Ernest Jones, August 10, 1913).[1]

NOTE

1. "Strike while the iron is hot" (Paskauskas 1993, p. 217).

Chapter 1

"A Pity to See History thus Unnecessarily Distorted"

> When a man begins with the pompous formula—"The verdict of history is"— I suspect him at once, for he is merely dressing up his own opinions in big words. (Trevelyan 1913, p. 49)

REMINISCENCES

In a short note, prefacing the 1945 M. D. Eder memorial volume, Sigmund Freud (1856–1939), as if writing from the grave, proclaimed David Eder "the first, and for a time the only doctor to practise the new therapy [of psychoanalysis] in England." (Hobman 1945, p. 9). In his contribution, "Eder as Psycho-Analyst," Edward Glover (1888–1972), claimed Eder's paper to the Neurological Section of the 1911 BMA Annual Meeting "the first public contribution to clinical psycho-analysis made in this country." (Hobman 1945, p. 89). Although Ernest Jones (1879–1958) remained silent about Glover's claim, he was furious at Freud's "statement," which he considered to be "quite incorrect" (Jones 1945b, p. 8).[1] But as Freud was dead Jones's only recourse was to write to Freud's daughter Anna, in an attempt to persuade her to let him use *her* name as a "counter-weight" to her father's authority. Jones's (1945a, italics mine) letter of April 28, 1945 is worth quoting extensively because it reveals, with singular clarity, just how Jones set about manufacturing his version of the early history.

> I heard recently, I am sorry to say, that your Father unwittingly did me a rather serious injustice in one of the last acts of his life, and think the best thing I can do is to write to you direct about it.
>
> I was indubitably the first person in this country (and, so far as I know, in the whole non-German speaking world) to assimilate your Father's work and to

practise psycho-analysis. In the conditions of 40 years ago [1905 pk] it was a considerable feat, and I suppose my reputation rests largely on it.

This honour your Father had strangely deprived me of in the preface he wrote for Dr. Eder's Memorial volume. In view of my unfaltering devotion to him you will understand when I call the act a strange one.

The facts themselves he had formerly known quite well. *I had told him* of my attempts to initiate Dr Eder into the elements of psycho-analysis, but he had been so unfavourably impressed by his writings that when Eder joined Jung and broke up our society by refusing to resign his office in it [Freud's] terse comment, in a letter I still possess, was simply "Um Eder ist es nicht schade."[2]

Since your Father was the very last person in the world anyone could suspect of either ingratitude or untruthfulness, the only possible supposition is that he allowed himself to be imposed on by one of two women,[3] both of which [*sic*] must have known that the statement was untrue. Dr. Glover had asked me what the facts were, but for some reason of his own had refrained from either getting the statement rectified or ~~conver~~ correc[ting] it himself in the psycho-analytic chapter he contributed to the book. I am not surprised at the behaviour of those three people, but I am bewildered by the thought that your Father (or you, yourself, if you happen to have known about it) did not think it worth while to verify the statement by inquiry of me, who was the only first-hand witness available.

Apart from my personal feelings it does seem a pity to see history thus unnecessarily distorted. With the weight of his authority behind it such a statement of fact, which would be supposed to be well within his personal knowledge, will be peculiarly hard to controvert. It will, of course, obtain wide publicity (Prof. Gilbert Murray, for instance, quoted it in the B[ritish] B[roadcasting] C[orporation] in the Brains Trust that followed the publication of the book).[4] Your name is the only counter-weight I can think of. If your love of truth, or desire to do justice to both myself and your father's memory, should move you to wish to rectify the statement, it would be open to you to do so in a note to any important periodical reviewing the book. (The New Statesman did this morning, hence this letter to-day).[5]

When Anna replied, on 7 May, she denied all knowledge of the affair but told Jones that she had asked Barbara Low, Eder's sister-in-law, to ask Hobman for "the original of [Freud's] letter" because she thought "it is just possible that there is a mistake, especially if the original letter should be in German." She also asked Jones to "collect the necessary dates and facts concerning you and Eder, regarding practice and public lectures."

By confronting them it should be easy to establish the true state of affairs and, through publication as you suggest correct the wrong impression which has been created.[6]

Although Hobman failed to return Freud's letter, he informed Anna that he had translated it himself and Freud had "approved of it." So Anna wondered if her father might have "meant the time in Dr. Eder's life when he was the sole representative of analysis in England while you [Jones] were in Toronto, and that this is badly handled in the translation," to which Anna then added, probably in response to a lost letter from Jones:

> I think that it is an excellent idea that you write a short article on the early history of psycho-analysis, and I think that an extract from that should then be used to appear as a letter in various papers; I am sure that also Mr Hobman would agree to include it in some way in the next issue of the book.
>
> Barbara Low tells me that Strachey will review the book in the next Journal. This, again, would be an occasion to present the historical facts as they are known to you and him. I, of course, have to rely entirely on these facts known to other people. And I do not know to what facts my father referred when he wrote the introductory letter.[7]

Although Jones (1945b, p. 8) subsequently claimed he had reluctantly accepted an invitation from James Strachey (1887–1967), editor of the *International Journal of Psychoanalysis* [*IJPA*], to reply to Freud's statement, the correspondence clearly reveals Jones took the initiative, wrote his own counter-narrative and sent it direct to Strachey suggesting that

> it would be of interest to have on record an outline of these early events before the memory of them pass away and the history of them be either defective or actually falsified. (Jones 1945b, p. 8).

On July 18, 1945, Strachey told Jones he had read his "historical sketch . . . with great interest: it seems to me just what is wanted."

> The only remarks I have to make are about the Primal Period: it seems to me slightly unjust to the shade of Fred Myers.

But before examining this comment, let us continue with Strachey's letter.

> I looked up the precise data at the B[ritish] M[useum] yesterday and they seem to me sufficiently striking:-
>
> On *April 21st 1893* at the 58th General Meeting of the S[ociety of] P[sychical] R[esearch] . . . Mr Myers read a paper on the 'Mechanism of Hysteria'. This was printed in full in the *Proceedings* . . . in *June 1893*. It contains . . . a detailed and eulogistic summary of the Freud and Breuer paper [*Preliminary Communications* 1893].
>
> On March 12th 1897 . . . 'Mr F. W. Myers delivered an address on "Hysteria and Genius"'. This was briefly summarized in the *Journal* . . . Vol. 8, April 1897. Pp. 55–56 . . . give an account of *Studien* über *Hysterie* [*Studies in Hysteria*]. A very much fuller account of it is of course contained in *Human Personality*,

Vol. I, pp. 50–56, published posthumously in February 1903 (Myers died in Jan 1901). This included summaries of Freud's case of Lucy R. and of Breuer's Fräulein O.

Strachey then detailed what he believed to be the SPR's subsequent interest in Freud.

> In *Proceedings* Vol. 24 (August 1910) is a paper by T. W. Mitchell on 'Some Recent Developments in Psychotherapy'. This includes a long abstract (pp. 673–78) of 'an excellent account' of the method of psycho-analysis 'given by Dr Ernest Jones of the University of Toronto in his contribution to the symposium' [on Psychotherapy, 1909]. . . . This no doubt paved the way for the publication in the *Proceedings* Vol. 26 (Nov. 1912) of Freud's own 'Note on the Unconscious in Psycho-Analysis'—'written' according to the footnote in *Collected Papers* IV, 22 '(in English) at the request of the Society for Psychical Research'.
>
> I have a personal feeling about this S.P.R. episode, as that was actually my own road of approach to [Psycho-Analysis]. The S.P.R was still very lively (and not at all exclusively spiritualistic) at Cambridge when I was an undergraduate (1905–1909),[8] and, though I was never spooky, I was very much interested. I read a lot of the current literature on abnormal psychology—Janet, Prince, Flournoy etc. But I remember quite well the impression made on me by Freud's paper in 1912—which was the first thing of his I ever read. It was because of that that I got hold of your *Papers on* [*Psychoanalysis* 1913a]
>
> I think it's a remarkable fact that the basic discoveries of [Psycho-Analysis] should have been accessible in print to English readers within six months of their first publication in German.[9]

Although Jones's original draft was probably destroyed, it is possible to reconstruct something of its contents if we recall that up until he sent that first draft to Strachey in July 1945. Jones held quite specific views about F. W. H. Myers (1843–1901) and the SPR. So, for example, Jones (1913a, pp. 12n and 259n) makes only two brief references to Myers in the first edition of his *Papers on Psycho-Analysis* the second being just an incidental footnote. More generally Jones (1911, p. 121) was dismissive of "the pronounced tendency of the members [of the SPR] to spiritism"—which can be read back into Strachey's defensive comment: "I was never spooky." Jones was also less than complimentary about Myers's "philosophical conception" of the "unconscious," dismissed its decidedly "mystical element," and even went so far as to lump Myers's writings together with Hartmann's and Jung's! (Paskauskas 1993, p. 136). These original views can also be read back into Strachey's comments: that the draft "seems to me slightly unjust to the shade of Fred Myers." We can assume, therefore, that it was Strachey's letter which persuaded Jones to alter his draft by obliterating all his previous criticisms of Myers and then incorporating *nearly* all of Strachey's letter into a revised draft which Strachey then published as "Reminiscent Notes on the Early History of Psycho-Analysis in English-Speaking Countries" [Reminiscent Notes].

Jones begins "Reminiscent Notes" by repeating *most* of Strachey's account but then adding:

> So we note the remarkable fact that the first new discoveries in what became psycho-analysis were accessible to English readers fifty-two years ago within six months of their being announced. . . . I think we may be sure that Myers was the first writer in English to give an account of the work by Breuer and Freud.

But in a subtle alteration of Strachey's letter, Jones (1945b, p. 8) adds:

> At least two later analysts, Dr. Mitchell and Mr Strachey, derive their interest in the subject from Myer's [*sic*] writing.[10]

This, of course, was *not* what Strachey said. Then having set out what would, from now on, become the Myers Myth Jones (1945b, p. 9) silently bypassed the Eder priority dispute by completely sidestepping Freud's 1945 claim and stating, instead, in a casual sort of way,

> I well remember the first patient with whom I practised the new therapy, surely the first person to be analysed outside the German-speaking countries (1905–6).[11]

Then, following further reminiscences, Jones (1945b, p. 10, italics mine) reiterated his original claim: "After practising psycho-analysis [in England] *for three years* I left for Canada in 1908 where I spent the greater part of five years." Jones (1955, pp. 31f) subsequently offers an almost identical version in Chapter three of the second volume of his three-volume biography of Freud [the Freud Biography]. Given that the two texts are almost identical we can safely assume that Jones probably incorporated Reminiscent Notes, more or less direct into his Freud biography. This was an astute, even brilliant rhetorical maneuvre, because by smuggling a fragment of his *own* autobiography into "the main, and as it were, official, biography" of Freud (Ellenberger 1994, p. 428), Jones has surreptitiously forced Freud to seal his own postmortem imprimatur on Jones's version while, at the same time, consummately censoring Freud's claim on behalf of Eder. This, in fact, was the final act in a long game stretching back some forty-five years to when Jones first attempted to bend psychoanalytic history. In a letter to Freud, written in January 1910, Jones claimed: "I think I can take a little credit in [Modena of Ancona] taking up the work [of psychoanalysis]." When Freud challenged him on the absurdity of this claim Jones wriggled: it was either his bad handwriting or a slip of the pen! (Paskauskas 1993, pp. 36, 41 and 44). Four years later, in May 1914, Freud sent Jones proofs of *On the History of the Psycho-Analytic Movement* [*On the History*]. In his reply Jones noted that he was never a pupil of Jung's and continued: "I got your book in 1906 and practised [psycho-analysis] (imperfectly, to be sure) for a year before the Amsterdam Congress in Sept. 1907, where I first met Jung and Gross. . . . " (Paskauskas 1993, p. 281). Although Freud (1914a, p. 31) removed the bit about Jones being a pupil of Jung's, he declined to add Jones's other correction so that a close reading of that silence in Freud's printed text reveals that Freud, for one, held that Jones had no interest in psychoanalysis prior to 1909; which means that Brill, who was already practicing psychoanalysis, must have trumped Jones. But it is also worth noting that Freud wrote Eder out of *On the History* presumably because, at the time of its writing, Eder looked as if he had converted to Jung. Thus once Freud's 1945 "Eder Preface" is recontextualized against this early history, it can also be read as a corrective to *On the History* and as a preemptive strike against any further attempts by Jones to bend that history.

In July 1953, Jones delivered a paper to the Royal Medico-Psychological Association, [the Association] and his talk, "The early History of Psycho-Analysis" [the Early History], was then published in the January 1954 issue of the Association's *Journal*. Although Jones delivered the Early History some nine years after "Reminiscent Notes," it was published about a year *before* the Second Volume of the Freud biography. There are significant discrepancies between the Early History (1954) and the 1945/1955 text(s) of "Reminiscent Notes" but the only one that need detain us is where Jones (1954, p. 202, 201) surreptitiously stakes his priority claim even further backward: "In 1905, forty-eight years ago, I ventured on the practice of psychoanalysis." This must imply that he was already reading Freud in 1904! But Jones also uses the occasion of his talk, delivered to psychiatrists, to stake his priority claim within the wider context of his own intellectual development *and* of the early history of British psychiatry. So he suggests, for example: "The science of neurology had decided that [psycho-neurotic] conditions were disorders of the brain, not of the mind, and therefore it was the brain that had to be treated." By suggesting this early-twentieth-century British neurological "group-think," Jones was clearly implying that as there was no British clinical psychology to speak of his early adherence to Freud was now even more remarkable.

According to Mervyn Jones (1959, p. 258), his father Ernest started working on his autobiography, *Free Associations*, sometime in 1944; that is about a year *before* 'Reminiscent Notes.' Mervyn also claims that when his father had completed the first eleven chapters, which constituted the first forty-one years of his life (1879–1918), Jones put away the manuscript to concentrate on the Freud Biography which, according to Maddox (2006, p. 259), he started writing in 1950. It was not until 1957, when "the biography of Freud was written and published," that Jones "tried to get on with his autobiography" but by then he "was suffering from a terminal cancer of the liver" and only had energy to revise the first seven chapters, that is from his birth up until his emigration to Canada in late 1908. Although *Free Associations* was published posthumously, in 1959, Mervyn's account suggests it must have been written mainly between 1944 and say 1949 which indicates that Jones was already working on *Free Associations* before he wrote "Reminiscent Notes." Thus *Free Associations*, generally considered the proof text for Jones's biography, and also for the early history, turns out to have been the first of Jones's late writings to be drafted but the last to be published. While there are important discrepancies between *Free Associations* and the other late texts the only passage that now concerns us is where Jones (1959, p. 159) describes his discovering the work of Freud.

> It was [Wilfred] Trotter who first mentioned [Freud's] name to me. Mitchell Clarke had published in *Brain* 1898[12] a review of his [*sic*] 'Studies in Hysteria', and Havelock Ellis had also alluded to him. The first of [Freud's] writings I came across was the Dora analysis, published in the 'Monatsschrift für Psychiatrie'. My German was not good enough to follow it closely, but I came away with a deep impression of there being a man in Vienna who actually listened with attention to every word his patients said to him.

It is worth noting, in passing, Jones's absurd and contradictory claim that the Dora analysis (not published until October–November 1905) was the first of Freud's writings he read! More remarkable, however, is the absence of any reference to Myers. This confirms that at the time of writing this passage Jones (1944a, p. 154) was still indifferent to Myers's writings and would therefore have written this passage prior to writing the first draft of "Reminiscent Notes" and, not catching his omission of Myers, he failed to rectify it before his death.

In his own autobiography *Chances*, Mervyn Jones (1987, p. 147) remembers his last meeting with his father on February 10, 1958. Although seriously ill in University College Hospital [UCH], Jones was still working on *Free Associations*.

> I saw him once more. He was dictating a sentence to my mother, to the effect that he had been the first person outside Vienna to take up Freud's ideas. When the sentence was read over to him, he decided that it was unfair to Jung.

> I suggested giving Jung a footnote: "too important," my father said. I tried to work in an extra clause: "makes the sentence clumsy," he objected. That was my last memory of him. Ernest Jones died the next day.

Surely this extraordinary deathbed vignette encapsulates two of the most abiding obsessions which ran through Jones's psychoanalytic career: his ultimate place in its history and what on earth was to be done with Jung.[13]

WRITING *THE* HISTORY OF PSYCHOANALYSIS IN BRITAIN

Despite significant inconsistencies and discrepancies between the various versions of Jones's late autobiographical, biographical, and historical writings [the late writings], it is relatively easy to sketch the essence of the Jones Account. Jones first heard about Freud in 1904, started reading Freud's writings, in the original, in October 1905 [*sic*] and was already practicing psychoanalysis by early 1906. Jones bolsters his claims with a number of assertions designed to reinforce his narrative and give further credibility to his priority claim. So it was his close friend, and future brother-in-law, Wilfred Trotter (1872–1939), who drew his attention to Freud's work in 1904 when "the ignorance concerning psycho-neurotic conditions . . . was truly abysmal." English physicians were parochial, had little or no interest in advances made in America let alone continental Europe and, worst still, most could not even read German. All this made it all the more remarkable that a Welshman should have been the first person in the non-German-speaking world to comprehend the genius of Freud and had the courage to throw in his lot with the founder of psychoanalysis. Jones (1959, p. 150) underlines this point by claiming that he was forced to resign from the West End Hospital when he attempted to psychoanalyze "a girl of ten with an hysterical paralysis of the left arm." His resignation, which he claims was manufactured by a Hospital Committee shocked at Freud's sexual theories, left Jones no option but to emigrate to Canada in late September 1908.[14] On his return to London, in 1913, and despite being blackballed because of his well-known "association with psycho-analysis," Jones (1959, p. 237) gathered around himself a small group of English physicians—Bernard Hart, Owen Berkeley Hill (1879–1944),[15] David Eder—all of whom, he claimed, had been pupils of his at one time or another.[16] Then, virtually single-handed, Jones established the British (then called London) Psycho-Analytical Society [LPAS]. Through an astute use of silences and omissions Jones leaves his readers under the distinct impression that his own unique relationship with Freud was already cemented by 1908 and that he was the only Englishman [*sic*] to have met and visited Freud prior to the 1914–1918 War [the War].

Although a handful of scholars have, from time to time, chipped at its edges, the Jones Account continues to dominate and beguile.[17] That his account has been taken so much on trust and for so many years suggests the revisions and revolutions in the history and historiography of psychoanalysis, first initiated by Ellenberger in the 1970s (Mayer 2013, pp. 3–4), have, like the angel of death, passed over Jones. With perhaps the single exception of Paskauskas (1988, p. 110), who recognized many years ago that "Jones's authority as historian and psychoanalyst has for the most part gone unchallenged," there has been no systematic or critical research into Jones's early medical career despite, or maybe because of, the biographies of Brome (1983) and Maddox (2006) which, for the most part, merely recycle and embellish Jones's own version of events. Yet without a detailed knowledge of Jones's early years (1901–1913) it is impossible to read Jones's late writings critically. This is an extraordinary state of affairs given that Jones played such a critically important role in shaping, making, and defining not just the history but also the historiography of psychoanalysis.

Perhaps one of the reasons why Jones's late writings have been accepted, more or less on trust, is because of how they became, from early on, the cornerstone of what Hinshelwood (1998, p. 87) has described as the "institutionalization" of British Psychoanalysis. By the early 1920s Jones had become a towering figure within the international psychoanalytic movement and, as "a ring bearer" in Freud's "inner circle" (Grosskurth, 1991), was invested with a power and authority which also extended into the heart of the BPAS. Falzeder (2015, pp. 59–62), for example, has revealed how Jones, together with Freud and other senior members of Freud's inner circle, had between them psychoanalyzed most if not all the senior members of the British psychoanalytic establishment thereby effectively investing Jones with extraordinary psychological authority over them.[18] Jones also wielded considerable economic powers of patronage with his ability to influence the election of new applicants, allocate the distribution of patients, and control the system of training analysis.[19] It is little wonder that Melitta Schmideberg (1971, pp. 62; and 63), the estranged daughter of Melanie Klein, should have experienced Jones's behavior as "patriarchal." But it was Jones's seemingly inviolable position which also ensured, as the heavily censored correspondence occasionally lets slip, that anybody who even thought of crossing him, especially in matters of doctrine or "priority," did so at their peril.[20] Thus, even before Jones started writing the early history, his Account had already become *the* history (Payne, 1946; Winnicott, 1958, p. 298).

When Borch-Jacobsen and Shamdasani (2008, p. 14) discuss "the direct linkages between [Freud's] interpretive procedures and [his] rewriting of history," they also, incidentally, offer a theoretical pointer to a more nuanced understanding of the motivations which drove Jones to write the early history—with those old scores still to be settled. Jones's obvious anger and distress at Freud's posthumous comments concerning Eder's priority; the rankling he still felt against Barbara Low; the sense of betrayal, through deceit, which he seems to have experienced from David and Edith Eder and also Edward Glover, to say nothing of Mervyn's memory of his dying father still grappling with the ghost of Jung some forty-five years after the "breach"—All this suggests Jones's late writings, including his biography of Freud, were more than just a "propaganda tool or an external rhetorical garment" which he had used to embroider his particularly narrow-minded, or monocular, vision of the early history. If an obsession with priority did ultimately drive Jones to write the early history then his late texts can also be read as his desperate attempts to "future proof" his legacy from oblivion. And once read through that lens it then becomes possible to identify how Jones employed a whole series of rhetorical strategies—obfuscation, misinformations, omissions, silences and lies—to distort the history in order to deflect whatever posthumous criticisms might be levelled against him. And it was this acute anxiety which impelled him to manufacture a series of foundational myths all of which revolved around himself.[21] And probably the most important of those myths was the Myers Myth. It was perhaps when reading Strachey's corrective account that Jones realized how Strachey had provided him, *subsequently*, with the almost perfect backward cover story which would allow him to bolster his questionable claims to have discovered Freud in 1904. By adding Myers, to Mitchell Clark and Havelock Ellis, Jones could now push the beginnings of *the* British Freudian journey backward to its very foundations, thereby subliminally suggesting, that Jones was also the natural heir of an English psychological tradition which could trace its affinities with Freud. This was a powerful rhetorical ploy and the real measure of its success lies precisely in the way in which it has remained unquestioned for so long. That the other myths have also continued to endure says as much about Jones's skills as mythmaker, propagandist, and rhetorician as it does about the countless historians, commentators, biographers, and psychoanalysts mesmerised by Jones's fantastical stories.

A QUESTION OF PSYCHOLOGY

If the writings of Chertok (1966, pp. 148–49; 1984, p. 224), Kline (1953, p. 2; 1955, p. 124), Bachner-Melman (2001, p. 39–40) and others hold good then the "problem" of hypnotism still remains largely tabooed from the psychoanalytic discourse. That Jones, as an historian, glossed it over in the early history, is particularly striking given that Freud (1910a, p. 197) not only regretted, for a time, "having given up hypnosis" but also acknowledged, on more than one occasion, that hypnosis had taught him that "somatic changes could after all be brought about solely by mental influences" and that "one could only describe [those mental processes] as 'unconscious'."

> It is not easy to over-estimate the importance of the part played by hypnotism in the history of the origin of psycho-analysis. From a theoretical as well as from a therapeutic point of view, psycho-analysis has at its command a legacy which it has inherited from hypnotism. (Freud 1923, p. 192)[22]

This intimate relationship between hypnotism and psychoanalysis has been examined, in depth by a number of historians not just through general historical surveys (i.e., Gauld 1992; Crabtree 1993) but also through specific studies. Smith (1992, p. 126), for example, has suggested that in the late nineteenth century there were "several well-established scientists who felt challenged both intellectually and socially by hypnotism." Borch-Jacobsen (1996) has argued, with detailed research, that hypnotism played a critical part in the early development of psychoanalysis, while Mayer (2013, p. 5) has identified "the emergence of hypnotism in the late nineteenth century as a key episode in the experimentalization of the unconscious mind." But these, and other studies, have focused almost exclusively on mainland Europe and, more or less, ignored the history of hypnotism in late-nineteenth- and early-twentieth-century Britain. Thus although Gauld (1992, pp. 385–402), E. W. Kelly (2007), Kelley and Grosso (2007) and others, have recognized the importance of the experimental and theoretical works of Edmund Gurney and Frederick Myers, they have tended to inoculate those experiments from their wider cultural context leaving the distinct impression that the early SPR hypnotism experiments were largely confined within the circles of British psychical research.[23] This neglect may be due, in part, to that widespread belief that hypnosis was tabooed by the British Medical Association [BMA] in the early 1890s (Chettiar 2012, p. 335), in which case there is nothing more to be said! Or it may even be due to Jones (1954a, p. 201) who claimed hypnotism was only taken up by a handful of British practitioners who "were looked at very askance by the medical profession, and their activities were regarded as closely akin to quackery," in which case it can be safely relegated to a footnote! But detailed studies, which I hope to publish separately, reveal that hypnotism, in late-nineteenth-century Britain was not just extensively discussed but also widely practiced therapeutically to treat both functional and organic diseases. And this meant there was little or no difficulty for those early-twentieth-century medical or lay practitioners who used curative hypnotism. Unlike the previous generation, who had to travel to France, Holland, or Sweden, this new, second-wave generation, discovered a ready-made and thriving homegrown "British" tradition supported by textbooks, books, and articles not just in translation but also written by the early first-generation British pioneering practitioners many of whom, like Tuckey, Wingfield, Bramwell, Cruise, Felkin and, for a time Kingsbury, continued not only practicing but also teaching and proselytizing the therapeutic benefits of hypnotism and suggestion. Even before the turn of the century those practitioners, loosely gathered under the sign of psycho-therapists (Shamdasani 2005), served as powerful subterranean drivers inspiring significant numbers of early-twentieth-century medical and lay practitioners, to experience, through hypnotism, the workings of the subconscious or hypnotic mind. And this, in turn, inspired a growing belief in the benefits to be derived from treating patients psychotherapeutically (Schofield 1904, p. ix). All this helps to explain why there were so many British medical men and women receptive to Freud's writings and willing to experiment with his theories.

During these early years, when psychoanalysis had not yet become an "intellectual development" (Schwartz 1999, p. 1), Freud's theories were considered to be another "positive curative measure" (Walsh 1912, p. 595) which might be used to ameliorate a wide range of psychoneurotic conditions. But Freud (1916–1917, p. 458) sought increasingly to extend those modest claims so that by the time he wrote his *Introductory Lectures on Psycho-Analysis*, he

> emphasized the fact that under favourable conditions we achieve successes which are second to none of the finest in the field of internal medicine; and I can now add something further—namely that they could not have been achieved by any other procedure.

Thus, from around 1908, when British psychotherapists and other medical psychologists began noticing "Professor Freud's system of psycho-analysis," they tended to view it, by and large, as just another of those "systems of treatment nowadays more or less popular, which invoke the mind to cure bodily ills" (*BMJ* March 29, 1913, p. 679). Those who expressed outright hostility to Freud or psychoanalysis tended to be hard-core neurologists, or old-school psychologists who, often on ideological grounds, refused to have truck with any kind of psychotherapeutics. Mercier (1851–1919) was one of them and Jones (i.e., 1954a, p. 205) subsequently delighted in presenting him whenever he wanted an exemplar of universal British medical bigotry. But Mercier was hardly representative because T. A. Ross (*BMJ* January 9, 1915, p. 94), for one, dismissed Mercier as "the writer of the comic column in the [*BMJ*]." The more serious criticisms of psychoanalysis came from the more open-minded critics, like L. Schnyder, who thought "Psychoanalysis is valuable in certain cases; but it is not indispensable to psychotherapy; and the Freudians run the risk of absolutism." (*Mind* 1913, Vol. 22, p. 452). The same can also be said about those who criticized the Freudian doctrine concerning the significance of "sex." Jones (1959, p. 237) was, of course, correct to note that there were those who thought the Freudians obsessed with sex as well as those who objected to the subject even being discussed. But such prudish views tended to be held only by a small vocal minority and the main strands of criticism came from informed observers and practitioners who objected not to the discussion of sex in the etiology of the neuroses but to the Freudian insistence that infantile sexuality was *always* the ultimate cause of *every* psychoneuroses. Thus by the time Jones returned to London, full-time, in the autumn of 1913 there was a general consensus about Freud's work which is nicely summed up by an anonymous reviewer who said of Brill's book on Psychoanalysis (1913):

> It is a very clear exposition of the views on psychology held by Dr. Freud, whose philosophy, with sex as the basis of a very large part of human activity, is greatly in vogue at present in many schools of thought. (*BMJ* January 10, 1914, p. 90).

NOTES

1. Jones was neither a signatory to the Eder Appeal (Einstein et al., 1936) nor a contributor to Hobman (1945) but did "receive" donations for the Eder library in Jerusalem (Paskauskas 1993, p. 755).

2. Perhaps a reference to Freud's July 10, 1914 letter, which is somewhat different (Paskauskas 1993, pp. 292–93).

3. Barbara Low and Low's sister-in-law Edith Eder who had recently died. What Anna probably did know was that in 1922 a woman in Derby, having read an article in *Lloyds*, loosely based on an interview with Low, wrote to ask Jones if he was "a pupil" of Eder's. Jones then made a vicious attack on Low for having dared to claim Eder "a leader of the movement" (Jones to Low February 12, 1922, BPAS, P04-C-D-03).

4. G. G. A. Murray (1866–1957) SPR President (1915–1916) known for his interests in parapsychology. Genome (2016) suggests Murray's comments, pre-recorded on 26 March, were broadcast on the "Home Service" on April 1, 1945. The programme included Kingsley Martin, editor of the *New Statesman*. Michael Osborn (Genome), to whom I am grateful, has suggested the recording was destroyed.

5. Harry Roberts, a contributor, also reviewed it for *News Statesman* (April 28, 1945, p. 278), but only mentions the chapter on "Eder as Psychoanalyst," in passing. A brief notice in *BMJ* (May 19, 1945, p. 701), probably written on the instructions of Jones, says: "Later [Eder] fell under the influence of Freud and Ernest Jones, then in Canada, and became one of the pioneers of psycho-analysis in this country." Jones (1936a, p. 295) offers a very different slant on Eder perhaps because Freud was still alive to read it!

6. Letter from Anna Freud to E. Jones, May 7, 1945 (Ernest Jones Collection, Archives BPAS P4-C-C-06). Jones wrote, in pencil, at the bottom: "Answered that teachers usually antedate pupils, in this case by [illegible] years."

7. Letter from Anna Freud to E. Jones, August 26, 1945 (Ernest Jones Collection, Archives BPAS P04-C-C-06). The review by Flügel (1945) makes no mention of the priority dispute presumably because it followed Jones (1945).

8. J. B. Strachey, Trinity College Cambridge, SPR member, December 1908 (*Journal* 1907–1907, Vol. 13, p. 314).

9. Letter from James Strachey to E. Jones, July 18, 1945 (Ernest Jones Collection, Archives BPAS PO4-C-E-14).

10. Strachey (1963, pp. 228–29) confirms that in 1912 he still had no idea about Myers's interest in Freud, while the absence of any reference to Myers in Rickman (1928, p. 187) also confirms this reading. Jones cannot decide between Myer or Myers which Strachey, as editor, also failed to notice!

11. Jones (1955, p. 31) is ambiguous as to whether this "first case to be analysed outside German-speaking countries" belonged to him.

12. The date, which is wrong, is reproduced in Jones (1945b) but corrected in Jones (1954).

13. See also Evans (1964, p. 119–20).

14. I offer a very different version (Kuhn 2015).

15. Freud (1914a, p. 30) refers to Hill, whose birth is usually given as 1874, as "an English neurologist in central India." Although Jones (1944b, p. 177) claimed Berkeley Hill "was one of the first Englishmen whose interest I had aroused in psycho-analysis, about the same time as the late Dr Eder," I have been unable to verify this. Compare, for example, the silence in Young (2016) with the comments by Nandy (1995, pp. 98–99).

16. Jones even claims, outrageously: "I was mainly responsible for trying to interest the late Dr Rivers in the subject of psycho-analysis" (*Times*, August 12, 1933).

17. That is, Paskauskas (1985; 1988), Johnson (1990, p. 210ff), Thomson (2001; 2011), Martindale (2003; 2004), Raitt (2004), Hayward (2014).

18. In October 1920 Jones noted: "As I know the private affairs of all the people I can say that those who have made [financial] sacrifices are Miss Low and Mrs. Riviere, and those the least Flügel and Mrs Porter" (Wittenberger & Tögel 1999, p. 119). See also Paskauskas (1993, p. 336).

19. In December 1925 Pryns Hopkins, "a former patient" of Jones's, funded the British Training Institute, aka The London Clinic of Psycho-Analysis (Paskauskas 1993, p. 588n; Grosskurth 1991, p. 86).

20. The list is too long; see however Roazen (1992, pp. 357ff); Falzeder (2007, p. 217 and n; 2015, pp. 81–82 and 234); Bakman (2013, p. 99).

21. Johnson (1990, pp. 24f) also notes Jones's skewing of history.

22. Freud (1910a, p. 215) suggests "Hypnosis showed itself at that time to be a therapeutic help, but a hindrance to the scientific knowledge of the real nature of the case, since it cleared away the psychic resistances from a certain field, only to pile them up in an unscalable wall at the boundaries of this field." See also Strachey (1966).

23. In drawing a distinction between experimental and introspective psychology, Myers argued that researchers, by concentrating on the former were in danger of sacrificing profundity for precision (Macdonald 1892, p. 289).

Chapter 2

Debatable Borderlands

> From a long series of investigations as to the phenomena of clairvoyance, telepathy, and hypnotism, Mr. Myers has come to the conclusion that there is a consciousness which lies below the surface of our ordinary waking life—a consciousness which at times comes into that waking life—but which apparently is not part of that life, but is existent independently of it. This consciousness Mr. Myers calls subliminal as distinguished from the ordinary or supraliminal. By the, "uprush" from the subliminal into the supraliminal, we get that kind of "sport" called genius which is, and has been, the despair of the evolutionist. Everyone will remember how Mr. Russell Wallace,[1] in his book on "Darwinism," showed that no theory of evolution would account for the sporadic appearance of the mathematical faculty for instance, and founded on this failure a claim for the existence of a spiritual existence outside the material. (*Light* September 12, 1892, Vol. 12, p. 450)

THE SOCIETY FOR PSYCHICAL RESEARCH [SPR]

According to Sage (1904) the SPR was established in 1882 "for the purpose of making an organized and systematic attempt to investigate various sorts of debatable phenomena which are—*prima facie*—inexplicable on any generally recognised hypothesis." Barrett (1911, p. 9) put it more succinctly: "To know something about the debatable borderland between the territory already conquered by science and the dark realms of ignorance and superstition." Myers (1888a, p. 365), in a moving tribute to his colleague Edmund Gurney (1847–1888), said the SPR "was founded, with the establishment of thought-transference—already rising within measurable distance of proof—as its primary aim, with hypnotism as its second study, and with many another problem ranged along its dimmer horizon." In his introductory comments to *Phantasms of the Living* [*Phantasms*], Myers (1886b, p. xlvi) noted:

> Throughout this treatise we naturally need a designation for phenomena which are inexplicable by recognised physiological laws, and belong to the general group into the nature of which we are inquiring. The term psychical (which is liable to misapprehension even in the title of our Society) can hardly be used without apology in this specialised sense. The occasional introduction of the word supernormal [beyond what usually happens] may perhaps be excused.

One of those debatable borderlands, which Myers and others sought to explore, was to be found in the relationships between "hypnotism, hysteria, and hystero-epilepsy" because, as Myers (1886b, pp. xviii, xlii–xliii) noted, the study of hypnotism offered "the strongest argument" for those who sought "to supplement and coordinate the somewhat narrower explorations of technical physiology" and because "the actual interest of the mesmeric or hypnotic trance . . . the central interest, let us say, of induced somnambulism, or the sleep-waking state—has hardly as yet revealed itself to any section of inquirers." The interest

> lies neither in mesmerism as a curative agency, as Elliotson would have told us, nor in hypnotism as an illustration of inhibitory cerebral action, as Heidenhain would tell us now. It lies in the fact that here is a psychical experiment on a larger scale than was ever possible before; that we have at length got hold of a handle which turns the mechanism of our being; that we have found a mode of shifting the threshold of consciousness which is a dislocation as violent as madness, a submergence as pervasive as sleep, and yet is waking sanity; that we have induced a change of personality which is not *per se* either evolutive or dissolutive, but seems a mere allotropic modification of the very elements of man. The prime value of the hypnotic trance lies not in what it inhibits, but in what it reveals; not in the occlusion of the avenues of peripheral stimulus, but in the emergence of unnoted sensibilities, nay, perhaps even in the manifestation of new and centrally-initiated powers.
>
> The hypnotic trance is an eclipse of the normal consciousness which can be repeated at will.

Although subsequent observers often criticize their methodology, and even point to their gullibility, Myers (1886b, p. xxxvi), and his other close SPR colleagues, always required their researches follow strictly established scientific protocols.

> And, again, we wish distinctly to say that so far from aiming at any paradoxical reversion of established scientific conclusions, we conceive ourselves to be

> working (however imperfectly) in the main track of discovery, and assailing a problem which, though strange and hard, does yet stand next in order among the new adventures on which Science must needs set forth, if her methods and her temper are to guide and control the widening curiosity, the expanding capacities of men.[2]

It was through those scientific investigations into the hypnotic "eclipse of the normal consciousness" that Myers came to develop his concept of the 'Subliminal Self,' a concept which he effectively articulated through a series of articles published in *Proceedings* between 1892 and 1895.

ON THE PSYCHICAL MECHANISM OF HYSTERICAL PHENOMENA

Gurney's and Myers's interest in "hypnotism from the point of view of psychical research" (Barrett 1911, p. 90) enabled them to forge important links with many medical psychologists: Richet, Charcot, Voisin, Liébeault, Bernheim and Janet, in France, William James,[3] and others in America, and Hugh Wingfield, Milne Bramwell, and Lloyd Tuckey in England.[4] Janet (1894, pp. 267–368; 1901, pp. 493–94; 1907, p. 7) originally praised Gurney and Myers "who have contributed much to the progress of these studies [on somnambulism] both by their own works and by the impulse they have given to the [SPR]." Janet also believed it was because of his interest in the psychological, as opposed to the physiological causes of mental "diseases," that Myers had "often expressed similar ideas [to his own] regarding the mechanism of hysterical accidents."[5] This, then, offers a brief background to "Psychology of Hysteria," the paper Myers read to an SPR General Meeting on April 21, 1893, and which was briefly summarized in the *Journal* (1893, Vol. 6, p. 78).

> [Myers] explained that his object was first to connect the various phenomena of hysteria, in so far as they fell under the domain of psychology, under a hypothesis which should include all their varieties; and secondly to show how this hypothesis itself confirmed and was confirmed by the general view of human personality which the speaker had already endeavoured to set forth. As the argument was a complex one, and the paper is intended so soon to appear in full, further account is reserved.[6]

That further account was published in *Proceedings* just two months later as "The Subliminal Consciousness." In examining "The Mechanisms of Hysteria," Myers (1893b, p. 4) was particularly interested in the problems of "motor automatisms."[7]

> The telepathic transmission of a message directly prompting to a motor act (as of writing) has no even apparent parallel in ordinary life.

Myers wondered "from what form of initial impulse these motor automatisms spring;" and drawing a distinction between the physiological and "the psychological end of the conscious spectrum," suggested examining

> the influence of motor and quasi-motor messages upon the organic functions before we analyse the intellectual contents of such messages, or discuss the source of such definite knowledge as they may contain.

Although Myers (1893b, p. 5, *italics* mine) had already discussed "the hypnotic stratum of the Self," he thought there was "one cognate topic of great importance—one repertory of subliminal messages especially of the vaguer organic type—" which he still needed to mention.

> I allude to the whole range of morbid interchanges or interactions between one section of the personality and another,—those 'self-suggestive maladies' or 'diseases of the hypnotic stratum,' as I have termed them. . . . 'whose differentia is an irrational self-suggestion in regions beyond the powers of the waking will;—a morbid or uncontrolled functioning of powers over the organism which effect profounder modifications than the empirical self can parallel.

Myers was, of course, referring to hysteria although he remained unhappy with the term because of all those popular misconceptions attached to it. He was also aware that there was no easy nosology of hysteria and suggested:

> If we would attain to a comprehensive view, we must seek it from some psychological standpoint.

Here Myers had in mind the current polarized debates concerning the cause, or causes of hysteria. On the one hand it was widely seen as a neurological condition, a "gross *organic* disease of the nervous system" which either, in reality or hypothetically, could always be traced to a *definite* cerebral or spinal lesion (Bastian 1893, pp. 2 and 2–5, italics mine). On the other hand there were those, like Janet (1895, p. 586), who now held that certain neuroses, such as hysteria, were "functional or dynamic disorders" with a psychological or psychical origin.[8] This distinction was critical because once hysteria was conceived as a functional rather than organic disease, it followed that the patient's condition might be amenable to some form of psychological intervention including psychical or psychological therapy. Myers argued that in many cases it was possible to identify

> a series of definite, objective lesions, inflicted upon the organism by some external injury, or by some internal operation of microbes, malnutrition, heredity disease, or senile decay.[9]

Generally speaking such lesions were not amenable to psychological intervention. But there was another series of lesions—*"phantom lesions"*—which although dependent, "of course, ultimately upon some cerebral conditions—hereditary, self-developed, or traumatic," were, in fact, *not* dependent upon

> injury to definite nervous centres or tracts, but as the apparently capricious manifestations of an injury presumably affecting some unknown seat of highest co-ordination; in short, as *perturbations of personality*, which work themselves out through some morbid process of self-suggestion, according to the laws of association cognisable by us, if at all, from the intellectual rather than from the anatomical side. (Myers 1893b, p. 5, emphasis mine).

Then drawing on Janet's work Myers (1893b, pp. 5–6) suggested those "phantom lesions" were "like some ignorant patient's objectified dream" in which the symptom, such as "hysterical patches of anaesthesia," correspond not "with any true areas of ordinary sensory innervation" but with "the patient's crude notions of where his limbs begin and end." And it was the "fundamentally psychological character of hysteria . . . which excuses, or rather compels, its study not only from the clinical, but from the psychological standpoint."

Myers (1893b, p. 7)[10] then criticized those who hold "the view that *any* perturbation of the ordinary personality is necessarily and in itself evil," and complained that the genius and the blank imbecile have been lumped together as "'hysterics.'"

> 'Les hystériques mènent le mond, says the French proverb. 'It is the fact,' says Breuer and Freud, 'that among the hysterics we find the clearest minded, the strongest-willed, the fullest of character, the most acutely critical specimens of humanity'.

This, Myers's first published reference to "Freud" is a reference to Breuer and Freud's jointly authored Über *den Psychischen Mechanismus Hysterischer Phänomene (Vorläufige Mitteilung)*—On the Psychical Mechanism of Hysterical Phenomena (Preliminary Communication) [Preliminary Communication]—which was published in the January 1893 issue of the *Neurologische Centralblatt.*

Myers (1893b, pp. 8–9) then continued with a meditation upon the fragility of the "Self" and "the supraliminal Self," noting those factors, such as "various intoxications" or "changes of trophic condition," which were sufficient "to produce a transient perturbation of personality of the most violent kind." And, to illustrate his point, he quoted from a long letter, dated Samoa July 14, 1892, in which Robert Louis Stevenson catalogued, in detail, three experiences in which he felt his mind starting to wander: "'It was as if there were two parts of him: the one part possessed; the other which was himself.'" Then, having discussed those cases which he had identified as "of definitely hysterical uprush from subliminal—as I have maintained, specially from *hypnotic* strata,"—Myers (1893b, p. 12) returned to that "important essay" by Breuer and Freud.

> I will begin by some citations from one of the best recent German sources, that the English reader may see that these observations are not peculiar to the French school.

In his detailed summary of the "Preliminary Communication" Myers (1893b, pp. 12–13) noted how the authors believed that it was a "distressing idea which caused the original lesion" and that it was the *idea* which then

> keep up irritation like a foreign body lodged in the organism, like a thorn in the finger. It must be brought to the surface and extruded;—the painful memory must be diagnosed in the hypnotised patient and then brought back to his waking consciousness and freely discussed, and thus reduced to its due proportions. 'A mere emotional recollection,' say Drs Breuer and Freud, 'is generally useless; the psychical process which caused the trouble must be again set on foot, brought down to its *status nascendi*, and then worked out (*abreagirt*) and talked away.' The neuralgia or the hallucination will thus recur once in full intensity and then disappear for ever. . . .
>
> 'It is not in the normal memory of the patient,' continue our authors, with emphasis, 'but in his hypnotic memory, that the recollection of the operative psychical lesion is to be found. The more we busy ourselves with these phenomena, the surer becomes our conviction that the sundering of consciousness which is so striking in certain classical cases of duplex personality exists in the rudimentary fashion in every case of hysteria.'

Then Myers (1893b, p. 13) noted how the authors, "who come to this discussion unpledged to any hasty theory," had suggested not only that the "'foundation'" of hysteria is to be found in "'the existence of hypnoid states,'" but also

> fully recognise the gravity . . . of that problem of the unique effectiveness and power of hypnotic suggestions, and of hysterical self-suggestions, for which so many pseudo-solutions have been based upon so much hypothetical cerebral physiology.

Breuer and Freud had wondered

> 'why it is that the pathological associations which form themselves in hypnoid states are so stable, and influence organic processes so much more profoundly than do the ideas or presentations of our ordinary experiences;—this question forms a part of the general problem of the efficacy of hypnotic suggestion in any case whatever.' (Myers 1893b, pp. 13–14)

Once we remember Myers's deep-seated interest in hypnotism, hysteria, and psychical research, it is not so surprising he should have been attracted to a title like "Psychical Mechanism of Hysterical Phenomena" or, that having read "Preliminary Communication" he should have become excited, most of all, by the fact that it seemed to offer him an "independent coincidence" with his own views because the Viennese had given

> emphatic support, from wide clinical experience, of the view of hysteria to which *my own observations* on different branches of automatism had already, by mere analogical reasoning, directed my thought. (Myers 1893b, pp. 14–15, italics mine)

Myers (1893b, p. 15n, italics added) also believed "Preliminary Communication" supported his own "Conceptions" of "stratified *consciousness*," a concept which

> *first presented itself* independently to three observers, as the result of three different lines of experiment. Mr Gurney was led that way by experiments on hypnotic memory; M. Pierre Janet by experiments on hysteria; and to myself the observation of various automatisms neither hysterical nor hypnotic.[11]

And then, as if to emphasize his point, Myers turned to a detailed discussion of Pierre Janet's *L'Etat Mental des Hysterique*.[12]

Reading Myers's 1893 essay, particularly in the light of the subsequent priority dispute(s) between Freud and Janet, reveals the extent to which Myers read "Preliminary Communication" in the lights of Janet's shadow. Indeed Freud (1893, p. 170) acknowledged as much when, in the 4th section of a paper, published in the July 1893[13] issue of *Archives de Neurologie*, he made it explicit that he agreed with Janet's belief that "The lesion in hysterical paralysis will therefore be an alteration of the *conception*, the *idea*, of the arm, for instance" (Freud 1910a, p. 191, 1914a, pp. 32–33; Macmillan 1997, p. 90; Ellenberger 1994, p. 819).

HUMAN PERSONALITY

Studies in Hysteria (Studien Uber Hysterie) [*Studien*],[14] coauthored by Breuer and Freud, was published in May 1895. That book consists of a reprint of "Preliminary Communication" together with a series of essays individually authored. Breuer had two contributions; the case history of "Anna O.," and a long theoretical essay. Freud had five contributions: four case studies and his own theoretical essay, *The Psychotherapy of Hysteria*. Some two years after its publication, Myers (1897, p. 51) read "the first part of his paper 'Hysteria and Genius'" to an SPR meeting on March 12, 1897. He "justified his topic on two grounds": that the psychological "cure of hysteria" had made great progress in recent years and because he felt a personal

> obligation to certain recent researches which have corroborated and completed in a welcome manner that general theory of the relations between supraliminal and subliminal strata of consciousness which already seemed to me to hold good in almost all those abnormal or supernormal states which enable us in some degree to analyse the elements of man's personality.

It was the "patient and penetrating observation" of men like "Dr. Pierre Janet and M. Binet, in France, and Drs. Breuer and Freud in Vienna," which had helped give a "rational interpretation .. to certain hysterical symptoms." Then, having discussed certain aspects of Janet's work, Myers (1897, pp. 55–56, italics mine) concluded:

> Notions like these, suggested to me largely by Dr. Janet's experiments, find (as seems to me) *a strange confirmation* in the more recent 'Studien über Hystérie' [*sic*] of Drs. Breuer and Freud. These physicians have had to deal, *most of all in Dr. Breuer's case of Anna O-* , with hysterics of much higher intellectual calibre than the patients of the Salpêtrière. . . .
>
> I repeat, then, that the collection of cases published by these physicians under the title 'Studien über Hystérie'[*sic*], seems to me to make it probable that all hysterical symptoms, without exception, have their origin in some localised and functional affection of the brain, of a type which the metaphors that I have been using set before us, perhaps, as plainly as is at present possible.

When Myers died, in January 1901, Richard Hodgson and Alice Johnson (1860–1940),[15] completed his unfinished manuscripts and published them, in February 1903, under the title *Human Personality*. In the second chapter of Volume 1, "Disintegration of Personality," Myers (1903, Vol. 1, pp. 35, 36 and 37) claimed

> we have no complete or unchanging unity, but rather a complex hierarchy of groups of cells exercising vaguely limited functions, and working together with rough precision, tolerable harmony, fair success.

He wanted to examine the "many disturbances and disintegrations of the personality" while, at the same time, speaking "of concurrent and alternating streams of consciousness,—of subliminal and supraliminal strata of personality." But he also wanted to look at consciousness from a psychological point of view.

> We come to regard consciousness as an attribute which may possibly be present in all kinds of varying degrees in connection with the animal and vegetable worlds; as the psychical counterpart of life; as conceivably the psychical counterpart of all phenomenal existence. Or, rather, we may say this of mind, to which, in its more elementary forms, consciousness bears somewhat the same relation as self-consciousness bears to consciousness, or some higher evolution may bear to self-consciousness.

These were, in effect, the introductory comments to Myers's idea (1903, Vol. 1, pp. 40, 41 and 42 emphasis added) that consciousness may disintegrate. And "the first symptoms of disaggregation," he discussed, was the *ideé fixe* which, as Janet had shown, "give rise to hysterical attacks" which may then be "removed by free discussion; 'talked out,' as Dr. Breuer has it." Myers also noted that emotions, such as fear, could also lead to fixed ideas and while they might take on a "morbid development" they could not necessarily be classed as brain disease. In these cases, "fixed ideas," for example, were of interest to the physician because they could be "*cured* by psychological means"; by which Myers meant the therapeutic use of (post) hypnotic suggestion which had already been used, for a number of years, by several British physicians including his two-fellow SPR Council members Drs. Bramwell and Tuckey. Then, having noted how "the distinction between functional and organic" disease "is not easily demonstrable in this ultramicroscopic realm," Myers turned to discuss the subliminal self.

> That is to say, we have to do with an instability of the conscious threshold which often implies or manifests a disorderly or diseased condition of the hypnotic stratum,—of that region of the personality which, as we shall see, is best known to us through the fact that it is reached by hypnotic suggestion.

Although Myers (1903, Vol. 1, p. 43) had already developed these views by 1892, he now wanted to see how far they corresponded with

> those modern observations of hysteria, in Paris and Vienna especially, which are transforming all that group of troubles from the mere opprobrium of medicine into one of the most fertile sources of new knowledge of body and mind.

Then, after surveying "Dr. Pierre Janet's admirable work, *L'Etat Mental des Hystériques* [Mental State 1894]" and discussing several of Janet's examples Myers (1903, Vol. 1, pp. 50–51) noted how the "notion of dissolutive hysterical processes" was also being "observed with closer insight than formerly, in certain great hospitals." And yet, he continued, there was now another group of patients, much smaller in number, "not from hospital wards, but from private practice." These were the patients who formed the basis for *Studien*. At this point Myers then discussed two of those case histories offering a detailed account of Freud's "Lucy R," followed by a detailed synopsis of the "still more remarkable" case of Breuer's Anna O.—in which Myers (1903, Vol. 1, pp. 53 and 55), once again, specifically quotes: "'The talking cure' or 'chimney-sweeping,' as Fraulein O. called it," while also noting how the cathartic method "was practically equivalent to confession under hypnosis." In other words Myers is reading *Studien*, just as he had read "Preliminary Communication," by reference to Janet's work, only this time more specifically in relation to the concept of disaggregation, which Janet (1894, p. 51; 1901, p. 53) had now developed through *L'Etat Mental*.

Although Myers (1903, Vol. 1, pp. 50ff)[16] more or less repeats what he had previously written about Breuer and Freud's "Preliminary Communication," *Human Personality* actually contains Myers's one and only reference to a work by Freud. This occurs in a passage where Myers (1903, Vol. 1, p. 465) draws a distinction between those phobias which "constitute then a special disease in themselves" and those which "constitute frequently but one out of many symptoms of a deeper nervous derangement,—neurasthenia." This is what he says:

> Freud has given to the state which is specially favourable to their evolution,—a state entirely distinct, according to him, from neurasthenia,—the name of *Angstneurose*. According to Hartenberg these phobies cannot be cured by suggestion, as their origin is to be found in organic derangements. However this may be, it is at least certain that the great majority of the phobies which have been cured by hypnotic suggestion are clearly *phobies neurastheniques*, and it is most probable that the removal of the phobia will arrest the development of the neurasthenia, and contribute largely to the restoration of neural stability.

Now there is no evidence that Myers ever read Freud's (1895b) paper, to which these comments clearly allude, so he must have gleaned his information from 'Névroses d'Angoisse,' Hartenberg's communication to the International Congresses of Psychology and Neurology (1900),[17] where Myers (1901b, p. 67) also delivered a paper (See also *Proceedings* 1901, Vol. 15, pp. 447–48).

The Myths of Myers, Psychoanalysis and the Subliminal Self

From this survey we can now conclude that Myers was only ever interested in the *product* of the Breuer—Freud collaboration and not with the writings of

"Freud" and certainly not with the idea of psychoanalysis. As Strachey (1955, p. xxi) has noted: "It is not easy to assign with certainty the responsibility for the origin of the various component elements of [*Studien*] as a whole," and it is only with the hindsight of Freud's later work that it becomes possible to distinguish the differences between the two authors. Perhaps even more telling I have only found one other reference to Breuer and Freud[18] in all the writings of the main SPR members either during Myers's lifetime or in the seven odd years following his death. It now seems clear that Myers's interest in Breuer and Freud was only ever focused on how the collaborative work of the two Viennese underlined his own and Janet's theoretical work.[19] But what also impressed Myers was how Janet's psychological work, originally conducted within the open gaze of the hospital ward, now seemed to have migrated into the enclosed, private space of the Viennese consulting rooms.[20] And it may well have been Breuer and Freud's privatization of the psychotherapeutic space which prompted Myers to equate their "talking cure" with the confessional.

Having challenged Jones's Myers myth we can now also read *Human Personality* for the absence of its reference to Freud's post *Studien* publications. This is important because if Myers had really been interested in Freud's work then surely he would have noticed, at the very least, Freud's three essays from 1896 (a; b; c) let alone *Die Traumdeutung* which was published several months before Hartenberg's communication to the Paris Congress.[21] Only an anachronistic reading could claim that Myers was "the first to introduce Freud and his ideas to the English-speaking world" (Crabtree 2007, p. 328).[22] Apart from the fact that nobody else appears to have picked up on Myers's reading of "Perliminary Communication" or *Studien* there is also that small technical, or pedantic point, that it was only in 1896, *after* the publication of *Studien*, that Freud first adopted the term psychoanalysis

> as formal confirmation that catharsis under hypnosis and suggestion had been dropped and that the obtaining of material would henceforth depend exclusively on the rule of free association. (Laplanche and Pontalis 1973, p. 367)[23]

On the other hand, if we now look at the obverse of Jones's counterfeit coin we can begin to detect the profound negative consequences which have flowed from the psychoanalytic obsession with the Myers' myth. First, there has been scant recognition of Myers's early pioneering work let alone his "services to psychology" (James 1911, p. 145). Second, the almost universal dismissal of Myers's theory of the "Subliminal Self," to be examined later, has meant that most historians have failed to appreciate that Myers articulated

> two forms of the subliminal: the subliminal as a region of the mind built up in the course of individual experience ["a store of submerged memories and

experiences"];[24] and that "profounder faculty" or "soul" which inhabits a metetherial environment. (Northridge 1924, p. 33; Myers 1903, Vol. 1, pp.34–35).

Because most students have only concentrated on the latter—"the real essential personality or soul which survives death" (*Journal* 1907, Vol. 13, p. 21)—they have assumed that the subliminal self simply "involves the hypothesis that we are living a life in two worlds at once; a planetary life in this material world, to which the organism is intended to react; and also a cosmic life in that spiritual or metetherial world, which is the native environment of the soul." (Myers 1903, Vol. 1, p. 151). Third, the absence of any detailed enquiries into Myers's and Gurney's pioneering experimental researches has resulted in a lack of understanding as to how members of the SPR not only intersected with the British medical profession but also helped shape the discourse on experimental and medical psychology during the 1880s and 1890s. Myers, for example, is shockingly absent from nearly all the psychology book indexes covering this period (i.e., Bunn et al., 2001; Ryan 2010).[25] Fourth, by fetishizing Myers's interest in Freud, historians have effectively ignored Myers's interest in Janet to say nothing of Janet's influence on Myers (*Journal* 1900, Vol. 9, p. 270). And this, unwittingly, or perhaps wittingly, has resulted in the repression, or concealment, of Janet's significance for the development of early-twentieth-century British medical psychology. By championing Janet's work, particularly *Mental States*, Myers helped prepare the psychological foundations for the British reception of Freud. And finally, in spinning the web of his narrative around Myers Jones effectively ignored, or wrote out of the history, those others who did actually help to bring Freud's work into the British psycho-medical discourse.

NOTES

1. On Wallace's comments see Lewis (1910, p. 57).
2. For detailed discussions on this see Sommer (2013b).
3. James (1926, Vol. 2, p. 154; Vol. 1, p. 57) was a good friend of Myers and respected his researches.
4. Goodrich-Freer (1899, p. 212), assistant editor of *Borderland*, noted: "It is, to say the least, suggestive that three of the doctors best known as making use of hypnotism as a means of cure in their ordinary practice should be all members of the [SPR], two of them holding office in the society and all contributors to its literature."
5. Crabtree (2008, p. 575) suggests Janet's idea of human psychology consisted of two basic elements: operating simultaneously—the conscious and the subconscious: the subconscious is "a region of multiple centres operating quite distinctly from each other and separately affecting conscious life."
6. Also Myers (1886a, i.e., p. 141).

7. The unwilled activity of hand or voice or "*motor automatism* will include messages written without intention (automatic script) or words uttered without intention (as in 'speaking with tongues,' trance-utterances, &c.). I ascribe these processes to the action of submerged or subliminal elements in the man's being" (Myers 1903, Vol. 1, pp. xv and 27).

8. Janet (1895, p. 586) noted it was often difficult to identify a lesion in the brain except *post-mortem*. Northridge (1924, p. 52) says: "The discovery that many forms of hysteria are wholly psychological took place in connection with the researches of a group of physicians into cerebral localization. These researches led to such interesting and valuable results that, as Jung says, 'everyone began to go in for post-mortem examinations'."

9. Hyslop (1895) has a good overview of the contemporary debates.

10. The quote is from Breuer and Freud (1893, p. 13).

11. Morton Prince mistakenly claimed "Myers's theories . . . are fundamental to Freud." (Prince to Putnam November 26, 1910 in Hale 1971, p. 324).

12. Myers (1894, p. 192) also mentions Breuer and Freud in passing.

13. The dating is Strachey's (Freud 1893, p. 158).

14. *The Athenaeum* (June 22, 1895, p. 802) notes *Studien*.

15. Alice Johnson, educated at Newnham College, Cambridge, became a demonstrator in animal morphology at the Balfour Laboratory. She then became Eleanor Sidgwick's private secretary in 1890, then editor of *Proceedings* and then also secretary to the SPR.

16. Myers (1901a, pp. 386–87) makes only a passing reference to Breuer and Freud.

17. Moll (1913, pp. 43–44) discusses Hartenberg's contribution.

18. Crookes (1898, p. 733). Bramwell (1903, p. 421) however references Freud's (1892–1893) paper on hypnotism.

19. "In the wonderful explorations by Binet, Janet, Breuer, Freud, Mason, Prince and others," thus (James 1902, p. 234) suggests a similar reading.

20. On this point see Mayer (2006).

21. Although Ellenberger (1994, p. 780) says Myers quoted "Pierre Janet, Binet, Breuer and Freud as authorities on hysteria," in his 'On the Trance Phenomena of Mrs Thompson,' this is not quite correct. (See Myers 1901b, p. 67; *Journal* 1903, Vol. 11, pp. 74–76).

22. Also Hinshelwood (1995, p. 135), silently following Jones (1945b), who said Myers was the first person "in England [who] was ready to take notice of psychoanalysis."

23. See Freud (1909b, pp. 155ff); *BMJ* (July 4, 1914, p. 47).

24. These comments are by F. C. Constable (*Journal* 1907, Vol. 13, p. 21).

25. Richards (2001, p. 38) notes: "The historiographical side-lining of the role of psychic research in the founding of psychology. . . ." An exception is Shamdasani (2003, pp. 125–27, 256n, 261).

Chapter 3

The 1898 BMA Hypnotism Debates

> By our various modes of suggestion, through influencing the mind by audible language, spoken within the hearing of the patient, or by definite physical impressions, we fix certain ideas, strongly and involuntarily on the mind of the patient, which thereby act as stimulants, or as sedatives, according to the purport of the expectant ideas, and the direction of the current of thought in the mind of the patient, either drawing it to, or withdrawing it from, particular organs or functions; which results are effected in ordinary practice, by prescribing such medicines as experience has proved stimulate or irritate these organs, thereby directly increasing their function, or which produce the reverse effect, either by direct sedative action on the organs, or by diminishing the heart's action, or by stimulating some distant part, and thereby producing revulsion. (Braid 1853, p. 87)

CONVERSIONS AND SUGGESTIONS

On May 28, 1897 Myers delivered his paper on the "Moral and Intellectual Limits of Suggestion" to a general meeting of the SPR. He took, as his starting point, "Hughlings-Jackson's scheme of centres at three levels of evolution" because he wanted to explore "the effects produced upon *highest level centres*, those which we imagine as governing moral and intellectual manifestations." Myers suggested that our "educative efforts are partly inhibitive and partly dynamogenic[1]; that is to say, we endeavour to check some impulses, and to stimulate and strengthen others." He believed it was now generally recognized that hypnotic suggestion could succeed where other means had failed. Thus, in the intellectual field, hypnosis or suggestion could be used to concentrate "attention either below or above the conscious threshold" thereby helping to foster "the self-regarding and the altruistic virtues," either through stimulation or by checking them.

> When we hear, for instance, of a patient raised by hypnotic suggestion from "moral insanity" to much-valued helpfulness as a hospital nurse,[2] we need not assume that she has attained any high pitch of self-devotion. There is a kind of ethical "position of stability" in the civilised world which implies adequate good sense and good will to others, but no heroic virtue.

Myers then drew upon the similarities between religious "Conversions" and "cures by suggestion" because he believed that, through both, "sudden and permanent changes for the better do frequently occur."

> But if it be true that *conversion* and *suggestion* are sometimes almost equivalent expressions for a change which seems profounder than the changes which mere reasoning inspires, this is not to say that the origin of either lies in some mere physiological trick or fortunate self-delusion. I believe that there is here a true dynamogeny, implying what must in some sense be an intensification of vitality. This—as I conjecture—comes in the last resort from a world of life, a *metetherial* environment,—some condition of things more fundamental and primary than the interstellar ether itself. In this energy, however defined or personalised, we live and move and have our being. Hence comes the vitalising or informing principle, which is nearer to its source, and can deal with the body more freely in its subliminal than in its supraliminal relations, can modify it more effectively in trance-states than in waking hours. (*Journal* 1898, Vol. 8, p. 83–85)

In the discussion which followed, Dr Charles Lloyd Tuckey (1855–1925), one of the leading British exponents of medical hypnotism and an SPR Council member, agreed that suggestion could help "develop" latent talents "and foster good qualities which were over-borne by evil tendencies." This meant "there was probably a great future for the judicious use of hypnotism as an educational agent." (*Journal* 1898, Vol. 7, pp. 85–86). Dr John Milne Bramwell (1853–1925), another leading British medical hypnotist, and fellow SPR Council member, confirmed "Myers's statements as to the value of suggestion in disease," because if one could "hypnotise a man of genius, questioning during hypnosis might possibly throw some light upon the subliminal origin of his inspirations." Bramwell cautioned, however, that hypnotism was not a cure-all because "as a rule the time and trouble required bore a direct proportion to the severity and duration of the disease and the mental instability of the patient." (*Journal* 1898, Vol. 7, pp. 86–87).

HYPNOTISM AND THE BRITISH MEDICAL ASSOCIATION

Just over a year later, in July 1898, the BMA published the programme for its Annual meeting to be held in Edinburgh at the end of the month. The Psychological Section [Section] was to have three separate discussions and the third, on "Hypnotism: Its Phenomena and Theories" was to be initiated by Drs Bramwell and John Francis Woods (1854–1947) and by F. W. H. Myers. There was also an impressive list of delegates indicating their intention of taking part: Professor Benedikt, Drs Kurella, Lloyd Tuckey, Yellowlees, Fletcher Beach, James Shaw,[3] A. R. Urquhart (president elect of the Association, and a co-editor of the *JMS*), Outterson Wood, and Fielding Blandford (*BMJ* July 2, 1898, p. 51). But first some brief historical background.

In 1869, Professor Thomas Laycock, then president of the Association, suggested to the BMA Council that "the scientific work hitherto transacted at the Association's annual meeting" might be transferred to the BMA's Annual Meeting. The Council agreed and at the 1870 Annual Meeting there was a Section "specially devoted to Psychological Medicine" and Laycock was elected its first president (*BMJ* August 13, 1870, p. 177). From then on the Section became a regular feature of the BMA's Annual Meeting so that when T. H. Tuke (1873, p. 189)[4] delivered his address, in 1873, he could claim, with justification, that the BMA had now made psychological medicine an integral part of its work. Although Tuke's understanding of psychological medicine was still deeply rooted in physiology and pathology those old hard-and-fast "materialist" definitions were already beginning to crack as medical psychologists, like D. H. Tuke (1827–1895)—no relation—became increasingly interested in the workings of the mind as well as of the brain. By 1898, the BMA Annual Meeting had become one of the major events in the medical calendar and when Sir John Batty Tuke (1898)[5]—no relation to the other Tukes—addressed the full Meeting, it was the second time that decade[6] that a BMA president had spoken on psychological medicine and his address received wide publicity.

Although the process of organizing the Annual Meeting remains somewhat opaque evidence suggests each Section remained autonomous so that once the 1897 BMA Council decided that its next Annual meeting was to be held in Edinburgh, it was in the gift of the Association to make all necessary arrangements for their Section. And because precedent dictated that the most senior member of the Association, based in or near the designated city, should be invited to preside, T. S. Clouston (1840–1915), Superintendent, Royal Morningside Asylum for the Insane [Morningside], was appointed president with George Robertson (1862–1933) being one of his *honorary secretaries*. It was then up to the president, vice presidents and honorary secretaries to

> constitute a Committee of Reference for that Section, and exercise the power of inviting, accepting, or declining any paper, and of arranging the order in which accepted papers shall be read. (*BMJ*, July 15, 1911, p. 133)

Robertson was born in India, educated at Madras College, St Andrews, where he graduated in 1885 before becoming resident physician at the Royal Infirmary, Edinburgh, and then assistant physician under Clouston at Morningside. In 1892 he was appointed physician superintendent at Murthly Asylum[7] and then in 1899 physician superintendent at Sterling District Lunatic Asylum, Bellsdyke [Larbert] before succeeding Clouston as physician superintendent at Morningside in 1908. Shortly before leaving Morningside, Robertson (1892b; 1893) had become an active advocate for the use of hypnotism in the Asylum and although his early enthusiasm was subsequently tempered, mainly because of his inability to effect the kind of therapeutic changes he had over-optimistically believed in, he continued with his interest. For his part Clouston (1897, p. 129), who had already earmarked Robertson as his successor, was clearly supportive of Robertson's hypnotic practices. So it should come as no surprise that hypnotism—supposedly tabooed by the BMA in 1890—should have appeared on the Section's agenda for the *sixth* time in nine years. But there were also other witting, or unwitting, dimensions at play. Although Bramwell, as one of the main speakers, now lived and worked in London, he was born in Perth, educated in Edinburgh and traced his own interests in hypnotism to his father who had seen many of James Esdaile's mesmeric experiments "and afterwards reproduced" them. But Bramwell was also inspired by Professor John Hughes Bennett (1812–1875) who used to give an "account of Braid's work," during his "course on physiology." By 1892, Bramwell was already known as a fine medical hypnotist and Robertson (1892a, p. 657), who clearly admired his work, believed that while still at Goole (Yorkshire) Bramwell had "acquired a reputation resembling Professor Bernheim's at Nancy."[8] For his part Bramwell (1903, p. 22), as an historian of the subject, also knew that James Braid, the so called "English surgeon," and by now generally considered the father of modern hypnotism, was in fact a Scotsman, born in Fifeshire, about 1795, educated in Edinburgh and, having qualified as a surgeon, had practiced "in Scotland for some years" before moving to "Manchester, where he remained up to the time of his death, gaining a high reputation as a skilful physician and surgeon,"—and hypnotist.

While it was logical that Bramwell, a member of the Association, with his Edinburgh connections, should have been invited to speak, this was certainly not the case for Myers who was neither a qualified doctor, nor a member of the Association nor even a member of the BMA. As such Myers's invitation would have needed special sanction from the BMA Council (*BMJ* July

16, 1898, pp. 160, 182) and while the notice announcing his paper appears anodyne—"Mr. F. W. H. Myers (Cambridge) has kindly consented to take part in this discussion" (*BMJ*, July 16, 1898, p. 182)—its phrasing suggests tensions within the Council, although these may have been more to do with protocol than hypnotism because, generally speaking, invitations to non-BMA or non-Association members, were only ever extended to foreign *medical* men of repute. Myers's invitation, which may have been something unique, clearly suggests that senior Association members, like Urquhart, Fletcher Beach, Percy Smith, and Conolly Norman, must have considered Myers one of the foremost authorities on the subject and that they had the necessary authority to persuade a possibly reluctant BMA Council to accept Myers's *bona fides*. If there were still vocal opponents of hypnotism within the senior ranks of the BMA there is no noticeable sign of a backlash against Myers's invitation, even from that handful of anti-hypnotism "campaigners," like our good friend Mercier,[9] thereby suggesting they would have been outflanked. Tuckey (1900, p. 5) was probably correct, therefore, when he said, following the 1898 meeting: "I think we may say that there is no longer any prejudice against hypnotism in the best medical circles." The third key note speaker was J. F. Woods,[10] Resident Medical Superintendent, Hoxton House Asylum (North London), and widely considered the main advocate for the use of hypnotism in the treatment of the insane. Thus in 1898 the Association had assembled three key note speakers who effectively represented the three different strands of British hypnotism: Bramwell, the specialist medical practitioner, Myers, the acknowledged theoretician and Woods, the foremost Asylum worker. Even more startling, all three men also happened to be senior members of the SPR.

After giving a brief account from his own "personal hypnotic observations" Bramwell (1898, pp. 669, 671) discussed "how far the theories of others [were] satisfactory" in explaining his own experiences.

> Up to the day upon which Myers propounded his subliminal-consciousness theory of hypnotism no scientific work on the subject had been done in any country at all comparable to that of Braid, and the Nancy school itself holds many views which Braid had demonstrated as fallacious. This is strenuously denied by Bernheim and others, but they are only acquainted with Braid's earlier work, *Neurypnology*, and are unaware that this was followed by many others, of which I have been able to trace thirty-five.

Then after briefly summarizing the more important points in Braid's theory Bramwell (1898, pp. 671–72) noted:

> Several of these views differ markedly from those expressed by Braid in his earlier work, but evidence is not wanting to show that they in their turn were undergoing modification. Thus, he referred to the complexity of the hypnotic

> condition; to the fact that mental and physical activity characterised certain of its stages, and to the phenomenon of "double consciousness." Above all, however, I wish to draw attention to the fact that he ceased to believe in an involuntary monoideism, and stated fully and forcibly that the volition was absolutely unimpaired. Not only could the subject resist attempts to induce hypnosis, but also, when hypnotised, could reject any suggestion disagreeable to him. The moral sense in hypnosis was raised instead of being lessened, and it was impossible to make a hypnotised subject commit a crime, or even any act which involved the slightest indelicacy. These statements Braid supported by repeated demonstrations.

Following these comments, in which Myers's SPR paper from May, was silently referenced, Bramwell (1898, p. 672) noted, in passing, that Elliotson and Esdaile, the forerunners of Braid, were also "two other Edinburgh graduates."

> Bernheim, in opposition to Braid, considers that suggestion practically explains all the phenomena of hypnotism. According to him, everyone is suggestible; you take someone and suggest to him to become more suggestible, and that is hypnotism. The success of suggestion depends, however, not on the suggestion itself, but on conditions inherent in the subject. In hypnosis the essential condition is not the means used to excite the phenomena, but the peculiar state which enables them to be evoked. Suggestion no more explains the phenomena of hypnotism than the crack of the pistol explains a boat race. Both are simply signals—mere points of departure, and nothing more. With Bernheim the word suggestion has become mysterious and all-powerful. It has acquired an entirely new signification, and differs only in name from the "odyllic" force of the mesmerists.

Then following further comments on the theories of Bernheim and the Nancy school Bramwell (1898, p. 673) noted:

> There is one other theory to which I wish to draw attention. This, instead of attempting to explain hypnotism by the arrested action of some of the brain centres which subserve normal life, would do so through the arousing of certain powers over which we normally have little or no control. This theory may be regarded, I think, as a development of Braid's latest views. Its earliest and clearest exponent is Frederic Myers, and, as he is here in person to represent it, I do not propose to say more than a word in reference to it, namely, that although it forms an advance on all previous theories, it does not fully explain two important points: (1) The origin of the powers of the secondary consciousness, and (2) the connection between the methods of inducing hypnosis and the extraordinary phenomena which follow.

With which Bramwell concluded:

> If Braid and Myers have done much towards giving us a clearer idea of the hypnotic state, they have also added to the difficulties of explaining it. A conception

> of hypnosis which limited its manifestations to simple automatic movements was comparatively easy to explain. The hypnotic subject who, while he has not lost the physical and mental powers of his waking condition, has acquired new and far-reaching ones, presents a very different problem. How he acquired these powers and why hypnotic methods should evoke them are questions by no means easy to answer.

We shall see shortly how the vast majority of practitioners and commentators on hypnotism would effectively ignore Bramwell's and also Myers's cautionary comments about "suggestion."

Myers in, "a very polished discourse," (*JMS* 1899, Vol. 45, p. 204), began his contribution by saying he had been asked to give

> a coherent psychological presentation of the multifarious and perplexing facts now commonly grouped under the name of hypnotism. Purely physiological explanations thereof have, by common admission, thus far failed; and little attempt has yet been made by the able practical hypnotists, to whom the recent advance in our knowledge is owing, to correlate their ever-growing observations from a purely psychological point of view. (Myers 1898, p. 674),

Originally Charcot, and his school, saw analogies between hypnotism and hysteria but looking "a little deeper into those analogies" reveals "the point at which they begin to be misleading—the point at which hysterical and hypnotic workings, although *in pari materiâ*, begin to be in effect almost exactly opposite the one to the other."

> In hysteria we lose from supraliminal control portions of faculty which we do not wish to lose, and we cannot recover them at will. In hypnotism we lose from supraliminal control portions of faculty which we wish to lose, or are indifferent to losing, and we can recover them the moment that we will.

Myers thought the best way of explaining this was to identify the "hypnotic stratum," which is where "the faculties submerged in hysteria sink [,] . . . . and to describe hysteria as a disease of that stratum." It was also possible to see this as "an undue permeability of the psychical diaphragm which separates ordinary consciousness from the deeps below." This would explain how this "or that group of sensory or motor ability drops out of waking knowledge or out of control of waking will." On the other hand, in the course of hypnotism, instead "of losing control over the supraliminal stratum, we gain control over the hypnotic stratum."

> We purposely increase the permeability of the psychical diaphragm in such a way as to push down beneath it various forms of pain and annoyance which we are anxious to get rid of from our waking consciousness; while, on the other

> hand, we stimulate in the depths of our being many sanative and recuperative operations whose results rise presently into the perception of our waking life. (Myers 1898, p. 674)

This relationship between "the patient's subliminal region of personality" and her "hypnotic stratum in particular" suggests how "hypnotism has exactly repaired the mischief which hysteria has done. It has acted on the same stratum, but with an increase instead of a diminution of central control." But Myers (1898, p. 675) also believed that while physical explanations of the mind might be useful they were ultimately inadequate because the

> present notion in which the terms upper and lower are used in a different metaphorical sense, this notion of a kind of stratification of the personality above and below the threshold of ordinary consciousness will be found to suggest new and practical questions to which it is possible to find some beginning of answer.

Myers then drew a distinction between the physician and the psychologist: "The more rare and useless the faculty, the more interest it has for [the psychologist] as a possible inlet into some human mystery yet unexplored." So too with genius where ideas, "matured by subliminal mentation, beyond the artist's conscious control," are "presented to him as finished products from his subterranean workshops." On the other hand, hypnotism

> lies in a still deeper evocation of latent faculty. The fact which is bringing hypnotism before the medical profession is not its power to imitate and in some sense to outdo the achievements of genius, but its power to imitate, and greatly to outdo, the achievements of sleep. . . .

Myers thought "trance" was a "better word" because "to identify hypnotic with ordinary sleep is to underrate the modifiability of this almost infinite complex of sentient units which we call a man."

> I have called the act of falling asleep a passage into another phase of personality; but such passages are like the irregular heatings and coolings of a molten mass; . . . Trance is a further stage of sleep in the sense that it accomplishes more powerfully sleep's characteristic task; the subliminal plasticity is more marked, the subliminal control intenser; until hypnosis sometimes seems to be to sleep what sleep is to waking.

Myers (1898, p. 676) then discussed the relationship between hypnotism and somnambulism, and touched briefly on multiple personality before suggesting that

> many of the sanative changes which hypnotism effects are morally and physically so profound as to deserve the name of regenerations. . . . And be it

> remembered that these sanative regenerations are both for physician and for psychologist the *leading facts* of hypnotism—the facts which call most pressingly both for explanation and for development.

As for the problems of "suggestion" and "self-suggestion," Myers thought Bramwell had

> demonstrated, with all the advantage of actual experience, what some of us foreshadowed long ago—I mean the absolute insufficiency at present of any purely physiological explanation. No such explanation, indeed, now survives with sufficient vitality to be worth the trouble of killing anew.

Most hypnotists now believed "that hypnotic phenomena are due to suggestion, almost or quite alone," but it was also the case, as Bramwell had pointed out, that suggestion "cannot mean . . . mere ordinary persuasiveness."

> Dr. Bramwell (to take his own instance) is not the first person who has advised the dipsomaniac not to drink. If he succeeds in reforming such a patient, it is because he has managed to touch not his supraliminal reason, but his subliminal plasticity. He has set going some intelligent organic faculty in the man which has laid dormant till that moment, and which proves more effectual for healing than the man's conscious will.

How has Bramwell done this? Either he has "infused power, or he has merely evoked it." In the latter case "he has simply started a self-suggestion; has unlocked, as I say, some fountain of energy which was latent within the man's own being." On the other hand, Myers did not altogether dismiss the *infusion of power* theory—which he also called "transmissive influences"—because he had come to

> believe that the great mass of hypnotic results can be, and are, accomplished without them, especially and manifestly in the fairly common cases where the subject can bring on the trance for himself, with no external suggestion to help him.

Thus Myers also believed that hypnotism could produce an increase in organic energy although he could, for the time being, only conjecture

> that it is from the subliminal region that any new energy or new modification of energy must needs proceed. Beneath the threshold of waking consciousness there lies, not merely an unconscious complex of organic processes, but an intelligent vital control.
>
> To incorporate that profound control with our waking will is the great evolutionary end which hypnotism, by its group of empirical artifices, is beginning to help us to attain.

And then Myers (1898, pp. 675–76) offered one of his extended metaphors.

> In waking consciousness I am like the proprietor of a factory whose machinery I do not understand. My foreman—my subliminal self—weaves for me so many yards of broadcloth per diem (my ordinary vital processes) as a matter of course. If I want any pattern more complex, I have to shout my orders in the din of the factory, where only two or three inferior workmen hear me, and shift their looms in a small and scattered way. Such are the confined and capricious results of ordinary hypnotic suggestion. At certain intervals, indeed, the foreman stops most of the looms, and uses the freed power to stoke the engine and to oil the machinery. This, in my metaphor, is sleep; and it will be effective hypnotic trance if I can get the foreman to stop still more of the looms, come out of his private room, and attend to my orders—my self-suggestions—for their repair and rearrangement.

How was it possible to make suggestion "effective" to "our subliminal selves"? The answer was to be found not only in the hypnotic clinic but in "all forms of self-suggestion" which can be "practically found to remove and soothe the pains and weariness of large masses of common men." This occurred not just through the recognized forms of hypnotic suggestion, carried out by medical practitioners, but also through those "popular forms of self-suggestion" which could be found, for example, in the healing fountain of Lourdes, or through the power of Christian Science, "or mind cure, to use its less presumptuous name." Then skirting the many questions raised by the cures from Lourdes, Myers (1898, p. 677) suggested that the "vaguer impulse which prompts to mind cure[11] may prove more capable of adaptation to whatever may hereafter be learnt as to the true relation between man's central will and his bodily organism."

> What is now to be desired is that medical science should recognise that a new task has opened before her; that these hypnotic artifices, empirical as they may be, do yet lie in the true path of therapeutic progress; that hypnotism is no more a trick than education is a trick: but that just as education develops observation and memory, through alert attention, so hypnotism develops organic concentration and recuperation, through their adjuvant phase of sleep.
>
> Finally, if beneath the fanaticism and the extravagance of men blindly seeking relief from pain some glimmering truth makes way, that truth also it must be for science to adopt and to utilise, to clarify and to interpret. By one method or other—and her familiar method of widespread cautious experiment should surely be the best—science must subject to her own deliberate purposes that intelligent vital control, that reserve of energy, which lies beneath the conscious threshold, and works obscurely for the evolution of man.

And then in conclusion Myers alluded, tantalizingly, to the *infusion of power* theory in which the "subliminal relations between man and man play a real part in the production of hypnotic phenomena" (*JMS* 1899, Vol. 45, p. 205).

THE HYPNOTISM DISCUSSIONS

In the discussions that followed Dr. Yellowlees (1898, p. 677), physician superintendent at Glasgow Royal Asylum [Gartnavel], who had expressed hostility to hypnotism during the 1889 BMA hypnotism debates congratulated both men. He had been persuaded by Bramwell's accounts of extraordinary cures because he, himself, had "obtained some remarkable results from [his] own endeavours." Ultimately, however, his own hypnotic work had "been disappointing, chiefly because" he had "failed to hypnotise the very patients" who would have benefited the most. He thought his failures were due to his not persisting "in [his] attempts more than six or seven times, and his attempts had been chiefly among the insane, hence perhaps the very partial success." Professor Benedikt (1898, p. 677), from Vienna, adopting his by now familiar absolutist position, reminded his audience that he had experimented with hypnotism thirty years ago and while he acknowledged its reality he opposed its use because it had become dangerous and, as a "scientific movement," had "produced mysticism propagated by novelists and other writers."[12] Furthermore it

> may become dangerous to the nerves, to the intellect, to the strength of will, and to the character of patients. Hypnotism is also dangerous for the physician because he is easily deceived by the patients, and because he is exposed to great delusions. As the cases benefited are rare, there is no place for hypnotic specialists.

Dr. Mercier (1898, p. 678) took issue with Bramwell because he believed a subject *could* be persuaded to commit a crime especially if the operator made him do something illegal under the impression it was innocent. After all "why should not a man be induced to sign an important document under the suggestion that he was signing something of a totally different character, and of no importance?"

In his talk, Dr Woods (1898, pp. 677–78) claimed he had "treated over a 1,000 cases of disease by so-called suggestion" and had found it a "potent remedy." But it was not just functional nervous disorders he had benefited.

> Let us not forget that the nervous system is implicated in almost all disease, and in so far as we can influence it for good we can benefit the disease. Take the case of organic heart mischief. At first sight it may appear irrational—I had almost said ridiculous—to treat it by suggestion. We must remember, however, that in all cases of serious organic disease of the heart there is a strong nervous element; the patient is apt to be agitated, perhaps he sleeps badly, or there may be pain. Now, if we can soothe the nervous system,—secure sleep, and remove pain—we can do all this—we are going a long way to improve the patient's condition. Moreover, in addition to these general effects we can produce a direct

> and specific effect upon the heart by placing one hand upon the epigastrium and suggesting that the heart shall quiet down, and beat more slowly and calmly.

It is worth noting how common it was, during this period, for hypnotic practitioners to lay on hands (Tuckey 1903a, pp. 350–51; Freud 1909a, p. 25; Forel 1906, p. 60), although perhaps without any conscious awareness as to its religious or spiritual significance Then having mentioned other organic diseases which had benefited from hypnotic treatment Woods (1898, p. 678) noted:

> One word as to the necessity of sending the patient to sleep. This is, in my experience, by no means essential. I have cured many cases without it; we may often succeed in getting the patient into a receptive condition by making him relax all his muscles to the utmost, and composing himself to complete mental and bodily inactivity. I do not agree with Mr. Myers that hypnotic phenomena cannot be explained on physiological lines. Mr. Myers would appear to assume that the subliminal processes to which he refers are purely psychic. I contend that they must have a physiological basis. Time does not permit me to say more than this concerning Mr. Myers's valuable and interesting remarks.

Following the discussion a *BMJ* editorial commented, testily, that as the Section "has once more left the subject in *statu quo*" it hoped the subject would not occur again "until there is evidence that the profession generally sees clearly that hypnotism can be adopted as a therapeutic measure which is trustworthy in operation and appropriate in application." Damming Bramwell and Myers with faint praise, the *BMJ* (Anon 1898, p. 735, italics mine) opined that there was little to be gained by introducing the term "subliminal consciousness." "We might more correctly and more suggestively speak of the "fringes of consciousness." Then directly addressing Myer's comments about "the infusion of power," the *BMJ* noted:

> We require further information as to this telepathy before we can allow it to override physiology and pathology. The latest theory of the mobility of the branching neurons, their tentacles withdrawing and breaking contact on exhaustion, is much more satisfactory to the physician *trained in exact scientific method.*

The *BMJ* was also dubious about Bramwell's case histories because "his records appear to be extremely meagre, and do not prove his main contention, which would ascribe the results [of cure] to hypnotism." Bramwell, who had failed to acknowledge that hypnotism threatened will power, had glossed its dangers. And the *BMJ* concluded by agreeing first with Mercier—"The exponents of the hypnotic faith cannot have it both ways; they cannot urge that hypnotism is effective and yet not effective as may suit the argument of the moment,"—and then with Benedikt—"that hypnotism may become dangerous to the intellect, the will, and the character of the patient; and not free from danger to the physician who practises it, since he is so easily deceived by his subjects and so liable to gross delusions" (Anon 1898, p. 736).

In fact this *BMJ* editorial exposes a profound rift within the medical profession. On the one hand the 1898 hypnotism debates reveal that a significant body of medical psychologists, and members of the Association, were increasingly receptive to the use of hypnotism for therapeutic purposes including senior members of the Association and, in particular, by senior Asylum physicians like Woods, Robertson, and T. B. Hyslop (1899, p. 783),[13] the latter being medical superintendent of Bethlem and an SPR associate member. The conversion of Yellowlees, for example, is perhaps indicative. Set against this sea change was a die-hard core of BMA members clinging to increasingly outdated anti-hypnotic and anti-psychological positions. Although the materialists had been roundly defeated during the 1890–1893 hypnotism debates, the *BMJ* still took it upon itself to articulate their views and present them as if they were representative of the vast majority of the medical profession. But, as we shall see shortly, their pontifications and admonitions did little or nothing to stem the tide running in hypnotism's favor because they clearly failed, for example, to prevent the subject being discussed, yet again, at the 1899 Annual Meeting when Bramwell delivered another key note paper this time on the "Mental Conditions involved in Post-Hypnotic Appreciation of Time."

THE BIRTH OF THE SUBCONSCIOUS

In *The Psychology of Suggestion*, which was completed shortly before Myers's address to the 1898 BMA Annual Meeting, Boris Sidis (1898, pp. 2–3, italics mine) said:

> Gourney [*sic*], James, Myers, and others, have done much toward the elucidation of the obscure phenomena of the subconscious. Psychology is especially indebted to the genius of Myers for his wide and comprehensive study of the phenomena of the subconscious, or what [Myers] calls the manifestation of the subliminal self.

Although Sidis acknowledged that Myers had "done much towards the elucidation of the obscure phenomena" which lay beneath "the ordinary threshold of consciousness" he could not accept the way in which Myers had theorized "'this unknown *quantity*, this lower level of mental life.'" As Sidis pointed out: "The only drawback in Myers's concept of the subliminal self is that he conceives it as a metaphysical entity, as a kind of a cosmic self."

Of course what he really meant was that Myers's concept of the subliminal self failed to conform to strict scientific criteria—or to the "algebraic"—as Maudsley (1867, p. 224) might have put it. And because Sidis believed that "the phenomena under investigation do not warrant the hypothesis of metaphysical entities" he preferred, instead, to use the concept of the subconscious which was quite different from Myers's concept of the subliminal. Sidis was not alone in these criticisms because there were other psychologists, perhaps following Sidis, who also wanted to strip Myers's Subliminal Self of its metaphysical components and then, having appropriated what was left of Meyers's "submerged life of the mind" (Jastrow 1906, p. 3), rebrand it under the sign of the Subconscious. Thus although Myers's "Subliminal Self" was to remain an essential theoretical tool for psychical researchers it was already a spent force by the time of Myers's death as increasing numbers of medical and experimental psychologists turned, instead, to Sidis's psychically liberated concept of the subconscious to explain and articulate that obscure region which lay beneath the thresholds of consciousness (Feilding 1899, p. 142). Herein lies the beginning of that apparently unbridgeable divide between the psychical and the psychological.

NOTES

1. Producing power or force, especially nervous or muscular power or activity. The concept, or theory, of the "inhibitory or dynamogenic faculty" was probably first developed by Brown-Séquard then taken up by Féré (i.e., 1886, pp. 212–14), Bernheim (1890, p. 138), Tuckey (1891a, p. 113) and others. See also Smith (1992, pp. 131–33).

2. The reference is to "the first insane patient treated by Voisin" in 1880 (Bramwell 1903, pp. 212–13).

3. J. Shaw (1902, pp. 355, 356 and 361) subsequently advocated "suggestion" and "hypnotism" where other means failed.

4. Thomas Harrington Tuke (1826–1888), Superintendent of the Manor House Chiswick, son-in-law of Dr John Conolly. No relation to D. H. Tuke.

5. J. B. Tuke, President Royal College of Physicians (Edinburgh), lecturer on Insanity at the School of Medicine (Royal College, Edinburgh).

6. Sir James Crichton (-) Browne delivered the address in 1890.

7. Robertson, who joined the Association in 1887, became its President in 1922.

8. Benedikt (1898, p. 677) says: "Then came the delirious epoch of Nancy, in which no nonsense was too great to be believed."

9. Ernest Hart, generally considered the main opponent of hypnotism, had died in January that year.

10. By 1911 Woods was a GP and head of a Nursing Home in North London.

11. Myers and Myers (1894, p. 161) suggest "*Mind-cure* denies that matter exists, or that evil exists, and heals the patient by inspiring him with the conviction that he is a pure spirit, unassailable by disease or pain. The *Faith-cure* teaches that pain and disease, although really existing, can be dispelled by an act of faith in the Divine power."

12. On this point see Bodie (1905, pp. 84f).

13. Theophilus Bulkeley Hyslop (1864–1933) was born in Inverness and in 1881, aged 17, was a medical student in Stretton House Private Asylum, Shropshire, owned and run by his father William. The 1881 Census lists 31 male patients variously described as lunatics, imbeciles and idiots. Hyslop subsequently worked in Wakefield and then as a Resident Physician at Bethlem and Superintendent at the Bethlem Convalescent Hospital. He was also a Lecturer on Mental Disease and Physiology at St Mary's. He was also President of the Society for the Study of Inebriety [SSI] (1910–1912), of which Jones was a member (1904–1907) Hyslop was also President of the Section at the 1910 *BMA* Annual Meeting. By 1911 he was in private practice in Langham Place, West London. A review of Hyslop's book, *Mental Physiology*, noted "Above all it may be looked upon as a kind of protest against the abject materialism which has become so much the fashion in psychology" (*BMJ* March 14, 1896, p. 666), while Stoddard (1933, p. 347) said of him: "It is therefore clear that [Hyslop] was regarded as a great authority on mental disease, and his lectures at St. Mary's Hospital achieved much popularity." Not to be confused with James Hyslop, secretary of the American SPR.

Part II

MIND CURES

Let me remind you, that improvement in medicine is not to be derived, only from colleges and universities. Systems of physic are the productions of men of genius and learning; but those facts which constitute real knowledge, are to be met with in every walk of life. Remember how many of our most useful remedies have been discovered by quacks. Do not be afraid, therefore, of conversing with them, and of profiting by their ignorance and temerity in the practice of physic. Medicine has its Pharisees, as well as religion. But the spirit of this sect is as unfriendly to the advancement of medicine, as it is to Christian charity. By conversing with quacks, we may convey instruction to them, and thereby lessen the mischief they might otherwise do to society. But further in the pursuit of medical knowledge, let me advise you to converse with nurses and old women. They will often suggest facts in the history and cure of diseases which have escaped the most sagacious, observers of nature. Even Negroes and Indians have sometimes stumbled upon discoveries in medicine. Be not ashamed to inquire into them. There is yet one more means of information in medicine which should not be neglected, and that is, to converse with persons who have recovered from indispositions without the aid of physicians. Examine the strength and exertions of nature in these cases, and mark the plain and home-made remedy to which they ascribe their recovery. I have found this to be a fruitful source of instruction, and have been led to conclude, that if every man in a city, or a district, could be called upon to relate to persons appointed to receive and publish his narrative, an exact account of the effects of those remedies which accident or whim has suggested to him, it would furnish a very useful book in medicine. To preserve the facts thus obtained, let me advise you to record them in a book to be kept for that purpose. There is one more advantage that will probably attend the inquiries that have been mentioned; you may discover diseases, or symptoms of diseases, or even laws of the animal economy, which have no place in our systems of nosology, or in our theories of physic. (Rush 1789, pp. 319–20)

Chapter 4

The London Psycho-Therapeutic Society (1900–1915)

'The perfect observer . . . will keep his eyes open in all divisions of knowledge, that they may be struck at once by every event which, according to accepted theories, ought not to happen, for these are the facts which serve as clues to new discoveries.' (Hallam 1900, p. 49)[1]

ARTHUR HALLAM AND THE HEALING FORCE OF THE ORGANISM

Arthur Hallam (1878–1948), the youngest of four children, was born in Leeds to Tom Steedman Hallam (1843–1921), a coachman in domestic service, and Mary, neé Cooper (b.1845). Shortly after arriving in London, probably in 1897, Hallam[2] began working as a journalist and, in his spare time, studied hypnotism and mesmerism. His researches prompted him to write a series of articles which were then published, in the *Humanitarian*,[3] under his own name, (Hallam, 1899a; 1899b; 1900; 1901a;1901b). However his first contribution may have been an unsigned review of Alice Feilding's *Faith Healing and Christian Science* (1899),[4] a book which both Barrett (*Proceedings* 1901, Vol. 15, p. 293n) and Paget (1909, p. 120) thought "admirable."[5] In her chapter on "Mental Therapeutics," Feilding offers an impressive survey of the history and positive state of "psycho-therapeutics," a discipline which she believed was now "honourably established in medical science" and "studied in all its forms by professional experts and specialists." In this respect, as well as others, Feilding's book offers an important corrective to those subsequent studies which have effectively dismissed or ignored the early history of this subject. In his review, Hallam (1899a, p. 374) noted the sudden upsurge in reports of faith cures which, he thought, were due, in part, to "the general re-action against that crude materialism which had so long held the field, especially in science." He also agreed, whole-heartedly, with Feilding who claimed that 'mind healing' was now firmly on the agenda and at last receiving "the scientific attention" it deserved. In discussing the wider question, which also included "so-called Christian Science," Hallam (1899a, p. 375), still following Feilding, suggested all types of faith healing operated with "the same underlying principle, the same basic truth—namely the power of suggestion, the superiority of mind over matter."

> Science has something to learn from, quacks, charlatans, Christian Scientists, Catholic-miracle workers and the rest. After examining and sifting the cures said to be worked by these, and making every allowance for fraud and trickery, no impartial investigator can doubt that remarkable therapeutic results are obtained, *and have been obtained*, by means other than those hitherto admitted by doctors to be rational, medical, and scientific.

But what Hallam failed to notice, perhaps because he did not know it, was that Feilding's interest in the subject had been aroused by her cousin, Lady Bath, who was "one of the earliest converts to [Christian Science] in this country"[6] (*Leeds Mercury* 14 October 1899, p. 17; *BCWG* 12 October 1899, p. 5) and that Alice's mother, Lady Louisa Feilding, was a member of the SPR.

In the first of his signed articles, published a few months later, Hallam (1899b, pp. 419–20) argued for the "adoption" of hypnotism "as a remedial agent" and pointed to the "overwhelming testimony from medical authorities that hypnotism may be safely employed not only as a curative agent but as a means of developing mental powers which are either weak or apparently non-existence." Hallam also discussed hypnotism from the theosophical point of view and although, so far as I can tell, he never openly proclaimed himself a theosophist the weight of his comments both in this and his subsequent *Humanitarian* articles strongly suggest he was, at the very least, a fellow traveller of the Theosophical Society.[7] Hallam (1899b, p. 421) explained that theosophists believe "we possess a consciousness independent of the body, and therefore a soul beyond all cavil or dispute." As there was "an asymmetry in evolution" men developed in different degrees leading, among other things, to an "asymmetry in mental energy" and this explained why it was possible for "one will to control another." But this imbalance had important ramifications because, according to the theosophist, when a hypnotist compels another to obey

> he subjects [that person] to an actual force conveyed by a vehicle of matter; or, in other words, the hypnotist directs a part of his own "nerve-fluid" upon and into the nervous system of his subject, where it remains an actual force, establishing new and modifying centres of vibration which act in obedience to the

ideation accompanying it. By this means the consciousness of the [subject's] ego is prevented from controlling its own sense organs; in fact it is a similar process to that which takes place when chloroform or morphine is administered.

It was this power of control which required theosophists to work with absolute integrity: "Purity of motive is therefore one of the first considerations in the practise of hypnotism or mesmerism." Hallam (1899b, pp. 421–22) also believed theosophists had to exercise extreme caution because once somebody had been "thoroughly hypnotised" they would never, again, regain "perfectly free will and entirely normal consciousness." And while Hallam (1899b, p. 422) acknowledged that most medical authorities claimed there was no evidence for this view, he, nonetheless, thought there was a path between these two diametrically opposed positions and pointed to the conciliatory approach set out, a few years earlier, by the blind American physician and homeopath Dr Cocke (1863–1900) who said

> that hypnotism is not a magical power by which one man can permanently control or rule the destinies of another . . . and yet certain states of mental enfeeblement may be produced, not by hypnotism, *per se*, but by the credulity which was a part of the subject's nature before he submitted to the process of hypnotization. (Cocke 1894, p. 57)[8]

Although Hallam (1899b, p. 422) accepted the theosophist belief that hypnotists had the power to make individuals commit crimes he believed its "real danger" lay "in its unintelligent use by those who do not understand its far-reaching effects, nor grasp the responsibility which the acquisition of these latent powers places upon them." Hallam (1899b, pp. 423–24) was, therefore, convinced, "from a theosophical standpoint," that one should only study and practice hypnotism from

> the purest motives, for it is motive alone which creates the distinction between black and white magic. There must be a perfect and complete altruism, an utter abandonment of self, before the induction of hypnosis can benefit either the operator or the subject, as the farther one retreats within the unfathomable depths of his being, the stronger and more powerful for good or evil becomes the forces which he employs.[9]

Thus once the operator accepts "as correct the theosophic principle," he must also accept "that in compelling another to obey his will the hypnotist transmits to the nervous system of the person influenced a part of his own 'nerve-fluid.'" It then "follows as a matter of course that the perfect health of the operator is essential to the well-being of the subject" because "there is an invariable relationship between condition of the blood and the 'nerve-fluid' possessed by the individual." If "the health of the hypnotist" is in any way imperfect "the persons coming under his influence would suffer thereby to a proportionate extent," and because being in the *presence* of a healthy person was often sufficient to confer health benefits on the sick it was also essential that no suggestion should ever be given unless agreed, beforehand, with the person to be hypnotized.

In his next article, exploring the differences between hypnotism and mesmerism, Hallam (1900, pp. 425–26) complained that the showmen had given mesmerism a bad name "and undoubtedly upon these men rests the responsibility of bringing mesmerism to a depth synonymous with all that was depressing and contemptible." As for hypnotism, Hallam noted that, at first, Braid "was disinclined to accept La Fontain's explanation that a subtle fluid passed from the mesmerist to the person operated upon" and this led Braid to conclude that, ultimately, any hypnotic "results obtained were due to physiological modifications of the nervous system." Braid called this new theory "hypnotism" although he also "found that suggestion was sufficient to produce hallucination, and it is this fact which had led later experimentalists to believe that to the feature of suggestion nearly all the 'fallacies' of the mesmeric theory are due." Hallam (1900, p. 427), however, also thought that as most adherents of Braidism believed that hypnotism's main function was as an anesthetic it was the introduction of chloroform that had propelled it into abeyance. Despite the current triumph of "hypnotism the old theories and practises of mesmerism remained and still had a claim to be taken seriously." Hallam (1900, p. 428) then turned to the "admirable treatise on 'The Rationale of Mesmerism,'" by the theosophist Alfred Percy Sinnett (1840–1921) whose book offered a radically different version of the history to the one written by the adherents of the Nancy School.[10] Sinnett (1892, p. 8) argued that Braid had

> invented a method of thinking which enabled people, thus inclined to handle and talk about some of the phenomena of mesmerism, without setting themselves in opposition to medical orthodoxy and without giving up the ungrateful cry that Mesmer was an imposter. . . . Mr Braid by a bold manoeuvre, possessed himself of some, at any rate among the facts, and, by putting a forged ticket upon them, justified himself before the world for continuing to vilify their real discoveries—for continuing to swim at ease with the stream of bigotry—and so afford his *confrères* an opportunity of escaping from the inconvenience of being at war with notorious experience, without incurring the humiliation of confessing they had previously been in the wrong.[11]

Hallam (1900, pp. 428–29), still following Sinnett (1892, p. 13), also claimed that Braid was simply "glorified . . . as the man who extracted the real truth of the subject from the confusion left by foolish enthusiasts or impostors." But Braid, in reality, had simply

> enlarged upon a portion of an old discovery, and presented it to the world in such a way as to make the whole proceeding most contemptible. As Mr Sinnett observes, the reasoning of Braid would have been blown to atoms by contemporary critics if it had been opposed to, instead of chiming in with, conventional prejudice. Far from placing the investigation of mesmeric phenomena upon a scientific basis, Braid and his successors have, in the opinion of mesmerists, degraded an inquiry which was opened in a scientific spirit, in an attempt to bolster up an unintelligent prejudice.

Hallam (1900, pp. 424, 425–26) claimed Braidists had built their theory upon purely physiological foundations and, by rejecting psychology, had failed to expand their researches.[12] Mesmerists, on the other hand, were able to "carry [their] investigations into a much higher region of consciousness" thereby enabling them to explore such phenomena as "clairvoyance," "somnambulism" and "trance."

> Mesmerism is therefore an important factor of psychological research and experimentation, for in the higher stages of the sleep we have at our command all the conditions necessary for minute observation and inquiry . . . the further one penetrates beyond the threshold of consciousness, the finer and more impressionable does the sensibility of the subject become. For this reason alone, the application of clairvoyance, mesmeric or natural, to personal or business ends is very undesirable."

Through, what appears to have been, his deep spiritual and theosophical beliefs, Hallam (1900, pp. 426 and 427) argued that mesmerism could only become recognized as worthy of serious investigations once the mesmerists had succeeded in eliminating "the pretensions of society entertainers, self-advertising 'professors' and individuals of this class." Arguing for the importance of mesmerism "as a remedial, educational and moral agent" Hallam nonetheless believed that its real power lay in "its capability of being utilised as a medium through which to study the human enigma, or the composite nature of man." Advances could only be made, therefore, when mesmerism, allied to experimental psychology, was placed "on an equality with physics and chemistry" so that scientists might then investigate the "phenomena concerning the superphysical realms of nature." Hallam's vision (1900, p. 429) appears to have been inspired by *The Philosophy of Mysticism* in which Du Prel (1889) argued that "man is possessed of a consciousness higher and more expansive than the one with which he is familiar in the normal state—in other words that the whole of the consciousness of the human being does not function through the waking brain."[13]

In the last of his signed *Humanitarian* articles, Hallam (1901b, p. 433) repeats his earlier claims that modern-day "hypnotists attribute all their phenomena to physiological modifications of the nervous system, the power suggestion has over a person in the semi-conscious, hypnotic state." At the same time, he also notes how Mesmerists had identified the "invisible magnetic fluid or subtle force, more or less universal in degree, which passes from them to the person operated upon." By juxtaposing the hypnotic and mesmeric systems, Hallam suggested that the dispute between them was not about the results they obtained but about their divergent explanations of the forces which brought about those results. His article, was, therefore, a plea to mesmerists and hypnotists to open their minds, learn from each other and thereby discover new and exciting areas for exploration. In the case of education, for example, hypnotism could help both adults and children to conquer bad habits and addictions. Here Hallam (1901b, pp. 435 and 436) thought suggestion was better than mesmerism because "Hypnotic suggestion appears to be of itself an educational force, by the application of which mental and moral energies may be given the desired trend—often with apparently miraculous results." But hypnotism had its limitations because it could only facilitate the release of talents and abilities already latent in the individual: it could not create or manufacture talents that did not already exist.

> It follows therefore, that to be successful the hypnotist should understand the factors which predispose persons to excess and abuse, so as to be able to exercise discrimination in the cases coming under his notice. (Hallam 1901b, p. 437)

Although Hallam claimed to offer a balanced view as between mesmerism and modern-day hypnotism, the weight of his arguments and his obvious affinity with theosophy, suggest that his sympathies lay squarely with the mesmerists. And although I have found no specific evidence to suggest that Hallam ever drew directly from Myers's writings, it is almost certain he was influenced by them. Myers, for example, had also insisted that as there was insufficient research to settle the hypnotism versus mesmerism debate it was imperative for researchers to do everything possible to keep both theories alive. Kelley (2007, pp. 90, 93–94, and 104), for example, has noted:

> Myers and Gurney believed that the mesmerists might have been on the right track, but that instead of being a physical phenomenon, the influence might be a psychological one, some kind of "a specialised relation between two minds," a resonant link, or a "subtle inter-communication" between subliminal minds.

The mesmerists described this "specialised relation between two minds" as *the rapport*, which Gurney and Myers subsequently articulated as: "This notion of a psychological link between minds," which then "became the basis of Myers's concept of telepathy, and indeed, his concept of all supernormal interaction" even though he realized that the nature of such a subtle intercommunication between two minds remained entirely unknown. Although essentially outside the scope of this study it is nonetheless worth contemplating how the mesmeric concept of *the rapport* might be heard to echo through those psychoanalytic explorations subsequently framed, or conceptualized, by reference to the theories of the transference and the countertransference. (Ferenczi 1916, pp. 31ff).

THE OLD MESMERIST: GEORGE WYLD

Although Hallam (1912a, p. 86; 1914, pp. 63–64) subsequently claimed that by 1900 he was already "seriously impressed with the necessity of establishing a society in London to deal exclusively with the subject" of psychotherapeutics,[14] the evidence suggests a more complex story. During the Spring and Summer of 1900 *Light*, the preeminent British spiritualist journal, founded by Dawson Rogers and W. Stainton Moses, ran a series of articles which discussed the growing trend of the "Mental Science school of thinkers and teachers" who now argued that

> "man is a spirit using a body"; that the centre of power and growth is within: that the mind can affect the body, and that by will-ability and psychic concentration we can largely modify adverse conditions in our physical form, contribute to our own restoration to vigorous health, and regain the power for natural enjoyment of life and its employments and beauties. (*Light* July 7, 1900, p. 322)

These articles, and the correspondence they triggered, can be read as part of a wider spiritual and religious challenge to that rampant late-nineteenth-century materialism, and which, in turn, inspired a number of correspondents to propose establishing some kind of Psychic Hospital in Britain. Although those proposals appear to have come to nothing, there was clearly something in the air which Hallam, through his particular genius, now sought to make concrete.

During October and November 1900, Mrs Jane Stannard (1865–1944),[15] a recent delegate at the August 1900 Psychological Congress in Paris (Stannard 1900a), was invited, by *Light*, to act as their Special Correspondent during the forthcoming International Spiritualistic and Occult Congress [Spiritualist Congress], also in Paris.[16] Stannard (1900d) subsequently filed five detailed and illuminating Reports from the Congress[17] and Hallam, for one, having become much interested in Stannard's description of the "Magnetic Section," wrote to *Light* (November 17, 1900, p. 551) pointing out how the "value of magnetism was first demonstrated in London by Baron Du Pôtet and

Dr. Elliotson" over sixty years ago, but had now fallen into obscurity. So he was moved to suggest the need for the "establishment of a society for the study and practise of magnetism" as a way of "bringing the subject more forcibly before the scientific world" and, at the same time, "to dissociate it in the minds of the multitude from trickery and superstition." Hallam also suggested that if there was a sufficient number who wished to meet and discuss the subject he "should be pleased to render what little assistance lay in [his] power." Apparently, the only reply came from Mrs Stannard, who offered her support if Hallam could arrange a meeting (*Light* November 24, 1900, p. 560). In a second letter, Hallam pointed "out that a meeting of two would not lead to very encouraging results" and he renewed his appeal for the setting up of "a magnetic society in London," which would help facilitate "an excellent opportunity to experts in the science to meet and compare notes" and which would, at the same time, help further undermine the "foundations of present day materialism." (*Light* December 8, 1900, p. 584). Although Hallam subsequently claimed nobody was willing to take the initiative, his second letter prompted not only a reply from E.C.C. of Guildford but also an editorial comment which noted that Hallam had received "interesting communications offering assistance in the formation of a Magnetic Society in London." (*Light* December 22, 1900, p. 615). This correspondence then prompted him to write a third letter defending himself by explaining that he had used the term magnetism in an attempt to avoid using the terms hypnotism and mesmerism which he thought would only alienate his readers. So he now appealed to the opposing schools of Mesmer and Braid to come

> together in a society which aimed at the elucidation of known facts, the discovery of new truths, and a fuller comprehension of the science in all its varying aspects. Rigid adherence to one particular theory, and unrestricted condemnation of all in opposition to it, have already been too long in vogue, and I sincerely urge all who have the interests of the subject, as a whole, at heart—no matter whether hypnotists, mesmerists, or magnetists, or merely students—to see if, by a careful discussion in meetings assembled, means can be devised to make a dawn of a new century also the dawn of a new era for this most interesting and important science. (*Light* December 29, 1900, p. 624)

Hallam (1912a, p. 86; 1914, pp. 63–64) subsequently claimed that when this letter produced no tangible results he tried "by private correspondence to induce some prominent persons to take the matter up." But William Crookes, A. J. Balfour, Sir Oliver Lodge, Professor Barrett, J. M. Bramwell, and Lloyd Tuckey all "courteously but firmly declined to have anything to do with the movement, although some of them cordially wished it success." It is noticeable that all the names Hallam listed were prominent SPR members which perhaps also underlines that Hallam was attempting to find ways of piecing together those fractional divides between mesmerists, spiritualists, theosophists, and psychic researchers who had effectively split asunder during the mid- to late 1880s. Ultimately, however, Hallam's only encouraging response came from Dr Wyld "who, after private interviews and friendly talks, offered the use of his drawing room in Westbourne Street and promised to provide tea if I would organise, at my own expense, a Sunday afternoon meeting."

George Wyld (1821–1906), yet another Scotsman, was born and educated in Aberdeen where he eventually qualified MD in 1851. While studying in Edinburgh, in the late 1830s, Wyld (1880, pp. 17, 19 and 118) met Mr John Dove who introduced him "to the marvels of mesmerism and clairvoyance" and, following these and other encounters, Wyld became interested in Spiritualism in 1855.[18] A founder member of the SPR, in 1882, Wyld served on its Council and, for a time, was secretary to its Committee on Mesmerism. Wyld subsequently said of himself that he had been "a practical mesmerist from the year 1839–40" but had never used it professionally choosing to make his living practicing medicine in London.[19] Some time around 1886, when it became clear that the differences between spiritualists and psychical researchers had become irreconcilable, many spiritualists severed their links with the SPR although Wyld appears to have continued his membership until early 1891.[20] Wyld was also an active theosophist and, for a short time, president of the British Theosophical Society (1880–1882) and although he broke with Madam Blavatsky, probably around 1883, he never abandoned his theosophical beliefs.

It is perhaps worth speculating why Wyld, retired but still widely regarded as the foremost exponent of mesmerism in Britain, should have been attracted to support Hallam. Apart from Hallam's undoubted enthusiasm there was clearly a shared vision which ran deeper than their mutual interests in Theosophy. According to Oppenheim (1985, pp. 139, 140, 232, 235) Wyld was a man of two parts; "utterly preoccupied with spirit as the 'fundamental substance of the Universe'" but also "a man of practical concerns who wanted to see a variety of social improvements, for reasons of man's health and moral well-being." To this end, Wyld "challenged orthodox views and assumptions" and having "fundamentally opposed any materialist interpretation of the body's functions" he "embraced . . . a view that emphasised the intangible vital essence of each person, the distinct mind existing apart from bone, muscle and flesh."[21] In many respects this could also describe Hallam. But also important, for this story, is that Wyld had been an active member of the short-lived London Hypnotic Society [LHS], inspired by Carl Hansen in late 1889 (*NR,* February 27, 1890, p. 103) and thus he may well have seen, in Hallam, the possibility for resurrecting the LHS, or something very much like it. But, for whatever reasons, Wyld agreed to lend Hallam his support. So Hallam placed an advertisement in *Light* (February 16, 1901, p. 81) and sent out innumerable cards of invitation with the result that on February 10, 1901, between sixty and seventy people gathered at Wyld's house

> to consider the advisability of establishing in London a society for the systematic study and investigation of Animal Magnetism, Mesmerism, Hypnotism, Christian Science, Faith Healing, and Higher Thought Healing.

But, as Hallam recalled, many years later,

> the practical result was almost *nil*, as Dr Wyld who presided, disapproved of [Hallam's] suggestion .. to form a committee there and then, and of course, in deference to the veteran gentleman, the matter was not pressed. Dr Wyld subsequently himself called a committee of six or eight friends (myself included) to further discuss the project but the meeting ended as it began, nothing of a practical nature being done.[22]

What Hallam (1914, p. 64) learned, however, was that among those who showed the most interest in the project

> there was a strong spiritualistic element, and a tendency to regard magnetic healing as part and parcel of, and inseparably connected with the spiritualistic movement. Dr Wyld, as a veteran spiritualist, adopted this attitude, and altogether failed to realise the importance of keeping the proposed new society free from sect or creed of any kind. He eventually declared himself in favour of the society being formed in connection with the London Spiritualist Alliance, a course to which I was very strongly opposed.

Shortly after the 10 February meeting, Hallam noticed that Mrs Stannard was booked, on 1 March, to speak to the London Spiritualist Alliance [LSA][23] on her proposal for "The Need of an Institute for the Psychical and Magnetic Treatment of Disease." He therefore immediately joined the LSA so he could attend and, if necessary, speak to that meeting. Dr Wyld was voted to the chair and, at the end of the discussion "to the astonishment of several, moved that a society be formed in connection with the Alliance and not left to those outside." Wyld's proposal was seconded and supported by several of those present.

> I had no alternative [said Hallam] but to speak against the proposal, pointing out that magnetic and mental healing, in fact psycho-therapeutics generally, were a separate and distinct science and to be associated with Spiritualism would not help to gain for that science due recognition; whilst above all, although there might be many spiritualists interested in healing, there were as many if not more, persons of other sects also interested, and in order not to alienate them it was essential that the new society should stand alone.

Despite Hallam's passionate arguments Wyld's proposal was carried although Dawson Rogers, President of the LSA, reminded the meeting that as the resolution was not binding the Council would have to give it further consideration.[24] Hallam now realized that if he was going to achieve anything he would have to move fast so, together with Mrs Stannard, he "drafted a scheme for the formation of a separate and distinct society "and, having secured promises from about a dozen people," arranged a meeting at the Frascati Restaurant where

> the scheme, aims and objects were adopted, and the organisation duly constituted under the title of the [London] Psycho-Therapeutic Society [PTS]. No more was heard of Dr Wyld's proposal; suffice it to add that notwithstanding his divergent views I cannot but feel grateful to him for coming forward at his advanced age and taking the interest he did in the movement.

At the first Frascati meeting, four people enrolled into the new Society: Arthur Lovell,[25] George Spriggs, Arthur Hallam and Jane Stannard. They were joined, not long afterward, by Mrs A. Gordon who "had seen Bernheim perform some remarkable cures." (*HR* May 1910, p. 51). Hallam, having been voted honorary secretary, sent out a circular letter to the Press asking for support. Somewhat exceptionally *The Lancet* (May 4, 1901, p. 1292), carried part of his letter:[26]

> that at a meeting of medical men and others interested in the study and application of psycho-magnetics, mesmerism, hypnotism, and kindred psychic and mental forces, held at the Frascati Restaurant,[27] London, on April lst last, it was unanimously decided to establish an organisation under the title of the London Psycho-Therapeutic Society. The society has in view, amongst other objects, the systematic study and investigation of the psychic and mental forces upon such lines as may be considered desirable, and it is hoped to establish central headquarters where the poor may be freed from those diseases especially susceptible to psychic and mental treatment. The society does not propose to be in any way antagonistic to existing scientific and sectarian bodies interested in these subtle forces. Rather it is desired to draw into one society representatives of all the various schools of thought.

But there was a sting in *The Lancet*'s tail when it delighted in pointing to the inaugural date—April Fool's Day! Hallam, however, saw it as a most "auspicious date" (*HR* April 1908, p. 41), and did not care they had been ridiculed in the Press because "those who were sufficiently interested" noticed the announcements and began contacting them (*HR* October 1901, p. 2).[28]

The PTS then made arrangements to use the London Reform Union's address, in Trafalgar Buildings, Charing Cross:

> Six or seven members would attend and discuss all manner of subjects excepting that for which the Society had been formed, and then depart no wiser than before. Indeed, at the outset it was most difficult to keep to the broad lines of scientific inquiry where so many and diverse views were represented and when the phenomena of mesmerism and hypnotism were but little understood. (Hallam 1914, p. 100)

GEORGE SPRIGGS, ARTHUR HALLAM, THE PSYCHO-THERAPEUTIC SOCIETY AND ITS JOURNAL

George Spriggs (1850–1912) was born in Greetham, Rutland (East Midlands), to George and Mary Ann Spriggs and was the second eldest of five sisters and a brother. The 1851 census records Spriggs' father, George senior, a farm laborer employed by his brother-in-law William Bothworth. The 1861 census notes him working as a wagoner. George (junior), probably left home during his early teens and, after periods living and working in London, Brighton and Tunbridge Wells, found his way to Cardiff, where, in 1875, he made the acquaintance of Charles Baker, an enthusiastic Spiritualist (*EE* August 12, 1892, p. 2). After several spiritualist experiences Spriggs met Mr Rees Lewis who invited him to join the Cardiff "Circle of Light" where Spriggs was "developed . . . [becoming] a medium for most marvellous and convincing materialisation phenomena." (TW nd, p. 13). In 1880 when John Carson returned to Australia from his trip to Cardiff he "reported what he had seen to his Spiritualist friends" and, between them, they invited Spriggs and Spriggs's friend Mr Smart to visit them in Australia and sent them £80 for the journey. After six years of working in Melbourne, Spriggs found that "the materialisation phenomena were waning, whereupon "séances were held for the 'direct Voice' manifestations, which were less exhausting."

> After a time Mr. Spriggs was given his choice by his spirit friends of either continuing his séances for materialisations or being used by them for diagnosis of diseases and healing. Wisely, we think, he chose the latter, and speedily an extensive practice was built up, hosts of persons receiving undoubted benefit from the advice and remedies they received. (*Light* March 16, 1912, p. 127)

Spriggs continued to cultivate and exercise "the clairvoyant power for the diagnosis of disease and the prescription of remedies, in which beneficent work he was so successful that for some nine or ten years he had to devote to it his whole time and strength." (*Light* March 30, 1912, p. 147). Spriggs subsequently recalled:

> I am not interfered with, and the doctors are, on the whole, more friendly than not.

> Some of them, indeed, occasionally seek my assistance. My work is almost entirely to diagnose and prescribe, both of which I do by the aid of my clairvoyant mediumship. I give prescriptions and supply herbal medicines, but write out for my clients what is to be obtained at the chemist's. (*Light* 26 October 1895, p. 520)[29]

After returning briefly to Britain in 1895,[30] Spriggs finally returned and settled in London in May 1900 (*Light*, April 21, 1900, p. 182; May 12, 1900, p. 219) whereupon he offered his services to the LSA as a medium for the diagnosis of disease.

> Every Thursday there is a little group of spiritualists waiting for the services of Mr. Spriggs at the office of the Spiritualist Alliance in St. Martin's-lane, and psychical diagnosis promises to become a popular feature of London spiritualism. According to the official announcement, 'no fee is charged, but Mr. Spriggs suggests that every consultant should make a contribution of at least 5s to the funds of the alliance.' (*Examiner* November 20, 1903, p. 3)

A large number of LSA Members and Associates were said to have profited from the advice received from Spriggs's "control."

From the beginning Hallam (1912, p. 138) and Spriggs developed an easygoing relationship working "together in perfect harmony": Spriggs concentrating on healing and Hallam on administration. Although occasionally offering healing Hallam devoted most of his energies to building the Society: organizing lectures, meetings, and classes; networking, campaigning, distributing publicity, and canvasing the local and regional press. So the *Cheltenham Chronicle* (June 8, 1901) commenting on Hallam's recent *Humanitarian* article noted:

> "Not only may dull minds be brightened, unbalanced minds adjusted, gifted minds empowered to develop their talents, but moral and social habits may be favourably influenced, evil-disposed tendencies permanently restrained and undesirable traits of character satisfactorily changed". . . . If this be so can anything be more desirable than the speedy application of hypnotism to some of the disreputable characters which are unhappily prevalent among us?

But Hallam (1914, p. 100) also had wider ambitions and, with his characteristic energy, enthusiasm and vision, he persuaded the new Committee to finance a Journal which he edited and published almost single-handed. This was the *Psycho-Therapeutic Journal* [*PTJ*] (1901–1906) subsequently renamed *The Health Record [HR]* (1907–1915)[31] which was launched in late 1901. The first issue, consisting of four pages, was published in October; the second, with eight pages, in January 1902 and thereafter it appeared monthly until 1912 when it started running into financial difficulties. From the beginning Hallam (1914, p. 100) saw the journal as a means for promoting, proselytizing, and campaigning not just for the society but also for his own particular vision of universal health which included psychical and spiritual healing. Spriggs (*HR* July 1910, p. 83) confirmed that the Journal "was a great advertisement for the society, and was doing splendid missionary work." And while it is difficult to gauge its reach the *PTJ,* and subsequently *HR*, appear to have had influence well beyond its circulation.

In the first issue Hallam set out what he saw to be the relationship between the PST and the medical profession claiming the PTS was a campaigning organization offering a radically different model for health. And being in the vanguard of a growing popular movement for mental healing, they welcomed open dialogue and cooperation with anyone who chose to engage.

> But with one or two exceptions the medical journals do not appear to regard the movement with any degree of satisfaction, seeing that it is not the entire creation of orthodox medical men. This irrational and prejudiced attitude is much to be regretted, for medical men might well devote more of their time to the investigation of psychic and mental forces generally, since it is they who are able to make the best use of them. Hitherto the majority of English doctors have maintained a stolid indifference to everything outside the pale of orthodox physical science, and it has been left to a few to experiment in connection with mesmerism, hypnotism and similar subjects. But the medical faculty as a body will eventually have to take cognisance of these matters if they intend to maintain their position, for increased sensitiveness and susceptibility on the part of the people is causing more interest to be taken in the affairs of the mind, and psychic and mental processes of healing are consequently receiving increased attention. (*PTJ* 1901, Vol. 1, p. 1)[32]

Those words would soon prove remarkably prescient. Not long afterward, a sympathetic journalist wrote an article, probably based on Hallam's briefing, describing how the PTS

> gives free treatment to the poor by the means of Psycho-magnetism, mesmerism, hypnotism or suggestion. When necessary, Mr. George Spriggs, whose clairvoyant treatment was so well known throughout the colonies, diagnoses and gives advice as to the mode of treatment and [illegible] to be followed. Mr. Spriggs has kindly placed his services unreservedly at the disposal of the Society he being also president. Although only established in 1901 for the scientific study and investigation of the psychic and mental forces, so great has been its success, that when the December [1903] journal was published arrangement was being made for getting larger rooms for treatment, meetings, lectures, &c. A large number of medical men and well known scientists lecture and much practical instruction is given. (quoted *FCP* March 31, 1904, p. 3)

In 1905 a reporter from *The Daily Chronicle* [*DC*] was clearly impressed with what she (?) saw and, although letting slip something of her class status, offered an unusually objective description of how the society worked.

> The waiting-room was crowded, the secretary busy taking names, and Mr. Spriggs, clairvoyant, who diagnoses disease, chatted cheerfully with the incoming patients, he and the other healers being at a slight disadvantage in that most of the cases are those given up by doctors. In another room patients were being treated by expert hypnotisers, some of them ladies, and certainly the methods "looked" pleasant. I sat and watched a treatment carried on for severe nervous shock, the patient being placed in an easy chair, the operator seated in front of her. First the thumbs were held until a throbbing sensation was felt, when the hands were lowered to the knees. The operator, talking in an undertone all the time about the treatment, asked the patient to put herself into a passive condition and keep her mind blank (not difficult for some people, one would imagine). The right hand was then quietly placed on the frontal region of the head with the thumb pressing gently between the eyebrows and the left hand over the heart. The patient began to look drowsy, and in a low monotonous tone the operator told her that her eyelids were going heavy she could not keep them open. "Now they are closed," said the operator; "you cannot open them. You are sound asleep, in a deep sleep and under my control—" Here the woman tried to open her eyes, but the gentle voice went on: "You can't open them. Don't try to. You are sound asleep." Then followed "suggestions" calculated to help her get rid of her complaint. It all looked very soothing. The woman slept on, but the talking had ceased. In a little while the operator said, cheerfully, "When I count three you will wake up feeling quite refreshed, quite strong and well. Now, one, two, three." The patient sat up in a rather dazed condition, but soon began to look quite spry, and told me she was gradually improving, after having unsuccessfully tried [orthodox] treatments. (quoted *BC*, June 26, 1905, p. 2)[33]

The same reporter also interviewed Spriggs:

> We don't arrogate to ourselves the power of healing but help people to help themselves . . . patients—good subjects—can be given power to suspend by their own volition the capability of feeling pain but seeing the faculty of feeling pain is too valuable a safeguard against injury the power is only given to prevent pain in an act to be performed such as a tooth drawing. The signal is very slight sometimes consisting in putting the thumb end for an instant between the teeth. A man once dropped some molten metal on his hand making a wound an eighth of an inch deep. It must, or rather would have been torture, but he remembered the signal and felt no pain. . . .
>
> Oh doctors as a body have all along been the bitterest foes of progress in this study though of course many of the leading ones are with us openly. The

amusing part is they now wish to put forward an exclusive claim to practising it, which is most undesirable because a knowledge of medicine is no guide to qualifications as a psycho-theraputist. The question would have to come before Parliament and we should have the inconceivable spectacle of the House discussing subjects in the existence of which 75 per cent of its members did not believe. But I must go to my patients now. Come along and see us any Monday or Friday. We have no mysteries and invite criticism. (*BC* June 26, 1905, p. 8)

Although the PTS's open psychotherapeutic space contrasts markedly with the closed, private space of many contemporary medically trained psychotherapists the matter is complicated by the uncertainty as to how many medical hypnotists followed the advise of Kingsbury, and others, "never to hypnotise a woman except in the presence of a witness." (*BMJ* January 28, 1893, p. 178). Thus the question as to how the presence, or absence, of a third person might define the nature of the psychotherapeutic space would merit further exploration.

Six years later, Lady Coomaraswamy (1911, p. 548),[34] honorary treasurer of the PTS, standing in for Spriggs who was ill, elaborated their position further.

The methods of the society consist chiefly of magnetic treatment, suggestion, and general directions for diet, hygiene, &c., given clairvoyantly by Mr. George Spriggs when diagnosing a case. Magnetic treatment is, perhaps, the principal means. Ten years ago it was a disputed question among many authorities whether such a thing as a magnetic current flowing through and from the human body existed or not, but today the human aura is no longer supposed to be an imaginary emanation, it has been publicly demonstrated to be a reality and made visible to all. It is also an admitted fact that the magnetic force emanating from the human body can be increased in strength by the will. It is easy, therefore, to see that, with this life current well under control, and guided by the intelligence of the healer, a change for the better is readily brought about in the patient whose own life forces have become weakened by ill-health. The sensitive aura of the patient responds at once and passes on the stimulus to the physical body, the healer having first taken care to remove the weak and useless matter in the patient's aura—for it is matter, though not usually visible matter, and may sometimes be felt as such in the hands of the magnetiser.

While the magnetic treatment is going on, the other part of the work must not be neglected. This is the opportunity for suggestion. Healthy, stimulating thoughts may be passed into the mind of the patient with ease while he is in the passive state, whether spoken articulately or not, and when the case is suitable an added power is given by the value of auto-suggestion being explained to the patient.[35]

For his part Spriggs worked tirelessly for the success of the Society.

Week after week found him at the society's rooms giving forth the healing light from his spiritual lamp. He was never too busy to lend his aid. Sympathy was

> the keynote of his character; he felt that he must use his life for the highest and holiest purpose—the lightening of the burdens of his suffering brethren. He has established a fact which deeply concerns mortals, that there is a world linked on to this from which comes oft-times healing for soul and body. That he will have his reward is not to be doubted. (*Light* March 16, 1912, p. 127; March 30, 1912, p. 147; *HR* April 1908, pp. 41–42)

A further tangible measure of the Society's continuing success can also be found in the opening of its new premises in April 1910 which, as we shall see, was a significant date in some of these other histories. And if the comments made during that opening were in any respects correct, the society's achievements were indeed remarkable. In the nine years from its inception, volunteers had seen around 2,500 patients and given over 200,000 treatments. Dr Joseph Stenson Hooker (1853–1946),[36] "expressed satisfaction that the medical men of to-day were beginning to acknowledge the tremendous power of mind over matter" and predicted that "the society's work would undoubtedly develop in view of increase in nervous disease." (*YPLI,* April 25, 1910).[37] And while the precise nature of the society's influence must remain debatable there can be little doubt that during the first decade of the PTS's existence its founder-members would have witnessed a profound transformation in "public opinion regarding the treatment of disease and health reform."

POLITICAL ECONOMIES OF HEALTH

In the first issue of the *PTJ* (1 October 1901, p. 2)[38] Hallam published a letter from a poor man in the East End of London desperately seeking a cure for his illness.

> Hospitals and dispensaries invariably pay little attention; give you medicine for a fortnight, perhaps, and as in my case, if no improvement change medicine with same result. Consequently, I have no faith in them, and do not intend to trouble them again. Private practitioners of the cheap kind cannot afford to give the time and treatment necessary; whilst the better class doctors, from whom I have received slight benefit, charge more than I can possibly afford to pay, as I have a family to support and am only a working man. Moreover, I have lately been suffering more and I am afraid of the future and the results to my family.

This was an age when there was no state-funded health care and systems of private health insurance remained uncertain particularly for those living at or below the margins. Even at this basic level the *PTS*, which "was based entirely on the voluntary system, everything being given free" (*HR* May 1910, p. 50; December 1911, p. 144) must have seemed like a god send.

Furthermore the PTS appeared not to carry the stigma of the typical charity institution or workhouse infirmary. It is hardly surprising, therefore, that the PTS, with its free treatments by donation, attracted patients, like the poor man seeking potential life lines after having been abandoned by an orthodox medical system which invariably measured health according to strict and often impossible pecuniary criteria (*BMJ* December 15, 1906, p. 333). This may well explain why the PTS appears to have grown so rapidly throughout the best part of the period under review (1901–1912).[39] Thus in its Annual Report, for 1905, the Society claimed to have treated "230 patients, compared with 141 in 1903–4 and 53 in 1902–3." (*OW* 4 October 1905, p. 41). In October 1907, *HR* (October 1907, p. 109), which now recorded details of some of the cases treated, claimed that in July and September (being closed in August), they saw 109 new patients and carried out 788 treatments on about 130 patients with a considerable number coming for a fortnight to three weeks, from outside London. In April 1911, during their tenth anniversary meeting at the Caxton Hall, Spriggs claimed

> that during the ten years of the society's existence some twenty-six thousand cases had been undertaken free, in many cases with very striking results. The society is supported entirely by voluntary contributions, and all members, including the medical staff, give their services free. (*Light* April 8, 1911, p. 165)[40]

A few months later, *Light* (November 18, 1911, p. 547) sought to explain the Society's success:

> I believe it is the only society in London where the whole of the healing work is done by voluntary workers, no one of whom receives any pecuniary benefit for the time he or she devotes to the society. This spirit it is which imparts such vitality to it, and which enables the unseen helpers to draw so near.

It is not surprising that this system of free treatments should also have provoked vehement opposition from many in the London medical establishments although, as we shall see shortly, their opposition tended to be expressed through the "silent treatment."[41]

Another measure of the Society's success can also be read, paradoxically, through a letter to the *BMJ* from Dr Hector Graham Gordon Mackenzie (1870–1930)[42] who, at the time, was actively researching "the subject of 'mental' and 'spiritual' healing" for his forthcoming contribution to *Medicine and the Church*. (Rhodes 1910b). Mackenzie was an important figure in the contemporaneous medical-clerical debates on "mind healing" (to be discussed in Chapter 6) and would serve on the Standing Committee on "Spiritual Healing," convened after the October 1910 Conference of representatives of the Clerical and Medical Professions (*Spiritual Healing* 1914, p. 7). It was probably sometime in December 1909 that Mackenzie (1910a, p. 783) heard, from a lady friend, about "the marvellous skill of a Mr S., an 'operator' of the [PTS] who (at a small charge) had diagnosed her condition with no hint from outside, and prescribed a most practical and successful line of treatment." Although Mackenzie's letter clearly suggests his "lady friend" was quite happy with this "practical and successful line of treatment" Mackenzie was clearly not impressed because he wrote to ask Mr S., obviously Mr Spriggs, if he could bring a patient to his afternoon clinic in Bloomsbury. Arrangements having been made Mackenzie arrived on January 12, 1910,[43] with one of his "Church Lads' Brigade lads . . . an exceptionally healthy youngster of 16 or 17" whom he had previously examined "with scrupulous care and could find no physical sign of any sort or description suggestive of disease. Nor were there any symptoms whatever" although Mackenzie did note "a small bony outgrowth just below the left knee" which a consultant had recently diagnosed as strained adductor tendons which the lad had suffered a fortnight earlier playing football.

> Mr. S. presented the appearance of an elderly gentleman of benevolent aspect and grave demeanour. He was commendably brief in his procedure. My friend was quite right. It was no part of his practice to ask for symptoms or to make an examination. He sat down in a chair, holding the boy's hand. The lad was seated opposite. The seer closed his eyes and began to recount the 'true inwardness of the condition.'[44]

Spriggs, "while in a kind of self-induced hypnotic trance," declared his diagnosis and "suggested the treatment" although he "required to be told no symptoms," made "no physical examination" but "merely sat in a chair holding [the boy's] hand, shut his eyes, and—well, the occult powers did the rest." At the end of the consultation, Mackenzie asked Spriggs about his diagnosis of "'slight congestion of the kidneys.'" Spriggs's reply was "most interesting and had all the charm of novelty."[45]

> He went on to advise a rather colourless dietary. It was obviously so much more the sort of thing which would appeal to a neurotic woman that I thought the seer was getting a bit lazy and was allowing his imagination to flag. Possibly he finds that his dupes swallow anything so greedily that it is lost labour to take trouble over his flies.

But then when Spriggs started prescribing medicine Mackenzie had clearly had enough and told him he would trouble him no more. "'Oh, but,' said a female amanuensis, in a tone of shocked surprise, 'this is a pure herbal mixture.'" Then having told Spriggs about his own diagnosis Mackenzie "retired [with the lad] from a rather silent room." This highly partial account, which clearly merits further detailed analysis would space allow, reveals something of the profound clash between two diametrically opposed systems; the spiritual and the orthodox. Furthermore Mackenzie's letter was one of the few occasions when the *BMJ*, let alone *The Lancet*, openly published criticisms of the working of the PTS and, as such, it also offers invaluable insights not just into the workings of the Society but also into the mind of an orthodox doctor with status and authority in both the medical *and* clerical worlds.

On November 9, 1911, the LSA, somewhat belatedly catching the mood of the times, organized a Symposium on "Some Unorthodox Systems of Healing" and invited expert speakers to give expositions on their different methods of working. Lady Coomaraswamy on "The Work of the [PTS]," W. S. Hendry on, "On Vital Magnetic Healing," Mrs Home on "The Principles of the Science of Being," and Percy Street on "Direct Spirit Healing." In his opening remarks Mr H. Withall, LSA vice-president, noted that Mr Macbeth Bain,[46] being out of London, would be unable to speak on "The Immanent Christ the Healer of Soul and Body." He also noted that despite their best endeavors they had failed to secure a speaker from Christian Science because

> the gentleman to whom he had applied wrote that 'under the rules of the Mother Church we are not permitted to make any addresses on the subject except under the auspices of Christian Science Churches.' That struck him as cruel to people who wished to become better acquainted with the subject, and he wondered whether such an attitude represented either the Christianity or the Science. (Laughter)

Having made what was, by now, a very old joke, Withall (*Light* November 18, 1911, p. 547) opened his address by pointing out

> that so long as man's personality was regarded as being confined to his body, orthodox medicine was held to be sufficient; but when it was seen that the mind had an influence on the body, that there was a part of ourselves which worked not only in the creation but in the upkeep of the body, and that that part, sometimes known as the subconscious, could be acted upon through the conscious, the discovery at once brought in new methods. The healers, instead of treating the result, treated the cause. All these new systems were due to the fact that man was considered as a spiritual being having a body, and not as being a body. Now, it was a psychological fact that persons who had a vested interest in anything were seldom able to see the necessity for any change. Having a monopoly, the medical profession, as a whole, were inclined to ignore the newer systems. We had to be content with the fact that anything that was really for the good of the people would live whatever the opposition might be.

In her address Lady Coomaraswamy (1911, p. 547–48) gave a brief overview of the work of the PTS.

From the first its purpose was single-hearted, and up to the present its objects and aims have remained the same. The cause of its existence was a great need to reawaken in men's minds the truth that the highest healing comes from the spirit. The means through which this healing can be attained has for thousands of years been known to mankind, but at times it has been clouded over and pushed out of sight by the greater belief in grosser and more physical methods of dealing with disease to which there has always been a tendency to revert. . . .

The objects of the society have all along been twofold. This has not been fully realised even by many of those who are most sympathetic. The first of these objects is to provide a suitable place where magnetic or psychic healers can receive and treat patients under good conditions, and where a clairvoyant diagnosis can be given when needed. . . . All who are in need of help are equally welcomed, and those patients who cannot afford to give even their mite to help on this work receive the same attention as those who give with a free hand. We have also many subscribers to thank for assisting us to give these free treatments.

The healing work is done by a staff of workers who are fighting for faith in the power of mind over matter, and who have attended the rooms of the society for ten years, at regular hours, giving of their best to those who asked for it, and always ready to take the bright view of life, their reward being that of seeing the result of their labours. But this reward is not trifling, as every healer knows whose heart is in the work. There are times when one is drawn into very intimate communion with the soul of a patient, so that the body is forgotten, and only spirit is realised and then arises a sense of oneness with the soul of the universe.

The society's second object—of equal importance with the first—is that of making its methods known as widely as possible. With this in view Mr. Spriggs and Mr. Hallam and others have for ten years held classes for Members and Associates in which instruction has been given in the various methods of healing and in medical clairvoyance.[47]

Lady Coomara, as she was often affectionately known, also stressed how important it was that the Society was "entirely unsectarian."

No worker is asked what his or her special faith or creed may be. All are welcome who will join in this work of love. This spirit removes all difficulties in dealing with patients of various faiths and nationalities. When a sense of spiritual oneness with our fellow beings is developed in a high degree, there is no room for criticism of these minor differences.

This same spirit of eclecticism can also be read through a report for the arrangements, probably initiated by Macbeth Bain, to establish a Psycho-Therapeutic Society in Brighton. Although the new group planned to work out of the Spiritual Mission in Manchester road, it was pledged to "be run on quite independent lines" and, following Spriggs's visit to bolster their work, *HR* (October 1907, p. 112) advised the Brighton Society to devote itself to psycho-therapeutics, pure and simple, without regard to any particular school, sect, or creed. This is as it should be, and so long as it is so conducted it will receive the countenance and support of the Committee of the London organisation.[48]

LECTURES

In her contribution to that November 1911 LSA Symposium, Lady Coomara failed to mention Hallam's increasingly successful series of lectures designed to educate the public, advertise the work of the society, promote its treatments, raise funds, and perhaps most of all, encourage engagement with the medical profession. The lectures were therefore an integral part of the Society's work. Surveying the series as a whole suggests Hallam was determined to create a programme that offered a voice to that ill-defined coalition of organizations committed to promoting Health through alternative or unorthodox means. In this Hallam appears to have developed an uncanny knack of also attracting qualified medical practitioners to attend and even to lecture. At first many of those who accepted might be considered on the fringes of orthodox medicine and yet, despite their unorthodox views, they were also qualified practitioners and, therefore, part of the medical establishment even if only tangentially; so their mere presence reveals something of the blurrings of those demarcation lines. So, as early as December 1903 L[yttleton] Stewart Forbes Winslow (1844–1913),[49] whose father Forbes Beningus Winslow (1810–1874) "'did more than anyone else . . . to popularise the term and concept of psychological medicine with all the implications of a recognised speciality'" (Tuke quoted Shepherd 1986, p. 640), spoke about "the treatment of inebriety by the use of suggestion."

> Years ago the idea that medical men should use hypnotism in the cure of disease would cause members of the old school to shudder in their shoes, but public feeling was turning round and they did not now regard those who practised hypnotism as charlatans but as scientists. . . . In treating these people it was necessary to suggest to their subjective and unconscious mind that they must take a dislike to alcohol, or that its actions would be that of an emetic.
>
> Winslow illustrated his meaning by hypnotising a male medium upon whom he said he had practiced in this way during the past ten years. With one wave of the hand the man entered a trance, and then drank some water which he believed to be whisky, and which he was told to dislike. The man's facial expression when he attempted to obey what seemed to him a repulsive request was quite startling. (*NZH* December 19, 1903, p. 6)

In May 1906 Dr. T. Stenson Hooker lectured at the Bedford Head Hotel, Tottenham Court Road. Hooker, who was now a PTS vice president, also sat alongside Mrs Stannard, Arthur Hallam and, for a time, George Spriggs, on the Executive Committee of the London Association for the Prevention of Premature Burial [APPB] whose interests, in part, overlapped those of the PTS.[50] In his talk Hooker said that although neurasthenia and neuritis were the curse of modern life, especially among brain workers, they

> were readily curable by diet not drugs. Music was waiting to be used for the cure of many diseases. We all know how soothing is the effect of sweet music, played by a soulful player. . . . colour will yet cure lunacy, certainly colour has a great effect on some people. Some colours make me feel quite bilious, others make me feel strange and unhappy; others bright and cheerful. The present-day passion for green in clothing and house decorations everywhere is a tribute to its soothing effect and distraught nerves. (*Sydney* May 1, 1906, p. 8)

But perhaps the most important turning point occurs in September 1906 when Hallam published an abstract of the article by Dr Edwin Ash (*PTJ* 1906, pp. 82–83) which had recently appeared in *The Lancet*. Although I have been unable to discover the history behind Hallam's publishing this article, the result was that Ash consented to deliver a series of lectures to the PTS. This was an extraordinary coup because, as we shall see in Chapter 9, Ash was, at the time, one of the best known of the younger generation proselytizers on hypnotism. What is more Ash was at the beginning of his medical career and still very much part of the orthodox medical establishment and his decision to speak to the PTS also coincided with the inaugural meeting of the Medical Society for the Study of Suggestive Therapeutics [MSSST], one of whose rules "expressly prohibited their members from speaking at any non-medical society promoting treatment by unqualified practitioners." (See Chapter 7)

Ash (1906c, p. 94) delivered the first of his PTS lectures in November 1906, a talk on "Modern Hypnotism" in which he explored the idea of a potent "Subconscious Mind" governed by the "Law of Suggestion."

> "In using hypnotism to cure disease" . . . "we are at present toying with a great force which we not fully understand [*sic*] and which we cannot entirely control. We certainly cannot control it sufficiently to govern the grosser forms of disease, and it is important to remember that nothing can do more harm to psycho-therapeutic methods than that one case treated by them, which should have been treated by surgical means, should go wrong."
>
> "Diseases which can generally be influenced by hypnotism are of the functional order, and not those associated with organic changes. It can, I think, be

> proved that it is possible by mechanical means and suggestion, without any personal influence such as magnetism, to mask the conscious mind of the subject and bring out some underlying consciousness. It can be demonstrated by experiments that the sub-conscious mind has stored up memories of events of which the conscious mind is not cognisant. It will be my aim in succeeding lectures to show the light in which hypnotism should be regarded, both as a legitimate therapeutic agent and as a necessary weapon in the armoury of research."

Ash then "experimented" upon a young man, whom he had brought with him. He "was a member of the auxiliary forces and Ash, having rapidly put him in a state of hypnosis," made him do a number of actions; going through the motions as if he was on the parade ground; driving the colonel's motor car and then making him act like a cat.

> "Hypnotism," Dr Ash said, "was not a thing to be played with. It was a great power which could be used with advantage if due care was taken, but it emphatically was not a thing for an amateur to trifle with."[51]

The *PTJ* (November 1906, p. 94) claimed this "demonstration of hypnotic phenomena formed the most important part of the proceedings." And when we come to explore the "hypnotic demonstration" in more detail we shall also see how Ash's lecture effectively replicated the one he delivered to the East Sussex Medico-Chirurgical Society in December 1905. But what is also noticeable is that *The Lancet* (November 10, 1906, p. 1308) broke with its previous "silent treatment" because it not only mentioned Ash's PTS lecture but also remarked upon the fairly large audience which "included members of the medical profession." If the old hypnotism Myths had been, in anyway correct, then Ash should have suffered adverse professional consequences not just for promoting hypnotism but also for associating with a society which many of his medical brethren considered a coven of quackery. Instead it seems as if hardly anybody blinked an eye!

In March 1907, Dr Bernard Hollander (1864–1934),[52] a member of the Association and associate member of the SPR, lectured on "Unorthodox Methods of Investigation and Treatment of Disease," by explorating the power of the mind. "We do not need to hypnotise a patient to show that the mental centres in the cortex have the power of directly influencing physiological function and tissue nutrition." This was why "psycho-therapeutics are successful when applied in conjunction with other treatment." Although Hollander (1907, p. 39) held, passionately, that it was the duty of the physician to study his "individual patient and relieve his symptoms" he also believed it was the "chief point to get at the cause of his trouble, which you must remove by all possible methods known to you."

> The old physicians were too much inclined to treat diseases; the modern physician treated the patient. Too little account was taken by the regular student of medicine of individual character. The physician should have a knowledge of human character and be able to read a man at sight. Physiologically the brain was the great regulator of all functions; and the ultimate court of appeal in every organic disturbance. For some persons a sound working mind and brain were a protection against disease. (*PBH,* May 4, 1907, p. 3)

In the discussion which followed Dr Abraham Wallace (1851–1930),[53] a spiritualist and former pupil of Lister's, noted that in his early career he had been an assistant to Thomas Laycock and, like Hollander, "was also interested in heterodox things."

> He did not think mere localization of the conditions of the brain would explain all our psychic phenomena. He adopted the spiritualistic hypotheses, not merely the materialistic one, and he had had experience with friends in that room. He saw present Mr George Spriggs, and he had not long ago a case which puzzled the diagnostic powers of most of the scientific men of the day; yet Mr Spriggs, in the condition of control, described the whole condition and symptoms of the man; and not only that, but he gave the exact details which could be afterwards made out by post-mortem examination. (*HR* April 1907, p. 40)

Wallace urged them to "maintain the scientific spirit" whenever they pursued their investigation.

> They had to show to the so-called orthodox people that there was something that could not be explained by mere microscopes and scalpels, and he was sure that Dr Hollander's scientific and interesting address would stimulate them to continue their noble work.(*HR* April 1907, p. 40)

In July 1907, Dr Robert Bell, a cancer specialist and formerly senior physician to the Glasgow Hospital for Women, lectured on Cancer which, he believed, was "'a degeneration of the thyroid gland. Cancer is not a disease caused by a microorganism because faulty diet and improper sanitation of the body breed this terrible scourge . . . the ingestion of too much red butcher's meat is the primary cause of cancer'" Bell's advise was

> careful attention to diet with plenty of vegetables and little or no red meat, strict supervision of all the sanitary eliminating functions of the body and the administration of thyrocal the active principle of the thyroid gland, to take the place of the vitiar secretion of the diseased gland. (*AG* July 18, 1907, p. 2)

Two of Bell's cancer articles had recently been published; one in the "orthodox" *MTHG*, the other in the "unorthodox" *Herald of the Golden Age*

[*Herald*] (1907, pp. 92–95),[54] edited by Sidney Hartnoll Beard (1862–1938). The *Herald* was the official Journal of the Order of the Golden Age, one of whose aims was "to advocate the Fruitarian System of living, and to teach its advantages." That Bell, a medical practitioner and Council Member of the Golden Age, had articles published simultaneously in the *MTHG*, *HR*, and *Herald* underlines, once again, the extent to which crossovers and alliances, albeit at the margins, were occurring not just between "alternative" practitioners but also across those supposedly impermeable barriers erected by the orthodox medical establishment in their attempts to inoculate themselves from the contaminations of unorthodox practices. These surprising and, at times apparently strange meetings, were in some respects inspired by that inclusive space which Hallam had facilitated in his attempts to create and promote vibrant dialogues as to how best to advocate, promote, and practice Good Health. It was probably no accident, therefore, that in January 1907 Hallam decided to drop the Journal's title of "psycho-therapeutic" and replace it with *Health Record*. And it was probably also no coincidence that in 1910 Beard added "and the British Health Review" to the original title of the *Herald*. A similar name change occured in 1910 when, as we shall see in Chapter 19, the MSSST changed its name to the Psycho-Medical Society thereby also removing "therapeutics" from its title.

In October 1907, Winslow, who also straddled the hetro/orthodox boundaries, delivered another talk, this time on "Hypnotism in the Treatment of Criminals and its Use in the Detection of Crime." Having ranged over many subjects, including references to his father's notes on Elliotson, Winslow concluded his lecture with

> an interesting demonstration of hypnotic phenomena, the experiments which he made upon a hypnotised subject being designed chiefly to show that whilst a person under hypnotic influence can be made by suggestion to perform a variety of acts, both serious and amusing, he cannot be made to do anything of a criminal nature. (*HR* November 1907, p. 124)[55]

In November 1907 Sidney Beard "instanced a remarkable case of longevity among fruitarians." (*EE*, January 7, 1908, p. 3),[56] while a few months later Dr Stenson Hooker, in a lecture on "How Not to Grow Old' gave, as his main advise, "Don't worry." He divided his talk into two parts: the first advocating a simple diet and more exercise, the second discussing "the mental aspect of the question":

> The whole world is in need of "suggestion treatment" in this respect, for it has somehow got it into its stupid head that we must be old men and women at, say, seventy years of age or even sooner. That is ridiculous, and the sooner a different

idea is driven into our sub-conscious minds the better. If a man thinks he is going to be old at sixty, he assuredly will be. Married people seem to live longer than single ones, therefore my advise is, "Get married." Also get a pension, and one which has been fairly earned. Never worry, for that is fatal; always be calm and serene. Be optimistic at all times. The miserable, croaking pessimist will grow old, and ugly as well, very soon. In a word be temperate, simple, cheerful, aspirational, charitable, and you will live to a great age. (*HS*, May 9, 1908, p. 4)

Simply to dismiss Hooker's ideas as banal, homespun medical advice would be to overlook the deeper political, moral and ethical significance carried by such messages especially when set within the wider context of the aims and ideals of those unorthodox organizations actively campaigning for radical changes to what they saw as a corrupt medical and social order. This was also set against the background where growing numbers had come to believe that the old order was beginning to fracture under the weight of widespread social, political, and economic unrest with mounting Suffragist protests; rising industrial actions; and the continuing reverberations of the political turmoil triggered by the 1906 Liberal Party Parliamentary landslide. This heady mix of rebellion and protest can also be read into the lecture Hollander delivered the following year (1908) because his lecture offers important insights into how those profoundly shifting attitudes and their consequent social, economic and inter-personal pressures could be seen to be bearing down on patients' health. But his lecture also offers, with its surprisingly contemporaneous feel, an insight into how Hollander (1908, p. 87) had come to perceive that newly constructed private psychotherapeutic space.

Often the patient will confess in the privacy of the consulting room the private sorrow which excited the present condition; much one may also ascertain through tactful questioning of the patient and his friends, much by careful observation of his and their demeanour to one another and their domestic relations. You are expected to recognise the depression caused by business cares, the sorrows of wounded self-esteem or checked ambitions of sensitive natures, the despondency caused by the expectation of a ruined career, of disappointed love, the care and worry of married unhappiness, the disappointed hopes of a parent who had ambitions concerning his children. You cannot remove these sorrows, but you can do something to soften their effects, especially when the patient has no one in whom he can really confide.[57]

In August Hollander lectured on "the value of mental suggestion in the cure of certain classes of brain troubles."

"Treatment by suggestion did not mean as many thought an attempt to plant a delusion in the brain of a person who was in a state of hypnotic sleep. Suggestive treatment of the insane was an endeavour to deflect the brain action

> into other than the morbid tracks and channels, and it was based on the idea that all thoughts, normal and abnormal, sunk into oblivion if not renewed. The part of the brain which was diseased could then be given a rest." Dr Hollander advocated a system of mental gymnastics for the patient, a systematic exercise of his will, by which he would gradually learn self-control, and the discipline of his thoughts and feelings. In many of the American mental hospitals these ideas have already been adopted, but as yet they have by no means been universally applied. (*NEM*, August 31, 1908, p. 2).

In the meantime Hallam continued extending the Society's reach. So, for example, in June 1908, Father Bousfield S Lombard, Vicar of All Hallows, Gospel Oak, and a previous warden of the Guild of Health,[58] spoke on "The Power of Silence" and argued "that excessive talking is responsible for the increase of insanity and nervous diseases in modern society." (*Auckland* June 13, 1908, p. 11; *HR* May 1908, pp. 49–51). We shall look at the Guild in Chapter 6.

In January 1909 Dr A. D. Deane[59] spoke of the difficulties of being a general practitioner "who believed in treatment by means of human magnetism, hypnotism, and suggestion." After his own experiences "had led him to follow up the power of thought and the finer of less evident forces of mind and body, some of the public had called him a quack. Nevertheless, he felt the principles of the Psycho-Therapeutic Society were sound." (*ST* February 19, 1909, p. 10).[60] In a lecture, delivered to the PTS in 1904, Deane, who had openly discussed his own nervous breakdown in 1902, said that he was now "changed as from dusk to daylight, like a passing from death to life." It was through that breakdown that "he became a convert to hypnotism" following his "reading American authorities" and he now used a combination of hypnosis and laying on of hands in his medical practice. (*YPLI* September 30, 1904, p. 4). Deane's 1904 talk also resonates with the almost contemporaneous accounts by Barker Smith, who, like Deane, struggled to articulate his own experiences of nervous break down partly as a way of making it public but also in an attempt to incorporate the experience into his own medical practice (*GP* September 10, 1904, pp. 577–78; *APS* 1908, Vol. 3, pp. 155–56).

The following month, in March 1909, Deane related some interesting cases of successful cures by suggestion one of which may even have been autobiographical.

> A man had got into a depressed condition; sleepless, melancholy something or somebody told him that he must destroy himself. Dr. Deane said to him: "Do not fight against the feelings, and the voices and suggestions," but as if you were talking to something or somebody beyond yourself, say, "All right, come along do your worst you cannot do me any harm. I am going to sleep. I have a power within me much stronger than you, so I do not care." He came about four times, and was now quite out of his misery. (*NZH*, May 5, 1909, p. 6; *Chronicle*, March 6, 1909, p. 2)

During the course of his April 1910 lecture, Winslow, now also a vice president of the PTS, discussed the work currently being carried out by Dr Bérillon[61] in Paris (*ME* April 16, 1910, p. 4).[62] Later that same month the surgeon, Mr. Dudley D'A. Wright [FRCS],[63] vice president of the Homeopathic Society, spoke of the effects of colored lights on the treatment of patients. He

> also brought out the striking fact that starving animals and entombed miners lived longer when deprived of light and remained in a state of complete rest. A further effect of the absence of light was the softening of the muscular tissues, and this fact was made use of by cattle and poultry farmers the stock being placed in badly-lighted pens and overfed for a few weeks before killing, whereby a more tender and rich condition of the meat was effected. (*EP* April 30, 1910, p. 10)

By early 1908 the monthly PTS lectures had become so popular that the Society "secured a large room at the Caxton Hall, Westminster," and later that year Hallam noted:

> Lecturers of authority are not difficult to secure now, like they were formerly, when the Society was looked upon with disfavour and suspicion by medical and scientific men. [All last session's lectures] were, in fact, arranged by the commencement of the session, which is an undoubted sign of progress, for whereas formerly the apparent insignificance of the organisation and the bitter hostility of orthodox institutions rendered it difficult for any prominent authority to venture upon our platform, today the Society has, despite prejudice and oppositions, attained for itself, a position of such standing and 'respectability' that influential speakers are more readily forthcoming and the old antagonism is changing to envious regard. It is believed that as time goes on the Psycho-Therapeutic Society will become more and more recognised as a valuable medium through which men of science interested in Psycho-Therapeutics may express their views. At all events, they can rest assured of obtaining in this way a sympathetic hearing, and their ideas are more likely to reach the public through this channel than through the old orthodox sources. (*HR* July 1908, pp. 73–74)

On May 8, 1911, during the discussion following Hallam's talk on "Mental Therapeutics," Ash, who was by now a regular attender, said that he had just listened to

> an extremely well-balanced and comprehensive lecture, and he hoped it would have a wider circulation than was possible through *The Health Record*. . . . He would like it printed in every medical and lay paper. He had not read anywhere an account of mental therapeutics which dealt with the subject in the way that it had been dealt with that evening. (*HR* May 1911, p. 54)

In November 1911, Ash (1911, p. 123) lectured, at short notice, on psychic influences and not having time to prepare a formal lecture for publication, wrote up his notes by way of a letter to *HR* which offers a glimpse as to why he was probably so attracted to the PTS.

> It seems to me now that, whilst suggestion certainly has an important part to play in life, both in health and ill-health (acting primarily on the mental planes), yet there is a far higher plane than the mental, and it is from that higher psychic plane, that we can look for the greatest benefits in the regeneration of mankind, either mentally or physically. It is quite possible that if such psychic or spiritual forces can ever by any means be made manifest in physical experiment it will be found that suggestion may have some what I may term "directing influence" in focusing its effects on particular parts of the body.[64]

In one of his own lectures, "Suggestive Therapeutics and Hypnotism," delivered on December 4, 1911, Hallam (1911b, p. 137)

> explained how suggestion, given to a patient in the conscious state, could be made a valuable force for good, and how it could often be successfully employed in cases where it was impossible to produce the hypnotic state. Where there was abnormal brain activity and complete lack of concentrative power . . . the hypnotic sleep could only be attained after a long series of treatments, which practically resolved itself into a course of mind-training or re-education. When this was completed there was really no need for hypnotism, the patient being cured in the training process, which gave him an insight into the meaning of his trouble, let him see new points of view, and introduced new ideas and feelings into his mind.
>
> This method of treatment had the advantage that nearly everybody could be subjected to it, but it did not suffice for all practical purposes. In obstinate cases the hypnotic sleep was necessary in order to increase the suggestibility of the patient and inhibit antagonistic ideas. Hypnotic suggestion was of the greatest value in the domain of functional diseases of the nervous system, whilst as an educational and reformatory factor it could not be over-estimated. . . . He had never seen the slightest untoward symptom result from the skilled use of hypnotism as a curative and educational agent, or any evidence that its alleged dangers, under these circumstances, had any existence, save in the brain of the novelist.

Hallam (1911b, p. 134) also spoke about suggestion in the conscious state and how important it was not to give direct suggestions as one would if the patient was in the hypnotic state.

> [Patients] cannot therefore take the direct form given in the hypnotic sleep; they have to be given indirectly and very carefully worded, otherwise the conscious mind, which recognises that they are only suggestions, is liable to reject them as such, and no good is done.

The whole point was to try and bypass the conscious mind because "the reasoning faculty is on the alert to analyse what suggestions are made." Although Hallam (1911b, pp. 134–35) acknowledged the benefits of suggestion he also believed hypnotism, particularly deep hypnosis, was the most effective because it "has the advantage that suggestibility being increased, and antagonistic ideas being dissociated or inhibited, the new ideas are more firmly implanted in the mind."

> It must be remembered that orthodox hypnotists attribute all their phenomena to physiological modifications of the nervous system in the first place, and, secondly, to the power which suggestion has over a person in the hypnotic state. Those who believe in human magnetism, however—and there are many practical experiments of this force now in existence—assign the benefit of the results they produce to the invisible magnetic fluid which passes from them to the person operated upon.[65]

Hallam (1911b, p. 135) went on to note that whilst magnetists and hypnotists might agree about the similarity of their results there was "a divergence of opinion as to the principles involved in the production of those results." Then, at the close of his lecture, Hallam (1911b, p. 137)

> gave a demonstration of hypnotic phenomena, his subject being a young lady who had volunteered her services. She was very easily hypnotised, and the cataleptic state was first produced, the muscles of the entire body being perfectly stiff and rigid. She did various odd and amusing things at her hypnotist's suggestion, but no amount of persuasion would induce her to steal [Mr Sprigg's] watch, showing that hypnotism cannot be used to compel persons to do what they will not do in the normal state. Finally, to show how suggestions can be given to take effect after waking, a valuable factor in medical treatment, Mr. Hallam told the subject that when she awoke she would shake hands with [Mr Spriggs] the president and ask him how he was; and this she did, much to the amusement of the audience.[66]

In early 1913 F. Gilbert Scott (b.1869)[67] argued that "There is no doubt that the subconscious mind can control the body" and gave examples of the appreciation of time under hypnosis. Although Scott's conclusions, more or less, followed those of Bramwell's he had clearly conducted his own experiments:

> Sometimes, of course, the experiments, especially when I quadruple them, do not come out right. But certainly there has been no fraud in these accurate experiments, and they do demonstrate the extraordinary powers which the subconscious faculties have over the conscious faculties and over the body, when they are properly treated and used. (*WN*, January 25, 1913, p. 28)

Then in late Spring 1913 Elizabeth Severn (b.1879),[68] aka "R.N.," subsequently one of Ferenczi's most significant analysands (1924–1932), delivered a "very able lecture on 'Colours and their Meaning.'" Severn lectured again, in November, on "Mental States in Relation to the Cause and Cure of Disease." (*HR* May–June 1913, p. 46; November 1913, p. 100). And finally in August 1913 Dr C. Muthu (1913),[69] of the Mendip Hills Sanatorium, who had also recently addressed the Royal Society of Medicine on Hindu Medicine, spoke about the four fundamentals for long life and health:

> correct breathing, abstinence, concentration, and control of will. Life is a series of breaths, and fresh air was life, and contained prana, the universal energy in a pure form. The civilised man had lost the art of correct breathing, upon which physical health very materially depended. Two meals a day, plain food, meatless diet, and fasting now and then kept the mind clear and open to intuitions and moral and spiritual perceptions. Yogi philosophy taught that man was not a mechanical machine, to be dosed and drugged and experimented upon as the Westerns thought, but was composed of living particles, conscious and intelligent cells, which were more or less sensitive, and obeyed the call of the mind. Thoughts were things, and as a man thought so he was. To get control of the body one should get control of the mind, which would be achieved by concentration and contemplation, and there should be set apart a room in every house for silence and meditation, and in every office, where clerks and other workers may throw themselves in a reclining chair and relax the tension of their muscles and nerves and regain their normal poise and repose. It was peace of mind and spirit that was the basis of all cure, and the want of it which was the cause of all disease, and which was to be sought for by concentration, contemplation, and communion. (*AS* August 9, 1913, p. 13)

DECLINING FORTUNES

The year 1910 appears to have been "a phenomenal" year for the PTS with the opening of its new larger premises at 34 Bloomsbury square,[70] together with "the creation of a special fund which resulted in £200 being raised in addition to the ordinary income." Increases in the donation boxes also suggested "how much the patients themselves appreciate what is done for them." There was a buoyant mood among members who genuinely believed their propaganda and philanthropic work, backed by the success of their lectures and the continuing poblication of their Journal, had effected "a great change in the attitude adopted towards the whole subject" of psychotherapeutics (*HR* July 1911, p. 74). Hallam even went so far as to claim that it was *HR*'s proselytizing and propaganda work which had enabled the PTS to bring about this favorable change in the public's mind. Hallam's growing confidence can also be read into the dramatic change he brought to the design of *HR*'s front cover in early 1911. It now shows a prominent representation of Hygeia, the ancient Greek goddess of health and symbol of the philosophy of hygiene. She is standing to the left of a proscenium arch and underneath the apex of its triangular roof is a dome, or globe, crowned with a cross. Underneath is: "The Health Record and Psycho-Therapeutic Journal edited by Arthur Hallam" and to the right of the arch a scroll printed in red, with the date of issue and then underneath in black, "Principal Contents of this Number." And underneath, in red, a list of contents and page numbers followed, in black, "Price Threepence: Annual Subscription 3/6 post free. At the base of the arch: "The Psycho-Therapeutic Society Ltd.," and their address. In 1914 Hallam replaced this last part with "Sane, Lively and Practical."

Although progress through 1911 might appear, at first sight, like an anti-climax there were alarming signs which suggest the Society's fortunes were already in decline. Despite, or perhaps because of their many successes, the Society's current account was sliding inexorably into the red with expenditure outstripping income received from subscriptions and donations. A significant part of the problem appears to have been their huge financial commitment to the rent on 34 Bloomsbury and, as the Committee grappled with the problem, they were forced to face the fact that they were likely to end the year with about £100 in debt. In an attempt to staunch the hemorrhage, they opened a special fighting fund (*HR* February 1912, p. 23). But then the following month the Society suffered an even greater blow with the death of George Spriggs. By August 1912, the situation had become critical and Hallam was forced to admit that the Society's financial difficulties had now impacted upon *HR* (p. 79). The Journal had been indispensable because it had

> fulfilled one of the principle objects for which the Society was founded; namely the dissemination of information regarding psycho-therapeutical methods of healing and the education of the public as to the importance of medical reform and the advantages to be derived from Psycho-Therapeutics in preference to the old and crude orthodox system of dealing with disease.

The problem was that the journal had never paid its way and because it had always relied upon subsidies from the Society the Committee now realized that if they were to avoid closing the organization altogether they would have no choice but to stop funding *HR*. This bland statement conceals what was almost certainly an acrimonious struggle inside the organization which Hallam clearly lost—a point he let slip in his May 1913 editorial.

> A year has now passed since we rescued the *Health Record* from the hands of those who were intent upon its destruction (*HR* May–June 1913, p. 43)

Hallam was clearly not prepared to let *HR* fold because he still believed it was critical not just for the Society's continued success but also for the promotion of his own vision for Health Reform. This was why he was so "anxious to continue it at all costs." Putting a brave face on what must have been a bitter defeat, Hallam acknowledged that the only way to save *HR*, and make it "free of cost to the society," was to carry the financial burden himself. So he detached *HR* from the Society, transferred it into the Heath Record Publishing Company [HRPC],[71] and then published it on "independent lines." Following these changes Hallam could no longer afford to issue the journal free to members (*HR* November 1912, p. 118; July–August 1912, p. 79) nor to send out complimentary copies as a way of promoting the Society or of drumming up support. (*Light* August 17, 1912, p. 394). Although little appeared to change on the surface it was not long before the Journal's financial plight started to bite. In October 1912, at a meeting of some 100 friends to inaugurate a "Health Record Propaganda Fund" [the Fund], Mr Hobbs remarked:

> Well, as they all knew, Mr Hallam had been the editor of the paper from the commencement and he naturally felt that to let it die altogether would be in the nature of a calamity, and therefore, emboldened by his own optimistic spirit and the encouragement of a few friends, he had decided to carry on the journal on his own responsibility. This they would admit was a very difficult task to undertake single handed, especially as Mr Hallam was not in a position to devote the whole of his time to it; and therefore he (Mr Hobbs) appealed to them most earnestly to give Mr Hallam all the encouragement and support that they could, both financially and otherwise. (*HR* November 1912, p. 116)

Despite good will from supporters and the occasional generous contribution Hallam struggled not only to keep the Journal going but also to fill its pages. What drove him, however, were the "words of sympathy and encouragement" he received, each month, from readers reminding him of his continuing and passionate belief in the Journal "the circulation of which is admittedly a philanthropic work of great importance to the education, well-being, and health of the community." By the end of the first year under his financial control Hallam was having to face the fact there were not enough readers prepared to buy the Journal and, unable to attract the necessary capital, he was forced to make, what was in effect, a final appeal to readers and supporters alike (*HR* May-June 1913, p. 43). In the Society's Annual Report for 1913, the Committee noted:

> Mr Arthur Hallam is making a brave attempt to continue the 'Health Record' on his own responsibility, and deserves all the support he can get for we know it must be an arduous and profitless task. (*HR* July 1913, p. 53)

But as kind words never put money into the account, Hallam was finally forced to fold *HR* following its final issue in January/March 1915.

There is little doubt that the Society was badly shaken by the death of Spriggs in March 1912[72] and then went "through somewhat troubled experiences" which Hallam referred to as a "period of transition." But there were also other losses because original workers died or, like Mrs Stannard, left to spread knowledge abroad. For his part Hallam remained determined to prove wrong those who said that the Society would cease to exist after Spriggs's death. Yet blows fell upon blows and in January 1913 the Society discovered they now faced a huge rental increase when their lease, on 34 Bloomsbury Square, came up for renewal at the end of April. But the Committee, having gone through yet another serious reassessment, eventually concluded they were still on the right tracks despite having lost, in Spriggs, their most significant healer. So they gave notice on 34 Bloomsbury Square and, having released themselves from its crippling rent, committed to premises at 26 Red Lion Square trusting this would help free them of debts (*HR* March–April 1913, p. 38). But the future remained bleak not least because the number of patients being treated continued to fall and Hallam, and the Committee, could only think the reasons were to be found in the enactment of the 1911 National Insurance Act "which practically compelled every wage-earner to join an 'Approved Society' of some kind" (Webb & Webb 1919, p. 498). Hallam thought that "the poorer classes, no doubt being obliged to pay for orthodox medical attendance, cannot [now] afford the additional expense of fares to and from the society's rooms." (*HR* June 1913, p. 53). But the reasons for the decline may also have been elsewhere.

The sudden disintegration of the relationship between Arthur Hallam and Edwin Ash offers a possible insight into one of the reasons why the Society appears to have declined so suddenly. At first the relationship between the two men was cordial, even warm until late 1912 when Ash, in an interview with the *Daily News and Leader* [*DNL*] spoke about the success of the new Liverpool psychotherapeutic clinic which offered "psychic treatment carried out by qualified medical men."

> Psycho-therapeutic treatment has suffered from constant association with the term hypnotism, which conveys to the mind of the public the use of a power for the inhibition of consciousness and the control of will in another person. As a fact, the best results in psychic treatment are being attained by suggestion without sleep or controlling the will. There is a world of difference between the quack hypnotism of the stage and of former times and the "New Hypnotism," or rational treatment by suggestion without sleep, as practised by well-known authorities today. (*HR* February 1913, p. 27)[73]

Although Hallam reproduced Ash's words in *HR* without comment, he was clearly upset by the fact that Ash had failed to mention how the PTS had "carried on functions similar to that of the new [Liverpool] institution for many years past." But it soon became clear that Ash was, in fact, now attempting to distance himself from his previous association with the PTS because several months later, in a second interview with the *DNL,* Ash spoke about his own newly created "London Nerve Clinic and School of Psycho-Therapy"[74] and yet again failed to make any reference to the work of the PTS. This was too much for Hallam who noted somewhat sardonically, "it would not do, however, for [Ash] to rob his new clinic of its professed originality by mentioning the actual facts." Ash took offense and instructed his solicitor, F. F. Palmer, to demand an apology certain that Hallam "did not wish to impugn [Ash's] honour in regard to this matter, and in view of the kindly spirit hitherto exhibited by Dr Ash towards the work of the Psycho-Therapeutic Society and the *Health Record*." But then, as if this condescending attitude were not bad enough, Palmer added:

> Dr Ash's observation on that occasion referred entirely to medical and hospital work, and he instructs me to point out to you that although psycho-therapeutic treatment is carried out at [Ash's] London Nerve Clinic, there can be no resemblance between the services of such an institution—carried out solely under medical supervision, for the examination and treatment of patients suffering from nervous disorders—and those of a society which apparently has no legal medical status and is not concerned with the duties of medically qualified experts in the examination of persons suffering from any form of disease, nervous or otherwise. (*HR* December 1913, p. 118)

In a contemporaneous letter to *The Lancet* (November 22, 1913, p. 1507), written in response to the debacle over the role of faith healing in the newly founded Medical-Psychological Clinic [MPC]—which we shall examine in Chapter 17—Ash wanted his readers to know that his own clinic

> is in no way connected with any organisation, institute, or clinic, staffed either by medical or lay workers, in which psychotherapeutic methods are carried out[.] Although offering treatment on psychological lines to patients of small means, as well as to the very poor, this clinic is entirely independent of outside financial support.

And then, in another cruel sideswipe, Ash rubbed more salt into Hallam's wounds because, in his new book *How to treat by Suggestion* (1914), he made no mention of *Health Record* or of the PTS, or of the kindly spirit which he once felt towards Hallam. But Ash was not the only one who set about distorting the history because, so far as I can tell, nearly all the qualified or unqualified practitioners who worked with or supported the PTS during this period, including Bernard Hollander (1910; 1912; 1920) and Elizabeth Severn (1913) effectively wrote Hallam and the PTS out of their history.[75] The boundaries between qualified and unqualified practitioners which had briefly become somewhat more permeable started, once again to ossify perhaps because medically qualified psychotherapists, feeling more secure in the mainstream, had come to believe that they no longer needed the PTS for the unique platform it had once offered them.

THE PTS IN HISTORICAL CONTEXT

In 1910, Winslow (1910, p. 28) noted:

> The progress of Psycho-Therapeutics in England is in many ways due to the energy and work of members of this present society, and I desire to congratulate them heartily on their progress and the success made. Many unbelievers in Psycho-Therapeutical treatment have been converted during the last few years, but the pioneers who have born the brunt and force of the battle, and who were bold enough to contend that cerebral influence exerted itself in a wonderful but inexplicable way over the bodily system, have had a hard struggle to contend against.

Dr Bell, speaking at the inauguration of 34 Bloomsbury Square, also noted the welcome change in public opinion which he thought was "brought about largely through the educational, philanthropic, and practical work accomplished by the Psych-Therapeutical [*sic*] Society." (*HR* May 1910, p. 51). For his part Hallam said

> For nine years they had struggled on, and he thought they could justly claim to-day to have healed the sick, educated the public, converted the Press, and transformed what was hitherto surrounded by mystery, quackery and superstition into a simple scientific art. (*HR* May 1910, p. 51)

Even the press had started to notice their work because the inauguration of 34 Bloomsbury Square was reported upon in many newspapers and journals including the *Medical Times* and *The Hospital*. Hallam thought such reports "distinctly encouraging" and "a sign that our good work and sincerity of purpose are even finding favour in orthodox medical circles." (*HR* May 1910, p. 55)[76] But here, once again, was the paradox, because as their pioneering work was increasingly taken up by qualified medical practitioners the PTS was no longer the main and only forum for public debate.

In one of his last editorials, which might also be considered his swan song, Hallam, perhaps with some bitterness, took issue with the huge resources "spent every year in trying to relieve people of symptoms and effects."

> Surely there is something wrong somewhere . . . would it not be better if the greater part of this vast sum of money were spent on teaching the people how to keep well, instead of waiting until they get ill; in enabling them to realise that disease comes in a large percentage of cases from their own folly, or lack of understanding; and it is just as easy by right living and right mental attitude to keep free from diseases, as it is by physical culture to develop muscular strength? We are almost all the makers of our own destiny so far as health and happiness are concerned, and if more were to grasp the principle underlying health and disease there would be much less sickness and misery in the world and prevention instead of cure would be the ruling rule. None who can realise how vastly more important the mind is than the body will deny that it is our absolute duty individually and collectively, to work to bring about a better condition of things so that the future generations may find better opportunities for harmonious growth and mental unfoldment. The crying need of humanity everywhere is knowledge of their own natures and of the real meaning and importance of human life.
>
> This is what *The Health Record* stands for and what it has now for twelve years strived to inculcate; and what more valuable and disinterested work could be undertaken in the interests of humanity? And yet we are lacking support. Thousands of pounds are annually flowing into the coffers of the hospitals and the well-to-do physicians and yet it is difficult to get pence to promote a much more deserving yet less known cause. The object of *The Health Record* is to teach people how to keep out of the hospitals and the doctors' hands, and how to be well and happy without recourse to medicines and drugs. Surely this is a work of first importance and one worthy of generous support. (*HR* September 1913, p. 79)[77]

Up until now Hallam has remained, more or less, a footnote in the history; partly because he seems to have suddenly disappeared after 1915; leaving few biographical traces behind him: and partly because his work was eclipsed by the far more charismatic Spriggs. Although Hallam failed in his ultimate ambition to create a Psycho-Therapeutic Hospital for the treatment of both in- and outpatients (*HR* July 1908, p. 76) that failure should not diminish his role as a significant and radical campaigner for health reform who was prepared to challenge the established medical order often single-handed,[78] not in a brash confrontational way but through quiet, persistent struggle, stolidly building foundations to underpin his dreams. Hallam's early positioning in the "mind healing" debates, his pioneering work in fashioning the *PTJ* (and *HR*) as a campaigning Journal, to say nothing of his energy and vision in building the PTS, especially through its lecture series, all helped encourage countless individuals to start contemplating the care of their physical and mental health by attending to their souls, spirits, minds, and/or, psyches. Through his early promotion of psychotherapy Hallam helped shift, and to some extent, shape the early-twentieth-century British debates on "pneumatology,"—that discourse on the soul. Thus Hallam can also be considered one of a handful of early-twentieth-century pioneers in the movement for health reform because his campaigning zeal and vision sit alongside, for example, the pioneers of the New Food Reform Movement—like Cobden-Sanderson, Sarah Grand, Charlotte Despard, Beatrice Webb and Seebohm Rowntree—whose aim was "'to enlighten public opinion on matters to diet' and 'to point out the dangers of our present system of food supply'" (Richardson 2014, p. 54). *HR* also sits alongside the *British Health Review [BHR]*,[79] edited by Lily Hodgkinson, whose first number appeared in April 1909,[80] and which, in July, published Stenson Hooker's "The delaying of Old Age" thereby, revealing, yet again, those informal crossovers between various reforming groups. But Hallam, and the PTS, also established something of an international reach because the Rev. Clinton A Billig[81] travelled to England specifically to study the methods of the PTS and, as one of its vice presidents, "returned to his church in America to put their ideas into practice." (Canney 1921, p. 296; *LAH* June 26, 1912, p. 22).[82] For his part Canney (1921, p. 296) noted that the PTS should be credited and remembered for being the first, and for a time, "The only Philanthropic Institution in the United Kingdom at which Free Treatment may be obtained along the above Psychological and Mental Lines."

From a wider historical perspective Hallam can also be seen as heir to that previous generation of British curative mesmerists who gathered around Carl Hansen when he founded the LHS which, for a brief time between 1889 and 1890, enabled mesmerists like Wyld, and the Rev. Tooth, to offer, free of charge, not only psycho-magnetic and mesmeric treatments but also public lectures and classes for training. Healers like Spriggs, Hallam, Miss McGrigor, Lady Coomara, and Dr Winslow should therefore also be situated within that older mesmeric, or magnetic tradition which has also, by and large, been written out of the history. Dr Wyld's brief cameo role in this chapter underpins this somewhat tenuous link in that silent historical discourse stretching between the old mesmerists and the new magnetic hypnotists with the latter seeking to reinvigorate and reinvent those older traditions. Whether wittingly or unwittingly Hallam, through his extensive reading, appears to have gathered up some of those old mesmeric residues and, if only briefly, found impressive ways to incorporate them into his own ideals and practice.

> Orthodox doctors and scientists are, I know, fond of trying to explain away all the claims of the early animal magnetists and the mesmerists and of attributing all the phenomena to suggestion, or, to be more precise, to 'a physiological process of the nervous system,' whatever that may be. Suggestion is another phase of Psycho-Therapeutics and a very important one which I shall deal with later. Suffice it to state here that it is unwise for the would be operator to entirely ignore any or either aspect of the subject. Human magnetism is a great reality, and treatment by suggestion is equally a fact, and the truest and the best course is not to ignore either side but to believe in both. The beginner will soon realise that the height of success in the practise of Psycho-Therapeutics means not the separate use of either one or the other methods, but a careful combination of what is good and appropriate in all of them. (*HR* December 1907, p. 147)

And finally it is instructive to note that Hallam's book, *The Key to Perfect Health* (1912), was favorably noticed and reviewed in a number of publications and, by way of a conclusion to this chapter and also as a link forward, it is worth quoting from the review in the *Leeds Mercury* (August 16, 1912).

> In no department is this new movement more in evidence than in the increasing readiness of the medical profession to consider the part which the Soul or Mind plays in the production of disease, as well as in its cure and prevention. The power of mind over matter, of the Soul over the Body, the value of psychotherapy as against serum-therapy, the use of what is somewhat clumsily termed animal magnetism, of hypnotism and suggestion, the efficacy of prayer as an aid to the cure of disease, and even the value of that bête-noir of the orthodox medicine man—Christian Science—all bulking more and more largely in the thought and even in the practice of the medical profession.

NOTES

1. This quotation, from Herschel's *Discourse on Natural Philosophy*, was widely used and varied during and beyond this period; e.g., Coates (1906, p. 33) and Barrett (1918, p. 20).

2. The 1901 census, enumerated on 31 March, the day before the founding of the PTS, lists Hallam a journalist, boarding at 23 Dante Road, Southwark. I have found very little information about him. Even his own biography of the PTS remained unfinished, a casualty of the sudden closure of *HR* in 1915. Hallam's colleagues also left few traces. Spriggs said: "No hours were too long or too late for Mr Hallam to devote to the Society, and but for him the Society would not have been in the position it was today," (*HR* May 1910, p. 50) while in a rare autobiographical fragment Hallam once said, of himself: "His position in the Society seemed to be somewhat akin to that of a man who ran a marionette show, inasmuch as he was the most at home when behind the curtain manipulating the wires . . ." (*HR* May 1910, p. 51).

3. *The Humanitarian*, founded July 1892 by Victoria Woodhull Martin (1838–1927) and her daughter Zula Maud Woodhull (1861–1941), was published in London and New York. It ran until 1901 and was regularly noted in *Light* (July 14, 1900, p. 326) although "not always quite to our mind." Z. M. Woodhull was a supporter of the *SPR*.

4. Although unsigned "The Bérillon System of Hypnotism," may also have been written by Hallam (1901b)

5. Feilding's (1899, p. 140n) unreferenced reference to "Breuer, Freud," was probably taken from Myers.

6. Moulton (1906, p. 33) notes the extreme secrecy surrounding the identity of members.

7. Although "Evolution in the Twentieth Century" by Hallam, appears in the *Theosophical Review* (1900, Vol. 27, December, p. 320) I have been unable to locate a copy. During this period there were a series of complex relationships between theosophists, spiritualists and psychical researchers, or as *Light* (February 17, 1900, p. 73) said: "The Spiritualist, the Psychical Researcher, and the Theosophist, are all on the same road. They differ only as to the distant view." Oppenheim (1985, pp. 159ff) has a good overview.

8. See also Alpheus (1903).

9. Similar ideas can also to be found in the Spiritualist's practice for mediumship. "For this simple reason alone, is it necessary for those who wish to develop their spiritual possibilities, to live upon a purely vegetable diet, whilst at the same time, it demonstrates to the thinking mind, that a life spent amidst the flowery fields and balmy glades, along with food consisting entirely of fruit, is the highest form of material existence." Those living in the cities surrounded by "sickly neighbours or relations . . . should avoid Spirit-mediumship, as they would a deadly reptile" (*OM* Vol. 1, July 1885, p. 45).

10. Sinnett's book was severely criticized in the January 1896 issue of *Borderland* (Vol. 3, pp. 111–12) on the grounds that it ignored "current history, current literature and current science."

11. Bodie (1905, p. 23ff) advances a similar argument.

12. Hallam (1900, p. 429) also argued that orthodox hypnotists still confined themselves to Braid's physiological hypothesis while mesmerists drew largely upon psychology. Bodie (1905, p. 75) makes a similar point.

13. In discussing "The health-prescription of somnambules" Du Prel (1889, p. 280) says: "It is not from the brain, the reflective activity of understanding, that the health-prescription flows, but from the organ of inner waking, the ganglionic system. This, as already noticed, experiences influences not accessible to the waking brain-life, from earthly substances; and it is therefore explicable that it may be able to feel the utility or hurtfulness of these substances."

14. Bampton (1907, p. 142) suggests that "therapeutic" intervention in disease was relatively new. "Barely 50 years ago belief in drugs and energetic treatment was the faith and practice of the majority of the profession. It was the rise of the pathological school and the study of morbid anatomy that shook the faith of the succeeding generation of practitioners, viewing only the last stages of disease and seeing structural

alteration in the *mass*. It was thought unreasonable to imagine that any pharmaceutical product could have any influence whatever on such profound structural changes in vital organs. It was argued that the cause of many diseases being unknown, therefore the remedies were irrational."

15. Mrs Jean Stannard "an excellent Psychometrix whose powers have been well received in France, in India and in England." Stannard was a pupil of Mr F. W. Thurstan, a Council Member of the LSA and was also "known as a writer to the Psychic Press and a lecturess of ability." (Coates 1906, pp. 155 and 129). After Mrs Stannard failed to be elected to the LSA Council in 1900 (*Light* March 17, 1900, p. 128) she became hon treasurer of the PTS and subsequently joined the SPR in February 1903 (Podmore, 1911, p. 184). Around 1910 she became a travel teacher, believer and active and energetic worker on behalf of the Bahá'i Faith. She taught in Calcutta and lived, for a time, in Cairo where she devoted herself to educating Egyptian women and girls. In 1925 she founded the International Bahá'i Bureau in Geneva which became a gathering place for Bahá'is visiting for the activities of the League of Nations. Her subsequent English translation of *The Hidden Words* was "highly appreciated by Shoghi Effendi." (Savi [nd], p. 355; David 2012, p. 51) See also *Star of the West (In the interest of the Bahai Movement),* (1911, Vol. 10). Stannard was the sister-in-law of Henrietta Eliza Vaughan Palmer (1856–1911), aka the novelist John Strange Winter, who had married Arthur Stannard (b.1854), a civil engineer, from Dorset.

16. *Light* (May 12, 1900, p. 220) has a short article on the programme for the Congress held between 17 and September 25, 1900.

17. Stannard (1900a) also had an article published prior to the Congress

18. George's brother, Robert Wyld of Edinburgh, was highly dubious about all things spiritual.

19. When Wyld moved to London he joined the Homeopathic Hospital as a physician to the outpatients. He became acting president of the British Homeopathic Society in 1876 (Oppenheim 1985, p. 231) and subsequently a Fellow of their Society.

20. *Proceedings* (Vol. 6, 1890), where Wyld is still listed as a member.

21. See also *Light* (April 2, 1881, Vol. 1, p. 102); *Journal* (1896, Vol. 7, p. 144); Anon (1906b).

22. See *Light* (March 2, 1901, p. 107).

23. The LSA, established in 1884, was "formed for the purpose of uniting together persons interested in the study of Psychical or Spiritualistic Phenomena, which throw fresh light upon the nature of man, and reveal him as surviving the change of death. It also provides opportunities of investigation, and affords Information by means of papers and discussions." (*Light* May 5, 1900, p. 216)

24. See *Light* (9 & March 16, 1901, pp. 115–17, 122–25)

25. Lovell, whose given name was David Coethyr-Williams (b.1864–), was a Spiritualist, contributor to *Light* and founder of the Vril-ya Club in 1903. He wrote a series of self-help books around the turn of the century. Fowler (2014, p. 145) credits him with having founded the London APPB in 1896.

26. The full text is reproduced in *Light* (May 4, 1901, p. 209)

27. PTS Committee members met regularly at Frascati's where Trotter and Jones (1959, p. 127) were also "in the habit of dining." It is intriguing to speculate whether their paths ever crossed.

28. A list of PTS Committee members, together with the objects, rules, and regulations can be found in *PTJ* (1 October 1901, p. 4).

29. On Spriggs see also Robertson (1908, pp. 351–52).

30. Bennett (1903, p. 29) notes the SPR refused to investigate what appeared to be a remarkable "cure of life-long disease or malformation of the leg and foot . . . by a well-known Australian healer, then in London." This was undoubtedly Spriggs.

31. For its full title see the bibliography.

32. See also Bodie (1905, p. 109).

33. Around this time PTS members, impressed by the work of Otto Wetterstrand, of Stockholm, discussed making "arrangements for the reception of patients to be treated by similar methods" (*Observer* [Adelaide] April 29, 1905, p. 21).

34. Elizabeth Clay Coomaraswamy (née Beely or Beeby) born in Greenwich and also known as Lady Coomara. Brief biographical details of her, her husband and son can be found in Kim (1999, p. 79).

35. Hallam (1910, p. 68), using the metaphor of a chauffer and his car noted: "Should he, however, have so lost strength in his ignorant struggles with the car as to be unable to make a fresh start alone when he has been taught to realise his faults, we give him that strength not by pushing at the car but by pouring into him from ourselves that amount of energy, nerve vitality, or human magnetism that he needs to give him fresh control over all the parts of the vehicle, the body."

36. Hooker, an SPR associate, ran the Grove Court Health and Rest home, in Totteridge, Herts which he described as "a refined holiday home for nice people. It is also excellent for convalescents who require rest, change and bracing up." The Home was taken over by Miss E. Mackay in 1913. (*HR* May–June 1913, p. 48). *The Lancet* (1904 and 1905) published Hooker's articles on psychic experiments with the spectrum of human rays. Hooker, who claimed some psychic powers (*Light* September 29, 1900, p. 471), was subsequently struck off, then restored to the Medical Register. See Fotherby (1907) and Brown (1991).

37. *HR* (July 1908, p. 76) claimed the Society had "nine eminent medical vice-presidents." In 1911 they boasted fourteen vice presidents five of whom were MDs and another five medically qualified.

38. This story is repeated in *PTJ* (July 1902, p. 52).

39. Maehle (2014, p. 13) notes "an official enquiry about the therapeutic value of hypnosis and the use of this method by lay healers, which the Prussian Minister of Education had sent to doctors' chambers and regional governments in April 1902." The reports "collected in the Ministry enquiry did not reveal cases of harm to health through hypnosis by lay healers." I have found no reference to this report in the lay or medical press.

40. There were, however, donation boxes on the premises. *HR* (July 1910, p. 82) notes that in the year to June 1910. "The contents of the donation boxes have gone down nearly £8, though the boxes have increased in number."

41. There were also issues of class because most doctors would probably have regarded spiritualists as their social and intellectual inferiors. There were probably also similar class divisions between Spiritualists and SPR members; for which see Noakes (2004, p. 55).

42. Mackenzie was born in Leamington, Warwickshire, educated at St. George School, Windsor, Winchester, and Oxford, where he graduated MA in 1897. He then studied at Edinburgh and Newcastle and qualified MB (1907) and MD (1913) from Durham. He was demonstrator in physiology at the Surgeons' Hall, Edinburgh (1902–3) and later served as assistant tuberculosis officer and clinical assistant at Charing Cross Hospital and clinical assistant at the Brompton Hospital for Consumption and Diseases of the Chest. (*BMJ* August 2, 1930, p. 197). Not to be confused with W. Leslie Mackenzie (1862–1935) an early reader of Freud (*Mind* 1913, Vol. 22, p. 136) and member of the LPAS and BPAS.

43. This suggests the PTS had already moved into their new Bloomsbury premises.

44. Another account suggests Spriggs "makes a diagnosis either from a personal interview or from a lock of hair belonging to the patient" (*Southland* August 17, 1907, p. 1).

45. Mackenzie says Spriggs told him he had received some medical training some time ago.

46. James L. Macbeth Bain (1860–1925) a well-known spiritualist and healer, author of *The Brotherhood of Healers* and, for a time, President of the Brighton Spiritualist Association. His wife was a psychic and healer and following her death Bain published her biography *The Lady Sheila*. During this period Bain, probably better known as a Scottish hymn writer, was a regular speaker at Spiritualist Society meetings. (i.e., *Light* March 2, 1912, p. 98; *Harbinger* February 1, 1912, p. 24; *Quest* Vol. 3, p. 186).

47. When Hallam (1912, p. 150) claimed to have cured a man failed by St. Thomas's Hospital the resident assistant surgeon demanded he withdraw the claim because they had no knowledge of such a patient ever having been treated by them. But when Hallam told them he had "in my possession a surgical casualty ticket relating to the patient in question" he heard nothing more.

48. Not long afterward the Brighton Society went through considerable turmoil (*HR* August 1908, p. 68).

49. Winslow, educated at Rugby and Downing College, Cambridge, a captain in the Royal Army Medical Corps during the Anglo-Boar War (1899–1902), carved out his reputation as an expert (medical) witness in a series of high profile criminal trials both in Britain and America. In 1890 Winslow established the British Hospital for Mental Disorders and Brain [or? Nervous] Diseases, a memorial hospital dedicated to his late father. Situated at 208 Euston Road it was established "for the treatment as 'out-patients' of poor persons mentally afflicted." According to Winslow (*The Times* January 2, 1907) 40,000 patients had been registered in the sixteen years since its inception. Three years later Winslow (1910, p. 26) suggested "upwards of 60,000 attendances." Bernard Hollander was one of its physicians. At Winslow's death the Hospital claimed "There have been on an average 3,000 'border-land cases treated annually." (*MCLGA*, 2 October 1913). Winslow (1910, p. 27) says he 'discovered 'the suggestive power of hypnotism when, attending an English Lady in Milan, he visited

Professor Lombroso who suggested 'suggestion by transference.' This prompted him to investigate the work of Luys. (See also *The Lancet* September 29, 1900, p. 982). Winslow, and his wife, became SPR Associates in June 1910. He is not to be confused with Henry Forbes Winslow or Lyttelton Francis Forbes Winslow.

50. On this point see *Occult Review* (November 1908, pp. 237–42). Also Bodie (1905, pp. 56 and 91) who mentions the dangers of the "death trance." *Light* (April 14, 1900, p. 176) considered premature burial as "the most awful of all deaths."

51. The article, from which I am quoting, differs from the *PTJ* report.

52. Hollander (1932, p. 602), who had been hypnotized by Hansen in 1879, was a phrenologist and prolific writer on mental disease.

53. Dr. A Wallace, a member of the SPR, not to be confused with Dr. Alfred R. Wallace.

54. The *Herald* ran monthly from January 1896 to December 1903, then quarterly until October 1918. "After 1910 the *Herald* added 'British Health Review' to its title while an advertisement in *The Temple* (December 1897), says the 'journal challenges the morality of Carnivorous Customs and advocates Practical Christianity, Hygienic Common Sense, Social Reform, Philanthropy and Universal Benevolence. It is opposed to War, Slaughter, Cruelty and Oppression, and is designed to promote Goodness, but not goody goodyism, and Orthodoxy of Heart, rather than Orthodoxy of Creed." (http://www.iapsop.com) For the full title see the bibliography. James Allen (1864–1912) worked as Beard's secretary before starting *The Light of Reason* (Woodcock 2003).

55. In February 1912 Winslow lectured to the SPR on 'The Need for Advance in Psychology,' whereupon W. F. Barrett invited him to repeat his lecture in Dublin.

56. *HR* (May–June 1913, p. 41) reports Dr Josiah Oldfield's lecture on 'Dietetics,' the benefits of fruitarianism, to the Lady Margaret Hospital, Bromley, Kent. Oldfield, a friend of Gandhi's, was instrumental in founding 'The Lady Margaret,' as a fruitarian Hospital in 1903 (*Herald* 1905, p. 15) and was Council Member of The Order of the Golden Dawn (founded in 1895).

57. A critical review of Hollander (1910) in *HR* (1910, 10 August p. 98), praised a number of its aspects before noting: "But while Dr Hollander has apparently been anxious to give such early pioneers as Mesmer and Elliotson their legitimate due he has—and one can understand why—omitted from his survey any reference to rational Psycho-Therapeutics upon the English public and professional minds. The work of the Psycho-Therapeutic Society, for example, is not even mentioned. Moreover Dr Hollander is imbued with the narrow-minded spirit that the practice of Psycho-Therapeutics should be confined exclusively to medical men, although upon his own showing their past attitude has rendered them anything but worthy of now assuming the monopoly." See also the scathing review of Hollander's *The Revival of Phrenology: The Mental Functions of the Brain* (1901) by McDougall in *Mind* (1902, Vol. 11, pp. 404–5). Mitchell (*BJMP* 1923, pp. 70–71) was subsequently unconvinced by Hollander's grasp of psychoanalytic theory.

58. I am grateful to Diane Rockell, Churchwarden All Hallows, for identifying Lombard, who resigned as secretary of the Guild in January 1908. (*CT* January 24, 1908, p. 107).

59. This could be Arthur Dorman Deane (b.1855–1916), a GP in Henley, Oxfordshire, at the time of the 1891 census; then Tendring, Essex, in the 1901 census; and Brentford Mddx., in the 1911 census.

60. *GP* (January 30, 1909, p. 71) reported this talk. Dr A. T. Schofield (1904), a minor but important physician, lectured, around this time, on the 'Unseen World.' Schofield (1894; 1896) was already discussing 'Mental Therapeutics' and the danger of 'quacks,' and then expanded the discussion, in 1896, to include the unconscious. Stenson Hooker talked about auras.

61. Bérillon, now the leading authority on Psycho-Therapeutics in France, ran the 'Établissement de Psycho-therapie' (Winslow 1910, p. 27).

62. Winslow lectured in February (*Light* March 11, 1911, p. 120).

63. Dudley D'Auvergne Wright, Past President of the Homoeopathic Society (1900) and Surgeon for Diseases of the Throat and Ear to the London Homoeopathic Hospital, and Consulting Surgeon to the Leaf Homoeopathic Hospital, Eastbourne.

64. Ash goes on to discuss what he calls "the Great Psychic Unseen."

65. Hallam (1912a, pp. 86–87) discusses 'Human Magnetism' in more detail. Shettle (1890) argues for a reasoned reassessment of the theory of 'Animal Magnetism.'

66. See also *Light* (December 16, 1911, p. 600).

67. Francis Gilbert Scott graduated from the London Hospital (1892), spent time as a District Surgeon in the Selangor Government Straits Settlement, and was, for a short time, a regular contributor to *HR*. Subsequently Hon. Sec. of the Electro-Therapeutic Society (1915) and President of the Section of Radiology at the 1923 BMA Annual Meeting. Haydn Brown (1921, pp. 222–23) discusses some of Scott's hypnotic experiments. One source has Scott a member of the Medical Hypnotic Society [*sic*] which I assume should have been the MPS although I have been unable to verify this. Scott was also a member of the SPR.

68. See Stanton (1991, pp. 157f); Dupont (ed. 1985); Fortune (1993, p. 3).

69. See also his letter to the *BMJ* (July 2, 1910, pp. 55–56).

70. *HR* (July 1910, p. 83) has a photograph of the building.

71. In January 1921 Hallam sold a 50% share in the HRPC to Thomas Hanson Lowe (b,1877), a fruit salesman in South Norwood. Then on March 21, 1921 Hallam assigned "the copyright . . . [of] '*The Health Record*' and '*The Key to Perfect Health* and the successful application of Psycho-Therapeutics" to the HRPC for £100. The Company was still on the register in 1926 but when the Registrar of Companies wrote to their trading office in Tooley Street, in 1928, a director of the London Fruit and Potato Company Ltd replied, on March 9, 1928, that he knew "very little about this firm and [did] not think it exists at the present time." On April 28, 1928 Lowe wrote to the Registrar "that no business has been done by the Company for the last few years and occupation of the offices has now been given up." The Company was dissolved on February 4, 1930 (*PRO*, BT31/26445/173050 C691524).

72. Mrs Cannock succeeded Spriggs "in the clairvoyant diagnoses which patients seek." (*HR* July 1913, p. 53).

73. Ash (1909, pp. 54–56) described rational treatment as rest, nutrition and suggestion.

74. *HR* (March–April 1913, p. 35) has another article by Ash this time advocating the use of electricity in conjunction with suggestion.

75. This tension is further complicated by the complexity in relations between members of PTS and the more orthodox medical fraternity. So, for example, Scott, a regular contributor to *HR*, referred one of his own patients to Tuckey (1913, pp. 76–77n).

76. *CC* (May 11, 1901) covered its inauguration, while several local papers covered *PTS* talks over the years although there was only a small spike in 1910. The PTS was still active in 1919 (*YPLI*, April 16, 1919).

77. Helen Boyle (1909, p. 687) makes similar points when stressing her attempts "to try to teach that mental hygiene as far as possible to the individual which, if generally appreciated, would result in national hygiene of the same kind."

78. Hallam also took up editorial responsibilities for the *Burial Reformer* [*BR*] a quarterly Journal founded April 1905, under the auspices of the APPB. The *BR*, which routinely carried advertisements for *HR*, folded sometime after March 1911.

79. The BHR was [probably] subsequently incorporated into Sidney Beard's *The Herald*.

80. Their issue of July 1909 carried 'The delaying of Old Age' by Stenson Hooker thereby, revealing, again, crossovers between various groups.

81. Billig was a wholesale grocer, a teaching fellow in economics and later assistant professor in marketing at Berkeley University. He gave up his business career to become a priest (Anon 1951, p. 16).

82. E. Percy Braid (d.1915) of San Bernardino was also an honorary vice president of the PST (*Los Angeles Herald*, December 28, 1914, p. 6).

Chapter 5

Walford Bodie and the British Institute for the Investigation of Mental Science

> Now there are always some objects that for the time being will not develop. They simply go out; and to keep the mind upon anything related to them requires such incessantly renewed effort that the most resolute Will ere long gives out and lets its thoughts follow the more stimulating solicitations after it has withstood them for what length of time it can. There are topics known to every man from which he shies like a frightened horse, and which to get a glimpse of is to shun. (James 1890, Vol.1, p. 421)

DR WALFORD BODIE'S ROYAL MAGNETIC COMBINATION

Samuel Murphy Bodie (1869–1939) was born in Aberdeen and by his early teens was already proficient "in sleight of hand magic," ventriloquism, and "debunking fraudulent spiritualists by demonstrating how 'voices' were really coming from behind the curtain!" Bodie performed one of his first professional magic shows in a small community theater in Banff before delivering a series of mesmeric entertainments in St. Katherine's Hall, Shiprow, where he appeared, in 1887, as Professor S. M. Walford Bodie (*AWJ* August 26, 1887). By 1891 he was drawing large audiences at the Alhambra, Aberdeen, where he was described as "also very smart as a mesmerist and last night he exercised the most complete control over the ten subjects whom he operated upon." (*AWJ* July 14, 1891). During the Summer of 1892, the "Bodie Show," also starring his wife and his sister-in-law, ran at the Grand Theatre of Variety in Liverpool, where it included "Hypnotism, Mesmerism and Animal Magnetism" (*Liverpool Mercury* August 4, 1892; September 5, 1892). Over the next two years, the "Bodie Show" alternated between Aberdeen and Liverpool where Bodie was described as a "capital ventriloquist, [who] introduces an array of life-sized figures worked by electricity" (*LM* April 24, 1894). In 1895 Bodie appeared at the Theatre Royal, Darwen, where he also gave "a highly successful private demonstration of hypnotism and dentistry before local doctors, and at the conclusion was complimented by them." (*Era* 19, January 1895). Such demonstrations were not that unusual during the early 1890s because, notwithstanding "professional" objections, many medical societies, and dentists in particular, invited music-hall mesmerists to demonstrate their skills. It may have been as a result of his success in Darwen that Bodie started incorporating, into his show, painless teeth extraction with the aid of hypnotism (*Era* June 22, 1895). By early 1896, Bodie was also using Professor Rontgen's X-Rays which he had modified in such a way as to allow him to demonstrate "the marvel of the mysterious X-Rays to 3,000 or 4,000 people at a time." One report even suggests he had patented his invention (*Era* 31 October 1896). Not long afterward Bodie, using his skills as an electrician, introduced the "electric chair" into his performances in order "to produce a mock electrocution, complete with sparks and lightning effects" which he then used not only on his assistants but also on volunteers who "would tremble, turn blue, become lethargic, and 'fry' but without (hopefully) actually dying." (Newton [nd]). Bodie's new turn was a sensation and, as a result, his fame spread rapidly through Scotland and the North of England. With his abilities to mesmerize, magnetize, and electrify his audiences, Bodie renamed his troupe "Dr Walford Bodie's Royal Magnetic Combination" and restyled himself president of the British Institute for the Investigation of Mental Science (*DC*, July 18, 1896, p. 4). As Newton (nd) has noted: "The Bodie Show was more than just novel, it was unique in that it's [*sic*] content was literally shocking. Audiences had never seen anything like it before. . . . and audiences were awestruck." And Bodie's popularity just kept on growing so when he appeared at the Alhambra at the start of a short season in July 1896 he "had a splendid welcome after an absence of three years. . . . A holiday audience filled the house from floor to ceiling and there was no mistaking the heartiness of the cheer with which the doctor was greeted when he made his appearance on the stage." (*AWJ* July 21, 1896). Although Bodie had incorporated X-Rays and electricity into his performances, his acts, more or less, followed in the well-worn tradition of the platform, or music-hall mesmerists who had gained such popularity during the early 1890s. But then something changed, around 1901, which led Bodie to begin incorporating psychic healing into his performances. And it is this new departure which makes him of interest to these stories.

The first signs of this change can be glimpsed, in 1902, in a review of Bodie's act for Ohmy's Circus in Preston.

> Bodie MD brought a mammoth programme to a close by his remarkable exposition of the powers of mesmerism and electricity . . . a human subject under

the doctor's power being tightly bound to the chair, while a tremendous force of electricity is thrown through his frame. A young man and two children belonging to Preston, who were suffering from paralysis, and whose names and addresses were read out to the audience were treated by Dr Bodie and were able to walk out of the arena, and the night's entertainment was brought to a close by the fun which Dr Bodie extracted from a number of subjects, whom he quickly placed under control. (*LEP* March 11, 1902)

The extent of Bodie's "healing powers" can be read more clearly in a review of his performance at the Manchester Free Trade Hall a few weeks later.

Dr Bodie makes the treatment of sufferers from paralysis a feature of his demonstration, and last evening he tried his skill upon a little boy from Patricroft, who after a few minutes under his hands, was able to limp across the stage without the aid of crutches. (*MCLGA* April 15, 1902).[1]

News of Bodie's curative powers spread rapidly and crowds started thronging to his performances. During a stroll through the center of Hull, in May 1902, one reporter noted

Gromston-street was a Via Dolorosa of rheumatics last week, and one threaded one's way past the "Empire" through crowds of cripples who came to submit their afflicted limbs to the Will of Dr Walford Bodie. (*HDM* May 19, 1902)

Reports of extraordinary cures followed:

A couple of paralytics on whom Dr Bodie had operated a few nights ago ran to and fro on the stage apparently greatly the better for his treatment. A little lad, George Wallace by name, and resident at 60 Summer Street, Aberdeen[2] was then brought forward. The boy who had been blind for several years, was operated on by the doctor, with the result that his sight was partially restored, he being able to distinguish objects a short distance off. A number of lads were subsequently mesmerised, and their droll and amusing antics were provocative of peals of laughter from the audience. (*Aberdeen Journal* July 29, 1902)

Toward the end of 1902, adverts in the local press proclaimed "Dr Walford Bodie, Modern Miracles. The blind made to see and the lame to walk" (*HDM* November 20, 1902) and by the summer of 1904 they had become even more extravagant, with one claiming, ahead of his run at the People's Palace, Bristol, that Dr Walford Bodie was

the most remarkable man on earth. . . . in his soul-stirring demonstrations that have created such a profound sensation all over the world. Science, mystery and fun. Hundreds of Dr Bodie's old patients testify nightly to his lasting and beneficial treatment. (*WDP*, June 25, 1904)

On the day of each performance Bodie set aside the hour, from twelve to one, to see patients suffering from paralysis: "Those given up by the doctors or discharged from the Hospital were specially invited." (*DEP* August 1, 1904). Although these consultations were free, Bodie clearly used them not just for publicity but also for identifying, or picking out, those patients he thought he could help. On the other hand, and if Bodie (1905, p. 45) is to be believed, once the evening performance was finished, he would remove his coat and "tackle as many of the cases waiting at the stage door as [he] could get through before the stage manager insisted on closing the theatre."

By 1904, Dundee had become another of Bodie's strongholds as huge crowds gathered nightly for admission to his shows. One report has Dr Bodie introducing "a young man of 23 named Alexander Farewell living in Walton Place, Arbroath, . . . who had been practically paralysed from birth."

> Farewell came onto the stage with his crutches and after being mesmerised by the doctor a big voltage of electricity was passed through the young man. After an application of several minutes he was aroused from his hypnotic sleep and being placed on his feet walked off the stage with the crutches over his shoulder. The sinews of the young man's leg were considerably contracted by their long spell of inaction. One could see that there was a great difference in them from the time he came onto the stage. (*DET* August 2, 1904).

Mrs Sturrock, twenty-nine years old from Wilkie's Lane, Dundee, who had been paralyzed for over seven years "was treated by Bodie in the same way as Farewell and being placed on her feet walked briskly off the stage amidst the loud applause of the spectators." Leaving aside, for the moment, the question as to whether or not these cures were genuine or how long they might have lasted, some of the press reports of Bodie's seemingly miraculous cures have uncanny echoes with some of the descriptions to be found in the contemporaneous orthodox medical literature. So, for example, here is an account from Dr Mitchell (1907d, p. 788), whose work we shall look at shortly:

> One day when I called to see this patient I found her afflicted with paresis of the right leg. She limped very badly, dragging the right foot as if it were quite useless. At this time I had had very little experience of the therapeutic value of suggestion, and I had not the courage to tell her to get up and walk forthwith. All I ventured was to assure her during hypnosis that her leg would very soon be alright. I was told next day that about ten minute after I had left she had greatly astonished her mother by running upstairs without the slightest trace of paralysis. There had been no return of the trouble up to the present time.

And even Ernest Jones (1959, p. 157), writing from many years distance, offers a similar dramatic account from 1905 in which he succeeded, "after some months of patient hypnotic treatment" in restoring his patient's "vision completely."

During 1905 Bodie, now routinely known as "The Modern Miracle worker of the North," was playing to packed houses. In Motherwell & Falkirk his "remarkable powers are the talk of the town. Audience convinced by his genuiness." (*HDM* March 6, 1905).[3]

> In the mysterious darkness [Bodie] passed thousands of volts through his system without any apparent discomfort. Dr Bodie claims to cure paralysis and produces unsolicited testimonials and local ones too that the cure is lasting. Before he displayed his powers at the first house on Monday two men stepped forward on to the stage and testified giving also their names and addresses. Then he demonstrated his cures. The first a woman of 32 who had to be carried on in a chair. She had been paralysed in her left side for 4 years. It seemed hopeless to attempt to restore the nerveless limb, but after charging himself with electricity Bodie brought his hypnotic force into play. Then he applied his treatment and when he awakened the woman she was able to walk off the stage and Dr Bodie received his first ovation of the evening. Peculiarly pathetic was his next patient a child of seven whose paralysis extended over the right side was of some standing. She was of too tender years to admit of hypnotism being exercised but this did not appear to effect the speedy working of the treatment which appeared most successful and cheer after cheer went up from the auditorium at the conclusion of these cures. (*HDM* March 8, 1905).[4]

Although significant hyperbole surrounded his claims—after all Bodie (1905, pp. 30–32) was not just a wondrous magician but also a consummate showman and publicist—it remains the case that tens of thousands paid good money to watch his demonstrations particularly during these years under review. One measure of Bodie's phenomenal success can be found in the occasional reports revealing, like a barometer, the steady rise in his fortunes. Having decided to make Macduff his home, and the center of his operations, Bodie started acquiring property in and about the town from around 1902. In 1905 he extended his holdings, buying the Fife Arms Hotel and a large property in Church Street. "This extensive purchase now makes Dr Bodie one of the largest proprietors of house property in the burgh." Besides the Fife Arms Bodie also bought "the Temperance Hotel and the Commercial Inn all valuable properties situated on the shore." (*Aberdeen Journal* March 25, 1905).[5] A "modern," let alone "post-modern" reader, might well point to the gullibility and naivety of the audiences, no doubt mainly working class, who were so "obviously" duped by Bodie's alleged therapeutic successes thereby assuming they must have been built on clever illusions and trickery. And yet a careful weighting of the contemporaneous evidence reveals Bodie's performances were far more complex than the mythical "post-modern" or "rationalist" reader might assume. For a start Bodie (1905, pp. 36–37, 183–84) returned to the same venues, year after year, and many of those he had helped or cured routinely returned to publicly attest to his miraculous cures and openly thank him for transforming their lives. This suggests, at the very least, that local audiences were convinced by the *bona fides* of those locals who gave testimonials and, with one exception, to be mentioned later, I have found little evidence to suggest that those unsolicited testimonials were ever seriously challenged or undermined. On the other hand there is now the unwitting testimonial of Dr J. W. Dawes, MOH of Longton, North Staffordshire, which seems to confirm that Bodie may well have effected at least one "miraculous" cure.

THE STRANGE CASE OF FRANCES OWEN

Mrs Frances Owen, forty-nine, wife of the bricklayer John Owen, lived in Longton, Stoke upon Trent[6] and probably worked in one of the local potteries. For some time she had been suffering from "partial paralysis" and, in the summer of 1903, Dr Dawes "advised her to undergo electrical treatment at North Staffordshire Infirmary." But because she was in a "weak state he advised that she should not go there then unless as an inpatient as the distance to the Infirmary was considerable." Although the reports remain silent on the matter there is more than a suspicion that Mrs Owen was reluctant to enter hospital not just because of the expense but also because of the loss of wages. Then Mrs Owen heard that Bodie had just started a six days' engagement at the Queen's Theatre and when she consulted him, that afternoon, he said he could help her. Later that day she

> was hypnotised by him, and had an electric current on the stage there the same night.[7] She walked away without assistance, and, contrary to [Bodie's] advice that she must keep quiet she attended to her household duties the next day, was in and out of the house all day and according to one or two witnesses was simply "dancing for joy." (*WC*, July 11, 1903)

She "was so delighted with the cure that on the same morning she walked three miles to carry her husband his dinner, walked two more miles after that, went to tell her friends what had happened . . ." (*HDM* August 2, 1903)

> On the night of that day she went to the Theatre to thank "Dr." Bodie for what he had done for her. There she would get on the stage and address the audience and very shortly after while she was still in the theatre she was seized with another fit and never recovered consciousness.

A postmortem revealed "a tremendous haemorrhage in the ventricles of the brain and diseased kidneys that would affect the blood vessels, and death by cerebral haemorrhage caused by over-excitement and over-exertion." The coroner ruled that the electric current Bodie administered—which Bodie said was no more than he would give a child—was not the cause of death.

> The only thing he could object to about her treatment by Mr Bodie was that it was performed in public, which was calculated to produce excitement. The jury returned a verdict of Death from natural causes and added a rider to the effect that they exonerated Dr Bodie from all blame in the matter. (*WC* July 11, 1903)

Making a number of assumptions and allowances—that Dawes was a competent medical practitioner; that Mrs Owen's condition had persisted for some time; that a coroner's court is not an unimpeachable seal of approval—it seems, on the face of it, that Bodie did cure Mrs Owen of her "partial paralysis."[8] But we can also read Mrs Owen's case in the wider context of the contemporaneous debates on "Mind Healing" and, in particular, in the light of one of the commissioned articles for the *BMJ*'s "Special Issue" on "Mind Healing" written by Mr Butlin, president of the Royal College of Surgeons, and president elect of the BMA. Although Butlin's argument (1910, p. 1467) concentrated primarily on "Faith Healing" and he almost certainly would not have had Bodie's performances in mind, he nonetheless makes some comments, apposite to Bodie's "miracle cures" when he argues that it was simply foolish to dismiss such cures with sloppy references to "imposture by wicked healers" or to patient's "feigning disease" or to other banalities because such rhetoric failed to explain the many instances of inexplicable cures. Taking, as his starting point, that such cures did not come through faith alone but through *the transaction* of "mutual faith" between the parties Butlin reminded his readers of those cases "treated by many physicians in many lands without relief, when suddenly, or rapidly, complete relief has resulted under the influence of faith."

> When such cures take place in the presence of vast masses of people, although it may be possible to explain all the steps through which the emotion has produced the "cure," how can we be surprised that the people fall on their knees before God and bless His holy name for the miracle which He has wrought? . . . There is therefore no excuse, in such a case as this or in ninety-nine out of one hundred cases which are cured by faith, to impute dishonesty and deliberate deception to the priests and people who proclaim such cures to be the work of God.

Mrs Owen's case, along with Butlin's warning, offers a caution against the easy dismissal not only of Bodie's "miraculous cures" but also of the thousands who left Bodie's performances transformed in the belief they had, indeed, witnessed miracles.[9]

DR. BATEMAN AND THE MEDICAL DEFENCE UNION

When Bodie first performed in London, probably in 1904, his advertisements proclaimed: "Dr. Walford Bodie M.D., F.S.Sc. The Most Remarkable Man on Earth. The Great Healer! Modern Miracle Worker of the North." Other extravagant claims promised Bodie's "performance" would incorporate "Bloodless Surgery!!! Bodieism or Bodic-Force" and that Bodie had "treated over 900 cases of Paralysis given up as hopeless and incurable, and discharged from the National Hospital, Great Ormond Street Hospital, Saint Bartholomew's Hospital, Guy's Hospital, Bloomsbury Hospital and all the London Hospitals." And of course his advertisements also offered free private consultations for those "suffering from Paralysis. . . . Infant Paralysis, and those given up by the Doctors or discharged from the Hospitals."[10] That summer *The Bodie* Show, which played in Hoxton, was a sensation and Bodie was immediately booked to return the following year.[11] But when those same or similar advertisements appeared in 1905 they became like red rags to the bulls of the London medical establishment some of whom now decided to take matters into their own hands.

On July 10, 1905, Bodie was summoned before Mr Francis, sitting at the Lambeth Police Court,

> to answer a complaint that on May 19th, at the Camberwell Palace of Varieties, he not then being a registered medical practitioner within the meaning of the Medical Acts of 1858 and 1866, unlawfully, wilfully, and falsely took and used the name, title, and addition of 'Doctor,' 'M.D.,' and 'Surgeon,' thereby implying that he was then registered under the Acts. There was a second summons charging the accused with pretending to be a doctor of medicine and a surgeon.

In fact the case had been brought by Alfred George Bateman (1853–1919), general secretary of the Medical Defence Union [MDU], a private company set up to insure its subscribing members "against the legal perils and dangers of a general practitioner's life." (*BMJ* March 7, 1896, p. 607).[12] As his obituarist and good friend John Tweedy (1919) remarked, Bateman's "acquaintance with the few 'black sheep' of the profession, with quacks, tricksters, and unqualified practitioners generally, was indeed extensive and peculiar." What is more Bateman

> seemed to have an instinct for finding out offenders and a genius for bringing them to justice. He spent months, and sometimes even years, in watching or tracking suspected persons, but he did not strike or invoke the help of the courts of justice or the higher medical tribunals until he was in possession of complete legal proof of guiltiness. The care and accuracy with which he prepared his cases gained him the confidence of the Public Prosecutor and other public and medical authorities. If some of the cases which he was instrumental in bringing

> to light were published, they would seem to belong to the realm of fiction and romance rather than to the ordinary world of sober fact.

Section 3 of the MDU's Memorandum gave it statutory authority "to suppress or prosecute unauthorised practitioners" and Bateman, as its representative, now brought a private prosecution against Bodie under the 1858 Medical Act which regulated "the Qualifications of Practitioners in Medicine and Surgery." Clause 3 of that Act had established the General Medical Council [GMC] which, having been defined by Clause 4, was now invested with statutory powers to police and regulate the conduct of qualified medical practitioners. Just as important Section 42 of the Act provided that: "Any sum or sums arising from conviction and recovery of Penalties" from any breach of the Act was to "be paid to the Treasurer of the [GMC]" which was then entitled to recover any sums incurred, by way of expenses, in "the execution of the Act." (*BMJ* 5 October 1889, p. 794). In other words once Bateman decided to prosecute his case the legislative cards were all stacked in his favor.

It is not surprising Bodie should have become a target for Bateman's "shrewd detective instincts" (*BMJ*, April 19, 1919, p. 504) because, so far as Bateman was concerned, Bodie, who was posing as a doctor, "was not entitled to use any medical degree," nor was he entitled to treat people on stage as if he had qualified "as a doctor."[13] Worse still: "By appearing as an artiste he was degrading the profession in the eyes of the public." Mr Avory, acting in Bodie's defense, said his client

> had no consulting room or surgery to which any person could go, nor did he charge any person for what he did. However much the medical profession might resent a person giving an exhibition of his art on the music hall stage and performing medical experiments, it was not forbidden by law. It might be inconvenient to the Medical profession that some of the things which had been done by this gentleman should be done on the music hall stage, but he was not to be punished because the medical profession did not like it.

Avory continued,

> the only offence that "Dr" Bodie had to answer was the technical one—which he admitted—of using the descriptions without the initials "USA" after them. The defendant never pretended that he was qualified to practice in this country. . . . He held medical degrees in America which entitled him to use the letters "M.D." and "C.M." but on the bills at Camberwell the initials 'USA' were omitted. (*DDT* July 11, 1905)

Although there were "a number of persons in Court who were discharged from hospital and by medical men, as incurable, but who have been treated by

[Bodie] with beneficial results," Mr Francis declined to hear their testimonies and brought the trial to a speedy conclusion.

> He was inclined to think this was not so bad a case as many which came before the Court, in which men practised as medical men and so infringed the Act of Parliament in the worst possible way. This was a case for a mitigated penalty. The defendant had no right to call himself "MD." He would have to pay £5 and £5.5s costs. (*BMJ*, July 15, 1905, pp. 165–66)

Under "Music-Hall Medicine," the *BMJ* (July 15, 1905, p. 47) complained bitterly that the verdict was not "commensurate with the gravity of the offence" because, in their opinion, Bodie had clearly set out to deceive the public by using medical titles he was not entitled to.

> He held himself out to treat the incurable by more or less occult arts. It is rather surprising that the magistrate should have considered that the circumstances of this case mitigated the offence committed. By assuming titles which he did not possess, for the purpose of imposing himself on the frequenters of music-halls, the defendant had brought an honourable profession into contempt, and the case might therefore have been deemed one for the infliction of exemplary punishment. Nevertheless, the Medical Defence Union has done a useful piece of work, for while Bodie will probably continue to give his "turns" at "music halls" and "palaces," the conviction will effectually prevent him from posing in the future as a member of the British medical profession.[14]

The *BMJ* was correct on one point: the fine and costs amounting to £10.5s., was hardly likely to deter Bodie who received "the unprecedented salary of £200 per week" when he had played in London the previous year and "£150 a week at one performance a night houses" with another £50 a week added to the salary "of this clever Macduff man whenever he appeared at halls where two performances a night are given." (*Aberdeen Journal*, July 19, 1904; January 25, 1907). As to the *BMJ*'s second point: it was highly debatable if anybody who attended Bodie's shows ever really believed him to be a qualified doctor let alone "a member of the British medical profession." Some five years later a House of Lords ruling, on Section 3 of the Dentists' Act, eventually exposed, serious flaws in the Medical Act and thus in underlining one of Mr Avory's arguments, must have sent shudders down Bateman's spine.

> So long as the unqualified person avoids the direct use of certain professional titles, he may use such other misleading descriptions as his ingenuity suggests, and the present law imposes no restraint upon him. (*BMJ* May 28, 1910, p. 313)[15]

In the meantime, Bodie's immediate response to his "conviction" was to publish *The Bodie Book* which, he claims, was already in Press but was delayed until after his trial so that he might add a chapter in his defense (Bodie 1905, p. 189). The book was probably completed on June 20, 1905, and officially published in September 1905 although the *Dundee Courier* (August 7, 1905), in reviewing an advanced copy, noted it had been

> written by Dr Walford Bodie, the well-known entertainer . . . and deals in a popular vein with electro-hypnotism, telepathy, mental suggestion, clairvoyance, magnetic touch, and various other occult subjects. It is dedicated to the British medical men—an interesting fact in view of the recent proceedings against Dr Bodie on the ground that he holds his diplomas from a United States University and not a British one.

For its part the *Edinburgh Evening News* [*EEN*] (September 4, 1905) commented:

> Dr Bodie, who explains frankly enough that his degree is an American one, has naturally no love for British doctors, many of whom are sceptical as to his cures, and critical as to his methods. . . . The book is a curious jumble of old and new, of facts that the regular practitioner unwillingly admits but which he cannot well explain, and assertions and theories of Dr Bodie himself. One has the impression that all through the writer is posing as a showman before an imaginary audience, and it is not easy to say how much or how little he believes himself.

According to Newton [nd], a professional magician himself, *The Bodie Book* "ran to ten editions and sold more than forty thousand copies." Somewhat ironically it was even noticed, although not reviewed, in the *BMJ* (September 9, 1905, p. 200). Ultimately however, it seems as if there was nothing the medical profession could do to block let alone topple Bodie who, by now, had become a household name.

> Wherever [Bodie] performed, and for no fee, he would spend the daytime helping the poor, in particular those with ailments who could not afford to pay medical bills. No doubt this afforded him a certain amount of free publicity, but he was also passionate about using hypnosis to cure a variety of ills. He practiced manipulation of the limbs and spine, and he had hands that were big enough and strong enough to do it. He combined these skills with hypnotherapy and electrotherapy. He even gave away tickets to those who otherwise couldn't afford to see him. And the public loved him for it—but not so the medical profession . . .
>
> As word of his miracle cures spread, so people flocked to see him. Bodie discovered that a mild tingling dose of electricity could alleviate all sorts of discomfort and ailment, especially those psychosomatic in nature. By this stage of his career Bodie was already wealthy, and yet he gave his time, free of charge to the poor of every town he played. I don't know many people today who would do that. In fact, I don't know of any at all. (Newton, nd)

But as Bodie's fame redoubled so too did the ire of the medical profession and so too the cunning wiles of Dr Bateman.

MRS HUDSON AND THE LEEDS INVALID CHILDREN'S AID SOCIETY

In early March 1906, when Bodie opened at the Leeds Tivoli Variety Theatre (*Leeds Mercury* March 6, 1906), a large group of Medical and University students—some reports suggested around 200—demonstrated "to show their lordly contempt for the 'Modern Miracle Worker.'"

> The prime movers in the hostile demonstration . . . were the would be physicians who gathered in secret conclave at the College on Tuesday [13 March] to discuss the best way in which the much discussed healer might be humbled. The method decided upon, it must be admitted, was questionable.

The "Medicals," leading the way, entered the Tivoli and started booing the moment Bodie appeared, but "loud and long clapping answered his bow and the rise of the curtain." When the medics continued booing and hooting "the cry 'Chuck 'em out' came from various parts of the audience," but the police, having anticipated trouble, moved in to remove the students who resisted. "During the mêlée people stood upon their seats urging the police to 'Do for 'em, lads', and all the while Bodie sat before a line of his cripples, smiling with an air of majesty and motioning with a sweep of his hands to those behind him as though saying, 'My cures are my answer.' The audience understood him and consequently redoubled their noise and shouts of praise to the constables." (*Leeds Mercury* March 15, 1906). When the students were eventually ejected they demanded their money back and caused further disturbances in the foyer and then set upon the police who were trying to bring order. One student, when interviewed, claimed he "merely went to 'boo' the show at which monstrous charges against men of national eminence were made and the students had a right with the rest of the public to show their disapproval. They were ejected by methods of sheer brutality." (*MCLGA* March 21, 1906)[16] This *vox pop* suggests the Leeds medical students were incensed by Bodie's claims to have cured patients, supposedly written off by some of the country's leading surgeons and physicians—"men of national eminence." The medical student clearly took this as a serious slur not just against his teachers but also against the profession he was striving to enter. Although this was not the first anti-Bodie demonstration—there had been violence in 1903 after he was heckled by medical students in Cardiff (*EE*, 17 June; July 7, 1903)—the Tivoli riots appear to have been of a different magnitude.

On March 19, 1906, just a few days after those riots, Mrs Hudson, president of the Leeds Invalid Children's Aid Society [LICAS], a local charitable organization, visited the Society's School at Clarendon House where she was met by a very angry Nurse Higgins. Having heard gossip at the School Higgins had gone to the Tivoli to see for herself.

> "Dr." Bodie came on the platform and explained some part of his electrical treatment. He performed operations upon two people and then said he would produce some of his cures among them being Edith Estill[17] and Rachel Schneider [*sic*] two of the girls from the Home. Bodie did nothing to the girls on the stage but simply exhibited his cures. He said Schneider had been discharged from the Infirmary as incurable and did not that night require either splints or crutches. The crutches had been chopped up for "piggies"[18] for her little brother. [Nurse] Higgins said she admonished the children in connection with the affair. (*HDM* August 3, 1906)

But what had really annoyed Higgins was that Bodie failed to tell the audience "that since the crutches had been chopped up, new ones had to be procured for the girl." Mrs Hudson subsequently claimed that Higgins had also "told her that the children had been paid; and further that one of the 'cures' which Bodie exhibited had never been treated by him before." The following day, March 20, 1906, at a LICAS meeting Mrs Hudson, in proposing a vote of thanks to the chairman, said:

> The committee were very sorry that some of the children had been taken to the Tivoli in connection with a certain show, and that some of the irons with which the committee had provided them had been exhibited as cruel things. [Bodie] had paid the man [*sic*] two shillings a night for the children to go there, but the parents had since been admonished. [Bodie] said . . . he had cured one child, but as a matter of fact the child had never been in his hands before. (*HDM* August 2, 1906)

On reading the press reports of the LICAS meeting Bodie contacted Mrs Hudson direct but when she refused to apologies or to publicly retract her quoted comments, he brought an action for slander against her, and her husband, Robert.[19] And the trial was set for Wednesday August 1, 1906 at the Leeds Assizes, Mr Justice William Grantham (1835–1911)[20] presiding. As Bodie was "fulfilling an engagement at Dundee, being under penalty of £300 if he chose to leave," William Mills Norman, his manager of nine years, travelled to Leeds to give evidence on Bodie's behalf. Although the trial was reported extensively and offers fascinating insights into aspects of Bodie's career, the burden of the case turned around the question of whether or not Bodie was a charlatan and whether or not he had effected the miraculous cures he claimed. Under examination Norman said that Bodie's turn usually lasted from fifty-five to sixty minutes. Patients were invited to assemble before the performance and Bodie picked out those he would cure.

> Many of those who had been cured on previous visits attended the demonstrations and paid testimony to [Bodie's] services. It was not true that [Bodie] paid 2s a night for children to be brought to him. The parents did not pay anything. The company got from 50–55% of the receipts according to the size of the hall. It is not true that Dr Bodie ever claimed to have cured a child that had never been under his care. Nor did he claim to cure people at a distance.[21]

Mr Scott Fox, Council for the Hudsons, asked Norman if he knew that one of the girls, Rachel Schneider, was suffering from hip-joint problems and had been diagnosed with tuberculous disease. "Do you know Dr Bodie took away her crutches, and sent her away without them? Do you know that the result of this was that the girl got worse and had to undergo an operation?" Although there is no indication of Norman's replies to these, presumably, rhetorical questions, when Fox then asked him how Bodie found out what the children suffered from, Norman replied "The same as other doctors do." (*Leeds Mercury*, August 2, 1906) At the adjourned hearing the parents of two crippled children, treated by Bodie, gave evidence as to how they had been benefited. The first, a little girl named [Violet] Hurley,[22] was told by a Leeds medical man that she would have to wear irons all her life. Bodie had operated upon her with electricity and since then she no longer had to wear irons, and Violet's mother, Mrs Emily Hurley, had often gone onto Bodie's stage to testify as to the good Bodie had done her daughter and had never been paid for doing this. Sarah Ellen Townsend said her nine year old girl[23] had worn wooden splints from the age of two and a half but since Bodie's treatment she had not used a stick or a crutch. Toward the end of the trial Fox, for the Hudsons, said if Bodie was to succeed in his action he had to show that he had suffered in his business.

> Now admittedly his business was that of a showman and it was not pretended that he had suffered in that capacity. Bodie was not a doctor and therefore it could not be said that his medical reputation, if he had any, could be injured in any way. [Mrs Hudson's] remarks were meant to allude to Bodie's pretentions as a doctor and nothing else and thus Bodie would suffer no injury in that respect because he did not now pose as a qualified doctor. Mrs Hudson uttered the words in good faith and thought that what she had said was privileged being in a private meeting.

Judge Grantham, having already ruled that the Society's meeting was not privileged, said there was a case to answer and, in summing up, argued strongly in Bodie's favor. He could understand "the feelings of nurses who were interested in these cases and who got angry if anybody took a different view from theirs" but "nothing more serious could be said about a man" like Bodie, than that he was a rank impostor. (*HDM* August 3, 1906) Mrs Hudson had practically admitted that the statement reported in the newspapers was true, and, what is more, also admitted a portion of that statement was false even though she believed it was true when she made it.

> That being so there was no doubt that [Bodie] had been slandered. He had been held up as an imposter and there was not a word of truth in the statement that he had paid children or parents to go onto his stage. Nothing could be more serious to Bodie than the statement alleged against him. Perhaps the method of treatment might not suit the tastes of all, and it might be better if the plaintiff did his work a little less publicly, but there was no doubt that he did a great deal of good. [People might regret, and he himself regretted that he did not carry out his cures in some other way; but so long as a man was making his living legitimately people had no right to call him a rank impostor because they disliked the way in which he carried on his work. It was well known that doctors were jealous people. . . . They called these men quacks but it was a fact that these men did things that doctors could not do.][24] In passing he reverted to the famous instance in which the cobbler had been successful as a bone-setter[25] in thousands of cases. Mr Little would himself have said that electricity was valuable in some cases, and although Bodie was not a qualified doctor he could not be stigmatised as a quack or an imposter. It was not for him to say how the cures were effected, but it was very hard if poor people were not to be allowed to consult him, as they had done with great success. The plaintiffs had unfortunately treated 'this man' as they called him, with the greatest contempt, and this was the more unfortunate, because the good lady [Mrs Hudson] having discovered her mistake could very easily have said she was sorry. (*Aberdeen Journal* August 3, 1906)

While the jury returned a verdict in Bodie's favor they assessed damages at only "a farthing," but Grantham then refused the defendants' application that Bodie should be deprived of costs. (*HDM* August 3, 1906). In reporting the case the *Medical Press & Circular* [*MPC*] (August 15, 1906, pp. 157, 166) noted

> The only comment we can make on the proceedings is that Mrs. Hudson has our sincere sympathy, and that, we are glad to see it already suggested in Leeds that her costs should be defrayed by public subscription.

But the *MPC*, like many in the medical profession, simply failed to address one of Grantham's central points: that "it was very hard if poor people were not to be allowed to consult" somebody like Bodie. But Grantham's comments also reveal how the Hudson case touched a number of other important questions. For example who was entitled to define and control the terms and nature of the medical discourse? How was society to deal with the socioeconomic issues of health, not just in respect of poor patients but also in respect of non-qualified "healers where class and status, and maybe even racial or national prejudice, supervened?[26] Something of this can be read back into Grantham's comments noting how Mrs Hudson, and probably also nurse Higgins, had referred to Bodie as "this man," thereby suggesting that they probably perceived him as, at best, working class. For their part the Hudsons, who were clearly a pillar of "polite" English Leeds Society, no doubt believed their wealth and philanthropic works entitled them to treat Bodie as a social, maybe even, racial inferior. Although further enquiries would take us too far from this study, it is nonetheless worth noting that Hallam and Spriggs, like Bodie, also came from working-class backgrounds and practiced their "gifts" of healing without any formal academic or medical training. Most members of the medical profession, including Mrs Hudson as a patron of LICAS, would, no doubt, have considered men like Bodie as interlopers seeking to appropriate, for themselves, some of the wealth, status, and privileges which they, as favored professionals, habitually took for granted. Thus Bodie's miracle cures also posed an existential threat to an established medical order fiercely protective of their closed guild status. This view might be read into a somewhat rambling *vox pop* quoted in an article following Bodie's visit to Cardiff in 1903.

> "If," said one medical man, "Dr. Bodie can effect the cures he asserts, why doesn't he take a suite of rooms in a London hotel and there receive patients? There are hundreds of wealthy paralytics who would pay him enormous fees if he could but restore them to health." It is admitted that Dr. Bodie's methods might be successful in the treatment of hypochondriacs, or hysterical folk, whose ill-health is almost entirely imaginary. So melancholy is the disposition of a great many women that they fancy themselves too ill to leave their beds when, as a matter of fact, if they would bestir themselves, they would be able to leave their bedchambers, get out into the fresh air and sunshine, and derive a fair average sum of enjoyment from life. This form of visionary ill-health is very much less common among men, although innumerable cases have been known. With regard to patients of this character, it is believed that the unwonted excitement of appearing on a stage and the force of suggestion (not necessarily hypnotic) would cause the patient to arise and walk. (*EE*, May 21, 1903)

It is difficult to imagine working-class women swooning in "bedchambers."

DOWN WITH BODIE!

At about the same time as his run-in with Bateman and the MDU Bodie established a head office at 163 Blackfriars, London (*The Era* June 24, 1905,

p. 26) where he set up the "Bodie Electric Drug Company, Wholesale Chemists, Druggists, Sundriesmen," a mail order business dispensing proprietary "quack remedies" which he advertised in local newspapers.

> Bodie's famous electric Liniment: kills pain in man or beast. The only sure cure for paralysis, rheumatism, sciatica, Rheumatoids, Atrophied Muscles, Locomotor ataxy, sore throat, coughs, colds in the chest [The quickest Healer of all Sprains] &c. The most powerful embrocation in the World. Thousands of Testimonials. May be had from all chemists at 2/9 and 1/1½ per bottle or post free. (*COMC* May 18, 1907; [*Cambrian*, November 29, 1907]; Bodie 1905)[27]

Meanwhile at the other end of the Kingdom the *Aberdeen Journal* (July 16, 1906), one of Bodie's long time supporters, reported him the toast of the town:

> He has just finished a fortnight's engagement at the Grand Theatre, Edinburgh where a large number of students were much interested in his operations. During the week close upon 500 cases passed through Dr Bodie's hands. The Grand Theatre was besieged daily by crowds of helpless cripples all eager to see Dr Bodie, who issued a challenge of £1000 stating that he would hand over this amount to the Royal Infirmary if anyone could prove that his cures were not genuine. (*Aberdeen Journal* July 16, 1906)

The contrast between the inquisitive Edinburgh students and their angry Leeds, London, and Glasgow counterparts could hardly have been starker.

Later that year (1906), while performing in Bradford, Bodie was summoned, by the local Council, under the 1903 Employment of Children Act on a complaint that children had been paid to appear on stage, two as cured patients, one as a patient. Bodie's defense was that the children had not been paid and even if they had there was no employment as defined by the Act. Although Bodie was found guilty and fined 37s 6d, including costs, or twenty-one days imprisonment, the magistrate granted his appeal on the grounds that this was the first case of its kind (*EE,* July 20, 1906).[28] And yet these set backs in Leeds and now in Bradford appear to have done little to diminish Bodie's popularity particularly the further north he travelled where his reputation remained largely untarnished.

Toward the end of 1906 Bodie issued a new set of provocative notices advertising his next London appearance: "Dr. Bodie, MDCM (USA) FRMS (London) the Electric Wizard."

> The Famous Bloodless surgeon, Electrical Anatomist, the Scottish Osteologist, and the most wonderful Exponent of Physiological Malformations the world has ever seen. Bloodless Surgery v. the Knife, introducing his Gorgeous Fit-up

> of Electrical Apparatus at a cost of £2,000. Marvellous Cures of the Paralysed. Modern Miracles performed in Full View of the Audience. Cheers, Tears, and Screams of Laughter Nightly. See Dr. Bodie passing Thousands of Volts of Electricity through his Body. Lighting a Cigarette with his Finger; Setting Fire to HandKerchiefs, &c. Important Notice.—Dr. Bodie will give Advice Free of Charge daily from 1 to 2 at the Theatre to the Hopeless and Paralysed. Children specially invited. Dr. Bodie has cured over 900 cases discharged from all the leading London Hospitals. (*EE* December 6, 1906)

This was clearly too much for some of the medical students from some of the principle hospitals of London who now assembled at the Hackney Empire to rag Bodie about those fake medical degrees which Bateman had exposed in July 1905. Although it "was announced that [Bodie] would 'cure' six patients with his electrical treatment" the students' hostility meant "he was only able to attend to one of them, a little cripple boy who was carried on the stage and who after treatment walked off apparently cured." Bodie's "appearance before the footlights was the signal for ironical cheering, amidst which was heard the question 'What does FRMS stand for?' Considerable uproar followed and when Bodie shouted 'A man is known by his deeds and not by the letters after his name,' there was much amusement amongst the hilarious students who continued to howl and 'boo.'" The *Leeds Mercury* (December 17, 1906) noted that when Bodie "refused to allow any of the students to examine his instruments or to have his electric current sent through his own body," his refusal "provoked further disturbances." In a subsequent interview Bodie said he believed the students were from the Charing Cross, the Middlesex and the London Hospitals and the demonstrators "had made up their mind to have some amusement at his expense." "'There were about a hundred of them seated in the stalls,' he said, 'but only about a dozen made any hostile demonstration. I invited them on the stage to test the electric current, but only one had courage enough to receive a shock. After remonstrating with them I was enabled to complete my operations, and the students at the conclusion of the performance gave three cheers for the orchestra. A theatre spokesman confirmed that as they were expecting trouble they took precautions in having additional policemen on duty.' In the end 'the doctor gave as good as he got.'" (*NEP* December 17, 1906).

From then on controversy and adulation dogged Bodie in almost equal measure. Back in Scotland he was fated with the *Motherwell Times* (23 October 1908) calling him an old favorite: "It may be taken for granted that the theatre will be crowded nightly, for everyone now admits that in drawing crowds Dr Bodie has few equals." Less than a year later there was a demonstration against him outside the Ardwick Empire, Manchester, and as he left the theatre with his wife and a medical gentleman "two young men supposed to be medical students threw a quantity of cayenne pepper at the party" (*MCLGA* May 12, 1909). Although such reports can be multiplied it is worth quoting from an astute comment in the *Luton Times and Advertiser* [*LTA*] (May 3, 1907) which noted that Bodie's mesmerism would be

> fairly familiar to all who have seen Kennedy and other mesmerists. . . . But after all the great interest lies in the more serious part of the Doctor's performance, namely his operations upon those suffering with various forms of paralysis and lameness due to malformations. The most sceptical cannot but be profoundly impressed when they see a child, discharged as hopelessly incurable from the local and London hospitals, wheeled onto the stage and submitted to Dr Bodie's treatment for a few minutes to not only kick vigorously with limbs that had been almost powerless, but walk off the stage pushing before it the invalid's chair in which it had been brought, helpless, to the theatre. And this is only one of quite a number of cases of "cure" that whatever be the explanation and whatever be the permanent results, are little less than miraculous.

Although there is evidence to suggest Bodie was still performing his weird and wonderful cures into the 1930s (*HDM* 11 October 1933, p. 11) the final part of this particular story occurred in November 1909, when Charles Henry Irving (b.1886) the son of a prosperous Cumberland farmer, brought an action to recover damages against Walford Bodie.

BITTER DEFEATS

Irving's case, which was heard in the King's Bench Division before Mr Justice Darling (1849–1936),[29] in late 1909, was that in 1906 Irving "bound himself to Bodie for a period of three years and paid him £1,000 premium" on condition that Bodie would "teach him hypnotism and mesmerism, bloodless surgery and medical electricity."[30] Irving claimed Bodie tricked him, personally and through the claims he made in the *Bodie Book*, that he was a qualified medical practitioner who could teach him everything he knew about the "medical aspects" of his art. In fact Bodie had taught him practically nothing "because his music hall exhibitions were mere trickery" and the *Bodie Book* a pack of lies (*Aberdeen Journal* November 3, 1909; *DET,* November 1, 1909). Mr Mellor, in assembling Irving's case, called Alfred George Bateman to prove that "all of Bodie's degrees," and especially the American ones from Barrett and Chicago Colleges, were fictitious. Bateman's appearance, as an expert witness, strongly suggests the MDU may well have been behind Irving's action and maybe even helping to fund it.[31] With his forensic evidence Bateman systematically revealed how each of Bodie's alleged American qualifications were entirely bogus. Bateman's evidence completely undermined many of the absurd claims Bodie (1905, pp. 190–92) had previously made and now cut a major plank from Bodie's defense. But Bateman's evidence would also, from now on, provide a powerful stick with which Bodie's enemies could beat him remorselessly. Following Bateman Mellor then presented evidence to show that the men who came up from the audience to be hypnotized, or to receive electric shock, were, as a rule, Bodie's men. "If a genuine member of the audience ever came up he was hustled about and knocked down." If true these, and similar allegations made during William Lovell's 1903 trial, reveal Bodie to be not just a skilful performer and "miracle worker" but also an adept at managing, controlling, and maybe even manipulating his audiences (*EE* June 10, 1903). In his evidence Irving, who had worked intimately with Bodie for a couple of years, claimed that Bodie employed a man named Giles who had a distinguished appearance and "usually posed as a doctor and was dressed in a frock coat and silk hat."

> As to the cures of paralysis. The patients were first seen at midday and only such as were able to walk off stage were chosen to attend evening performances. The patients except as had crutches were then carried on to the stage. Bodie broke down any particular adhesion that might exist[32] and passed an ordinary magnet over the affected limb. The lights were lowered a mild current of electricity was applied and the patients passed off as cured. (Laughter)

Irving also claimed that the same people "appeared at hall after hall as patients cured of paralysis" (*MCLGA* November 2, 1909) while others were manipulated into claiming disabilities they never had and a number of them then were called to corroborate Irving's claims.[33] In his evidence William Lovell said he had known Bodie for seventeen years, been in his employ, on and off, for some eight years, and did a little boxing between times.

> He was engaged as a hypnotic subject[34] with a number of others whose duty it was to pretend to be hypnotised by Bodie. But he was never hypnotised. He had also appeared as a subject cured of what Bodie described as catalepsy in a diseased form from a dreadful malady which would yield to nothing but mesmerism. The witness who said he usually paid at the door and took his place among the audience said on one occasion he was found out. He dressed as a sailor procured what he thought was a midshipman's uniform but unfortunately for him some stripes were sewn on the sleeve which would have taken him 20 or 30 years to earn. So when he went on stage for the usual purpose the sailors in the audience spotted him—there was also a disturbance at Cardiff in the quelling of which he had the misfortune to strike a man so hard as to break his jaw. He was committed to Quarter Sessions for that. [Lovell] denied that he was dismissed for drunkenness and insubordination and made threats against Bodie.[35]

For his part Bodie's Counsel admitted his client was an entertainer, there was no doubt about that; but his client had also cured cases and, to this end, he called a number of patients and parents of patients to testify.

> Cecilia Goulding[36] a machinist of 59 Church-street Stoke Newington was paralysed in her lower limbs from infancy and had to use double leg irons. She was treated in infancy at a hospital without effect. In August 1904 when she was 17 years old she was treated by Dr Bodie at a music hall in Shoreditch and never after had to wear the irons but could walk quite well. She walked across the court and shook hands with Bodie. She had testified at several music-halls to Dr Bodie having cured her because she could never do enough to thank Dr Bodie for what he had done for her. (*MCLGA,* November 3, 1909)

Henry Smith, of Barclay Road, Leytonstone, then told the court that "his boy who had suffered from rickets and was for two years at Great Ormond Street Hospital was unable to walk till he was treated by Bodie. 'Now' said the witness 'I have to pay for three windows he smashed at football' (laughter)." (*MCLGA* November 3, 1909) Finally Bodie, called in his own defense,

> said that he had been touring music halls for the last 23 years and had visited the same places over and over again. He was greatly against taking the plaintiff as pupil at first but then consented to do so. He denied that he had ever told the plaintiff that he was a qualified medical man in this country. (*MCLGA* November 3, 1909)

Somewhat surprisingly the judge allowed Bodie to give a private demonstration before the jury with Mr Arthur Stritch, an electrical engineer, acting as expert witness. As the trial drew to a conclusion Mr Powell, probably in his summing up, said his client, Bodie, had to contend with an enormous amount of prejudice.

> What about the people who climbed to power by the use of terminological inexactitude? He derided the suggestion that [Bodie] ever supposed he was a duly qualified medical man. It was for stage purposes only that he held this qualification. The allegation that he was not skilled in hypnotism had failed on the evidence brought forward . . . a serious question for consideration was whether the defendant was a quack in the popular sense. He submitted no one could pretend that Bodie failed to possess the skill to which he laid claim.

In reply Mr Mellor, for Irving, said Bodie's "business was . . . absolutely dishonest and fraudulent." In his summing up Mr Justice Darling, suggested "a person who performed hundreds and thousands of operations, as defendant declared he had, might be able to bring persons to Court to say he had cured them. It would have been well, however, if a little more had been known about the nature of these person's afflictions." (*DET* November 4, 1909).

The jury's verdict, in Irving's favor, unleashed an extraordinary wave of pent up anger against Bodie. A group of students made an attack on the stage when he performed at the Glasgow Coliseum music hall shortly after the trial (*SET* November 12, 1909; *Motherwell,* November 12, 1909) and, in the riot that followed, Bodie's wife, La Bella Electra, was seriously injured. Shortly afterward Bodie "himself also suffering from a serious and dangerous physical breakdown," was forced to cancel his performances issuing a doctor's medical certificate: "'Dr.' Bodie was suffering from extreme neurasthenia bordering on collapse . . . [and] was quite unfit for work of any kind and it was necessary that he should have rest." (*DET* November 15, 1909). Although Bodie was forced to cancel his London performances for later that year, his absence did not prevent a wave of anger from sweeping through the medical and electrical faculties.

> A large body of students made their way to 'Dr' Bodie's drug store in Blackfriars road London where stones were thrown and windows smashed. Other demonstrations were made by bands of students as they marched from South London to the West End and in Piccadilly Circus where 10 of their number were arrested.[37]

At another demonstration "large numbers of medical students marched on the Canterbury and Paragon Music Halls . . . [where] there was considerable disorder, eggs being thrown." (*Aberdeen Journal* November 16, 1909). In Glasgow the authorities got wind of a large demonstration being organized by a joint group of medical and engineering students and although they persuaded the medical students to disperse about 200 engineer apprentices marched to Gilmorehill[38] where they staged Bodie's mock burial. (*DET* November 16, 1909). There were also disturbances, the following year, when Bodie, now back to work, appeared at Princes' Theatre, Preston, and about 100 pupils, workmen and others from the electrical works[39] in town "arranged to pay a visit to the theatre but police got wind of what was happening and although they were present in force there were wild scenes of uproar" with seven arrests. (*SDESG,* June 8, 1910). But then another heavy blow against Bodie occurred in February 1910 when his appeal against Mr Justice Darling's decision, was summarily dismissed with an excoriating judgment by Sir Herbert H. Cozens-Hardy, (Master of the Rolls).

> [Mr Justice Darling] in the Court below took a strong view that it was an incongruous mixture to attempt to exercise the healing art upon the music hall stage, after having given some kind of electrical performance. The learned judge indicated that he did not like that kind of thing and that was particularly noticeable in his summing up. There was no doubt that Bodie did publish himself as a showman.
>
> According to the evidence given at the trial [Bodie] had actually cured a great many persons suffering in various ways. He was not exactly a bone-setter,

> but was a person who claimed to afford considerable benefit to children suffering from infantile paralysis. He was undoubtedly a showman and the plaintiff wanted to follow him on stage.
>
> To allege possession of a qualification is a very different matter. Bodie's counsel says that although Bodie's book was full of lies it could not be seen as misrepresentation which induced the plaintiff to enter into a contract.
>
> [The Master of the Rolls] said that he could not but admire the courage and ability displayed by Mr Powell in presenting [Bodie's] case to the court. A more hopeless appeal it had never been his misfortune to have heard. In substance the appellant's case rested solely on the ground of misdirection of the learned judge. But he wished to say that he had seldom or never heard or read a more clear or explicit judgement, or one more directed to the real points of the case, or one more free from objection . . . Bodie told the plaintiff that he was a duly qualified medical man and in his Lordship's opinion a more gross lie could not possibly be imagined. The statements made by Bodie were absolutely unfounded, and at the time when he got this £1,000 he was an ignorant, unscrupulous quack." (*YPLI* February 25, 1910) "It would be a waste of words to say more. [Bodie] was a swindler and [Irving] had been swindled by him." (*DC* February 25, 1910)

Although a serious set back for Bodie's credibility the Irving case ultimately turned around "breach of contract" with the jury finding that Bodie had deliberately deceived Irving into believing that his bogus medical qualifications were in fact real. It followed, therefore, that because Bodie claimed medical qualifications to which he was never entitled,[40] he had effectively induced Irving to part with his £1,000 under false pretenses. On the other hand the whole question as to the status of Bodie's "miracle cures" remained largely unresolved and the matter was not helped by the fact that even the Master of the Rolls grudgingly accepted that Bodie "had actually cured a great many persons suffering in various ways."

NOTES

1. "A young girl was also placed in a trance in full view of the audience and Dr Bodie stated that she would remain in a condition of artificial catalepsy until next Saturday night. She is, he said, to be watched each night by a committee of ladies." (*MCLGA*, April 15, 1902).
2. No record in the 1901 census.
3. The Bodie sensation coincides, for a time, with the mass "awakening" of Evan Roberts and the Welsh Revival Movement (1904–1905) for which see the excellent account by Hayward (2007, pp. 107f). Bodie, who actively took against Roberts, sent one of his pupils to hypnotize Roberts "in order to drive the Welsh revivalist out of Liverpool." (*Aberdeen Journal*, May 1, 1905, p. 4).
4. Bodie (1905, pp. 36ff) offers a detailed description of one of his performances.

5. Bodie (1905), who rented the Fife Arms as a going concern, advertised Macduff (fifty miles north of Aberdeen) as "The Greatest Health Resort in Scotland."

6. There are discrepancies between the coroner's court report and the 1891 census. The latter has Frances Owen (b.1855) the daughter-in-law of John Owen a general laborer. Frances was probably married to John's son William who also worked in the potteries. I am following the newspaper reports.

7. "Mrs Owen was the first person upon whom Dr Bodie operated on Monday for paralytic cure with his electrical apparatus." (*WC* July 11, 1903).

8. See, however, the more complicated case of Mrs. Taynton, of Wellington-street, Canton, whom Bodie claims to have helped but Dr O'Donovan "absolutely denied that he had regarded the case as incurable. (*EE* May 21, 1903).

9. Also Bodie (1905, pp. 135–36). For an insight into this world see for example, Randi [nd].

10. Leaflet in the John Johnson Collection.

11. Bodie (1905, pp. 64, 175) probably played at the Britannia Theatre, Hoxton, East End of London. "That he has made a triumphant beginning there can be no gainsaying, nor can it be denied that he has won the hearts of the rough-cut East Enders—who, by the way, prefer ocular rather than oral testimony of what appear to be little less than miracles in the healing of the halt and the lame, who for years past have led unhappy lives, some in dingy tenements in the none too salubrious atmosphere of Shoreditch, Whitechapel . . . and other similar neighbourhoods" (*The Era*, quoted Bodie 1905, p. 175). Bodie (1905, p. 181) may also have played the Paragon Theatre, in the Mile End Road.

12. An Occultists' Defence League was established to defend prosecuted members (*Light* August 18, 1900, p. 396; December 15, 1900, p. 604).

13. Although it was common for mesmeric entertainers to pass themselves off as "professor," it would seem that the stage designation of "Dr." went beyond the pale.

14. Bodie (1905, pp. 189–93) offers his own version of the case.

15. For a detailed survey of the law in this area see Anon (1911a).

16 Although John Spink, a young traveller for a type writer agency, sued the police for illegal arrest, imprisonment, and assault, Judge Greenhow, sitting in Leeds County Court, dismissed the case (*Leeds Mercury* June 16, 1906).

17. This could have been Edith M Estill (b.1893) living with her widowed mother Rose.

18. As far as I can make out this was a form of skittles.

19. Robert Hudson (1840–1912) and his wife Hannah (b.1853) had three sons, also mechanical engineers, who probably all worked in their father's company making wagons and other railway plant. The Hudsons had five live-in servants (*YPLI*, April 16, 1912, p. 7).

20. Grantham was a Conservative MP who resigned in 1886 on being appointed a judge. "Mr Justice Grantham . . . enjoys the distinction of being, we believe, the only judge within living memory whose conduct has been called in question by Parliament . . ." (*MPC* August 15, 1906, p. 157). The *MPC* failed to mention, however, that Grantham was censured because of his decisions on petitions following the 1906 Parliamentary elections.

21. This was probably a reference to Bodie's "battle" with Evan Roberts, for which see above.

22. Probably Violet M Hurley (b.1898), eldest daughter of William (b.1877), an Iron Planer, and Emily (b.1876) living in Leeds from around 1899. There is no indication of a disability in the 1901 census.

23. Probably May Townsend (b.1899) eldest daughter of John (b.1876), a coal hewer, and his wife Sarah (b.1878). There is no indication of a disability in the 1901 census.

24. *HDM*, August 3, 1906.

25. As there was a long tradition of bone-setting in Scotland it was probably "a survival of a tradition rather than a deliberate creation of modern social demands." In Glasgow, from around 1910, there was a firm of American practitioners "calling themselves 'Oseopaths'" (Fitzroy 1910, pp. 54 and 55).

26. The medical profession believed, almost unanimously, that "gratuitous" treatments tend "to diminish the thrift and self-respect of the public, lessens the esteem in which medical science is held, and has a detrimental effect upon the position of many members of the medical profession." (*Lancet*, December 15, 1906, p. 1680).

27. At an inquest into the death of Elizabeth Ann Morgan her husband, who had purchased "a phial of Dr. Bodie's electric life pills," originally thought the "electric life pills" were the cause of her death. The coroner, Dr Macartney, told the court that "Morgan had told [the police] that he considered Dr Bodie was a clever man; no doubt he was, or he would not have sold pills for 1s 1½d a phial which cost him only a penny to make. As long as the public would buy these pills Dr Bodie and his race would exist and get fat" (*EE* January 17, 1908).

28. I have been unable to discover how this case ended.

29. Like Justice Grantham, Charles John Darling was originally a conservative MP who resigned on being appointed a judge in 1897.

30. Irving first saw Bodie perform in 1902, or 1903, and wanted to join him but being under age his parents refused to give him the £500 Bodie demanded. When Irving came of age, in 1906, he persuaded Bodie to hire him and a contract was drawn up in which Irving, having paid £1,000, was to receive "a salary of £2.10 a week . . . during his term of pupillage." (*EEEM*, November 2, 1909, p. 2).

31. *MPC* (August 8, 1906, p. 132) took an uncompromising position against "irregular medical practice and quack medicines."

32. On this point see Bodie (1905, pp. 38, 173–74).

33. In 1906 Ernest Miller, aged twenty-five, who simulated deafness, pleaded guilty to stealing a watch and chain. He told the judge he worked for Dr Bodie and the detective, in evidence, said Miller "used to go on [stage] and hop about and make out he had been cured. The next night he would be carried on again. The Judge: he was one of the sham cures?—Yes, my lord, and he got worse every night" (*EE* May 23, 1906).

34. According to Hart (1896, pp. 169f), there was a highly profitable trade in professionally trained hypnotic subjects during the 1890s.

35. Probably William Lovell, born Glasgow 1887. He and his brother Christy described themselves as showmen in the 1901 census. William, described as a stage

assistant, was found guilty of assaulting Edward Nelson on May 29, 1903. The reports contradict Lovell's account. Nelson, a well-known tobacconist, had gone to see Bodie's show. While hypnotising his subjects Bodie, heckled by medical students, started "calling people present all manner of names and himself creating a good deal of the excitement that was going on." As this continued for a long time Nelson called out "Why don't you go on with the show?" Lovell, sitting behind, came up and "put his face in front of Mr Nelson and told him to shut up." An altercation started whereupon Lovell suddenly struck Nelson between the eyes. The wound "which bled profusely .. was such that the medical evidence showed could not be due in whole to a fist." Lovell, already in remand, was imprisoned for a day (*EE* 17 June; July 7, 1903)

36. The 1911 census has Cecilia, born 1888, as a sewing Machinist.

37. Had this been a few years earlier Ernest Jones might have been one of those who took part (*LES* March 12, 1900, p. 8).

38. A large college at Gilmorehill, with engineering laboratories, opened in 1901. Engineers were probably involved in the demonstrations not just because Bodie was alleged to have faked his electrical apparatus but also because he had made derogatory remarks about Gilmorehill.

39. Opposition to Bodie from electricians can be traced to Cardiff in 1903 but these tended to be no more than bad tempered heckling. Mr How's Cardiff protest against Bodie (*EE* May 25, 1903) was offset by the warm welcome he received when he appeared in Swansea (*Cambrian* September 27, 1907). Serious demonstrations by electricians, in alliance with doctors, appear to have only started after 1907.

40. Although never quite explicit Bodie (i.e., 1905, p. 165) suggests, surreptitiously, that he was a doctor.

Chapter 6

The Medical, the Clerical, the Spiritual

> When the even were come they brought unto him many that were possessed with devils; and he cast out the spirits with his word, and healed all that were sick, that it might be fulfilled which was spoken by Esaias the prophet, saying, 'Himself took our infirmities, and bore our sickness' (Mathew 8; 16–17).[1]

THE CRUEL CREED OF THE "PECULIAR PEOPLE:" CHRISTIAN SCIENCE IN THE DOCK

On Wednesday February 7, 1900 Mr Justice Ridley, congratulated the Grand Jury because the list he was to put before them was "especially light" and the cases they were required to try were "of a simple nature."

> He need only refer to that in which Wm. Henry Barnes and Mary Ann Barnes, members of the sect called Peculiar People, were charged with the manslaughter of their daughter, Lois Mary Barnes, who was about 14 years of age. The Peculiar People,[2] as no doubt the Grand jury were aware, had a religious tenet that it was not lawful to employ a physician. Instead of doing so they considered that the Bible enjoined them to elect people as elders, who might have any other occupation in life, and if any were ill the proper course was to send for an elder to anoint them with oil and to call upon the name of the Lord. In many cases, unfortunately, "this cruel creed not only caused suffering to the children but had also cost them their lives." This was one of the instances in which death had occurred.

Justice Ridley said, if there was "the probability that medical science would have saved the girl's life" then the parents would have to answer a charge of manslaughter. If, on the other hand, they thought that the girl would have died anyway, then the parents would have to answer a charge of cruelty and neglect under the 1889 Prevention of Cruelty to Children Act (*CC*, February 9, 1900). The Jury having decided there was a case to answer Mr and Mrs Barnes were sent before Mr Justice Bingham at the Essex Summer Assize, whereupon on Wednesday June 20, 1900, the prosecution withdrew the charge of manslaughter and the parents, having been found guilty of causing their daughter unnecessary suffering, and were fined £5 each with the alternative of a month's hard labour (*ESWS*, June 23, 1900).

A few weeks later *The Lancet* (July 14, 1900, p. 119) linked the death of Lois Barnes[3] with the recent acquittal of the defendants charged with the manslaughter of Harold Frederic, an American novelist living in London. *The Lancet* now claimed that the Christian Science movement in America was such "that the danger has there reached a point at which it must be taken seriously."

> With us, however, the danger is not a serious one as in the States owing to the craze not having "caught on" to the same extent, while, as we have seen, the fear of prosecution has a restraining effect in the case of children. Besides which a little reliance on the good sense of the average Englishman and Englishwoman and a glance at the congregation as it files into the "Christian Science" services in London alike tend to reassure us.[4]

Apart from its assumed superiority of "Englishness" the article also oozed class prejudice, and, no doubt assuming their readers knew William Barnes was a farmer, suggested that such a case was hardly likely to happen in London where the congregation of "Christian Scientists" was made up of

> smartly dressed ladies who sing hymns to the accompaniment of a grand piano and are soothed by solemn rigmarole in the comfortably furnished room in Bryanston-street.

The breeding "of well-to-do people," as opposed to the ignorance of the Peculiar People, would surely never allow such things? (Moulton 1906, p. 22; Gartrell-Mills 1991, p. 70). Arthur Hallam (1899a, p. 374), also thought: "It is a fact also that this sect [of Christian Science] has drawn to it many from the educated and intellectual classes . . ." On the other hand the *JMS* (1899, Vol. 45, p. 353), in commenting on the Harold Frederic affair, was far more uncompromising and ranted: "This farrago of pitiful nonsense, falsely heralded as Christianity and Science, is a very definite evil." Feilding (1899, p. 60), in her more measured tones, called Christian Science "a kind of metaphysical mysticism."

A couple of years later although still pointing to the spread of Christian Science[5] and its "murderous heresy," *The Lancet* (September 27, 1902, p. 884) still saw it as a product of "the degenerate side of the American mind—its megalomania and shoddy mysticism." Just two months later, however, there was a subtle shift in tone when *The Lancet* (November 22, 1902, p. 1409), reviewed the recently published translation of the pamphlet in which Albert Moll (1902) "admits that Christian Science may improve the symptoms even when serious anatomical changes are present. But so, also, he says, will ordinary psychotherapy and suggestion." The significance of *The Lancet's* intervention, at this precise moment, lies in its unquestioned acceptance of "psychotherapy" and of the way in which Moll (1902, pp. 24–25) had framed the "obscure or mystic powers" of Christian Science by reference to "well-known natural forces." In other words to *suggestion* which had now become a "kind of generic term for all sorts of things, and includes many complicated psychic processes." For his part Moll defined *suggestion* as "the production of a desired state by awakening the conviction of its existence," which included "hypnosis" because it "enhances susceptibility considerably." Suggestion would explain those faith cures where a person was "firmly convinced that this particular treatment will benefit them." But Moll also extended *suggestion* to include other "motives" such as emotion.

> The anticipation of coming events is the father of diverse sensations. According to Carpenter, anticipation may produce functional changes in the human system, even without the aid of direct suggestion.[6]

It was Moll's (1902, p. 25) extensive researches into Christian Science which had led him to conclude:

> But one thing is certain: that if, under ordinary circumstances, psychical influences offer advantages in the treatment of disease, it is quite unnecessary to resort to Christian Science for that purpose, or, in other words, to engage the sudden and direct intervention of Mrs. Eddy or her emissaries between God and the patient.

By early 1903 the dangers feared, even anticipated, by the local reporter who had covered the Barnes trial three years earlier, had now not only reached the capital but were also beginning to infect sections of the metropolitan élite. So *The Lancet* (March 21, 1903, p. 823; March 28, 1903, p. 922) reported that the Rev. John Bond had recently preached against Christian Science in a sermon, delivered at St. Mary Plaistow, in the East End of London: and the following week J. Johnson Abraham urged readers to take Christian Science seriously:

> Its interest—and, I may add, its danger—lies in that it professes to be much more than a religion: it claims to hold the keys of health, to check disease, and to place the patient under treatment on the high road to health, not by drugs or any physical method of treatment, but simply by a sustained effort of the will.

The Christian Scientist "who professes to cure diseases of which he can have no practical knowledge" was not just a danger to the patient but also the State! Two years later *The Lancet* (November 18, 1905, pp. 1485–86) signalled yet another shift in attitude when it warned against "the widely-spread poverty" that now existed in London, and many other great industrial centers and feared this would inevitably produce, or aggravate, illness thereby

> increasing the demands made upon hospitals at the very time when their funds must inevitably suffer from the competition of organisations [charities pk] established for the relief of ordinary distress.

These comments were ostensibly inspired following a generous gift from her Majesty the Queen in her attempt to help alleviate poverty at a time when the onset of winter suggested that an already difficult situation would turn into a crisis where

> sickness will follow in the wake of famine. Insufficiency of clothing will tell upon both children and adults. Injuries will be less easily recovered from, infections will be more rapidly diffused. The general result must, as we have said, be an increased demand upon hospitals; and it is certain that the governing bodies will, in the majority of cases, recognise the duty of dealing with this increased demand as with an emergency for which they are bound to provide, even at the cost of a mortgage upon the future liberality of their supporters.

Although the article went on to urge parochial (i.e., local) medical officers, teachers and MOs of schools to be particularly alert to the growing dangers of poverty, it also struggled with those anxieties triggered by the ingrained belief that increased charity to the sick would be seen an assault on the natural order because it was widely believed that charity undermined not only laissez faire but the entire free market.

> At all events, during the present period of stress, the benefits of supporting the children against the effects of insufficient food are likely, we think, altogether to outweigh the evil consequences which may possibly be attendant upon the process [of diminishing the parental 'sense of responsibility' by distributing charity.]

And then "by an easy chain of association" the article (*ibid*, p. 1485) attacked the Bishop of London who, in a recent discussion on "a paper on the Truth and Error of Christian Science" had seemed to suggest that "he was in agreement with the Christian Scientist." This juxtaposing of the two issues—poverty and Christian Science—strongly suggests *The Lancet* feared that impoverished parents of sick children would be driven into the clutches of those "who profess to exercise gifts of healing of a very remarkable character." Perhaps not surprisingly there was no discussion as to problems relating to the relationship between poverty and unqualified practitioners: a subject rarely articulated let alone discussed but which nonetheless runs like an invisible thread through many of these stories.[7]

A year later, in November 1906, Dr. William Graham (1861–1917),[8] Resident Medical Superintendent District Lunatic Asylum, Belfast, and subsequently a member of the London Psychoanalytic Society [LPAS], spoke on "The Psychology of Christian Science" to an Irish Divisional Meeting of the Association, held in Dublin. He

> traced the growth of the cult in spite of argument and ridicule, and expressed the view that, though seven tenths of the so-called recoveries must be rejected, there existed a grain of truth in Mrs. Eddy's teachings, that grain being the power of the mind to control the bodily state, a power recognised by all who practise suggestion.

Dr Drapes agreed and recounted the case "of a man suffering from hay fever who improved after writing to a Christian Science expert, but relapsed on finding that the latter had not received his letter." Dr. Nolan spoke of a "case of a tabetic patient who was judged by an eminent medical man to be dying, but who walked into his study three weeks later after a visit to St. Winifred's Well." Nolan said it was difficult to understand such cases but "thought that the interest, other than metaphysical, of the new faith [of Christian Science] consisted in the vogue it had attained" and gave, as an example, a patient who "improved greatly without aid at all." Dr. Rainsford thought these "Christian Science 'cures'" could be explained by "the large nervous element in disease." (*JMS* 1907, Vol. 53, pp. 224–25)

Latent fears of Christian Science were now becoming palpable. In his contribution to the Bath & Wells Diocesan Conference Stephen Paget (1855–1926), one of their fiercest critics, said: "He longed to have Christian Science opposed with regular fury, to have a downright battle out in the open with all their artillery pounding away. . . . What they wanted was furious hating attack." (*MT* June 5, 1909, p. 452). But Paget (1909, p. vii) also warned that Christian Science was "widespread . . . in this country" and his claims were underlined by the growing number of books and articles on the subject and by the increased attacks against it. In a wide ranging article, commissioned by the *BMJ* for its Special Issue on "Mental Healing," the anonymous author (Anon 1910, p. 1494) noted:

> We need say only one thing more about Christian Science, which, to speak plainly, is a repulsive subject, inasmuch as it shows in a way no other form of

spiritual healing does the depths of degradation to which the human mind can sink under the weight of superstition.

But then the author could not resist adding:

In one thing Christian Science has probably a unique record of achievement: Beyond any sect or system that we know of it has succeeded in exploiting human imbecility and turning airy nothing into solid cash.[9]

The author had a point because their emphasis on faith also "involved payment for treatment" (Gartrell-Mills 1991, p. 70).

THE GUILD OF HEALTH

In late 1906, Mr W. N. Miller (1837–1913), First Reader at the Bryanston Street Church addressed a meeting in Bristol on "The Necessity for Christian Science and its Practical Application," in which he said Christian Science was based on the teachings of Mrs Eddy and because the doctrine taught "the understanding of the 'Allness of God'" it was faith which cured sin and sickness. Its spectacular results proved its necessity. Then having given examples of cures wrought through Christian Science, Miller claimed

> that the religion which produced such results must emanate from God, and therefore must be a necessity for mankind, while the failure to heal the sick and reform the sinner stamped as unbelievers those who did not procure those results, no matter what their pretensions might be. . . . An outside testimony to the necessity for the healing was afforded by some earnest Church of England clergymen organising a society called the "Guild of Health," to find out how the healing was effected, so that they might bring it into their own church. . . . (*WDP* December 14, 1906)

Miller's explicit claim that Christian Science had helped conjure the Guild of Health into being was not altogether self-serving hyperbole.

Over the Winter of 1902–3 F. W. Puller (1904, p. 3), of the Society of St. John the Evangelist, which had been established for mission work at home and abroad, "delivered a course of four lectures on the Anointing of the Sick." Puller then enlarged and annotated those lectures and published them in 1904. In their review the *London Daily News* [*LDN*] (September 10, 1904) noted that Puller "argues for a revival of the Sacrament of Unction whereby a priest might use the holy oil without a bishop's consecration." Another review noted the explicit connection between Puller's pamphlet and a new organization, called the Church Guild of Health [The Guild], which was now being formed and whose objects were:

> The cultivation of personal and corporate spiritual health; the restoration throughout the [Anglican] church of the scriptural doctrine and practice of Divine healing and the study of the influence of spiritual on physical well-being.

Another report explained how a number of clergyman and laymen inside the Anglican Church had formed the Guild

> as a way of countering the significant advances being made by the Christian Scientists in England whose numbers were much greater than was realised. Although membership of the Guild was confined to communicants in the Church of England there would be occasions when non-Anglicans would be invited to join their meetings. (*LDN* 6 October 1904)

The Guild's inaugural Council of Management was composed of the Revs. Percy Dearmer, Conrad Noel (1869—1942) and B.C.L. Courthorpe and, according to their press release, all members of the Church of England who accepted the Guild's "objects" were eligible to become members. (*YPLI* 4 October 1904). In his preface to the 1923 American Edition of Dearmer's book *Body and Soul*, (1909, p. xi), the Rev A. J. Gayner Banks noted that the Guild was

> an English Society for the promotion of Spiritual Healing . . . [which unlike] the many healing cults which have sprung up during the decade . . . sought to promote their objects by conservative methods and have attempted to correlate the best modern thought of Religion, Philosophy and Science in the great task of healing the sick and ameliorating the sufferings of mankind.

In fact the Guild was strategically placed within the Anglican Church which, at the time, was beset by groups and pressure groups often fiercely conflicted. Percy Dearmer (1867–1936), first chairman of the Guild and Vicar of St. Mary the Virgin, was a lifelong socialist and secretary (1891–1912) to the London Christian Social Union [CSU]. Dearmer, who was also an SPR member, was, in effect, an Anglo-Catholic, who favored ritualism although he denied the existence of the supernatural because he believed all spiritual healing and miracles, could be explained by natural law and that spiritual healing was more potent than materialist psychology because belief evoked far greater suggestive powers than did "mental healing." (See also Root 2005, p. 197n; Gartrell-Mills 1991, p. 153). Although the CSU is marginal to this story it had the support of the bishops of London and Worcester as well as Canon Scott Holland (1847–1918) and thus it occupied an important position within the Anglican Church, having originally emerged from the Christian Social Movement, one of whose aims was to find ways to "apply the moral truths and principles of Christianity to the social and economic difficulties of the present time." (Canney 1921, p. 104). Generally considered "left wing" the CSU was, in effect "socialist only in so far as socialism expressed the antithesis of *laissez-faire* individualism" (Inglis, 1963, p. 278). Although a fuller understanding of these tensions within the Anglican Church would require a book in itself, it is nonetheless important to bear in mind that many of the conflicts, often couched in theological terms, were also determined by the spirits of deeply divergent views concerning the Church's position on the political, economic, social, and moral questions of the moment. In other words the increasingly burning issues of faith healing, raised not only difficult theology and liturgical questions but also fed into deeper ideological divisions. The Guild's early history is therefore also of interest because of the ways in which it sought to reach across the religious and spiritual spectrum. For example its Annual Report reveals

> The following had addressed meetings of the Guild:—[Lombard] on "The Power of Silence," Mr. G. K. Chesterton, on "Cheerfulness," Rev. H. E. Gunson on "The Battle of Pain," Rev. F. Boyd on "Christian Science—a Criticism," Professor Barrett, F. R. S., on "Telepathy," Dr. A. T. Schofield on "The Psychology of Personality," Dr. Felkin on "Master Mind," Rev. A. W. Robinson, D. D., on "The Church and the Sick," and the Rev. Conrad Noel contributed a criticism, of the "New Theology" from the Guild's standpoint. (*CT* July 12, 1907, p. 42)

Although the Rev. Bousfield S. Lombard,[10] vicar of All Hallows, Hampstead, and nonorary secretary was inaugurated warden of The Guild in early 1908 (*CT* January 24, 1908, p. 107) his tenure was brief and in late 1908 the Rev F. Boyd, of Clifton, Bristol, was appointed the new warden and claimed they already had a membership of 700 (*GE* November 17, 1908).[11] But as Boyd began to consolidate and extend the work of the Guild he started ruffling medical feathers. And then matters, which had clearly been rumbling for a time, came to a head in August 1910 when Stanley Bousfield (b.1872),[12] a general practitioner in Lee, Kent, warned readers of the *BMJ* (August 20, 1910, p. 464) against the Guild because although it appeared to have the active support of fifty-three ministers of religion, it had "no names of medical men" on their list.[13]

> It is particularly important to draw attention to this guild as it has at its head as warden a clergyman [Boyd] who also occupies an active position in the Church of England.

Although the barb was probably as much political as medical what appears to have angered Bousfield was that Boyd had recently "treated" one of his (Bousfield's) patients and, following an unsatisfactory response to a private exchange of views, both in writing and, on one occasion, in person, Bousfield now felt impelled to publish his attack on Boyd. Setting out the facts concerning Boyd's treatment of his patient Bousfield concluded:

> I hope I have said enough to make us give a wide berth to this guild or to any similar society that may spring up in the future. I offer this criticism because such societies can only tend to retard that most desirable greater union of religion and medicine in a combined attempt to help the physical and mental health of mankind. If our profession has been backward in the past in securing the great help often obtainable from ministers of religion, yet the latter should not approve of attracting men and women to undergo 'spiritual healing' by their colleagues through the medium of any such society as the Guild of Health. (*BMJ* August 20, 1910, p. 465)

In his reply Boyd refuted all Bousfield's criticisms and claimed to be

> "working quietly in my capacity as a clergyman under proper conditions in conjunction with medical men." I neither call myself nor wish to be called a "spiritual healer"; I merely attempt to supply that contribution of spiritual energy in the work of healing sick people which the Church ought to supply, and which I believe the majority of sensible Christian doctors would welcome. (*BMJ* August 27, 1910, p. 572)

Lombard, who had lectured to the PTS in June 1908, joined the debate in his capacity as past Warden of the Guild. He deplored Bousfield's attack on Boyd. He, at least, had no hesitation in admitting he had practiced "spiritual healing" for the last fifteen years.

> In his attempts to undermine the Guild of Health, Dr. Bousfield is attacking one of the sanest and most practical societies of late years. It is the Church's own effort, inside the Church, to bring together thoughtful men and women to study their Gospels and learn therefrom the message in time of sickness. It constitutes a wise provision on the part of Church people against the onslaughts of the many fallacious cults, such as Christian Science, which with dangerous philosophy and still more dangerous action often neutralize medical treatment, and by raising false hopes bring about the very form of physical excitement that is most antagonistic to beneficial results. (*BMJ* September 17, 1910, p. 822)

Then in a second repost Boyd denied having undermined Bousfield's medical authority because when the patient

> in question first came to me she told me she was not then under any doctor; that she had been to many but that there was no treatment of any kind, and that the last time she had seen a doctor she was told that nothing more could be done for her. Under the circumstances I did the only thing I could do. I consulted a

> medical friend of mine, who told me all that is, I believe, known about the disease. If I had been told that Dr. Bousfield was her doctor, I would certainly have communicated with him. I do not know what difference it would have made or what 'medical control' he would have exercised. The point is simply this, that I am just as opposed as any of your readers could possibly be to any one attempting to heal by any means whatever who is not himself qualified or is acting in co-operation with some one who is qualified. (*BMJ* 1 October 1910, p. 1002)

Charles Buttar, dispensing with all the usual courtesies, then weighed into the debate wielding his cutlass.

> For the information of Mr. Boyd [*sic*] and his fellow "healer," Mr. Lombard [*sic*], may it not be stated that the medical profession cannot accept the assistance of ignorant free lances who presume, on their own initiative, to treat disease of which they know nothing? Nor can medicine accept the assertion of the existence of "special gifts of healing" on the unsupported testimony of professed healers. (*BMJ* September 24, 1910, p. 911)

Buttar continued his attack in a second letter.

> I hardly like to suggest that Mr. Boyd is making use of this correspondence as an advertisement for his methods, but I am sure that until he repents, deals honestly with himself, and attempts to use his reason, neither the Guild of Health nor its warden will succeed in awakening the interest or enlisting the sympathy of thinking men. (*BMJ*, 8 October 1910, p. 1099)

Although Boyd, and many other clerics, clearly wished for a more open dialogue with representatives of the medical profession their conciliatory approaches were not always reciprocated, particularly from those more militant doctors, like Bousfield and Buttar who, deeply suspicious of any clerical motives *whatsoever*, remained adamant that they would only accept "spiritual" intervention on the sole understanding that the role of the "priest" was to be precisely circumscribed by *their* own medical understanding of the demarcations between theology and medicine. One cannot help feeling there was also more than a little church politicking beneath Bousfield's and Buttar's angry letters.

THE ANGLICAN COMMUNION

During the 1906 annual London Diocesan Conference,[14] William Macdonald Sinclair (1850–1917), the Venerable Archdeacon of London, moved a resolution condemning Christian Science "as antagonistic both to Christianity and to Science."

> Faith had much to do with recovery from illness, of course, but faith would not cook our food, cleanse our rooms, provide sanitation. The works necessary to faith in illness were the accumulated experience and skills of the physician, surgeon and nurse.

Although I have been unable to find a detailed record of the discussions which followed there are sufficient pointers to suggest the ensuing debate was acrimonious (*CT* May 25, 1906, p. 695; June 8, 1906, p. 760). First, it took place against the backdrop of the trial of Dr. George Robert Adcock, a "medical Christian Scientist" accused of the manslaughter of Major J. N. White through wilful neglect (*WG* May 25, 1906, p. 10). Thus there were those in the Conference who feared Sinclair's original motion would be misunderstood as condoning Christian Science. Second, there was a minority, including Lord Halifax, who strongly believed that: "If the Church was to be true to herself and her tradition she ought to restore the anointing of the sick." Dr. A. F. Winnington Ingram (1858–1946), the bishop of London, and a supporter of the Guild, vehemently disagreed. "The Roman Catholic doctrine of extreme unction was an entire perversion of the Church's teaching in regard to it." It is important to note, however, that Ingram, like other members of the Guild, drew an important distinction between "Extreme Unction," which was the "anointing at the point of death" and the Act of Unction which was "anointing people in sickness for health" and it was the latter which had been abandoned while the former had been "substituted" instead. (*CT* November 24, 1905, p. 662).[15] In drawing the debate on Christain Science to a close Ingram said

> the other day he described Christian Science as a gigantic heresy. He did not withdraw from that, but he had to say that he felt it was due to admit on the other side that just as every heresy called attention to some forgotten truth, so he felt that this gigantic heresy had brought to light several truths. The first was influence of mind over matter. Then they must admit the sacredness of the healing art which had been so much left out of use in modern times. (*MCLGA*May 18, 1906, p. 9)[16]

Dwelling further on "the influence of mind over matter" Ingram urged the clergy to work together with the medical profession. "He had seen instances which convinced him that if we work with the doctors, using every physical means, the prayer of faith does help on the sick person." (*The Lancet* June 2, 1906, p. 1548). Sinclair's original motion was then amended and the following bland statement adopted unanimously:

> That this conference, while emphasising the power of faith in healing, views the main outline of the teaching and attitude of Christian Scientists as antagonistic both to Christianity and science. (*WDN*, May 18, 1906, p. 5; *The Times* May 18, 1906, p. 4).[17]

The Lancet (June 2, 1906, p. 1548), glossing the acrimonious debate, was clearly satisfied.

> On the whole the feeling of the conference appears to have been that modern Christianity had not laid sufficient stress upon the importance and practice of faith, especially in illness, and that the Scriptural rite of unction should be restored. Moreover, it was allowed that 'Christian Science' had laid hold of a truth in its insistence upon faith. There is no medical man who will deny that if a sick person has hopes of recovery or some definite stimulus to desire recovery he is much more likely to get well than if he had no such belief. . . . Faith of this kind is of the utmost assistance to the medical man in whose hands lies the conduct of the case.[18]

Ingram's role in these, and other discussions, is important because he was probably instrumental in pushing "faith healing" onto the agenda that year.[19] This would have been characteristic of the man who chose to confront rather than avoid difficult issues. For example, the previous evening, having invited George Lansbury (1859–1940)[20] to open a discussion on Socialism, Ingram introduced the session with these stirring words:

> I believe in burning subjects . . . Everyone knows that Socialism is very much in the air. We all know that many of its chosen representatives from the Labour party who are in Parliament have Socialism prominently in their minds. Then in God's name, let the Church of God discuss it, thrash it out, and find what the real truths about it are. (*Wells* May 24, 1906, p. 6)

Ingram, who would subsequently become a president of The Guild was, in fact, credited by Ellis Roberts (1910, p. 236), as being "one of the first [church leaders] to recognise the reality of the need for a greater recognition of the place of psychic healing." On the other hand Ingram, and other church leaders, may well have been pushed in that direction by Archdeacon Colley's *Healing Mediumship in the Church of England*[21] which consisted of two letters, one each to the bishops of London and Worcester, and was Colley's most recent attempt

> to arouse public interest and clerical interest in spiritualism, which he, speaking from an almost life-long experience, contends is a force which had been in the past, and must in the future, be recognised as having a distinct bearing on religious life. (*LSC* May 25, 1906, p. 3)

Colley, of Stockton Rectory, who had long-standing contacts with Spiritualists (i.e., *Light* March 12, 1889, p. 104; January 23, 1909, pp. 46–47) had, in fact, published his pamphlet from "the office of *Light*," the main Spiritualist

Journal. It was perhaps bending to these and other pressures that senior clerics in the Church of England decided to appointed the Right Rev. H. E. Ryle,[22] bishop of Winchester, to chair a Committee of Enquiry[23] into "the subject of Ministries of Healing," and their report [Ministries of Healing], issued in time for the 1908 Lambeth Conference,[24] was extensively discussed during the session of Friday 10 July. In its preamble, Ministries of Healing confessed itself

> at a disadvantage in discussing phenomena which only in recent times have been the subject of scientific investigation. In the present stage of knowledge it would be premature for any except experts to hazard an opinion upon such topics as the powers of "Mental Suggestion" and the range of "Subliminal Consciousness,"[25] or to attempt to forecast the possibilities of "Mental" or "Spiritual Healing." (Winton 1908, p. 133)

Such caveats, which clearly signal significant concessions to orthodox medicine, also reveal, between their lines, how the established Church was not just anxious about Christian Science but all other types of mental healing, in all their different guises. This point is further underlined through the somewhat confused section suggesting that the church had lost its way because "sickness has too often exclusively been regarded as a cross to be borne with passive resignation, whereas it should have been regarded rather as a weakness to be overcome by the power of the Spirit." (Winton 1908, p. 134).

Although Ministries of Healing argued in favor of prayers for the restoration of health, including "the apostolic act of the Laying-on of Hands," it took an ambiguous attitude toward the Unction—the belief "that these prayers [for the sick] should be accompanied by the anointing of the sufferer with oil." (Winton 1908, p. 137). Part of that ambiguity may have been because the bishops of Durham and London (*The Times* May 18, 1906, p. 4) had recently set up an historical investigation into the whole question; and although their investigation would eventually raise serious questions about the liturgical validity of the ritual their enquiry still remained inconclusive at the time of the 1908 debate. Ministries of Healing, therefore, remained reluctant to place the Act of Unction under outright ban so it offered a compromise: that unction could only be used in those cases where it had been specifically requested by the sick person *and* where the request had also been approved by the Bishop of the Diocese. (Winton 1908, p. 138). Ultimately, however, Ministries of Healing, both in tone and content, was specifically framed to address not just the clergy but also the medical profession (*MT* June 5, 1909, p. 452): and while one of the original catalysts may well have been the fear of Christian Science, with its "pseudo-spirituality," the more astute church leaders, like Ingram, had also come to realize that if the Church were to thrive in a materialist age, and also in competition with a growing anti materialism, it would have to find new ways of incorporating the spiritual into its ministry (Anon 1920, p. 123). This articulation of what might be considered a new turn in Church theology can also be read into the contemporaneous sermons of leading clergymen, like Dr Pigou, the dean of Bristol Cathedral (*WDP* June 25, 1907, p. 3) who believed that the Church, having seriously neglected "the importance of spiritual forces in the work of healing and in the promotion of happiness" (Anon 1920, p. 123), had effectively abandoned her healing ministry not just to the medical profession but also to her religious, spiritual and psychic rivals. Ultimately, however, Ministries of Healing was treading a fine line because in seeking to distinguish psychic from spiritual forces, it also felt the need to caution that the ability to heal by faith should not be "regarded as gifts of a special or supernatural character, whereas they are rather to be looked upon as natural gifts in the same category as art or music" (Winton 1908, p. 135–36). Thus Ministries of Healing urged the Church and all who professed a gift of healing,

> diligently to fit and prepare themselves, by constant prayer and by scientific medical study, for its proper and safe exercise, in order that there should be no room for reproach or suspicion on the ground of ignorance or inexperience; and it is of extreme importance that, if not medically qualified to practise, they should act with the approval, or under the supervision, of qualified medical practitioners. (Winton 1908, p. 136)

This concept of "spiritual fitness" appears remarkably similar to the theosophical views of Hallam (1899b, pp. 423–24) who urged: "There must be a perfect and complete altruism, an utter abandonment of self, before the induction of hypnosis can benefit either the operator or the subject." It also chimes with the spiritualist belief in "the right preparation" for mediumship, and it even echoes, the somewhat later psychoanalytic caution as to the dangers of the transference and countertransference. We shall see shortly how these points of intersection between theosophy, theology, spiritualism, psychotherapy, and psychoanalysis, run considerably deeper than might at first appear.[26]

But Christian Science, and contested points of theology, were not the only drivers for change because the growing debates around psychological medicine had also encouraged some of the more enlightened clergy that "they ought to take more account of the recent growth of knowledge about the power of spirit and mind over body" (Anon 1920, p. 15). Several years later R. T. Davidson, then archbishop of Canterbury (1903–1928), perhaps with Ingram's previous comments in mind, wrote, in his Encyclical Letter to the 1920 Lambeth Conference:

> On the other hand, it must not be forgotten that these movements [Christian Science and Theosophy] are very largely symptoms and results of reaction against materialistic views of life. We cannot but sympathize with persons who seek a refuge from the pressure of materialism. It is the part of the Church to afford such a refuge, and, if it fails to do so, there is something wrong with its own life. (Anon 1920, p. 15)

Thus the more enlightened Church leaders had come to realize that if they were to succeed in their mission they would have to find new ways of (re) introducing spiritual healing into the sick room. The results of their deliberations, often buried in private undocumented discussions and debates, suggest that senior Anglican clerics came to understand that if they were to regain ground from the spiritualists, materialists, theosophists, and all the other 'ists', they would need to establish a unified position: and this meant choosing either a radically isolationist policy, which would alienate the medical profession and and thus by default drive the Church toward the absolutism of Christian Science, or they would have to ally themselves with the medical profession in which case they would have to find ways to work with them. Having chosen the latter the Church then set about trying to persuade the medical profession that it was in their joint interest to unite, on common ground, because only in that way could they hope to tackle head-on not just Christian Scientists but also all the other pseudo-spiritualists and unqualified mental healers who clearly threatened both institutions. But as members of the Guild had already discovered this strategy of "co-operation" was also fraught with dangers.

DISSENTIENT DISSIDENTS

Mr James Moore Hickson (1868–1933), was born in Mansfield, Victoria (Australia) and shortly after arriving in England with his wife, in 1899, became "a layman" practicing "healing activities in the poorer areas of south London, using prayers, laying-on of hands and anointing" (Gartrell-Mills 1991, p. 155). Robinson (2014, pp. 102–3), following Mullin, suggests that by the early 1920s Hickson "had become . . . 'arguably the most famous proponent of Christian healing in the English-speaking world.'" In 1905, with the active support of Bishop Mylne and others, Hickson founded the Society of Emmanuel—not to be confused either with Christian Science or the Emmanuel Movement, of which more shortly. The Society of Emmanuel aimed "to bring together Christians 'who were in sympathy with the Scriptural practise of the laying on of hands with prayer for the sick in the name of Jesus Christ'" and also to strive to bring "together in partnership the work of the medical profession and the ministry of healing through the laying on of hands." (Anon 2015). Some time around 1908 Edward George Henry Montagu, 8th Earl of Sandwich [Lord Sandwich] (1839–1916) became worried about his butler George Andrews who was "suffering great pain after an operation," and having heard of a "so-called faith healer" by the name of Hickson Sandwich travelled to London in the hope of inducing Hickson to help Andrews.

> I called . . . on Mr. Hickson in Talbot Square. He immediately, on my introduction, said, 'You have the same power that I have.' I was so astounded that I asked no questions.' (Erskin 1919, p. 263)

Hickson then visited Sandwich in Hinchinbrook and treated Andrews. Thus on May 11, 1908, Sandwich took the opportunity to ask

> Mr. Hickson how he had known so quickly that the same power had been given to me as to himself. His answer was: "I cannot tell you, except that I saw it at once in your personality." (Erskin 1919, p. 264; *BMJ*, June 18, 1910, p. 1496)

After Hickson returned to London Sandwich started exploring his newfound gifts and had some success in helping Andrews and other workers on his estate. But the real impetus to Sandwich's calling, as a healer, occurred in early 1911 when a Mrs Charlotte Herbine, an American, came to stay.

> She has a remarkable psychic gift, and has communicated with a spirit calling himself Dr. Coulter ever since she was a child. This spirit always told her that she would come to England. . . . Almost from the first interview with Dr. Coulter, [Sandwich] became convinced of the truth of [Coulter's] words and the importance of the message he had to bring. One of the first requests made to him by Dr. Coulter was that he should continue his healing, assuring him that it would have no bad results to his own health. This [Sandwich] readily consented to do, and from that time to within four days of his death it was seldom he had less than six or seven cases on his hands. (Erskin 1919, p. 266)

In July 1908, not long after Hickson's visit to Hinchinbrook, there was a meeting of "spiritual healers" in Pinner, North London [Pinner Meeting], which was probably organized to coincide with both the Lambeth Conference and the somewhat earlier Pan-Anglican Congress at Kensington Town Hall.[27] The Pinner Meeting was attended by the Rev. C. H. Boutflower (1863–1942), Bishop of Dorking, the Duchess of Bedford, Lord Radstock, and a Miss Eleanor M. Reed MD. Although I have been unable to find detailed information about the Pinner meeting the fact that it was reported in *The Healer*, suggests it was probably organized by Hickson who was subsequently described, somewhat dismissively, as "a gentleman who probably at one time devoted his energies to massage," but was now "another professor of spiritual healing" (*BMJ* January 9, 1909, pp. 109–10; *The Lancet* January 9, 1909, p. 110). Sandwich,[28] who was subsequently described as an "Independent Spiritual Healer" (*BMJ* June 18, 1910, p. 1496) was also present, probably as Hickson's guest.

The Society of Emmanuel was, in many ways, a very English organization deeply rooted in the Anglo-Catholic tradition and with a committee composed of people drawn from "polite society" (Robinson 2014, pp. 102–6). Apart from Hickson (President), there was Bishop Mylne (1843–1941), who had been the bishop of Bombay but was now Rector of Alvechurch, Worcester (1905–1917): Adelaine, duchess of Bedford,[29] the Countess Beauchamp, Mrs Edward Trotter, the Revs. Maurice Bell and George Trevelyan, W. M. Wroughton, Lady Somerset, Lady Mosley, and Mrs Dickin who was also editor of the Society's official Journal *The Healer*.[30] Mark Hutchinson (2014), in a remarkeable paper, reveals the extraordinary web of interconnected relationships between members of the committee and the upper echelons of the Church of England. From this he concluded: "Between them, the English Duchess and the Indian Bishop had access to most of the Anglican hierarchy" while, through the rest of the Committee, "we see a slice of contemporary High Church society." It is hardly surprising, therefore, that by March 1909 Hickson had already had a series of interviews with the Archbishop of Canterbury (Root, 2005, p. 192).

The Society of Emmanuel claimed, as one of its aims, "to develop the Divine gifts . . . especially the gift of healing by prayer and laying on of hands" not just "for the healing of the body, but as a means of drawing the souls of men nearer to God." Even before he had established the Society Hickson had planned to open

> a hostel, especially for poor gentle folks, a class who are beyond the reach of ordinary help where their cases may be diagnosed by duly qualified medical men, and where a band of healers may develop and use their gifts to further the work. (Quoted *BMJ* January 9, 1909, p. 109; June 18, 1910, p. 1495)

In their Annual report, for the year-end June 1909, Hickson confirmed that they had now opened the hospice, "for the reception of [8] in-patients," on the outskirts of Regents Park[31] and that, on May 26, 1909, it had been "'dedicated and set apart for the Glory of God and for the service of our acting brothers and sisters' by . . . Bishop Mylne." That same report also noted that the hospice had been more or less occupied since it was opened.

> It cannot be too strongly emphasized that a home such as ours, with its chapel for private prayer, devotional meetings and intercessions, its band of helpers,

> the visits of the clergy for administration of the Sacraments and spiritual work in preparation for healing, may, under God's blessing, foster to the full an ideal spiritual atmosphere for the Healing Gift. We hope that all our members will come forward to take some active part in this work. We are glad to be able to report that all the healing that has been done in the hospice has been duly certified by qualified members of the medical profession. Dr James Moorhead and Dr. Rowse have examined the in-patients each week. We owe them a hearty debt of gratitude for their devoted and ungrudging services in connexion with this part of our work.

Another report (Anon 2015) noted how the two doctors "worked in fellowship and faith with members of the Society for those who were sick," while Dr Moorhead,[32] in remarks attached to the 1909 Report, claimed Hickson, as their main "healer," had been "the means of bringing much comfort and help—physical and spiritual—to several sufferers" and had cured or alleviated "cases of both organic and functional disease." Moorhead even claimed that Hickson had succeeded in a number of cases where eminent surgeons or physicians had failed and, gave as example, a patient with locomotor ataxy who having been "discharged from two hospitals as incurable" had "undergone a remarkable improvement" under Hickson's treatment. The *BMJ* (June 18, 1910, pp. 1495–96), in noting one of those claims, declined to comment on this and several other of Hickson's "cures," because, as we shall see shortly, they were currently under investigation by a BMA sub-committee. On the other hand the *BMJ* had no hesitation in reporting that the patient, recently referred to by Bishop Mylne in his sensational account of a remarkable cure from cancer, was "absolutely incorrect." (Mackenzie 1910b, pp. 142–45). By early 1911 the BMA had clearly lost patience with Drs Moorhead and Rowse suggesting "that they were 'covering' unqualified practice, and so exposed themselves to action on the part of the Medical Council." As a result they withdrew their cover and the hospice was forced to close on the basis that it was "against the principles of the Society to carry on this branch of its work with a house full of invalids without, proper medical supervision." (*CT* May 19, 1911, p. 667; Anon 2015).

Hickson, who clearly had significant funds at his disposal, may well have been inspired by the work of the PTS and there were certainly similarities in their models of "health care" not least because both organizations were fronted by charismatic "spiritual healers"—Spriggs and Hickson. On the other hand the PTS, perhaps because it only treated outpatients, was never particularly intent on attempting to attract medical men to offer cover, or legitimacy, for their work and thus they appear to have had few problems by operating outside of orthodox medicine. There were also other notable differences: the Society of Emmanuel, with its upper class membership, appealed to "poor gentle folks" while the PTS, with its lower middle-class membership, tended to appeal to the "poor man." Strange to say class distinctions remained stubbornly resistant in the theological and spiritual worlds.

THE CHURCH MEDICAL UNION

On November 16, 1908, following the 1908 Lambeth Conference, there was a joint meeting of clergy and laymen at Sion College, Victoria Embankment, London [Sion College], to consider "matters connected with healing by other than physical means." Hickson spoke about the Society of Emanuel who "were in sympathy with all kinds of healing, which they considered to be a gift of God, but they wished for a more spiritual atmosphere around the patient." Dr. Armitage Robinson, dean of Westminster, said that although "he was a believer in healing by divine intervention . . . [i]t was necessary to have some test of the nature of the cases dealt with, as had been adopted by the Roman Catholics at Lourdes." There may even have been one or two dissentient voices at the meeting, such as Archdeacon Cunningham (1849–1919), who said, during the Pan-Anglican Conference,

> that cures effected by psychotherapeutic methods were dangerous and that the church should refrain from encouraging them. It was, he said, a complete reversal of Christianity to make physical health a supreme end, and to regard spiritual power as merely the means of attaining it. Common sense held that physical evils could be met by appropriate physical remedies (i.e., by the medical profession). (quoted Gartrell-Mills 1991, p. 160)

Ultimately, however, as there was little or no direct opposition to the idea of closer cooperation with the medical profession, the delegates passed the following unanimous resolution.

> That in the opinion of this conference the time has come to form a Central Church Council in the Diocese of London for the consideration of questions connected with healing by spiritual means, and that the Bishop of London be respectfully asked to nominate the members of the council. (*MCLGA* November 17, 1908, p. 10; *LDN* November 17, 1908, p. 9)

The Lancet (November 21, 1908, p. 1539), probably unaware of Hickson's role in the meeting, was "glad that the Church is taking up this question for the amount of evil done by unlicensed and quack professors of 'faith-healing' is incalculable."

> So long as the skill of the physician is not neglected there is no reason why the offices of the Church and their effect upon the mind of the patient who believes

> therein should not be used. Every medical man knows perfectly well that a patient who desires to, and believes that he will, get well is far more likely to recover than one who, owing to carelessness or despair, meets death half-way.

The *Church Times* (*CT* November 20, 1908, p. 671) in acknowledging their own growing anxieties at the "rapidity" in which "Christian Science is taking hold upon the well-to-do class in this country," expressed satisfaction "that some of the London clergy are taking up the question of spiritual healing in real earnest."

At about the same time as the Sion College meeting a group of laymen and clergyman formed the Church and Medical Union [CMU]

> with the object of promoting the co-operation of the Church and the medical profession in the healing of the sick. The principles on which the union professes to carry on its work are those embodied in the report of the [Ministries of Healing]. (*BMA* January 9, 1909, p. 108)

By early 1909 the CMU, whose lay secretary was Mr Geoffrey Rhodes, had set up offices in Gerard Street and was already collecting "as much evidence as possible in regard to the various healing movements both within and without the orthodox Christian Churches." Having then discovered "what was good in them and what was not" they issued their manifesto:

> (1) to establish head quarters in London where books and literature may be consulted, and where persons may come for advice and information; (2) to canvass the clergy and medical men generally all over Great Britain with a view to obtaining their co-operation; (3) by means of literature, lectures, and meetings, to obtain support for the [CMU] and the objects for which it has been formed; (4) to recommend courses of reading. (*BMJ* January 9, 1909, p. 108; Canney 1921, p. 106)

The CMU also believed "that sickness and disease are in one aspect a breach in the harmony of the Divine purpose, not only analogous to, but sometimes at least caused by, want of moral harmony with the Divine Will; and that this restoration of harmony in mind and will often brings with it the restoration of the harmony of the body." They also went on to claim "that medical science is the handmaid of God and His Church, and should be fully recognized as the ordinary means appointed by Almighty God for the care and healing of the human body." (*BMJ* June 18, 1910, p. 1495). In an interview with the *Daily Mail* (quoted *BMJ* January 9, 1909, p. 109) Rhodes noted

> 'Men and women will be in attendance at our head quarters to interview the patients, who will be asked to give a certificate from the doctor who is attending

> the case. Then we will arrange for the patient to be seen by a clergyman—if possible by his parish priest. The clergyman of the future will have to study psychology, and it is our intention to have lectures and classes on mental therapeutics, where the clergy will learn how they can help those who need their aid.'

Although the *BMJ* gave the CMU considerable publicity it nonetheless remained distinctly unimpressed and, through its restrained comments, implied that Rhodes was treading on dangerous ground because he had given no indication as to what he meant by "mental therapeutics" nor was there any information "about Mr Rhodes's special qualifications for the task."

> Till satisfactory information on these points is forthcoming, the medical profession, however much individual members thereof may sympathize with its objects, will be well advised not to give any active support to the union. (*BMJ* January 9, 1909, p. 109)

Shortly afterward the *BMJ* (April 24, 1909, p. 1023), almost as if it were unable to leave the matter alone, abstracted "Medicine and the Church," the talk Rhodes had recently delivered to a CMU meeting in which he had argued that "the discoveries of psychology showed that mind and body reacted on one another."

> In considering the question of mental healing, a sound conclusion was most likely to be reached if the lines of careful theological study and close scientific research were followed. These they would get in the deliberations of their spiritual leaders and medical men. There was a danger of people being led off the track by unqualified healers. They were not to neglect natural means in the hope of a miracle being performed. They were bound to consider themselves humbly as students, but they could express firm belief in the vital principle that the doctor of medicine and the clergyman should work in all cases in the closest consultation.

Despit offering the CMU yet more publicity, the *BMJ* remained distinctly unimpressed.

> We have no doubt of the excellence of the intentions of the promoters of the movement, but their notions of the end they have in view and of the means by which they are to reach it seem to be vague to the degree of mistiness.

But the *BMJ* also warned that "the close alliance with the medical profession which the [CMU] professes to desire may easily be used as a means of 'covering' unqualified practice," a warning which can also be understood in the context of the BMA's continuing fears about the proliferation of unqualified practitioners.

Canney (1921, p. 106) thought the inspiration for the CMU was "suggested by the work of healing [originally] carried on at the Emmanuel Church, Boston" [Emmanuel Movement] which advocated "for the cure of non-organic diseases by mental and moral treatment." (*BET*, November 26, 1906, p. 5). The Emmanuel Movement, which took its name from the Emmanuel Church, in Boston, Massachusetts, where it had originated, was founded in 1905 and had been inspired by the collaboration between Dr Joseph H. Pratt (1872–1956), of Massachusetts General Hospital, and the Rev. Elwood Worcester (1862–1940) of the Emmanuel Church. "The success of this enterprise convinced its promoters that the Church has an important mission to discharge to the sick, and that the physician and the clergyman can work together to the benefit of the community." The Movement's aim was "to bring into effective cooperation the physician, the psychologically trained clergyman, and the trained social worker in the alleviation and arrest of certain disorders of the nervous system which are now generally regarded as involving some weakness or defect of character or more or less complete mental dissociation." The Rev. Worcester was also supported by his assistant the Rev. Samuel McComb and both men insisted their spiritual work was always "under strict medical control." (Anon 1910, p. 1494; Ryle, 1914, p. 43). That there were links between the Emmanuel Movement and the CMU is underlined by the CMU's recommendation of two books recently published under the auspices of the Emmanuel Church. The first, by Worcester et al. (1908, p. 1) was the result of a collaboration between "three friends" which described "in plain terms the work in behalf of nervous sufferers which has been undertaken" by Emmanuel Church workers. That book, which incidentally has a couple of passing references to Freud, was reviewed by the *BMJ* (November 21, 1908) and then by T. W. Mitchell (1909b) in the *Journal*. The second book, *The Healing Ministry of the Church*, also published in 1908, was edited by Samuel McComb. Perhaps, not surprisingly, the *BMJ* (January 9, 1909, p. 110) was left somewhat confused.

> We do not know how far these various representatives of spiritual healing agree with each other; we think it not unlikely that they hate each other with the fervour which is generally proportionate to the intensity of theological belief. If all or any of them can show that they have discovered a new force, or a new method of applying one already known, to the cure of disease, rational medicine will welcome a new weapon.

The *BMJ* may well have had a point because the CMU, the Emmanuel Society, the Emmanuel Movement and the Guild, had all emerged out of very different theological, ideological, and even national traditions, and, thus effectively occupied different positions inside the wider Anglican Movement. The situation was soon to become even more complex, however, when members of the British medical profession began to realize that there was now outright condemnation of the Emmanuel Movement among a significant number of their American brethren. According to the *New York Times* (December 28, 1908, p. 7)

> the general opinion [in medical circles] is that the [Emmanuel] Movement has bolted with its promoters and is running riot, and doing much harm.

Worcester et al. (1908, p. 2) had given the clear impression that the highly respected J. J. Putnam of Harvard Medical School, who had "presided at the preliminary meeting," was still closely associated with the Movement. But Putnam, an early reader of Freud, had now protested, "against the use of [his] name in any matter in connection with the so-called Emmanuel Movement" because now he "considered the whole affair an injury to the progress of scientific medicine, especially to neurology, and to the intelligence that has made possible the recent discoveries in this delicate branch of medical science." (*ibid*; *BMJ* January 16, 1909, p. 171). The *BMJ* (January 16, 1909, pp. 171–72), perhaps unusually, took a more conciliatory line when it agreed with Dr Allen Star

> that the medical profession is ready to welcome the co-operation of the clergy in dealing with certain kinds of nervous disease so long as they do not step outside their proper sphere of purely spiritual ministration.

The *Medical Times* (June 9, 1909, pp. 452–53) was far more militant. In reporting on the recent Bath and Wells Diocesan Conference, they noted Paget's "vigorous denunciation of so-called Christian Science" (*CT* May 21, 1909, p. 690) and also his ridiculing of the whole idea of closer co-operation between clergy and doctors. What Paget wanted to know was "what the clergy were going to do."

> We fully agree with Mr. Paget that active co-operation with clergymen in healing the sick is impracticable. . . . Moreover any such co-operation would no doubt be held as unprofessional by the [GMC].[33]

But Paget (1909, pp. 187–88) went even further when he lumped *all* faith healing together and let rip in what was to become his much referenced and highly acclaimed attack on Christian Science.

> Once a man thinks that he can heal by prayer, and laying-on of hands, and anointing, nothing will stop him. Not only will women, more than men, practise the new faith-healing, but all, Christian or not, who discover a gift that way. "The impulse

becomes almost irresistible," Mr. Hickson says, who is the chief of these healers. I am well aware that he has a beneficial influence; but his account of his work and of his cases is too like Science and Health[34] for me. "The patient," he says, "must come in an attitude of passivity and receptivity. . . . It is not his part to contribute ideas and suggestions. To doubt the healer is to set up a condition of inharmony and friction, thus wasting precious time to both healer and himself. Even Christ could not heal some, because of their unbelief." The hands are Mr. Hickson's hands, but the voice is the voice of Christian Science. The very words, *inharmony, friction, and waste of precious time*, and the reference to *unbelief*, remind me of her.[35]

INVESTIGATING THE SUBJECT OF 'SPIRITUAL HEALING'

The BMA's 1908 Annual meeting, held in Sheffield, opened on 24 July, just two weeks after the Lambeth Conference had discussed Ministries of Healing. On the eve of its opening the bishop of Sheffield held a special service in the Parish Church for BMA delegates.

> He regretted that the admission of the clergyman into the sick room was so often regarded as a signal of the grave nature of the case, that the prayers of the Church were looked upon almost as the sentence of death instead of being for the comfort and relief as intended. But there seemed a danger now, not of the exclusion of the clergyman from the sick room, but of the medical man. Christian Science, faith healing and the unction of the sick were strongly in evidence. He agreed with Sir Oliver Lodge[36] that we could believe as little in the efficacy of prayer without drugs as in drugs without the prayer. We needed a combination of faith and works. (*Dominion*, September 12, 1908, p. 6; *BMJ* August 1, 1908, p. 272)

Although "Spiritual Healing" was not openly discussed during the BMA Sheffield Meeting reports of the November 1908 Sion College meeting on "so-called spiritual or faith healing" became the subject for discussion at the November 1908 meeting of the Council of the Metropolitan Counties' Branch of the BMA [the Metropolitan Branch][37] where members expressed concern that "efforts" were being made "by certain persons to secure the support of the Established Church for what is termed 'spiritual healing.'" In what appears to have been a deliberate preemptive strike the Metropolitan Branch passed a resolution which

> noted that a meeting of clergy and laymen had asked the Bishop of London to form a Central Church Council in the Diocese of London, for the consideration of questions connected with healing by spiritual means, and was of opinion that the subject was of sufficient importance to the [medical] profession as a whole to merit careful consideration.

Armed with this Resolution the Metropolitan Branch approached the bishop of London "to secure that proper inquiry should be made into the subject" and having received a favorable response they then submitted their Resolution to the BMA's Central Council (*BMJ* July 3, 1909, p. 15). It was surely no coincidence that at the same time Drs Lullum Wood Bathurst and Charles Buttar, the latter being honorary secretary of the Kensington Division of the Metropolitan Branch, wrote, in their private capacities, a joint letter to the *BMJ* (November 28, 1908, pp. 651–52) in which they noted that there were no medical representatives at Sion College and expressed concern at the role played by the Society of Emmanuel.

> It seems to us a little curious that although this spiritual healing movement has been in existence in this country for at least three years and although it is very evident that the idea has made great strides amongst the clergy, no notice has yet been taken by the medical profession of the great dangers involved.

It was "high time that the leading members of the medical profession in this country should show that they can in no wise 'lend their sanction and aid to such a dangerous enterprise.'"

The pressure from the Metropolitan Branch resolution, the Bathurst and Buttar letter, the militancy of Paget to say nothing of other rumblings now forced the BMA Council to take note of a subject "which was apparently arousing considerable interest among religious bodies." So they referred the matter to their Medico-Political Committee who, in turn, in January 1909, appointed a special sub-committee [BMA Sub-Committee], to investigate. That Sub-Committee was deliberately composed of "representatives of the different branches of the profession" so as to include general practitioners, physicians, neurologists and alienists.[38] By May 1909 the BMA Sub-Committee, having finished their initial investigations, concluded there was "the necessity for a careful professional investigation into the subject at its present early stage of development." (*BMJ* May 22, 1909, p. 292). So they appointed

> A Special Investigation Sub-Committee [BMA Investigation Committee] . . . to inquire into cases brought to its notice, which have been treated by so-called 'Spiritual Healers'; with instructions to call to its assistance any members of the profession specially qualified for the purpose, and to collect for comparison cases of mistaken diagnosis. (*BMJ*, July 10, 1909, p. 49)

The BMA Investigation Committee made slow progress and although the BMA Council, announced, in May 1910, that they hoped "soon to be in a position to report" (*BMJ*, May 21, 1910, p. 274) the investigations dragged on until July 1911 when the Committee finally issued their "Report on the

Subject of 'Spiritual Healing'" [BMA Spiritual Healing]. The Medico-Political Committee having discussed the report recommended that the "[BMA] Council be instructed to take steps to give [BMA Spiritual Healing] general publicity." (*BMJ* July 8, 1911, p. 70; July 22, 1911, p. 102).

BMA Spiritual Healing admitted that despite extensive reading and researching the members of both the BMA Sub-Committee and the BMA Investigation Committee had no "clear idea of what was understood by the term 'Spiritual Healing' by those who used it." So, in an attempt to clear up the confusion, the BMA Investigation Committee sent questionnaires to a number of those "known to be interested in the subject": Geoffrey Rhodes of the CMU, the Rev. F. Boyd of the Guild, and both Mr Hickson and the Rev. Maurice Bell, of the Society of Emmanuel. In other words, and perhaps quite pointedly, the Investigation Committee approached only that narrow band of men known to have affiliations to the Anglican Communion thereby completely ignoring the opinions and experiences of other organizations. In their questionnaire the BMA Investigation Committee asked respondents to explain the difference between "Spiritual Healing," "Faith Healing," and "Psychic Healing," but although they had received many and detailed replies they discovered that

> most of the writers experienced considerable difficulty in defining the difference between "Spiritual Healing" and other forms mentioned. The communications showed, however, that there was a general desire on the part of those interested in the matter for guidance on the technical side of the question.

These comments reveal, once again, how that narrow band of respondents were quite happy, and willing, to defer to medical opinions. But the BMA Investigation Committee also did not have much success in their investigations into "healing" cures because they "found great difficulty in obtaining cases for investigation and in following up the cases submitted." Although they had spoken and written to a number of people—again within that narrow band—those respondents

> did not see their way to put the Sub-Committee in touch with patients treated, or with those treating them. The only cases actually seen were provided by the Society of Emmanuel through the intermediation of . . . [Hickson and Bell]. The Rev. F. Boyd, Warden of the Guild of Health, also submitted some details of cases in writing to the Sub-Committee. The Investigating Sub-Committee spent two afternoons at the Hospice of the Society of Emmanuel and personally examined ten patients, afterwards communicating, where possible, with the former medical advisers of the patients seen. The patients, of whose cases particulars were given but who were not seen, were written to and their statements compared with those of their former medical advisers. In each of the cases

> submitted a personal examination was made as far as possible, and the diagnosis verified by reference to the records of previous medical advisers or of hospitals. Three of the cases were seen a second time at an interval of four months. Opportunity for subsequent examination, though requested, was not permitted. The Sub-Committee also elicited by interviews and by correspondence the views of certain medical practitioners specially interested in healing by mental suggestion and hypnotism. (Anon 1911b, p. 125)

Despite, or maybe because of, their enquiries the Sub-Committee concluded "there is no difference in kind between 'Spiritual Healing,' 'Faith Healing,' 'Mental Healing' or 'Psychic Healing,' because, in their view, the essential factor in all forms of psychic healing is mental suggestion, which has been used from remote periods, although more fully explained by modern psychology." Finally BMA Spiritual Healing concluded:

> c) That there is abundant evidence of the efficacy of mental suggestion in the treatment of many [functional] disorders. . . .
>
> (d) That the benefits of hypnotic suggestion or waking suggestion can be obtained from qualified medical practitioners whose training enables them to distinguish the conditions which are amenable to this kind of therapy from the conditions which should be dealt with by other kinds of medical or surgical treatment.
>
> (e) That, in accordance with the principle that for the protection of the public the diagnosis and treatment of disease are best left in the hands of those whose training has fitted them for that calling, any formal co-operation of clergymen and medical practitioners in the treatment of disease is to be deprecated. All the benefits which may undoubtedly accrue from the assistance given to sick persons by the ministrations of the clergy in suitable cases may be obtained in a way which will not give rise to dangerous misunderstandings on the part of the public. (Anon 1911b, p. 126)

Then on July 22, 1911, during the BMA Annual Meeting, in Birmingham, Mr Verall, chairman of the Medico-Political Committee, moved to adopt BMA Spiritual Healing. Dr Helme, who had served on the Sub-Committee, moved "that expression of opinion be postponed pending the receipt of replies from the Divisions." It is unclear whether there was a serious debate on Helme's motion before that substantive motion was agreed: "That the report on spiritual healing submitted to the Council be approved, and that expression of opinion be postponed pending receipt of replies from Divisions" (*BMJ* July 29, 1911, p. 224). This was *the* classic BMA procedural tactic, often used by a minority of "backwoodsmen," in their attempts to stall or burry a report with which they disagreed. At best Helme's resolution was bound to delay, for at least another year, the adoption of BMA Spiritual Healing. More to the point, however, it effectively stifled debate because convention dictated that the *BMJ* (March 9, 1912, p. 553) would not comment on an official Report until it had been adopted. Although the report was now sent to the Divisions only a handful took the motion seriously because BMA Spiritual Healing was only read and approved by the Monmouth Division of the South Wales and Monmouth Branch (*BMJ*, August 19, 1911, p. 310), the Jersey Division of the Southern Branch (*BMJ* 21 October 1911, p. 402) and the Altrincham Division of the Lancashire and Cheshire Branch (*BMJ* February 24, 1912, p. 245). Somewhat ironically the Marylebone Division of the Metropolitan Branch, where the impetus for the Report more or less began, prevaricated: so Dr Forbes Winslow proposed their discussion be postponed (*BMJ* November 18, 1911, p. 516). And with that Dr Helme and his supporters had effectively succeeded in burying BMA Spiritual Healing almost exactly as their reactionary predecessors had buried the revised 1893 Hypnotism Report. And yet it is worth noting that despite the politicking BMA Spiritual Healing, just like the revised 1893 Hypnotism Report unanimously approved "the benefits of hypnotic suggestion or waking suggestion" in the hands of "qualified medical practitioners" (See i.e., *BMJ* August 5, 1893, p. 324).

A SECOND SPIRITUAL HEALING REPORT

On June 18, 1910, Dawson Williams, editor of the *BMJ*, published a series of specially commissioned articles on what he considered to be the general and convenient term of "Mental Healing." That Special Issue[39] contained papers by eminent medical men like Clifford Allbut, Henry Morris, H. T. Butlin, and William Osler. In "Mental Healing," one of the articles already referred to, the Anonymous author (1910, p. 1493), in a detailed and wide-ranging survey from antiquity to the present day, argued that various descriptions of "miracle" cures from the past were strikingly similar to many of the interesting cases discussed by Hack Tuke (1873) in his *Illustrations of the Influence of the Mind upon the Body*. As there was no suggestion "of thaumaturgic influence" in Tuke's cases, "one can hardly avoid the conclusion that the mechanism is the same in the one class of cases as in the other." Thus Anon argued that "faith" and "spiritual" cures could all be explained by reference to suggestion. Despite being severely criticized by Myers and Bramwell, the suggestion theory actively promoted by Moll (1902) had now become the stock explanatory "mechanism"—the predominant medical-scientific paradigm—and routinely used to explain those apparently inexplicable cures. Stephen Paget (1909, pp. 202–4), the militant materialist, had made the same assertion the previous year and this same paradigm would also be used in

BMA Spiritual Healing when it was published the following year. And it was this same "suggestion" paradigm which also informed *all* the contributions to the *BMJ*'s Special Issue on "Mental Healing." Thus although Williams subsequently claimed (*BMJ* March 9, 1912, p. 553) that the Special Issue had re-ignited those "Mental Healing" debates, which had lapsed "for a time into a state of suspended animation," it would be more prudent to suggest that the Special Issue galvanized a number of different strands thereby acting as a catalyst for that Conference on Spiritual Healing, which was convened in October 1910, in order to try and bring together "prominent members of the clerical and medical profession" so that they might jointly "consider the asserted results and the rapid development of so-called 'spiritual' or 'faith-healing' movements."

Delegates to that October 1910 Conference then appointed a Clerical and Medical Spiritual Healing Committee to be composed of more or less equal numbers of medics and clerics but to be chaired by Dr Ryle, dean of Westminster. The Ryle Committee was then charged "to consider and report upon the possibility and the best methods of closer co-operation between the two professions in their respective spheres." During the course of 1911, the Ryle Committee held twenty-two sessions and corresponded with and interviewed many eminent medical practitioners, "some of whom had made the relation of mind to body their special study." They also held discussions with a number of clergymen as well as "many persons associated in one way or another" with so-called "spiritual" or "faith healing." Then having accumulated a large amount of material the Ryle Committee convened a second conference, for October 1911, where it presented its preliminary conclusions which "were unanimously adopted, published and forwarded to the Diocesan and the Medical Corporations." At the same time the Conference also agreed to enlarge the Ryle Committee into a Standing Committee so that they might continue their investigations into how to guard against "the dangers connected with ['faith'] treatments by persons not medically qualified," and how best to "promote all legitimate co-operation between the two professions and, so far as may be, to influence opinion and correct false impressions in regard to irregular and unqualified attempts at 'healing' in the name of religion." But as the Ryle Committee (1914, pp. 7–8) made clear, in its interim report, the parameters for its further investigations were to be tightly circumscribed because

> any attempt on the part of the clergy to enter into competition with the medical practitioner by any separate and independent treatment of the sick is to be strongly deprecated, not merely on practical, but also on religious grounds. For there is a serious danger lest the association of physical healing with the work of the ministry should divert attention from the primary purpose of that ministry, and prove injurious to individual faith.

This medical orthodoxy is hardly surprising given the names of many of the medical practitioners who served on the Standing Committee such as Stanley Bousfield (Hon. Secretary and Treasurer), Charles Buttar, T. B. Hyslop, H.G.G. Mackenzie, J. A. Ormerod, and Sir T. Clifford Allbutt all of whom, with perhaps the exception of Hyslop, had, in their own ways, argued for a more rigid medical control over matters related to spiritual healing. The Committee held nineteen meetings and interviewed a number of qualified practitioners who had practiced or made special study of "the treatment of physical disorders by spiritual or mental influences," including Drs. Bramwell, Tuckey, and M. B. Wright. And yet the Ryle Committee, which continued to avoid any kind of dialogue with unqualified practitioners, also appears to have virtually ignored the contemporaneous work of the BMA Investigation Committee; perhaps because the BMA Spiritual Healing report had not yet been adopted. And because the Ryle Committee travelled much the same path as BMA Spiritual Healing it is hardly suprising that both Reports reached similar conclusions although the Ryle Report (1914, pp. 15–16), given its clerical chairman, was couched in somewhat more theological terms being

> of the opinion that the physical results of what is called "Faith" or "Spiritual" healing do not prove on investigation to be different from those of Mental healing or healing by Suggestion. The term Suggestion is used in this Report in a wide sense, as meaning the application of any natural mental process to the purposes of treatment.
>
> They recognise that Suggestion is more effectively exercised by some persons than by others, and this fact seems to explain the "gifts" of a special character claimed by various "Healers." It is undoubtedly due to the striking benefits which sometimes result from Suggestion that the belief in such claims has been fostered.

Although the Ryle Report clearly deprecated "the independent treatment of disease by irresponsible and unqualified persons" and stressed the primacy of the medical practitioner, it also expressed the "desire to see an increased importance attached to spiritual ministrations as contributory means to recovery." But then, perhaps turning the orthodox medical arguments on their head, Ryle (1914, pp. 7–8; *BMJ* March 23, 1912, p. 687) urged all medical men to be sensitive to the intervention of the clergy because "the calming and strengthening effects of spiritual ministrations may be a valuable auxiliary to ordinary medical methods." Ultimately, however, the Committe concluded that as this was clearly a complex problem they should continue their investigations so that: (1) they could draw up guidelines for closer cooperation "between Ministers of Religion and members of the Medical Profession;" (2) continue investigating those "Spiritual" or "Mental" claims for cures of organic diseases; (3) investigate "the degree of success resulting from the medical practise of the various methods of treatment by Suggestion"; (4) issue publicity, in the form of lectures and articles, to inform and "to warn the public of the serious dangers incident to the many irregular and often ignorant efforts to heal the sick"; (5) to promote the formation of a Joint Committee of Clergy and Doctors "as a means of advancing knowledge and forming a sound public opinion." (Ryle 1914, pp. 18–19). If a skeptical reader were to borrow from the conclusions which the *BMJ* (March 9, 1912, p. 555) drew following its lengthy review of Rhodes (1910b) she might conclude that the Ryle Report "may, perhaps, be not unfairly described in one sentence as a plea for the restoration of miraculous powers to the Anglican Church."

SOME CONCLUSIONS

Root (2005, pp. 202–3) suggests that the medico-religious collaboration throughout this period was

> always overtly unequal, with the Church predominately accepting medical strictures, medical language and medical explanations. The reason for this inequality was that the Church proved to be far more anxious to attain secular medical approval than the medical establishment was to give such approval. In order to preserve their credibility and establishment authority the Anglican Church judged that their healing ministry required medical backing to a significantly greater extent than the medical profession would ever have believed that they required any religious involvement in medicine. . . . As a result of this need for medical approval. . . . Anglican healers were far more likely almost than any others to accept the common medical argument that the efficacy of spiritual healing could be explained materially through psychological suggestion.

And yet there were voices raised against this seemingly cozy accommodation between the Anglican and Medical hierarchies. Rhodes (1910a, p. 1497), for example, cautioned: "For what is the miracle of to-day is often found to be the ordinary working of a scientific law, to-morrow." Podmore (1910, p. 250), perhaps with a touch of irony, said: "Science and Superstition can now almost shake hands, so narrow is the ditch that divides the two camps," while J. H. Hyslop introduced a more cautionary note.

> "Suggestion" has become a universal solvent when a man wants to get out of a difficulty. It was never, in fact, an explanation of anything, and I doubt if any man, living or dead, could tell exactly what he means by the term; but it is very useful for throwing dust in the eyes of the public. It names no known cause, and only increases mystery instead of removing it. But it keeps the public at bay,

and that is its chief function. As a means of frightening away false ideas it is, and has been, useful; but as a means of explanation it is absolutely worthless.' (Quoted Cobb, 1914, pp. 204–5; see also Root, 2005, p. 284)

Miss Eleanor M. Reed went even further and "accused the Anglican Church of neglecting its duty towards the sick in its obsequious attitude towards orthodox medicine." And she added, "that 'where the clergy and the doctors needed to meet was in the homes of the sufferers, and not merely at the bedside of the dying.'" (Root 2005, p. 181) For his part C. H. Lea (1913, p. xii), who converted from an enquiring "Free Churchman" into a Christian Scientist, noted that while the Ryle Committee were tasked with investigating the whole subject of faith healing "Christian Science did not come within the terms of its reference," and, perhaps plagiarizing Hyslop, Lea accused Ryle of "throwing dust into the eyes of both press and public as regards the true facts of spiritual healing." (Gartrell-Mills 1991, p. 170). If Lea had been less partisan he would surely have also noted that Ryle's other silences cast all faith and spiritual healers beyond its pale.

NOTES

1. Bible (2006, p. 1557).

2. The term alludes to Titus (2:14)—"and purify unto himself a peculiar people, zealous of good works." Here the Greek *periousios* could also mean for one's own special possession. Although the Peculiar People were a small English sect, quite distinct from Christian Scientists, the fact that both sects held similar beliefs in relation to faith healing meant that they were often seen as interchangeable.

3. In another case Thomas George Senior was sentenced to 4 months of hard labour "for the manslaughter of his child because he had not sought medical aid or medicine, although aware he/ she would probably die." (*JMS* 1899, Vol. 45, p. 354).

4. Christian Scientists had probably been working in London since the early 1890s (*Pall Mall* February 14, 1891). By 1908 there were 64 registered CS healers in London, 10 in Manchester and 9 in Brighton. All CS healers were trained to take cases and had "made formal declaration that they use, as their only text-books, the Bible and Mrs. Eddy's writings, and that they are not engaged in any other profession or vocation than healing." (Paget 1909, p. viii).

5. Feilding (1899, p. 60) calls it "a kind of metaphysical mysticism."

6. The reference is to Carpenter's physiological theory of 'unconscious cerebration' (See i.e., Hyslop 1895, pp. 165f).

7. See however a BMA debate on the subject where Eder, as a loan voice, called for "the nationalization of the whole medical profession" (*BMJ* December 15, 1906, pp. 330f).

8. Graham graduated in 1882, studied mental disease in London and then on the continent, before joining the Association in 1887. He was appointed resident medical

superintendent of the County Armagh Asylum in 1884. (*BMJ*, November 17, 1917, p. 674).

9. Root (2005, p. 239) suggests: "It was arguably Christian Science which was at the root of most of the escalating popular, medical, and religious interest in spiritual healing during this period."

10. Lombard was Curate at All Hallows (1897–1899), Vicar (1900–1908), Chaplain to the British Embassy, St Petersburg (1908–1918) then to the Baltic Fleet. I am grateful to Anne Layzell for this information (e-mail to the author September 27, 2015). Lombard was involved with the Guild from its inception in late 1904 (*CT* November 18, 1904, p. 675).

11. Stanley Bousfield, quoting from the 1909 Annual Report, suggests a membership of 429 (*BMJ* August 20, 1910, p. 464).

12. There is brief reference to him speaking at the opening of the refurbished Enterprise Club for women working as clerks in the City of London (*LDN*, April 18, 1904, p. 8). Not to be confused with Paul Bousfield who became interested in psychoanalysis during the War.

13. Although strictly correct there were doctors, like Greville Macdonald of Harley St., who were active supporters of the Guild.

14. Christian Science was discussed at the 1905 Weymouth Church Congress (Gartrell-Mills 1991, p. 158).

15. Lombard went even further: "I am inclined to think that imposition of hands as a healing method may prove to-day to be more efficacious in most cases than anointing with, oil, though, undoubtedly, the latter has been of much value" (*CT* November 24, 1905, p. 662).

16. *CT* (May 25, 1906, p. 695) takes up this argument.

17. The original motion said: "That this conference, while considering that Christian Scientists are justified in emphasising the power of faith in healing, views the main outline of their teaching and attitude, as antagonistic both to Christianity and science.' (*The Times*, May 18, 1906, p. 4).

18. Although *sub judice The Lancet* (July 28, 1906, pp. 237–38) had in mind the trial of George Robert Adcock, subsequently acquitted of the manslaughter of Major J. N. Whyte. Adcock was defended by [Dr] George C. Kingsbury a pioneer medical hypnotist in the 1890s, but now standing council for Christian Scientists. See also *BMJ* (July 7, 1906, pp. 56–57).

19. Root (2005, p. 180), following Stuart Maws, says the subject was placed on the agenda following a "request" from the "American bishops who wanted to co-ordinate their response to the [Christian Science] movement."

20. Landsbury, an active campaigner against vested interests, became a socialist in the early 1890s and was elected Labour MP in 1910. He resigned his seat in 1912 to campaign for women's suffrage. His socialism was underpinned by his Christian beliefs.

21. Thomas Colley, somewhat of an eccentric, managed to straddle the orthodox and the spiritual but was eventually forced to resign because he had himself carried around the aisles in a glass coffin, raised the lid and said the benediction. In his will he asked that his remains be sent to the Medical Faculty at Birmingham for dissection and his bones wired together and the skeleton sent to the Psychic Museum in

Leamington. (*SMH* February 8, 1912, p. 9). See also *APS* (1906, Vol. 4, pp. 135 and 333f).

22. Root (2005, pp. 193 and 199) suggests Ryle, a renowned Old Testament biblical scholar, was "a broad-churchman favouring a liberal and rational interpretation of church doctrine."

23. A full list of members can be found in Anon (1908c, p. 133n).

24. The Conference occurred between 6 July and August 5, 1908.

25. A rare reference, outside psychical research publications, to the 'Subliminal Consciousness' rather than the sub- or unconscious. There were at least 53 Revs. listed as SPR members in *Proceedings* (1911, Vol. 25, pp. 478–519).

26. Gleig (2012) offers an important insight into the current debates around psychoanalysis and spirituality.

27. Miss E. Read spoke at the Conference, so too Dr. McComb (*WDP* June 18, 1908, p. 10), Hickson and Bishop Mylne (Gartrell-Mills 1991, p. 160).

28. Sandwich appears again in Chapter 20.

29. Adelaine was also a member of the SPR.

30. *The Healer: A Monthly Record of Spiritual Healing*, had its offices at 22 Talbot Square.

31. Maurice Bell (1862–1931) [High Church] Vicar of the inner city parish of St Mark's Regents Park (1904–12), was formerly officially connected with the Guild of Health and a close associate of Percy Dearmer (Hutchinson [nd]).

32. James Moorhead (1851–1918?) born in Ireland, a retired (Lt Colonel) from the Indian Medical Service where he had been posted c.1880.

33. See also Hill (1901, p. 964).

34. The reference is to Mary Baker Eddy (1875) the founder of Christian Science.

35. 'Her' is Mrs Eddy.

36. A respected scientist and active member of the SPR.

37. The Metropolitan Counties Branch, was composed of the following local branches or divisions: Kensington, Richmond, Chelsea, City of London, Hampstead and Walthamstow. Given its geographical spread and membership this was a particularly powerful lobby.

38. The sub-committee comprised E. H. T. Nash, chairman of the Medico-Political Committee, H. W. Armit, Drs Chas Macfie, Chas Buttar, E. F. Buzzard, T. A. Helme, J. A. Macdonald, D. G. Thomson, J. F. Woods and Mrs Mary Scharlieb (*BMJ* May 7, 1910, p. 213) A slightly different membership is given in *BMJ* (May 1, 1909, p. 214). Armit, who was a member of the Hampstead Branch, was appointed to the Medico-Political Committee in December 1908.

39. Root (2005, p. 236) notes the lengthy correspondence most of which welcomed the *BMJ*'s "spirit of inquiry."

Part III

THE PSYCHICAL, THE PSYCHOLOGICAL, THE PSYCHO-THERAPEUTICAL

> The greater part of the "philosophy of the unconscious," as taught by Schopenhauer and Hartmann, deals with those deep subconscious phenomena that do not rise to the level of the throne of reason, but which, nevertheless, as they show, really give the bent to human action and human history. They represent the *natura naturans* and are the unseen forces that are at work below the surface, shaping events in apparent opposition to the wishes and intentions of men. They thus appear unconscious or even supernatural, but in and of themselves they as really [*sic*] involve the principle of consciousness as do the often less wise and less successful decrees of the developed brain. (Ward 1911, p. 123)

Chapter 7

The Medical Society for the Study of Suggestive Therapeutics

> As seen nowadays, the influence of mind as a therapeutic agent was chiefly practised under the term 'suggestion'; and it was familiar under the term 'hypnotic suggestion,' though all suggestion was not of the hypnotic form. Let them have a clear conception of what was meant by 'suggestion.' It was the insinuation of a belief or impulse into the mind of a subject by any means, as by words or gestures, usually by emphatic declaration; also the impulse of trust and submission, which led to the effectiveness of such incitement. According to Dr. MacDougall: 'Suggestion is a process of communication resulting in the acceptance with conviction of the communicated proposition in the absence of logically adequate grounds for its acceptance.' (Shaw 1909, p. 1352)

THE GENERAL PRACTITIONER

In early March 1891 George Brown (1844–1917),[1] then editor of *The Medical Times & Hospital Gazette* [*MTHG*], invited "a few medical men" to discuss the possibility of forming a society for "the improvement and advancement of the medical profession." Brown's ambition was to create

> a bond of union between general practitioners, whom it would weld together through the sympathy of their calling, their common wants, and their varied and too many grievances. (Alderson 1894, pp. 1–7)

The original impetus for Brown's suggestion was a House of Lords Select Committee examining serious allegations of abuse of hospital charities which, if proved correct, would be "so injurious to the well-being of the medical profession, and so hurtful to the public."[2] From that meeting there emerged the Medical, or General Practitioners Alliance (*BMJ* July 2, 1892, p. 40), aka the Incorporated Medical Practitioners' Association [IMPA] with George Brown, as its first president, and a Council of "men well known as earnest reformers in the medical profession." Although the *MTHG* advertised itself as the "General Practitioner's Journal" it was also, for a time, the de facto Journal of the IMPA which, amongst other matters, campaigned for "increased and more efficient representation on the General Medical Council, especially for bringing pressure on [the GMC] to exercise its power in suppressing illegal medical practice."[3] In 1892, a total of 30,000 medical men formed the "profession," with the majority being GPs and yet the GMC was "composed . . . chiefly of delegates from the various teaching corporations" which meant that the interests of the GP, already poorly served by the BMA, were largely ignored.

> [The GMC] have allowed the profession to suffer in dignity, public estimation, and in pocket by their want of spirit and business enterprise.
>
> On all sides are to be found flourishing, at our expense, unqualified practitioners, quacks, bonesetters, herbalists, and prescribing chemists. The majority of the men on the senates and councils of our colleges and corporations are not personally affected by these hardships, and the great bulk of the profession has no opportunity of bringing any pressure to bear on them. (*BMJ* May 21, 1892, p. 1113)

The IMPA also wanted power to "supervise all legislative propositions calculated to affect the interests and prospects of that bulwark of the profession, the general practitioner, and to deal with all matters affecting the well-being of men in general practice." Brown's ambition was that the IMPA would

> become a not unworthy second to that greatest of all medical societies, the British Medical Association . . . [and] jealously guard the interests of the profession, and to hold intact our too limited privileges, of which it behoves us to watch and see that there is no encroachment . . .[4]

Following a rather public falling out between the IMPA and the *MTHG*, Brown resigned from the *MTHG* and, in 1900, founded *The General Practitioner* [the *GP*],[5] which he established as "the official journal of the [IMPA]." Although Brown continued fiercely defending and trying to extend the rights and privileges of GPs what is of interest here is Brown's changed attitude toward hypnotism because by the early 1900s Brown, who was also a member of the GMC, had drastically modified his previous, apparently implacable, hostility to hypnotism (*BMJ* March 8, 1890, p. 573; July 30, 1892, p. 258). This change of heart and mind, which also included a more benign attitude towards psychical research (*GP* February 7, 1903, p. 79), may have been due, in part, to Brown's growing friendship with the Croydon-based GP, Percy Allan (1869–1927).[6] Allan (1925, p. 116), who became Brown's editorial assistant in 1903, was also, by then, good friends with Lloyd Tuckey and therefore one of a number of practitioners whom Tuckey had taught and encouraged, over the years, to use curative hypnosis and suggestion as part of their *armamenta medica.*

Charles Lloyd Tuckey (1855–1925),[7] was educated at Kings College London [KCL], then Aberdeen, and worked for a time (c.1880–1889) at the London Homeopathic Hospital until his growing theoretical interests in hypnotism drew him, in August 1888, to travel to Nancy to investigate the matter further. By the time Tuckey (1888, p. 839; 1889a, p. 365; 1907b, p. 335) returned to London, he was convinced of the therapeutic benefits of hypnotic suggestion and, by his own account, was already using it "seriously and systematically" by November 1888 (Anon 1892a, p. 459). Tuckey's article, describing, what was in effect, his conversion to hypnotism, was published in the December 1888 issue of *The Nineteenth Century* and by January 1889 he had completed what was to be the first edition of *Psycho-Therapeutics, or Treatment by Sleep and Suggestion.* Many medical practitioners, as well as subsequent historians, have traced the birth of the British Psycho-Therapeutic Movement to 1888 and that moment of Tuckey's conversion. Although it is difficult to weigh the impact of Tuckey's book, which went through six revisions between 1889 and 1913, it was still widely considered, in 1919, to be "a standard treatise on the subject." Tuckey's significance can also be found in the impressive array of signatures to a Memorial requesting that he be granted a civil list pension because serious illness had forced him "to relinquish his medical practice, and owing to this is now in very straightened circumstances." (Mitchell 1919). It is probably no exaggeration to claim that Tuckey's influence, through lectures, articles, and practical teaching, inspired a whole generation of medical and lay practitioners, including clergymen and school masters, who now took up hypnosis for curative and educative purposes and moral improvements. Kingsbury (1891, p. 14) claimed Tuckey was "The first English medical man . . . to take up the Nancy treatment"[8] while many others acknowledged him as "the pioneer in this country of the revival of Hypnotism and Suggestion as therapeutic agents in medical practice." (Mitchell 1919). As Wingfield (1910, p. 119) noted it was

> Lloyd Tuckey's perseverance and Bramwell's determination and courage in advocating the claims of the new treatment that hypnotism chiefly owes its recognition in England as a legitimate addition to our armoury of healing.

Significant evidence reveals that interest in, and practice of, hypnotism as a psychotherapeutic, was already relatively widespread in Britain by the turn of the century and there is little doubt that Tuckey's writings, especially in the *GP*, were to be a significant factor in its growing popularity during the first long decade of the new century. In June 1903, the *GP* published a substantial article by Tuckey (1903a, pp. 350–51) outlining the case in favor of hypnotism, although Tuckey still saw it very much in physiological terms.

> A most important response to suggestion is the sensation of warmth which follows the laying of the hand over the epigastrium or other part. The warmth is a glow or flush, and is due to action on the vaso-motor nerves. It means a flow of blood to the parts that the sympathetic system is more or less under control, and that local circulation and nutrition can be influenced. When pain is a leading symptom it can generally be relieved, at least temporarily, by suggesting this local warmth.

There is no mistaking the "laying on of hands,"[9] even when dressed up in physiological garb. Tuckey also spelled out what he saw as the physiological mechanisms of hypnotism with the idea that it "seeks to influence function and nutrition through the highest cerebral centres which besides being the seat of intelligence and imagination are also able to exercise a controlling power over organic life." In the case of pain it relieved "symptoms probably by direct inhibitory action on the pain centres" and with "nervous breakdown, from overwork or shock hypnotism is, I think the remedy *par excellence*, for it goes direct to the root of the trouble by its effects on the highest cerebral centres." Tuckey's (1903a, p. 367) physiological model was further reenforced by his belief that suggestion would not work in the treatment of organic mental disease. "The insane and imbecile are rarely hypnotisable, and as our object is to act on the organism through the highest centres it is not possible to get the curative action of suggestion when they are primarily diseased. . . . Hypnotism has perhaps won its greatest triumphs in the borderland cases occupied by dipsomania, morphinomania and kleptomania."[10] Then after detailing some of his own cases Tuckey (1903a, p. 384) concluded, no doubt with the PTS very much in his mind,

> a great change is apparent in the attitude of the profession towards hypnotism within the last few years; and if it can only be kept out of the hands of quacks I feel convinced its future position in therapeuticsis [*sic*] secured.

But Tuckey (1903a, p. 367)[11] was also repositioning himself not just in relation to quacks but also in relation to the medical profession as a whole.

> The trusted family physician seemed the proper person to carry out [hypnotism] to his own and the patient's advantage. But it was gradually borne in upon me that there were many reasons against the general use of hypnotism by the

> profession. In the first place the process takes up a great deal of time, more than can be spared by the busy practitioner. Secondly, it is found that suggestions come with more weight from comparative strangers and that the patient who is accustomed to look to his doctor for ordinary drug treatment often fails to appreciate suggestion from him even when it is possible to hypnotise him. I have frequently found this in the case of old patients of my own, whereas, if called in as a 'specialist' one is at a great advantage. Thirdly, there is still much prejudice and misconception in regard to hypnotism, and the ordinary practitioner cannot run the risk of scandal and misrepresentation to which its use might subject him.

At first sight it might seem as if Tuckey, from his widely acknowledged status as one of the foremost psychotherapist specialists, was touting for business by advising GP's, of whom he used to be one "to abstain from using hypnotism" with their "own patients."[12] But his comments can also be seen to represent an important marker indicating his belief that psychotherapy should no longer be an adjunct to general practice but become a specialism in its own right and that the psychotherapist should now become its acknowledged specialist. This often unspoken assumption was, also subsequently, to define the role of the psychoanalyst.

Tuckey's (1903b, p. 607) second article was a response to an article on hallucinatory voices by the fascinating Dr. Barker Smith (b.1846) who, unfortunately will have to be placed in this footnote.[13] Tuckey claimed that he (Tuckey) and F.W.H Myers had finally managed to profoundly hypnotize a lady "who thought herself mesmerised by a Sheffield quack whom she had once consulted." In a third article, discussing sexual perversion,[14] Tuckey (1903c, p. 703), reveals a good working knowledge of the current British *and* foreign literature on the subject and claims that although the tendency was to ignore the issue, "in the interests of public morality," there was sufficient evidence, particularly in the press, to make it

> clear that sexual perversion is of much more common occurrence than is generally supposed. Some authorities have estimated the proportion of sexual perverts or 'urnings' [homosexuals] to normal men as high as five per cent., but this is, I think, altogether too high, and one per cent. would, I consider, be much nearer the mark. Even this figure is sufficiently startling and makes one *furieusement á penser*.[15]

After ten years of working in this field, Tuckey (1903c, p. 704) had concluded that "the moral tone varies in different cases, and how unfair it is to class all sexual perverts in the same category of depravity." And yet by conflating indecent child sexual assault with homosexuality Tuckey was led, perhaps not surprisingly, to support the current law which criminalized all homosexual acts. But he was also driven by a sense of "moral repulsion" which led him to believe "beyond dispute that no form of vice is so anti-social and so destructive of the very foundations of civilization." This was why it was necessary that "the pervert must suffer in the interest of the community." On the other hand Tuckey also sought to distinguish "between the real 'urning,' who inherits this idiosyncrasy," which Tuckey believed "to be hereditary in certain families," and the debauchees. Aware that young boys could also be "corrupted" by pederasts, Tuckey (1903c, p. 704) suggested that while hypnotism held out the only possible cure for a genuine urning, that cure could only come through suggestion "administered in the deepest hypnosis."

> It has unfortunately happened that not one of the sexual perverts I have hypnotised has proved susceptible to the required extent. But my faith in the remedy is unshaken and I look forward to lighting upon an urning who is also a 'somnambule' any day. As the only possible remedy it should certainly be tried in these cases.[16]

Following one of those three articles W., a general practitioner in a northern manufacturing town, wrote, in late 1903, to tell Tuckey about some very interesting cases of hypnotism in his own practice. Tuckey replied by suggesting W., should send them to the *GP* because the editors, Brown and Allan, were "sufficiently open-minded to print them." In reply W. said that he could not afford to publish the accounts "in his own name as the prejudice against hypnotism is still very strong in the provinces." He had recently treated a girl successfully but her parents promptly removed her from his care (*GP* January 30, 1904, p. 72). While there is no reason to doubt W.'s account there is, as we shall see, ample contrary evidence which shows that hypnotism was now widely discussed and used in a number of very different medical settings. For example Bolus (1903, p. 379), during a relatively long article on hypnotism in the prestigious *Guy's Hospital Gazette* [*GHG*] noted: "Minor operations have been performed in this hospital without pain under hypnotic influence." More important, for this chapter, is the close relationship between Tuckey, the acknowledged advocate for the Nancy School of hypnotism, and Drs. Brown and Allan, the open-minded editors of the *GP,* because it was this alliance which now served as a powerful driver for the spread of hypnotism among an ever increasing number British GPs.

BETTS TAPLIN AND THE LIVERPOOL CONNECTIONS

On April 19, 1906, Dr. A. Betts Taplin (1856–1939),[17] a Liverpool GP, and soon to become an important figure in the emerging psychotherapeutic movement, gave a talk on "Treatment by hypnotic suggestion" to the Liverpool Medical Institution [LMI]

> [He] said that hypnotism was generally acknowledged to be a physiological and not a pathological condition, and to be absolutely free from danger in competent hands. It had been found most useful in cases characterized by pain, spasm, or other nervous phenomena in which no organic cause could be found, and for which no other therapeutic measures seemed to be of any avail. The time for its study and reception by the medical profession was ripe, and, to prevent its possible abuse in ignorant or unscrupulous hands, it was much to be desired that, as soon as possible, its use should be limited by legal enactment to properly-qualified persons under proper control.

Taplin probably had in mind not just Christian Science but also the PTS and maybe even Walford Bodie who had performed in Leeds about a month earlier. In the discussion which followed Grossman noted that 18 years ago he had given an account, before the LMI, of his visit to Charcot "and a stay at Nancy, where he studied the methods and saw the patients of Dr. Liébeault and Professor Bernheim." He, himself, "had no difficulty in hypnotising subjects, but he had never seen any therapeutic results in his cases." Dr A. E. Davis (1926), soon to become an important figure in the Liverpool psychotherapeutic community, agreed with Grossman "that subjects often deceived the hypnotiser" but he could not "accept the statement made by one of the speakers that hypnosis was produced in hysterical neurotic soil. In his experience this was the least fruitful of all." He agreed there were many problems with hypnosis—"The objection of males to try hypnotism was a great drawback to its practice and study"—and yet he "had repeatedly produced trophic changes." Dr. S. Whitaker[18] thought "a better description of the treatment desired would be 'treatment by suggestion with or without hypnosis.'"[19]

> It was usually unnecessary to hypnotise the patient more deeply than the lightest lethargic stage when he would accept suggestions, and the operator could obtain good therapeutic results. During treatment there should be no distracting sounds and sights. He used the method of 'monotony' . . . and, so far as this element existed, it was possible to benefit the patient. He had obtained excellent results in the palpitation of exophthalmic goitre, headache, insomnia, and pain generally.

Dr. C. T. Street (b.1858),[20] the proprietor of Haydock Lodge Asylum in Newton-le-Willows, Lancashire, also wondered if "treatment by suggestion without hypnotism" was preferable and thought suggestion with the insane could be beneficial. "The result from this form of treatment might be slow, but it was certainly more sure and lasting than that produced by hypnotism." (*BMJ* April 28, 1906, pp. 979–80). This discussion clearly suggests that by April 1906 there was already an informed interest in hypnotism, at least in Liverpool, even if the consensus tended to be on its physiological rather than psychological benefits. But this LMI debate can also be seen as a first tentative step toward the founding of the Liverpool Psycho-Therapeutic Clinic in November 1912.

It may have been the report of the LMI meeting which inspired Dr. Douglas Bryan (1879–1955),[21] a GP in Leicester, and subsequently a member of the LPAS, to write up some "remarkable instances of the use of hypnotism in ordinary medical practice." And because his own experiences had been so successful he was now inclined "to believe that hypnotism and hypnotic suggestion, so little recognised by the greater number of medical men, are a thoroughly legitimate and valuable therapeutic adjunct." So Bryan (1906) sent some of his notes to the *MTHG* where George Brown, now once again its editor, published them. This tentative chronology offers a possible explanation as to how Taplin, a GP in Liverpool and Bryan a GP in Leicester, came to discuss the possibility of forming some kind of hypnotic society.[22]

THE MEDICAL SOCIETY FOR THE STUDY OF SUGGESTIVE THERAPEUTICS

Some time during the Summer of 1906, Betts Taplin and Douglas Bryan approached Frederick R. Cruise (1834–1912), consulting physician to the Mater Misericordiae Hospital, Dublin, to ask if he would become president of their proposed medical society for the study of hypnotism. In the early 1890s, Cruise, already a highly respected Dublin physician, was an early pioneer of hypnotism, along with Tuckey, Kingsbury (1861–1938), Bramwell, Felkin (b.1853)[23] and others. But Cruise[24] declined on the grounds of old age and too many other commitments so Taplin and Bryan then approached Tuckey (1907a, p. 210) who, at first, also declined. But they eventually persuaded him to change his mind and a meeting was convened, for November 8, 1906, at Tuckey's residence in London

> with the object of forming a Society of Registered Medical Practitioners who are interested in the study and practice of hypnotic suggestion: the aims of such society being to facilitate the study thereof, and bring its claims as a therapeutic agent more prominently before the profession at large. (*GP* November 24, 1906, p. 748; *Journal* SPR, 1908, Vol. 13, p. 14)

During a well-attended inaugural meeting, there was a discussion about the name but when somebody suggested the "Psycho-Therapeutical Society"[25] Tuckey, and, no doubt others, reminded them that this had already been taken "by another society chiefly of laymen and women who run a dispensary and a quasi-medical journal in Bloomsbury." Somebody may then have suggested the Medical Hypnotic Society but Bramwell (1909, p. 164), for one, would probably have argued that they should avoid using hypnotics or hypnosis in their title because he and others had now dispensed with hypnosis altogether. "The essence of the whole condition, then, is an increased suggestibility; the production of a preliminary imitation sleep is not necessary, and is simply a waste of time. . . . I commence curative treatment at once, and obtain quicker results." So Bramwell proposed, instead, "The Medical Society for the Study of Suggestive Therapeutics" [MSSST],[26] which Felkin seconded and so the name was adopted and Tuckey unanimously elected their first president. Following further discussion Bramwell proposed, Felkin seconded, and the meeting agreed, probably unanimously:

> That the membership of the society be limited to registered medical practitioners; and secondly, that no such shall be eligible for membership *who are connected in any way* with any non-medical society which has for its object the treatment of disease by unqualified persons, whether by hypnotism or otherwise. (*GP* November 24, 1906, p. 749; *Journal* 1908, Vol. 13, p. 14, italics mine)[27]

Following the meeting Tuckey approached Percy Allan, now sole editor of the *GP*, to ask if he would publish articles and communications relating to the work of the Society. Allen not only promised to publish their papers and give them every assistance but also "expressed a wish to join the society." (*GP* November 24, 1906, p. 749). There are now two points to note. First, From its very inception the MSSST had effectively secured the active support of a well-established publication. Second, because a significant number of its founding members were also members of the SPR—Bramwell and Tuckey even sat on their Council—the MSST also had access to the *Journal* and other SPR facilities, including the use of the SPR Offices at 20 Hanover Square. Thus from its very inception the MSST effectively inherited the kind of ready-made institutional framework which might otherwise have taken them years to establish.

One of the stated aims of the MSSST was to promote the therapeutic values of hypnotism and suggestion, through lectures and articles and, in particular, to point "out the fallacies which abound and to give an intelligent, practical, and useful idea of the subject" (Bryan 1907, p. 490).[28] To this end, the Society initiated a series of public lectures which were then published or extensively abstracted in the *GP*. While the titles of these papers will offer a flavor of the topics presented and, at the same time, serve as comparison with the PTS lecture series organized by Hallam, the names of the authors of those talks reveal the full extent of the intertwinings and symbiotic relationships between the MSSST and the SPR. So on 25 October 1907, Wingfield [SPR] read "Results of experiments with Cambridge Undergraduates: being mainly an attempt to determine the Waking States of Hypnotism;"[29] On January 16, 1908, William McDougall [SPR], Professor of Physiology at Oxford, read "The Physiological Theories of the Hypnotic State" (*Journal* Vol. 13,

p. 192);[30] On May 1, 1908, T. W. Mitchell (1908) [SPR] read "Hypnotism and Hysteria;" On 30 October 1908, Bramwell [SPR] read "Obsessions and Their Treatment by Suggestion;"[31] In January 1909, Taplin [SPR, 1913] read "Methods in the Treatment by Hypnotic Suggestion"; On July 8, 1909, Dr Albert E. Davis [SPR, 1915] read "Some Observations on Suggestive Therapeutics in General Practice" (*GP* September 4, 1909, pp. 562); On July 15, 1909, Dr Walters spoke about his use of suggestion in nervous and organic diseases (*GP* August 14, 1909, pp. 514f.); On 26 October 1910, J. W. Astley Cooper (1910) read "The Treatment of Alcohol Inebriety by Psycho-Therapy" at a meeting in Liverpool.[32] Then from about July 1909 the meetings, which remained open to the public, appear to have assumed a more specialist orientation with speakers encouraged to report specific cases of interest although it remains unclear as to whether or not subjects, let alone patients, were ever "shown." In the meantime a growing interest in hypnotism and suggestion also spread beyond the confines of the MSSST and SPR as other organizations also started exploring the subject in more detail. Most important, for this study, is that hypnotism remained very much on the BMA agenda. So in his presidential address to the Section of the 1907 Exeter Annual Meeting, T. C. Shaw (1907a) who was soon to become actively interested in psychoanalysis, spoke on "mental healing" by way of introducing J. F. Woods (1898), whom, it will be recalled, had spoken on hypnotism at the 1898 Annual Meeting. Now in 1907, Woods told his audience about

> his experience, extending over a period of fifteen years, of the therapeutic value of hypnotism in insanity. Most of the patients were treated in asylums, others in private. He finds the treatment most efficacious in borderland cases. Illustrative cases are given with details of the method employed. (*BMJ* July 27, 1907 p. 64)[33]

The report in the *BMJ* (September 18, 1907, p. 812) suggests the tone of the discussion was measured and respectful and although Yellowlees cautioned against the dangers of hypnotism there is little indication of any voice raised against its medical uses. Indeed, in his summing up, Shaw concluded by

> affirming his belief that states of mind had an enormous influence on states of body, although they had to confess their ignorance of the underlying connexion.

CONSTRUCTING THE HISTORY AND HISTORIOGRAPHY OF HYPNOTISM

Despite his early reservations, Tuckey (1907b, p. 247) threw himself into the cause, thanking Taplin "for his energetic initiative" and suggesting the new society "is a move in the right direction."

Within three months of its foundation . . . it numbers about thirty members, and bids fair in time to rival in influence and utility its prosperous French forerunner, La Société d'Hypnologie et de Psychologic, founded 1890. The English society will, we hope, afford encouragement and support to those medical men who are fighting as pioneers against lay and professional prejudice, and will enable us to collect and compare experimental and clinical results.

By late 1907 the MSSST claimed "members from all parts of the United Kingdom (Bryan 1907, p. 490): by early 1908 membership was 50 (*GP* February 1, 1908, p. 72; *Journal* 1908, Vol. 13, p. 192; GP May 9, 1908, p. 301): by 1909 about 90 (Mitchell 1909c, p. 60): and by 1913, it had risen to 150.[34]

In the fifth revised edition of his book, Tuckey (1907b, p. vii), offered this somewhat parochial assessment.

The formation of an English society, composed of medical men interested in the theory and practice of suggestive therapeutics, will afford the encouragement and support so much needed by isolated practitioners, and will bring to light much excellent material which is being lost for want of collection.

Bramwell (1908a, p. 61), originally a GP in Goole (Yorkshire), and the second MSSST president, was more low key:

A society of medical men interested in hypnotism has recently been formed, and already numbers over fifty members. Most of these are general practitioners, and some of them have obtained as good results as I got in Yorkshire some nineteen years ago.[35]

On March 30, 1907, Tuckey (1907a, p. 211)[36] delivered the first presidential address.

I was for a long time, I confess, opposed to the formation of a new society, for I had the feeling shared by many, that medical and special societies have been overdone in the past and that hypnotism would be adequately considered by the existing societies and journals. As a matter of fact we have nothing to complain of in the treatment of the subject by the medical authorities and societies. I have been present at interesting debates at the Harveian and Hunterian Societies of London and one of our members, and a most prominent exponent of hypnotism, Dr Woods, has been recently president of the latter. We are often asked to speak at local medical societies, and are always accorded a fair and sympathetic hearing. My only regret, on those occasions when I have been the spokesman, has been that the cause was so inadequately represented.

Tuckey admitted that he had been lucky because he "was already in London and in a fairly independent position" when he first took up hypnotism. "Even so I often found it an uphill battle to combat misrepresentation."

> The struggle must have been harder in the provinces. I have heard of a good many men during the past 20 years being forced to give up the practice especially when they realised that to continue would mean the loss of their livelihood. I know at least half-a-dozen men now in good practice who confess to this experience.[37] Two or three of them have now revived their interest and joined our ranks. I recognise the importance for encouragement. Occasional visits to Bérillon[38] or the reading of Forel's book or the kind appreciation of friends like Cruise and Taplin have put new life and energy into me.

In his book Tuckey (1907b, p. 209n) spelled out what he believed to be the rationale for the new Society, which he mistakenly called The Medical Society for the Study of Hypnotism. It was started, he said,

> with the idea of giving backbone and support to doctors who are handicapped in their researches by being isolated and cold-shouldered. Dr. Hugh Wingfield, of Winchester, in joining the society, writes : I hope [it] will succeed in removing the prejudice against hypnotism in England. . . . I am very glad it has come at last.' He adds : 'I make use of hypnotism a good deal in cases of dipsomania, and the results are to me astonishing' (*vide* p. 245).[39]

Significantly Tuckey presents a somewhat optimistic overview of the history of hypnotism during the 1890s:

> So we have no martyrdom to chronicle like that which befell Elliotson in the early Victorian period. Elliotson's downfall resulted from his own errors of judgement as from the vindictiveness of his opponents. He allowed himself to be made a tool by spiritualists and cranks and aroused the prejudices of the profession by his intemperance of his advocacy. His fate has had a considerable inhibitory influence to this day.

Tuckey's reference to spiritualists as well as his peculiarly physiological language of "inhibitory influence," to described the perceived deadweight of Elliotson, runs like a silken thread through his estranged history of English [*sic*] hypnotism. And although not always easy to catch, Tuckey's physiologically inspired history will also silently and surreptitiously define how other qualified medical psychotherapists, like Bramwell and Mitchell strove to represent themselves in the history of hypnotism and of psychotherapy. This can also be seen, through that part of Tuckey's presidential address where he mounts an attack on the press, who remained "heavily subsidised by the advertisements of the purveyors of [useless medicines and quack] nostrums,"[40] as a prelude to a wider attack on psychical quacks.

> Christian Science is now the fashion and all over the country we see people adopting the grotesque teachings of Mrs Eddy and her imitators. The public are the chief sufferers, but medical men feel the unscrupulous competition.[41]

Tuckey, therefore, urged his fellow members to explain to the public why some psychic nostrums seem to work. “Suggestion acting on a prepared and a receptive mind is, we maintain, the explanation of most of these cures, and I hold that the medical student should be taught something of the nature and value of suggestion for the preservation of health and the cure of disease.” Leaving aside that thorny question of “suggestion” Tuckey's campaigning message was not that dissimilar to the one advanced by Arthur Hallam in his promotion of the curative benefits of hypnotism and mesmerism.

THE PALMER AFFAIR

On Friday, 25 October 1907, the 3rd MSSST Council meeting convened at Tuckey's residence where those present discussed applications for membership and added new names to the role. Then Bramwell accepted the invitation to become next year's president (1908) with Tuckey vice president and Bryan continuing as honorary secretary with elections for the Council planned for the next public meeting, to be held on January 24, 1908, in Hanover Square. (*GP*, 19 October 1907, p. 662; November 9, 1907, p. 716).

A few days before the October 1907 Council meeting, Ernest W. J. Ladell (1907),[42] a Southampton GP, and active member of the MSSST, could not help but crow over what he saw as the triumph of reason in the recent BMA hypnotism debate at Exeter, and his letter to the editor of the *BMJ* was published on 19 October 1907 under the title “Hypnotism as a Therapeutic Agent.” In referencing Woods's (1907) lecture, and the discussion which followed, Ladell claimed the conclusions drawn by the section would “go far towards removing any lingering doubts in the minds of the majority of medical men as to the power for good which the process undoubtedly possesses.” But his main reasons for writing were not to meet the “suspicion” that still existed among “many of our professional brethren,” who still needed educating on the subject, but to address the even bigger problem of a lay public who were “more difficult to deal with.” Glossing over what he saw as upper- and lower-class attitudes to hypnotism, Ladell focused on “the middle-class man, who prides himself on his common sense and freedom from superstition, and declares that he will not let any man tamper with his free will if he knows it.” Ladell then gave two examples, presumably from his own personal experience, of patients who had chosen operations rather than submit to hypnotic treatment. “All this shows that the amount of prejudice to be overcome is still very considerable, and it seems almost a pity that some new name has not been applied to medical hypnotism to distinguish it from music-hall hypnotism.” And then extoling the virtues of hypnotism as a curative agent and urging his fellow practitioners to put hypnotism “nearer the top of the list of remedies than right at the bottom,” Ladell endorsed

> Dr. Woods's opinion that no harm has ever come of hypnotism in intelligent hands, and that to be applied intelligently each patient must be studied and treated as an individual. At the same time I think there is no doubt of the value of hypnotizing new patients in the presence of old habitués; a greater percentage of successes will occur under such conditions.

This ringing and some might say uncritical endorsement of hypnotism was clearly too much for Dr James Foster Palmer (b.1848),[43] a GP in Chelsea (London), who now took upon himself the mantel of "one of those benighted persons"—referred to in Dr. Ladell's letter—"who view with suspicion hypnotism in all its forms."

> The "risk" of an operation is the loss of life. The "risk" of hypnotism is the loss of reason; and I have not yet seen the man, woman, or child who would not rather part with life than reason.

Palmer believed hypnotism was simply "the loss of certain cerebral functions, either of will-power, or of sensation, or of special sense."

> I know this is unpopular in these days, but I am convinced that when the conscience of the nation (I do not refer to the antivaccinator's nor to the passive resister's conscience) is duly aroused, the artificial induction of delusions, by whatever specious name it may be called, and whether practised in the music-hall, the operating theatre, or the bedside, will be recognized as a criminal act. That it is not so already is due to the fact that the great bulk of the medical, and practically the whole of the legal, profession either ignore the existence of hypnotism or are absolutely uninformed on the subject. This position is perhaps justified by the extremely limited scope for the exercise of its action. (*BMJ* November 30, 1907, pp. 1621–22)

At the next MSSST meeting, which had been rescheduled to January 16, 1908, Bramwell, as their new President, drew attention to Palmer's recent letter in the *BMJ* which,

> contained gross misstatements regarding hypnotism as a therapeutic agent and at the same time cast serious reflections upon those medical men making use of hypnotism in the treatment of disease.[44]

Bramwell then informed the meeting that Drs Wingfield, Ladell, and Bryan had all written letters of protest to Dawson Williams but Williams had declined to publish any of them despite the fact that Wingfield and Ladell were also members of the BMA. Williams had effectively denied his members the right to reply to Palmer's outrageous charges. Following a full discussion the meeting

> decided to send a letter to the President of the BMA[45] drawing his attention to the facts of the case and to record the dissatisfaction of the Society at such unfair treatment of certain of its members. (*GP* February 1, 1908, p. 72)

Percy Allan, who took up the cudgels in a *GP* editorial, said he made no apologies for "references to suggestion in the matter of therapeutics" and claimed credit for "publishing papers and reports of cases treated by suggestion," because he believed they were in the vanguard of those who were attempting "to educate the profession with regard to the therapeutic use of hypnotism." Although matters had certainly improved since Tuckey was [allegedly] heckled while speaking on the subject in the early 1890s

> medical opinion has generally remained pretty much the same with regard to treatment of disease by suggestion . . . Meanwhile Christian Science has come to stop; regular practitioners and quacks are making handsome incomes by relieving patients of their real or imaginary ills by means of suggestion; while the ordinary practitioner is, by all accounts, in a worse monetary and social position than [he] has ever been.

By attacking "suggestive therapeutics" and branding it "as a criminal act" Palmer had "cast reflections on those who practised hypnotism." Now Drs Wingfield, Ladell and Bryan, who "felt personally aggrieved," had been "refused publication" of their letters (*GP* February 1, 1908, p. 73). As we shall see shortly Allan's trenchant comments, with his references to "Christian Scientists . . . regular practitioners and quacks," helps to illuminate the wider background against which members of the MSSST perceived what would now become the Palmer Affair.

On May 1, 1908, following an MSSST Council Meeting,[46] held in Leicester, members removed to the YMCA for their general meeting, but before Mitchell delivered his paper on "Hysteria and Hypnosis," Bryan raised the matter of the Palmer Affair.

> [He] had not received a reply to his letter addressed to the President of the [BMA]. . . . This apparent discourtesy gave rise to some surprise and not a little indignation among both members and non-members present and it was decided after some discussion to ask [Bryan] the Secretary to repeat his communication . . . and in addition to address two others, one to the Chairman of the [BMA] Council and the other to the Chairman of the representative meeting. (*GP* May 9, 1908, p. 301)

I have been unable to discover how, or even if, this matter was ever resolved although strictly speaking it was Ladell who had started the ball rolling with his trenchant defense of hypnotism and his veiled attack on those who still needed "education on the subject." Assuming Palmer had read Ladell's letter as a personal insult then it could be argued that Palmer had been goaded into sending his intemperate reply and that Williams, seeing it as such, was not inclined to encourage further intemperate locking of horns. Thus one letter apiece was about right.

But the anger of MSSST members went deep: and was aimed first at Palmer, then at the editor of the *BMJ* and then at senior members of the BMA. But it would miss the point to see the Palmer Affair as some kind of war being waged between an enlightened vanguard and a reactionary medical establishment determined to censor the rational psychotherapists' counterblasts against Palmer's rather silly "knee-jerk" attack on all aspects of hypnotism. A close study of the history of British hypnotism, from the late 1870s, reveals that it does not fit into those neat historiographical myths, advanced by Cruise, Bramwell, Tuckey, Felkin, and others, which paint the early medical hypnotists as a small beleaguered group struggling manfully against prejudice and ignorance. The plethora of early-twentieth-century articles and discussions, to say nothing of the many psychotherapeutic practitioners of hypnotism and suggestion, effectively destabilizes that myth and serves to further underline how it was Palmer's reactionary views which were now in the beleaguered minority. Within a year of its founding there was clearly widespread support for the MSSST, as evidenced, for example, by a 30 October 1908 meeting of the LMI reported in the *GP* (November 14, 1908, p. 747)

> It may be noted as a sign of the times, at any rate in Liverpool, that the audience included many of the leading hospital physicians, and was unanimous in its sympathy with the objects of the Society.

This, and other evidence, to be discussed later, reveals no real objective reasons for MSSST members to have feared ostracism from the majority of their medical brethren, notwithstanding Palmer's bigoted views. The fiercely fought hypnotic battles of the early 1890s had, as we have already seen, been all but won by 1898 and what was now left were local skirmishes and the Palmer Affair was one of them. In fact, as Allen let slip, the Palmer Affair served as a useful scape goat for the growing fear, among psychotherapists, that "Christian Scientists . . . regular practitioners and quacks" were enticing their patients and stealing their incomes. Palmer's bigoted attack, which painted all forms of hypnotism as criminal, was perceived, therefore, as a potentially destabilizing force against those who argued for the efficacy of suggestion because Palmer's attack had exposed a potentially uncomfortable truth: that there was, essentially, little or no difference between the hypnotic skills of the qualified and of the unqualified practitioner especially when it came to matters of "suggestion." Charles H. Melland (1872–1953), consulting practitioner and physician to Ancoats Hospital, although probably not a member of the MSSST, articulated something of those fears in his paper "The Role of Suggestion in Treatment," delivered to the Clinical Society of Manchester in February 1908.

> The success of the quack mainly depends on the overweening self confidence with which he proclaims his special gifts, and the occasional coincidence of the cure of some functional ailment with the use of his nostrum. The same must be said of other methods of cure which have much in common with quackery viz., faith-healing in various forms, including 'Christian Science.' That certain diseases may be cured by purely psychical methods every medical man will admit, but the different schools of faith-healing have ignorantly transgressed the limits of the possible, whereas had they confined themselves, *guided by medical skill and knowledge*, to teaching that imaginary diseases have no real existence they would have done well. (Melland 1908, *italics* mine)

The Palmer Affair therefore serves to illuminate how qualified practitioners were struggling to legitimize and justify their use of suggestive therapeutics while Palmer's attack served to further blur the lines making it harder to persuade doubters and waverers not to flee into the arms of the unqualified practitioner. Left unanswered Palmer's bigoted views would be seized upon by their enemies and thus further undermine their attempts to draw precise and inviolable boundaries around their own "legitimate," qualified practices. This, after all, helps explain why, at its inaugural meeting, the MSSST passed its rule forbidding membership to anybody "*connected in any way* with any non-medical society which has for its object the treatment of disease by unqualified persons. . . . " Such fears, inscribed in the MSSST's constitution from the very start, not only surface through the Palmer Affair, but can also be detected in articles written by individual MSSST members and in off-the-cuff derogatory comments by "'medical men' against 'quack practitioners' Tuckey (1891c, p. 279) had already cautioned against the dangers of itinerant mesmerists and urged that "the better comprehension of its uses by the profession, and of its dangers by the public, will, it is hoped, soon stop this abuse of a therapeutic agent." More recently Ash had expressed his own anxiety at "the ever-growing systems of so-called religious treatment which are now so much in vogue." (*The Lancet*, January 9, 1909, p. 132). Of course Hallam, as one might imagine, had a somewhat different understanding:

> It is quite true that all these things do belong undoubtedly to rational medicine, but who is it that has all along blindly refused to recognise this fact, and unhesitatingly condemned these "certain forms of treatment" as utter rubbish? Why, of course, the very orthodox medical man who is now under the cloak of "public good," advocating that these things should be captured for his own benefit. (*PTJ* November 1906, p. 97)

In delivering the Harveian Oration in October 1909 T. C. Shaw (1909) chose as his subject "The Influence of Mind as a Therapeutic Agent." In welcoming the audience Charles Buttar, president of the Society, noted how the growing interest in various forms of mental healing "made it incumbent upon the medical profession to take cognizance of the trend of public opinion, and to ascertain how far suggestion may operate in the treatment of morbid conditions." (*BMJ* November 6, 1909, p. 1352). Buttar's challenge, and Shaw's paper, were widely taken up and discussed in the lay and medical press, while the subject was more generally taken up when Dawson Williams published the special issue in June 1910. But long before then no serious commentator, observing the changing landscape, could afford to ignore the very real practical and theoretical problems raised by "mental healing." To this extent, at least, it was now incumbent upon qualified medical psychotherapists to articulate and theorize their various mind healing practices and, at the same time, seek to discover ways of defending or cooperating, or uniting, around a common standard. Slowly, uneasily, and sometimes even reluctantly practitioners were drawn to the *ersatz* sign of suggestive therapeutics not least because the MSSST was now seen as the most efficient organization to advance their cause.

NOTES

1. Born in Cornwall, studied at Charing Cross Hospital School of Medicine, where he was appointed house surgeon in 1873. Resident MO at the North-Eastern Hospital for Children 1874, Prosecutor of Anatomy Royal College of Surgeons 1874, and Demonstrator of Anatomy Westminster Hospital Medical School 1873–1874. A GP for nearly thirty years he was founder and editor of both *MT* and *GP*.

2. See *GP* (August 30, 1902, pp. 545–46).

3. The problems faced by GPs included "'the ever increasing competition of unlicensed quacks, who are permitted to carry on their nefarious practices at the cost of the legitimate and State recognised medical practitioners'" (*PTJ*, September 1905, p. 75).

4. The relationship between the BMA and the IMPA was not always cordial (*GP* September 8, 1906, p. 568).

5. Not to be confused with *The Practitioner* (1861–).

6. Arthur Percy Allan educated Birkbeck and Guy's Hospital where he became House Physician. Subsequently vice president of the University of London Graduates' Association. He edited the *GP* for five years and was subsequently a member of the SPR.

7. Tuckey's father, Charles Caulfield Tuckey (?1819–1895), born in Ireland, was a Surgeon at the Manchester Homeopathic Hospital, Physician at the Preston Homeopathic Dispensary and member of The Northern Homeopathic Medical Association.

His son C. L. Tuckey attended The International Homoeopathic Convention in London between 11 and July 18, 1881. (*HC*, 1881, p. 202). Owen (2004, p. 125) suggests that in the mid 1890s Tuckey was briefly a member of 'The Hermetic Order of the Golden Dawn' while Hayward (2014, p. 23) suggests he was also a member of the Isis Urania Lodge.

8. Tuckey (1903a, p. 350) suggests Sir T. Lauder Brunton also went to Nancy.

9. This can also be seen in Woods (*BMJ* November 6, 1909, p. 1355).

10. There is a similar argument in Schofield (1904, pp. viii–x).

11. Bramwell (1908a, p. 61) makes a very different point: "It is the general practitioner, who can choose suitable cases from amongst his own patients—patients whose confidence he has already gained."

12. This is contradicted by Tuckey (1900, pp. 62 and 328n).

13. Over several years J. Barker Smith noted, and published, accounts of his own hallucinatory experiences. The *GP* (February 6, 1904, p. 82) having decided reluctantly to publish yet another of Smith's accounts, noted: "The mental state of Dr Smith is certainly one of a most unusual kind, and he would, we think, act wisely were he to seek and follow the advice of a professional brother experienced in such abnormal conditions." Smith (*GP* September 10, 1904, pp. 577–78) held very specific views about the cause and treatment of the psychoneuroses having been inspired by an article in *La Presse Mèdicale* by André (-Thomas) (1904) who, at the time, was working with Déjerine. Smith believed the various symptoms of the psychoneuroses point to "physical or moral shock; and the discovery of this traumatism is a matter that concerns the physician and his success in the application of psycho-therapy." In a further communication, stressing "that persuasion is altogether superior to suggestion," Smith recounts (*GP*, September 17, 1904, p. 593) the treatment carried out in the Pinel Ward at the Salpêtrière, where in conjunction with isolation: "The physicians examine and interrogate the patients during the first few days of their admission, and endeavour to obtain their confidence, and to discover their moral torments or physical suffering. These psycho-therapeutic conversions are of the first importance; when the confidence of the patient is obtained the cure is, in some degree, assured." Smith, who was probably familiar with Myers's account of *Studien*, also believed the medical profession should take an interest in "psychic phenomena." Although an important, if forgotten figure, I must reluctantly leave Dr. Smith on the edge—in all senses—of this story.

14. *GP* (September 26, 1903, p. 606) takes a surprisingly sympathetic view of Dr W. Maunsel Collins, convicted and imprisoned in 1893 for procuring an abortion. "Most of us in private practice must have had at different times to refuse to help our patients in such difficulties as led to Dr Collins' incarceration."

15. 'Think hard.'

16. Referencing *Psychopathia Sexualis*, the "well-known book" by Krafft-Ebing (1893, p. 351) Tuckey (1898, pp. 80–81) thought hypnotism was "the only remedy which holds out any prospect of cure in perverted sexuality, I have seen a number of these cases (twelve). In only one has it proved curative. This morbid condition is evidently very much more common than is generally supposed, for the patient keeps his secret to himself unless he has some hope of cure."

17. Taplin worked in business before obtaining his Edinburgh licentiateship in 1883 and establishing himself as a GP in Liverpool. (*BMJ* September 9, 1939, pp. 587–88). Haydon Brown (1921, p. v) speaks of Taplin in glowing terms.

18. This may be Sydney Morgan Whitaker, MO to the North Homoeopathic Dispensary, and a member of the Liverpool Branch of the Homoeopathic Society from 1900.

19. Bramwell (1910, p. 138) says Braid abandoned "the old idea that patients must be placed in some condition of artificial sleep before being treated by suggestion."

20. Charles Tidbury Street, a member of the Association, worked as a resident clinical assistant in Bethlem before running two private asylums; the other in Liverpool.

21. Clement Arthur Douglas Bryan, married with two children, worked as deputy to his father Clement Frederick Bryan and, on his father's death in March 1914, became interim workhouse MO (Negrine, 2008, p. 228). Bryan, a member of the SPR, would become Hon. Secretary of the LPAS, and co-translated, with Alix Strachey, Karl Abraham's *Selected Papers* (1916). For a time he was a member of the Leicester Choral Combination, which comprised thirty-six solo voices under the bâton of Mr Fred Stork (*MS* 17 October 1908; p. 254).

22. Tuckey (1913, p. 256) suggests the founding of the MSSST was due to the "energetic initiative" of Bryan and Taplin. See also *SFC* (Vol. 100, no. 45, July 15, 1906).

23. Robert W. Felkin, lecturer on Tropical Diseases, Edinburgh Medical School, was also involved in Stella Matutina, one of the sects that broke from S. L. M. Mathers's Golden Dawn in 1900 (Sumner [1915], p. 44).

24. That Cruise was not a GP suggests Taplin and Bryan may have originally wanted to create a society with a wider reach.

25. Robertson (2000–2005) has suggested the name was taken from "an influential book by Bernheim (1884)," but see Shamdasani (2005).

26. A full list of the original members were: Drs Tuckey, London; A. Betts Taplin, Sefton Park, Liverpool, (elected Hon. Secretary); Bryan, Leicester; Bramwell, London; Ash, London; Felkin, London; Percy Allan, Croydon; Stanford Read, London; Francis Cruise, Dublin; J.C. McClure and Alexander MacLennan, Glasgow; J. Norris, Birmingham; George Kerr, Edinburgh; Graham Martin, Liverpool; Adam Pearson Hope Simpson, Liverpool; MacClelland, Liverpool; [Richard?] Humphreys, Liverpool; Easton Scott, Surrey; Crichton Miller, Inverness-shire; Montague Rust, Newport, Fife; Peddie, Lancashire. (*GP* November 24, 1906, p. 749). There was also a Henry M'Clure of 30 Portland Court, Portland Place, who joined the SPR in 1913. A. P. H. Simpson was educated in London and Dublin, late House Surgeon & Physician Liverpool Royal Infirmary & Hon. Assistant Surgeon Children's Infirmary, Liverpool. Stanford Read would subsequently become a member of the BPAS. Technically Ash should have been debarred from the MSSST because of his involvement with the PTS.

27. Although Bramwell (1910, p. 9), Tuckey (1907b, p. 247), Craig (1910, p. 435) and others acknowledged that lay people cured patients whom doctors diagnosed as incurable they argued that "the number of such 'cures' is very small when compared with the vast amount of disease . . ."

28. Bryan (1907, p. 490) believed that "medical men in general practice had greater opportunities for observing ["that the mind of an individual has an influence over the bodily function"] than those doing hospital work."

29. Although the meeting expressed "a unanimous desire that the paper should be published" (*GP* November 9, 1907, p. 716), I have been unable to trace it.

30. McDougall was elected to the SPR Council in April 1913 and became their President (1920–1921). I have been unable to trace a copy of his paper.

31. Although *GP* (November 14, 1908, p. 747) said the paper was "to be printed in pamphlet form, and sent to each member as the first quarterly issue of the Transactions of the Society," I have been unable to trace it.

32. This meeting may well have been the catalyst for the Liverpool Branch of the PMS (*Proceedings* 1912–1913, Vol. 26, pp. 373–74) which, in turn, led to the creation of the LMPC.

33. At first Woods "invariably practised hypnotic sleep. . . . Later on he gave up the use of sleep, and treated the patients by suggestion alone. His practice was to place his patient in an easy chair, sit by him, and induce him to relax his muscles and quieten his mind. Sometimes he put his hand on the patient's epigastrium, so as to suggest tranquillity and warmth. The patient was told to remain in that condition until he returned, and, on returning, he generally found him to be fast asleep." (*BMJ* November 6, 1909, p. 1355).

34. Although it is difficult to track all the new members, Astley Cooper was elected in May 1908: others include Drs Holt, The Lodge, Middleton; H. Halton, 97 Hartington Road, Liverpool; V. D. de Boinville, South Grange, Aigurth Road, Liverpool; J. W. A. Bryden, The Priory, Godalming Surrey (*GP* May 9, 1908, p. 301).

35. Bramwell (1909; 1921) fails to mention the MSSST in his two books.

36. Unless otherwise stated the following is taken from Tuckey (1907a).

37. For one of these see Tuckey (1913, pp. 211–12 and n).

38. *HR* (October 1907, pp. 110–11) has an anonymous first-hand account of Bérillon.

39. Wingfield (1910, p. 161), co-opted to the SPR Council in February 1891 (*Journal* 1891–1892, Vol. 5, p. 20), took a referral from a Dr. Dill (1895, p. 304) and also helped the children's nurse of his friend Dr W. H. Gaskell.

40. One such nostrum was "Clarke's World-Famed 'Blood Mixture,' . . . for Scrofula, Scurvy, Eczema, Bad Legs, Ulcers, Glandular swelling, Skin and Blood Disease . . ." etc. A testimonial from E. Taylor, of Halifax, says after eighteen months of suffering he was turned out of hospital "incurable, as I would not consent to have my leg taken off." A friend suggested Clarke's Blood Mixture and after taking a large bottle "I was able to go about on my crutches. I had another bottle, and by the time I had finished it my leg was quite well, and I am able to go to my work" (*EEN* February 3, 1898). Compare this with Bodie's adverts.

41. See also the criticisms of Christian Science by Hallam (1911a, p. 53) and Morris (1910, pp. 1462–65).

42. Ernest William Julius Ladell (1879–1932?) born in Kent; not to be confused with R. Macdonald Ladell who practiced psychoanalysis after the War.

43. Born in Norfolk. The 1891 census records him married with eight children.

44. There is another Foster diatribe against hypnotism in *The Lancet* (December 4, 1909, pp. 1707–8).

45. Dr Henry Davey, physician of the Royal Devon and Exeter Hospital, was President for 1907–1908. The President elect for 1908–1909 was Simeon Snell

(1851–1909), Ophthalmic surgeon at the Royal Infirmary Sheffield and Professor of Ophthalmology, University of Sheffield.

46. The Council included Drs. Bramwell, Tuckey, Bryan, Stanford Read, Deane Butcher and Taplin.

Chapter 8

The Evils of the Unqualified Medical Practitioner

THE INQUIRY

In November 1907 the GMC, under mounting pressures from the Medical and Surgical Colleges and the Medical Universities [Medical Corporations] convened to consider "the evils that attend the unqualified practice of medicine." And they passed a Resolution empowering themselves to appoint a Committee to advise on the situation and "ascertain what legal provision existed in the Colonies and Dependencies of the Empire and in Foreign Countries for the prevention of medical practice by other than legally qualified persons." It is often forgotten that the extraordinary reach of the early-twentieth-century British Empire was also effectively replicated through those various professional organizations, like the BMA, whose influence, under the Imperial flag, stretched into nearly every corner of the world where British doctors practiced privately or in an official or quasi-official Colonial or Imperial capacity. So the Foreign, the Colonies and the India Offices all became involved. But as the bureaucratic Whitehall wheels creaked slowly, it was not until some time in 1909 that the Privy Council discussed the November 1907 GMC resolution and

> deemed it expedient in the first instance to have recourse to ordinary means of information, and caused letters to be addressed to the [English] Local Government Board, the Scottish Office and the Irish Government, enclosing copies of the [GMC] Resolution and asking that a circular might be issued to the Medical Officers of Health [MOHs] in each country inviting their opinion as to whether the practice of medicine and surgery by unqualified persons is assuming larger proportions and as to the effect produced by such practice on the public health. (Fitzroy 1910, pp. 2–3).

So the GMC then appointed a Committee under Dr. Langley Browne (1848–1928) [the Browne Committee], which then composed a questionnaire which they sent directly to all British MOHs. And having received replies the Browne Committee collated them into a tabulated appendix and having attached it to their Report, it was then published as a Command Paper [Fitzroy] through His Majesty's Stationary Office. Fitzroy (1910, p. 4) concluded:

> It is difficult to say, categorically, whether the practice of medicine and surgery by unqualified persons is increasing. In some districts the evidence is distinctly in this direction, while in others there seems to be very little of such practice.

Fitzroy also noted a patchy picture because

> unqualified practice increases in large centres of population, attracting dwellers in the smaller urban area and rural districts. This is assisted by the ready means of access to the towns which now exist, by the extensive advertising in newspapers and magazines which brings quackery of all kinds under the direct notice of all classes; and by the facilities, extensively used, of obtaining advice and medicine through the post.

At first Fitzroy implied that it was only the lower classes who were likely to be duped by unqualified practitioners but then it made its prejudices explicit:

> While the educated classes, as a rule, are not deceived in this respect, it is probable that a large number of people among the more ignorant sections of the community *are* deceived into the belief that the person they consult is, in some way or other, qualified to give medical or surgical advice. The fact that many [health insurance] societies accept certificates of unqualified persons, doubtless assists this belief, which is further strengthened by the practice of some Registrars of Deaths in accepting certificates of death granted by unqualified persons without further inquiry, and entering them up as uncertified deaths.[1]

Ultimately, however, Fitzroy, with its barely concealed distain for the BMA, reveals far more about the bigotry, bureaucracy, and incompetence of the GMC than it does about the unqualified practitioners it was tasked to investigate. Their own remit was far too vague; if not absurd, covering inter alia, "Chemists, Herbalists, Bonesetters, Dentists, pedlars of Proprietary Medicines, Abortifacients, the illegal practices of abortionists, the treatment of Venereal Diseases, Eye Diseases, Infectious Diseases, Cancer treatments, Consumption, Hydropathic Establishments, Domestic Remedies, Old Women and witchcraft." Their brief section on "Christian Scientists, Faith Healers and Spiritualists" was more than useless. Occasional individual answers suggested practices were "increasing among the more important districts . . . Sunderland, Manchester, Rochdale, St Marylebone [London], County of East Sussex, Halifax and Bradford, while others suggested that there was no increase and not much local practice although there were 'visits to non-resident quacks who have acquired a reputation.' (Fitzroy 1910, p. 39). The MOH for Halifax reported an increase, especially with spiritualistic healers (*ibid* p. 40), while the MOHs from Lowestoft and Middlesbrough reported: "Such [unqualified] practice is enormous in extent" (*ibid* pp. 40 and 44) although the Middlesbrough MOH also reported "no evidence of recent increase" and remained silent about spiritual healers &c. The MOH of St. Helen's (Lancashire) reported, rather elliptically "that in which healing is not the object sought is increasing" by which he probably meant abortions which were a criminal offense at this time (*ibid* p. 48). The MOH from Sunderland reported "so-called faith-healers, practice of great extent" also of "Electro Masseurs—a new form of unqualified practice." (*ibid* p. 50).

Fitzroy, in its brief reference to Christian Science, noted that it was strongly condemned by some MOHs: "Malignant and other serious diseases are treated by Christian Science [without qualified doctors] and the 'effect in serious cases is too obvious to need emphasis.'" But Fitzroy also made it clear that there was no reason to take this further because the effects of such treatments "are only on individuals, and not on the public health as such." Here then was one of the major flaws in Fitzroy's methodology because the main function of an MOH was to focus only on matters which adversely affected Public Health so, short of mass hysteria, it is difficult to see why an MOH might have been persuaded to investigate Christian Scientists let alone individual unqualified mind healers. And yet despite, or maybe because of, its many absurdities Fitzroy, was eventually tabled at a GMC meeting in December 1910, three years after it was first mooted. Then Langley Browne moved, and it was agreed, that their Report "be received and entered on the minutes." And there being nothing else to discuss that was the end of that! Unless some GMC member nursed the vein hope that some future Government might appoint a Royal Commission to investigate the matter further. (*BMJ* December 3, 1910, p. 422).

READING THE REPORT

One of the problems with Fitzroy was that the Browne Committee decided to by-pass the BMA and communicate direct with the MHOs, most of whom, especially in urban districts, were full-time *public* officials, no longer in general medical practice and therefore too busy with their own quotidian duties. For a start this did not help the already strained relations between the GMC and the BMA (*BMJ*, December 3, 1910, p. 1784). The typical MHO, many of whom used to be GPs, had effectively exchanged local for district knowledge and rarely had contact with individual patients. What is more most MOHs only had time to "tick" the boxes or pass the questionnaire down the line either to local GPs, the local BMA division, or to other local medical societies. For their part most GPs were far too busy to care about a questionnaire from the GMC, for whom there was no love lost, so they tended to complete their answers according to hearsay or impressions. And even if those impressions were accurate they were not quantified or recorded as changes over time. Most answers, therefore, were meaningless. The situation was very different, however, in Scotland where MOHs were still part-time and answered direct to the Local [Scottish] Government Board. They were also under attack from the BMA who wanted to replace them with full-timers (*BMJ* February 5, 1910, p. 352) and as this was causing a lot of anger and uncertainty it might explain, in part, their unique response to the GMC questionnaire.

In a Memorandum attached to their Report the Scottish MOHs made it clear they were unimpressed with what had been asked of them.

> The limits of "Medicine and Surgery" are so vague; the boundaries between what is medical and surgical in the technical sense and what is "hygiene" are so constantly shifting; the increase of medical discussions and medical directions in the lay press has recently been so great; the frequent acceptance by the medical profession of ideas and methods first elaborated by "unqualified persons" is so striking,—that the difficulties of any inquiry into the nature and limits of "practice by unqualified persons" must be almost insuperable. (Fitzroy 1910, p. 54)

But being public servants they had little choice but to make the best of a bad job so they concentrated on what *they* considered to be the "well-known classes of 'unqualified practice'" which meant that the only reference to faith healers was a note to the effect that a large number of people from Kilmarnock were "treated by a clergyman in Glasgow for cancer, consumption &c." (Fitzroy 1910, p. 58). Perhaps not surprisingly all traces of this angry but insightful Scottish Memorandum were disappeared by the time Fitzroy was abstracted for the *BMJ* (November 26, 1910, p. 1729; December 3, 1910, pp. 1784–1785). And yet not everything could be brushed under the orthodox carpet.

Given that the BMA's nose had been put out of joint and that the *BMJ* (November 26, 1910, p. 1729) probably felt constrained to print an absurdly bland synopsis of the Fitzroy Report, Dawson Williams may have taken some subsequent satisfaction in publishing a long and at times angry article from J. H. Taylor (1911, pp. 1243, 1246), general secretary of the Salford Division of the joint Committee of the Manchester and Salford Division of the BMA. Taylor made his feelings crystal clear.

> A more incomplete report has rarely been issued from any public department, for, while on the one hand it contains practically but little information as to the extent and effects of unqualified practice on the public health beyond what any man of the street could have put together with little trouble, on the other hand the replies of several of the medical officers of health to the questions addressed to them were evidently written without having made any serious attempt to obtain first-hand information.

Having highlighted the Report's methodological flaws Taylor, claiming intimate knowledge of his local district, noted:

> The fact is Manchester is simply the great breeding place for quacks of every description, and thousands of people from the rural districts and the smaller towns of Lancashire, Cheshire, Derbyshire, and Yorkshire flock to Manchester, where they can find a quack specialist for almost every variety of disease.

And after having painted a disturbing picture of many widespread abuses, Taylor noted:

> The itinerant quacks of the market-place still flourish as much as ever, but the characteristic of the day is the phenomenal growth of the large and well-organized schemes and companies carrying on their business on a scale almost incredible, and in most cases succeeding in defrauding the public into the belief that their treatment is in the hands of qualified medical men.

Although Taylor thought the current Government scheme for "sickness insurance"—subsequently the 1911 Act—might go some way to ameliorating the situation, what was really needed was a Royal Commission *and* a wholesale reform of the Medical Act.

Taylor also pointed to other flaws in the GMC inquiry. For example Fitzroy made no attempt to explore, let alone explain, how unqualified medical practices, including faith and spirit healing, might operate within specific local political economies of health. Apart from two MOHs in Ireland—Monaghan and Youghal—there was no attempt to understand why people were driven to consult unqualified practitioners. Was it tradition, habit, ignorance, poverty, or just gullibility for the clever and deceptive marketing of astute businessmen? (Taylor 1911, pp. 1245 and 1246). Or perhaps some people were enticed because of "a certain fascination in secrecy" (BMA 1909, p. v). There was also hardly any consideration of questions of costs particularly as they might, or might not, have been related to poverty.[2] And there was no discussion of nostrums, proprietary medicines, or of self-drugging let alone the widely recognized fact that patent and other medicines were a highly profitable business not just for the manufacturers and the chemists who dispensed them, or the "quacks" who sold them, but also for the newspaper proprietors who received a considerable proportion of their revenue from advertising them. Even the *BMJ* who, from the early 1890s, had actively campaigned "against the proprietary medicine trade," was not immune from such suspicions and criticisms (Bartrip 1990, pp. 190–96).[3] And finally there was no mention of the social, moral, and legal pressures which drove many to seek out unqualified practitioners; for example women seeking abortions, or married men afraid, or ashamed, to consult their "ordinary medical attendant" because they feared they had contracted venereal disease. And finally there was virtually no discussion of the potential financial damages inflicted upon doctors forced to compete with "unqualified practitioners."[4]

NOTES

1. This chaotic state of affairs prompted the APPB to invite Arthur Hallam in 1905, to establish the Burial Reformer (*Aberdeen Journal* April 24, 1905) which he then edited alongside *PTJ/HR*.
2. "Comparatively large sums are spent [on proprietary medicines] by people almost destitute." (Fitzroy 1910, p. 81).
3. See also BMA (1909).
4. The *BMJ* (May 27, 1911, pp. 1217–88) devoted a whole issue to quackery.

Part IV

FOUR PSYCHOTHERAPISTS

But here an objection arises, and I do not wish to elude it. Bourget has defined it in a jest equally smart and unjust, by saying that the doctor's dream has always been "to substitute a box of pills for the Gospel."

It must be acknowledged, however, that the higher hygiene which I propose can only be exercised efficaciously by a tête-à-tête in the consulting-room of a specialist, and that it actually is lay confession without prestige and without poetry, at the tribunal of a priest who takes money for his "opinions," does not wear a habit, does not claim to represent God, and has no power to 'bind or loose' souls. (Fleury 1900, pp. 222–23)

Chapter 9

Edwin Ash

Edwin [Lancelot] Ash (1881–1964)[1] entered Owens College, Manchester [Owens] in 1890 and then worked, for a time, as a house surgeon at the Royal Infirmary, Wigan. Around 1903, when he was a "some-time" demonstrator of physiology, and house physician, at St. Mary's Hospital in London, he tried to hypnotize "hysterical patients of a somewhat low order of intelligence" without success but "a good deal of amusement among [his] friends." That a relatively junior physician in one of the larger London hospitals should be openly experimenting with hypnotism suggests a very different atmosphere from the early 1890s when Cruise (1907, p. xxii), already a highly respected physician, was alleged to have been "kindly warned to abandon a dangerous subject."[2] Following his failures Ash (1906b, p. 501) adopted the position of an "antagonistic sceptic rather than an unprejudiced investigator" and continued studying the literature and undertaking "experiments with healthy male subjects." Although Ash (1906c, p. 93) never reveals what originally drew him to hypnotism it is possible to speculate that, like a significant number of his generation, and despite his supposedly "thoroughly sceptical scientific training," his interest may well have came through osmosis! Hypnotism was in the air. That Ash had been educated at Owens is perhaps also significant because in 1885 Walter Whitehead, then president of the Manchester Medical School, had invited Kennedy, one of the foremost platform mesmerists of his generation, to lecture and demonstrate to staff and students and Kennedy's visit clearly made a profound impact on many of those present (*BMJ*, 10 October 1885, p. 722). In 1886 William (Billy) Sterling (1851–1932), succeeded Arthur Gamgee as Brackenbury professor of physiology and, like Gamgee, took an interest in mesmerism and hypnotism and almost certainly incorporated it into his physiology lectures. Fraser (1920), who was taught by Stirling in Aberdeen in 1884, recalls how he traced his own "life-long interest in psychotherapy" to one of Sterling's Aberdeen lectures. Edwin Goodall (1863–1944), another early exponent of hypnotism was also at Owens during this period, working as a demonstrator of pathology, while T. B. Hyslop, another exponent of hypnotism, may even have been working at St. Mary's when Ash was there (*MA* 1903, p. 868). In a slightly more speculative vein Ash may even have attended one of André's famous mesmeric performances at the Free Trade Hall Assembly Rooms in Manchester in October 1891 (*MT*, 9 October 1891). Ultimately, however, Ash's early writings suggest he probably taught himself through the many readily available 'English' language texts—articles in medical periodicals, Christian Herter's translation of Bernheim (1890) and, of course, books by Braid (Robertson 2013), Tuckey (1900) and Bramwell (1903). Indeed some of Ash's early ideas can probably be traced to what Bramwell (1898, pp. 671–72) suggested were Braid's early theories of monoideism.

In late 1905, Ash (1906a, p. 217, italics mine) carried out a series of experiments on porters and patients at the East Sussex Hospital, in Hastings, where he was then working.

> The method used at first was fixed gazing at a small polished disc set in the centre of a larger disc of ebony. But it was soon found that by diverting the subject's attention to one hand which I slowly moved from the height of about 18 inches from the forehead down to the level of his eyes and then rapidly past them hypnosis was as readily produced in susceptible people. Sometimes the condition could be better induced in the first instance *by placing the whole hand firmly on the head* and vigorously pressing, the centre of the forehead with my thumb, the subject being seated in a comfortable chair with a head-rest.

With his first subject, a 29-year-old porter, Ash (1906a, pp. 217 and 219) produced "complete analgesia and anaesthesia" and induced "in him the deepest stages of somnambulism." In the second, a 26-year-old porter, his attempts were unsuccessful. With the third, an 18-year-old youth convalescing after an operation for acute appendicitis, his experiments were by and large successful. The fourth, a 13-year-boy, was hypnotized almost immediately. "On several subsequent occasions I made experiments with him and found myself able to obtain a deep yet alert stage of somnambulism with sometimes complete amnesia on waking." Although Ash had little success with his fifth subject, a slightly deaf 25-year-old man, he was more successful with a 19-year-old railway porter. Thus he concluded that

> deep hypnosis was produced in three, a moderately deep stage in one, and two appeared to be unaffected. One of these latter was the only subject whose health was at all enfeebled, he being under treatment for extensive tuberculous adenitis. The rest may be said to have been quite healthy. . . . . In all four of the susceptible subjects analgesia was produced and it is certain that operations of

> considerable extent could at any time be performed upon either of them whilst in the hypnotic state without any need of an administered anesthetic. And as in each I was able to produce pain by suggestion, I take it that certain forms of headache or neuralgia could be relieved by a similar process.

Although his experiments lead him to believe that deep hypnosis could produce pain-relief the matter was complicated because

> there seems to be no means of gauging the susceptibility of a patient beforehand and consequently at present one cannot have much confidence that analgesia will be produced in any given case. (Ash 1906a, p. 219)

Following these experiments Ash was invited to give a demonstration, in the Hospital, to the East Sussex Medico-Chirurgical Society and, by his own account, his talk, on December 19, 1905, was a great success not least because, in one case, several gentlemen, at Ash's request, failed to wake the subject and also tested for cataleptic rigidity.

> In addition I suggested anaesthesia of one hand and hyperaesthesia of the other with convincing results. Various hallucinations were then produced, for the most part indicated in the first instance by various members, such as the *presence of a caged lion*—he evidenced great objection to going near the cage, asserting that the brute was both large and furious; *that he had just met a friend*—he shook hands, carried on a conversation, and eventually said good-bye in quite a natural manner. On being questioned he mentioned some name as that of his friend and told us where she lived. He had apparently imagined he heard his friend's voice during this hallucination. Other suggestions were that *he was smoking*, had been *bitten by a gnat, was sliding on a frozen pond*, and so on, to all of which his behaviour indicated a response. I was then asked to produce some simple reflex by suggestion so I told him that something was tickling his nose and that he would sneeze directly. Having made a wry face he sneezed once quite naturally. I then produced a very deep stage of hypnosis and endeavoured to get this man to go through some scene of his past life and as he had served in the recent South African campaign I suggested that he should open his eyes and find himself in action against the Boers. He immediately began to act in a remarkable manner. Apparently he was at once seeking cover from the enemy and executed movements as if he were using a rifle, repeatedly raising and ducking his head behind some imaginary protection and occasionally making some remark to his comrades in arms. During this experiment I found it impossible to make him conscious of my presence and it was only by vigorously shouting at him that I could elicit any reply to questions. At times he seemed to think that he was being addressed by some officer, as he would then rise to his feet and salute. His actions were only stopped by placing my hand over his eyes and telling him to sleep, which he did almost immediately, having to be assisted back to his chair. (Ash 1906a, p. 219)

Following further demonstrations involving post-hypnotic suggestions, which he thought ought to be called post-hypnotic *influences*, Ash (1906a, p. 220) was asked to hypnotize his subject once again.

> It was then suggested by the chairman that as this man had allowed himself to be thus made use of without hope or idea of reward he should be made to take a collection for himself whilst in a condition of hypnosis. This was done and I told him that he had been given a number of counters which he was to put in his pocket. When awakened he had no idea of what had happened and later had an agreeable surprise when told to examine his pockets. The meeting terminated with a discussion of the phenomena observed.

Ash's account is of particular interest for several reasons not least because he had framed it from the standpoint of a physician delivering a clinical lecture on hypnotism. On the face of it this framing device replicated the standard clinical lecture whereby a doctor presents a patient to a group of colleagues in order to illustrate particular points for discussion or to elicit responses and advice for further treatment. But here there is also a subtle subtext because Ash, with the collusion of his audience, also assumes the persona of a skilful hypnotist apparently exercising some occult magic over his "subject." This was clearly the view of a number of readers who, according to Ash, wrote to him in the belief that he must be "a person endowed with some mysterious power." This was not the view which Ash, a "thoroughly sceptical" scientist in the early stages of his medical career, would have wished to cultivate, or at least not in public! But Ash's lecture and demonstration also unwittingly, or perhaps wittingly, mimics the standard and well-worn format of the platform mesmerists of the 1890s who mixed their "scientific" lectures with demonstrations which displayed their hypnotic or mesmeric "powers" for the amusement and the elucidation of their audience. The way in which Ash used his unsuspecting subject—who derived no obvious benefits from the demonstration—would have evoked memories of the music-hall mesmerists, at least among the older members, thereby offering tantalizing glimpses of hypnotisms potent mix of science and mirth.[3] Finally, although Ash's lecture was delivered and framed from the physiological point of view his demonstration suggests that in exploring his subject's hallucinations he was already aware of the psychotherapeutic potential of hypnotism.

In August 1906, *The Lancet* published a second article by Ash (1906b, pp. 501ff) written in response to the large correspondence he had received, and which revealed a widespread interest "coupled with an extraordinary ignorance of the huge literature that deals with this condition and, in some quarters, expressed by a still more extraordinary scepticism as to the existence of such a mental state." He wanted his readers to know that

> an expert hypnotist is not a person endowed with some mysterious power, but is somebody who has taken the trouble to study carefully the psychology of his subjects, with the object of ascertaining what means are likely to succeed best in bringing about in them a state of mental rest, suiting his methods to every individual case. Psychologists define 'Attention' as mental activity which raises certain sensations or ideas in point of intensity and completeness, with a corresponding lowering of simultaneously presented impressions—a process familiar to everybody in daily life.

Then dwelling upon the concept of "Attention," as a physiological rather psychological condition (Cole 1913, pp. 67–68), Ash set out detailed instructions as how best to hypnotize and conduct experiments "to obtain certain phenomena." Although he focused on experiments in respect of the induction and phenomena of hypnosis in relation to analgesia, there is a hint, near the end of his article, that Ash had already started using hypnosis psycho-therapeutically. For example, he mentions, in passing, having tested "the efficacy of suggestion during hypnosis in several cases presenting various functional neuroses" and claims he was "more than satisfied with the results." He also noted how he preferred using hypnosis in a quiet room, apart from other patients, because it was difficult, if not impossible, to induce it in a busy hospital ward. By the Autumn of 1906, Ash appears, therefore, to stand on the threshold of that private psychotherapeutic space which Myers, and others, equated with the confessional.[4]

It is remarkable that *The Lancet*, supposedly one of the most conservative of medical publications, with its highly questionable past relationships to mesmerism (Winter 1998, pp. 96f) and its apparently fiercely materialist intolerance for any kind of "metaphysical medicine," should have offered space to a relatively junior physician not only to discuss the therapeutic benefits of hypnotic suggestion but also, actually, to explain how to use it. This seemingly radical shift in medical opinion is also reflected in two letters from John R. O'Brien, a general practitioner in North Kensington, already deeply interested in the works of Janet and the Nancy school (*BMJ* March 22, 1947, p. 389). O'Brien claimed he started using hypnosis around 1892 and having already treated "a large number of cases in general practice" (*Lancet* February 10, 1906, p. 402) urged Ash to

> hold a demonstration to the Medical Society at St. Mary's Hospital, to which a number of outside medical practitioners should be invited; that this procedure

> would be productive of good there could be no doubt. In May I gave an address on hypnotism to the Medical Society at the Middlesex Hospital, at which other medical men were present;—the various phases of hypnosis were practically demonstrated on several subjects; that enthusiasm and interest were shown, was proved by the number of questions asked and the discussion that arose on the various points. This is far better than laying down hard-and-fast rules in writing. (*Lancet* September 22, 1906, p. 830)[5]

From this wider perspective it is no longer surprising that Hallam, an astute student of the subject, should have noticed Ash's second *Lancet* article, abstracted it extensively in the September 1906 *PTJ* (pp. 82–83) and then invited Ash to lecture on the subject. For his part Ash (1906c, p. 94) stated, in the introductory remarks to his first PTS lecture, in November 1906,

> I feel particularly happy in addressing the members and associates of the Psycho-Therapeutic Society on the subject of Modern Hypnotism, as I know that my audience will be in sympathy with me. Usually one's audience are so distinctly sceptical towards hypnotic phenomena that a vein of antagonism runs through an address; the fighting spirit is roused, and bitter things said on both sides that do a good deal to harm the cause we all have at heart. To-night I can safely say, in the phraseology of the old Greek orators, I speak to those who know.

Although these remarks appear to contradict Ash's positive experiences during his December 19, 1905 talk to the East Sussex Medico-Chirurgical Society they tend to underline Hallam's claim that one of the attractions of the PTS was that it offered "a valuable medium through which men of science interested in Psycho-Therapeutics may express their views." (*HR*, July 1908, pp. 73). And this also suggests yet another mismatch between the rhetoric and the practice of qualified medical hypnotists, like Ash (1914, pp. 55, 31 and 55) who consistently claimed, for example, that "for the great bulk of the medical profession the subject [of hypnotism] is almost as much a closed book as ever": while the actual evidence suggests a very different story. There is no indication, for example, that practitioners like Ash or O'Brien were ever prevented from lecturing or demonstrating on the subject. Nor is there evidence that they were prevented from using it medically because Ash, and others, would occasionally be asked to hypnotize patients prior to surgical operations. Thus from 1905 Ash, who would from now increasingly employ suggestive psychotherapeutics in his general practice, was to became one of the preeminent practitioners and proselytizer in the British psychotherapeutic movement. Ash is also of interest not just because of the nature of his relationship with Arthur Hallam, for which see Chapter 4, but also because he appears to have been one of the few psychotherapists who were never particuarly attracted to psychoanalysis.

NOTES

1. Ash, was a prolific writer on psych-therapeutics before and after the War. His main publications are (Ash 1907a; 1910a; 1910b; 1913; 1914; 1919; 1920; 1922). Other articles also include *BMJ* (22 October 1910), *MT* (1909 Vol. 37, 35–54) and *Nursing Mirror*. See also his book on Faith Healing (Ash 1912). According to Hayward (2014, p. 25) Ash "held a private surgery at Harley Street, where he combined suggestive therapy with Christian instruction in the hope that the subliminal mind could be encouraged into the rescue and healing of the damaged body." Ash married Mabel Ethel Streeter (d. 1957) on December 14, 1907 and they had two sons, Charles Seymour Cromwell (b.1910) and Geoffrey Glanville Cromwell. Charles would subsequently become a physiotherapist. Ash officially changed his name to Edwin Lancelot Hopewell-Ash in 1927 (*LG* February 4, 1927, p. 807).

2. Reading the contemporaneous evidence reveals this Cruise story a hypnotism myth constructed after the event (Kuhn 2016).

3. For example compare Ash's lecture with the description of Kennedy's performances (*York* 27 October 1890, p. 3). Ash could have picked up stories of Kennedy's memorable Owens College visit.

4. On this point see Brabant et al. (1993, p. 417). Ash's (1914, p. 26) first attempt at curative hypnosis might have occurred in the Outpatient Department at St. Mary's in January 1906.

5. Ash (1914, p. 53), like Crichton Miller (1912, pp. 212–13), advocated "soporific drugs as an adjunct to" hypnotism especially in the "refractory patient."

Chapter 10

T. W. Mitchell

A SIMPLE COUNTRY DOCTOR

Thomas Walker Mitchell (1869–1944), was the second youngest of eight children born to Robert and Isabella, prosperous drapers and grocers in Avoch, Ross-shire. He was educated in Scotland and graduated MD in 1890 from Edinburgh University & School of Medicine and, the following year, worked as house surgeon in the County Hospital of Huntingdon. Thereafter, having made no returns to the *Medical Directory*, Mitchell disappears from the official medical records until 1903 when he is listed as a fellow of the Royal Medico-Chirurgical Society living in Hadlow, a village near Tonbridge, in Kent and some thirty-five miles south-east of London.[1] Mitchell (1907c) reveals that he started working as a GP in Hadlow in 1894 and the 1901 census lists him as boarding with Dr. Henry Major Lawrence (1846–1929), Mrs Lawrence and their three children. Dr Lawrence, MOH for Kent,[2] and also Edinburgh educated, had set up general practice in Hadlow in 1868 where he remained until his death in 1929. Mitchell follows a similar trajectory because he, too, was deeply rooted in his local community—he was, for example, active in the local cricket club—where he continued living and working until he retired in June 1939 following forty-four years of medical practice in the district (*SCKA* June 30, 1939).

Mitchell (1907d, p. 754) suggests that like many doctors of his generation he was "sent out into the world qualified to practice all branches of the healing art, without having received the slightest instruction as to what place suggestion may or may not hold as a therapeutic agent."

But this is too simplistic because it masks what appears to have been an important trend during this period for although Mitchell claims he found his own way to have hypnotism so too did a significant number of his contemporaries; Jones, Ash, Eder, Taplin, and Bryan to name but a few. Interestingly there were a significant number of early-twentieth-century psychotherapeutists and medical psychologists who received their training in Scotland, particularly in Edinburgh, where there was obviously a strong hypnotic tradition. The trajectory of Mitchell's biography also undercuts that stereotypical view advanced, for example, by Tuckey and Wingfield, that country and provincial doctors faced prejudice, hostility and ostracism if they tried to use hypnosis because there is no indication that Mitchell ever suffered such difficulties. Mitchell like many of his contemporaries also never mentions a eureka moment although, in his case, as with Ash and Jones, there are sufficient clues suggesting how he might have found his way to discovering the therapeutic benefits of hypnotism. But first a rare glimpse into Mitchell's pre-hypnotic career.[3]

In February 1901, a local paper carried the report of an inquest into the suicide of Miss Ellen Everest, a butcher in Hadlow. Mitchell had attended Miss Everest between 5th and 15th January 1901.

> She admitted that she had been drinking, and said that business troubles drove her to it. [Mitchell] asked her to give it up, and pull herself together. She recovered very rapidly, in four or five days, and when he left her she was fit and well. He was sent for at half past six [on 31st January] and found [Miss Everest] lying in her bedroom dead in a pool of blood. . . . Mr Russell did not think that [his sister-in-law] had given way to drink since Dr. Mitchell had left her. (*KSC* February 8, 1901, p. 6)

In 1894, shortly after settling in Hadlow, Mitchell started treating Lizzie B., and continued treating her, periodically, until 1901 when she had "an exceptionally severe series of epileptic attacks." Only then did Mitchell notice she was unable to stand straight but he was unable to help her with her posture until after he "began practising suggestive therapeutics." A more precise chronology can be found in Mitchell's account of his treatment of Amelia Geraldine P. [Amelia], a 29-year-old unmarried woman living at home with her father and two sisters.[4] Mitchell (1912b, pp. 287–89) was first called to see Amelia, in February 1901, after she had developed "a paroxysm of coughing" which Mitchell thought "was of hysterical type." It is worth noting that Amelia's attack, which occurred around the time of the suicide and inquest of Miss Everest, may have been more than coincidental because Amelia's father, like Miss Everest, was also a butcher. Over the next nine days Amelia developed a series of symptoms which "began to abate, and in their disappearance they followed the exact order in which they had come on." Although Amelia continued to suffer "complete anaesthesia with loss of muscular sense of the whole of the right arm with the exception of the thumb and index finger" the majority of her symptoms had more or less disappeared after three weeks and by the end of July 1902 she appeared "practically well." While there is no indication that Mitchell made any conscious psychotherapeutic interventions during this period there are clues suggesting he was already inching his way toward this end. So, in relation to Amalia's "word-blindness," Mitchell (1912b, pp. 292–93) says, "One day after much trouble I taught her to pronounce the letter *p*, and the curious fact was observed that from that day she could use the *p* sound in speech, could read the letter in print and in writing and could use it in writing spontaneously or from diction." But Mitchell was quite clear that "re-education had little to do with her recovery, although she had lessons every day."

> During the whole course of this illness of eighteen months, and after recovery had taken place, the interpretation of the case was exceedingly difficult. The symptoms pointed to serious organic disturbance of the brain, combined, however, with a large functional element whose extent it was impossible to determine. The acute condition at the beginning corresponded to no known affection, and the long duration of the word-blindness was opposed to the view that it was of a purely functional nature. Yet it was almost impossible to understand how the various peculiarities of the case could be accounted for by any definite organic lesion. The fact that the patient could write, although she could not read, except by kinaesthetic impressions, showed that her word-blindness conformed to the type of "pure" word-blindness first described by Déjerine in 1892,[5] but with regard to certain letters of the alphabet there was not only "blindness" but agraphia. (Mitchell 1922, p. 77)

Although written up many years later, and without any references to external texts, the trajectory of Mitchell's intellectual development suggests that by 1902 he was already familiar with the rudiments of the French literature on hysteria. Amelia then fell ill again, on December 3, 1904, when she developed a series of symptoms, including almost total word and letter blindness with the climax occurring at the end of March 1905 whereupon she remained more or less ill "throughout April, May and June 1905." In July Mitchell (1922, pp. 78–79) suggested a holiday in Folkestone and when she returned, a fortnight later, she was "improved in health." In October and then again in December 1905, there were sudden improvements in her condition so Mitchell (1912b, pp. 295–96) concluded

> there was hardly any doubt as to the nature of the troubles from which the patient was suffering. Every fresh symptom helped to strengthen the conviction that all the peculiar phenomena which I have described were of functional or hysterical origin, and were not dependent on any organic lesion whatsoever.

Following her recovery, Mitchell did not see Amelia again until November 5, 1908, a few weeks after she had fallen ill with "headache and general *malaise*, and had a temperature of 100 F." But by then Mitchell (1912b, p. 297) was using hypnosis.

> I tried to hypnotize her, but with little apparent success. Every day for a week I went through some brief hypnotic process, but thinking there was little probability of inducing a true hypnosis, I confined my attention almost entirely to making suggestions with regard to the headache and obsessions. During this treatment the headache got well and the obsessions became much less troublesome; but she developed many of her old hysterical symptoms.[6]

In his paper "The Appreciation of Time by Somnambules," which he read to an SPR meeting on May 16, 1907, Mitchell mentions F. D., "a delicate girl whom I had relieved of some functional troubles by hypnotic suggestion." The evidence suggests F.D. was probably one of the first patients upon whom Mitchell made his hypnotic experiments,[7] and as this occurred toward the end of March 1906 Mitchell (1922, p. 16)[8] probably first started using hypnotic suggestion some time in early 1906, not long after he stopped treating Amelia in late December 1905. As Mitchell leaves no clues as to what led him to start using hypnosis we can only guess that he must have developed his interest through extensive reading of the literature and that Bramwell's article on "Hypnotism" in the *Encyclopaedia Medica* (Watson 1900, pp. 88f), with its added Scottish connections, may perhaps have been an important early source. An early account of his hypnotic "technique" suggests that like many of his contemporaries Mitchell (1907d, p. 754; 1921, pp. 9–10) at first took up "the Nancy method."

> I stand immediately in front of the patient who is seated in an unconstrained attitude. I take his head between my hands in such a way that while my fingers rest lightly on the sides of his face and temples, my thumbs can, with ease, be placed on his closed eyelids. Bringing my face to within a foot from that of the patient, I say to him, 'Look steadily into one of my eyes—very steadily—and your eyes will get very tired—your eyelids will get very heavy—so heavy that you cannot keep them open—you will get very sleepy—you will go to sleep—sleep—sleep.' If the eyes do not close I put my thumbs gently over the eyebrows and slip them down over the eyelids as if to close them. In most cases this produces a closing of the eyes.[9]

A subsequent description of Eder's hypnotism technique (Hunter & MacAlpine 1953, p. 66) also resonates with this. But what appears to be unusual about Mitchell (1907d, p. 755–56) is that he immediately started exploring states of consciousness from a psychological rather than physiological point of view.

> In deep hypnosis a great change in consciousness occurs; but not in even the most profound hypnotic sleep can it be said that the subject is unconscious.

> The hypnotic state is always a conscious state. The subject is at all times in relation with the operator, although he may apparently have lost touch with other people and his surroundings.

It may well have been this line of enquiry which first led him to believe that the beneficial effects of suggestion could be accentuated by their postponement, or in popular terms, through post-hypnotic suggestion.[10] And this may have inspired Mitchell (1907d, p. 787) to use curative suggestion for hypnotic amnesia in order to help his patients forget physically painful experiences, such as a tooth extraction, as well as psychologically distressing memories. So, for example, Mitchell (1907d, p. 819) relates how a patient, when two months pregnant, suffered extreme fright on seeing a large spider and then became obsessed with the thought that her own terror would permanently damage her unborn child. Mitchell hypnotized her in order to persuade her "in the future she would have no fear of spiders at all, and, further that when she awoke she would have lost all recollection of having been frightened by a spider in the past." This therapeutic intervention clearly resonates with Janet's "substitution theory" whereby Janet, having

> discovered some of the lost memories connected with the hysterical symptoms . . . endeavoured to modify those which he found charged with painful emotion, by substituting for the painful ideas other ideas associated in the patient's mind with memories that were pleasant (Mitchell 1921, p. 148).[11]

This point is critical because it strongly suggests that as late as 1907, and despite being an SPR member, Mitchell had still *not* discovered Breuer and Freud's theory of treatment by cathartic confession [cathartic theory] thereby suggesting that he had still not read Myers's commentary on Breuer and Freud's *Studien* where Myers (1903, p. 56, italics mine) had expressly contrasted Breuer's cathartic theory with Janet's substitution theory in which Janet seeks to suggests a "new and false, but helpful memory."

> In Fräulein O.'s case *no deception* was needful. All that was necessary was to make her see past events in their true proportion. The confession was cathartic; it cleared away the morbid products and strengthened the coherence of the sane personality; it restored Fräulein O., to mental and bodily vigour.

THE APPRECIATION OF TIME BY SOMNAMBULES

On becoming interested in curative hypnosis Mitchell (1922, pp. 6 and 60) started exploring some of the theoretical conundrums of divisions of consciousness which then led him to study and repeat some of those hypnotic experiments on somnambules' appreciation of time [the time experiments] originally conducted by Edmund Gurney, Milne Bramwell[12] and Joseph Delboeuf (1831–1896) during the late 1880s and early 1890s. It may even have been his researches into the "psychical" phenomena of hypnotism, rather than its therapeutical uses, which first drew Mitchell to join the SPR in late 1906,[13] not long after obtaining his M.B. (1st class honors) from Edinburgh (*Journal* Vol. 13, p. 2; *MD* 1906). Mitchell's time experiments,[14] which began in March 1906, ran for about a year and culminated in the paper he read to that SPR General Meeting in May 1907. That paper was abstracted in the *GP* of August 1907 and published, in full, a few months later in *Proceedings*. A brief summary (Anon 1907b, p. 83), in the June 1907 issue of the *Journal*, noted how Mitchell (1907a; b) expressed

> his adherence to the view that subconscious cerebral activity in hypnotic somnambules is not merely physiological but has a psychical concomitant coexisting with the supraliminal consciousness known to us by introspection during waking life.

This marks another critical point because it reveals that Mitchell (1922, p. 4), having become an exponent of "the reality of subconscious mentation," was now an opponent of those, like Münsterberg and Ribot, who believed "that all subconscious activity is merely physiological."

In the discussion on Mitchell's paper Tuckey "was inclined to think that the appreciation of time by somnambules was a kind of instinctive faculty, akin to the homing instinct of animals" although he also thought, like Mitchell, that

> estimation of time might in some cases be done by counting the number of respirations or heart-beats. Any such process would be facilitated by hypnotism, by which all the subliminal faculties tend to be exalted. (Anon 1907b, p. 85)

Gerald Balfour, who chaired the meeting, summed up his own response.

> What had specially interested him . . . was the indication they afforded not only of the existence of one subliminal region of consciousness such as was now generally recognised—but that within this region a number of more or less separate strata of consciousness or psychic centres were contained. (*ibid* p. 87)

It is worth noting Balfour's and Tuckey's phrasing because although Myers's concept of the "subliminal consciousness" still continued to shape the SPR's discourse Mitchell is using the terms "subconscious," and "secondary consciousness." These and other fragments suggest Myers's theory of the subliminal-self was not nearly as dominant as commentators like Cerullo (1982, p. 103) suggest.[15] We shall examine this later.

By Spring 1907 Mitchell (1907a; 1907d; 1907e; 1908), having concluded experimenting and theorizing the appreciation of time, was now routinely using "curative suggestion" as part of his medical practice. That Summer he was elected a member of the South-Eastern Branch of the BMA (*BMJ* July 27, 1907, p. 79) and, by late autumn 1907, had become an active member of the MSSST, and having become a passionate advocate for curative hypnotism, was proselytizing in the lay and medical press (Mitchell 1907d; 1908).[16] In an article in *Quest*, edited by G. R. S. Meade (1863–1933),[17] Mitchell (1909, pp. 48 and 49, *italics mine*) argued that hypnosis was a psychological not a physiological phenomena.

> Almost the only hypothesis which seems applicable to the whole range of hypnotic phenomena is that which postulates in the mind a region of subconscious or subliminal activity to which access can be obtained by employment of those artifices which are made use of in the induction of hypnosis. The most elaborate presentation of this hypothesis is to be found in the writings of F.W.H. Myers. But although in the particular field of research in which Myers was especially interested, his doctrine of the Subliminal may appear to be, *as he himself claimed*, a limiting and rationalising hypothesis, it is felt by many to be extravagant and needless in so far at least as the explanation of hypnotic phenomena is concerned.

Mitchell also juxtaposes Myers's theory to Janet's "hypothesis of mental dissociation" and although Janet's theory had now become the dominant discourse, it did not necessarily explain all the facts because it was "prone to exaggerate the resemblance between hypnotic and hysterical states." Mitchell thought it was "indeed easier to believe that the waking consciousness is a split-off portion of the total consciousness potential in man than that the hypnotic consciousness is a split-off portion of the waking consciousness." (*ibid* p. 51) Mitchell had also become impressed with how the power of suggestion could influence conduct and this was why hypnotism was an important area of study for "all students of psychology, ethics and religion." (*ibid* p. 54). And yet, like many contemporary psychotherapists, Mitchell could not resist complaining that so few medical men acknowledged the therapeutic value of suggestion which made the present situation not that different from the days of Mesmer and Braid although opposition was now driven by prejudice and not ignorance (*ibid* pp. 56–57).

At first Mitchell seems to have held the experimental and therapeutic sides of hypnotism in uneasy tension but by 1912 he had started to synthesize his medical, psychotherapeutic, psychical, and experimental work. Quoting approvingly from Myers (1890a, p. 200) Mitchell (1912b, p. 286) now argued that mental diseases

> are not pathological phenomena but pathological revelations of normal phenomena, which is a very different thing. The gearing of the hysteric's inward factory is disconnected; the couplings are shifted in all sorts of injurious ways; some of

the wheels are standing still, and some are whizzing uselessly round and round. But the wheelwork is still all there; and by observing the various hitches and stoppages which are now taking place we can get a better notion of the way the power is applied than the smoothly working, carefully-boxed machinery of the healthy subject is likely to give us.

NOTES

1. The 1911 census suggests Hadlow had a population of c.3,500.
2. Lawrence also worked at the Foundling Hospital.
3. Mitchell (1907d, p. 773) says a 20-year-old woman went into labor with her first child: "And the midwife who was attending her sent for me in conformity to that generous provision in the Midwives Act which insures that in cases of difficulty a medical man may be sent for, regardless of the expense, which nobody pays."
4. This was probably Ada Peckham (1873–1936) daughter of John Peckham (1833–1911) a successful butcher in Hadlow. Ada had three sisters Sarah (b.1869), Jane E. (b.1875) and Amy Eliz (1876–1881).
5. 'Contribution à l'étude anatomo-pathologique et clinique des différentes variétés de cécité verbale. *Mémoires de la Société de Biologie* (1892, Vol. 4, pp. 61–90).
6. Mitchell (1910c, p. 682) said; "When for any reason hypnosis can not be induced" he would encourage his patient to enter into the hypnoidal state as advocated by Sidis. Mitchell probably started studying Sidis in 1909 and remained open to Sidis's theories.
7. Bramwell (1898, p. 669) was clear on this point: "Here it may be well to state that I have made it the rule to keep my therapeutic and experimental work apart. Most of the experiments were conducted on healthy males, and never without express consent having been given in the waking state. Former patients, after restoration to health, have occasionally, under similar conditions, been the subjects of experiment. I feel strongly, however, that patients, above all others, should be regarded as sacred, and nothing should be suggested to them except what is necessary for the relief or cure of disease."
8. I am following Mitchell (1922, pp. 1–68) which reproduces 1907e.
9. On another occasion Mitchell (1922, p. 84) says: "All you have to do is to sleep a little more deeply, and they will stop of their own accord. Now, I am going to stroke your face, and at each stroke you will go more and more deeply asleep." Compare this with Liébeault (1891, p. 275) and Woods (1904, p. 491).
10. In discussing post-hypnotic suggestion Mitchell (1907d, p. 757) attacks: "The pernicious teaching of the Charcot School as to the nature of the hypnotic state, the error of the Nancy investigators in failing to allow for the importance of auto-suggestion in connection with the fictitious crimes by the investigation of which they tried to elucidate the relation of hypnotism to real crimes, the totally false views in regard to the possibilities of hypnotism promulgated in popular fiction, and in the daily press, and the disgusting platform exhibitions of some of the most trivial phenomena manifested in the somnambulic state, have all tended to bring hypnotic practice into such

disrepute that the practitioner who ventures to employ this therapeutic method is often shunned by the public and looked at askance by his professional brethren."

11. On Janet's "altering" memories see Hacking (1995, pp. 195–96). In a slightly later work Mitchell (1909b, p. 101), referring to the majority of American neurologists, says "although its supporters maintain that the manifestation of subconscious phenomena is not necessarily an indication of abnormality, it differs very little from the opinion of Professor Janet, who regards every manifestation of subconsciousness as proof of pathological dissociation. Its weakness as a hypothesis lies in the difficulty of applying it to the description or explanation of all the observed phenomena."

12. See that is, Bramwell (1897, pp. 179ff; 1898, p. 670; 1900b).

13. He is listed a new member in January 1907 (*Journal* 1908, Vol. 13, p. 2). From December 1909 Mitchell was regularly co-opted onto the SPR Council.

14. Somnabules, the term for subjects in which "post-hypnotic amnesia was complete." (Mitchell 1922, p. 1; see also Mitchell 1921, p. 12; Bramwell 1900b, p. 161).

15. Allbutt (1910, p. 1456), somewhat unusually for a non SPR member, uses "subliminal self."

16. Having been invited by the secretary of his local BMA Sevenoaks Branch to give a talk on hypnotism it was then published in the November issue of *GP* (Mitchell 1907d). Although I have found no prior notice for Mitchell's lecture it was probably part of an ad hoc series on psychological medicine. Another lecture was from White (1907; 1918), professor of Psychological medicine at KCH and subsequently Consultant in Mental Diseases to the Western Command.

17. Meade, ex-associate of Madam Blavatsky's, helped publish and then edit *Lucifer*. Then in 1909 he started The Quest Society along with other disillusioned Theosophists.

Chapter 11

Alfred Ernest Jones

THE FARRINGDON GENERAL DISPENSARY AND LYING-IN CHARITY

Alfred Ernest Jones (1879–1958), the eldest son of a mining engineer, was born in Rhosfelyn (aka Gowerton) in Wales, some six miles between Swansea and Llanelly.[1] Jones began medical studies at the University College of South Wales in 1895, and then at University College Hospital, London [UCH] in 1900 where, the following year, he obtained a scholarship and gold medal in obstetric medicine (*LDN* December 12, 1901). In the Summer of 1902 Jones worked, for a time, as a resident surgeon (*EPG* June 7, 1902) which is probably how he first met Wilfred Trotter (1872–1939) who was soon to become a close friend and, subsequently, his brother-in-law. Assuming Jones went through the conventional UCH medical training he would have attended the short course in neurology and psychiatry taught by Julius Mickle (1848–1918),[2] Superintendent Grove Hall Asylum, London, who was described, by his good friend F. W. Mott (1853–1926), as "an alienist physician" who "would seek where possible a material cause of mental disorders." (Mott 1918, p. 103). Jones (1901b) would have gained only limited neurological experience during 1901 working under John Rose Bradford (1863–1935), and then for a short time in 1902, as a part-time clinical assistant to Charles Beevor (1854–1908)[3] who, shortly before his death, claimed he had never studied psychotherapy let alone any of the French books. (*JNMD* 1908, Vol. 35, p. 784). In fact a composite of Beevor, Mickle and Mercier, may well have served as the template for that 'average legend' (Freud 1939, p. 10) of that "old school" neurologist who would subsequently infect Jones's historical memory. Although Jones (1959, pp. 123 and 114) claims to have made occasional Sunday afternoon visits to various London asylums, it is unlikely these would have been to "'play cricket with the patients,'" as he claimed. More likely they were to visit the pathological laboratory at Claybury. This then would have been the sum total of Jones's clinical and theoretical education in neurology and/or psychiatry. There is no evidence Jones ever treated neurological or psychiatric cases while acting as Kingston Fowler's house physician at the Brompton Chest Hospital (1903) nor when he was Resident MO at the North-Eastern (Jones 1959, p. 111). Then following his enforced resignation from the North-Eastern, in late 1903, Jones spectacularly failed to secure another Hospital post until January 1906 when he was appointed lecturer for the short neurology course at the Seamen's Hospital, Greenwich [Seamen's],[4] before becoming a part-time assistant physician on the wards under R. Tanner Hewlett (1865–1940) who was essentially a pathologist and bacteriologist with no apparent interest in neurology or psychiatry (Hewlett 1914). Jones may have occasionally worked under Guthrie Rankin (1854–1919), who wrote on nervous diseases from a neurological point of view (Rankin 1903, 1909), but there is no evidence that Jones ever treated any of Rankin's patients. In short there is absolutely no evidence to support Jones's (1954, pp. 199; 1959, p. 114) highly inflated autobiographical claims that by January 1904 he was already an exceptionally qualified neurologist.

Having failed to secure a full-time hospital post Jones (1959, pp. 126, 132), perhaps somewhat rashly, established himself, in early 1905, as a glorified GP[5] working out of Harley Street. But without the necessary experience, let alone connections, he was forced to supplement his income with a series of part-time jobs: working as an ad hoc clinical assistant, a tutor coaching students for medical examinations, reviewing and digesting medical literature and as a medical researcher (Jones 1959, pp. 118f, 135f; Maddox 2006, pp. 33–34).[6] One of those part-time jobs was working as an Honorary Physician, each Thursday afternoon, at the Farringdon General Dispensary and Lying-in Charity [the Farringdon], situated in Holborn, London. Jones (1959, p. 133) recalls the Farringdon as

> one of those curious City institutions that had survived in seclusion the original need for them. It still catered, nevertheless, for the class of people intermediate between hospital and private practice. It provided me, not only with further experience, but also with cases of special psychological interest that I could investigate at more leisure at home.

Jones probably first started at the Farringdon on Thursday May 12, 1904 although his precise duties remain unclear. On 8th September 1904 a 44 year old solicitor's clerk "presented himself" and told Dr Parry (1866–1945),[7] one of the senior part-time physicians, that he was "desperate for help" having been plagued by acute tinnitus for about eight years. He was depressed, had lost weight and his life had become so unbearable that he "was willing to undergo any treatment to give him even partial relief." Parry referred him to Jones who "placed [the patient] on a simple mixture of bismuth carb., grs.xx and pot. brom., grs x., three times a day before food." The patient returned, on 15 September, then again on 22 September, and both times reported feeling better and thought "the medicine had done him good." But when he returned on 29 September his situation had deteriorated. The "tinnitus" had been very bad that day "and 'giddiness [had] occurred on and off all day yesterday." At this point, reports Dr. Parry (1905, p. 478),

> Dr. Jones suggested treatment by hypnotism, which [the patient] said he would be willing to try. Dr Jones then shone a reflected light by means of an ophthalmoscopic mirror[8] from an electric throat lamp into his right eye, and was speedily able to throw him into a drowsy condition. When in this state Dr. Jones made the suggestions that the giddiness and sickness would disappear. The patient was particularly susceptible to hypnotic influence. I timed the experiment and found it took [Jones] one and a half minutes to place the patient in a cataleptic state.

On 6 October,[9] Jones hypnotized the man again into "a cataleptic state and the impression that giddiness and vomiting should cease was again imprinted upon him in the sub-conscious state." The patient's condition improved over the next few weeks whereupon Jones hypnotized him again on 1 December. "The former suggestions were strengthened and a new suggestion was made—viz., that the tinnitus should be no longer heard." From that time until 25th April 1905, when Dr Parry wrote up his account for the medical press, the patient had made an extraordinary recovery and had "been perfectly free from vertigo and vomiting that were so persistent during the last eight years while the tinnitus which he has is bearable and in no way interferes with his carrying on his work as a lawyer's clerk." Some two years later, in a further communication, Parry (1907a, p. 337), reported that the patient continued to lead a bearable life. "I must here repeat that the whole honour of this case belongs to Dr Jones and none to myself. I am merely the scribe."

Although it is unclear why Jones decided, apparently quite suddenly, to use hypnosis, it is possible to speculate that, like Ash or Mitchell, Jones was drawn to hypnotism through osmosis. UCH was thick with the ghosts of old mesmerists and the rise and fall of Elliotson remained an essential part of the Hospital's cultural mythology (Winter 1998, pp. 73ff; Kuhn 2015, p. 45n). On a more prosaic level Victor Horsley (1857–1916), Jones's old UCH surgical teacher, and subsequently friend and mentor, may well have reminisced about his own role in the SPR's 1883 physiological experiments with subjects hypnotized by the great Carl Hansen (Tuke 1884a, i.e., pp. 69ff; Kuhn 2016). Following his patient's first visit Jones may also have decided to research the subject of tinnitus and drawn details from Tuckey (1900, p. 204) who discussed Bramwell's "therapeutic uses of hypnotism" in "four cases of Ménière's disease" in which "great improvement was brought about in the hearing, and the vertigo was almost entirely removed." Although Bramwell (1903, p. 185) made no reference to Ménière's complex of symptoms he had previously discussed it in one of his talks (*BMJ*, February 28, 1891, p. 468). Furthermore in 1897, at Purves Stewart's invitation, Bramwell had successfully administered hypnotic treatment to a patient in one of Gowers' wards, at Queen's Square. This 'audit trail' now reveals that Sir William Gowers (1845–1915), "one of the greatest neurologists of his age," must have permitted one of his juniors to call upon Bramwell in a refractory case. And this was not the only time Bramwell (1900, p. 93) had been called into Britain's preeminent neurological Hospital. Hypnotism was, therefore, not just in the air but also firmly in the wards of Queen's Square and thus, presumably, also in the consciousness of Gowers (1909, p. 280) who subsequently advocated its use, albeit in certain limited cases. And Jones (1959, p. 119; 1906, p. 527), in fact, appears to have started using hypnosis at more or less the same time as he "was engaged that year (1904) on an arduous piece of research" for Gowers! Such subliminal thoughts and memories may even have been triggered when Jones saw the patient again, on September 29, 1904, and realized there was nothing to lose by resorting to hypnotism in such a desperate case.

On 9 October 1904 Parry received a letter from a 41 year old hospital nurse who had "been suffering from Ménière's complex of symptoms" for the past three and a half years. She was recently treated as an inpatient at Queen's Square but without success. When Parry examined her, presumably at Farringdon, he told her about some "encouraging" results he had obtained from the use of hypnotism and "recommended a trial of this treatment in her case." The nurse agreed.

> An attempt was made twice by a medical man [Jones pk] to hypnotize her, but without any definite success, and the patient soon affirmed that she felt unfit to make weekly journeys to town to follow this treatment. (Parry 1907b, p. 1109)

TOM ELLEN

On Thursday morning, March 18, 1899, Tom Ellen (1874–1945), a 'letter sorter' living with his wife and daughter in Church-road Islington, was involved in a train crash near Babworth, Retford.[10] On being taken to Doncaster Infirmary Ellen was found to be "suffering from the effects of concussion of the brain, an abrasion on the right side of the face and a slight injury to the right ankle." First reports suggested his condition "so serious that at present he cannot be spoken to" (*YH* March 17, 1899, p. 3). But then Ellen made a surprisingly quick recovery and, having returned to work, reached a settlement with the Great Northern Railway Company [GNRC] who paid him £190 for the injuries he had sustained. Not long afterward Ellen's eyesight deteriorated and in 1900 he lost his job "on account of eye problems" and, shortly thereafter, became "quite blind and destitute." So Ellen sued the GNRC for "damages to the amount of £3,000" and following a complex legal battle the Company probably settled out of court after loosing its appeal against Mr Justice Bucknill's ruling that Ellen's compensation case should be heard before a jury. (*YPLI*, March 11, 1901; *HDM* March 11, 1901).[11] It was probably this new settlement which enabled Ellen to seek specialist medical help and, having been referred to UCH, he came under the care of Dr John Rose Bradford (1863–1935) who diagnosed "hysterical right hemiplegia of traumatic origin" (Wilson 1907a, p. 229; 1907b) and then referred him to Jones (1909b, p. 501).[12] Jones (1901b; 1959, p. 159) was originally taught by Bradford (1900–1902) and by 1905 the two men had become good friends after Bradford started visiting Wilfred Trotter (1872–1939) who had taken up residence with Jones in Harley Street (Jones 1959, p. 126). Bradford, who was clearly fond of Jones and respected his abilities, would have known that Jones was currently researching "the onset of hemiplegia in vascular lesions" and, therefore, possessed the necessary "qualities of an investigator."[13] He also knew Jones had time to devote to a private patient suffering from a series of complex symptoms which Bradford had diagnosed as functional rather than organic. (Jones, 1906; Gowers 1907, p. 2; Jones 1959, pp. 119–20) And he would also have known of Jones's recently discovered abilities to alleviate symptoms by hypnotic suggestion (Parry 1905; 1907a). Bradford's referral was not just a practical solution but an inspired one because, by his own testimony, Ellen said that Jones had

> eased [his] pain; made the dark way seem light, brought tranquillity, to a mind that had nearly lost all hope of human aid. . . . I never think of you without a feeling of deep love and intense gratitude for all the love, respect and brotherliness you have shown me.[14]

The evidence, suspiciously fragmentary for such an important patient, suggests Jones treated Ellen, on and off, between early 1905 and Spring 1907 and then whenever Ellen suffered a relapse. The two men even kept in touch after Jones emigrated to Canada in September 1908 and, on a brief visit to London, in August 1910, Jones invited Ellen to visit. But Ellen's case was also significant for Jones (1909b, p. 502)[15] because Ellen's "courageous endurance and clear-sighted intelligence" offered Jones "invaluable aids" and "an introspective analysis" into what Jones had now come to believe was "that very rare condition pure hysteria."

When he first consulted Jones, in early 1905, Ellen was suffering from analgesia,[16] kinaesthesia[17] and allochiria,[18] but under treatment began to improve although in a somewhat unusual way because he experienced "a great variety of abnormal sensations" especially when Jones "stimulated" the parts in question. This strange constellation of symptoms fascinated Jones (1959, pp. 157–58) because they

> provided . . . an interest which was not only theoretical, but also personal and dramatic. It was thrilling, for instance, after some months of patient work, to restore [Ellen's] vision, completely: first in a blurred fashion, then clearly except for faces, all of which looked like plain white paper, then for faces as well.[19]

Even after some fifty years, Jones's description of Ellen's cure, with his sense of personal thrill, is reminiscent of accounts of miracle cures described in the religious and spiritual texts. Although Jones claimed (1959, p. 157), on more than one occasion, that he "intended to write a book on [Ellen's] case, which it richly deserved," he never fulfilled that promise.[20] But he did publish six Ellen inspired papers [the Ellen papers] between 1907 and 1909 (Jones, 1907a, 1907c, 1908a, 1908f, 1909b, 1909c). Reading the first four, together with his contemporaneous *psychological* publication (Jones 1907f), will help illuminate the fascinating trajectory of Jones's intellectual development during this critical period of his *pre-Freudian* career.

MENTAL DISEASE FROM THE PHYSIOLOGICAL POINT OF VIEW

Jones's first Ellen paper, 'La Vraie Aphasie Tactile,' was written in French and published in the January 1907 issue of the *Revue Neurologique* [*RN*], edited by Edouard Brissaud and Pierre Marie, two of Charcot's disciples. In that paper, probably completed toward the end of 1906, Jones claimed his patient [Ellen], "a man with hysterical right hemiplegia of traumatic origin and of seven years' duration," was perhaps "the first true case of tactile aphasia ever recorded." He made this bold claim by way of intervention in an ongoing debate between Raymond, Déjérine and Claparède, on the question of whether a patient, shown recently at the Neurological Society of Paris, was suffering cerebral monoplegia or tactile aphasia.[21] Jones's paper is framed, therefore, within the context of a disagreement between Déjérine and Marie concerning the precise localization of language in the cortex: whether it was in "the third frontal convolution" or only in "Wernicke's zone." (*BMJ* December 29, 1906, pp. 1879–80; *JNMD* 1908, Vol.35, pp. 110–14).[22] In the course of his paper Jones noted that under "treatment [Ellen] began to improve steadily." Although Jones (1959, p. 158) remains silent as to the nature of that treatment we can assume he used a mixture of hypnotic suggestion, faradism and galvanism.[23] And as this treatment was probably carried out according to a physiological rather than psychological conception of hysteria, Jones may well have drawn from Mickel's (1892) essay, 'The Traumatic Factor in Mental Disease', as well as other texts from the dominant British neurological tradition grounded in the theory of localization as articulated, particularly, by Hughlings Jackson. This was the tradition Jones would have learned at medical school (Bastian 1893, pp. 40–48; Buzzard 1891; *BMJ* August 9, 1902, pp. 386–87; Horsley 1909).[24] By the time Jones (1907a, p. 5, italics mine) came to write up his first Ellen paper he had already started wondering if Ellen's neurological condition "might, *perhaps*, also be considered from a psychological point of view."[25] Once read within the context of his second Ellen paper, to be discussed shortly, these comments can be seen as Jones's first published foray into the field of psychopathology thereby revealing that in late 1906 Jones was only just beginning to feel his way out of the "British" neurological tradition and toward the French School of psychology which had only started to gain currency in Britain at the turn of the century (Buzzard 1902, p. 1401). These paradoxical tensions between the physiological and psychological conceptions of mental illness were rather nicely articulated by Sidis & Prince (1904, p. 675, italics added) who observed that the new (French) conception of "hysteric anesthesia" no longer held it to be "due to inhibition of sensory centers or any kind of suppression of their activity; . . . but is due to *a dissociation of consciousness*, probably corresponding to a *functional* dissociation of systems of cortical neurones." This might also be applied to the question whether the loss of comprehension of language was due to a lesion (in which case it was neurological) or to an intellectual defect (in which case it was psychological), or to a combination of both.

"PROFESSOR JANET'S REMARKABLE ESSAY"

In September 1907 Jones attended the First International Congress for Psychiatry, Neurology, Psychology, and the Nursing of the Insane [Amsterdam Congress] where he delivered his paper 'The Clinical significance of Allochiria,' which was then published in *The Lancet* and the *Conference Proceedings*. Jones (1907c) claims that this, his second Ellen paper [the Amsterdam paper], was the result of two years "*detailed investigation* of some cases of allochiria" and was "a preliminary communication containing a summary of [those] results." In other words although Jones's Amsterdam paper (1907c, p. 830) might have been inspired by his treatment of Ellen it is only a summary of his *researches* into "the clinical significance of the condition" together with some thoughts on the theoretical issues raised as a result of his extensive reading of the literature. It is not surprising that Jones failed to discuss the "pathogenesis" of Ellen's illness, nor the detail of Ellen's treatment because, as late as September 1907, Jones still had only limited experience of treating "functional psychopathic cases."[26] With this in mind it is now worth noting that Jones (1907c, p. 832) set out two specific but interconnected positions. First: he attacks the orthodox neurological tradition which, he believed, had over-emphasized the *physiological aspects* of nervous diseases, in particular hysteria, at the expense of the *psychological*. Second: he makes it clear that his psychological discourse was now informed by the writings of Janet thereby suggesting a shift from the mainly neurological discourse in his first Ellen paper. When set within the context of his paper's publication in *The Lancet*, Jones's comments can also be read as a veiled attack against "the physiological conception of insanity" which, according to Bernard Hart (1911, p. 90, italics mine), "had until *within recent years*, dominated almost the whole field of psychiatry."[27]

But the silent references in Jones's Amsterdam paper only become explicit in his third Ellen paper which is, in effect, an expanded version of the Amsterdam paper. That third paper, 'The Precise Diagnostic Value of Allochiria,' was completed before the end of October 1907[28] and then published in the January 1908 issue of *Brain*, the house journal of the Neurological Society. Jones's third Ellen paper now reveals, particularly through its footnotes, the full extent of the influence of Janet's theories. First; Janet's book *Névroses et Idées fixes* [*Névroses*], especially the chapter on Allochiria,[29] helped Jones fashion his *subsequent* understanding of Ellen's condition (Janet 1898, pp. 235ff; Jones 1908a, p. 530; 1908f, pp. 429, 433).[30] Second; Janet's book *The Mental State of Hystericals* [*Mental State*], helped Jones shape the *subsequent* theoretical framework for his diagnosis and treatment of Ellen. *Mental State*, Caroline Corson's translation of Janet's 1893–1894 État mental des hystériques [État mental],[31] published simultaneously in America and England (1901), had become, by 1906, probably the most important English language conduit for Janet's work. Jones probably acquired his copy in July 1905 not long after he started treating Ellen.[32] By 1907 Jones (1907c, p. 832), was now firmly under Janet's influence, and had come to believe dyschiria, one of Ellen's symptoms, was not "due to a defect in the excitations that reach the mind from the periphery" but "rather to an incapacity on the part of the mind to appreciate the excitations, which are themselves unimpaired."

> As Hysteria is purely a mental affection, and certainly is not associated with any defect in the peripheral afferent system, we therefore have strong grounds for supposing that Dyschiria is likewise a mental phenomenon. In two cases of Hysteria Allochiria has been artificially produced during hypnosis so that here we have positive evidence of its mental origin.[33]

Reading the first three Ellen papers reveal that when Jones first started treating Ellen, in early 1905, he was relatively ignorant about functional neuroses in general and hysteria in particular. Jones probably began to acquire a working knowledge of the French "psychological" literature while researching on behalf of Sir William Gowers although it was his treatment of Ellen which made him realize that if he was to understand hysteria he would need to study "the French School of Morbid Psychology . . . initiated under Charcot and Ribot" and which "culminated in the work of Janet," (Hart 1910b, p. 432). This was because it was the French school of psychology, mainly the disciples of Charcot, who, at the time, "led the way for the work on [hysteria]." (Coriat 1910, p. 236). Jones may have learned about the "French School" from Paton's text book on Psychiatry (1905, pp. 9–10, 14–15, 192 and 494f),[34] which he probably acquired in July 1905. Jones's (1907a, p. 6) *unreferenced* reference to "la théorie de M. Pierre Janet," in his first Ellen paper, further suggests that he only realized the full significance of Janet's work when nearing completion of that first paper in late 1906. This suggests, in turn, that Jones probably did not start seriously reading *Névroses* and *Mental State* until early Spring 1907 and yet by the Summer of 1907 *Névroses* and *Mental State*, in particular, had become the most significant *proof-texts* for Jones's growing interest in psychological medicine and should therefore, now be considered important influences on his intellectual development.[35] All this suggests a very different story from the one originally offered by Jones (1959, p. 162), then recycled by Brome (1983, p. 45) and then again by Maddox (2006, pp. 39–40).

THE AMSTERDAM CONGRESS 1907

According to Ellenberger (1994, p. 797) Janet's prestige at the time of the Amsterdam Congress was considerable. He was the star-guest, read his paper in person and many delegates, including Jung, openly acknowledged his contributions to the burgeoning field of psychopathology.[36] All this would have confirmed Jones (1959, p. 158) in his belief that he was now working at the cutting edge of a new discipline and following "the most distinguished worker we had yet seen on the experimental aspects of medical psychology." There is nothing in the record that even hints at the possibility that Jones's admiration for Janet was, in any way, diminished by his experiences in Amsterdam. In fact there is clear evidence that Jones (1910d, pp. 247ff; 1910f, p. 123n) remained very much under Janet's influence until at least late December 1910. On the other hand all the contemporaneous evidence, *contra* evidence, and subsequent evidence also suggests that Jones had no interest in let alone knowledge of Freud or of Freud's work, prior to Amsterdam.[37] We can venture, therefore, that it was during the Amsterdam Congress that Jones had his first encounter with Freud, or to be more precise with the *presence* of Freud, whose work was openly discussed and where "as many [delegates] were for as against Freud." (Ellenberger 1994, pp. 875n216, 797f).[38] We can even speculate that Jones's first encounter with the works of Freud occurred during the morning of September 4, 1907 when, by Jones's own account, he attended the session where Aschaffenburg and Jung debated Freud's theory of hysteria (Jones 1913a, p. 57; 1911b; Wayenburg 1908, pp. 271–84; McGuire 1974, pp. 83–85). Jones was probably at that debate because it followed immediately after Janet's lecture which Jones would surely have attended.

In his debate with Aschaffenburg Jung offered his audience a comprehensive review of how Freud's theories had developed over time; from Freud's 1893–1895 collaboration with Breuer through to Freud's most recent work. But it was with the publication of *Die Traumdeutung*, in 1900, that Freud had made his most significant theoretical departure and, by 1904, had officially adopted the psychoanalytic method in which "[a]ll suggestion is now discarded." Jung (1908a, pp. 276–77, 280; 1908b, pp. 14–15, 18–19, emphasis mine) also discussed Freud's *Three Essays on the Theory of Sexuality* [*Three Essays*] and stressed the importance of "the sexual components of psychic life." Although Jung's "lecture" was "broken off prematurely," because he over-ran his allotted time (McGuire 1974, p. 84), those present, who also understood German, would have gained a good understanding of Freud's theories. During the adjourned discussion, the following morning, Janet criticized Breuer and Freud [*sic*] for having placed too much emphasis on the sexual etiology of hysteria.

> Mais pourquoi donc généraliser ces observations vraies d'une manière tout à fait demesurée pourqui déclarer que toute l'hystérie consiste dans cette pertubration génitale de quelques malades? (Wayenburg 1908, p. 302)

Jung subsequently noted in a letter to Freud, that

> Janet couldn't help letting it drop that he had already heard your name. He knows absolutely nothing about your theory but is convinced that it is all rubbish. (McGuire 1974, p. 85).

Jung had a point because Janet, who struggled with German, had to rely upon French and English commentators (Ellenberger 1994, p. 818; Janet 1913) and, like other non-German readers at the time, would have had little or no knowledge of Freud's post 1895 writings. Subsequent events suggest Jung's Amsterdam lecture had no immediate impact upon Jones (1959, p. 163) maybe because he was still struggling to comprehend spoken German or may just because he had not yet appreciated the importance of Freud's work.

With one exception, to be discussed later, Jones had little or no contact with the British contingent at Amsterdam all of whom, with the exception of Tuckey (1907c), worked in the Asylum and were, therefore, also members of the Association. (See i.e, *JMS* 1907, p. 861; Wayenburg 1908; p. xix). This, in itself, is significant because it underlines how Jones was outside any formal British association or organization, and therefore detached from the vast majority of those involved in psychological medicine. Paradoxically it may have been his free lance position which encouraged him to network with some of the 'foreign' delegates. Thus it was probably in Amsterdam where Jones first met Carl Jung and also, most probably, Otto Gross (Ellenberger 1994, pp. 796–98, 875n; Wayenburg 1908; McGuire 1974, p. 86; Paskauskas 1993, p. 281), who delivered a paper and made a couple of interventions in defense of Freud's therapy, one being during the discussions following the Aschaffenburg-Jung debate (Wayenburg 1908; pp. 298–99, 598–599; Gross 1908). Amsterdam was also where Jones almost certainly had his first meetings with some of the American psychologists soon to become of singular significance for him: William James, Joseph Jastrow, Stewart Paton, G. W. Spiller, S. E. Jelliffe, Adolf Meyer and W. A. White were all listed as delegates (Wayenburg 1908, pp. xv–xvi, xxvi; i.e, Paskauskas 1993, p. 13–16). This powerful American contingent also strongly suggests that it was also at Amsterdam where Jones first discovered the *Journal of Abnormal Psychology* [*JAP*], founded and edited by Morton Prince (1854–1929).[39] Thus it is hardly coincidence that Jones should have had a paper published in *JAP* just a few months after Amsterdam.[40]

A SEVERE BRIQUET ATTACK: PIERRE JANET, WILLIAM SPILLER AND THE 'BOSTON SCHOOL'

Although Jones's first *JAP* paper was published in December 1907 he probably dispatched the manuscript to America toward the end of September. This chronology is underscored by its strap-line which makes no mention of Jones's new appointment at the West End which was privately confirmed on 4 October 1907. On the other hand, Jones's third Ellen paper, published in *Brain* (January 1908), announces his new appointment thereby suggests Jones completed his *JAP* paper *after* Amsterdam but *before* completing his third Ellen paper. In fact Jones may even have written his *JAP* paper at the invitation of Adolf Meyer, one of the Associate editors, who was also listed as a delegate at Amsterdam.

The title of Jones's first *JAP* paper, 'Mechanism of a Severe Briquet Attack as Contrasted with that of Psychasthenic Fits,' immediately announces its indebtedness to Janet who had recently introduced the "conception of psychasthenia" into modern psychiatry (Paton 1905, p. 15; Blumer 1906, p. 338). Jones's paper (1907f, p. 221) turns around a brief case history of Wm. C., an eighteen year old "man-of-war's man" who had been admitted to the Seamen's in March 1907 after "He was found unconscious in a garden." In his prefatory comments Jones notes the difficulty of "distinguishing an epileptic from a hystero-epileptic fit"[41] and makes passing reference to "the writings of certain German and French workers in the important group of conditions characterized by transitory affections of consciousness." The German workers were Hoche,[42] Heilbronner[43] and Oppenheim,[44] all of whom had looked at the problem from a psychiatric or neurological point of view; although Oppenheim, perhaps with a nod toward psychology, had introduced "the expression *psychasthenic* convulsions." But Jones (1907f, p. 218, italics added)[45] also noted how Spiller, thinking Oppenheim's expression "too limited," had suggested, instead, "the term psychasthenic *attack*." Jones's footnote reveals how his introductory comments were drawn mainly from Spiller's (1907, pp. 256f) February 1907 JAP article, "*Psychasthenic Attacks Simulating Epilepsy*" which was originally delivered as a talk to a Joint Meeting of the New York and Philadelphia Neurological Societies and which had generated an interesting discussion (*JNMD* 1907, Vol. 34, pp. 411–19).

William Spiller (1863–1940), editor of the *Journal of Nervous and Mental Disease* [*JNMD*],[46] was a highly respected neurologist and neuropathologist (UP 1912, p. 19) who had recently become interested in the psychological, or functional, aspects of certain neurological conditions mainly because of

> a growing tendency to recognise that amongst the cases generally classed as epileptic, there are to be distinguished certain groups which are of a distinctly different pathology (Thomas 1908, pp. 131–34; Paton 1905, p. 517)

In the course of his *JAP* article Spiller surveyed those recent French and German writers who had discussed the difficulties of determining whether epileptic-like symptoms were organic (epilepsy) or functional (hysteria). Having defined his paradigm Spiller introduced two of his own cases which, although they resembled epilepsy, were "neither epilepsy nor hysteria." Thus he had written them up "in the hope that they may draw attention and discussion to the subject of *psychasthenic attacks*."[47] Although Spiller glossed the tensions between the German psychiatric and French psychological writings his own theoretical framework was informed mainly by Janet's concept of psychasthenia (Spiller 1907, pp. 262, 259 italics added: Janet 1901, pp. 519f) probably because Janet offered the best framework within which to grapple with those psychiatric conditions which straddled the borders between neurology and psychology. By 1907 Janet had become a powerful presence in American psychiatry particularly among members of the so-called Boston school,[48] and his influence, which I think Caplan (1998, p. 114) underplays, can be traced back to at least 1904 when, having delivered a paper to the Boston Society, Janet (1905a) was invited, along with Binet, to serve on the advisory board of the *Psychological Review* [*PR*]. Janet's (1905b) subsequent lecture to the Congress of Arts and Sciences was then published in *PR* and, in late 1906, Janet delivered his inaugural lecture at the Harvard Medical School. His short teaching appointment, at the Lowell Institute in Harvard University, led to the almost immediate publication of those lectures in the *Boston Medical and Surgical Journal* [*BMSJ*], and their re-publication, the following year, as *The Major Symptoms of Hysteria* (Janet 1906b, 1907). And, as if to underline Janet's (1906a) full significance his paper, "The Pathogenesis of Some Impulsions" was the first, or lead, paper when *JAP* was launched in April 1906.[49] This helps explain not only why Spiller was interested in Janet but also why Jones was interested in Spiller because Spiller's article offered him not just a reference point for his own continuing migration to psychology but also a theoretical framework from which to write up his treatment of Wm. C.

Although Jones, more or less, followed Spiller's general argument, modifying it to account for some of the differences between his own and Spiller's patient(s), a close reading of both texts reveals how Jones uses a surprising number of the same references as Spiller. So, like Spiller, Jones refers to the articles that White (1902) and Parker (1902) contributed to Sidis (1902). Like Spiller Jones references the exact page number (p. 93) of Janet's (1905b) article in the *BMSJ*, even though Spiller's reference was only to its first page.[50] Like Spiller Jones references Janet (1903) but, unlike Spiller, failed to cite any page number. Like Spiller, Jones refers to 'Hysteria from the Point of View of a Dissociated Personality,' the article by Prince (1906b), published in *JAP*. And, like Spiller, Jones also references Putnam and Waterman's 1905 article in the *BMSJ*. All this might be considered tedious if it were not that Spiller made a critical mistake in his Putnam and Waterman reference where, having noted the correct page number (p. 509), he cited the wrong Volume—CLII *not* CLIII. And Jones faithfully reproduced that mistake (Spiller 1907, p. 260; Jones 1907f, p. 221). Thus although Jones appears to be well versed in the writings of the Boston School his slavish following of Spiller strongly suggests his knowledge of their work was not quite as extensive as it seemed. But Jones's use and misuse of Spiller's *JAP* article also reveals the extent to which Jones did *not* read what Spiller had written. Toward the end of his article Spiller (1907, p. 265, italics mine)[51] makes some comments about "the occurrence of [a patient's psychasthenic] attacks in proportion to the frequency of [his] masturbation."

> Freud has called attention to *the importance of sexual errors* in the etiology of the neuroses. There is in this case something very much like a subconscious working and made evident without the use of hypnosis, and it in itself makes a diagnosis of epilepsy improbable, as does also the cessation of all attacks during a period of several years under psychotherapy. Possibly the condition may be explained, as is done for many other peculiar mental states, as a dissociation of the personality.

Although Jones follows Spiller's arguments religiously whenever they turn around Janet's theories, he remained conspicuously silent, even blind, to Spiller's comments concerning a possible link between masturbation and psychasthenic attacks. In other words Jones has completely ignored Spiller's reference to Freud's theory concerning the sexual etiology of hysteria; a point Jung subsequently noted after reading Jones's article (Kuhn 2014a, p. 32).

A SEVERE BRIQUET ATTACK: PIERRE JANET AND THE "ZURICH SCHOOL"

In the prefatory remarks to his first *JAP* paper Jones (1907f, p. 221) says his purpose was to "study, through the subconscious memory . . . the immediate cause of a given fit" so as to extend the possibilities for differentiating "between hysteria and psychasthenia." He then discusses the 18 year old Wm. C., who had been admitted to the Seamen's in early March 1907 following some kind of fit.[52] Once under his care Jones (1907f, p. 222, italics added) encouraged Wm. C., to enter into some form of hypnotic trance.[53]

> As his pain was so severe, I asked him to lie down *and closed his eyes* [*sic*].[54] His limbs almost at once relaxed, and he began to talk—reluctantly at first—in a quiet monotone. He then disclosed in a rambling fashion the following details.

Having recounted those details Jones (1907f, p. 223–24, italics mine) concludes:

> Here was a case of major hysteria in the making. A definite focus of *disaggregation*, invested with a *powerful emotion-complex*, had been rapidly growing in the past few days and had reached the surface for the first time only a few hours ago. If the boy were merely allowed to recover from his crisis and to return to work, we might expect, within perhaps a few weeks, some major manifestation

> of hysteria to develop, possibly paraplegia, *blindness* or hystero-epilepsy. Recovery from the crisis meant merely the submergence of this dangerous focus, which sooner or later would again exert its devastating influence on the mind.

The sub-text here is an unambiguous reference to Ellen who appeared, at first, to make a rapid and natural recovery but having received no psychological intervention, suddenly developed major manifestations of hysterical trauma. So now, in Wm C.'s case, Jones (1907f, p. 224) "therefore employed a little suggestion along the obvious lines" to prevent further "disaggregation" and to "reunite the focus to the main mental content and so prevent further insulation of the powerful body of emotion." Jones's attempt to effect "the dissolution of the [patient's] fixed ideas" through (post) hypnotic suggestion was clearly based upon Janet's well-known "substitution theory." (Ellenberger 1994, p. 367f).[55] Jones's conceptual language—"subconscious," "disaggregation," "psychasthenia," and "submerged memories"—are all taken, more or less, straight out of Corson's translation of État Mental (Janet 1901, pp. 251, 53, 102, respectively).[56] Thus at the time of writing his first *JAP* paper, in late September 1907, Jones clearly reveals the extent to which he has drawn from Janet's therapeutic methodology and theoretical framework as well as his conceptual language.

But there is another thread running through Jones's *JAP* paper which reveals that he has now started engaging with the writings of the 'Zurich School,' particularly the *early* writings of Jung, and Jung and Riklin, in an attempt to synthesize their theories with those of Janet's.[57] So, for example, Jones imports, into his *JAP* paper, the concept of "the emotion-complex" which he almost certainly drew directly from Jung & Riklin's 'The Associations of Normal Subjects' (1904, p. 72; Jones 1907f, p. 223). And this is further underlined in that passage where Jones attempts to "consider a point in the differentiation of some cases that belong to" the psychoneuroses rather than epilepsy (Jones 1907f, pp. 218, 220, italics mine).

> Heilbronner,[58] for instance, refuses to diagnose epilepsy in absence of the characteristic mental changes found in that condition apart from fits. In the differentiation and analysis of hysteria during the interval period, Jung and Ricklin [*sic*][59] have obtained very striking results by the application of the Association-reaction method. *Without the use of some exact method of investigation such as Jung's* there is of course the great difficulty that two conditions such as hysteria and epilepsy may coexist.

Although Jones's interest in Jung and Riklin might be traced back to Amsterdam what probably attracted him, as it did with many other British physicians at the time, was their *scientific* attitude,[60] and in particular the "scientific aura," surrounding the Galvanometer, or the 'Soul Machine' as *Harper's Weekly* called it *(ARR* 1909, Vol. 13, p. 298). Jones may even already have been familiar with "the value of the so-called 'psycho-physical galvanic reflex'" from Peterson's and Jung's (1907, p. 492) article in the July 1907 issue of *Brain* and with the claim, made by Peterson (1907a, p. 449, italics mine; 1907b), during his BMA talk, that the Galvanometer—which measured physiological reactions associated with the word-association method—was "*an instrument of precision* in psychophysical research." Thus Jones was probably attracted by the promise of "scientifically useful material" which it was now believed could be harvested from patients' "reactions" to the word-association tests which Jung and Riklin (1904, pp. 3 and 152)[61] had claimed to be "an extraordinarily sensitive test for affective processes in particular and the individual response of the subject in general." As we shall shortly Jung's word-association tests, which Freud (1910a, pp. 199), himself, originally recommended as a quick and easy way of obtaining "a preliminary knowledge of the patient's repressed complexes," were about to become *the* critical pathway for those British psychotherapists looking to migrate from psychotherapy to psychoanalysis. On the other hand Jones would also have had strong affinities with Jung's early work because of its echoes with Janet's.

> As to Pierre Janet, with whom Jung studied for a semester in Paris,[62] *his influence on Jung was considerable.* From him Jung learnt about 'psychological automatism,' dual personality, psychological strength and weakness, the 'function of synthesis,' the *abaissement du niveau mental*, and 'subconscious fixed ideas' (which Jung later identified with Ziehen's 'complexes' and Freud's 'traumatic reminiscences'). Jung learnt Janet's distinction of the two basic neuroses: hysteria and psychasthenia (to which he substituted the distinction of extroverted hysteria and introverted schizophrenia). (Ellenberger (1994, p. 727; also pp. 149, 406, 694, 742n,[111] italics added)[63]

What is also noticeable is that the 'Zurich School' articles, to which Jones refers in his first *JAP* paper, make no reference to Freud's post *Studien* (1895) publications thereby suggesting that even if Jones had already started engaging with Freud—for which there is still no evidence—he would have been left with the distinct impression that Freud's and Janet's work dovetailed. (Jung 1902, pp. 154–55; Jung & Riklin 1904, p. 191n; Janet 1901, pp. 495–96). This was also the view taken by Clarke (1896, p. 414) who, along with Myers (1903, p. 299) and Ellis, was the only other early British commentator to have discussed or abstracted *Studien*.[64] This absence of (almost) any reference to Freud is highly significant. So, for example, in his attempts to identify "the immediate mechanism of an individual fit" Jones (1907f, pp. 226, 224) asks: from which of the two main "psycho-neuroses—hysteria and psychasthenia"—the patient might have been suffering? This was the classification

Janet had articulated several years previously and which now formed the basis of his "psychological analysis" (Ellenberger 1994, pp. 375f; Janet 1901, pp. 519f). If Jones had been at all interested in Freud he would surely have examined Wm C. according to whether he was suffering from hysteria or from an obsessional or anxiety neurosis and would then have explained his patient's condition by reference to "the psychical mechanism of (unconscious) *defense*" (Freud 1896b, p. 162; anon 1905). Jones also treated Wm. C., through suggestion and hypnotism as well as with the more "orthodox" psychotherapeutic procedures such as faradism, galvanism, and hydrotherapeutics (Paton 1905, p. 514; Rachford 1905, pp. 348f).[65] If Jones had been practicing some form of psychoanalysis he would surely have known, what most informed English language commentators already knew (i.e., Ellis 1906 p. 406; Anon 1908a, p. 103; Putnam 1906, p. 30), that Freud had abandoned hypnotism several years earlier (Freud 1904, p. 250). In fact Jones (1910d, p. 271, italics mine) subsequently confirms this same point when he says:

> Like the great majority of the Freud school, *I had practised for some years with various forms of suggestion and hypnotism before I learned the psycho-analytic method.*

Perhaps even more crucially Jones also completely ignored what most informed commentators also understood to be Freud's belief that "*a sexual element is almost an essential factor of hysteria* and allied neurotic conditions, such as the liability to causeless fright (Angstneurose)." (Ellis 1898c, p. 851, italics mine; Ellis 1901b, pp. 155f; Ellis 1907c, p. 834; Wolfstein 1905, p. 139; Anon 1908a). Jones's silence on this is all the more striking given that the 'sexual question' was discussed in at least one other article Jones consulted (i.e., Putnam 1906, p. 27). But perhaps most telling of all Jones now reveals his almost total ignorance of Freud's work what is probably his first published reference to Freud.

> It is, by the way, interesting to note [the fit's] relation to dream states in this instance, in view of the importance attached by Freud to dreams in this connection.

To which Jones (1907f, p. 226) has added, by way of footnote: "Freud, Traumbedeutung, Wien. 1900." Of course he should have written *Die Traumdeutung*. Once Jones's mistake is set within the context of his intellectual development it would be difficult to argue that this must have been a printer's error. The Freud reference, at this point, also makes no sense given that *Die Traumdeutung* has nothing to say about 'fits' in relation to dreams, thereby suggesting Jones must have thought Freud's book was about the meaning rather than the interpretation of dreams and that not knowing its argument he had assumed *Die Traumdeutung* was probably interchangeable with most standard accounts of dreams.

In *Text-Book on Psychiatry*, which Jones acquired in July 1905, Paton (1905, p. 504), who was also an associate editor of the *JNMD*, suggested that:

> According to Sollier [in *Genèse et nature de l'hystérie*, Paris 1897] hysterical patients are always in a pathological state of dreaminess, and this drowsiness and the anaesthesias are practically one and the same.

Janet (1901, pp. 495, 496, 516–17, italics mine) made much the same point when, after praising the "independent researches" of Breuer and Freud, he said: "The most common accidents of hysteria, even hyperaesthesias, pains, commonplace attacks, should be interpreted in the same way as the accidents of traumatic hysteria—*namely, by the persistency of an idea or a dream*." And Spiller (1907, p. 258), in the article from which Jones drew so heavily, says, in relation to mistaking a psychasthenic attack for epilepsy: "I am inclined to think that the danger of mistake is especially great as regards the dreamy state of epilepsy described by Hughlings Jackson under the name of 'uncinate group of fits.'" All this makes it possible to speculate that in the course of writing his *JAP* article Jones realized that men like Jung, Putnam and Sidis considered *Die Traumdeutung* a seminal book and, as such, he ought to at least reference it. So Jones turned, not to the book itself, but to a second-hand source, which is suggested by the almost casual way in which he introduces his first reference to Freud—"It is, by the way, interesting to note . . ." Jones may even have included it as an after-thought and then (mis)referenced it when he assumed it fitted within the wider context of the psychological discourse with which he was already familiar (Jones 1954a, p. 199).[66] So from where did Jones glean this mis-information about *Die Traumdeutung*? I have been unable to find any direct discussions or reviews of Freud's book in either the British or American literature between 1900 (the date of its publication) and late September 1907 when Jones was completing his paper.[67] A wider trawl of the review literature suggests only two possible sources: Sidis's (1906) review of *The Psychopathology of Everyday Life*, where Sidis refers specifically to "'Traumdeutung,'"[68] and Putnam's critical essay on Freud. Although Jones makes no reference to either it is interesting to note that Putnam made a similar mistake when he referred, also in passing, to "'Traumdeutungen'" (Putnam 1906, p. 26).[69] So we can now speculate that when Jones decided to make what would become his first Freud reference he alighted on Putnam's article but then failed to check the reference just as he had failed to check the Putnam & Waterman reference when following Spiller.[70]

FROM MUNICH TO ZURICH TO PARIS (VIA VIENNA)

Despite his growing interest in psychopathology Jones was also beginning to achieve something of a reputation in the field of pathology, a subject he first started studying in 1901 when, under the guidance of Bradford, he delivered a paper to the Pathological Society of London on the "calcification of the pericardium." This was published in the Society's *Transactions* (Jones 1901a) and can be counted Jones's first medical publication while his membership of the Pathological Society (1903), was probably the first of the many medical societies he joined. From time to time Jones travelled to Claybury from where F. W. Mott (1853–1926), the chief Pathologist to the LCC, and a highly respected figure in the asylum system (Mould 1902, p. 1201), had issued an open invitation to all serious researchers to use the "well-equipped laboratory" (Anon 1909b, p. 1014). By 1907 Jones (1954, p. 200; 1959, p. 123), had come to know Mott well and subsequently remembered him with affection, calling him, with good reason, "the real Father of the Maudsley Hospital."[71]

At Amsterdam Jones stood at a cross roads having so far failed in his ambition to secure a full-time physician's appointment in a London Hospital. The subsequent chronology suggests that he talked this problem over with Mott, who was also at Amsterdam, and that Mott advised him that if Jones still wanted to secure a job as a psychiatrist then he should enter the profession through pathology because, as several commentators had already noted, "the pathological laboratory [was] the hub of the asylum universe" and nowhere more so than in Britain (Hart 1908c, p. 474). Mott therefore probably advised Jones to take a short post-graduate course at Kraepelin's Clinic in Munich rather than continue his ad hoc independent researches at Claybury because Claybury, unlike Munich, was a stand alone facility and not being integrated into a Hospital would not offer Jones ready access to patients. Furthermore because Kraepelin's system was now becoming well known in Britain a short training in Munich would enable Jones not only to develop his pathological skills but also obtain the necessary qualifications to enhance his career prospects. There seems little doubt that by the time he left Amsterdam Jones had resolved to pursue a full-time career in pathology.

As Jones had been a clinical assistant to Harry Campbell at the West End since 1905 he would almost certainly have heard, through the grape-vine, that the West End Medical Committee was about to set up a new pathology department, run on Kraepelin-lines, and would shortly be advertising for a full-time pathologist to run that department (Kuhn 2014a, pp. 29–30; Jones 1959, p. 163; Paskauskas 1985, p. 181).[72] We can now assume that Jones applied for the Kraepelin course on his return from Amsterdam because on being offered the new post of pathologist at the West End he immediately requested, and was granted, a month's leave of absence, during November

1907, to study in Munich. While in Munich Jones met, or re-met, Otto Gross (1877–1920), who, at the time, was working as an assistant in Kraepelin's clinic. It was probably Gross who encouraged Jones to curtail his studies in Munich, take advantage of his close proximity to Zurich, and visit Jung at the Burghölzli Psychiatric Clinic [Burghölzli]. Jones arrived in Zurich (probably) on November 25, 1907 and spent the next five days working at the Burghölzli (McGuire 1974, p. 97; Jones 1955, p. 43; Paskauskas 1993, p. 281). A close reading of Jung's letters to Freud—outwith Jones's (1955, p. 43) subsequent contrary comments—clearly reveals that what prompted Jones's visit was not his interest in Freud's work, about which he still knew little, but his desire "to get himself initiated" in the psychological investigations carried out by Jung and his colleagues. (McGuire 1974, p. 97. See also Paskauskas 1993, p. 281).[73] And what attracted Jones, above all, were the word-association experiments, which he had discovered while researching his first *JAP* paper and which his visit to the Burghölzli now allowed him to study and use in *situe*. Paradoxically this now suggest that Jones was, for a short time at least, a pupil of Jung's although Jones subsequently tried to conceal this 'fact' through a number of deflections. First; by claiming that he was already practicing psychoanalysis "(imperfectly, to be sure) for a year before" Amsterdam, and second with what now looks like his highly questionable May 1914 claim that while in Munich, in November 1907, he had "learnt more there from Gross than I ever learnt form Jung."[74] (Paskauskas 1993, p. 281; Kuhn 2014, p. 31).

On March 12, 1908 Jones, who had been working for just over four months as *the* full-time pathologist in the West End, a busy London children's hospital, attended a meeting of the Neurological Society of which he had been a member since 1903. Drs F. E. Batten (1866–1918) and Campbell Thomson (1870–1940) each presented a case. Batten's patient had a tremor of the right arm associated with epilepsy, Thomson's had *hemiplegia* with involuntary movements. In the discussions which followed Jones (1908c) ventured to suggest that both cases might be diagnosed hysteria and, in Thomson's case, "[a] diagnosis [of hysteria] could be obtained by a psychological examination." Charles Beevor (1855–1908),[75] in the chair, and an old teacher of Jones's, intervened: "He could not agree with what [Jones] had just said as to complete loss of consciousness, biting of the tongue, relaxing of the sphincters, being associated with hysteria, and he could not let that statement pass." Beevor believed that in Thomson's case "there must be some gross lesion in the cortex."[76] Gordon Holmes (1876–1965) agreed: "He did not think there was any ground for saying those symptoms occurred in functional disease." In reply Thomson said he had carefully considered the possibility of a "functional disease" but having observed the *fit* in hospital was persuaded "the symptoms enumerated . . . sufficed for regarding the case as organic"

(Nachbar 1907–1908, pp. 54–57).[77] Against this somewhat hostile background Jones presented his own case, a 12 year old boy with "primary spastic paraplegia." What is significant here is that although Jones had already published three overtly psychological papers and was even prepared to argue psychological explanations for Batten's and Thomson's patients, he had chosen, for his own presentation, a case that was undoubtedly organic and probably hereditary, thereby offering him no possibility of elaborating a psychological discourse.[78] This small vignette reveals two interesting points in relation to the contemporaneous tensions between neurological and psychological medicine. The first, articulated with great clarity, was made by Beevor just before his death, in his contribution to the May 1908 meeting of the American Neurological Association where he claimed, quite erroneously, that "psychotherapy .. had not yet invaded England's shores." Beevor also went on to say,

> he must confess that he has not studied the French books, and he doesn't know that any of the English have very much, but they still use the Weir Mitchell treatment. They use it with the greatest success in the world and as far as psychotherapy is concerned he does not know of any *neurologist* who uses it in England. (*JNMD* 1908, Vol. 35, p. 784, italics mine)[79]

The second point concerns Jones's uncertain standing within the Neurological Society. Not withstanding his "psychological" intervention in the meeting Jones may have felt it inappropriate for a pathologist to present a psychological case study to senior members of the neurological establishment. But this point must remain mute not only because there is no further information about Jones's patient but also because, just eleven days later, Jones was accused by a young female patient at the West End of improper sexual behavior and, her allegation having been taken seriously, Jones was forced to resign on March 27, 1908 (Kuhn 2015, pp. 25–26). Given the seriousness of the charge let alone that this was now the second time he had been accused of indecently assaulting a child; and that this would now also be the second time that he had been forced to resign a hospital post Jones realized, no doubt correctly, "that all hope vanished of ever getting onto the staff of any . . . hospital in London" (Jones 1959, p. 151; Paskauskas 1993, p. 110). He was clearly left with little option but to try and find work abroad.

Although Jones was busy trying to secure an appointment in Canada during the weeks following his 'resignation' he still had time, and money, to travel: First to Salzburg where, on 27 April, he delivered a paper to the 1st International Psycho-Analytic Congress [Salzburg Congress]:[80] then to Vienna, in the company of Brill (1874–1948), whom he first met at the Burghölzli in November 1907. Jones (1955, p. 43) and Brill then dined with Freud on 30 April (E. L. Freud 1970, p. 283) and attended, as Freud's guests, at the

6 May meeting of the Vienna Psychoanalytic Society (Nunberg & Federn, 1962, pp. 392–96). The two men then travelled to Budapest where they visited Ferenczi, on 8 May, and they then returned to Munich where they parted company. Brill most probably returning to the Burghölzli while Jones remained in Munich where he was already working at Kraepelin's clinic by 13 May. Jones then left Munich on 27 June and, following a two day visit to Zurich, returned to London for a week before going to Paris to study for six weeks under Pierre Marie (1853–1940). It is worth noting that Marie, a pupil of Charcot's, was not only a neurologist but also a distinguished pathologist and had recently been appointed to the chair of pathological anatomy at the Faculty of Medicine (*BMJ* January 18, 1908, p. 173). Jones (1959, p. 175), therefore, would almost certainly have studied pathology under Marie *not* neurology as he subsequently claimed. This, in turn, suggests that Mott, who met Marie in late 1904 when the latter visited the Pathological Laboratory at Claybury (*BMJ* 15 October 1904, p. 1034), may well have made the original introduction for Jones.

Although Jones only discovered about the works of Freud during the Amsterdam Congress in September 1907 he was, by then, set upon establishing a career in pathology and that commitment held fast at the time of his emigrating to Canada, in September 1908. I have argued elsewhere (Kuhn 2014a, pp. 44–45) that Jones only started taking an active interest in psychotherapy "'carried out by the Freudian methods,'" after he had arrived in Toronto. What is more if Jones (1955, pp. 31f) had really been "practising psycho-analysis for three years" before he left for Canada in 1908,—as he subsequently claimed—then it seems strange that he did not take the opportunity of studying psychoanalysis in Vienna, Budapest, Berlin or even at the Burghölzli during those six months between his resignation and his emigration.

NOTES

1. Rhys Dafis informs me that "Welsh-speaking people nowadays normally refer to it as 'Tre-Gwyr' and that "The anglicized spelling of 'Llanelly' changed back to the Welsh spelling 'Llanelli' in the 1960s.
2. Mickle, born and qualified MD in Toronto, arrived in England in the late 1860s and studied at St. Thomas's. He became Medical Superintendent at Grove Hall Asylum, Bow, which housed around 200 men and 45 women. Mickle's speciality was the pathology of general paralysis, particularly the aetiological significance of syphilis in the production of organic disease of the nervous system: hence his close friendship with Mott. Jones was unlikely to have asked Mickle for help once he had decided to 'emigrats' to Toronto in 1908.
3. Jones subsequently claimed "he had been Dr. Beevor's assistant for a couple of years." (*Medical Record* August 6, 1910, p. 256).

4. The Seamen's Hospital Society had two hospitals;The Dreadnought at Greenwich, with 225 beds, and the Branch Hospital in the Royal Victoria and Albert Docks with 50 beds. There were also 2 Dispensaries: in the East India Dock Road, and at Gravesend. The School Buildings, Laboratories, Museum Library, etc. were in the grounds of the Branch Hospital, in Connaught Road. The Seamen's also offered the chance of "studying diseases incidental to Tropical Climates and also Practical Surgery before entering the services or going abroad. (*BMJ* September 3, 1904, p. 532).

5. Although Jones would have resented this label it cannot alter the fact that his Harley Street address, usually reserved for senior London Consultants (Maddox 2006, p. 37), effectively concealed his lowly position.

6. Jones probably also received financial support from his father (Maddox 2006, p. 37) and then also from Loe Kann with whom he had a seven year relationship (1906–1913).

7. Dr. Thomas Wilson Parry, a GP in North London, subsequently President of the North London Medical and Chirurgical Society, although better known for his extensive practical research into Neolithic trephination instruments and techniques. (Guthrie 1945, p. 7). "His status as an anthropologist secured his election as a Fellow of the Society of Antiquaries, and he became the leading authority on prehistoric trephining." (Langdon-Brown 1945).

8. During their Bethlem experiments (1888–1889) Smith & Myers (1890, p. 210) used a laryngoscopic mirror.

9. Parry has 7 October but as Jones only seems to have worked Thursday afternoons I have altered the date.

10. I am grateful to the anonymous reader of Kuhn (2014a) who originally identified the dates and place of the train crash. The 1901 census confirms T. E. J. Ellen, of 26 Charles Square, Shoreditch as blind, and registers his birth as 1875 although his birth certificate has 1874. Tom and his wife Mary Ann had three daughters.

11. The hotly debated question as to whether an external trauma could cause disease of the nervous system was further complicated by compensation claims for damages. Ellen's case, however, turned on whether the original document he had signed and agreed with the GNRC was a contract or merely a receipt for the money.

12. The correspondence suggests Jones was already treating Ellen in May 1905 (Ellen to Jones May 6, 1905, BPAS, PO4-C-F-05).

13. The quote is from Bradford's June 8, 1908 job reference for Jones (BPAS PO4-G-C-01). Jones (1906) was abstracted by Jelliffe (1907, p. 215) who called it "an extremely interesting paper."

14. Ellen to Jones, August 16, 1910 (BPAS, PO4-C-F-05). The 1911 census confirms Ellen's occupation as Oilman.

15. Jones (1909b, p. 516) treated a similar case in April 1907 whilst working at the Seamen's.

16. A deadening or absence of the sense of pain without loss of consciousness.

17. The sensation by which bodily position (weight, muscle tension, and movement) is perceived.

18. Obersteiner says allochiria is "a condition in which, 'though the sensibility is retained more or less completely, the patient is not clear, or is frequently, if not

constantly, in error as to which side of the body has been touched.'" (Quoted Jones 1908a, p. 492)

19. Jones (1959, p. 158) could not resist adding: "With the sole exception of his wife's!" This subsequently re-constructed rhetorical device nicely reinforces his deception that Ellen's treatment was an early step on his seamless psychoanalytic journey. Reading Jones (1954, pp. 201–2) appears to confirm this reading.

20. Jones told Putnam, in July 1910, that only "a tithe" of his work on allochiria and hemiplegia had been published (Hale 1971, p. 221; See also Jones (1908d; 1908e)

21. See Coriat (1907) and Wilson (1907b) for brief summaries. For a detailed discussion see Prince (1908).

22. Prince (1908b, p. 230) suggests the matter was further complicated because: "It is well known that not rarely motor aphasia clears up." Shortly after Jones completed his paper Marie said "that in his opinion all the current doctrines concerning aphasia need reconsideration." (*BMJ* December 29, 1906, pp. 1879–80).

23. The application of alternating electrical current and direct electrical current for therapeutic purposes.

24. See also Knapp (1907). Although Paskauskas (1985, pp. 85–86) discusses this point I think he misunderstands the nature of Jones's early medical training.

25. The phrase is: "beaucoup d'avantage à considérer la question à un point de vue plus psychologique." See also Jones (1908a, p. 491) and Wilson (1907a). The February 1907 issue of *JAP* also carries an abstract of this debate (Coriat 1907).

26. This term, used by Sidis & Goodhart (1905, p. vii), meant hysterical conditions which had no obvious organic cause.

27. Jones (1911a, p. 121–22) subsequently claimed "clinical psychology . . . is viewed with a cold antipathy" in English "scientific circles" unlike America where there was "a widespread cordiality towards the subject." Hart (1925, p. 238) referred to this period as "the arid days of the academic psychology with its meticulous introspective description of mental processes . . ."

28. In the strap-line Jones notes his new job, at the West End, which he was offered on 4 October 1907.

29. Spearman (1905, pp. 304–5) discussed one of the mysteries of Allocheria, from the 'organic' point of view.

30. Had Jones known of *Studien* he might have drawn certain conclusions from Breuer and Freud's discussions of hemianaesthesia, for which see Clarke (1896, p. 410).

31. Jones (1908a, p. 530) makes an explicit reference to Corson's book. Corson died on May 21, 1901 shortly after completing her translation but before correcting the proofs.

32. Jones's name and date of acquisition are inscribed on the fly-leaf of the copy in the IPA Library in February 2003. Paskauskas (1985, p. 116–17) assumed that dates written into Jones's books signified when he acquired *and* read them. There is clear evidence that some of those dates were predated either by Jones or somebody else.

33. This would have been Janet's view, for which see Hart (1925, pp. 234f).

34. Reading Paton's (1905, pp.494ff) chapter on Hysteria suggests it was particularly significant for Jones's 1907–1908 psychological publications. Paton has several passing references to Freud but nothing specific. A reviewer of Paton (*JMS* 1907,

Vol. 53, p. 166) thought him "an earnest student of Kraepelin," which is not quite my impression. (See i.e., Patton 1905, pp. 13–14). Jones may have first learned of Kraepelin from Paton.

35. Another stepping stone may have been Wetterstrand (1902 [1897]); which was still in Jones's library in February 2003.

36. Jung to Freud September 4, 1907 (*McGuire* 1974, p. 83).

37. This may raise eyebrows; but only for those who take on trust Jones's autobiographical claims that he was already "practising [Freud's] method at the end of 1906." (1959, p. 162).

38. Freud was only mentioned, in passing, during a cursory report in *The Lancet* (September 21, 1907, p. 861).

39. Morton Prince, a significant figure in American and European psychology, was Professor of Diseases of the Nervous System at Tuft's Medical School and Physician at Boston City Hospital.

40. Following its launch, in April 1906, *JAP* had only minimal publicity in the British medical press (*JMS* July 1906, p. 580) and few seem to have known of its existence until late 1909.

41. Putnam & Waterman (1905, p. 509), whom Jones (1907f, p. 221) appears to quote, state that "the term hystero-epilepsy is a misnomer and should in the future be disused."

42. Alfred Hoche (1865–1943), professor of psychiatry at Freiburg and by 1906 "an outspoken adversary of psychoanalysis" (McGuire 1974, p. 9n).

43. Karl Heilbronner (1869–1914) psychiatrist and director of Utrecht University Clinic.

44. Herman Oppenheim (1858–1919) a Berlin neurologist who, according to Jung, maintained a "benevolent neutrality" toward Freud but "show[ed] signs of sexual opposition" (McGuire 1974, p. 86).

45. Jones's reference has the wrong page number, which should be p. 258.

46. The *JNMD,* founded in 1874, had close links with *JAP.*

47. Hart (1907, p. 390) notes the "close relationship between psychasthenia and epilepsy" but draws mainly from Janet (1903).

48. Hale (1971, p. 16) says Morton Prince "deliberately refrained from creating a 'school,' lest the hostility of the medical profession be increased." Members tended to refer to themselves as the Boston Group, or the Bostonians (Paskauskas 1985, p. 138f)

49. Paskauskas (1993, p. 8n. 10) says Freud refused to contribute to this inaugural issue.

50. Spiller says Janet's article appeared on 19 January which Jones silently corrects to 26 January.

51. Spiller's reference is to Freud's *Sammlung kleiner Schriften zur Neurosenlehre* (1906) but has no page number.

52. Apart from Ellen and Wm. C., I have only identified two other cases of hysteria treated by Jones during this period. The first; a "young lady" briefly mentioned in a letter to Freud (Paskauskas 1993, p. 105). The second; Lizzy Spalding the sister of a nurse employed by Jones's friend Ivor Tuckett who asked Jones to treat her in July 1906. (Tuckett to Jones July 11, 1906, BPAS PO4-C-H-06; Jones 1909b, p. 502). Tuckett (1873–1942), educated at Cambridge was subsequently a physician at UCH

and also a member of the Physiological Society where he and Jones probably met. Jones's interest in hypnotism may even have come through Tuckett (1911) who subsequently gained a reputation for exposing false claims by Spiritualists.

53. Jones (1907f, p. 224), probably following Sidis, believed his patient probably entered a "hypnoidic" state.

54. On this point see for example, Bramwell (1921, p. 340).

55. In his early practice Freud, following Breuer (Breuer & Freud 1895, p. 101), often resorted to "suggestion" but there is no indication Jones would have known this not least because if he had been at all interested in Freud he would have known, from reading Corson, that Janet (1901, p. 412) had reservations about Breuer and Freud's cathartic technique.

56. Janet (1901, pp. 369–79) has a section on "Briquet" attacks which was the main subject of Jones's paper (1907f).

57. Jones may have subsequently discovered A. M.'s review of Jung & Riklin in *PB* (1905, Vol. 2, pp. 242–59).

58. Jones's reference to Heilbronner is probably drawn straight from Jung & Riklin (1904, p. 43).

59. Hoch (1906, p. 98), who reviewed some of Jung's works in June 1906, also miss-spells Riklin, thereby suggesting Jones may have been following Hoch's review.

60. Jones subsequently told Freud, in November 1913: "Your own rigid adherence to [the scientific attitude] has always called forth my admiration." (Paskauskas 1993, p. 240).

61. Jung was still checking "galvanic oscillations during the association experiment" in 1907. Ellenberger (1994, p. 742n111) says Jung's concept of the "complex . . . preceded the foundation of psychoanalysis." Walter Whately Smith (aka Whately Carington) subsequently suggested using "the word association test" in Psychic Research (*Proceedings*, 1921, Vol. 21, pp. 401f).

62. This throws doubts on Jones's subsequent claim that Janet did not accept pupils (i.e., Brome 1983, p. 62).

63. Janet (1901, p. 375) asks: "Have we not the right to say that an association of ideas has induced, at the sight of a little flame, the reproduction of the emotion he experienced in seeing the kitchen fire?" Jones may have associated this with Jung's Association Experiments.

64. Jones (1945, p. 9) claims to have read both accounts in 1903 for which there is simply no evidence.

65. Jones probably used the more "orthodox" psychotherapeutic procedures such as faradism, galvanism, and hydrotherapeutics, for which see Paton (1905, p. 514) and Rachford (1905, pp. 348f.)

66. Mickle (1901, p. 13), Jones's old neurological teacher, noted: "I think we do not assign to dreaming states in disease all the importance they really possess, whether as symptoms, prodromic, or of the established malady; whether as modifying, enhancing, or precipitating scenes and acts in the morbid drama of delirium, or of insanity."

67. Ellis (1901a) reviewed *Ueber den Traum*, but makes no useful comments about *Die Traumdeutung*.

68. Sidis (1906, p. 101) mentions Freud's theories concerning the "analysis of the mechanism and interpretation of the meaning of dreams" and notes: "This mechanism of the dream is not by any means unique, for it is similar to what we observe in the various forms of the psychoneuroses, hysteria, etc.!"

69. Putnam has pluralized the noun, Jones substituted a very different one.

70. Although Jones (1959, p. 142) prided himself "in the art of accurate bibliographical work" there is sufficient evidence, here and elsewhere, to undermine his claim. Of the 30 citations in Jones's 1907 *JAP* paper a handful have no specific page references—"Traumbedeutung" being one of them—and there are several others which appear not to exist. See also Ellenberger's comments in Micale (1993, p. 61).

71. Although Edgar Jones (2010, pp. 376ff; 2014) has published a number of articles on Mott they tend to focus on Mott's War and postwar period.

72. Jones would have heard officially about the vacancy in early September 1907 (*Lancet*, September 7, 1907, p. 745) or earlier through Harry Campbell.

73. Freud originally believed Jones had studied psychoanalysis in Zurich and was, therefore, Jung's pupil but Jones contradicted him and Freud, having deferred to Jones's 'memory,' excised this statement from the history. Compare Paskauskas (1993, p. 281 and n.2.) with Freud (1914a, pp. 26–27 and 31) in which Jones does not appear until the Autumn of 1909!

74. While I am indebted to Gottfried Heuer for having originally drawn my attention to Gross's importance for Jones I am now inclinded to believe that Jones overplayed Gross's significance in order to diminish the importance of Jung. See, however, the recent and important study on Gross by Heuer (2016).

75. Beevor died on December 5, 1908 (*BMJ* December 12, 1908, pp. 1785–86).

76. Thomson (1903) said existing treatments for epilepsy should be supplemented with psychical methods which would encourage patients to control the inhibiting impulse and drew on Drs J. J. Putnam, White and Sidis.

77. Just over two years later Campbell Thomson (1910) delivered a paper to the Hampstead Division of the BMA in which he discussed "Freud's and other methods of treatment." Although Thomson and Jones dined together in November 1913 (Paskauskas 1993, p. 242n) nothing seems to have come of their meeting.

78. This may have been more complex than I have allowed because if the boy was a patient at the West End then Jones, as the Hospital's pathologist, might have been constrained by his seniors, Campbell or Savill, as to his presentation.

79. Jones (1911a, p. 123) makes a reference to a meeting of the Neurological Society on January 30, 1908 during which a number of doctors spoke about tics but "nothing new was brought out." This was not the case. See, for example, the comments by Head (1908, p. 44).

80. I have argued elsewhere (Kuhn 2014a, pp. 37–40) that Jones's 1908 Salzburg paper reveals only a limited knowledge of Freud's work.

Chapter 12

Montague David Eder

EDER'S EARLY MEDICAL CAREER

Montague David Eder (1865–1936) entered Bart's in October 1890, qualified B.Sc. in 1891 and MD in 1895. While at Bart's Eder made the acquaintance of an American post-graduate student, Dr William Conyers Herring (b. 1863), and, shortly afterward, Eder started a relationship with Herring's wife Florence (née Ida Murray, b.1866) who subsequently divorced her husband amicably in 1894. A checkered medical career followed as Eder and Mrs Herring moved first to Johannesburg, then Columbia and finally Bolivia.[1] Eder eventually returned full-time, to England, around 1905 where he set up medical practice with his cousin Dr Bernstein, at 55 Commercial Road, in the East End of London (*BMJ* December 15, 1906, p. 333; MD, 1905).[2] In early 1906 Eder took "up an appointment as a school medical officer in Poplar" (Thomson 2011, p. 67) and then enrolled for the Diploma of Public Health [DPH] at Weymouth's University Examination Postal Institution, in Southampton Street. Weymouth "ran an extensive business of coaching for medical examinations" and Jones (1959, p. 117), who had qualified DPH in 1903, was now coaching the course (Jones 1959, pp. 121–22).[3] This then was probably where Jones and Eder first met because Jones (1959, p. 137) recalls that while coaching he made "a number of friends . . . The closest of them was M. D. Eder, although he was one of the very few I was unable to get through his examination." As with most of Jones's claims there is no independent verification on this point.[4] However there is an extant letter from Eder to Jones confirming the two men already knew each other in late April 1906 and that the connection was through Weymouth's College. Technically speaking, therefore, Eder was Jones's pupil but only in respect of the DPH examination as we shall see, in respect of psychoanalysis.

By 1907 Eder, now estranged from Mrs Herring,[5] was in relationship with Mrs Edith Clara Guest (1872–1944), the estranged wife of Leslie Haden Guest (1877–1960).[6] At first Edith and her two sons moved into 46 Fitzroy Square (Kerr & Wallis 1907, Vol. 3, p. 116) with Eder before the four of them moved around the corner to 2 Charlotte Street. In a letter to Freud, dated July 1912, Jones claimed he had treated Mrs Herring "four years ago" (1908). But if this was the case then it would have been before Jones left for Canada; so the treatment was probably medical, maybe psychotherapeutical but certainly *not* psychoanalytical, as Jones implied. Jones also claimed, in that same letter, that Mrs Herring had "committed suicide when [Eder] left her and ran off with another man's wife" (Paskauskas 1993, p. 145). But this is also questionable because it seems as if Mrs Herring might still have been alive in 1911, a full four years *after* Eder and Edith started living together and two years *after* Eder and Edith married in late 1909, following Edith's divorce from Haden.[7] There are, however, a number of uncanny similarities between Eder and Jones, particularly during this early period when their medical and social lives intertwined through coincidences and shared networks. Both would subsequently prefer favoring their middle names, both were school MOs, Jones a quarter-time temporary local assistant MO (1905–1907) in South East London (Kuhn 2002, p. 351), Eder an MO working in Poplar and, presumably, in his spare time, at the Margaret McMillan Clinic—aka the London School Clinic for children—which was also based in the East End.[8] (Hobman 1945, pp. 73–74; Simkin 2013; Thomson 2011, p. 69; Jones, 1936, p. 296). Both men were also active in the Society for the Study of Disease in Children [SSDC], which Jones had joined in 1904: and both reviewed for its *Journal*, although Jones was by far the more prolific. Both men also knew Dr James Kerr, Chief MO of Education for the LCC and while Jones's relationship with Kerr was somewhat short-lived Eder subsequently collaborated with Kerr, first in organizing the Second International Congress of School Hygiene (Eder 1907b, c), and then in establishing *School Hygiene*, a monthly journal which first appeared in 1910 (Hobman 1945, p. 75).[9] Eder's and Jones's medical colleagueship also played out through their social lives because Jones (1959, p. 139) claimed it was "through Eder"[10] that he first met Louise [Loe] Dorothea Kann (1882–1944) with whom he lived for seven years. Loe was the rich daughter of a Dutch Jewish industrialist and she and Jones would routinely pass themselves off as man and wife (Paskauskas 1993, p. 96; Maddox 2006, pp. 66–67), which was was not dissimilar to Eder and Mrs Herring and then, for a time, Eder and Edith Guest. This digression has been necessary because even Thomson (2011, p. 62), in an otherwise important contribution to Eder scholarship, failed fully to confront the relationship between Eder and Jones even though he recognized that "it does not help that Ernest Jones, the man who shaped the archive and historical image of the early British psychoanalytic movement, had a strong personal interest in downplaying the role of Eder."[11] On the other hand many years later, perhaps when he thought his status finally secured, Jones (1959, pp. 137–38) chose to remember Eder with a certain fondness: He "had a heart of gold and serious concern for the future of socialism, so that I was doubly drawn to him." All of this makes Jones's *animus* against Eder all the more fascinating.

EDER'S FIRST DISCOVERING FREUD

In his paper to the Section of the 1913 BMA Annual Meeting in Brighton, Eder (1913c, p. 1214) claimed he "first came across Freud's work in 1905" but his "resistance [to Freud's sexual theory of the neuroses] was so strong that it was not until several years later, after further experiences in psychotherapy, that I could return to Freud's writings without prejudice." Given that the Eder archive is so sparse I can only speculate as to how Eder became interested in psychotherapy. Having found no obvious signs of a tradition of hypnotism at Bart's during the late 1880s and early 1890s, I have assumed, following Ethel Mannin (Thomson 2011, p. 66) that Eder discovered hypnotism and suggestion during his South American adventures in 1903 or 1904. This makes it plausible that Eder could have come across a reference to Freud in some of the early psychotherapeutic literature (e.g. Anon 1895; Schaffer 1895) not least because he was an active reader of the *BMJ* (e.g. Eder 1907a, 1911a) and also interested in psychology (Hobman 1945, p. 43) and sociology (Eder 1907d). There is even circumstantial evidence that Eder read the 1905 *BMJ* review of Löwenfeld's *Die psychischen Zwangserscheinungen* and this might have inspired him to investigate further. As Eder spent part of his school years in Frankfurt he "was unusually familiar with the German language" (Jones 1936b, p. 145; Hobman 1945, p. 34) and, therefore, quite capable of reading Freud in the original; something which Jones was probably unable to do much before late 1907 (Kuhn 2014a, p. 37).[12] Given his varied interests—he "was both shrewd and cultured" (Wilson 2009, p. 65)—Eder may also have heard discussions of Freud's work among his wide circle of friends; perhaps in the Fabian Society, where he met his first "psychoanalytic patient" (Hunter & MacAlpine 1953, p. 64); or in the Independent Labour Party;[13] or among those "radical" friends surrounding his cousin Israel Zangwill (1864–1926) or Zangwill's wife Edith Ayrton an activist in the women's suffrage movement. Or he may even have come across a reference to Freud through his interest in children's medicine, or school hygiene as it was also known, which suggests he may even have been familiar with the *Pedagogical Seminary*, founded and edited by Stanley Hall (1844–1924). Hall, was an early reader of Freud and, in fact, it was Hall who invited Freud to lecture at Clark University in September 1909. Eder could also have heard about Feud through meeting Dr. Maurice Eden Paul (1865–1944),[14] yet another of those buried links in the Freudian chains of transmission. Paul was a Dorset GP, a member of the Association and, being an active reviewer of foreign literature for the *JMS*, was familiar with contemporary German and French psychology. In fact Paul was particularly interested in children's medicine (i.e., Engel 1912) and, like Ellis, with whom he was in touch (Kurella 1911, p. vi), took a keen interest in "works on the psychology of the child," particularly German sexology. We know Freud sent Ellis (1939, p. 312) a copy of *Three Essays* shortly after its publication, in 1905, so it is quite possible that Ellis discussed Freud's book with Paul shortly thereafter. We also know that, around this time, Paul, with the active encouragement of Ellis (1907, p. 639), was working on a translation of Bloch (1907; 1908, pp. 413–14, 456, 464–65),[15] who had discussed Freud's work in general and his sexual theories in particular. And Paul was probably already familiar with Moll (1912, p. 14; Freud 1905) whose book he would soon translate. Eder's fragmentary memory from 1905 makes it just possible that the *Three Essays* may well have been the publication which both attracted and repelled him. But whatever his alleged early resistances to Freud's sexual theories Eder (1908, pp. 6 and 15) appears to have overcome them by the summer of 1908 because his pamphlet, *The Endowment of Motherhood*,[16] which was probably published in September (*BMJ*, 3 October 1908, p. 215), reveals that he had now started engaging with Freud's sexual theories even if only theoretically. Here are the two relevant passages:

> One of our leading neurologists, Professor S. Freud, points out our danger: "Concentrating our attention upon what is distinctive in nervous diseases, all the disastrous effects of civilisation can be essentially reduced to the harmful repression of the sexual life among civilised races (or classes) owing to the prevalent 'civilised' sex-morality."
>
> Little wonder that many medical authorities now regard all hysterical diseases, all neuroses, as grounded upon some sexual disturbance in childhood or puberty. This is the standpoint of Freud, Janet, Muthmann, and many other psychiatrists of the first standing. As Professor Freud aphorises it: "Without repressed sexual events, no hysteria."

The second reference to Muthmann and Freud's aphorism; '*Without repressed sexual events, no hysteria*' is, as we shall see shortly, an almost direct quote from the article, 'Professor Freud and Hysteria,' published in the *BMJ* in January 1908 (Anon 1908a, p. 103) which, perhaps, might suggest a precise moment when Eder first started seriously engaging with Freud's work.

EDER DISCOVERING PSYCHOANALYSIS

Although Eder leaves no indication as to how or when he first started using psychotherapy in his general medical practice there is an early autobiographical fragment which suggests he first started using psychoanalysis in May 1910; a date which coincides, among other things, with Hart's (1910b) paper to the BPS in Oxford. Eder claims that his psychoanalytic journey began when a 25-year-old man, an acquaintance from the Fabian Society, visited by appointment. Following a physical and psychological examination Eder (1911, p. 752) thought his patient's "pain of long standing which showed no physical sign . . . was hysterical in nature," so he told the man that "his pain was of nervous origin, that he was 'an interesting case of psychosexual inhibition'" and would benefit from "'a course of psycho-analysis.'" (Hunter & MacAlpine 1953, pp. 65, 64).[17] Eder began the treatment with a series of word-association tests which, it seems, he had already incorporated into his psychotherapeutic practice. Like other psychotherapists during this early period Eder, who had clearly already accepted the idea of the subconscious, would have needed little persuasion to see how "the application of the association method to *unconscious* mental processes" confirmed Freud's researches and offered the psychotherapist an important diagnostic tool with which to map and explore his patient's unconscious complexes. (Jung 1919, pp. v–vi). For his part Jones (1910e, p. 240), who probably only started s using the word-association test sytematically sometime in early 1909 subsequently claimed that his own

> experience has fully confirmed that of Jung and his pupils as to the great practical value of the word-association method in enabling one objectively to determine the nature of the mental conflicts in which psychoneurotic symptoms take their origin.

It seems, at first sight, as if Eder, like other British psychotherapists, might have discovered the word association tests through Jung and Riklin (1904) via Peterson's and Jung's (1907) *Brain* article and perhaps also through Peterson's BMA paper (1907a; 1907b). On the other hand the test words which Eder used in May 1910—although he did not published them until September 1911—bear a remarkable similarity to the test words which Jones (1910e, pp. 221–22) used in his early psychoanalytic practice but which he did not published until November 1910, suggesting a link which I might have failed to identify.

Having analyzed the results of the association tests Eder believed they revealed a number of phobias which he suspected had "some sexual basis" although he subsequently discovered "[t]he explanation was different" for one of them because he was able to trace it back to when his patient had fallen into a stream at the age of two and "[t]he fright had set up the fear of water."

As the psychoanalytic treatment progressed Eder began exploring his patient's homosexual and incestuous obsessions by reference not only to his patient's dreams but also to Freud's *Three Essays* which he had probably already read, in the original and therefore *before* Brill's 1910 translation.[18] As Eder noted: "The interpretation of the dreams and the word associations were the chief helps in the patient's analysis. Assistance was obtained by notes and observations about himself that he gave me." The treatment was "twice weekly for three months" with "each visit lasting an hour to an hour and a half." Eder (1911, p. 752) claimed that "there was at first an exacerbation of the patient's woes . . . [t]hese gradually ceased and the patient was cured of his difficulties." Many years later that same patient told Hunter and MacAlpine (1953, pp. 64 and 66) that he remembered how Eder had hypnotized him at the last session.

> 'Dr Eder was almost on top of me: I could feel his hands pressing on my head; although I do not know what actually happened while I was under, I know he must have been very close to me, because all the time I distinctly heard his pocket watch ticking.' (Hunter & MacAlpine 1953, p. 66)

The patient also subsequently revealed that during "the last session . . . it was suggested to him [under hypnosis] that he was cured; an incident which was found to have considerable significance for him." (Hunter & MacAlpine 1953, p. 64). He also remembered that although the fees for his treatment "amounted to only about two shilling per session it was a considerable expense" because he was "at that time earning a weekly wage of twenty-three shillings." He also recalled that when he asked to settle the bill "Dr Eder replied: 'As regards the account, if it makes your life more pleasurable (people seem to vary in this respect), why you shall have it . . . but you are under no obligation to pay this now or at any time.'" (Hunter & MacAlpine 1953, p. 64). Apparently buoyed by what he saw as his first psychoanalytic success Eder (1911, p. 752) now claimed he started treating men and women for a series of "troubles . . . which were clearly due to repressed wishes, mostly of a sex nature." If this was the case then it was unlikely to be through psychoanalysis, because as Eder himself claimed, in a subsequent talk, he had few opportunities for treating patients psychoanalytically especially in a working-class district where most patients could barely afford one visit to the doctor's let alone twenty-four.

INTERIM CONCLUSIONS

Reading Jones's contemporaneous publications strongly suggest that Jones did not discover Freud until September 1907 and that he only started practicing psychoanalysis seriously, after he emigrated to Canada in September 1908 (Kuhn 2014a, pp. 15–16). On the other hand Eder claims, in his contemporaneous publications, that he first heard about Freud in 1905, did not start engaging with Freud's work until around February 1908 and only started using psychoanalysis in May 1910. It is no longer possible, therefore, to accept Jones's (1936a, p. 143; 1936b, pp. 295–96) claims that he "gradually aroused Eder's interest in psycho-analysis, to which he sympathetically responded." The chronology also makes it highly unlikely that Jones and Eder would have had any meaningful discussions about Freud's work in the period between late November 1907, when Jones returned from his short trip to the Burghölzli, and late April 1908 when Jones effectively departed for the Continent prior to his emigration to Canada in September 1908. Although there still remains that short five months period, from December 1907 until April 1908, when Eder and Jones might have had the opportunity to discuss Freud's work there is evidence to suggest that Eder was probably abroad for most of that time (Hobman 1945, pp. 71–72).[19]

NOTES

1. See also Kuhn (2014b, pp. 193–94).
2. Although Jones (1959, p. 137) says Eder "ran a queer little practise in Soho among foreign waiters," this may well have been an under-hand dig given Eder's passionate commitment to socialism and "[t]he nationalization of the whole medical profession" (*BMJ*, December 15, 1906, p. 333).
3. Eder to Jones 30 April [1906] (BPAS P04-C-B-14). I am grateful to Rosie Musgrave for tracking down the Weymouth information.
4. After consulting the Bart's Student Signature Book (SBMS/S/1/3, p. 72), Kate Jarman, Deputy Archivist, Bart's Health NHS Trust (e-mail to pk, November 11, 2015) noted: "Some students at this date took less than five years to complete medical training and qualify MD, but this was not unusually long, and does not suggest any significant delay to [Eder's] studies." Eder's alleged exam problems did not prevent him passing the CEPM in 1914 thereby enabling him to join the Association.
5. I have found no evidence suggesting Eder and Mrs Herring were married.
6. L. H. Guest was a regular contributor to *The New Age* (August 15, 1907, pp. 253–54). See also *Light* (28 October 1911, p. 514). L. H. Guest would subsequently become a physician and LCC School's Inspector.
7. More to the point Jones may have projected onto Eder his fears that Loe Kann would commit suicide if he ended their relationship (Paskauskas 1993, p. 96).
8. The Clinic was formally opened on July 15, 1910 (*School Hygiene* 1910, Vol. 1, pp. 468–70).
9. Although Thomson (2011, p. 70) suggests Eder used the Magazine "as a vehicle to spread his growing enthusiasm for psychoanalysis, with articles from Ernest

Jones and other psychoanalysts," the evidence does not support this. Eder published articles by Jones and Pfister in 1910, to offer readers "some opportunity of arriving at an understanding and perhaps at a valuation of the methods [of psycho-analysis] so far as children are concerned." Those two articles were followed, in 1913!, with reviews of Jones (1913a) and Pfister's *Die Psychoanalytische Method* (*School Hygiene* 1913, Vol.4, pp. 56–57 and 238–39).

10. Maddox (2006, p. 47) says "Eder introduced [Jones] to Loe" but this is not quite what Jones says.

11. See also Turner (1995, p. 291).

12. Eder translated Freud's *Ueber den Traum* (1914), and Jung's *Diagnostische Assoziationsstudien* (1919). See also Steiner (1987, pp. 51–52).

13. The Medical Socialist Society (aka The Socialist Medical League) was inaugurated on June 25, 1908 under the chairmanship of Dr A Salter with Eder as secretary (*New Age* June 20, 1908, p. 150; *GP* July 4, 1908, p. 421).

14. Paul, was the son of Charles Kegan Paul, clergyman, publisher and author and of Agnes Colvile, novelist: born in Dorset, educated at University College School and the London Hospital where he worked as a house physician before qualifying MD (Brux) in 1891. Paul then worked for a time in various jobs in the far East before returning to England where he established himself as a GP in Parkstone, Dorset. He joined the Association in 1905, was a regular reviewer for the *JMS* (1907–1912), wrote for the *Open Review* and translated Bloch (1908) and Moll (1912). He was a prolific translator, during and after the War together with his wife Cedar, and the two of them are now forgotten figures in the early history.

15. Bloch was a Physician in Charlottenburg, Berlin, specialising in Diseases of the Skin and of the Sexual System. Paul's translation, which I discuss in Chapter 19, was first advertised in *The Lancet* (10 October 1908, p. 1118).

16. Hunt (1996, p. 139) suggests: "Endowment of motherhood in its most limited form" was a demand for "a maternity benefit for women while bearing and suckling children." She suggests Eder's pamphlet gave an "impetus for the debate within the Social Democratic Federation."

17. The patient said he decided to consult Eder because he had met him "'casually at lectures at the Fabian Society. I was attracted by his very interesting face, particularly after he shaved off his moustache'" (Hunter & MacAlpine 1953, pp. 64–65).

18. The *BMJ* offered an informative and positive review of Brill's translation of Freud's sexual theory: "Once Professor Freud's point of view is adopted, the facts fall into their proper place as matter deserving of careful study." (Anon 1911c, p. 1337).

19. A review of Jones (1913a), which points to its many "noteworthy omissions," says "Freud's important theory of sex is only briefly delineated, and even on the clinical side there is no account of the theory of hysteria, of obsessions, or paranoia" (Anon 1913a, p. 37).

Part V

DISSEMINATING THE WORKS OF FREUD

And I cannot refrain from one last quotation in which [McDougall] comments on the relation between the conscious and the subconscious. 'We must recognize' he writes, 'that the relations of subconscious operations to conscious thinking are in many cases so intimate, so much of the nature of participation in the working out of a single purpose, that any such division of the mind into two unlike parts, such as is commonly implied by names of the kind mentioned above, appears wholly unwarranted.' This is a reminder that many theorists on the subject would do well to heed. (*Mind* 1913, Vol. 22, pp. 583–84)

Chapter 13

The *British Medical Journal* 1904–1908

DISCUSSING FREUD

Within days of the death of Ernest Hart (1835–1898), in January 1898, the BMA's Journal and Finance Committee recommended Dawson Williams (1854–1928) as the new editor of the *BMJ* with Charles Taylor as his assistant (Bartrip 1990, p. 91). At the time the *BMJ* (June 11, 1898, p. 1536) had a print run in excess of 21,000 copies a week and, as Williams noted, "it forms the most effective link between our scattered members and Branches, while affording a means of intercommunication and of advancing the scientific work of the profession by bringing to its members the new discoveries, new theories, and new observations of clinical and pathological workers not only in the British Empire but throughout the world." Thirty years later Rolleston (1928),[1] the highly respected medical writer, historian and bibliographer (Anon 1944, p. 452f), said: "The power [Williams] gradually acquired of forming and directing a right medical opinion was very real, and the affectionate regard inspired by his upright character enabled him to obtain leading articles and signed reviews from prominent and busy members of the profession."[2] We have already seen how Williams helped steer and shape the "mind-healing" and psychotherapeutic debates particularly with the 'Special Issue'. In this chapter I will now examine how Williams, through the reviews and articles he published, and no doubt occasionally commissioned, helped steer and shape the British debates around psychoanalysis. This stands in stark contrast to the many silences carved out by *The Lancet*.

In late April 1904 the *BMJ* (30 April, p. 1060) carried a note under 'books received: "Zur Psychopathologie des Alltagslebens [Everyday Life], von Dr. Sigm. Freud. Berlin: S. Karger, and London: Williams and Norgate. 1904. 3s." Several months later there appeared a lengthy unsigned review of 'Everyday Life.'[3]

The severance of normal from morbid psychology has for long been maintained by the psychologists of the schools, who, for reasons into which it is unnecessary to enter here, have for the most part and—in no question more than in the great free-will controversy—tacitly ignored the bearing upon normal psychology of the phenomena of morbid mentality. That this separation, however, though of practical use, is arbitrary and essentially factitious, and that there is an unbroken continuity of phenomena and a fundamental conformity of law between these two apparently dissimilar bodies of knowledge, has been successfully urged by modern psychopathologists. The gap is being daily filled up by studies in degeneracy, criminal psychology, and kindred subjects; and, Professor Freud's interesting book on the *Psychopathology of Everyday Life* is a small contribution to the evidence for the fundamental solidarity of normal and morbid mental states. The subjects under investigation are occurrences apparently trivial, but, inasmuch as they throw light on obscure mental processes, of importance; occurrences which every one must have encountered, such as slips of pen and tongue, solecisms, and mistaken and apparently accidental actions. These incidents, in the main personal experiences of the author, are subjected to searching examination, and their mechanism explained. Throughout all these apparently accidental happenings, whether the forgetting of a proper name—the subject first discussed—the insertion of a wrong word in speaking or writing, or a mistake in conduct, any one of which may or may not be instantly recognized as faulty by the subject, accident or chance, the author maintains, has no place. 'I believe, indeed' he says, 'in external (real) accident but not in internal (psychic) chance.' He relates in detail numerous instances in illustration of his contention that all such mistakes are 'motived' subconsciously, and are generally related to a definite disturbing influence outside the intended action and connected thereto by some process of association. These views are ingeniously worked out at a length which here precludes a more detailed account. One of the most interesting chapters—the keystone, indeed, of the whole work—is, that on determinism and superstition, in which the results of the preceding chapters are summed up; and it is shown that the common characteristic, of all these phenomena is that they can be referred to incompletely suppressed psychical material which has become detached from consciousness without, however, being deprived of every possibility of expressing itself. Even the apparently random choice of a name or number is thus, he contends, subconsciously determined. He makes a suggestive comparison between this subconscious determination in the normal and the characteristic attribution by paranoiacs of extraordinary significance to unimportant details in the conduct of others. The category of the fortuitous, of unnecessitated motives, which the normal man predicates of part of his mental processes, is rejected by the paranoiac in the psychical processes of others; that is, Professor Freud says, he probably projects into the mental life of others what is present in his own subconsciousness; or, to put it otherwise, the nexus of determined action and thought, which in normal states remains unconscious or subconscious, rises in the paranoiac into the conscious field. This outwardly projected psychology is also for Professor Freud the cause of a large part of the mythological conceptions of the universe which, he affirms, still

> persist in the most modern forms of religion. This book deals with a fascinating subject, but it is rather the sidelight thrown on graver issues than the ingenuity displayed in elucidating everyday occurrences which make it noteworthy. (Anon 1904, pp. 691–92)

About a year later, in March 1905, Williams published 'The Phenomena of Obsessions,' being a review of Löwenfeld's *Die psychischen Zwangwserscheinungen* (the Mental Phenomena of Obsession).[4] In the course of very positive comments on Löwenfeld's work in general, and this current book in particular, the reviewer noted:

> In 1895 Freud [1895b] wrote an interesting paper in the *Neurologisches Centralblatt*, contending that the phenomena of obsession belong to two different neuroses, the compulsive-neuroses (*Zwangsneurosen*) and the phobo-neuroses (*Angstneurosen*), separable from the other neuroses by their different etiology; the phenomena of obsession in these classes having, for Freud, a particular connexion with an inhibition of normal sexual function, an accumulation of sexual energy and, in consequence, persistent impressions upon the subconscious field. Loewenfeld has been entirely unable to substantiate this, and allies himself with Kaan, Thomsen, Krafft-Ebing, Mendel, Donath, and many others in regarding these phenomena from the symptomatological point of view, as being of very varied origin, as occurring in the course of many forms of disease, neurasthenia, hysteria, epilepsy, etc., and therefore neither to be generalized under degeneration nor separated as exclusively distinct neuroses. (Anon 1905, p. 661)[5]

Despite, or maybe because of, these apparently negative comments concerning Freud's generalizations about the importance of the sexual function in the etiology of the neuroses,[6] this review marks an important juncture in the dissemination of Freud's writings because Löwenfeld's book, which was to become "the standard work" on obsessional neurosis (Freud 1909b, p. 221n), also contains the 'Mitteilung des Autors,' Freud's own communication concerning his "psychoanalytic Method [Methode]" being Freud's first account of his new psychoanalytic technique. There is circumstantial evidence that several British commentators, drawn to Löwenfeld's book, would have read Freud's contribution thereby enabling them to disseminate Freud's new "psychotherapeutic procedure." (Löwenfeld 1904, pp. 545–51; Freud 1904a, pp. 247–54; p. 249).[7]

Just over a year later, in June 1906, Williams published 'Expression of the Emotion in Disease,' and this review of Bleuler's *Affektivitat, Suggestibilität, Paranoia*,[8] contains a brief mention of Freud.

> Now, it is precisely on such controversial questions as these that careful observation of the expressions of the emotions in morbid disintegrations or alterations of the personality in the insane, hysterical, and neurasthenic is likely to shed

> much light. *In this field, Janet, Freud, Loewenfeld, and others have done distinguished work*, and to these names must be added that of Professor Bleuler of Zurich, whose small book on affectivity, suggestibility, and paranoia has lately appeared. (Anon 1906a, p. 1531, italics mine)

Bleuler's book, which "repeated Freud's theories" also discussed "the role of Freudian mechanisms in symptom formation." (Kerr 1994, p. 110 and 127) Then a couple of months later Williams published a review of Morton Prince's *The Dissociation of a Personality* (1906a/1908), which also made brief reference to Freud.

> Dr. Prince's observations throw considerable light on the mechanism of dream states, and further afford possible explanations of many other abnormal phenomena, such as hallucinations, fixed ideas, aboulia and obsessional states, already so ably investigated by Janet, Freud, and many others; phenomena occurring not only in the hysterical but in the insane, and in what Soukhanoff[9] has well termed the ideo-obsessive constitution. (Anon 1906c, p. 381)

In July 1907 *Brain*, the official Journal of the Neurological Society of London, edited by Henry Head, carried an article, coauthored by Peterson and Jung (1907a, p. 492), which discussed "the value of the so-called 'psycho-physical galvanic reflex' as a recorder of psychical changes in connection with sensory and psychical stimuli . . ." and offered some conclusions, from their joint researches, undertaken between January and March 1907, upon normal and insane individuals (*BMJ* 26 October 1907, p. 1175).[10] In the section "Association Experiments" Peterson and Jung (1907a, p. 526) concluded:

> it is extraordinarily common for the subjects to be unconscious of the complex disturbed by the stimulus-word, and to be unable to answer questions relating to it. It is then necessary to employ the psychoanalytic method, which Freud uses, for the investigation of dreams and hysteria. It would carry us too far to describe here the details of this method of analysis, and readers must be referred to *[Die Traumdeutung]*

This fairly unambiguous statement, which clearly indicates how Jung's word-association tests were to be considered a precursor-procedure to Freud's psychoanalytic method marks yet another critical moment in the dynamic of this story.

Shortly after this *Brain* publication Peterson, yet another forgotten figure in the dissemination of Freud's work,[11] addressed the Section of the 1907 BMA Annual Meeting in Exeter. In his paper, which he delivered shortly before Wood's paper on Hypnotism, Peterson (1907b, p. 804) spoke about his researches and, in particular, the galvanometer "as an instrument of precision in psycho-physical research." He claimed to have "demonstrated it to be a far more accurate instrument for recording physical changes associated with mental function than any apparatus heretofore employed, such as the plethysmograph, pneumograph, and the like." Although Peterson (1907b, p. 805) did not mention Freud by name he did discuss, in some detail, how he and Jung had used the galvanometer together with word-association tests to reveal unconscious complexes.[12]

> How far this method of study with galvanometer and word association may prove useful in attaining to a knowledge of hidden matters in the minds of neurasthenics, hysterics, the insane, and criminals, it is impossible to foresee; but that it is a new and valuable method of exploration in psychology is already beyond question.

Although Peterson's paper was reported in *The Lancet*, the *BMJ* simply noted that it "was listened to with great interest" but "evoked very little discussion." This cursory dismissal must have caused some upset because in October 1907 Williams published a very different version in which the anonymous reviewer, noted that Peterson's address "aroused great interest in the Section," and advised readers, who wanted to know more, to read the *Brain* article itself. Then Anon (1907b, p. 1175) continued:

> Perhaps the most interesting part of these investigations is concerned with the authors" association experiments in combination with galvanometrical tests. It will be remembered that since Galton, Wundt, and Kraepelin employed these simple association tests, which consist in presenting, orally or visually, words—as a rule substantives—to the test person, who must respond as quickly as possible with the first word which occurs to him. This method of psycho-analysis has undergone great development at the hands of Sommer, Ranschburg, and others, and has given valuable results. The employment of the galvanometer in these association experiments, however, undoubtedly endows them with additional value, and for this reason it may not be amiss to outline the main point of the authors' discussion of their results.

The article then continued:

> Freud has shown that in hysteria and obsessional states there are always certain hidden 'thought-complexes' associated with strong emotional tone which dominate the individual and decide the symptoms, powerful emotional associations, and constellations dwelling in the subconscious which had their origin in real life possibly years before, as Morton Prince in *The Dissociation of a Personality* has shown. Boris Sidis in his *Psycho-Pathological Researches* has called them 'resurrected moments.'[13]

And after raising questions associated with the Jung-Peterson experiments, Anon (1907b, p. 1176) concluded:

> It certainly appears as yet uncertain whether, as a means of discovering the underlying mechanism of mental disorders, the galvanometer will give information which cannot be more easily obtained by the ordinary psychoanalytic methods.

It is highly likely that a number of psychotherapists would have read this review and, as a result, were inspired to start incorporating the word-association test into their psychotherapeutic practices although, no doubt, without using the galvanometer. On the other hand the reviewer's comments concerning "this method of psychoanalysis" can also be read as a short-hand, increasingly used by psychotherapists, to describe those suggestive therapies which now incorporated the word-association test into their practice. It is important, therefore, to beware anachronistic interpretations framed through the *subsequent* "propagandism" of the Freud school. (Ellenberger 1994, pp. 539–40; Jones 1913a, p. 242; Jones 1923, pp. 40f) because despite Freud's contribution to Löwenfeld (1904a) there was, at this time, no uniformly accepted psychoanalytic procedure even among the early psychotherapeutic practitioners of psychoanalysis. The perceived complexity and difficulties of the free association technique, which took time and skill to master, meant that an increasing number of psychotherapists would find their way to psychoanalysis through the short-cut of Jung's word-association tests which, before long, were to become an integral part of the preparatory work for what most commentators would now understand as a psychoanalysis. The significance of the Peterson and Jung article and of Peterson's Exeter paper,[14] therefore can not be over-estimated.

The galvanometer, with its promise of "great precision" (Mayer, 2013, p. 212) also offered British psychiatrists, physiologists, pathologists, neurologists and psychologists, the prospect of establishing a bridgehead across what many considered to be that unbridgeable gulf between physiological and psychological medicine.[15] This particular reading can be traced, for example, through the contemporaneous writings of Drs. Shaw and Mott. Thomas Claye Shaw (1841–1927) has recently retired as Medical Superintendent at the London County Asylum, Banstead (Surrey) although he continued to lecture in Psychological Medicine at Bart's.[16] As President of the Section during the 1907 BMA Annual Meeting Shaw took a keen interest in Peterson's experiments, although from a physiological rather than a psychological point of view. In a paper, delivered a few weeks later, at the September 1907 Amsterdam Congress, Shaw (1907b, p. 1308) noted:

Simple change of idea did not cause any elevation in the curve, but when the idea was associated with emotion the result was manifest and immediate. To have got so far is, however, not enough. We want to know what are the conditions which make the cell discharge more suddenly, be less tolerant of tension.

Although the evidence remains sparse a subsequent publication suggests Shaw's interest in Peterson's talk probably served as a stepping stone for Shaw's interest in psychoanalysis. In his January 1911 Address to the North-London Medico-Chirurgical Society, subsequently published in *The Lancet*, Shaw (1911, p. 354) mentioned Freud's insistence on the importance of the "sexual element . . . in the mental life of the individual." And although Shaw thought "Freud's process is tedious and complicated" he nonetheless believed that it

brings out clearly two factors which did not previously receive the attention which they merited—viz., that much of what we feel, say, and do is determined by basic conditions which exist in a subconscious area and are therefore not at once perceived, either by the patient or by the examiner, as being vital to the true conception of the subjective position. It is these deep complexes which must be got at, and it is only after considerable practice and with much application that success can be achieved. Another thing upon which Freud insists, and the importance of it cannot be over-estimated, is the frequent presence of a sexual element in the subconscious area which is of the greatest possible influence as a disturbing factor. I have been much interested in finding how often a sexual element is discovered to be of the greatest importance in the history of a case where it was before examination either unsuspected or ignored.

This suggests, at the very least, that by 1911 Shaw was testing and maybe even using, psychoanalysis in his private and maybe even his Hospital practice. He may even have briefly discussed Freud with his students prior to his retiring from lecturing in 1909.[17]

Mott (1908, pp. 857–58) who was also present at Peterson's Exeter talk, was particularly interested in what Peterson had to say and like Shaw, thought Peterson's researches might serve to bridge physiological and psychological medicine.

Every thought tends to activation, and thoughts based upon the revival of memories of past experiences are more or less suffused with affective tone, according to the nature of the experience and the temperament of the individual. There will thus be a tendency to revival of the physical concomitants (emotions) of that affective tone. It does not require a delicate instrument to prove the truth of this statement. In many instances, for we know that the recollection (revival in consciousness) of a great sorrow or injustice will awake sometimes a more violent emotional discharge than actually occurred at the time it was experienced.

> The experiments of Féré, Tarchanoff, Veraguth, and Jung and Petersen [*sic*] tend to support this conclusion. . . . The inference is that the psychical change produces some physical change by which the current passes less readily, or more readily through the body. . . . Jung and Petersen [*sic*], who have repeated and elaborated the above experiments and applied the method of investigation to cases of dementia praecox, conclude that the change in resistance is due to the relative condition of secretory activity in the sweat glands.[18]

PROFESSOR FREUD AND HYSTERIA

Perhaps because of his astute knowledge of the medical world, Williams now invited one of those prominent and busy members of the profession to write an article on Freud which he then published, on January 11, 1908, under the heading 'Professor Freud and Hysteria.'

> For some time past a particularly interesting and lively controversy has been in progress concerning the teaching of Professor Sigmund Freud of Vienna on the etiology of hysteria, and more particularly as to the value of his method of psycho-analysis. (Anon 1908a)

The article noted how Freud's theories had been "rejected by Kraepelin" and "stigmatized by Bumke[19] as 'simply a horrible old wives' psychiatry,'" and Freud's "method of psychoanalysis" had been criticized by Aschaffenburg[20] "as 'in most cases incorrect, in many hazardous, and in all dispensable.'" On the other hand Freud's theories, "though perhaps not in their entirety" had "found warm adherents in Janet, Jung, Hellpach[21] and many others." There were also studies by Freud's followers, like Sadger and Muthmann,[22] supporting his theories. "In these circumstances . . . a brief outline of Professor Freud's views may not be out of place." Then following brief comments on Freud's work with Breuer, the anonymous author noted how Freud's views had "since undergone considerable development" because he now

> maintains that at the time of the original psychic trauma an adequate and fitting individual reaction was denied the subject, either through force of circumstances or by its voluntary suppression on the subject's part, and that as the consequence of this denied relief, and the voluntary suppression or displacement (*Verdrängung*) from the field of conscious mentality of the painful impression with its persistent affective colouring, these latter take on an independent, 'split-off,' subconscious existence, making their own hidden associations and resulting in a more or less fixed psychic dissociation.

According to Freud, and others, "this split-off complex is inaccessible to the waking consciousness, though it may be revived in hypnotic or hypnoidal states and may give the framework to dreams."

> Yet it has its outlets, nevertheless, in bodily form by means of what Freud calls 'conversion of the sum of excitation.' "The sum of excitation,' he says in his *Studien über Hysterie* 'which may not enter into psychical association, takes the wrong road, to bodily innervation all the more readily. The repression of the idea could only be due to an unpleasant feeling, to incompatibility between the idea to be repressed and the dominant ideational mass of the self. But the repressed idea avenges itself by becoming pathogenic.' In this transformation, then, of psychical excitement into persistent bodily symptoms, or, perhaps, better in a bodily compliance or undue facility of somatic outlet of repressed psychic processes, Freud finds the essential characteristic of hysteria as contrasted with other neuroses and psychoneuroses.

Freud believes that for "repression and conversion to come about there must be a native individual predisposition." Originally Freud "disallowed the necessity for any hereditary or constitutional factor, and declined to recognize Janet's '*affaiblissement de la faculté de synthèse psychologique*' in hysteria." More recently Freud

> has attached greater importance to the hereditary factor . . . and this is the most important point of his whole later teaching—this hereditary or constitutional factor takes the form in hysteria of the 'sexual constitution.' Not only in hysteria but in neurasthenia[23] and the obsessional and phobic psychoneuroses the disorder is rooted, he maintains, in disturbances of the sexual life. 'With a normal *vita sexualis* a neurosis is impossible.' Further, in hysteria, with which only we are concerned, the exciting moments are referred back to the childhood of the subjects. 'Without repressed sexual events of early childhood, no hysteria.' Here, then, is a frank return, though in sublimated form, to the fond conceptions of a thousand years ago, whose revival in cruder form than those of Freud's led, not so many years ago, to the frequent performance of öophorectomy[24] for the relief of purely hysterical symptoms.

The author claims that this "brief account" of "Freud's theoretical teaching" will help explain "the form which his method of diagnosis, or *Deutekünste*, published in 1905 [*sic*], must naturally take." This mistaken reference, which should have been to Freud (1904a) was, perhaps an unwitting reference to the *review* of Löwenfeld's book, published in March 1905! The author continues: Freud's method

> consists of an exhaustive interrogation of the patients as to the recollected events of their whole past life of the most intimate kind: of the search for subconscious thought-complexes by the study of reaction times to questions, lengthy reaction times being accepted as indices of strongly emotionally tinged complexes;[25] of the detailed recital of their dreams by the subjects, dreams being for Professor Freud a direct route to the subconscious; and also, by some of his followers,

> though this has lately been abandoned by Professor Freud himself, the revival of forgotten scenes under hypnosis. So exhaustive an investigation must needs take time, in fact Professor Freud states that a complete psycho-analysis of any case will take from six months to three years.

It was not, however, a question of time but "other, more obvious and certainly graver reasons."

> Although the patients are directed by Professor Freud to relate the incidents which come into their mind 'without selection,'[26] the whole trend of the interrogation is, as Professor Aschaffenburg pointed out in the article already mentioned, in one direction, and that a very undesirable one. Further, it is to be remembered that the whole therapeutic aim is the revival of repressed and long-forgotten sexual incidents and their assimilation by the waking consciousness in the hope of bringing about their adequate motor expression. How far this process of revival is likely to benefit the subjects we leave to others to imagine. It is evident from the foregoing that in these inquiries Professor Freud usurps the confessional, and that the therapeutic result, when obtained, is only the medical equivalent for absolution; and, though we earnestly wish to avoid any disparagement of the views of one whose psycho-pathological researches place him in the ranks of the most eminent, we cannot but agree with Professor Aschaffenburg that this method of psychoanalysis is 'in most cases incorrect, in many hazardous, and in all dispensable.' (Anon 1908a, p. 103–4)

A reader might, at first, instinctively focus on the author's explicit agreement with Aschaffenburg's condemnatory views as to Freud's sexual theories. On the other hand it is also important not to forget the wider context from within which this article was written, published and read because, through its sub-text, it also articulates a barely concealed anxiety that Freud's apparently modern ideas on hysteria, "though in sublimated form," now threatened a return "to the fond conceptions of a thousand years ago." This, at first, seemingly bizarre connection to the medieval witch-craze—which Freud had also originally made, albeit in private (Mason 1984, pp. 224–25)—touches a fear that Freud's procedure, which "usurps the confessional" and becomes "the medical equivalent for absolution," might feed into those wider debates concerning Faith and Spirit Healing. Concealed within these remarks, therefore, is the author's concern that one "of the most eminent" psychotherapists might end up summoning through the back door the very worst aspects of medieval religion. A few years later Ormerod (1911b, p. 693) articulated these same reservation although in more moderate terms.

> This curiously revives the old conception of the sexual origin of hysteria, and of the efficacy of the confessional; but in this novel confessional the doctor is the priest, listening to subjects of extremist privacy, while the penitent does not even

> know what he is about to confess, and his confession (a sceptic might add) may be purely the result of imagination or of suggestion received from without.[27]

Even the work of Freud and psychoanalysis were now being read in the lights of the faith and spirit healing deabtes. The following month, in early February 1908, Williams published "Hysteria and Dementia Praecox," a review of Janet's *The Major Symptoms of Hysteria* (1907) and of Jung's monograph *Ueber die Psychologie der Dementia praecox* (1907). Although the juxtaposition is significant—given Janet's influence on Jung—it will be sufficient to note the almost unreserved praise for Janet's book before turning to the comments on Jung's latest work which the reviewer saw as "another most suggestive and stimulating illustration of the benefits to be obtained by the application of modern methods of psychological analysis to psycho-pathological states." (Anon 1908b, p. 325) The author praised Jung's monograph as "a notable exposition of psycho-analytical methods, and one which throws much light upon many of the apparently inexplicable processes manifesting themselves in the symptom-complexes united under the category of dementia praecox." Then, following a brief résumé of Jung's book, including a reference to Freud's theory of "split-off thought complexes," the reviewer noted:

> In these chapters [Jung] follows and corroborates the work of Freud and others, and shows, in the same way that they have done in hysteria and dreams, that in dementia praecox there are severed complexes—which may be discovered by the method alluded to above—which live a more or less independent existence. The difference, however—and this is the main result of the fourth chapter and the pivot of his whole argument—is that whereas in hysteria the split-off complex is still susceptible, with proper treatment, of proper co-ordination with the other complexes of mentality, in dementia praecox the complex or complexes dominate the whole individuality, are fixed and inveterate. From this dominating complex the mind of a precocious dement never frees itself and improvement is only attained by the destruction of the complex, involving a permanent loss to the personality, or, expressed otherwise, recovery with defect. The cause of this radical distinction is yet to seek, but the author suggests that it may be found in the presence of metabolic or toxic alterations in the subjects of precocious dementia.[28] The lack of any argument in support of this suggestion is perhaps the only weak spot in a book which from the psychological standpoint is of outstanding merit. (Anon 1908b, p. 326)

Several months later, in September 1908, Williams published 'The Galvanometer and Subconscious Ideas.'

> In a subsequent article, dealing with a paper by Dr. C. G. Jung and Dr. Peterson, published in *Brain*, we alluded to the results obtained by the authors with the galvanometer in disclosing the 'subconscious thought complexes,'

whose existence Freud, Sommer,[29] Ranschburg,[30] and others claim to reveal by psycho-analytic means, mainly by reaction times to test words. There is, however, a considerable difference of opinion as to whether any such processes as subconscious ideas—that is, co-conscious processes of which the subject is unaware and which yet manifest themselves in intelligent action—ever exist at all. Professor Ziehen, for instance, scouts utterly the doctrine of subconscious processes, and it is still widely held that the so-called subconscious manifestations are the result of physiological—or, more straitly still, physical—processes, devoid of any ideal content or association whatever. To put the matter to the test, (Drs. Peterson and Prince [*sic*]) have carried out some experiments with the galvanometer in a case of multiple personality, which experiments are discussed and published in a recent number [June–July 1908] of the *Journal of Abnormal Psychology* (Anon 1908d, p. 943)[31]

Following a brief discussion of the Prince and Peterson (1908) article the Reviewer summarized their conclusions:

(1) That in certain pathological conditions, active, subconscious processes—that is, memories of some kind which do not enter into the conscious life of the individual, may exist. (2) Memories of conscious experiences which the subject cannot consciously recall—that is, for which he has amnesia—may be conserved and give rise to the same galvanic reactions which are obtained from conscious emotional states. (3) The reactions are compatible with, and, so far, confirmatory of the theory that these subconscious processes are psychical (co-conscious). (4) To explain these reactions by the theory of physiological reactions is possible, but far-fetched. (Anon 1908d, pp. 943–44)

FREUD ENTERED INTO THE DISCOURSE

Reading the *BMJ* between 1904 and 1908 reveals that even before Jones embarked upon his self-imposed exile to Canada in September 1908, there was already a growing awareness, among readers of the *BMJ*, of whom Jones was certainly one, that Freud and his psychological theories were of significance. But what this survey also reveals is that, by and large, the various *BMJ* reviews and articles were supportive, complimentary and informative. Even the Anonymous author of the January 11, 1908 article, who strongly objected to Freud's dogmatic insistence on the aetiological significance of sex, still acknowledged the importance of Freud's work and reviewed it, generally, in an open, if critical spirit. Although the *BMJ* articles and reviews were, no doubt, written by only a handful of aficionados or experts on medical psychology and psychotherapy, this should not obscure the fact that they were published in (probably) *the* most important British medical journal which, by late 1910, had a circulation rising to 25,500 (Bartrip 1990, pp. 184–85).

And while these articles and reviews may not have been closely followed by many *BMJ* readers they nonetheless would have received wide currency. As I have already suggested there is some evidence that Eder, for one, might have been influenced by them generally and by the January 11, 1908 article in particular. But a measure of the growing currency of Freud can also be found in the intellectual inquisitiveness of Joseph A Ormerod (1848–1925), the eminent Queen's Square neurologist, who took a very different attitude from his younger colleague Beevor. Ormerod (1911a, p. 1), in his November 1910 Presidential Address to the Neurological Section of the RSM was already sufficiently aware of the growing interest in Janet and Freud to have acknowledged to his audience that "some of you, I know, . . . have already studied these [striking] theories in detail" (Ormerod 1911a, p. 1). Less than four years later Ormerod (1914), then Registrar to the Royal College of Physicians, devoted his entire third Lumleian Lecture to a detailed and critical discussion of Freud which was then published in *The Lancet*. Reading Ormerod (1911b, p. 693) suggests that his deep and critical engagement with Freud's work probably began even before he wrote the 'Hysteria' entry for *A System of Medicine*. Ormerod, however, was just one example of this rapidly growing interest in Freud which is also rather nicely illustrated through two books reviews published in late 1909. In the first, from August, the reviewer of the 27th edition of *The Medical Annual*—"written for practitioners, students and especially post-graduate students"- noted, without comment, that "Freud's psycho-analytic method of treating hysteria is described" (*The Lancet*, August 17, 1909, p. 1118; MA 1909, pp. 376–79).[32] In the second, from October, a brief anonymous (1909c, p. 990) review of Professor C. S. Myers's recently published *Textbook of Experimental Psychology*, noted:

> The work of Jung and Peterson it is true is included in the bibliography, but the valuable results of word-pairing methods and the light which modern psychoanalysis throws on hidden and subconscious effective processes are nowhere discussed. Breuer is mentioned only in connexion with labyrinthine sensations, and we have looked vainly for the name of Freud.[33]

NOTES

1. Humphrey Rolleston (1862–1944) originally assisted Clifford Allbutt "[i]n the preparation of [Allbutt's] famous *System of Medicine*," which was first published in 8 Volumes (1896–1899) before Rolleston became co-editor for the second edition with 11 Volumes (1906–1911). Rolleston's obituarist claimed "[*System of Medicine*] still holds its place among the chief encyclopaedic medical works in the English language." Rolleston who gatherered many honours, including President of the Royal College of Physicians (1922–1926) was also a highly respected historian, writer, bibliographer and biographer (Anon 1944, p. 452f).

2. Despite Rolleston's comments all the Freud reviews and articles during this period were anonymous.

3. Kiell (1988) omits this review but notices Middlemiss (1904).

4. Bleuler, who was already interested in Freud, reviewed Löwenfeld's book in 1904 (Mason 1984, p. 461n).

5. The reference is to Löwenfeld (1904, pp. 318–19 and 294–98).

6. Reading contemporaneous articles reveals questions relating to sex were not nearly as tabooed as the Freudian myths assume. So Schofield said "Sexual excesses, both natural and unnatural, should be carefully inquired into and treated in neurasthenic cases. The treatment should be varied to suit the patient and not vice versâ. (*The Lancet* August 10, 1901, p. 389)

7. Löwenfeld's book (1904), also published in Glasgow, would have been relatively easy to obtain in Britain.

8. Halle a S., Carl Marhold 1906.

9. Serge Soukhanoff of Moscow University and contributor to the *Journal of Mental Pathology*. The reference is obscure.

10. Janet (1914, pp. 12–13) subsequently suggested Jung's word-association tests were a revival and an attempt "to use clinically an old experiment of the psychological laboratory." This probably also reflects the views of a number of British physiologists and psychologists who understood the Peterson-Jung association experiments in the context of the association researches being conducted in European laboratories of experimental psychology (See Akavia 2013, p. 75n; Jung 1905b, p. 224). Brown (1924, p. 145; 1936) says something similar when he says: the "well-known association test, first suggested by Sir Francis Galton and developed by C. G. Jung . . ." See also the comments by Mott below.

11. It was Peterson who advised his student Brill (1939, pp. 318–19n.) to go and study "the Freud work in Zurich."

12. "In many cases word associations were used." (Peterson 1907a, p. 449).

13. According to Mitchell (1911b, p. 340) Sidis was influenced by Janet and then McDougall (1908, p. 243).

14. A close reading of Forsyth (1913, p. 14) suggests he might have started his psychoanalytic journey during the Exeter BMA Annual Meeting where he delivered 'The Relations between the Thyroid and the Parathyrold Glands,' to the section on pathology. (*BMJ* July 20, 1907). I discuss Forsyth in Chapter 15.

15. In relation to this point see Hart (1908c, pp. 479–80).

16. Shaw also delivered the 1909 Harveian Society Lecture.

17. I am grateful to Kate Jarman, Deputy Archivist, Bart's Health NHS Trust for information concerning Shaw's course on Psychological Medicine (Jarman to pk, June 10, 2014).

18. Although Mitchell (1938, p. 182) erroneously refers to the early BPS as "an association of Academic Psychologists," Mott and other physicians were also early members (Edgell 1947, p. 115). Pear (1941, pp. 7ff and 11–12; also 21) suggests it was only after the War that psychotherapists and psychoanalysts became detached "from the field of general psychology" thereby effectively ignoring "the antecedent labours of [psychologists]." While J.C. Flügel was "a notable exception," most British psychoanalysts effectively ignored the works of McDougall, C. S. Myers, Rivers,

Stout and Ward. There is an interesting note of a quarterly meeting of the Association on February 23, 1909 when "Dr. Rivers [a member of the Association since 1893] had been, kind enough to offer to show any members over his laboratory, and display his various apparatus for conducting psychological experiments." Drs Rivers and Myers [who was not a member of the Association] then showed "a number of pieces of apparatus." (*JMS* 1909, Vol. 55, p. 392). C.S Myers was a member of the SPR, in 1913, as was G. F. Stout.

19. Oswald Bumke (1877–1950) German psychiatrist and neurologist.

20. Gustav Aschaffenburg (1866–1944) professor of psychiatry and neurology in Heidelberg.

21. Willy Hellpach (1877–1955).

22. Probably a reference to Arthur Muthmann's recent book (1907) which Freud praised as "good, fine case histories, excellent cures, dignified and modest; I have hopes that the man will become a staunch collaborator." (McGuire 1974, p. 64).

23. Taylor (1911, p. 1245) says "unqualified specialists" claiming to be able to treat venereal diseases "hid their real character by only advertising remedies for 'loss of manly vigour or 'neurasthenia.'"

24. Removal of the ovaries.

25. Richet's experiments in reaction times with subjects under hypnosis were already being studied in early twentieth-century Britain—"By reaction time I mean the interval between the application of a sense stimulus and the external sign caused by it." (Bolus 1903, p. 378). There was also the work of Stephen Hall (unidentified) and Dr. H. J. Watt, lecturer on psychology in the University of Glasgow (LHSA, GD15/1/13, March 19, 1909).

26. This suggests the anonymous author had in mind Freud's contribution (1904, p. 251) to Löwenfeld's book (1904, p. 547) while his earlier reference to "reaction times to questions" suggests, like many of his contemporaries, he also had Jung's association work in mind.

27. Jung (1931, p. 7338) noted: "The first beginnings of all analytical treatment of the soul are to be found in its prototype, the confessional. Since, however, the two have no direct causal connection, but rather grow from a common irrational psychic root, it is difficult for an outsider to see at once the relation between the groundwork of psychoanalysis and the religious institution of the confessional." I am grateful to Melanie Rein for drawing this to my attention.

28. I explore this point in Kuhn (2000).

29. Robert Sommer (1864–1937) professor of psychiatry at Giessen University and a founder, in 1904, of the Gesellschaft für experimentelle Psychologie. He may have taught Tom Pear.

30. Paul Ranschburg (1870–1945) head of the Medico-Pedagogic institute of Budapest. The reference may be to Ranschburg & Hajós (1897).

31. This was only the third reference to *JAP* in the *BMJ*. This changed dramatically from around 1910 when, as we shall see, *JAP* was to become another important conduit for the dissemination of Freud's work into Britain.

32. The article in question is 'Hysteria,' by Purves Stewart (1909). The following year Pierce & Kemp (1910, pp. 448–50; 1911) began their detailed discussion of psychoanalysis by quoting "extracts from the able summary of the subject by Ernest

Jones." The following year their revised entry took account of new developments. Although Hart (1940, p. 1154) suggests "[f]or a long period . . . [Devine] was responsible for the psychiatric sections" of the *Medical Annual* I have found no evidence for this and suspect Hart probably had in mind the postwar *Journal of Neurology and Psychopathology* (Wittenberger & Tögel 1999, p. 220).

33. The reviewer remained unimpressed with the reasons Myers (1909, p. vi) gave for his exclusions: "That owing to unsatisfactory methods and insufficient knowledge of subconscious and abnormal states, these subjects are as yet too controversial in character to come well within the scope of an elementary textbook."

Chapter 14

The *Journal of Mental Science* 1898–1911

THE HAVELOCK ELLIS REVIEWS (1898–1908)

The Association of Medical Officers of Asylums and Hospitals for the Insane [the Association] was founded in 1841. In 1854 Association members established their own 'House Journal', the *Asylum Journal of Mental Science*, and appointed John Charles Bucknill (1817–1897) its editor.[1] In 1861 Bucknill rechristened it *The Journal of Mental Science* [*JMS*][2] and, following his retirement (probably in 1863), all subsequent issues carried an extract from Bucknill's original preamble: "We profess that we cultivate in our pages mental science of a particular kind, namely such mental science as appertains to medical men who are engaged in the treatment of the insane." For most of this period under review the *JMS* was co-edited by Henry Rayner (St. Thomas's Hospital, London), A. R. Urquhart (James Murray's Royal Asylum, Perth), and Conolly Norman (Richmond Asylum, Dublin),[3] thereby indicating its British rather than English reach. Following Norman's illness and untimely death (1852–1908), his post was filled by James Chambers (1853–1938), Medical Superintendent, The Priory, Roehampton. Although the Association changed its name in 1865 to the Medico-Psychological Association, it retained its roots in the asylum system and only admitted, as members, those who were professional practitioners in the treatment of the insane *and* had passed the Certificate of Efficiency in Psychological Medicine [CEPM] (Anon 1896, p. 590).[4] By the turn of the century many of the doctors working in the Asylum, as well as the many British hospitals specialising in the treatment of functional nervous diseases were likely to be members of the Association[5] and therefore regular subscribers to the *JMS* which contained a mixture of Association business, original articles, book reviews and epitomes of current English and foreign literature. The *JMS* was, therefore, an important conduit for the transmission of news and information for the vast majority of medical men, and women,[6] engaged in the treatment of mental illness according to the principles of psychological medicine.

Although Havelock Ellis (1859–1939) never worked in an Asylum, nor a hospital for nervous diseases and, so far as I can tell, was never a member of the Association, he was nonetheless a regular and prodigious *JMS* reviewer, a role he probably assumed through his friendship with Hack Tuke (1817–1895) who had become joint editor in 1880 (Grosskurth 1985, p. 180).[7] By the mid 1890s Ellis had already established his significant European reputation as an expert in criminal anthropology, sexology and insanity and, as an omnivorous reader, was equally familiar with the English, Italian, French and German literature. In his tribute to Freud, probably written shortly before his own death in 1939, Ellis (1939, p. 311) said: "It was natural . . . that I should have obtained [*Studies on Hysteria*] on publication and found it of great interest." He also claimed, with good justification, that he had "recognized [Freud's] importance [from the very] first."

> It has always been a satisfaction to me that [my *Studies in the Psychology of Sex*] was the first book in the English language in which Freud's name was introduced and his work (in its immature stage) expounded. It was evidently also a satisfaction to Freud himself to receive this early recognition. He entered into correspondence with me and sent me his books as they appeared: the friendly relations thus set up continued unbroken, although my attitude was always somewhat critical. (Ellis 1939, p. 312)

Apart from having seriously misreading Ellis's *Studies* (1900a, b; 1905), Jones also completely censored out any references to the *JMS*, from his published writings, until, that is, Jones delivered his Maudsley Bequest Lecture to the Association in 1953. Jones simply wrote Ellis and the *JMS* out of the early history.[8]

In an unsigned review from October 1898, but almost certainly written by Ellis,[9] the author discusses Felix Gattel's *Ueber die Sexuellen Ursachen der Neurasthenie und Angstneurose*. In a passage, much along the lines of Ellis's contemporaneous article in the *Alienist and Neurologist* (1898a; 1898b), the author notes "the remarkable investigations of Breuer and Freud" and that Gattel, "much impressed by Breuer's and Freud's results," had tried to discover the extent to which the sexual history of a number of patients played a part in their nervous disorders. But Ellis (1898c, pp. 851 and 852) remained unconvinced by Gattel's findings.[10] In April 1901 Ellis, having returned to writing under his own name, offered a positive but critical review of *Ueber den Traum* (Ellis 1901a).[11] Five years later, in April 1906, and only a few months after its publication, Ellis reviewed *Bruchstück einer*

Hysterie-Analyse, the so-called Dora Case, in which he noted that even now, ten years later, he still considered *Studies* "an epoch-marking book in the history of hysteria." Ellis (1906, p. 407) was of course aware that Freud had since then "very considerably developed the technique of his analytical process," and had abandoned hypnosis. He was also clearly impressed with Freud's new work because while "a cautious and critical reader" might view it "with suspicion" the clues Freud draws "prove such excellent guides that one hesitates to condemn them on account of their extreme tenuity." Ellis, who had clearly also read *Die Traumdeutung* although, so far as I know, never reviewed it, informed his readers of Freud's insistence on the "very great importance" of dreams "in the interpretation, not only of hysteria, but of all allied psycho-neurotic conditions; without a study of dream-life, indeed, [Freud] believes we can make very little progress in this field." Ellis thought some readers would probably find the Dora case study "unsatisfactory, trivial and unwholesome" but in that case, he ventured, they were like "the little girl who criticized the operations of the Divine mind with the remark that 'it must be fiddling work making flies.'" And Ellis concluded: "People of this mental type cannot . . . be advised to study hysteria." In January 1907 Ellis reviewed Freud's *Sammlung Kleiner Schriften zur Neurosenlehre* "an admirable introduction to Freud's work" which revealed the changes Freud's thinking had undergone during the past fourteen years. And having discussed some of those changes, Ellis (1907a, p. 173) concluded: "Freud's style is always clear, attractive, and sincere, and his book is well worth the perusal of all who desire to become acquainted with the work of one of the subtlest and most original investigators in a difficult field." Several months later, in October 1907, Ellis (1907c, p. 834) reviewed the second edition of Freud's *Psycho-pathology of Everyday Life*[12] as well as 'The Value of Freud's Psycho-analytic Method' by Isidor Sadger (1867–1942), a long time exponent of "Freud's doctrines and "perhaps the ablest and the most enthusiastic of Freud's pupils." (1907d).[13] And finally, for this survey, Ellis (1908a, p. 588), in reviewing "Freud's Doctrine of the Sexual Aetiology of Neuroses," noted that although Friedländer was complimentary about some of Freud's work, he remained critical of Freud's view that the psychic traumatism is "always sexual."

It is of course impossible to know how many *JMS* readers would have noted, let alone read, Ellis's reviews, but we can be pretty certain their number dwarfed those handful who might have acquired a copy of Ellis's *Studies in the Psychology of Sex* because that book, with its detailed discussion of Breuer and Freud's "really important contribution to our knowledge of hysteria" (Ellis, 1901b, pp.149ff), had been seized by the Watford police, shortly after its publication in late 1899, and all copies destroyed by order of the magistrates (*WO* January 6, 1900).[14] Although we can only speculate as to the likely impact of Ellis's Freud reviews there can be little doubt that Ellis was held in high regard during this period and that his work, including his *JMS* reviews which continued for many years, commanded attention.[15] But Ellis, apart from being an important early disseminators of Freud's work, was also a significant, if understated cultural figure who helped shape and influence a general climate of changing opinions not just through his writings about the significant developments in psychological medicine taking place in Vienna, Paris and Italy, but also through his many personal contacts including with Tuckey, Bryan and Eden Paul.

THE BERNARD HART REVIEWS: (1905–1911)

Bernard Hart (1879–1966) was also, for a time, a prolific *JMS* contributor having some forty reviews published between 1905 and 1911. At first Hart concentrated on the French literature, particularly the works of the French School of psychopathology and then more specifically on Pierre Janet (Cameron & Forrester 1999, p. 68).[16] By early spring 1908 Hart (1908d; 1908e) had clearly mastered German sufficiently because he now started reviewing its literature, and, as the content of his reviews reveal, he also started taking a strong interest in the works of Jung and the Zurich School for which he clearly had some admiration. It may well have been this early interest which prompted him to travel to Europe, in the spring of 1908, during which time he probably visited Kraepelin's Clinic in Munich, Freud in Vienna and Jung at the Burghölzli. (Paskauskas 1993, p. 2).[17] Hart's intellectual journey from 'Paris' to 'Munich' to 'Zurich' and then from 'Zurich' to 'Vienna' mirrors, more or less, the intellectual journeys, if not the physical journies, undertaken, around this time, by a number of others like Jones, Eder, Devine and Middlemiss (1879–1954).[18] In his July 1908 review of Jung's *The Psychology of Dementia Praecox* (1907) Hart (1908d, pp. 584–85) praises Jung's "work on associations, which are of such importance as to practically revolutionise many of the older theories." And while clearly recognizing Freud's significance for Jung's investigations Hart also believed "the validity of Jung's work is by no means entirely dependent upon that of Freud." Hart's deepening knowledge and growing, if critical, appreciation of Freud's work, and of its wider significance, particularly for medical psychology generally, becomes manifest in his essay 'A Philosophy of Psychiatry,' published in the July 1908 *JMS*. In this carefully reasoned paper Hart (1908c, pp. 485–86) lays out the arguments for a clear delineation between the studies of the brain (physiology) and of the mind (psychology) while also arguing for the acceptance of "the concept of the 'subconscious,'" which he believes to be "a most potent weapon in enabling us to comprehend abnormal mental phenomena." Hart (1908c, pp. 483 & 476) now believed that anybody interested in mental illness, be they psychologist, psychiatrist or alienist, would, from now on, have to engage in a rigorous scientific investigation of the concept of the subconscious as "a mind fact" much in the same way as physiologists or pathologists studied the brain. Only through "the principles, methods, and aims of modern science" could psychologists ever hope to become proficient in the theoretical and practical applications of their subject. In the course of his essay Hart (1908c, p. 487) is critical of Kraepelin's methodology, which he thought had "[t]he essential disadvantage . . . [of] the more or less unconscious tendency to make the patient fit the disease" On the other hand Hart (1908c, pp. 489–90) praised "the strictly psychological researches of Janet, [and] those of Jung and the Zürich school," and stressed the need for a far more rigorous investigation and defense of psychotherapy which, he acknowledged, "is still in a nebulous stage."

> In the hands of men like Janet, Freud, and Jung, psycho-therapy has been rationalised to a certain extent and systematically employed with the most striking results. The classification of cases adopted in the best English asylums, the endeavour to segregate the curable from the incurable, and to provide the patients with a cheerful and stimulating environment, is another example of this same method. As a science it is still in its infancy, but that a vast field of potent therapeutics is now opening before us in this direction cannot be doubted by any impartial observer.

"A Philosophy of Psychiatry" was the first of five philosophical, theoretical and historical essays [the five essays] which Hart published in various journals between 1908 and 1911. The others were: "The Conception of the Subconscious," published in the February–March 1910 issue of *JAP*; 'The Psychology of Freud and His School', published in the July 1910 issue of *JMS*; 'Freud's Conception of Hysteria,' published in the January 1911 issue of *Brain*;[19] and finally 'The Psychological Conception of Insanity,'' published in the 1911 issue of *Archives* which appeared alongside Jones's "A Review" (1911a) and a psychological paper by Hart's Long Grove colleague Barham (1911). And then a year later Hart (1912b) published his book *The Psychology of Insanity*. This brief listing of titles offers a flavor of the depth and breadth of Hart's early engagement with the new developments in psychotherapy and reveals the extent to which he recognized the significance of Freud. But Hart (1912, pp.vi-vii) is also important because of the way in which he sought to situate the new Freudian psychology not just in its broader psychotherapeutic setting but also in its philosophical, theoretical and historical contexts. But there is, however, also evidence which strongly suggests that many of Hart's ideas penetrated into the writings of his contemporaries, and that even Jones, for a time, fell under Hart's spell and from which he then found it difficult to extricate himself. So, for example, Freud told Jones, in April 1910, that he had just read Hart's (1910a) paper on the 'Subconscious' which was "the best on the damned topic of the Unconscious I had read in the last years and enormously superior to Morton Prince's trash" (Paskauskas 1993, p. 51). But Jones failed to embrace Hart's critical researches and wide ranging spirit of enquiry because he distrusted Hart's fierce empirical independence and, at the same time, feared that Hart's growing intellectual stature might threaten his (Jones's) own precarious status as Freud's English *nuncio*. And this, in turn, would then undermine Jones's determination "not only to direct the external side of the [psycho-analytic] movement, but also to coordinate the internal, scientific side." (Paskauskas 1993, p. 340). Jones was clearly ruffled when Hart told him that while he was "definitely prejudicial in favour of Freud" he was not "prepared to substitute [Freud] for the Bible of my early youth."[20] John Forrester thought Jones's interchange with Freud over Hart's essay was

> a key moment when Jones [was] trying to assert his position over another competitor. I formed the view that Hart, Jones and Eder were the English that Freud looked to, for very different forms of support and 'linkage', and that Jones needed to win those fraternal battles, and saw this very early on.[21]

I think that it was perhaps this combination of jealousy and threat which impelled Jones (1959, pp. 238–40) to side-line Hart first from the LPAS, then from the BPAs and finally to effectively write him out of the early history.[22] As with the reassesment of Jones's relationship with Eder this brief chronology now also undermines another of Jones's claims; that Hart was one of his "most illustrious students." (Robinson 2013, p. 182n). But, as we shall also see in Chapters 15 and 17, Hart's role in disseminating Freud's work went far beyond his writings.

SOME CONCLUSIONS

The reviews of Ellis and Hart, which echo and complement the concurrent reviews and debates in the *BMJ*, suggest that even by the end of 1908 there would have been a significant number of medical psychologists, many of whom also read the *BMJ*, who, at the very least, would have known something about Freud and Jung and of the significance of their work, irrespective of any prejudices they might have held on the matter. Thus by early 1909 there would have been a small but significant number of non-German speakers who, having read all the available English language texts, would have been keen to read more. It is against this background that Brill's authorized translations appear in quick succession: *Freud's Selected Papers on Hysteria and Other Psychoneuroses* which was enlarged and re-issued three years later (Freud 1909a; 1912c);

the *Three Contributions to The Sexual Theory* (Freud 1910b);[23] and finally, *The Interpretation of Dreams* (Freud 1913). But there was also Brill's (1913) exposition of Freud's work;[24] Jones's *Papers* (1913a) and Hitschmann's (1913) book on Freud to say nothing of those other significant translations including Peterson and Brill's *The Psychology of Dementia Praecox* (Jung 1909b) as well as Eder's translation of *On Dreams* (Freud's 1914a). Paul Roazen (1992, pp. 380–81; 2006, p. 390), for one, has noted how Brill's translations were heavily criticized over the years, especially by Jones.[25] But as Jones was closely involved with their production his subsequent criticisms were probably more on 'political' than linguistic grounds (Steiner 1987, pp. 59–60). And then with the publication of the *Standard Edition*, Brill's translations were all but disappeared, at least in Britain. And yet their being written out of the history should not conceal their full significance because with the growing interest in Freud they were to become a crucial catalyst for the further dissemination of his writings (Ormerod 1914, p. 1299, Steiner 1987, pp. 70f). This point is rather nicely illustrated by two reviews. The first being of Brill's translation of the *Selected Papers*: "There can be no doubt that they will meet with the grateful recognition they deserve" (*BMJ* December 18, 1909, p. 1756). The second; being Barham's *JMS* review of Brill's 1913 exposition of Freud's views on psychology: "To Dr Brill we are already indebted for placing some of Freud's own writings within the reach of those, in England and America, who are unable to read these works in the original German." (Barham 1913, p. 666).[26]

NOTES

1. Bucknill was a co-founder of *Brain* in 1878.
2. Volume 7 records the change.
3. Edwin Goodhall was also briefly co-editor of *JMS*.
4. See also *BMJ* (September 9, 1911, p. 574).
5. Although there were many neurologists who had more than a passing interest in psychological medicine—J. Mitchell Clarke, H. C. Bastian, E. F. Buzzard, S. K. A. Wilson, A. Turner and Purves Stewart—they were members of the Neurological Society which, at the time, was considered far more prestigious than the Association. Jones, who was never a member of the Association, was however elected one of its Honorary Members in 1935 (Paskauskas 1993, p. 738; Jones 1954a, p. 198). This may help explain why Jones effectively ignored the *JMS* and the Association.
6. There were a significant number of women members of the Association, for example Helen Boyle, medical director of the Lady Chichester Hospital in Brighton: Adèle De Steiger who joined in 1901, Kathleen Dillon in 1909, Constance Robertson in 1905 ,Emily Dove in 1897, Laura Davies in 1914, and Winifred Muirhead in 1908, to name just a few.

7. Ellis's long articles, 'Criminal Anthropology' and 'The Influence of Sex in Insanity' are in Tuke (1892, Vol. 1, pp. 288–92; Vol. 2, pp. 1152–56).

8. Jones probably only started reading *JMS* after he returned to London in 1913 (Paskauskas 1993, p. 246).

9. The editors were happy for Ellis not to sign his name because, at that moment, his book, *Sexual Inversion* (1897), was implicated in George Bedborough's prosecution for selling indecent literature (Grosskurth 1985, pp. 193ff).

10. On Gattel's book see the ambivalent comments by Freud (Masson 1984, pp. 297 and 314). On Gattel's work in general see Macmillan (1997, pp. 226–27 and 634–35).

11. *On Dreams* was listed under books received by *The Lancet* (February 16, 1901, p. 522) but not reviewed.

12. First published 1901 in *Monatsschr. Psychiat. Neurolog.* then as a book in 1904.

13. This comment was made in the context of Ellis's review of Magnus Hirschfeld's *Jahrbuch für Sexuelle Zwischenstufen* where Ellis (1908b, p. 754) also makes a brief mention of Freud's theories.

14. Tuckey (1903c, p. 703) was one of probably only two British physicians to cite Ellis's book; the other being J. Barker Smith, an old student friend of Ellis's (*GP* February 6, 1904, p. 81).

15. Raitt (2004, pp. 67–68) is one of the few commentators to have noted the "approving reviews, often by Ellis."

16. Hart (1910a, p. 370) says: "But whatever the ultimate verdict on these theories may be, Janet's indestructible monument will always be his vindication of the psychological method, his demonstration of the phenomena of dissociation, and a description of the facts of hysteria which has never been excelled in the history of psychiatry." See also Hart (1927, p. 32).

17. Although Jones confirms Hart was in Munich on May 13, 1908 the rest of Hart's itinerary is speculative and based upon his obituary (Anon 1966).

18. James Ernest Middlemiss was born in Bradford, the eldest son of a photographic apparatus manufacturer and was educated in London before he joined the Association in 1910.

19. As Hart's essay appeared alongside Ormerod's 'Two Theories of Hysteria' (1911c) and Wilson's 'Some Modern French Conceptions of Hysteria' (1911) it would have been widely read thereby further helping to disseminate Freud's work.

20. Bernard Hart to Ernest Jones, November 6, 1910 (BPAS, PO4-C-G-02, p. 1).

21. John Forrester to pk (e-mail August 18, 2013).

22. See also W. Clifford M. Scott to R. Steiner, September 2, 1994 (BPAS, P28-A-01).

23. *The Lancet* (May 21, 1910, p. 1424) said Freud's work "was comparatively unknown in this country" but Brill's translation "will no doubt serve to give [it] an impetus . . . in England and America."

24. Brill was also co-translator, with Peterson, of Jung's *The Psychology of Dementia Praecox* (1909b).

25. “There is no need for me to stigmatize Brill’s translations; others have done so freely enough” (Jones 1955, p. 50).

26. In reviewing Vol. 1 of Freud’s *Collected Papers* (1924a; 1924b), edited by Jones and with the translation supervised by Joan Riviere, Mapother (1925, p. 181), challenged Jones’s claims that Freud’s work “‘should for years . . . [have] remained buried in a foreign tongue,’” by noting: “This remark does not seem particularly applicable to the present volume [as] most of its contents have for long been available in English since their publication in the ‘Nervous and Mental [Disease] Monograph Series,’ and are familiar to all seriously engaged in the study of neuroses.” The JNMD series was edited by Smith Ely Jelliffe & Wm. A. White. For a discussion of the series and of the significance of Brill see Meynell (1981, pp. 306ff) & Roazen (2006).

Chapter 15

Some Early Practitioners of Psychoanalysis

BERNARD HART AND THE LONG GROVE PSYCHIATRISTS (1907–1912)

Following the 1888 Local Government Act, responsibility for the care of pauper lunatics and the management of the County Asylums was transferred to the jurisdiction of the newly formed County and Borough councils. As a result the new County of London Authority [LCC] took responsibility for five of the six lunatic asylums on the outskirts of London, including Colney Hatch and Cane Hill (Commissioners 1914, pp. 7–8). On July 1, 1889, the LCC, through its Asylums Committee, embarked upon an extensive programme of refurbishing, rebuilding and building to create a modern system of mental asylums around London.[1] The first, at Claybury, in Essex, was an existing site with the old mansion redesigned and rebuilt to accommodate all the latest thinking in the care and treatment of the insane, including electric lighting, smaller wards and increased numbers of nursing staff. Dr. Robert Jones (1857–1943),[2] its first Medical Superintendent, noted:

> it is hoped that the success of this experiment may encourage the [LCC] to provide further for a class of patients above the pauper class, but who can ill afford to bear the cost of a private asylum, and who may find comparative quiet and comfort; perhaps even a touch of 'home' in such an institution as the Claybury mansion-house. (R. Jones 1897, p. 48)

Claybury also became the site for the new pathology department designed to serve the entire London Asylum system and Frederick Mott, the chief LCC Pathologist, was put in charge of that "well-equipped laboratory for the study of the pathology of insanity" (Anon 1909b, p. 1014).[3] The Claybury complex, opened in May 1893, accommodated some 2,500 patients (half male, half female) and employed around 250 staff. (Jones 1897, pp. 55–56).[4] Long Grove,[5] "the sixth asylum erected by the [LCC],"[6] was built on the Horton Estate, near Epsom and opened in June 1907 with the most up to-date facilities and accommodation for 1,600 patients (800 of each sex) on the main site, and a further 400 patients in eight detached blocks, or villas, and a number of "chronic but quiet cases" in smaller units (Anon 1907a).[7] It is well to remember that the vast majority of patients admitted to Long Grove, and other asylums, were paupers.[8]

Hubert Bond (1870–1945),[9] Honorary and General Secretary of the Association (1906–1912), became the first Superintendent of Long Grove (1907–1912), an appointment whole-heartedly supported "as a practical endorsement of the Association's choice of him to follow Dr. Robert Jones." (*JMS* 1907, p. 202). By 1907 Bond had become one of the most important figures in the Asylum system and wielded considerable power and influence. He was previously Medical Superintendent at The (Epileptic) Colony, Ewell, in Surrey,[10] where, by all accounts, he had introduced a progressive and enlightened regime (*JMS* 1906, p. 182) which he then carried into Long Grove. What is more he collected around himself some of "the ablest and most enlightened of the Medical Superintendents in the Council's service": men like Bernard Hart, Henry Devine (1879–1940), Guy Foster Barham (1873–1944)[11] and Edward Mapother (1881–1940),[12] all of whom subsequently rose to prominence in their respective specialisms in mental health. Under Bond's leadership

> [the] chief line of interest was the relation of mental illness to philosophy and psychology, and especially to the novel findings and theories of Janet and Freud. Although the neuroses were still regarded as lying in the province of the neurologist, the Long Grove group of psychiatrists had acquired, through reading and untutored experiment, a familiarity with the problems of neurotic behaviour that equipped them to deal with the disorders of that nature brought to the surface in the First World War.

When Mapother first arrived at Long Grove, as a *locum tenens*, probably in May 1908,[13] he "found an intellectual climate which was more like that of a University than of a mental hospital." (Bewley n.d., pp. 2 and 4; See also Jackson 2012; Anon 1966; Lewis 1969, p. 1350).

Bernard Hart was born in Hampstead, the second youngest of six children whose father George Hart, was a musical instrument-maker. Hart was virtually the same age as Ernest Jones[14] and, like Jones, was educated at UCH although they probably lost touch when Jones was appointed Assistant MO at the Brompton in September 1902 and Hart continued at UCH until he was appointed House Surgeon at the East London Hospital for Children in 1904.

It was probably during that appointment that Hart resolved to specialize in psychological medicine and, on being appointed RMO at the York Dispensary in 1905, joined the BMA and the Association, having qualifying CEPM. In 1906 Hart became Assistant MO at the Herts County Asylum, in St Albans, where he worked under Arthur N. Boycott another important and enlightened Superintendent. The following year Hart, who was probably hand-picked by Bond, was appointed assistant MO at Long Grove shortly after it opened in June 1907.[15] Despite comments by Jones (1911a, p. 121) and Hart (1911, p. 90) that "the physiological conception of insanity" dominated the discipline of psychiatry in early-twentieth-century Britain, this current study suggests a far more complex picture. By 1911 the balance of the dynamics, with its deep fissures separating the discourses of neurology and psychology, were already tipping dramatically; a point nicely illustrated by comparing the entrenched views of Beevor as opposed to the enquiring mind of Ormerod. A new generation of medical psychologists, or psychiatrists, at Long Grove, Wakefield, York and even Bethlem, all significant British Asylums, were increasingly adopting different psychotherapies as part of their curative treatments. And this was complemented by a younger generation of neurologists, like Wilson and Stoddard who by 1910 would have vehemently denied Beevor's implied claim that there were no neurologist, in Britain, interested in psychotherapy. (JNMD 1908, Vol. 35, p. 784). This new atmosphere, also increasingly reflected in the pages of the *BMJ* and the *JMS*, brought radical changes to the treatment of mental illness especially at Long Grove where Bond appears to have kept abreast of all the latest literature and actively encouraged his staff not only to explore all the latest intellectual currents in psychological medicine but also to put them to the test through experimentation in their clinical practice (Devine 1909, p. 310).

Although the early evidence remains fragmentary—almost the entire Long Grove Archive appears destroyed—early published material suggests that by the time Hart's first philosophical essay appeared in July 1908, Hart, Devine, Barham, and Mapother, were already routinely using various forms of psychotherapy in the treatment of some of the inpatients under their care (Devine 1909, pp. 305–6). The various therapies included hypnotism, suggestion and post-hypnotic suggestion, the Breuer-Freud cathartic treatment and Jung's word-association tests (Barham 1911, p. 106). These "procedures" which they used in various degrees of combination, were increasingly described under the sign of psychoanalysis especially after they started to incorporate dream analysis and free association.[16] As Barham (1911, pp. 104–5, 117) said: at Long Grove they all worked at trying to encourage patients to have "a deeper insight into the factors conditioning [their] trouble."[17] Hart's own development is worth following because he articulated, more than the others, his belief that it was paramount to test all possible therapies scientifically.[18]

It seems inconceivable, therefore, that Hart would not have tested different and sometimes competing forms of psychotherapies, including those of Janet, Jung and Freud, and that he, and the others, would not have discussed their practices on a regular basis. This reading can be traced through Hart's five essays which, although essentially theoretical and historical, remain highly suggestive of his deep commitment to verifying the "scientific" benefits of different therapies particularly psychoanalysis. So, for example, in his Oxford May 1910 BPS talk Hart (1910b, p. 446)[19] stressed the importance of testing Freud's theories "empirically":

> Almost everyone who had taken the time and the trouble to master Freud's technique—a task, by the way, of no mean difficulty—has confirmed his results in all their essential details. But, even if all this be admitted, there is still room for doubt. The initial method of non-critical associations might be reasonably established by proofs of this kind, but the *Deutungsverfahren* [method of interpretation] introduces a conveniently mobile factor which inevitably arouses some distrust.

Although Hart's comments might be voiced through the persona of the rational scientific investigator they reveal, through his eliding of the personal pronoun, that he, too, "had taken the time and the trouble to master Freud's technique," while his phrase, "almost everyone," suggests he is also talking about his colleagues at Long Grove. This suggests, at the very least, that Hart, Mapother, Devine (1909; 1911b-d) and Barham (1912) were all using various forms of psychoanalysis by 1910. Subsequent papers, which we shall look at shortly, will confirm this reading. In the meantime the paper Hart (1912a, p. 243) read to the Association in February 1912 clearly reveals that he had psychoanalyzed a 26-year-old man and "that the analysis was brought to a successful conclusion." Mapother suggests Hart started treating the patient in February 1911 and that he was well on the way to recovery by July (Graham 1911, p. 396): while *The Lancet* (June 8, 1912, pp. 1555–56), reporting Hart's paper, said:

> It is to be hoped that Dr. Hart will take some opportunity of recording the psycho-analysis of this case in detail, for it cannot fail to be instructive.

Hart's significance, therefore, is not just confined to his published writings but also to his early therapeutic work which clearly inspired the other Long Grove psychiatrists to explore psychoanalysis.

But Hart also played an active role in disseminating Freud's writings through his work in the Association. When Hart and Devine were elected joint honorary secretaries of the Library Committee in 1910 they collaborated to expand Tuke's Library, recently gifted to the Association by his widow.

Some of the books they acquired, during their first year in post, are instructive: Janet's *The Major Symptoms of Hysteria* (1907), Brill's translation of Freud's *Selected Papers on Hysteria* (1909a), Freud's *Die Traumdeutung* and Peterson and Brill's translation of Jung's *The Psychology of Dementia Praecox* (1909) (*JMS* 1910, Vol. 56, pp. 386–87). But they also sought to expand the Association's policy of making library books, and foreign journals, available on loan to members. In this their work parallels the endeavors of William Brown, the new BPS librarian (Edgell 1947, p. 119), who, as we shall see, was also becoming increasingly interested in the works of Freud. But there is also evidence that apart from his organizational abilities Hart was offering practical and educational assistance to both Association and BMA members keen to know more about the works of Freud and Jung. This is revealed, in 1912, through an interesting fragment of an exchange in the *BMJ* (May 25, 1912, p. 1224, italics mine) under its "Questions" column:

> Psychoanalysis who wants to know [*sic*] if there is anyone working with stammering along analytical lines, as suggested by Professor Freud of Vienna, and to know whether there is any one in this country working and practising on those lines whose experience might be available, or to hear of any one who has had experience of Professor Freud's method.

J. E. Middlemiss (1912), AMO of the Gartloch Hospital for Mental Diseases, a practitioner of hypnotism and an early reviewer of Freud (1904) replied:

> 'Psychoanalysis' is probably acquainted with Brill's translation of Freud's work, *Selected Papers on Hysteria and other Psychoneuroses*, which gives a first-hand account of the Freudian theory and procedure; if not, I shall be happy to lend him the copy which I have in my possession. . . . there is also a very instructive exposition of Freud's method by Dr. Bernard Hart of Long Grove Asylum, Epsom, in one of the recent issues of the Journal of Mental Science, and that [I have] been much indebted to Dr. Hart for much assistance in the study of the subject.

Although it is difficult to know whether Middlemiss's experience was an isolated example it nonetheless highlights, in its own small way, Hart's significance for the spread of psychoanalysis[20] and his willingness to share his new knowledge.

HENRY DEVINE

Henry Devine,[21] was born in Bristol on May 2, 1879, the second son of a civil service clerk, and was some two months younger than Hart and some three months younger than Jones. But unlike Hart and Jones, Devine studied medicine at University College Bristol and then, from 1902, worked as a house physician at Bristol General Hospital before obtaining various junior appointments at the Chelsea Hospital for Women, Mt. Vernon Hospital for Consumption and Wakefield Asylum. It may have been his experiences at Wakefield which prompted him to enroll at KCH where he qualified M.B.B.S. in 1905 and then, having entered the LCC's mental hospital service, he joined the Association and obtained a post at Cane Hill Asylum. In late 1907 Devine was appointed to Long Grove where he continued working until (probably) early 1911 when he was appointed senior assistant MO at the West Riding Asylum, Wakefield (Anon 1940; Hart 1940, p. 1153). Circumstantial evidence suggests that before joining Long Grove Devine, like Jones, also studied at Kraepelin's clinic.[22] And it may have been while studying Kraepelin's theories on dementia praecox that Devine discovered Jung whose work he probably started reading from around 1908 (*JMS* 1909, Vol. 55, p. 81).[23] In late 1907 or early 1908 Devine began treating a fifty-five year old woman following her admission to Long Grove in October 1907. Although she had been in and out of Asylums since she was first detained in 1902 Devine resisted treating her condition as the manifestation of a "neuropathic heredity"[24] and concluded "her cravings are purely accidental in origin and imply no original and inherent moral defect."[25] Although this initial framing was Janet's Devine now set about diagnosing her condition not just through the conceptual framework of Janet (1898 & 1903) but also through Freud's French paper 'Obsessions and Phobias' (1895a) and, most striking of all, through Freud's *Die Traumdeutung* (1900) and Jung's *Über die Psychologie der Dementia Praecox* (1907b). In a subsequent paper Devine (1909, p. 305n) suggests that he treated this patient according to the Freudian dream mechanism, whereby "[i]t is more usual . . . for the complex to express itself symbolically rather than directly" and that he also followed Jung's (1907b) suggestion that one should attempt to link the significance of dreams to the emotional complex revealed through the use of "stimulus word[s]."[26] Although Devine's 1909 paper might not be considered a psychoanalytic account, in the strictest sense of the term, there can be little doubt, as his subsequent papers reveal, that by January 1908 Devine was exploring different forms, or variants, of psychoanalytic treatment. But Devine's 1909 paper is also significant because it was published in the *Archives* and not in the *JMS* where Devine was a regular reviewer and would probably have been offered automatic rights of access.

Mott, the founder and driving force behind *Archives*, had recently added "and Psychiatry" to the original title which, as one reviewer noted (Anon 1909b, p. 1014) indicated "an enlargement of the scope of the publication, which seems to be warranted by the increasing readiness of MOs of asylums to contribute scientific papers bearing upon the causation, treatment, and pathology of insanity." In fact Mott had already signalled this change in his Preface to the previous volume: "Early cases of uncertifiable mental affection termed neurasthenia, psychasthenia, obsession, mild impulsive mania, melancholia, hysteria, etc., if studied carefully by trained medico-psychologists, could not fail to yield valuable results in regard to our knowledge of the causation, prevention and cure of insanity." (Mott 1907, pp. v–vi). This now explains why medical psychologists, like Jones, Barham and Hart, started submitting articles to *Archives* which was considered, until then, an absolute bastion of physiological, pathological and neurological research. That Devine's article was the first of these psychological studies suggests that Mott,[27] clearly sympathetic to these new currents, may even have invited him to submit it specially. But whatever Mott's impetus here is another indication of the profound shift in attitudes as neurologists and pathologists, particularly of the stature of Mott, became increasingly aware that "psychological conceptions [might] throw light on problems hitherto incomprehensible" (*JMS*, 1909, Vol. 55, p. 81). Devine's 1909 paper is therefore an important sign of this significant step-change. Furthermore Devine was a high-flyer in the Association and with the active support of many senior members, including the new President Bevan-Lewis (*JMS* 1909, Vol. 55, pp. 764–65), and with the imprimatur of Bond, who had encouraged and supported his work, Devine's paper would have been guaranteed wide circulation and attention.

In April 1911 the *JMS* published 'Abnormal Mental States Associated with Malignant Disease,' in which Devine (1911a, pp. 353–55 and 356–57), who had recently left Long Grove for the prestigious post of senior MO at the Wakefield Asylum, explored how a potentially life threatening illness, like cancer, "must constitute a particularly painful emotional complex in the mind of the sufferer." In speculating how patients might deal with this kind of psychological trauma Devine listed a number of possible options, one of which was an escape into psychosis—a form of insanity—which "served the purpose of explaining away what was so patently obvious to anyone but the individual concerned." And then commenting on a woman suffering from psychasthenia noted:

> A little investigation showed, though she confessed it with resistance and hesitation, that she had recently heard of several friends who had been operated upon for cancer of the uterus, and associating this with some irregularity of menstruation, she had feared that she had been suffering from the same disease. This concealed complex had therefore been instrumental in producing the various neurotic symptoms which have been indicated. When it was explained that her irregular periods were due to a physiological epoch, and that since she had had no children the possibility of cancer was remote, the psychasthenic reactions were largely ameliorated. (Devine 1911a, p. 358)

On April 27, 1911 Devine (1911b) delivered his paper, 'Pathogenesis of a Delusion,' to the Northern and Midland Division of the Association [NMD Association] and although that paper was not published until the July 1911 issue of the *JMS* it was briefly reported in the May 1911 issue of the *BMJ* which noted that Devine (1911b, p. 1180)

> described a case in which a young lady had developed the delusion that she was suffering from an infectious disease, and that those around her were in danger of becoming affected. A psycho-analysis was undertaken to trace the source of this delusion. By means of Jung's association experiment it became manifest that underlying the delusion was a concealed complex giving rise to feelings of shame and self-reproach. This was found to depend on an experience with her lover a short while before. She accused herself of having acted wickedly. Since, however, her behaviour had not been open to criticism it became obvious that her self-accusation was itself a delusion covering a deeper complex. Further analysis revealed the fact that the patient had determined to avoid marriage on the ground that she had an insane heredity. The psychosis had therefore arisen out of two conflicting wishes: (1) Natural sex instincts, and (2) a wish to remain single. The delusion was the symbolic representation of her original determination and enabled the patient to gratify her ideals and solve the conflict in a manner impossible in contact with reality. The analysis was also a method of treatment, a form of re-education. As the mechanism became obvious to the investigator it was possible to lead the patient back to reality once again.

When Devine's (1911c, p. 463) April 27, 1911 talk was published in the *JMS* in July 1911 also revealed, in considerable detail, the psychoanalysis of a twenty-five year old woman who had been admitted to the Asylum "in a state of diffuse anxiety and unrest." In setting its theoretical context Devine said:

> In order to trace the connection between the manifest symptom and the complex from which it is derived, some form of *psycho-analysis* must be undertaken. Freud's technique for such an investigation is very complicated and laborious, but considerable assistance may be obtained by the use of association experiments, which have been brought into prominence in this connection by Jung . . . A number of words are called out by the investigator, and the patient is required to give the first word that comes into his mind. The reaction time of the response is estimated by means of a stop-watch, and when the list of words has been completed the experiment is repeated and the responses again noted.

Devine (1911c, pp. 469–70) then listed 50 of the 100 stimulus words, reaction words, time and repetitions of the test, by way of illustrating and discussing them in relation to their associated complex. With this he then revealed how the patient's perfectly natural sexual impulse was opposed by conventional views on sex relations.

Since, however, the patient's behaviour (sex-impulse expression) had not really been reprehensible at all, even judged by rigid standards, one could only suppose that the patient was possessed of a pathological degree of primness and viewed her own conduct from an abnormally rigid standpoint.

Further analysis then led Devine (1911c, p. 470) to conclude:

Two entirely antagonistic wishes are present: on the one hand we have the natural sex instincts and desire for marriage, and on the other what might be called her conscience, consisting of motives which render marriage repugnant.

It was clearly the "theoretical and practical experience of psychiatry" which Devine acquired at Long Grove through extensive reading and untutored experiments which had initially encouraged him to begin psychoanalyzing his patients.[28]

SOME OTHER EARLY PRACTITIONERS OF PSYCHOANALYSIS (1908–1911)

Sometime in April or May 1910 Bedford Pierce (1861–1932), Medical Superintendent of The Retreat in York, since 1892, and thus another significant member of the Association, delivered a paper to the Leeds and West Riding Medico-Chirurgical Society [LWR] in which he drew on 200 "consecutive cases observed between the years 1898–1908." Then, having detailed the various causes of the patients' depressions he said:

It would lead me too far from my subject to discuss Freud's hypothesis of the causation of psychasthenic states. Suffice it to say that my experience confirms his views of the importance of the sexual element. The physician will in not a few cases succeed in clearing up difficulties arising from past experiences of this kind and so remove a chronic source of mental irritation, with the result that the patient is permanently relieved and the obsessions and the imperative ideas disappear.

Pierce (1910, p. 1335) also discussed two case histories by way of illustration. In one the patient needed hospitalization.

The obsessions were clearly the cause of the depression. It would have been an interesting case for Freud's psycho-analysis, as in all probability the cause of the strange dislike of dogs could have been discovered and the chance of a future relapse greatly reduced. Unfortunately this method of investigation was not generally known when this patient was under care.

Then on November 22, 1912, Pierce (1912a, p. 1551) delivered a second paper to the LWR, this time "On Psycho-analysis," in which he outlined its principles and criticized it "as a method of diagnosis." He made it clear, however, that he was not criticizing psychoanalysis as such, but questioning whether it could ever be used as a diagnostic tool. In the discussion which followed Devine "urged its value both in diagnosis and treatment" while Dr. Botham, from Darlington, "was of opinion that unless the mental attitude of the patient were changed in the process of psycho-analysis, further treatment was necessary in the direction of re-education."

Although it is difficult to piece together Peirce's intellectual development the fragmentary evidence suggests he had studied medicine in Vienna and, like a number of other British psychiatrists, was influenced by Kraepelin (Whyte 1910; Ion and Beer 2002, pp. 422–23; Kuhn 2014a, pp. 29–30). But as he was not averse to employing different forms of treatments he started exploring aspects of psychotherapy and, from early 1909, was probably already using variants of psychoanalysis although only in a limited number of cases and only after having diagnosed them according to Kraepelin's criteria. Pierce's initial interest in psychoanalysis, like Devine's, probably emerged through his interest in Kraeplin's investigations into dementia praecox which, like Devine, led him to study Jung and, to the conclusion, that Jung's writings would complement his own Kraepelin-inspired methodology. This reading is supported by the articles on 'Psycho-Analysis' which Pierce wrote for *The Practitioner's Encyclopedia* (Murphy 1912, pp. 502–5; see also p. 484),[29] and also for the *Medical Annual* (Pierce 1912b; 1914). And, more tenuously, through his subsequent relationship with H. G. (aka Peter) Baynes. (*Lancet*, August 21, 1920, p. 404; *JMS* 1921, Vol. 67, p. 104).

In July 1911 Dr William Graham delivered a paper on "Psycho-therapy" to the Association's Annual Meeting in Dublin. Graham (1911, p. 396) discussed the different therapies that might be used in the treatment of mental disorders and suggested psychoanalysis was one of several options.

> This method (identified with the name of Professor Freud) rested on the view that many disorders arose from the inability of the personality to assimilate certain experiences, such as those of a painful emotional character, and from the conflict thus set up between opposing groups of thought. The therapeutic consisted in making clear to the patient the source of this conflict by bringing into the clear light of consciousness the submerged factor, and in thus re-establishing mental unity and integrity. The cases in which this method had given best results were those of long-standing obsessions, psychasthenias, phobias, hysteria, and paranoid states. Freud's view overemphasized the element of sexuality. The method was applicable only to some types. The modern tendency to confine psycho-therapy to this one method must therefore be rejected.

Despite his conception of psychoanalysis, with its mixture of suggestion, word association and the original Breuer-Freud cathartic method of treatment, Graham also seems to express an underlying anxiety, even fear, that psychoanalysis—at least as he understood it—which was now widely discussed both within the Association and other medical societies, was going to become the *psycho-therapeutic* treatment of choice. But Graham's view was challenged in the discussion which followed. Dr. Bond said "a large proportion of the work which was attempted at Long Grove was more or less along the lines indicated" by Graham's paper: by which he meant a mixture of suggestion (including hypnosis and post-hypnotic suggestion), therapeutic conversation, psychoanalysis, occupation and re-education. And although the precise meaning of Bond's subsequent comments remains unclear—perhaps because of a faulty short-hand note—the context suggests that what Bond said next was: "The method [psycho-analysis?] brought one into touch with one's patients in a way which no other method did. But if such means were to be carried out to any extent in asylums, there must be a great extension of asylum staffs." Mapother, who was still at Long Grove, "said he knew that his colleague Dr. Hart had treated one case for an hour every day for the past six months, and that patient was now on the way to recovery. But in another case which he [Mapother?] had seen he did not think improvement could be said to have occurred." (Graham 1911, p. 396).[30] Mapother's reference was probably to the case Hart (1912a) subsequently read to the Association in February 1912 and to which I have already made reference. Then just over two years after he had delivered his paper Graham's somewhat uncertain attitudes to psychoanalysis must have changed because on 30 October 1913 he become a charter member of the LPAS (Paskauskas 1993, p. 233n).

On August 5, 1911 the *BMJ* published "Four cases Illustrative of Certain Points in Psycho-Analysis," by Hugh Wingfield (1863–1925), Consulting Physician at the Royal Hants County Asylum. Wingfield, who had started using and experimenting with hypnosis as early as 1886, outlined some of Freud's theories as they had impacted upon the treatment of several of his own patients. Wingfield's language suggests he was working primarily from Brill's translations particularly of *Studien* and "The Defence Neuro-Psychoses" (Freud 1909a, pp. 121f).[31] Although his idea of psychoanalysis included "suggestion" and "abreaction," there can be little doubt that by late 1909 Wingfield (1911, p. 256; 1910, pp. 126f, 129–130) was also already using variant forms of psychoanalysis, including free association, as a sort of bolt-on technique for discovering the origin of his patient's trauma in order that he could treat it. Wingfield believed that "the mere discovery of the original cause of the condition did little or nothing to relieve the patient's condition; but suggestion during hypnosis directed against the ideas, when they were brought to light, produced instant amelioration." Thus while

Wingfield adopted an eclectic approach—mixing early Breuer and Freud with Janet's substitution theory—he nonetheless remained convinced that without discovering the original cause of the problem he would only ever be able to deal with the symptoms. He noted one case in particular, which "*conforms completely with Freud's theory*, the mere recalling of the fact to the conscious memory and the discussing it with someone else being sufficient to dissipate the emotional idea which formed the core of the mischief." But Wingfield (1911, p. 257, italics mine) also used hypnosis to "unearth" the distressing cause of the symptoms now buried in the unconscious.

> Cases of the kind described above seem to show the paramount importance of a really accurate diagnosis in many such instances, if we hope to cure them at all. Sometimes, as in the second case, the actual diagnosis and discovery of the hidden cause is sufficient to effect a cure. For other patients suggestion is needed, but is often of use only if directed against the actual morbid subconscious idea. And, as a rule, that idea must be discovered by some process of psycho-analysis, different methods being applicable to different cases. But the time which this treatment takes is often a bar to its use. Thus Freud often consumes more than a year in completing an analysis. The instances given above took only a very short time, and may, I hope, encourage others to apply the same principle to similar cases.[32]

Two years later, during the course of a discussion on Constance Long's paper 'Complex Formation in Relation to Hysteria and the Psychoneuroses,' Wingfield suggested:

> Psycho-analysis should only be tried as a last expedient owing to the long time and considerable expense incurred. He described the conditions essential for successful hypnosis and his own method of induction. In his opinion the two chief essentials were concentration of attention and limitation of consciousness. (*The Lancet* December 27, 1913, p. 1824)

Wingfield (1910, pp. 129–30) might also have suggested, as he had previously done, that Freud's psychoanalysis

> requires powers of insight, deduction, and sympathy amounting to a kind of genius. As every patient shows unconscious resistance to the demand for recollection, and as many subjects intentionally withhold the crucial fact when it *is* remembered, the personality of the physician counts for more in this form of treatment than in any other.

Finally, in October 1911, Dr William Aldren Turner (1864–1945),[33] outpatient physician at Queen's Square, against whom Jones (1959, p. 166) takes an apparently uncalled-for sideswipe, delivered a paper on 'Neurasthenia, hysteria and allied neuroses' to a joint meeting of the Nottingham BMA and the Nottingham Medico-Chirurgical Society. In his paper Turner (1911), who was soon to collaborate on a psychoanalysis with William Brown, having considered Freud's views, concluded:

> Freud's organized system of psychoanalysis would, no doubt, in the future prove of value in certain types of case. But as the method was slow and often wearisome, inapplicable to patients below a certain level of intelligence, and liable to place sexual matters in the causation of functional nervous disease upon a pinnacle which further investigation might not entirely endorse, it was unlikely to be as commonly used as its advocates anticipated.[34]

THE POVERTY OF PRIORITY DISPUTES: OR THAT 1911 BMA MEETING

By 1911, if not earlier, psychoanalysis had become a topic of debate in a number of medical societies where, on the whole, discussions were conducted in an enquiring spirit with psychiatrists and psychotherapists exploring the costs, benefits and utility of using psychoanalysis for treatment. It should come as no surprise, therefore, that the subject should appear on the agenda when the BMA held its 79th Annual Meeting in Birmingham in late July 1911 despite the fact that Edwin Goodall (1863–1944),[35] Medical Superintendent of the Cardiff Mental Hospital, was to be President of the Section. Although Goodall (1890a; 1890b, p. 1119; 1890c., p. 369), was for a time, involved with the Smith and Myers (1890) Bethlem hypnotic experiments, and then with his own hypnotic experiments at Wadsley Asylum, near Wakefield, he was now a recognized toxicologist and his 1911 address on toxicology set the tone for three days heavily dominated by discussions on neurology and pathology, including contributions from Professor Oppenheim, on 'Disseminated Sclerosis' and F. W. Mott (1911) on 'The Relation of Head Injury to Nervous and Mental Disease'. Although Mott's BMA paper can not be considered 'psychological' he had become, by 1911, increasingly interested in psychoanalysis particularly as a "means of a study of unvolitional trains of thought, time reactions and the examination of dream states, as well as the more ordinary methods by which attempts are made to obtain knowledge of individual character." (Murphy 1912, p. 498). It was not until the last session, on Friday afternoon, that the two psychology papers, slated for the agenda, were read; perhaps by way of complementing, or challenging, those physiologists, although decreasing in number, who still tended "to ascribe a physical causation to abnormal mental states" and who were therefore inclined to overlook "the significance of *the actual content of a psychosis*" (Devine 1911d, p. 747, italics mine). The second of those psychology papers was *that* paper by M. D. Eder which Glover subsequently claimed "was the first public contribution to clinical psycho-analysis made in this country" (Hobman 1945, p. 89).

However the first psychology paper on the agenda was Henry Devine's "On the Significance of Some Confusional States." A brief summary noted that Devine

> gave details of several cases showing that certain confusional states would be found to depend on the general tendency of human nature to evade real issues and take the line of least resistance. When reality so often proved painful and difficult, the individual might seek to gratify his desires by turning away from facts as they existed, and taking refuge in certain inferior mental operations. Freud had shown that dreams had a similar significance, as they represented the 'living through,' or fulfilment of a wish which could not obtain normal gratification (*BMJ* August 5, 1911, p. 279)

A longer report, published several weeks later, reveals that Devine (1911d, p. 748) discussed four cases each of which, he believed, confirmed Freud's concept of a "'defence neurosis,'" that is "a defence against reality."

> In all these cases, then, it will be seen that the psychosis fulfils a definite function. The contents are not entirely meaningless, but they bear a definite relation to circumstances in the patient's life. They may be described as prolonged dream states or reveries, and serve exactly the same purpose to the individual. The difference is one of degree, not of kind. The type of reaction varies from a purely hysterical delirium to the acute hallucinatory phases of dementia praecox, but in all cases the biological significance is the same.

In all four cases "the antagonism between desire and circumstance was quite apparent" although there were other cases where

> a more elaborate investigation was necessary, and the significance of the psychosis more obscure. Jung has furnished very striking examples in some of his monographs. . . . It is hoped, however, that the cases which have been described will serve to illustrate the fact that a confusional delirium may fulfil a definite purpose and constitute one form of reaction to experience.

Once Devine's BMA paper is set within the trajectory of his NMD Association paper from April 27, 1911 there can be little doubt that he would have explained, at least in outline, the forms of psychoanalysis he had used in each of the four cases he had identified. That Devine (1914, p. 92) was discussing psychoanalysis is also confirmed through a subsequent paper about a case "which has recently been engaging my attention" and in which: "The analysis has been undertaken by means of 'word association' tests and the method of 'free-association,' upon the lines indicated by Jung [1907b & 1910]."

Following a paper by Dr Winifred Muirhead on 'The Wasserman Reaction in Insanity', Eder delivered his paper, 'A Case of Obsession and Hysteria treated by the Freud Psycho-Analytic Method.' This was an account of his treatment of the patient who had consulted him in May 1910 and whose case was discussed in Chapter 12. After detailing his patient's history Eder told his audience how he had carried out the "Association tests" which had "produced interesting results." At first he "worked with a stop-watch" but finding it too distracting he simply noted "down whether the reaction time was long or short." He had conducted those tests on two occasions and used "[a]ltogether 200 words" following the criteria set out by Jung.

> To quite a number of words the patient could give no reaction word. But in these cases his whole demeanour betrayed some powerful reaction. There were twitchings of the face, stroking of the chin; sometimes he would rise from the chair, excitedly raise his hands, or cry out in despair, 'Well, why does nothing occur to me'?

Having gathered up "all the words that produced a long reaction time," Eder (1911, p. 751, italics mine), then set about encouraging his patient to "concentrate his mind upon the ideas that presented themselves in the order of their appearance, so that I obtain a number of *what the psychologists* call 'free associations.'" Through this process Eder discovered, or perhaps encouraged, his patient to discuss his hidden sexual life and, in the course of the 'analysis', two phobias emerged, one of them which Eder linked to "some sexual basis," the other to a very real fear of water. Having finished his clinical account Eder (1911, p. 752) then discussed Freud's theory of repression so as to explain how the patient's energy "found an outlet in a somatic manifestation. There was conversion, to use Freud's term, to something assimilable in consciousness—pain in the neck to be put down to 'rheumatism' or what not." Then Eder, having briefly outlined Freud's current theories on sexuality—making reference to Brill's translation of *Three Contributions* (Freud's 1910b; 1905), concluded: "The interpretation of the dreams and the word associations were the chief helps in the patient's analysis. Assistance was obtained by notes and observations about himself that he gave me." But as there was little time remaining for Eder (1911, p. 752, italics mine)[36] to explore the deeper theoretical points he concluded by urging a more compassionate response to others, like his patient, who suffered from all sorts of anxieties which were "clearly due to repressed wishes, *mostly of a sex nature*."[37] There was however one problem: "Patience and resource are required to treat these cases. I found that when I was myself not very well nothing was elicited. It is a severe tax upon time, and for that reason I have not undertaken this treatment of many patients."

Now according to Edward Glover: "When Eder had finished speaking the Chairman [Edwin Goodall pk] and the entire audience, numbering about nine, rose and stalked out without a word." (Hobman 1945, p. 89). Jones (1955, pp. 99–100; 1945b, p. 10) tells this same story in two separate accounts which I have merged into one: "Eder had an audience of eight, but they left the room when he came to the sexual aetiology"—"almost visibly wondering who had got among them." The question remains as to the origin of this Eder Myth. Although the Jones account(s) were published after Glover's claim, it is quite likely that Jones (1945a) was the origin of the myth not least because Jones always claimed to have been "the only first-hand witness available" to speak of these 'pre-historic' times not withstanding that he was in Toronto at the time of Eder's 1911 talk (Paskauskas, 1993, pp. 108–14). It is also noteworthy that Jones (1936a, p. 296) makes no mention of the 1911 'walk out' in his Eder obituary but merely suggests Eder's 1911 paper was "I believe, the first [psycho-analytic] lecture . . . in England." A moment's reflection should now reveal the total implausibility of the Eder Myth which has gulled even an astute commentator like Thomson (2011, pp. 70–71). If the audience had really taken against Eder's paper then they would have voiced opposition rather than walked out leaving Eder's account unchallenged.[38] Although there is no list of those actually present for Eder's talk there is a list of those who originally indicated their intention to attended, either as speakers or delegates: Professor Hermann Oppenheim (from Berlin),[39] Risien Russell, F. E. Batten, F. W. Mott, T. B. Hyslop, assistant physician of Bethlem and also a colleague of Stoddart's, Dr. G. M. Robertson (Edinburgh),[40] Edwin Bramwell,[41] and Professor J. J. Putnam, who, it will be recalled "'was not only the first American to interest himself in psycho-analysis but soon became its most decided supporter and its most influential representative in America.'" (Freud, quoted in Jones 1945, p. 9). And then, of course, there was Henry Devine who had just presented his own talk on psychoanalysis. It is inconceivable, therefore, that many of those listed, most of whom were already interested in and discussing psychoanalysis, would have walked out of Eder's talk in disgust.[42] Quite the opposite because, given the general climate, there would have been a number of delegates interested in hearing Eder's first-hand accounts of a psychoanalysis. But we don't need to speculate because if Eder had been given the cold and silent treatment in 1911 then he would hardly have been invited to present a talk on "The Present Position of Psycho-analysis" to the 1913 Annual Meeting (*BMJ*, June 28, 1913, p. 604; Eder 1913c). Even more telling however, *The Lancet* (August 19, 1911, p. 515), in reporting on the Section, noted "Dr T. Gwynne Maitland (Sutton) [43] made a few remarks on [Eder's] paper."

SOME CONCLUSIONS

If this book were at all obsessed with priority disputes then Devine's April 1911 paper to the NMD Association would trump Eder's BMA paper by several months and therefore qualify, under Glover's definition, as the first British 'public contribution to clinical psycho-analysis.' And yet, as this book suggests, the early histories of psychoanalysis did not run on straight teleological lines because it now turns out that there were *two* psychoanalytic papers delivered at the 1911 BMA Annual Meeting; one by Eder, a GP, the other by Devine, a medical psychologist (psychiatrist). This underlines how by 1911 Freud and psychoanalysis had become an important topic of discussion in local, divisional and national meetings not just within the Association but also within the BMA itself as well other medical societies as a small but significant number of branches and divisions began discussing the merits or otherwise of psychoanalysis in the treatment of the psychoneuroses. But what is also noticeable, and worth stressing once again, is that the tone and tenor of those debates and discussions were, by and large, measured and civilized and most definitely *did not* involve wholesale negative reactions. In fact I have found very little evidence to support the claims, advanced by Jones (1959, pp. 204–8), that there was considerable resistance to the Freudian emphasis on the sexual theory of the neuroses, a point to be discussed further in Chapter 19. Where there were challenges to, and criticisms of, Freudian theories they tended to center on a certain distaste for the way in which a number of Freudians insisted upon their absolutist claims that "sexual matters" explained *all* psychoneuroses. However, for the majority of physicians, interested in the subject, the practical and utilitarian issues were far more important as they weighed up the feasibility of employing psycho-analysis either in general or Asylum practice. In the latter case, for example, there were inmates, already deeply disturbed and often below a certain level of intelligence, which suggested it was impossible for psychiatrists, already over-worked and, no doubt under-paid, to engage in such intensive interventions. Bedford Pierce (1912b, p. 460), who was clearly sympathetic to psychoanalysis, identified the problem.

> Hence the practical question arises. How is it possible to provide treatment of this kind for those who are not wealthy, unless the physician takes the case up as a matter of scientific interest? It would seem clear that if psycho-analysis is to be generally useful, some simplification of technique must be discovered. As it is, the methods in use require so much special study and experience as to place the treatment out of the reach of the general practitioner.

And yet despite such practical problems a spirit of enquiry was clearly abroad because increasing numbers of physicians and psychiatrists now started taking up psychoanalysis. One example was David Forsyth (1877–1941),[44] who began his psychoanalytic practice around 1912 having already studied it for some time. Forsyth (1913, p. 14; 1922, p. viii) certainly liked to claim that he was completely self-taught—"there was no one in this country to turn to for assistance"—which was, of course, clearly disingenuous because apart from the general climate Forsyth would have already known of Jones and, no doubt Eder, because of their previous shared interests in children's medicine. It was no accident, therefore, that both Forsyth and Eder were to become members of the LPAS. In fact Freud actually spotted Forsyth's *BMJ* article on psychoanalysis almost immediately on its publication in July 1913 and alerted Jones accordingly. Freud (1933, pp. 47–48) was also sufficiently impressed with Forsyth to have agreed to analyze him shortly after the end of the War, an "honour" he never bestowed upon Jones (Paskauskas 1993, pp. 212, 350, 355, 357; Roazen 2000, pp. 41–42). Another convert was W. H. B. Stoddart (1869–1950)[45] who made virtually no reference to the psychological causes of insanity in the 1908 edition of his Text-Book where he simply exhorted: "Hysteria must be fought on its own ground. Suggestion causes it and counter-suggestion will cure it." (Stoddart 1908, p. 376). But in the second, 1912 edition, Stoddart (1912, pp. viii & 165f; 1914; Anon 1950) noted that: "The study of the subconscious by psycho-analytic methods has become sufficiently important to justify the addition of two chapters on this subject." And then having become an enthusiastic exponent of the "psychoanalytic points of view" promptly joined the BPAS after the War. Thus by 1913 there were significant numbers of psychiatrists, physicians and psychotherapists practicing psychoanalysis. Practitioners like Hart, Devine, Mapother, Graham, Wingfield, Forsyth, Stoddart, Middlemiss, Pierce, Long and Eder, to name just a few of those early pioneers who were more or less nearly all disappeared from the Jones Account.

NOTES

1. In 1896 London had four 'Asylums' (Jones 1897, p. 47).
2. Robert Jones, later Armstrong-Jones when he added his wife's family name was Superintendent of the L. C. C. Asylum, Claybury, for nearly twenty-four years; also honorary general secretary to the Association and its president in 1906. Robert Jones and F. E. Batten (1866–1918) were also joint secretaries of the Psychological Section of the International Congress on School Hygiene (London in 1907) in which M D Eder was involved. R. Jones also lectured on mental diseases at Bart's and contributed 'Insanity and Epilepsy' to Allbut & Rolleston (1911, pp. 941–61) See also *JMS* (1917, Vol. 63, pp. 302–3).
3. Hart (1908c, p. 474) said in Britain, "and to a large extent in Europe also . . . the pathological laboratory is the hub of the asylum universe."

4. In 1907 'Ward K.' housed on average about fifty-five epileptics out of sixty-two patients (Barham 1907, p. 362).

5. The Archives relating to Long Grove are sparse and, apart from various 'book-keeping' registers, only sixteen patient case files remain, all of them still closed.

6. Although the *JMS* (1906, p. 179) says it was the tenth of the new LCC Asylums I suspect the larger figure includes the four asylums the Council inherited in 1888.

7. See also Jackson (2012).

8. See that is, 'Long Grove Asylum: Females, transfer admissions' (6251/4/4).

9. Dr. Charles Hubert Bond, trained in Edinburgh, was formerly Medical Superintendent Ewell Epileptic Colony, Senior Assistant MO at the Heath Asylum, Bexley, formerly Assistant MO at Banstead Asylum, and Clinical Assistant at the National Hospital, London, at Wakefield (1892) and at Morningside Asylums (Anon 1903). Bond was President of the Association (1921–1922) and appointed a Commissioner in Lunacy in 1912 in which capacity he served until shortly before his death. (Anon 1945). Bond was succeeded at Long Grove by David Ogilvy (d. 1934).

10. The Colony was opened in 1903 (Commissioners 1914, p. 8).

11. Barham studied medicine at Cambridge University, then at the London Hospital where he qualified MD 1903. Formerly house surgeon at the Poplar Hospital before moving to Long Grove as Senior MO. He subsequently became Medical Superintendent at Claybury. There is a brief obituary of him in *BMJ* (23 September, 1944, p. 420).

12. Mapother qualified from UCH in 1908 and became a member of the Association in 1909. Although he had "developed a keen interest in psychotherapy while working with Bernard Hart at Long Grove, yet he was never a convert to Freudian doctrine." (Hayward 2010, p. 72). In 1923 Mapother became Superintendent at the Maudsley Hospital. See also Lewis (1969).

13. Long Grove, Post Mortem Register, Male No.1 (6251/4/100).

14. Jones was born on January 1, 1879; Hart on March 24, 1879.

15. Hart was already working at Long Grove by October 1907 (Long Grove 'Post Mortem' Register Male (1) 6251/4/100).

16. "She replied willingly, the attention being well maintained and the reaction not delayed. . . . The prevailing affective tone was one of mild depression and anxiety." (Barham 1911, p. 106, italics mine). See also the comments on Barham's paper (1912, pp. 230–31) by J. R. Lord, Medical Superintendent Horton Asylum, Epsom: "With regard to the symptomatology of the condition, not all had the ability or the opportunity to enter into a psycho-analysis of the character which the meeting had had the pleasure of listening to from Dr. Barham. If he were to insist upon that analysis in all his admissions, he would have to ask his Committee to give him as many medical officers as there were patients."

17. Barham suggests, in the context of the two cases he had been discussing, that Freud's concept of the unconscious mind and its conceptual mechanism offer a better account than Janet's. These comments may well have been influenced by Hart. Although one of Barham's patients was already in Long Grove in 1907, and re-admitted in 1909, his paper, discussing her case, was not published until 1911 so it is difficult to know when exactly he started using psychoanalysis.

18. Bernard Hart to Ernest Jones November 6, 1910 (BPAS, P04-C-G-02, p. 1).

19. This same narrative can also be read into Hart's collaboration with Mapother which he acknowledges in the preface to his *Psychology of Insanity* (1912, p. vii).

20. Although Middlemiss (1914, p. 460) used aspects of psychoanalysis he adopted a pragmatic approach: "I submit that at the present juncture, when the whole subject of psycho-therapy is, so to speak, in embryo, it is premature to arrogate such claims in favour of any particular procedure." See also Middlemiss (1942).

21. Educated at KCL, Bristol and Munich, Devine was variously clinical assistant at Chelsea Hospital for Women, Junior RMO at Mt. Vernon Hospital for Consumptives and Casualty House Surgeon and Hospital Physician at Bristol General Hospital. Devine joined the Association in 1905 and in 1909 won the Association's Gaskell prize and gold medal when he was also awarded MD from University of London in the division of psychiatry (*JMS* 1909, Vol. 55, pp. 764–65). In 1916 Devine was appointed assistant editor of the *JMS* becoming a co-editor 1920–1927 (*BMJ* May 11, 1940, pp. 792–93; Hart 1940).

22. Hart (1940, p. 1153), whose memory was not always reliable, suggests that while at Long Grove Devine "obtained a grant of special leave to attend Kraepelin's clinic at Munich."

23. The reference here refers to an animated discussion on dementia praecox in November 1908 (*JMS* 1909, Vol. 55, pp. 170–71, 179). Jones reveals Jung's work was already being discussed in Kraepelin's Clinic (Paskauskas 1993, p. 2).

24. Although Devine's paper implicitly attacks Mott, the acknowledged authority on neuropathic heredity, Mott, as editor, nonetheless published it.

25. Devine (1909, pp. 305–6) is following Janet.

26. See also Jung (1909b, i.e., pp. 50f; 1909a, pp. 223–26 & 264).

27. In 1909 Mott suggested Dr [Rae?] Gibson, from Edinburgh, should study with Jung (McGuire 1974, p. 221).

28. See also Devine (1914). Devine would join the LPAS in 1913 (Paskauskas 1993, p. 233n) and subsequently attend the inaugural meeting of the BPAS on February 20, 1919, but would then resign in March 1920 (*IJPA* Vol. 1, 1920, pp. 118 and 363) Although Devine, like many others, has been all but written out of the early history, in his case it is not only Jones to blame because Hart (1940, p. 1154) also buried Devine's early interests in psychoanalysis under the following: "Devine was pre-eminently qualified to undertake a work of this kind [*Recent Advances in Psychiatry*], because he had always steadfastly avoided attaching himself to any one school of thought, but maintained a balanced and impartial attitude, ready to examine and appraise every alleged advance." This was probably also an apt description of Hart himself. See also Bellamy (1915, p. 44).

29. The article on Hysteria, which also discusses Freud's work in detail, was written by Craig & Macnamara (Murphy 1912, pp. 491–94). Maurice Craig, educated at Cambridge and London, joined the Association in 1892 and was, for a time, 2nd Assistant MO at Wakefield then Senior Assistant Physician at Bethlem before becoming physician and lecturer in Mental Physiology [subsequently Mental Diseases] at Guy's (*GHG*, September 17, 1910, p. 349). Craig, along with Rayner, Medical Superintendent, Hanwell and lecturer at St. Thomas's held special classes, with clinical instruction, at Bethlem (*BMJ* September 3, 1904, p. 532). An active member of the

MSSST Craig's (1905; 1912) text book, *Medical Psychology*, remains largely dismissive of hypnosis in cases of insanity.

30. This is further confirmation that Hart was using psychoanalysis at Long Grove although it does not exactly indicate when. Mapother's comments also suggest that he, too, had tried psychoanalysis, but without success. Another contribution, from Dr. Robertson, suggests he too had tried psycho-analysis but "had had failures from the method under discussion." (Graham 1911, p. 396).

31. Compare, for example, Wingfield (1910, p. 128) with Freud (1909a, p. 2) although the reference here was to Breuer's Anna O.

32. Wingfield was now "more interested in the experimental than in the clinical" and increasingly thought "psycho-analysis . . . was impossible in general practice" (Anon 1913b, p. 1312; Wingfield 1910, pp. 129f).

33. Turner was educated at Edinburgh where he obtained a gold medal in 1892. He went on to study at Bart's and Berlin and although essentially a neurologist, specializing in epilepsy, he increasingly took a keen interest in psychology and psychoanalysis.

34. See also Turner (1920, pp. 6–8) and the comments by J. R. Lord who also appeared to have been practicing psychoanalysis, but found it was not always appropriate because "it required too much time." (*BMJ* March 23, 1912 p. 673). Lord, who was assistant editor of the *JMS* (1900–1911) became a joint editor with Thomas Drapes in 1911.

35. After studying at Guy's and Tübingen, Goodall became pathologist and assistant MO to the West Riding Asylum [Wakefield]. Coincidentally Devine, who delivered a paper on the last day of the proceedings, was now Senior Assistant MO at Wakefield.

36. Following Eder's talk there were papers by E. R. Schuster (possibly), R. V. Stanford and Dr Bryer before the session ended and the Meeting closed.

37. About a year later Eder said: "In analysis so much as is required for the solution of the conflict must be taken up—somewhere or other it will necessarily lead to the sexual sphere, *but not everywhere nor always*." (Mitchell 1913, pp. 18–19, italics mine) See also Eder (1917, p. 8).

38. A far more prosaic scenario is that there was little time for discussion because it was late Friday afternoon, there were still other papers to be heard and many delegates were keen to return home for the weekend.

39. Although Abraham complained, in October 1910, about Oppenheim's "resistance" they nonetheless had cordial relations and Oppenheim, who "sent [Abraham] a patient for psychoanalysis" in June 1908, seems to have been generally supportive if critical of Abraham's psychoanalytical work (Falzeder 2002, pp. 46, 64, 82, 93, 118)

40. See Graham (1911, p. 396).

41. Edwin Bramwell, Assistant physician Edinburgh Royal Infirmary, On the death of Alexander Bruce (1854–1911), who had published Middlemiss's review (1904) of *Every-Day Life*, Bramwell became assistant editor of the RNP which, in 1910, published two of Jones's quasi-Freudian essays.

42. The *BMJ* (March 25, 1911, p. 146) lists a number of those who indicated they would attend the Section: David Blair, (County Asylum, Lancaster), W J Middleton, Dr. Shuttleworth, (late Medical Superintendent Royal Albert Asylum, Lancaster),

Byrom Bramwell (Edinburgh Royal Infirmary), Dr G. Robertson (Edinburgh), James William Russell, Cuthbert S Morrison, James Craig, S. A. Kinnier-Wilson (Queen's Square) and Henry Shaw (County Asylum, Stafford). Most of them would have already known of Freud's work, maybe even used psychoanalysis, and would therefore have been interested in Devine's and Eder's talks.

43. Maitland (1875–1948) born Merthyr Tydfil, Wales (Anon 1948).

44. Graduated from Guy's in 1902, elected to the visiting staff at Charing Cross, and later the Evelina where he worked as an outpatient physician. Forsyth was an inaugural member of the BPAS, a long-term member of the IPA and like Jones and Eder was also a member of the SSDC (Anon 1941, p. 652).

45. Stoddart, assistant physician at Bethlem and subsequently its Resident Physician and Medical Superintendent. By 1912 he was lecturing on Mental Disease at Westminster Hospital, Royal Free Hospital and London School of Clinical Medicine. He was also the educational secretary of the Association and, like a number of early British psychoanalysts, a member of the BPS (Edgell 1947, p. 121).

Chapter 16

T. W. Mitchell, Discovering the Works of Freud

"AS A SEA OF SUBMERGED IDEAS AND EMOTIONS"

In November 1908 Mitchell (1912a, p. 270), whose early writtings we looked at in Chapter 10, realized that Amelia, the patient he first started treating in 1901, had "a hypnotic personality, claiming to be co-conscious." Although already familiar with the literature on double and multiple personalities Mitchell was prompted to return to Sidis & Goodhart (1905) and also to Morton Prince's *The Dissociation of a Personality*, a copy of which was entered into the SPR Library shortly after its publication in 1906 (*Journal* 1906, Vol. 12, p. 348).[1] That McDougall (1907a; 1907b) had recently written extensive reviews of both books for *Proceedings* (See also *Journal* 1908, Vol. 13, pp. 20–23) suggests that multiple personality was, at this time, actively discussed in SPR circles. If, as the evidence suggests, Mitchell started re-reading Prince (1906a), in late 1908, this now helps to explain how Mitchell came to read Prince's latest work (1908–1909), a long monograph on 'The Unconscious.' The first part of Prince's paper appeared in the October-November 1908 issue of *JAP*. Although still relatively unknown in Britain at the time, Mitchell probably came across a reference to *JAP* when reading 'The Galvanometer and Subconscious Ideas,' which was published in the *BMJ* in September 1908. This was a review of a recent *JAP* article, written by Prince and Peterson (1908) discussing their experiments to determine if "subconscious ideas—that is, co-conscious processes of which the subject is unaware and which yet manifest themselves in intelligent action—ever exist at all." (Anon 1908c, pp. 943–44).[2] As an habitually curious reader, particularly of the *BMJ*, Mitchell would have noted the reference not least because *JAP* was edited by Morton Prince who was also an Honorary member of the SPR. If Mitchell still did not know about Freud's post 1895 (*Studien*) writings in November 1908 then all this would have changed, dramatically, once he had read Prince's monograph, which Jones advised Freud to read because of its severe criticisms (Paskauskas 1993, p. 14). Discovering *JAP* was another critical moment in Mitchell's intellectual development because it not only inspired him to abstract the April–May 1909 issue for the June 1909 issue of the *Journal* (1910, Vol. 14, p. 110) but also because it alerted him to the significance of Freud through its numerous references and articles. And tracing Mitchell's discovering *JAP*, in late 1908, reveals how 'Freud' and 'psychoanalysis' *did not* enter into the SPR discourse through Myers's reading of Breuer and Freud but through Mitchell's reading of *JAP*.

Following Myers's 1903 posthumous discussion of *Studien* there are no references to Freud in the SPR literature until April 1909 when Mitchell makes a passing reference to Freud in his review of the February-March 1909 issue of *JAP*. After commenting on Prince's monograph on 'The Unconscious,' Mitchell (1909a, p. 80) noted that the article by W. D. Scott

> defends the thesis that the psycho-analytic method [of Breuer and Freud (see *Human Personality*, Vol. I, p. 50)] is nothing more than an unusually skilful application of the method of suggestion, and that it offers no proof for the existence of subconscious complexes of suppressed emotional ideas.

Although Scott (1909, p. 372) was clearly familiar with Freud's more recent work he, like many others at the time, assumed that psychoanalysis also included hypnotism, re-education and suggestion.[3] Mitchell not only ignored these errors but—and this is the critical point—he also *misquoted*, or more probably *miss*-read, what Scott had written because it was Mitchell, and not Scott, who had inserted that Myers's reference to *Studien* which I have enclosed in square brackets. This misreading suggests that as late as March 1909 Mitchell was still ignorant of Freud's post *Studien* writings while his miss-quoting Scott, by coupling Breuer and Freud with Myers, would have been instinctively understood by his SPR readers. Then in June 1909 Mitchell (1909b) reviewed, in detail, *Religion and Medicine* (Worcester et al. 1908) which, as we have seen, was reviewed by the *BMJ* earlier that year. Reviewing that book, which described "in plain terms the principles underlying the new medico-religious effort which goes by the name of the 'Emmanuel movement,'"[4] Mitchell noted how Worcester and Coriat took very different views as "to the psychological status" of the "'subconscious.'" Worcester believed each of us has a subconscious mind which is a normal part of our spiritual nature and therefore "more amenable to external control than our ordinary consciousness." Coriat (1875–1943), on the other hand, "regards the subconscious as being always due to a dissociation of consciousness; and to a subconsciousness so originating no peculiar powers can be ascribed." Mitchell suggested Coriat's view was the one held by the majority of American neurologists. More to the point, however, Mitchell makes no reference to Coriat's brief reference to Freud's *Everyday Life*, nor to McComb's reference to Freud's "Neurosenlehre" (Worcester et al. 1908, pp. 206 and 281).

Then just over a year later, in the July 1910 *Journal* there appeared 'Notes on Current Periodicals,' another of Mitchell's occasional reviews which, this time, was inspired by the April 1910 issue of the *Psychological Bulletin* [*PB*] and particularly Jones's essay on 'Freud's Psychology.' In his review Mitchell (1910b, pp. 353–56) takes as his starting point, Jones's prefaratory remarks which caution that it was extremely difficult "to give an intelligible account of Freud's work" because his views have undergone significant changes over the last twenty years and could only be understood "in the light of its historical development."

> Another and greater difficulty is that Freud's Psychology involves a radical change in our attitude towards the questions of the structure and functioning of the mind. Its applications are exceedingly diverse, and much of the cogency of Freud's arguments is derived from the confirmation and mutual support that the application of them receives from widely different fields of study, such as psychopathology, dreams, wit, mythology and every-day life.

Passing over Jones's claim as to Freud's 'radicalism,' Mitchell offers, instead, his own understanding of Freud:

> The conception of the Unconscious (*Unbewusstsein*) as a sea of submerged ideas and emotions interacting with and determining the course of events in the consciousness which we know by introspection forms the foundation on which Freud's psychological superstructure rests. Freud's Unconscious is in truth not very different from Myers's Subliminal, but it seems to be more acceptable to the scientific world, in so far as it has been invoked to account for normal and abnormal phenomena only, and does not lay its supporters open to the implication of belief in supernormal happenings.

Perhaps, somewhat ironically, it may have been Jones who unwittingly signalled this particular reading of Myers's because in his text Jones noted: "Unconscious memories are those that cannot be spontaneously recalled by the subject, but which can be evoked by the use of special methods (hypnosis, psycho-analysis, etc.). . . ." And to this Jones (1910c, p. 111 & n.) added, by way of a footnote:

> It will be noticed that by definition [these unconscious memories] resemble Myers's subliminal process, Prince's co-conscious, and Janet's *subconscient*.

> There exist, however, fundamental differences between Freud's views on the subject and those of other writers; these have been strikingly discussed in a recent article by Bernard Hart [1910a] in [*JAP*] Feb.-March, 1910.

Reading Jones's footnote suggests that Jones's 'reading' was almost certainly gleaned *not* from his reading of Myers but from his reading Hart's essay 'The Conception of the Subconscious,' in which Hart (1910a, p. 363) notes:

> Myers ascribes to the subconscious various supernatural properties which take his conception altogether beyond the limits of science.

But even more striking is that Mitchell's use of the phrase, "Unconscious (Unbewusstsein) as a sea of submerged ideas and emotions," echoes Hart (1910a, p. 365) who says:

> The subconscious (unbewusstsein) is regarded as a sea of unconscious ideas and emotions, upon whose surface plays the phenomenal consciousness of which we are personally aware.

And, in using the metaphor of the sea, Hart has unwittingly—or maybe wittingly!—returned this image full circle to Myers (1903, Vol. 1, p. 51) who, in discussing Breuer's case of Fräulein Anna O., says: "These submerged ideas, these hidden ulcers of the mind, become, so to say, *confluent*." Thus although Mitchell appears to have introduced "Freud" into the SPR's discourse through his review of Jones's essay on "Freud's Psychology," it is, in fact, Hart's *conception* of Myers's concept of the subconscious [*sic*] which now enteres into that SPR discourse. Or to be even more precise the Hart / Jones conception of Myers's concept of the (~~subliminal~~) unconscious, as "altogether beyond the limits of science," can be traced even further back to that long critical obituary of Myers by McDougall (1903, pp. 514ff) who, in turn, may well have taken his argument from Sidis (1898, p. 3).

Whatever the ultimate source for this negative *conception* of Myers's concept of the unconscious Mitchell's July 1910 review marks the precise moment when Freud's concept of the unconscious enters into the SPR's discourse *and* when orthodox 'scientific' psychology—as advanced by Sidis, McDougall, Hart and Jones—formally distances itself from the contamination of psychical research. It is at this moment that the British psychic and psychological discourses bifurcate. This can be traced, for example, through to 1912 when Jones openly expressed his fears of being 'misunderstood' if he should accept an invitation to write an article for the SPR (Paskauskas 1993, p. 136); and then through to 1945 when Strachey, having admitted to being a member of the SPR in 1908, immediately felt it incumbent upon himself to reassure Jones, "I was never spooky." But it can also be read through the almost total absence of any references, let alone discussions, of the SPR in the orthodox histories of psychology, framed, as they invariably are, by the 'psychologists.' (Bunn et al. 2001). But there is another significance in Mitchell's July 1910 review because it intersects with three other important publications: Hart's May 1910 BPS Oxford lecture, subsequently published as 'The Psychology of Freud and his School': The April / May 1910 publication of the first English translation of Freud's 'The Origin and Development of Psychoanalysis,' which was published in the *AJP*'s "famous special number," and which, as we shall see shortly, was to have such a profound impact on British experimental psychologists. And finally it intersects with the publication of the June 1910 *BMJ* 'Special Issue' on Mental Healing which we have already looked at, in some detail, in Chapter 6.

FROM MYERS TO FREUD

On May 6, 1909 a symposium on Psychotherapy was arranged to coincide with the Annual meeting of the American Therapeutic Society in New Haven where Morton Prince had gathered together nine speakers "learned in modern psychology, expert in neurology, skilful in psychotherapy." These included Prince himself, Gerrish, Jones, Sidis and Putnam. And all their papers, save Putnam's,[5] were then published in the June–July (1909) issue of *JAP*. 'Some Recent Developments in Psychotherapy,' Mitchell's long review of that issue, was then published in the August 1910 issue of *Proceedings*.

Mitchell (1910c, p. 665) begins his review by reminding his readers that:

> Myers's conception of the Subliminal Consciousness was in no small measure influenced by the work of investigators who were primarily interested in psychopathology and psychotherapeutics. . . . The psychological and therapeutic aspects of hypnotism have ever been closely associated, and the further developments of a subject for which Mr Myers and Mr Gurney did so much should be of interest to all who are interested in psychical research.

Mitchell then offered a brief discussion of Gerrish's paper, a much longer discussion of Morton Prince's paper, as well brief discussions of the papers by E. W. Taylor and G. A Waterman. But he reserved the core of his review for "the method of psycho-analysis elaborated by Professor Freud, of Vienna, of which an excellent account is given by Dr Ernest Jones . . . in his contribution to the symposium." This, incidentally, was the review which Strachey mentioned in his 1945 letter to Jones.

> The psycho-analytic form of psychotherapy is specially applicable to those psycho-neuroses in which a mental complex has become dissociated from the personal consciousness, and it is carried out by simultaneously laying bare and remedying the pathological mechanism at the base of the malady. Hysteria may

be taken as the type of these psycho-neuroses, and in order to understand what is meant by psycho-analysis it is necessary to have some knowledge of Freud's views on the nature and causation of hysteria. (Mitchell 1910c, p. 673–74)

Mitchell then noted how "the majority of modern observers" acknowledge "that the occurrence of hysterical symptoms is associated with a splitting of consciousness and the subconscious functioning of dissociated mental states." Then, in a passage worth quoting at length, Mitchell (1910c, pp. 674–75) added:

Myers regarded stratification of consciousness as part of the normal structure of the mind, and he ascribed hysterical manifestations to a dream-like action of the subliminal consciousness at the hypnotic level, whereby powers of faculties that ought to be retained in the supraliminal become submerged and lost to the waking self. According to Janet hysterical symptoms are the result of a splitting of consciousness, and all subconscious manifestations are due to pathological dissociation. In people who are lacking in capacity for psychic synthesis, in whom there is a narrowing of the field of consciousness, some of the ideas that enter into the formation of personality tend to become dissociated from the waking consciousness and to take on independent functioning on their own account. Inability to keep a hold on the whole of the conscious field is the cause of the splitting of consciousness, and the stigmata of hysteria are the consequences. Freud's views regarding the origin of the mental dissociation manifested in hysteria are quite different from those of Myers or Janet and in some respects are totally opposed to them. Far from thinking it due to a dream-like action of the subliminal at the hypnotic level, or a merely accidental result of *misère psychologique*, Freud believes that the splitting of consciousness met with in hysteria is caused by a deliberate act of will on the part of the patient. He does not, of course, mean to imply that the patient intends to produce a splitting of consciousness. The patient's intention is different, but in trying to attain its aim it provokes a splitting of consciousness.

Psychic health may exist so long as there is no hopeless incompatibility between the ideas which enter into consciousness. But it may happen that an experience or an idea or a feeling may arise which is so incompatible with all the ideas and feelings that enter into the formation of the personality, that a psychical pain ensues which is felt to be unbearable. If this unbearable idea is fairly faced, and if it can by any means be adjusted within the personal consciousness, no harm will follow; but if such adjustment cannot be effected, if the personal consciousness will have nothing to do with the idea that has arisen, the unbearable idea is repressed by an act of will. The personal consciousness tries to forget it and to treat it as if it had never occurred. This can only be done by taking away from it the emotional excitement which adheres to it, thereby changing the strong idea into a weak one which will have little claim on the associative process. But the sum of the excitation thus freed must be utilised in some other direction, and in people who develop hysterical symptoms there seems to be

> some psycho-physical adaptation which enables the emotional excitement to be transformed into bodily innervation. In hysteria the unbearable idea is rendered psychically harmless because the sum of excitation is transformed into physical manifestations. This transformation, for which Freud proposes the term *conversion*, is to be regarded as a defence reaction of the Ego against unbearable ideas. If there does not happen to be any adaptation for conversion to take place, and still for the purpose of defence a separation of the unbearable idea from its painful feeling-tone is necessary, the emotional excitement must remain in the psychic sphere. But it separates from the unbearable idea and attaches itself to some other idea not in itself unbearable, and in this way gives rise to obsessions or phobia. From his later work Freud has come to the conclusion that the repressed idea is always of the nature of a wish, and that the hysterical symptom is a symbolic expression of its realisation. A wish whose realisation would be incompatible with the whole personality of the patient is realised symbolically as a tremor or a paralysis, and the hysterical symptom serves as a sort of unconscious gratification to the patient. When an unbearable idea is successfully repressed a splitting of consciousness takes place, the repressed complex takes on an automatic activity, and its functioning is manifested in the symptoms of the psycho-neurosis.

Mitchell suggests the aim of psychoanalysis was "to discover the repressed complex which underlies the hysterical symptoms, to reveal it in all its relations and to bring it back into the waking consciousness of the patient." Once the patient's defenses are overcome and conversion has taken place "the repressed wish and the circumstance under which it came to be entertained may be completely forgotten by the patient and the distorted form in which the activity of the repressed complex becomes manifest forms the chief difficulty in discovering the real nature of the wish which is thus symbolised." (Mitchell 1910c, pp. 675–76). The usual procedure for "resuscitating forgotten memories related to the repressed complex is to ask the patient to concentrate his mind on a given idea, generally one in relation to a symptom, and to relate in the order of their appearance all the thoughts that come to his mind. If he does this quite honestly and without reservation, important clues as to the nature of the disturbing complex are very soon discovered." Then Mitchell turned to Jung's recent work and, after describing his method of word association, gave an "instance taken from Jung." Although Mitchell offers no reference he had obviously drawn from Jung's (1907a, p. 249) article in the February 1907 issue of *JAP*. But Mitchell (1910c, pp. 677–78) also referred to the use of the galvanometer and also to the Coriat and Prince & Petersen experiments.

> Suffice it to say that by the methods just outlined, combined with an analysis of the patient's dreams by means of the special technique introduced by Freud, it is possible to trace the origin of a symptom to its underlying complex, and the

> advocates of psycho-analysis as a therapeutic method maintain that by bringing submerged complexes to light and by enabling the patient to understand and appreciate their significance in relation to his malady, 'he is able to free his personality from the constraining force of these complexes, and by taking up an independent attitude towards them, to gain a degree of self-control over his aberrant thoughts and wishes that was previously impossible.'[6] The repressed complex, after being dissected and analysed in all its relations, becomes assimilated by the personal consciousness and the patient is cured.

Mitchell (1910c, p. 678) then discussed the significance of accurate diagnosis in the treatment of disease.

> The psycho-analytic procedures elaborated by the Vienna and Zurich schools are the most delicate instruments of psychical diagnosis which we at present possess and their value in this connection can not fail to be recognised;[7] but when it is maintained that these procedures are in themselves curative as well as diagnostic there are good grounds for disputing the validity of the claim. To trace the psychogenesis of a symptom is not in itself to modify the complex which causes it, and if the psycho-analysis can not be successfully performed without at the same time so modifying the complex that the symptom disappears, the influences which lead to such modification—whether rational explanation, persuasion or suggestion—must be given their share of credit in regard to the therapeutic result.

Mitchell then went on to discuss those therapies which use "the artificial induction of more or less profound alterations of consciousness" and then noted the many benefits to be derived from hypnotic suggestion even "when no objective signs of hypnosis can be discovered." And, at this point, Mitchell (1910c, pp. 679f) turned to discuss the theories of Boris Sidis whereupon he concluded his article with a general discussion and defense of hypnotism.

Reading Mitchell's August 1910 review reveals that he drew not just from Jones's contribution to the Symposium (Jones 1909a) but also from Jones's *AJP* article on Hamlet (Jones 1910a, p. 73), from Jung's *JAP* article (1907a) and from Brill's recently published translation of Freud's (1909a) early work. As Mitchell was a voracious reader it is also quite likely that by the end of 1910 he would have read most, if not all, the available English language texts on Freud, including the April 1910 Special Issue of *AJP* which carried not only Freud's and Jung's September 1909 Clark Lectures but also important articles by Jones (1910b) and Ferenczi (1910). Mitchell may even have attended Hart's May 1910 BPS Oxford lecture and would almost certainly have read it shortly after its publication in the *JMS*. There can be little doubt, therefore, that by July 1910 Mitchell had a good working knowledge of Freud while his detailed reviews and active presence in the SPR would have had a significant influence on a number of its members.[8] These speculations find support from Alice Johnson (1918, p. 33) who says: "From 1910 onwards, some valuable discussions of psychoanalysis have been contributed to the *Proceedings* by Dr. Mitchell and Dr. Woolley (1879–1966)."[9] But to further understand this trajectory we will need to return to Mitchell's treatment of Amelia, the patient he "had under observation" since 1901 (Mitchell 1912b, p. 286; Anon 1910a, p. 264) and whom, as it now appears, he started treating again, for a third time, in November 1908.

A STUDY IN HYSTERIA

On March 31, 1910[10] Mitchell read "A Study in Hysteria and Double Personality, with Report of a Case," to a Private Meeting of the SPR. Although briefly summarized in the April 1910 *Journal* the full paper was not published until November 1912 when it appeared under the slightly but significantly altered title: "A Study in Hysteria and Multiple Personality, With Report of a Case" ["A Study"]. "Double" had become "Multiple." Then on 31 October 1911, Mitchell read "Some Types of Multiple Personality" ["Multiple Personality"] to a Private Meeting of the SPR. "Multiple Personality" and "A Study," can be considered companions,[11] because they were published simultaneously in the November 1912 first Special Medical Issue of *Proceedings* (Mitchell, 1912a, b) appearing alongside Freud's (1912a) 'A Note on the Unconscious in Psycho-Analysis' and Sidis's (1912) 'The Theory of the Subconscious.'

Multiple Personality,' in which Mitchell discusses, at length, some of the theoretical issues raised by double and multiple personalities, particularly "dissociation" and "the unity of consciousness," was clearly inspired by his long-term treatment of Amelia, whose case history forms the focus for 'A Study.' Our interest, however, lies in the period after November 1908 when Mitchell (1912b, pp. 296f) started treating Amelia yet again. At first he failed to hypnotize her and "thinking there was little probability of inducing a true hypnosis, I confined my attention almost entirely to making suggestions with regard to the headache and obsessions." (*ibid* p. 297). Within three weeks Mitchell "discovered that [Amelia] now went into what seemed to be a genuine hypnosis with amnesia on waking" although he "was disappointed that her speech affection . . . did not respond to my suggestions of recovery." While trying to tackle Amelia's various symptoms through hypnosis and suggestion Mitchell (*ibid* p. 298) became increasingly "struck by the unequal response which attended his efforts." Some symptoms "disappeared instantly at the first suggestion. Others . . . seemed to be quite unaffected, no matter how often or how impressively appropriate suggestions were given."

> It soon became evident that the symptoms which were easily relieved were those which, in her waking state she *asked* me to relieve, or those to the relief of which I had gained her free and unqualified assent during hypnosis.

With this in mind Mitchell (1912b, pp. 298–99 and 301) then tried "inducing" Amelia to ask him "definitely to relieve those symptoms which most seriously impaired her bodily and mental health." By the middle of December (1908), following a series of successes, Amelia's

> chief disabilities having been removed, she very soon recovered her health .. although for many weeks she provided me with a variety of hysterical symptoms on which to exercise my therapeutic ingenuity.

Mitchell's chronology suggests he must have stopped treating Amelia no later than the end of March 1909.

As already noted Mitchell read 'A Study' to an SPR meting on March 31, 1910 which was briefly reported in the April 1910 *Journal* [the Report].

> From the beginning of this last attack [Amelia] was treated by hypnotic suggestion, and Dr. Mitchell said he was struck by the unequal response to therapeutic suggestions which he met with in this case. It seemed to him that the resistance encountered in connection with particular suggestions was the deliberate act of a second personality which was brought to light by the induction of hypnosis. Only when the hypnotic personality so pleased were suggestions for the relief of any particular symptom of any avail. (Anon 1910, p. 264)

There are two points here. First; the word resistance. Although Freud (1910a, p. 192) "based [his] theory of the psychic process of hystericals" on the idea of resistance it is unlikely Mitchell was using the term in its Freudian sense when he delivered his talk in late March 1910. Second; the absence of any reference to Freud or Freud's work in the Report stands in marked contrast to the detailed discussion of Freud's work which appeared in 'A Study' when it was published in November 1912. This chronology, which dovetails with what we now know about Mitchell's reading during this time, suggests that when Mitchell read his paper in late March 1910 he had only just started to appreciate the importance of Freud's work but had not yet started the process of incorporating it into his own psychotherapeutic practice. This transition can also be read through that part of "A Study" in which Mitchell (1912b, pp. 301–301) reflects upon the end of his treatment of Amelia.

> As I have already said, I was very much struck by the unequal results produced by suggestion in this case. Hypnosis was apparently profound; post-hypnotic

> amnesia was complete; the disabilities I was anxious to remove were obviously of a functional nature; all the conditions favourable to the speedy removal of any particular symptom seemed to be present; yet it was clear that to most of my suggestions there was some resistance of a kind quite different from the mere failure of response to suggestion that may be met with in ordinary psycho-therapeutic work. It is difficult to account for such resistance to therapeutic suggestion as was met with in this case. Obstinacy was certainly a very marked characteristic of the hypnotized patient, but we feel that there must be some good reason for unwillingness to accept curative suggestions. It seems to me probable that the resistance to which I have referred may be related to the resistance met with by Freud in the practice of psycho-analysis in cases of hysteria.

In discussing Freud's views on repression[12] Mitchell frames his comments through Brill's translation of 'The Psychotherapy of Hysteria,' the theoretical essay in *Studien* by Freud (1895, pp. 253f; 1909a, pp. 75f). But Mitchell chooses, in particular, to reference the passage where Freud (1909a, pp. 98–100) affirms the success of "the pressure procedure" whereby the doctor, or analyst, attempts "to overcome [the patient's] continued resistance .." in order to "obtain [the patient's] collaboration" and above all, to induce them to reproduce and utter "under emotion" the "causal pathogenic impressions" linked to the hysterical symptom.

> Now if Freud's views on the causation of hysterical symptoms are correct, it would seem that when a hysterical symptom is removed by suggestion, the disappearance of the symptom must be accompanied by its re-conversion into some other symptom or into the original unbearable idea. And just as the 'repugnance of the ego' to the unbearable idea may lead to resistance in psycho-analysis undertaken to disclose it, so the same psychic force may lead to the rejection of suggestions directed towards the removal of the hysterical symptom. (Mitchell 1912b, p. 302)

At first Mitchell speculated that Amelia's resistance to his curative suggestions may have been due to the fact that "somewhere in her mind there was some sort of prevision that the removal of" a symptom would result in great mental distress. If this was correct then

> there would be good reason for her prolonged rejection of my curative suggestions in regard to this symptom, and this rejection may be regarded as being due to the same cause as that which leads to resistance in psycho-analysis.

But Mitchell (1912b, pp. 303 and 303–4, italics mine) curtailed these speculations because he wanted "to describe how the resistance to suggestion met with *in this* case appeared to me *at the time*."

> In the course of treatment it seemed to become more and more apparent that there was a wilful rejection of certain therapeutic suggestions and an exercise of choice and discrimination as to what suggestions were to be allowed to be effective. Here was no passive state in which every suggestion is readily accepted, but rather a very obstinate and capricious person, who seemed to have some unusual kind of control over her own bodily organism. The rejection of therapeutic suggestions appeared to be the deliberate act of a second personality brought to light by the induction of hypnosis.

And this other personality was

> different from that of a mere state of hypnosis, and it seemed to persist throughout waking life as a co-conscious personality capable of acting on its own initiative, and also capable of taking possession of the bodily organism at will. (Mitchell 1912b, p. 305)

Then, following a brief discussion of the differences between Janet's and Freud's views as to the cause of hysterical symptoms, Mitchell (1912b, p. 308) concluded:

> In view of the remarkable findings of Freud and his pupils in regard to the pathogenesis of hysteria, I decided to analyse [Amelia] in the hope that I might be able to achieve the complete restoration to health which suggestion alone seemed unable to effect. For various reasons I adopted, to begin with, the technique used by Freud in his earlier work, making use of the hypnotic state as a means of facilitating the analysis. At a later period this was supplemented by word-association tests in the waking state and other measures.

Given that Mitchell appears to have stopped treating Amelia some time in early 1909 and appears not to have discovered or read the works of Freud and Jung until around June 1910 it is difficult to square Mitchell's chronology other than to suggest that he must have written up Amelia's treatment retrospectively or, which is more likely, that she returned to him for a fourth time, maybe in the Summer of 1910. If the latter then the "various reasons" as to why Mitchell only followed Freud's earlier work are quite simple. He did not read German and so had to rely on Brill's recently published translation of Freud's (1909a) early work.

SOME CONCLUSIONS

When Mitchell first started using Freud's ideas in his own psychotherapeutic practice he probably trod the route followed by most, if not all, the other early

British practitioners with or without a working knowledge of German. So he began using the 'cathartic method' which he was able to study through Brill's translation of *Studien* and, in particular, Freud's (1909a, p. 100) theoretical essay 'The Psychotherapy of Hysteria.'

> The aim of psycho-analysis is to recover the repressed ideas in their entirety, to bring them back into consciousness, and to let the feelings connected with them have their proper emotional expression. According to Freud, 'a patient can rid himself of a hysterical symptom only after reproducing and uttering *under emotion* its causal pathogenic impressions.' (Mitchell 1912b, p. 302, italics mine).[13]

When Mitchell subsequently turned to Freud's later work he felt confident enough, like Eder, Wingfield, Jones and others, to start incorporating Jung's word-association tests into his psychotherapeutic practice. We know Mitchell (1910c, pp. 676–77) had already discovered Jung's "series of test words," by August 1910, although he may originally have thought that they were dependent on "the galvanic current of low tension" and so only started using them manually, so to speak, in late 1910, perhaps as a result of reading Wingfield (1910, pp. 126–30) which was briefly reviewed, probably by Mitchell himself, in the January 1911 issue of the *Journal* (Vol. 15, pp. 15–16).[14] There seems little doubt that by early 1911 Mitchell was already using those variants of psychoanalysis common at the time: a combination of word-association tests—to discover the underlying complex—together with hypnosis and suggestion, where hypnosis was used primarily as a way of resuscitating memories forgotten in the waking state.[15] Or, as Mitchell (1912b, pp. 309 and 310–11) said: he used hypnosis or the "verbal suggestion of sleep combined with light passes with contact on the face," to help facilitate the psychoanalysis.

> According to Freud, the pathogenic psychic material which has been crowded out of the ordinary consciousness in hysteria may be shown still to exist in an orderly form; and again and again in the course of psycho-analysis undertaken in the waking state, Freud seems struck by the appearance of its being in the possession of a second intelligence. He says: "One receives a delusive impression of a superior intelligence, external to the patient's consciousness, which systematically holds a large psychic material for definite purposes. . . . I presume, however, that this unconscious second intelligence is only apparent." [ft] In another place [Freud] says: "The pathogenic psychic material appears as the property of an intelligence which is not necessarily inferior to the normal ego. The semblance of a second personality is often most delusively produced." [ft]
>
> There are some grounds, I think, for demurring to Freud's view that this semblance is necessarily delusive. It seemed to me that in the case of [Amelia] the induction of hypnosis brought me into touch with a series of personalities who

> held in their possession a vast amount of psychic material of which the waking consciousness had lost all knowledge, and of a kind which, on Freud's own showing, must be regarded as hysterogenic.[16]

Although Mitchell was obviously, by now, inspired by Freud's work he was not prepared to relinquish hypnosis and suggestion because, as he noted. "Very likely from the Freudian point of view the analysis was incomplete, but I had attained my end, and [Amelia] became to all appearance a normal healthy woman. And so she remains." (Mitchell 1912b, p. 311; also Mitchell 1911b, p. 348).

NOTES

1. See also *Proceedings* 1933, Vol. 41, p. 58.
2. Prince and Peterson (1908, pp. 130–31) also discussed Jung's word-association tests.
3. Scott's paper, a confusion of different therapies, reveals a highly disturbing insight into a male therapist's emotional abuse of his female patient.
4. See Craig (1910, p. 437).
5. I have been unable to locate Putnam's essay which appears never to have been published.
6. The quote is from Jones (1909a, p. 147).
7. The *Journal* (1912, Vol. 15, p. 101) suggests using the psychoanalytic method to understand the "scripts" which had been published in *Proceedings* (1911, Vol. 25, pp. 120ff.)
8. As the subsequent review essay by Mitchell (1918, pp. 142f and 157) suggests this marked an important shift in Mitchell's thinking. In discussing Freud's theories, he says: "The unconscious is psychical but it has a dynamic character which distinguishes it from the relatively static systems of psychical dispositions." And, "There is no conception more fundamental to the psychoanalytic psychology originated and developed by Freud than the conception of 'Repression.' By repression alone is the existence and nature of the unconscious of Freud explained, and the overcoming of the resistances is the one aim of his psychoanalytic therapy."
9. Victor James Woolley born East Suffolk qualified MD Cambridge and St Thomas's (1911) where he then lectured in pharmacology. A member of the Physiological Society and of the SPR from 1906. He married the German born Henrietta (b.1887) and they had a daughter, Stella Margaret (1910–). The Woolleys lived in Chislehurst some thirty miles north-west of Mitchell.
10. This meeting was originally planned for March 15, 1910.
11. When Mitchell republished these two papers, in 1922, he split them across three chapters.
12. Myers (1903, Vol. 1, p. 173) links repression with stimulus: "Repression is needed long before moral teaching begins, from the mere fact that all kinds of

impulses tend to express themselves in act,—and that many of the resultant acts, if often repeated, are unbecoming or injurious."

13. The Freud (1909, pp. 100–101) text continues: "Yet the therapeutic task merely consists in inducing him to do it, and once the task has been accomplished there remains nothing for the doctor to correct or abolish . . ."

14. Wingfield (1910, p. 128), in discussing abreaction, seems to dispense with the original Breuer-Freud idea of an emotional discharge or catharsis: "Yet, however long [non-abreacted ideas] have persisted, once they have been discovered, restored to the primary consciousness, normalized by becoming part of that, and made to abreact by discussion in ordinary conversation, they cease to be noxious, and the symptoms dependent on them must vanish." See also Wingfield's letter to the *BMJ* (November 5, 1910, p. 1470).

15. Brown (1913b, p. 1218) used: "Psycho-analysis, in the form of word-association tests" and then hypnosis, using "the *hypnoidal* state" with post-hypnotic suggestion.

16. I have glossed Mitchell's descriptions of the different personalities and phases of the hypnotic state.

Chapter 17

Bernard Hart, Charles Spearman, and the British Psychological Society

> After the mind has become thus stored with knowledge the time at length arrives when it begins to work upon its own materials. The psychologists tell us how this is done. This is a strictly creative process. By ransacking, as it were, every corner of the brain certain likenesses are discovered between images impressed upon different areas, or cells, or what not, and these are confronted and scrutinized, and their relations discovered. Something new results, something different from any of the separate items of intelligence that had been acquired during the receptive period. It may have no resemblance to any of them, yet it results from them. It is a relation subsisting between two or more of them, but it is real and definite, and constitutes a tertium quid, created by the brain's own activities. The mind knows it, so that it is an additional item of knowledge, but it did not come directly from the external senses; only its elements thus came. (Ward 1911, p. 439)

PSYCHOLOGY, EXPERIMENTAL AND MEDICAL

At the turn of the century Charles Spearman (1863–1945) gave up philosophy and went to study psychology under Wilhelm Wundt[1] in The Psychological Institute of Leipzig. Following two years interruption, serving as the British Staff Officer for Guernsey during the Boer War, Spearman (1930, pp. 301–9) completed his Ph.D. in 1906 and, following studies in various German centers, returned to England in 1907 where he was appointed reader in experimental psychology at UCL, replacing William McDougall who returned to Oxford. Because Spearman's "function was to supplement the work of . . . Carveth Read,[2] who held the chair in General Psychology," Spearman had time to concentrate on research until Read retired in 1911 and "the experimental and general psychologies were united under a single chair" to which Spearman was elected. Around 1909 J.C. Flügel, an associate member of the SPR, and subsequently a member of the BPAS, became Spearman's "right hand in the laboratory almost from the beginning." Francis Aveling (1875–1941),[3] having been appointed lecturer in Analytical Psychology, at about this time, also joined Spearman (1930, p. 309) and although Aveling subsequently acquired "his own independent department" at KCL, probably around 1914, he and Spearman continued the intimate relationship they had already forged.

It was during his time in Leipzig that Spearman (1904a, 1904b) completed some of his most important work. Following his study into the mental ability of children he concluded there were two factors involved in measuring intelligence and published his findings in two separate articles. In the first, 'The Proof and Measurement of Association Between Two Things' [Proof and Measurement], which appeared in the *AJP*, Spearman "developed his Theory of General Ability, or Theory of Two Factors, as it is alternatively named," and by 1921 that theory, "at least in England, [had] ever since dominated *correlational work* in its applications to psychology." Spearman's idea

> was to measure a number of mental abilities, some of them school subjects, others artificial tests, in a number of persons, and calculate the correlation coefficients of each of these activities with each of the others. These correlation coefficients, he then noticed, had a certain relationship among themselves, a relationship which may be called hierarchical order. . . . He saw, quite rightly, that the presence of a general factor would produce this hierarchical order among the coefficients, and, reversing this argument, he concluded that the presence of hierarchical order proved the existence of a general factor. (Brown & Thomson 1921, pp. 164, 154, 165)

Although most commentators focus on the first of Spearman's paper, it is his second, "'General Intelligence' Objectively Determined and Measured" [General Intelligence], published just three months later, which is of particular interest. In 'General Intelligence' Spearman discusses a range of topics: "The correspondence . . . between Intelligence and 'Reaction Time'" (1904b, p. 208); Binet and Henri's article on "'the relations that exist between different psychical processes'" (*ibid* p. 210); the problems faced by researchers, such as Kraepelin, who sought to devise tests for intellectual health and disease (*ibid* p. 218); and the difficulties faced by those who tried to test the general intelligence of students or sought "to find [a] correspondence between the psychics of the Laboratory and those of Life" (*ibid* p. 221). Essentially Spearman wanted to devise a theory that would allow for the accurate measurement of *psychological phenomena* by preventing one set of measurements from being wrongly connected to another apparently similar set.

> But in psychology . . . persons may honestly endeavour to appraise the same mental faculty, and yet, owing to diversity of procedure and ignorance of organic uniformities, they may really obtain measurements of quite independent function. In such cases, the sets of measurement, however accurate they may be, will show no correspondence with one another; and if the functions are even only partially different, the measurements will correspond with one another to that extent less than they would by reason solely of errors of observation. (*ibid* p. 254)

Some time in late 1907, or maybe early 1908, Spearman and Hart began a relatively short but fruitful collaboration to extend Spearman's 1904 researches. Although it remains unclear as to how, or even why, their collaboration began,[4] it is possible to speculate that Spearman, a reader in experimental psychology at UCL with time for experimental work started forging close, but informal links, with the London medical schools of UCH and KCH, where Hart and Devine, respectively, had been educated. Devine, who worked with Hart at Long Grove during this period, had probably studied experimental psychology at KCL, where William Brown was lecturing,[5] while Hart may even have studied under Spearman (1930, p. 309) who subsequently said of him: "Bernard Hart I am proud to claim as having at one time been both my student and collaborator." It is also possible to venture that the collaboration between Spearman, the experimental psychologist, and Hart, the medical psychologist, might even have been inspired by the collaborative researches of Peterson and Jung (1907, p. 492) whose work on the "physical experiments on the subject of emotion" (Shaw 1907b, p. 1308) were, as we have seen, very much to the fore between July and November 1907. Informal and semi-formal relationships were also being discussed in other British institutions, so while asylum doctors like Hart and Devine became increasingly interested in the experimental works conducted in the psychological laboratory, experimental psychologists, like Spearman, McDougall (1871–1938), C. S. Myers (1873–1946), Cyril Burt (1883–1971),[6] T. H. Pear (1886–1972), William Brown (1881–1952)[7] and J. C. Flügel (1884–1955),[8] some of whom were also medically trained and qualified, were becoming increasingly interested in extending their psychological researches into the Asylum.[9] Spearman's own researches in the Leipzig Nerve-hospital,[10] was perhaps an early example. For his part Bond would almost certainly have encouraged the Spearman-Hart experiments at Long Grove and it may well have been this cooperative venture which Spearman had in mind when he claimed, in 1913, that several years earlier: "The notion . . . was started *by some medical practitioners* who, working with myself, realised the great change that is coming over psychology" and so discussed with him the possibility of founding "a department for the study of psychotherapy." Or as Hector Munro subsequently put it, to bring about "a practical alliance . . . between psychotherapy and general psychology" (*The Lancet* December 20, 1913, p. 1803). We shall examine this further in Chapter 20.

Although Hart and Spearman's original aim was "to determine to what extent certain psychological tests can be applied to the insane" (Commissioners 1910, p. 75) they subsequently appear to have modified their research. At first they devised a number of tests "in order to obtain an accurate introspective knowledge of the mental processes involved in them." Then they applied those tests to sixty-eight inmates in Long Grove who "were selected as presenting fairly typical cases of certain kinds of insanity *according to current classification*."[11]

> Care was taken to render them as homogeneous as possible with regard to previous education and intelligence; all had reached the sixth or seventh standard in the elementary schools, or had done something equivalent. All were specially examined as to acuity of vision; this was found indispensable; the results got from several patients before we realized this necessity had to be discarded. Although the testing extended to three days, surprisingly few patients who once began were unable to finish. In spite of our losses in this way and of the cases discarded on account of defective eyesight, sixty-one out of the original sixty-eight patients furnished complete usable results. (Hart & Spearman 1915, pp. 227–28, italics mine)

Hart then tested a number of "English Asylum attendants" and when the final results were tabulated they found "the two groups performed in a remarkably similar manner."

> Those who have been accustomed to regard lunatics as completely different beings from themselves may be surprised to find that there is no very clear distinction here. In every performance there are many insane who surpass many sane. But still, even the best of the insane are almost always far behind the best of the sane. (Hart & Spearman 1915, pp. 228 and 229)

In January 1911 Spearman and Hart read 'Mental Tests applied to the Insane,' at a BPS meeting held at UCL (*BJP*, 1911, Vol. 4, p. 126) and although their paper appears to have been lost a trace can be found in Commissioners (1911, p. 81) where it is referenced as 'Mental Tests in the Sane and Insane.'

> It was a preliminary communication giving the results of research carried out at Long Grove during the years 1908–1910. A number of Individuals, including both sane and insane were subjected to tests of various kinds. The results were investigated mathematically. The conclusions reached support those arrived at by Dr Spearman in his previous experiments with normals.

Although Spearman (1929, p. 1145) subsequently claimed it was Hart who "had shown that G [general ability; a genuine faculty—i.e., one possessing functional unity] was just the factor which was predominantly influential in the pathological state known as amentia or dementia," their published work offers few further clues as to the nature of their experiments, or as to exactly what they hoped to achieve.[12] This may be due, in part, because their joint research was cut short when Spearman encountered an unspecified problem—perhaps when Read retired in 1911 thereby forcing Spearman to curtail his experimental research. And because then in late 1912 Hart left Long Grove to take up an appointment as "Superintendent of a private asylum." And while this left him more time "to do private practice" (Paskauskas 1993, p. 144) it probably also meant he now had little time or opportunity for further research and experiment.[13] On the face of it the Hart-Spearmen project appears to have ended in a cul-de-sac and their work more or less disappeared from the medical-psychological discourses, a point underlined by the fact that Hart makes no further reference to his collaboration with Spearman. It may also have been a victim of the apparent bifurcation of the two psychological discourses—the medical and the experimental—which appears to have been accelerated by the War. On the other hand Brown & Thomson (1921, p. 172) claim: "Many experimental researchers were inspired by" Hart and Spearman's work and it was cited for some time to come.[14] More to the point, for this story, Hart's active collaboration with Spearman, one of the leading psychologists of his generation and a man admired as much by his peers as by his students, was to have unexpected ramifications because it was probably as a result of their relationship that Hart was invited, by the BPS, to deliver what would turn out to be his seminal lecture on Freud.

THE BRITISH PSYCHOLOGICAL SOCIETY

In a reminiscent note, written in 1961–1962, T. H. Pear[15] recalled that in the early years of the BPS, founded in 1901, philosophers, neurologists, psychiatrists, educationalists and anthropologists would often attended meetings.[16]

> From 1910 onwards, following Freud's visit to Clark University, and the subsequent publication of the famous special number of the *American Journal of Psychology, there was daily talk of [Freud] among the younger English psychologists,*[17] but I doubt if the new ideas disturbed the oldsters much. Certainly not Ward. (Pear 1962, pp. 226 & 223; See also Pear 1941, pp. 12–13, italics mine)

While Pear notes the significance of the "special number" he failed to note two salient points. First, that apart from Freud (1910a), the special number also contained translations of Jung (1910) and Ferenczi (1910) and papers by Stern (1910) and Jones (1910). And second, he failed to note the context within which Freud's *Five Lectures* appeared.

As the *AJP* was an American publication and "the famous special number" was only published in April 1910, the journal, which many British psychologists routinely consulted (Pear 1921, p. 352)[18] probably did not start circulating until the beginning of May,[19] which coincides, almost exactly with 'The Psychology of Freud and his School,' the talk Hart (1910b) delivered to a BPS meeting in Oxford on 7 May [Oxford paper] (*BJP* 1909–1910, Vol. 3, p. 348). Hart's paper was then published in the July 1910 issue of *JMS*. This coincidence of timing suggests that Hart's paper helped not only contextualize the psychologists' reading of Freud but also facilitated their enthusiastic reception of his work. It is perhaps also no coincidence that the first published reference to Freud in the *BJP* should have appeared in October 1910 at the end of a paper which McDougall (1910, p. 266; 1911, pp. 327–28) delivered in July to a joint meeting of the BPS, Aristotelian Society [AS] and *Mind* Association [*M*A]. And it was not long after that Freud's work was being referenced and discussed in the pages of both *Mind* (1911, Vol. 20, p. 103) and the *BJP*.[20] In fact Pear (1960, p. 227) appears to confirm the significance of Hart's Oxford paper when he recalls that while he was working in Würzbürg, in 1909, he had heard nothing of Freud. "The first article I remember reading on Freud—in the psychiatric clinic at Giessen[21]—was by my English friend Bernard Hart." Although Pear failed to identify which Hart paper had inspired him we know Pear was in Giessen in 1911 (Forrester 2006, p. 68) which makes it possible that he *was* 'thinking' of 'The Psychology of Freud and his School' which Hart had delivered in Oxford in May 1910. And if this was the case then Pear's discovering Freud occurred, more or less, through the same channel as the other English psychologists if only several months later than he had half-remembered it happening. Now Pear (1914a, pp. 281n, 288 & n; 1960, pp. 228–29) also claimed that he first started analyzing his own dreams "at a time when I knew only the bare outlines of Freud's theory," and that his apprenticeship in dream interpretation was one and a half years *before* he delivered his paper on dreams to the September 1913 meeting of the British Association.[22] This suggests Pear probably started reading *Die Traumdeutung* around March 1912; about a year after he had discovered Freud.[23] Pear (1914a, p. 281) also noted: "Since the publication of Freud's theory [in Brill's 1913 translation], however, the study of dreams has naturally received a great impetus."[24] Here, then, is yet another reminder of the significance of Brill's translations for those interested in Freud (1913, p. xi) but "handicapped by their inability to read fluently very difficult German."

Pear[25] was not the only psychologist to credit Hart with the dissemination of Freud's ideas because W. H. R. Rivers (1920, p. 85) also pointed directly to the importance of Hart "who more than any other English writer has made the psychology of the unconscious part of general knowledge." Rivers (1864–1922), who would become an Associate of the BPAS in 1919, was thinking of Hart's book, *The Psychology of Insanity* (1912), which also had an important influence on Arthur Tansley (Cameron & Forrester 1999, p. 68; 2000, p. 229) before it was published let alone reviewed by Bernard Muscio in *Mind* (1913, Vol. 22, pp. 410–12). Thus prior to Jones's *Papers on Psycho-Analysis* (1913)[26] being noticed, let alone reviewed, the growing interest in Freud's work had already spread from the medical to the experimental psychologists. So, for example, Brown (1913a; 1921, p. 17), a fluent German speaker, claimed his interest in Freud began in 1912 when he started reading *Die Traumdeutung* (Brown 1921, p. 17), and by early 1913 he had published a long, two part article, on Freud's 'Theory of Dreams,' in *The Lancet*. But by then Brown was also completing a long paper on psychoanalysis, part of which he delivered to the July 1913 BMA Annual Meeting (Brown 1913b) and part of which he delivered on Tuesday September 16, 1913 to a British Association meeting in Birmingham. And then having submitted the remaining manuscript to the *BJP* in late November 1913 it was published some three months later (Brown 1914). Pear (1914) followed close on his heals when he delivered his talk, 'The Analysis of some Personal Dreams with reference to current theories of Dream Interpretation,' to that same September 1913 BA meeting (Anon 1914, pp. 688–89). And then having amplified that talk and modified its title, from 'Current Theories' to 'Freud's Theory,' he then sent it on December 6, 1913 to the *BJP* where it was then also published in February 1914.[27] Edgell (1947, p. 117) may have unwittingly drawn these same connections when she noted that in March 1913—just three years after Hart's paper,

> Mr Pear gave the Society 'An Analysis of some Personal Dreams, with Special Reference to Freud's Interpretation' and at the same meeting Dr W. Brown spoke on 'The Psychological System of Sigmund Freud, as set forth in Chapter VII of Traumdeutung'.[28]

All this will now help explain why Jones reported to Freud, in July 1914: "I have excellent news from the English psychologists, which confirms my expectation that they would prove more accessible than neurologists" (Paskauskas 1993, p. 290).[29]

NOTES

1. Pointing to the explicit fissures between Wundt and the SPR, Sommer (2013a, pp. 27 and 36–37) highlights the growing rift between German academic psychology and spiritualism. Münsterberg insisted: "It was the responsibility of scientific psychologists to publicly demarcate their work from the "unscientific" investigations of the psychological societies in Berlin and Munich." Myers (1893a, p. 95) says "There

unfortunately exists at present a certain degree of severance between the right and the left wing of experimental psychologists;- between those who cling to the established methods of the psycho-physical laboratory, and those who follow the wider vistas which hypnotism and kindred studies seem now to be opening up."

2. Not to be confused with Stanford Read an early member of the BPAS.

3. The Rev. Francis Arthur Powell Aveling for a time Prebendary and [Catholic] Cathedral Chaplain subsequently joined the psychological staff of the MPC and along with Burt, Flügel, Murray, Turner, Carveth Read, Homer Lane, Stoddart and others were on the Council of The Society for the Study of Orthopsychics (*The Lancet* May 6, 1916, p. 970).

4. Anon (1966) noted: "Hart had a clear understanding of scientific method, and collaborated with Charles Spearman in a rigorous inquiry into the measurement of dementia by psychological tests . . ." but then added, erroneously:—"They also wrote jointly a learned and closely reasoned paper on the existence of a general common factor of intelligence." This error is now habitually reproduced in the secondary literature.

5. As Devine's biography is unclear I have assumed he studied with Brown after Brown became a lecturer in psychology at KCL in 1908 and where Brown (1913b, p. 1217) then worked under W. Aldren Turner who took an interest in Brown's study of psychoanalysis.

6. In 1908 Burt became lecturer in physiology and experimental psychology under Sherrington in the University of Liverpool. It is not clear when Burt (1916), an early member of the BPAS, first started his interest in Psychoanalysis.

7. Born in Slinfold, Sussex. Following his studying mathematics and philosophy at Oxford, and post-graduate studies in Germany, Brown graduated MD from KCH. "[A]t the instigation of his teacher William McDougall [Brown] worked with Burt, Flügel and, later with Spearman, to produce, for the committee of the British Association, the Spearman-Brown formula for the checking of mental tests in the assessment of intelligence, which he applied in 1908 as head of the psychological department at [KCL]." During the war Brown worked at Maghull and Craiglockhart Hospital for Neurasthenic Officers.

8. Flügel was a member of the SPR and BPAS.

9. Pear (1941, p. 7) says "professional psychotherapists—not psychoanalysts only—. . . have few chances to know, still less to study, normal people intimately and sympathetically."

10. In 1904, Professor Flechsig, director of the Leipzig Nerve-hospital, permitted Spearman (1905, p. 289) to quantitatively test a patient's power of localization over a four month period.

11. These classifications may have been Kraepelin-inspired, for which see the table of classification in Hart and Spearman (1915, p. 259).

12. It seems that they used calculations and memory (Hart & Spearman 1915, p. 258); also "crossing out rings," as a way of "measuring quickness of sensori-motor coordination" and testing general ability "by 'tapping'" in order to measure feats "of the attention for ' backward '" adults (Abelson 1911a, pp. 273 and 300; Abelson 1911b).

13. In 1912 Hart took up a new appointment, perhaps because he heard Bond was about to leave Long Grove. Then in 1913 Hart was appointed Physician-in-charge of

the Out-Patient Department for Mental Diseases at UCH. As Spearman was clearly unable to conduct the bulk of the experiments and Hart was now overstretched their collaboration petered out (Hart & Spearman 1915, 217n).

14. Hart and Spearman published two papers; the first in the *BJP*, the second in *JAP*. Hart and Spearman (1913) also delivered 'An Experimental Investigation into the General Nature of Dementia' to the 1913 International Congress of Medicine (*JMS*, July 1913, p. 539).

15. I am indebted to the late John Forrester for having suggested Pear's importance for this narrative.

16. Three of the original founders of the [BPS] were also members of the Association: W. G. Smith, F. W. Mott and Robert Jones (Bunn 2001, p. 28n).

17. See for example, Alexander (1911, p. 259), Read (1911, p. 351), Brown (1921, p. 17).

18. Most British Psychologists routinely consulted *AJP* (i.e. Burt 1909, pp. 107 and 122n), which was founded by G. Stanley Hall (1844–1924) and linked to the APA which Hall founded in 1892. Hall, an early pioneer of psychotherapy (Caplan 2001, p. 98) also founded and edited the *Pedagogical Seminary* which Eder and Kerr may have read. Hall, as President of Clark University from 1889, was responsible for inviting Freud and Jung to lecture in 1909.

19. Freud had still not received his copy by 15 April (Paskauskas 1993, p. 51; Brabant et al., 1993, p. 161). Although Jones wanted to translate Freud's 'Clark Lectures' the task was organized by the University and offered to Harry W. Chase, who worked under Freud's supervision. (Paskauskas 1993, pp. 37, 38n, 41; Steiner 1987, p. 71).

20. Although Forrester (2008, pp. 38–39) suggests that C. S. Myers was already interested in abnormal psychology the review of Myers (1909) by Anon (1909b) suggests otherwise. Forrester also notes that in 1913 Myers explicitly recognized "the importance of psychoanalysis in his formal speech at the opening of the Laboratory [for psychology in Cambridge]," which parallels Brown's lectures at KCL.

21. The Clinic was opened in 1896 and Peterson, who visited in 1899, considered it the best of the major European psychopathic hospitals (*The Lancet* June 29, 1901, p. 1841).

22. Although Pear (1960, pp. 228–29) says he "discussed Freud's dream theories" at a BPS meeting I have been unable to verify this and suspect he may have confused it with the British Association meeting.

23. Freud (1910a, pp. 200f) offers the first comprehensive English outline of *Die Traumdeutung* which may also help to explain why the 'Special Number' had such a profound impact upon its early readers and why so many of those readers—especially the experimental psychologists—then took up the study and interpretation of their own dreams.

24. A copy of Freud (1913) was received by the *BJP* (Vol. 6, p. 262) some time in the Autumn of 1913 "A very readable translation of Freud's best-known work." It is also worth noting, however, that "The sale, by the way, is restricted to members of the medical, scholastic, legal and clerical professions . . ." and the book was published by George Allen & Co. (*OR* 1913, p. 185).

25. When Jones met Pear in July 1914 he called him this "clever young psychologist" (Paskauskas 1993, p. 291).

26. Although the preface to Jones (1913a) is dated London September 1912 Jones suggests his book was already in print by the end of January 1913. (Mitchell 1913, p. 13n) This may have been the same for the book by Hitschmann (1913, p. iii) which offered "a synthetic presentation of the Freudian theory."

27. These papers were followed, in October 1914, with 'An Inquiry into some questions connected with imagery in Dreams," E. Roffe Thompson's attempt (1914, p. 300) "to consider certain problems which have been suggested mainly by a study of Freud's well-known book *Die Traumdeutung*." I am assuming E. Roffe Thompson would have been inspired to study Freud while working under Pear in the Psychological Laboratory at Manchester University.

28. Brown's and Pear's papers were delivered on March 8, 1913 (*BJP* 1914, Vol. 6, p. 136). Brown's (1913, pp. 1182f) was probably based on the lecture he read before the Listerian Society at KCL on January 21, 1913. See also Paskauskas (1993, pp. 290–91).

29. These early meetings between clinical and experimental psychologists would bear fruit during and after the War: for example, through the *BJP Medical Section*, edited by Mitchell; and when Rivers, Burt and Flügel joined the BPAS (*IJPA* Vol.1, 1920, p. 116, 118; Edgell 1947, p. 121).

Chapter 18

Disseminating the Works of Freud

T. W. Mitchell and the SPR

> He must confess that all these questions of words derived from psyche, which seem to have such a mystic and wonderful significance, to him were often a little fatiguing. He had had assistants who had become most enthusiastic over psychoanalysis and psychotherapy and yet who found it impossible to test the knee jerks properly or to test sensation correctly. In the craze for matters psychical they have neglected the fundamental principles of the art of medicine. The whole tendency of this present move in favour of psychoanalysis and psychotherapy has been to neglect, as Dubois cheerfully neglects, the physical basis which is so often at the bottom of the nervous disorder.
> (Dr. P. C. Knapp, *JNMD* 1908, Vol. 35, p. 785)

THE MEDICAL SECTION OF THE SPR

In 1911 the SPR Council Report for the year 1910, claimed that "psychical research is influencing contemporary thought all over the world." And to support their claim pointed to Dr [T.F.] Gardner's Presidential address to the Dorset and West Hants Branch of the BMA, in which "lengthy and emphatic reference was made to the great services rendered to psychology by the scientific treatment of it by the [S.P.R]." Gardner (1910, p. 363) believed it was the study of psychology "from a scientific standpoint" which had rescued "the wheat of psychological therapeutics from the chaff and humbug of Christian Science and spiritualistic knavery."[1] Although Gardner praised the 'scientific' positioning of the pioneer work of the SPR he only hinted at the extraordinary network of relationships that now existed between qualified medical practitioners and psychical researchers. By 1910, there was already a significant group of qualified medical practitioners who were members of both the MSSST and the SPR and thus, in theory at least, shared common commitments to the study and practice of both psychical research and psychotherapeutics. This group, which constituted a powerful presence both within the SPR and the wider field of psychotherapy, were, in effect, bringing about profound changes to British psychological medicine. Varying, somewhat, the words of Garner (1910, p. 364), it was this new movement which had now given

> pause to the fossilized conservatism of the older therapeutic school and shake to their foundations the old dry-as-dust ruins of the blue pill and black draught school of therapeutists.

In 1912 the *Journal* (1912, Vol. 15, pp. 41 and 44), continuing something of this theme, claimed, with some justification,

> the altered attitude of the profession is no doubt partly due to the efforts of the [MSSST] some of the leaders of which were recruited from the ranks of our Council; Dr. Lloyd Tuckey having been elected as President in the first year of its existence, Dr. Bramwell in 1908, and Dr. Mitchell in the current year (1911).

It was against this background that a number of SPR medical members submitted "A scheme for the formation of a Medical Section of the Society" which, following discussions, was adopted by the Council on March 28, 1911. And an announcement was then made, in the April 1911 issue of the *Journal*, for the formation of a new Medical Section of the SPR [Medical Section], open to any Member or Associate of the Society "who is a qualified medical practitioner." The objects were:

2(a) To promote the study of the psychological side of medicine, especially the principles underlying different forms of treatment by suggestion and other psychotherapeutic measures, dissociations of consciousness, and analogous problems.
(b) To publish original contributions by medical men on these subjects in special medical Parts of the *Proceedings*, to appear from time to time.
(c) To consider the possible bearings of these studies on Psychical Research proper.
3. That the affairs of the Medical Section be managed by a Committee of medical men, appointed by the Council who shall recommend what papers to publish in the special medical Parts of *Proceedings*.
4. That the Committee consist of Drs. J. Milne Bramwell, C. Lloyd Turkey, T. W. Mitchell. H E Wingfield, and Maurice B Wright. Dr. Mitchell acting as its Hon. Secretary. (*Journal* 1912, Vol. 15, pp. 51–52).

One of the main and indeed unambiguous reasons for establishing the Medical Section was to "induce others to join [the Society]" in the hope that this would "lead to further co-operation with the medical profession, in so far as the subjects dealt with by it and by the [SPR] trench on each other's provinces." The strategy clearly bore fruit as can be seen in the 1911 Annual Report, published in March 1912 (*Journal* 1912, Vol. 15, pp. 215–16).

> One of the most important events of the year has been the formation of a Medical Section. . . . There is already a considerable increase in the number of medical members, the list of accessions including more than one distinguished American and Continental name, and it is hoped that, as the Section and its work become better known, and as medical men become more interested in the study of suggestion and the psychological side of medicine, many more will join it. The problems of suggestion and of multiple personality and minor dissociations of consciousness are of far-reaching importance in psychical research; they press on us, indeed, more and more urgently as our work advances, and especially in relation to the growing evidence obtained through automatic writing relating to the survival of personality after death. In automatic phenomena, as Mr. Myers long ago pointed out, the normal types and the abnormal or pathological types throw light on one another; in both cases we see certain extensions and certain restrictions of faculty, and it is conceivable that further knowledge may lead to a more complete control over the whole field of mental life, which will enable us to cultivate the favourable and check the injurious processes of automatism.

The Council meeting, on 31 October 1911, announced three new medical members: Percy Allan; Douglas Bryan and Sándor Ferenczi (*Journal* 1912, Vol. 15, p. 138). Not long afterward Taplin, now Chairman of the Liverpool Psycho-Therapeutic Clinic (*Journal* 1912, Vol. 15, pp. 271–72) was elected a member and Sigmund Freud a corresponding member. Hayden Brown then joined in June 1913, Constance Long, Jessie Murray and A. E. Davis,[2] now director of the Liverpool Psycho-Therapeutic Clinic, were elected in November 1913, with Hector Munro, May Sinclair and F. G. Scott joining around July 1914. Save for Ferenczi and Freud all those new members were also significant figures in the British psychotherapeutic movement. The Annual Report for 1912, published on January 31, 1913, suggests, without too much exaggeration, that the SPR was now at the heart of the British psychotherapeutic movement:

> Much advance has been made in [hypnotic research] of recent years, and it is extremely important that the Society should keep in touch with all the new work, much of which has a close bearing on the most obscure problems of psychical research.

On the other hand the 1913 Report also struck a more cautious note when it insisted: "The therapeutic side of hypnotism must for the most part be left to the medical profession": but then, no doubt remembering its own history, realized that it did not want to exclude informed laymen like Mr. Bayfield, who had recently delivered a paper "to a meeting of the Society" in which he had "reported some cases of the removal of pain and induction of sleep by suggestion."[3] But then, as if to emphasize its point, it added: "In the most serious case the sanction of the patient's doctor was obtained," while also announcing: "A series of interesting and instructive experiments in self-suggestion" would, it was hoped, "form the subject of a paper to be presented to the Society within the next few months."[4] Such convoluted contortions, clearly echoing similar prevarications from elsewhere, reveal that even the SPR was also concerned not to be seen encouraging quack practices. Ultimately, however, the Council remained upbeat, acknowledging the significance of the work of the Medical Section while also noting that SPR members had at their disposal "what is probably the best collection in England" of English and foreign "books dealing with the psychological side of medicine" (*Journal* 1914, Vol. 16, p. 23). Thus on the eve of the outbreak of War the SPR Medical Section had arguably become the most impressive group of psychotherapists working in Britain notwithstanding the tensions which no doubt emerged whenever SPR members sought to discuss their scientific investigations into "the survival of personality after death."

NEGOTIATING THE FERENCZI PAPER

During their meeting of October 1911 the SPR Council agreed that as part of their strategy to grow the Medical Section they would devote the next issue of *Proceedings* entirely to the first Special Medical Part [Medical Part]. It was also agreed, at that meeting, that the first contribution should be 'Types of Multiple Personality,' the paper Mitchell (1912a) had read just prior to the Council Meeting. With that decision having been made it seems reasonable to assume that the Medical Section met, shortly afterward, to discuss what other contributions they would like for the Medical Part. Given that Mitchell had now become the most prominent and respected member of the Medical Section, it should come as little surprise that the meeting resolved to invite Freud, Jones and Ferenczi to contribute papers. As we have already seen Mitchell now believed Freud's work to be singularly important and also that Jones was a good expositor of Freud's writings. The trajectory of events now suggest Freud was invited to contribute a paper sometime in late 1911 because Freud told Ferenczi, on January 23, 1912, that he was about to start work on "an English essay on the 'Unconscious' for the [SPR]." On January 28, 1912 Freud told Ferenczi he had finished the paper which he had written in English (Brabant et al. 1993, pp. 334, 338): and on February 24 Freud told

Jones that his paper had already been "mildly corrected by one of the Society's members." Although Freud also told Jones that he had written the paper because he wanted to try "to explain our points of view to English readers and in English words,"[5] it is by no means certain that it was Freud who chose the the subject of the 'Unconscious' not least because Freud also said: the SPR which "has prevailed upon me to send her a paper on the 'Unconscious in [Psychoanalysis]" (Paskauskas 1993, p. 133). In fact Mitchell (1938, p. 183) appears to confirm this "other" reading when he says: "And we asked [Freud] to contribute a paper on his use of the word 'unconscious' in his writings." It makes sense that it was Mitchell, rather than Freud, who suggested the topic because, as we shall see shortly, the problem of the "subconscious" had now become a burning issue in psycho-therapeutic circles and Mitchell, who was well aware of the nuances in the debates, would have thought it useful to invite Freud to explain, for himself, not only "'what the term 'unconscious' has come to mean in Psycho-analysis and in Psycho-analysis alone" but also why the 'Freudian' concept of the unconscious was so different from the concepts of the subconscious as used by other psychotherapists.

Although Jones was also invited to contribute it remains unclear as to when his invitation was sent because, in his March 15, 1912 letter to Freud, he simply says: "I heard about your contribution . . . for the secretary told me about it when asking me for one also." But, as Jones also told Freud, he had "refused to send [the SPR a contribution], for I think that you can afford to do things that someone in my junior position cannot without being misunderstood." (Paskauskas 1993, pp. 133 and 136).[6] Ferenczi, who was probably already considered "a favourite pupil of Professor Freund [*sic*]" (*BMJ* June 21, 1913, p. 1349), was also invited to contribute because he told Freud, on April 23, 1912: "The [SPR] requests that I write an article for the Proceedings. I want to deliver to them a paper on 'A New Conception of Hypnotism and Suggestion." Although it might appear as if Ferenczi, chose the subject himself the matter might not be that straight forward. We know Mitchell was an astute reader of the psychotherapeutic literature and being a passionate advocate of hypnotism and suggestion it is quite likely that he had already read 'The Action of Suggestion in Psychotherapy,' where Jones (1910d, p. 221) discussed Ferenczi's "recent illuminating essay," 'Introjektion und Uebertragung' [Introjection essay], criticizing hypnotism and suggestion from the psychoanalytic point of view. Furthermore Mitchell would also have known of Ferenczi's Introjection essay because there was a detailed abstract in the July 1911 *AJP* (Vol. 22, pp. 433–37, 437–38): which also sat alongside an abstract of Jones's (1910d) paper.

Although it remains unclear as to when exactly Ferenczi received his invitation there are three reasonable chronological possibilities: In late 1911, which coincides with the SPR's invitations to Freud and Jones: in late March

1912, after Jones had declined his invitation; or in late April 1912 when Ferenczi first told Freud about his invitation. The answer, however, must be left hanging. Now Ferenczi says, in a letter to Freud dated 28 October 1912: ". . . and the just received note from Miss Johnson, which contains a polite rejection of my paper on hypnosis by the [SPR]." To which Ferenczi adds:

> So, English prudery even finds something offensive in very temperate communications.—Do you think that I should give the article to the 'Psycho-Medical Society' (which is completely unknown to me)? I think it would be foolish to pretend that I am insulted—What we have here is clearly a psychologically understandable symptom of resistance. Or do you think that we should use the occasion to have an educational effect on England?—The question concerns the propaganda of [Psycho-Analysis] and for that reason I don't want to settle it on my own. (Brabant et al. 1993, p. 420)

In a late text Mitchell (1938, p. 183) appears to give credibility to Ferenczi's reading of Alice Johnson's letter when he recalls that Ferenczi's paper, 'The Psycho-analysis of Suggestion and Hypnosis,' was not published in *Proceedings* because

> [i]t was thought inadvisable to do so in a lay publication because of the attitude of public opinion at that time towards Freud and his work, and with Ferenczi's consent his paper was handed over to the Psycho-medical Society and was published in its *Transactions*.

Of course Ferenczi's narrative fits comfortably into that orthodox Freudian story in which Jones (1959, p. 237), and others, claim: "In those days the conception of sex simply did not exist in scientific circles, as Havelock Ellis had long ago found out to his cost." And yet a moment's pause reveals not just the absurdity of Jones's claim but also that Ferenczi's gloss on Alice Johnson's polite rejection makes little sense.

We can now assume that Ferenczi received his SPR invitation no later than late April 1912, and thus in good time to complete his essay. On the other hand the trajectory of the evidence—"the just received note"—suggests Ferenczi did not send his paper to the SPR until late October 1912 and so it would have been far too late for it to have been translated *and* ready for inclusion in the Medical Part due for publication in early November.[7] That Mitchell had a second paper in that Medical Part supports this reading. Now as Mitchell was clearly the de facto editor of the Medical Part and almost certainly the prime mover behind the invitations to Freud, Jones and Ferenczi, we can safely assume that it was Mitchell, as editor, who instructed Alice Johnson, as secretary, to 'reject' Ferenczi's paper and that it was also Mitchell, as President of the Psycho-medical Society [PMS] who, at the same time, asked Alice Johnson to invite Ferenczi to send his 'rejected' paper to the PMS instead. As we shall see, in Chapter 19, Ferenczi's 'rejected' paper was not only read at a PMS meeting but then both the paper and a transcript of the discussion were separately published in *Transactions*. Furthermore by 1912 there were already a significant number of psychotherapists and psychologists who were not only aware of Feud's sexual theories but also had little or no problems openly discussing sexual questions even with 'ladies' present! This now invites a very different reading *for* the subsequent comment by Mitchell (1938, p. 183, italics mine) that "[i]t was thought inadvisable to [publish Ferenczi's paper] *in a lay publication* because of the attitude of public opinion at that time towards Freud and his work." There was no explicit law, during this period, preventing the British medical press, nor indeed the legal or clerical press, from openly publishing articles discussing sex and sexuality: after all Eder's 1911 BMA paper, with its references to masturbation and incest, was not only paraphrased in *The Lancet* (August 19, 1911, p. 515) but also extensively abstracted in the *BMJ*. These and other examples suggest that if Mitchell 'rejected' Ferenczi's paper because of 'sexual considerations' then the question needs to be examined differently.

In 1898 George Bedborough was arrested and charged with selling obscene literature but Bedborough plea-bargained and just prior to his trial admitted three of the eleven counts one of them being that he had sold a copy of Havelock Ellis's *Sexual Inversion* to a policeman disguised as a member of the public. The precise question as to what constituted obscene literature was therefore never tested in the criminal courts so thus the *status quo* remained.[8] The complexities of what exactly constituted an obscene publication are rather nicely revealed in the history of the publication of Eden Paul's translation of Bloch's *Sexual Life of our Time* (1907; 1908). In August 1908, not long after Paul's translation was first published, a complaint was lodged at the Home Office who passed it to Scotland Yard who sent a detective-inspector Lawrence, 'disguised' as a member of the public, to visit the publishers where he then bought "the [book] in the ordinary way, without any inquiry being made." If Lawrence had been challenged to identify himself and to justify why he wanted the book then "proceedings might never have been taken." But as no questions were asked, or proof required, the Police were granted a search warrant which allowed them to raid the publishers and seize all 272 copies of Bloch's book whereupon the magistrate then summoned the publishers to show cause why all those copies should not be destroyed. Following lengthy arguments on both sides:

> The magistrate remarked that there was no doubt a great deal in what had been said with reference to a change in opinion with regard to such matters, but he was bound by the decision of the High Court which made it absolutely clear that

> this book came within the definition of obscene then given. It was true that it was published with the very best intentions, but it was sold to anybody who asked for it, and it could not be said that a book of that character should be so sold.[9]

As I have found no evidence that Rebman & Co., the highly respected publishers, ever appealed the decision, it is reasonable to conclude that a private arrangement was made between Rebman and the Home Office which allowed the publishers to circumnavigate the magistrate's decision and reprint the book *but* with certain modifications. So Paul's original Preface[10] and the three Bloch Prefaces were excised and, at the same time, the following added: "Publisher's Note to the English Edition."

> The subject is no doubt one which appeals to and affects the interests of all adult persons, but the publishers have, after very serious and careful consideration, come to the conclusion that the sale of the English translation of the book shall be limited to members of the legal and medical professions. (Bloch 1909, p. i)[11]

The *BMJ* (April 10, 1909, p. 904, italics mine), in its review of the 'reprint' remained studiously silent about the magistrate's decision although it is inconceivable the anonymous reviewer would have been ignorant of the case. So while Anon recognized Bloch's book as an important addition to "the library of physiology and frenzy which are already groaning under the weight of Krafft-Ebing, Albert Euenburg, Magnus Hirschfeld, Havelock Ellis, and other introspective philosophers," he (?) also felt it incumbent upon himself to point out:

> [Bloch's] appeal to all earnest men and women was re-echoed in England by the translator in the following words: "It must be clearly understood that this is a work belonging to the category of 'adult literature.'" *With this reservation* we may commend the book, which appeals especially to members of the learned professions, medical, legal, and clerical, and next, perhaps, to responsible persons engaged in the instruction of youth, the final appeal of the work being to all those who hold that "the proper study of mankind is man." The sale of the volume being limited, as is customary with such works in this country, to members of the learned professions.

The Bloch case, also set against a growing battle over censorship,[12] now helps to set the context for Alice Johnson's "polite rejection." Although the *Journal* was "for private circulation among members and associates only," and might therefore have been theoretically immune from prosecution, *Proceedings* had always been for general distribution. What is more the editors of the Special Medical Part were also determined that it should receive as wide a circulation as possible. At the same time because Ferenczi's paper had arrived so late there was little or no time to seek legal opinion as to whether or not to risk its publication. Ferenczi's paper was, therefore, far more likely to have been rejected on the grounds not of prudery but prudence.

The first Medical Part was published at the beginning of November 1912 (*Proceedings* 1913, Vol. 26, pp. 257–374) and contained: Two essays by Mitchell: "Multiple Personality" and "A Study in Hysteria", Freud's "A Note on the Unconscious in Psycho-Analysis", and Sidis's, "The Theory of the Subconscious." It also contained G.W. Balfour's lengthy Review of McDougall's *Body and Mind* (1911), Woolley's review (1912) of Bleuler's "sympathetic pamphlet on 'Freud's Psychoanalysis,'"[13] Tuckey's review of Ash's *Faith and Suggestion* (1912), and a short article by Taplin on the Liverpool Psycho-Therapeutic Clinic which was to be opened on November 11, 1912 and, perhaps with the PTS in mind, was hailed as "the first Clinic of this kind in Great Britain *under the direction of medical men* for the treatment of the sick poor [*sic*]." (*Proceedings* 1913, Vol. 26, p. 374, italics mine). The Issue appears to have been a great success, promoting the Medical Section and, at the same time, boosting the circulation of *Proceedings*. As the *Journal* (1914, Vol. 16, p. 23) reported:

> A number of appreciative comments on it have reached us, and [it] has already had a considerable sale to outsiders. We hope that it will play a part in stimulating the scientific study of hypnotism and suggestion by medical men and psychologists a study which in the past has owed so much to the [S.P.R], in particular to the labours of Mr. Gurney and Mr. Myers.[14]

A NOTE ON THE UNCONSCIOUS OR THE POLITICS OF PSYCHOANALYSIS

It remains unclear as to the immedicate effect Freud's paper might have had on members of the Medical Section let alone the SPR membership at large. As we know Strachey subsequently remembered "quite well the impression made on me by Freud's paper in 1912—which was the first thing of his I ever read," a comment worth noting given that some of Freud's work had been available in translation since 1909. Strachey, listed as a member in December 1911 was, however, no longer a member in the July 1913 list. We also know that Freud's paper did not just drop into a vacuum because, as we have already seen, there were a significant number of SPR members who were already familiar with Freud's work, through Mitchell's reviews, and also, like Wingfield, Wright[15] and Long, using variant forms of psychoanalysis in their medical practice. Keeley (2002, p. 134; 2001, p. 776) is therefore mistaken to suggest that Freud was motivated to write his paper for *Proceedings* because he "had to be irked by his perception, around 1912, of Myers's presenting in his theory of the 'subliminal self' a rival theory to psychoanalysis," or

> that it was Freud's perception of rivalry with Myers's psychology of the subliminal self that spurred Freud to his first systematic theorization of the unconscious in "A Note on the Unconscious in Psycho-Analysis. (Keeley 2001, p. 772)[16]

Although the superstructure of Keeley's thesis might, at first, seem ingenious its structure is built on quick-sand because, by the turn of the century, the term "subliminal self" [the subliminal], if it was used at all, tended to be used "as a synonym for subconscious" and, anyway, most informed commentators would have argued that Myers's concept of the subliminal carried a very different meaning from, say, the subconscious of Janet or Prince. What is more, as we have already seen, Myers's subliminal was effectively excluded from the discourse which concentrated on the competing but "dominant theories of the subconscious" of which Münsterberg et al. (1910, p. 14) said there were three but to which Prince added "three other meanings of the subconscious." Thus, while the term subconscious might have become widespread by 1907 it was not sufficiently applied or understood. And, what is more, there was "no consensus of opinion . . . as to the class of phenomena to which the term 'subconscious' shall be applied or, as to the interpretation of these phenomena." It was mainly to address this confusion that Prince organized a symposium on the subject to which he invited contributions from himself, Hugo Münsterberg, Théodule Ribot, Pierre Janet and Joseph Jastrow. Prince then published those contributions in the April–May and June–July 1907 issues of *JAP* (Vol. 2, pp. 22–45, 58–80). When the subliminal was mentioned, which was rarely, it was summarily dismissed. Ribot thought it "bears the stamp of a peculiar biologic mysticism" while Prince suggested:

> Above all it is a wasteful expenditure of intellectual energy to indulge in metaphysical speculations regarding the existence and functions of a mystical subliminal self (Myers), transcending as it does all experience and everything that even a 'subconscious self' can experience. (Münsterberg et al. 1910, pp. 35 & 74)

Sidis (1898, p. 3), having already dismissed "Myers's concept of the subliminal . . . as a metaphysical entity," presumably felt no need to mention it further. Jastrow and Janet also remained silent on the matter. Thus by 1907 there was no interest in the subliminal amongst most American psychologists, a point confirmed, perhaps, by Caplan's (1998) silence on the subject. Then some three years later Prince published Hart's, 'The Conception of the Subconscious,' in the February–March 1910 issue of *JAP*. In that paper Hart, perhaps following Prince, merely suggests: "Myers ascribes to the subconscious various supernatural properties which take his conception altogether beyond the limits of science." (Münsterberg et al. 1910, p. 127). Later that year Prince added Hart's paper to the five 1907 *JAP* papers and published all six under the title *Subconscious Phenomena*. Reading that collection confirms that none of the mainstream American medical psychologists paid any attention to the subliminal. But it is also worth noting that none of the original five American contributors, from 1907, made any reference to Freud, so that anybody reading that book in 1910 would only have known about Freud after reading Hart's essay discussing Freud's conception of the subconscious, or rather "the 'unconscious,' the literal translation of the German *Unbewusstsein*," which Hart thought was "surely very different from anything that we have hitherto considered." (Münsterberg et al. 1910, pp. 130 and 137). A similar Symposium, organized in May 1909 under the auspices of the American Therapeutic Society, reveals much the same point because none of the contributors, including Prince, Gerrish, Jones, Sidis and Putnam, made any reference to Myers or to the subliminal. (*JAP* 1910, Vol. 4, pp. 69–199). These silences are perhaps explained by Prince (*JAP* 1909, Vol. 4, pp. 70, italics mine) who, in his introductory comments, said that he had convened the Symposium because: "The time seemed opportune for a careful, serious, *scientific study* of the subject by this society" and because they were "under a peculiar obligation to the profession" to counter the "grotesque mixture of fact and fancy, of truth and error, the good and bad" which made "the product [of psycho-therapy] at once alluring and dangerous to *untrained minds*." For these reasons they "ought, as far as possible, to correct the misapprehensions which prevail concerning psychotherapy, and accord the sanction of its interest and influence to this valuable form of treatment." Thus by 1909 the subconscious, both as linguistic sign and as therapeutic concept, had been effectively appropriated not just by "medicine" and "science" but also by psychotherapists and experimental and medical psychologists who were now using it in an attempt to distance themselves from anything remotely smacking of religion, mysticism or spiritualism. The hegemonic power of the concept of the subconscious, riding on the coat-tails of the new psychotherapeutic movement, had all but obliterated the medical psychologists' interest in the subliminal,[17] while those silences on the subject further re-enforced the belief that the subliminal was hidebound in metaphysics. Freud's (1912a) paper on 'The Unconscious in Psychoanalysis' appears, therefore, within that space defined, not by the subliminal, but by the subconscious which was, itself, defined by a series of competing (sub) theories which had "suddenly transformed psychology from a purely theoretical science, a preoccupation of the learned, into a powerful instrument for the improvement of human life" (Worcester et al. 1908, pp. 14–15) Freud's paper therefore needs to be read within this context. Furthermore the silences in the Freud—Jones correspondence add further proof that both men remained totally indifferent, even oblivious, to Myers let alone his theory of the subliminal. They were far too preoccupied with other more important battles including those real or imagined "hostilities" (Falzeder 2002, p. 71) from those other psychologists and psychotherapists. But even those paled into insignificance when it came to the question as to what to do with Jung (Paskauskas 1993, p. 188).

THE SELF, THE SUBLIMINAL SELF AND THE UNCONSCIOUS SELF

Although most early-twentieth-century British orthodox psychologists, medical and experimental had, by and large, buried Myers's concept of the subliminal the concept nonetheless remained current within SPR circles where it continued to inform the work of psychical researchers such as Mrs A. W. Verrall, aka Margaret Verrall (1857–1916),[18] a lecturer in classics at Newnham College and long-standing member of the SPR. In an important, but neglected paper, Verrall (1906, p. 6) seeks "to give as complete an account as possible of the phenomena of automatic writing which have occurred since I first found myself able to produce such writing, in March, 1901." Verrall (1906, pp. 29, 59) assumed that the 'scripts,' produced through her automatic writing, had come from, or through, her subliminal rather than her conscious self. Here Verrall is using Myers's concept of the "subliminal self" to conceptualize and, at the same time, define that specific site of the subliminal for further investigation, exploration and mapping. It was as if Verrall conceived her subliminal self as a separately connected site (*locus*) distinct from and yet also intimately connected with her conscious self. It was as if there were these two different sites separately connected. On the other hand Verrall (1906, pp. 32 & 59) also saw the subliminal self as being stratified; which meant that "the subliminal strata trapped, so to speak, in the automatic writings are not those reached by the usual ways of dreaming or semi-conscious thought."[19] So Verrall was perplexed, for example, that French "which has for me long and deep associations of familiarity and sentiment should altogether fail to appear" in her scripts, which then prompted her to make deeper investigations into the relationship between her own knowledge of languages and those language(s) which appeared in her scripts. And this, in turn, encouraged her to explore the nature of what she now understood to be the 'free associations' that occurred in her subliminal self. If this were re-translated a few years forward Verrall might have conceived herself exploring those different 'streams of consciousness' running through or between her own subliminal strata. Ultimately, however, Verrall (1906, p. 80) concluded that her automatic writings and the scripts *it* or *she* produced had given her access into her own 'unconscious.' In one instance, for example, a script revealed a distinction "not consciously observed by me" but "recognised by my subliminal self." Verrall (1906, p. 92) was also interested in questioning her own "disposition to attach value to the communications of the script and to attribute them to some external cause rather than to my own subliminal self." Although Verrall failed to explore these particular questions any further she was well aware that they touched upon those debatable borderlands between clairvoyance and introspection and this made her wonder to what extent the "subliminal however unconscious" was, in fact, "derived from my normal experience or knowledge," rather than from some mystical other self. From here she was then led to ponder the possible connections between forgotten dreams and the scripts she had written thereby leaving her to imagine whether, if her "subliminal self continued on the same lines [as a dream now forgotten] when it got the chance of writing automatically," she could then reproduce that dream (Verrall 1906, pp. 122, 153).[20] Verrall's paper, which was a serious and systematic introspective attempt to explore what might be happening beneath the threshold of her own [subliminal] consciousness, hardly fits Strachey's spooky wing of Psychical research.

In a somewhat later discussion Lodge (*Proceedings*, 1909, Vol. 23, p. 138), in the same vein of enquiry, wondered if the control of Mrs Piper, the medium, "is merely a personation by Mrs. Piper's subliminal consciousness, or is a telepathic influence from living persons acting upon it, or whether it is really some surviving influence of the departed intelligence who is the ostensible communicator." For his part Pigou (*Proceedings* 1909, Vol. 23, p. 293) thought there was evidence suggesting "the subliminal self of one person is sometimes capable of influencing the perceptions of another apart from conscious will." If articulated somewhat differently these, and similar discussions during this period, would raise potentially profound questions as to the nature and the workings of the unconscious—or the subliminal self—particularly whenever two individuals engaged in the psychotherapeutic or psychoanalytic, encounter. In other words what happens to those neglected, or repressed or habitually unspoken inter-psychical communications which occur during the therapeutic encounter and which, even when noticed, are often too easily dismissed under the negative psychical signs of 'telepathy' or 'thought-transference', or under the problematic psychological sign of 'suggestion,' or even the psychoanalytic signs of the 'transference,' and 'counter-transference'?[21]

That the psychical and psychological might still overlap during this period is rather nicely demonstrated in 1914 when Miss Helen de Gandrion Verrall (b.1884), Margaret Verrall's daughter and collaborator,[22] and also cousin of Joan Riviere's, accepted the post of honorary assistant demonstrator in Psychology at KCL "with a view to keeping in touch with modern developments in psychology which may bear on psychical research" (*Journal* 1914, Vol. 16, p. 202). And, in a final post-*script* to this chapter, there is that interesting trance utterance from a Miss Rawson, dated Jan. 30, 1901,' in which she claims that Myers, although he had died in Rome just thirteen days earlier, had now become her 'control' and had already returned to offer us this post-mortem message.

> I understand now the full meaning of what I had only half realised in the subliminal consciousness. I can separate the two now, and know how far conscious thought and unconscious thought are dependent one on the other, and I can fully apprehend their indivisibility. That's where I made my mistake. I believed them to be separate, but now find they are merely two sides of the same thing—the unconscious self is the sleeping conscious self, and the conscious self is the reflection of the spiritual man, and that light, reason, and discernment come from one and the same source. (quoted Lodge *Journal* 1909, Vol. 23, p. 222)

NOTES

1. This was only a partial reading. Gardner's (1910, p. 363) talk, especially when set in its (1910) context can also be read as an acknowledgment of the changing climate in psychological medicine in which patients were now seen as "psychical personalities possessed of capability of answering to suggestion and hypnotism, and with attributes of mind and power of mind over those bodies little suspected when Mesmer talked of fluid magnetism, and spiritual phenomena were the sole possession of charlatans and quacks, quick to trade on the susceptibilities of a gullible public."
2. Albert E. Davis, born 1864 in Liverpool, married Annie Louisa, and they had three children. Davis (1926) was also to become chairman of the renamed Liverpool Psychiatric Clinic, which was still active in 1939.
3. The tile was 'Some Cases of the Relief of Pain by Non hypnotic Suggestion' (*Journal* 1914, Vol. 16, p. 28).
4. This may be the paper by Woolley in which he "discussed a number of the cases from a psycho-analytic point of view showing how they illustrated some of the normal processes of dream-formation" (*Journal* 1914, Vol. 16, pp. 202–3).
5. Keeley's (2001) argument is based upon the assumption, which can be traced back to Jones, that somehow Freud needed to answer Myers's 1897 reading of Freud!
6. This was an extraordinary misreading of the Society whereby Jones admitted that his "curiosity about telepathy [was] no doubt inhibited by prejudice." (Wittenberger and Tögel 1999, p. 179).
7. The translator, A. Newbold, appears to have been a close associate of Felkin's (Ehrlich & Hata 1911; Hilger 1912).
8. I discuss this in Kuhn (2012).
9. Undated and unidentified newspaper cutting tucked inside a copy of the book.

10. Paul (1908, italics mine) says in his Prefatory Note to the first edition: "That the publishers have determined that the sale of the English edition *shall not be restricted* to members of the medical profession."

11. After quoting a similar publisher's warning from Moll (1912), the reviewer said: "We strongly recommend all parents and eugenists who have not the good fortune to belong to one of the favoured professions to overcome this difficulty by borrowing it as soon as may be from someone who does" (*Eugenics Review* 1912, Vol. 4, p. 319).

12. From around 1909 a consortium of lending libraries surreptitiously started removing books which, in their "opinion [were] likely to prove offensive to any considerable section of our subscribers." (*The Times* 12, September 1913, p. 4). Not long afterward a powerful delegation from the National Council of Public Morals urged McKenna, the Home Secretary, to introduce a Bill to clarify the meaning of 'obscene.' Their proposals, which McKenna received enthusiastically, entailed creating an elaborate system of local censorship (*The Times* January 24, 1912, p. 10).

13. Bleuler's article was originally a reply to Kronfeld (*Mind* 1913, Vol. 22, p. 459).

14. The Special Medical Part was noticed in *The Athenaeum* (December 14, 1912, p. 733).

15. Wright (1945), a good friend of Mitchell's, who joined the LPAS, would then become an associate member of the BPAS in 1919.

16. Although Freud (1900, p. 14) was aware of Myers's work on hypermnesic dreams he says: "But these are unluckily inaccessible to me."

17. Jung, however, was aware of its significance and would discuss it in his paper, "The Significance of the Unconscious in Psycho-pathology," delivered to the BMA Annual Meeting (*The Lancet*, September 5, 1914, p. 650).

18. Margaret's husband, Arthur Woollgar Verrall (1851–1912), was a well-known classics scholar at Trinity College Cambridge while Joan Riviere, A. W. Verrall's niece, was a discrete member of the SPR who tried table tilting with her cousin Helen when she visited her aunt in Cambridge. *Proceedings* (1913, Vol. 26, pp. 44–46 and 371). Riviere would subsequently join the BSPA.

19. On this more generally see E. F. Kelly (2007, pp. 584ff).

20. See also the comments by Pigou (*Proceedings* 1909, Vol. 23, p. 295) and E. F. Kelly (2007, pp. 592ff).

21. For a brief introduction to this subject see, Paskauskas (1993, p. 592); Schröter (1996, pp. 138–39, 142); Timms (2012, p. 8); Gyimesi (2012); Pierri (2010, p. 747); Massicotte (2014, p. 99n).

22. I am grateful to Andreas Sommer for alerting me to this. Miss Verrall was an SPR Assistant Research Officer.

Chapter 19

T. W. Mitchell and the Psycho-Medical Society

> But as a matter of fact it is only when [hypnotism] is used in the great variety of bodily and mental disorders which come under the care of the general practitioner that the extent of its field of usefulness becomes clearly manifest. It is then also that its limitations become accepted in the same spirit as are the limitations of other therapeutic measures. (Mitchell 1910c, p. 666)

THE PSYCHO-MEDICAL SOCIETY

Some time in 1910 members of the MSSST resolved to rename themselves the Psycho-Medical Society [PMS] (*Journal* 1912, Vol. 15, p. 15).[1] Although I have been unable to discover why this particular name was chosen it is worth noting that it almost mirrors the Medico-Psychological Association [the Association] which represented the vast majority of medical psychologists working in the Asylum. If this was the case then it suggests attempts by members—primarily GPs also practicing psychotherapeutics—not just to widen their reach but also to put a more acceptable professional stamp upon their medical and psychological credentials thereby enabling them to further distance themselves from the non-medical or quack practitioners of psychotherapy. The name change may also signify a deliberate attempt to move away from the vaguely defined concept of suggestive therapeutics and toward a more "scientifically robust" designation. But it may also, in part, have been an attempt to accommodate the growing interest in psychoanalysis especially if psychoanalytic members objected to being shoe-horned into a society with the catch-all name of 'suggestive therapeutics.' Apart from its name change the PMS appears to have continued seamlessly adopting the same organizational and structural model, with its quarterly Council meetings coinciding with public lectures which were then published in an individual pamphlet-style fascicle [*Transactions*] for distribution to members.

It is difficult to reconstruct a detailed biography of the Society because of gaps in the record, including missing issues of *Transactions*. I have assumed, however, that the first in a new series of *Transactions* was Vol. 2(1) which contained Van Renterghem's January 1910 talk. Van Renterghem (1910, p. 23), from Amsterdam, who was a long-standing exponent of hypnotism (Tuckey 1907, p. 2) and a member of the SPR, told his audience that he no longer relied exclusively on treatment by suggestion because he also used "moral treatment, re-education and the cathartic treatment known as psychoanalysis." He described how he used this treatment, first discovered by Breuer but since perfected by Freud, "chiefly in the so-called waking state, which is however, really a true passive state analogous to hypnosis." Mitchell (1911b, p. 348) would make a similar point when he delivered his PMS Presidential Address the following year. Although van Renterghem (1910, pp. 23–24), called it psychoanalysis he believed its aim was to revive some old experience long since relegated to the subconsciousness of the patient. As those experiences had not been allowed free vent at the time of their occurrence they acted as a psychic traumatism which remained buried in the subliminal consciousness; like a foreign body which irritated the psychic organism and caused hysterical symptoms producing morbid expressions. Reporting on van Renterghem's talk, in the July 1911 issue of the *Journal*, Mitchell (1911, p. 110) said it was "of great importance to physicians and the public" alike because in recent times, there had "been a diminution of the esteem in which the medical profession is held by the public." Van Renterghem, who was subsequently in analysis with Freud (Falzeder 2015, p. 59), also examined the causes of this "evil" and proposed remedies.

> He says that at the present day the general practitioner has to fight for his very existence against the encroaching army of specialists and a growing horde of quacks and charlatans. He thinks specialism tends to produce a class of men who are wanting in that broad outlook on life and disease which was so characteristic of the great physicians of former times, and he is not surprised that the specialist often fails to cure the patients who consult him. But a patient who finds that the specialists can do nothing for him is apt to lose all faith in official medicine and soon drifts into the hands of the charlatan or faith-healer. Not infrequently these succeed where the specialist has failed. . . . the specialist's failure in these cases is due to his ignorance or neglect of the mental aspects of the disorders which he has been called upon to treat, and the success of the charlatan is to psychical influences consciously or unconsciously employed. He believes that suggestion, direct or indirect, is the curative agency in all these cases.

The (?) third publication, Mitchell's Presidential Address, delivered on January 26, 1911, appeared as Vol. 2(3) of *Transactions*. Tuckey (1913, p. 182) suggests T. B. Hyslop gave a talk in 1911. Although I have been unable to verify this it is worth noting that Hyslop (1910, pp. 101–13), an early exponent of hypnotism, who had also collaborated, for a time, with Bramwell (1903, pp. 321–23; Hyslop (1895, p. 424) was then medical superintendent of Bethlem, an active member of the Metropolitan Branch, and a contributor to *Medicine and the Church*. There then appears to be a significant gap until late 1912 when Eder (1912) delivered what was considered, by many at the time, to be an important paper on Freud's theory of dreams which was then published as Vol. 3(3). Eder subsequently sent the paper to Freud who thought it "an excellent article." (Brabant et al. 1993, p. 423). Although Eder's paper appears to have been lost it was extensively reviewed in *The Universal Medical Record* [*UMR*][2] which, in singing its praises, suggested that it "is, perhaps the first exposition in the English language—or, at any rate, the first exposition in England—of the teachings of the 'Traumdeutung'; and British scholars are therefore under considerable obligation to Dr Eder." (Anon 1912c, p. 307). Ferenczi's paper, "The psycho-analysis of suggestion and hypnosis" was then published as Vol. 3(4), and the subsequent January 30, 1913 discussion,[3] published as Vol. 4(1) thereby suggesting *Transactions* was issued quarterly. Following the Ferenczi discussion Jung (1913) spoke to a PMS meeting in August 1913 and his paper "General Aspects of Psycho-Analysis," was then published as Vol. 4(2). According to Long (1913, p. 358), there was also a paper by Jones subsequently published as Vol. 5(1), but I have been unable to verify this.[4]

At their first Annual Meeting, in May 1910, the American Psychopathological Association [APA], founded in 1909, voted to adopt *JAP* (1911, Vol. 5, p. 91) as its official Journal and, shortly thereafter Jones, still living in Canada, became an assistant editor. Mitchell (*Journal* 1912, Vol. 15, p. 12) thought: "This change in the status of the Journal will, it is anticipated, lead to the publication of articles of a more distinctly medical kind than those which have hitherto appeared." Some three years later, on 30 October 1913, Jones, having just constituted the London Psycho-Analytic Society, then attended a "'Psycho-med. dinner'" (Robinson 2012) thereby, as we shall see shortly, cementing his nascent connection with members of the PMS. In a letter to Freud, written a few days later, Jones said: "I am arranging to make [*JAP*] the official organ of the [PMS] here, which will help to bring a wider circle under *our influence*" (Paskauskas 1993, p. 233, italics mine). The subsequent negotiations, which deserve a paper of their own, were eventually concluded so from April 1914 *JAP* also became the official organ of the PMS with Jones appointed the assistant editor for 'the British Isles' in May 1915 (Vol. 10), a position he held until he retired some time in 1920 (see i.e., *JAP* Vol. 16) after which time he seems to have severed all editorial connections with his only subsequent contribution being a single short book review (*JAP* 1922, Vol. 16, pp. 280–81).

FERENCZI'S PAPER: "THE PSYCHO-ANALYSIS OF SUGGESTION AND HYPNOSIS."

Mitchell, as President, and Bryan as vice president, were the main driving force behind the PMS during the four years of its prewar existence. It is hardly surprising, therefore, that they should have invited psychotherapists, with an interest in psychoanalysis, to deliver talks: van Renterghem, Mitchell, Eder, Ferenczi, Jung and Jones. Thus despite gaps in the record it is still possible to obtain a detailed snap-shot of the Society's workings through an examination of Ferenczi's 'rejected' paper, subsequently delivered to the PMS, and the discussion which followed.

Although Mitchell, as editor of the Medical Part, had 'rejected' Ferenczi's paper he persuaded Ferenczi to submit it to the PMS instead. So Ferenczi's paper was then translated, published and circulated to members, probably some time toward the end of 1912, not long after the publication of the Medical Part for which it was originally written.[5] In his paper Ferenczi (1912, pp. 3–4) argued

> Psycho-analysis was originally tried on hypnotised neurotic patients. After sleep had been induced by the usual methods, the increased power of memory—hypnotic hypermnesia—possible in this state, was utilised to arouse those active but unconscious memories which are at the root of hysterical symptoms and the knowledge thus gained was used in the cure of those conditions.

Ferenczi continued first historically and then from his own personal practice:

> But it must be admitted that psycho-analysis is indebted to hypnosis, not only for the opportunity thereby afforded of going through its first stages, but also for the fundamental views as to the nature of the unconscious psychical conditions.

However the relationship between the two did not last long because psychoanalysis, having explained "suggestive and hypnotic psychical processes," could now dispense with hypnotism. That first step was made by Freud (1910b, p. 15n) himself, when he said, in a short note to his *Three Essays,* that "the nature of hypnosis is attributable to the unconscious fixation of the libido on the person of the hypnotiser (by means of the masochistic components of sexual desire)." It is worth noting that this particular interpretation had already entered into the British discourse via a footnote in Brill's translation of the second edition which notes: "Ferenczi connects this character of suggestibility with the 'parent complex.'"[6] Taking "this supposition of Freud's" as his starting point Ferenczi (1912, p. 4) claimed that having confirmed it he thus made all previous scientific explanations of hypnosis inadequate. Charcot's theory explained nothing; Liébeault and Bernheim's theory of suggestion was an advance; so too Janet's. But all those theories try to explain one 'unknown,' hypnotism, by another unknown, 'suggestion'.

> They all give a very inadequate explanation of the cause of that "dissociation," and while overestimating the effect of the suggestor, they take too little account of the very variable individual disposition of the "medium" to be hypnotised.

Psychoanalytic investigation proves "definitely that the efforts of a hypnotist are not necessary to induce a 'condition of dissociation' in the medium" because "the mind of every individual is always 'dissociated' in a certain sense as conscious mental processes are going on simultaneously with unconscious ones." Thus work is going on in the individual being hypnotized while the hypnotist becomes the object "grasped and utilised by the medium, according to the individual and temporary disposition of his Unconscious." In other words "there exist in the Unconscious complexes of sensations and ideas, which may explain the inclination of certain people to be hypnotised or rendered suggestible." And because ideas are repressed out of consciousness they can appear in consciousness at any time whenever intentional thinking is purposely dropped. Ferenczi (1912, pp. 5 & 6) then discussed the repression of childish impulses in relation to that stage in a child's development when he has

> an overwhelming desire to believe blindly, obey without criticism and to be in subjection to a higher power. The power to which the child first submits with such ardour is always that of his parents (or of persons who have authority over him), the motive of this devotion being his intense desire to gain their affection.

Then, adopting what would soon become the orthodox oedipal framework, Ferenczi (1912, pp. 6 & 7) noted how the inherent tension between wanting maternal reward and fearing paternal punishment were subsequently sublimated into other signs of authority, such as God or the Sovereign.

> *Suggestibility* is really the unconscious desire thus originated to believe blindly and obey without criticism, to be persuaded by love, and intimidated by an imposing appearance, with opinions and actions easily influenced by both: it is, in short, a fragment of infantilism. . . . in other words behind suggestibility, psycho-analysis always detects libidinous impulsive emotions towards the

> person by whom the suggestions are given. After having got at this definition and at the genealogy of suggestibility, it was easy to recognise that *hypnosis* is a special form of artificially increased suggestibility.

Following comments concerning the external attributes for a good hypnotist, Ferenczi (1912, pp. 7 & 8) discussed the two methods of inducing hypnosis. The first involved bringing a patient into a condition where he obeys and believes blindly: these are the conditions of fear and love. The second involved stroking and the darkened room which "are merely new editions of the scenes enacted perhaps hundreds of times at the child's bedside between him and his gentle mother, while she sang a lullaby or told him fairy stories." In this case "the hypnotic condition is specially suitable for recalling the fantasies of childhood and awakening the latent imperative infantile obedience in the unconscious mind." This method of inducing hypnosis was therefore, "very appropriate for reawakening infantile memories and sentiments."

> Hypnotisation in our opinion is the intentional restoration of conditions under which the desire to believe blindly and obey without hesitation—a remnant of infantile love and fear of the parent—can be transferred to the person of the hypnotist and made manifest. Although generally present in man, this desire is usually unconscious or latent. (Ferenczi 1912, p. 9).[7]

Once his own psychoanalytic experiences had led him to these conclusions Ferenczi realized his techniques of hypnotism "were derivatives of unconscious impressions made upon the child by the severe, but beloved father." For those who were bad mediums it could be shown, psychoanalytically, that they were obstinate children and this "prevented the production of latent masochistic fixation (suggestibility)." But Ferenczi (1912, p. 10) also argued that auto-suggestion, or post-hypnotic suggestion, like going to sleep, was also related to childhood.

> In our opinion, the hypnotist acts merely as a *releasing cause* of the hypnotic manifestations, while the most important conditions for the production of suggestion—the hypnotic phenomena—are to be looked for in auto-suggestive mechanisms, *i.e.* in the psychical life of the 'medium' himself, and can be demonstrated psycho-analytically to a form of devotional love."

The doctor, therefore, holds a unique position in the life of the child because of the child's blind confidence in the doctor's abilities which means "the doctor has an enormously calming effect on his patient and his successes are due to a very large extent to suggestion." Ferenczi (1912, pp. 10–11) agreed with Charcot that "*Hypnosis is an artificial hysteria.*"

> Behind the hysterical symptoms, psycho-analysis has everywhere proved the existence of the same infantile and unconscious desires of a sexual kind, and of the same mechanism of repression that we postulate here for hypnosis and suggestion. Further comparison of the motor sensory and psychical phenomena of excitation and paralysis which may be produced in hypnosis with the symptoms of hysteria indicates the similarity between the nature of the two. This is not contradicted by the fact that so many 'healthy' persons are hypnotisable, as neurotic disturbances can be shown to exist in all those who are mentally healthy. In many cases of hysterical automatism I was able to demonstrate analytically that the symptoms were due to commands received in childhood. For instance, a hysterical patient was compelled, by internal voices, to leave his bed every night and do certain things while in a somnolent condition. It was found that these voices were repeating orders his father had actually given him when a child, twenty years previously. Consequently, his father's suggestion had persisted through life as an auto-suggestion, and had produced somnambulic (as well as other hysterical) phenomena.[8]

THE FERENCZI DISCUSSIONS

In late January 1913 Mitchell opened the discussion on Ferenczi's paper by welcoming 'Ladies and Gentleman' to the PMS meeting. Although we know some of the gentlemen, because they spoke in the discussion there is no record of any of the Ladies present. And yet an informed guess reveals a potentially large number of female psychotherapists who might have already been interested in Freud or would soon to take up psychoanalysis. Constance Long, who was already in the process of completing her chapter on psychoanalysis for the sixth edition of Tuckey's book (1913) had been using psychoanalysis for some time and would soon become a charter member of the LPAS; May Sinclair (1863–1946), who was fluent in German, may already have been interested in psychoanalysis;[9] Jessie M. Murray (1867–1920) who was already interested in psychotherapeutics and probably knew Constance Long, as well as Long's long-term friend Kate Haslam, through their mutual connection with the Women's Federation League and the Women's Tax Resistance League (Valentine 2009, p. 149); Edith Eder, David Eder's wife who, it is often forgotten, was a keen student of psychoanalysis and regular attender of LPAS meetings (Paskauskas 1993, p. 266); Edith's sister Barbara Low (1874–1955),[10] who was to become an important figure in the BPAS; Elizabeth Severn (1913, pp. 84–85) whose book, *Psychotherapy*, reveals she was already familiar with Freud's work, in translation, and using variant forms of psychoanalysis in her practice;[11] What is more we know that she would lecture to the PTS in late Spring 1913; Joan Riviere (1883–1962) who would become a significant member of the BPAS and an important translator of Freud's work and who attended several MPS meetings (Hughes 1991, p. 15);[12] Violet Evans [Dion Fortune] (1890–1946), who enrolled as a lay analyst at the newly formed London Medical-Psychological Clinic [MPC] in June 1914 (Selby 2008, pp. 132 & 410). And maybe Sylvia Payne (1880–1976) who, at the time, was working as a house surgeon and assistant anesthetist at the Royal Free Hospital (Nölleke 2016). And then there was Estelle Maude Cole (neé Aikin, 1874–1958),[13] and maybe even Agnes Savill (neé Blackadder) widow of T. D. S. Savill,[14] a physician of note, an active supporter of the suffrage movement and who took a critical, but informed, interest in psychoanalysis (Savill 1916).

Following his welcome Mitchell (1913, pp. 2–3) opened the discussion by suggesting their attitude to Ferenczi's paper would very much depend upon their attitude to Freud's work and, he guessed, that most of those present would adopt an "attitude of impartial investigation" although he thought repressed complexes would always influence how one looked at any question.

> We must admit, if only for the purpose of this discussion, that a good case has been made for the main tenets of the Freudian psychology, and we must be willing to apply its conceptions as tentative hypotheses in the interpretation of the phenomena of suggestion and hypnosis.

There were many concepts to grasp in order to understand the nature of the problem:

> But, above all, it is necessary that we should know Freud's views on the nature of what he had called 'infantile sexuality' and on the importance of psychosexual activities in relation to the flow of mental life.

Mitchell (1913, p. 3) then ventured that it was

> this unusual use of the word [sexuality] that is mainly responsible for much of the opposition which exists in many quarters to Freud's work. It seems to me hopeless to try to get people to understand or use the words sex and sexuality in any other sense than that which they bear in ordinary speech.[15]

Then having summarized aspects of Freud's sexual theory by relying on Brill's translation of Freud (1910b), Mitchell (1913, p. 4) turned to discuss the 'Oedipus complex,' because Ferenczi had approached "the problem of the nature of suggestions and hypnosis" "from the standpoint of the knowledge of the Oedipus complex derived from psycho-analysis." Because information about the 'Oedipus Complex' was not yet to be found in any of the extant translations of Freud's work, Mitchell had probably read about it in Jones's (1910a, p. 97) essay on Hamlet, published in the January 1910 issue of *AJP*.[16]

Then, having reprised something of Ferenczi's arguments, Mitchell (1913, pp. 5–6) spelled out his "own attitude towards the work of Freud and his school."

> I have already practically admitted that it is one of suspended judgement. I am convinced of the great importance of the principles which Freud has enunciated and of the methods of investigation which he had elaborated. I am also convinced of the truth of many of the most important conclusions that have been arrived at by means of psycho-analysis. But I cannot, at present, follow Freud the whole way, and still less can I keep company with many of his followers. For even if all that they mean to imply in their writings should ultimately prove to be, in some sense, truth, there must surely be something wrong with an exposition of the truth that it leave such a bad taste in the mouth of almost everyone who tries to assimilate it.[17] I have already suggested that the greatest mistake in the exposition of the Freudian psychology is the extension given to the connotation of the words sex and sexuality. It may indeed be right and profitable to trace the connections and inter-relations of the various forms of pleasure-pain feeling and of the different conative tendencies that arise in the course of experience; and if the evidence points to their correlation with, or their common origin in, the feelings and tendencies that accompany the furthering or frustration of sexual impulses, no one need object to such a conclusion. But it seems to me that no good purpose can be served by grouping so many divergent forms of feeling and conation under a common term which had from the beginnings of speech been appropriated to designate certain specific kinds of mental and bodily activity. It seems to me to be due to such misuse of language that however carefully and sympathetically we try to read the works of Freud and his followers, we feel that we are being asked to believe that the innermost and most secret chamber of the mind is a sort of brothel, and that all the saints and martyrs of history are no better than the harlots and profligates of the streets.[18]

But Mitchell (1913, p. 6) was also concerned that Freud's theory of sublimation led to the belief that "so much of what is best in man" is "nothing but the by-products of activities designed primarily to ensure the continuity of biological existence."

> And if the mental and moral attributes of man which we value most highly can only be attained through the sublimation of sexual impulses then sublimation should not be regarded merely as a harmless outlet for unsatisfied sexual desire. Rather should it be considered a normal and necessary part of the evolutionary process by which man rises above the level of the brutes and gets glimpses of a destiny that lies beyond the range of his vision so long as he is imprisoned in the underworld of purely sensual life.

Then, taking issue with Ferenczi's arguments concerning the origin and nature of suggestion, which he thought were built upon a logical fallacy,

Mitchell (1913, pp. 7–8) ventured that suggestion was "action prompted by the herd instinct as opposed to purposive action of the personal will;" thus he thought Ferenczi's view of the state of subjection was too narrow. Rather than seeing it as a stage in the normal psychical development of the child "I am inclined to see in it a phase of personality normally evocable at all ages by appropriate circumstances and having no constant or necessary relation to psycho-sexual activities." Ribot had described it as one of the primary emotions under the name of negative self-feeling while McDougall, following Ribot, had described it as the emotion of subjection which accompanies the activity of the primary instinct of self-abasement or subjection. "Subjection as instinct and emotion is on this view to be regarded as being almost as primordial as the sex instinct itself." Psychoanalysts forget that what they teach is only the result of interpretation and they assume their interpretation of the facts is the only possible one. Ferenczi had argued that the absence of suggestibility was due to the child's defiant relations with her parents: "But instead of considering the absence of suggestibility in the adult as a consequence of the obstinacy of childhood, is it not possible that both may be due to some common cause, such as for example, a defective development of the instinct of self-subjection?" Mitchell (1913, pp. 9–10) thought "the most striking peculiarity of the hypnotised person is not so much his blind obedience as his apparently super-normal power over his own organism" and Ferenczi's theory failed to throw any light on this particular aspect of hypnotism.

Ernest Jones (1959, p. 229), who was just then passing through London, and would subsequently give a very different account of this meeting, said he was honored to be invited to take part in this important discussion and wanted to compliment Mitchell

> with all respect, on his admirably suave and lucid exposition of a subject that is admittedly thorny . . . and in his striving towards impartiality the President has set us an excellent example. Much of the criticism he urges against the psychoanalytical position seems to me to be very much to the point, but before discussing this I wish to say a little about some misunderstanding concerning which it is essential to be clear if we are to grasp the position in question. (Mitchell 1913, p. 10)

Freud's discussion of sex was not a novel use of language, but a recognition that sexual processes occur in childhood.

> When [Freud] calls certain infantile processes 'sexual' he does so because he believes that they are inherently of the same nature as the processes that everyone calls sexual in the adult; whoever thinks that the differences between Freud and his critics can be reduced to a matter of terminology is under a serious misapprehension. . . . In other words whether he knows it or not, the patient is

always in love with his hypnotist. The special contribution that Ferenczi made, one in my opinion of the highest value, was the identifying this attitude and its accompanying obedience, with the attitude of the normal child towards its parents . . . (It is, I think, accepted by every psychologist that the action of the mind on the body . . . is predominantly due, not to the influence of pure ideation, if indeed such a thing ever exists, but to that of emotional processes). This is in harmony with the general experience that the more removed is such a process from the sphere of pure ideation, the more automatic and less under the control of the will it is, the deeper in the mind and particularly in the unconscious, the greater is its capacity to affect bodily processes; for instance, a sudden and involuntary emotion may effect the beating of the heart in a way that no voluntary idea ever can. That it is solely the idea suggested by the hypnotist that produces such extraordinary results, therefore, is a conception that cannot be brought into harmony with the rest of our psychological knowledge; the apparent absence of any motive force makes the whole occurrence quite unintelligible. The psycho-analytic view on the other hand, makes plain the tremendous emotional forces engaged, just those which, in the unconscious, are in the closest relation to the involuntary functioning of the sympathetic and vaso-motor systems. (Mitchell 1913, pp. 11, 12–13 and 14)

Then Jones continued;

To my mind the most valuable part of the President's criticism, and one which alone would raise his address far above the usual criticisms of psycho-analysis, is that in which he suggests that suggestibility, and the tendency to self-effacement, may not be of sexual origin at all, but the manifestation of some primary instinct, such as the herd instinct, which imposes obediency as a measure to ensure the protection of both the individual and the race. (Mitchell 1913, p. 15)

While Jones thought this to be speculation he also thought there was much that pointed toward this conclusion and he was prepared to assent to this view as a probable one but with this important modification:

[that] there can be no doubt that one of the most striking characteristics of the psycho-sexual group of instincts is the tendency these show to extend their influence from their own proper sphere onto that of other neighbouring instincts, in a sense to exploit these for their own purposes and it is likely that we have here an example of this very process; in the same way I hold that morbid anxiety ('nervousness' and phobias) represents an exploitation of the fear instinct by the sexual one . . . whether the part played by the sexual instinct represents a secondary invasion or a primary process it is one of very greatest significance for the understanding of psycho-pathology . . . [but ultimately] the greater part is certainly derived from the psycho-sexual instinct and that it is this latter which is essential for the producing of therapeutic effects in hypnotism. (Mitchell 1913, pp. 15–16)

William Brown (1913b, pp. 1218–19), who would shortly publish his own account of a psychoanalysis,[19] said Mitchell's remarks were "of exceptional value to the discussion since it brings up-to-date psychological knowledge and sound psychological judgement to bear upon a subject which is too often treated in complete disregard of generally accepted psychological views and modes of thought." He was in close accord with what Mitchell said about Freud's views of the sexual element although the question was perhaps one of terms because, he said,

> I can not help thinking that Freud and his followers unduly, or at least unnecessarily, extend the connotation of the term 'sexual' in their psychological system. With the President I prefer to follow Ribot, Shand and McDougall[20] in holding that the sexual instinct and emotion is only one among a number of equally fundamental and equally important primary conative tendencies, such as positive and negative self-feeling, curiosity, fear, disgust, etc., and that the effects of hypnotism are more plausibly explained in terms of positive and negative self-feeling than by reference, however indirect, to sexuality. (Mitchell 1913, p. 16)

Brown thought Freud's theory

> is valuable as in showing the presence of the sex-element where previously no one has thought to look for it, and especially in emphasising the existence of infantile sexual tendencies and demonstrating their fundamental importance in the mentality of later life, especially in certain cases of mental derangement. Its defect lies in a too ready generalisation from facts of abnormal psychology to those of normal consciousness. This seems to me especially apparent in Freud's theory of dreams. . . . With this exception, I find myself in close sympathy with the Freudian psychology, and regard Freud's general theory of the unconscious as one of the most brilliant and important contributions to modern psychology. (Mitchell 1913, p. 17)

Then Brown, who had started reading *Die Traumdeutung* in 1912, discussed something of his own dream analysis:

> A careful study of my own dreams by the method of psycho-analysis has certainly convinced me that in many cases my dreams represent the disguised fulfilment of repressed and unconscious wishes, and these wishes are often sexual in nature and show a reference to infantile wishes of a similar kind. But in the majority of cases these wishes have no reference to sex, and cannot by the widest stretch of the imagination, or the most thorough going application of the method of psycho-analysis, be made to have them. (Mitchell 1913, p. 17)

Now the presence of William Brown, an academic psychologist, is clearly important not least because Mitchell (*Proceedings*, 1922, Vol. 32, p. 379) subsequently suggested Brown's "attitude towards Freudian doctrine is of particular interest because he was one of the first academic psychologists in this country to give sympathetic consideration to the views of the psycho-analysts and to expound their teachings." But Brown's presence also suggests Mitchell may have met him in Oxford, in May 1910, and on assuming the role as PMS President, invited Brown to the discussion in order to try to bridge the divides between medical and experimental psychologists: a tack he strove to continue during and after the War.

Maurice Wright, who would also soon become a member of the LPAS, thought: "The term sexual as applied to feeling, is to my mind, made by the Freudians to cover a much wider range of sensations than is warranted by the accepted use of the word. This, to my mind, misuse of the term sexual arouses in many people resentment against Freud's theories." (Mitchell 1913, p. 17). Then Eder said that just as some had underestimated Freud's theories so others were in danger of overestimating them. He could speak with some authority because he had recently talked over the subject with Freud who shared his "rather conservative views, that instruction in the school is more likely to be harmful than useful." And then after discussing his own views on sex education for children[21] Eder said

> The President . . . questions the wide influence which Freud attributes to the sexual instinct, or rather he suggests that it is largely a question of terminology. From this view I dissent. The influence of sexuality is the core of Professor Freud's doctrine in regard to the neurosis. He gives the term a wide connection but not wider than the material warrants

On the other hand Eder took issue with the use of the term polymorphic pervert as descriptive of the child's sexual activities (Mitchell 1913, pp. 18 and 19).[22]

SOME CONCLUSIONS

This vibrant and highly important discussion of Freud's work sits in stark contrast to the Jones Account (1959, pp. 228–30) which suggests a London medical society intellectually sterile, barren of any serious discussion on psychopathology, let alone psychoanalysis, and with "no other practitioners" save Eder and Forsyth. The Ferenczi discussion is also important because it reveals glimpses of those battle lines which were to emerge, in sharp relief, both during and after the War. Apart from the manifest tensions around hypnosis and sexuality Mitchell also touched the nerve of another important fault line when he raised the question of "action prompted by the herd instinct."

At first sight Mitchell's comments might be considered an explicit reference back to Trotter's essays in the *Sociological Review* (1908; 1909) but as those *original* essays appears to have sunk, virtually without trace, and as there is no evidence that Mitchell had, as yet, read Hart's *The Psychology of Insanity*, it is far more likely that Mitchell's reference to the herd instinct was drawn from an earlier paper by Hart (1910b, p. 444) who, so far as I can tell, was the only pre-war British psychologist to have noticed Trotter's sociological work.[23] On the other hand Jones would have picked up Mitchell's reference to the herd instinct because Jones, who was living with Trotter at the time of its writing, would have discussed Trotter's work in progress and read it on publication. This apparently obscure subtext was to become manifest some three years later when Trotter expanded his original essay into *Instincts of the Herd in Peace and War* and, following its publication in 1916, it had not only "an enormous popular impact" (Johnson 1990, p. 226) but also a profound influence on the many and often acrimonious debates concerning the nature and importance of various instincts in the diagnoses and treatment of shell shock, or the traumatic War neuroses (i.e., Bernard 1923; *JAP* Vol. 17, pp. 226–27; Erős et al., 2013, pp. 37–38). But the discussion is also important because Eder now reveals that he had recently returned from Vienna where he had originally gone in the hope of being analyzed by Freud. But Freud, pleading overwork, directed him to Tausk although this may have been Freud's diplomatic excuse as he no doubt wanted to avoid antagonizing Jones. (Paskauskas 1993, p. 190). This now suggests that Eder was the first British 'analyst' to have undergone a psychoanalysis, even if only for three weeks.

NOTES

1. The talk by Van Renterghem (1910) suggests the name change occured in January 1910.

2. From its very inception, in 1912, the *UMR* reviewed and promoted Freud's work; see that is, Anon 1912a; 1912b, 1912c, 1913a.

3. Although Jones made no mention of this discussion to Freud either in the short letter he wrote to him that day, or subsequently (Paskauskas 1993, p. 190–91) an anonymous report of the meeting appeared in the July issue of the *IZAP* (1913, Vol. 1, pp. 404–5).

4. Several issues of the *Transactions* were published in Cockermouth, near Astley Cooper's home, suggesting Cooper may have been involved in organizing its printing. The PMS also had a library (Tuckey 1913, p. 5).

5. Ferenczi briefly mentions his paper in the January 1913 *IZAP* (1913, p. 94).

6. Ferenczi's reference is to the section on 'Anatomical Transgression; Overestimation of the Sexual Object.' (Freud 1910b, p. 15 and n). Brill translates the original footnote as "the blind obedience evinced by the hypnotized subject to the hypnotist"

whereas Strachey translates Freud (1905, p. 150n) as "the credulous submissiveness shown by a hypnotised subject towards his hypnotist."

7. The theory of the transference touches on those problem, articulated many years ago, by Holland (1852, p. 288): "In considering these general attributes of the nervous power, a question of much interest still occurs to us; viz,, whether this element, so generated within the living body, and distributed to all parts of it in connexion with their several functions, is capable of any kind or degree of diffusion beyond this limit, so as to produce direct influence on other living organisations without?"

8. This seems to be the view taken by Chertok (1984, p. 227).

9. Martindale (2003, pp. 5, 84 and n, & pp. 18–19) suggests Sinclair "declared in a letter that she had begun to study psychoanalysis in 1913 or 1914." See also Rapp (1990, p. 220).

10. Barbara Low was born Alice Leonora Loewe, the youngest of eleven children in a Jewish family (Nölleke 2016)

11. A copy of Gerrish, ed. (1909), accessed from archive.org is inscribed: "May 1916, Elizabeth Severn."

12. See however Bakman (2013, p. 95).

13. Born in Arabia, she subsequently gave her birth date as 1882. She married Philip Henry Cole (b.1874), an electrician, in 1896. An Associate of the BPAS in 1919 she was also a member of the BMA although her book *Education for Marriage*, was roundly criticized in the *BMJ* (December 17, 1938, p. 1263).

14. I discuss T.D.D. Savill as an early reader of Freud (Kuhn 2015, pp. 30f).

15. Hitschmann (1913, p. 4) notes: "A part of the antagonism is explained by the fact that Freud is compelled by his investigations to use the word sexuality in a broader sense than usual, giving it about the same meaning as the word 'love' in the German language, thus asserting the underlying unity of all love from the grossly sensual sexual intercourse to the most unassuming exhibition of affection. The use of the term sexuality in the Freudian sense is justified psychologically and brings forward a most fruitful point of view. It is also obvious that not only the actual activities of the sexual life but also its phantasies are to be considered. Freud refuses to countenance the narrow and degraded use of the word sexuality on which a part of the antagonism rests."

16. Although Freud (1913, pp. 212ff) discusses the Oedipus Complex Brill's translation only appeared after the Ferenczi discussion.

17. These are similar sentiments to those made by Bernard Hart in his November 6, 1910 letter to Jones (BPAS, PO4-C-G-02, p. 1).

18. Podmore (1911, p. 18) made a similar point: ". . . search in the attics or the lumber-room might bring to light now and again curious and antiquated things, some of them even now good enough for the drawing-room. But groping in the dust-bin after jewels would be likely to prove unprofitable."

19. Rapp (1990, p. 221) suggests that Brown's January 1912 article in the *Strand* was "possibly the first reference to psychoanalysis in a British large circulation general interest magazine."

20. All three were SPR members; Ribot (1839–1916) a corresponding member; A. F. Shand (1858–1936) a Council member and also secretary and treasurer of the BPS.

21. See Eder's comments in *School Hygiene* (1910, Vol. 1, p. 529).

22. See also a summary of the discussion in *IZAP* (1913, pp. 404–5).

23. Hart (1912, p. vii, p. 133) acknowledges his indebtedness to Trotter's "extremely suggestive and stimulating articles;" whilest Stoddart (1915, pp. 583f) only references them.

Chapter 20

Jones Returns to London

> Especially have the writings of Ernest Jones brought down the wrath of the heretics upon the head of this self-appointed and altogether arbitrary high-priest of the psycho-analytic cult in America. (McDonald 1911, p. 517)

FOUNDING THE LONDON PSYCHOANALYTIC SOCIETY

Having spent time in Rome over the New Year (1912–1913) Jones travelled briefly to London so as to make arrangements for his eventual and permanent, return 'home'. Although it was probably mere coincidence that he was in London for the Ferenczi discussions it was clearly fortuitous and helps explain why, when he returned, some nine months later, he was already relatively well informed as to the main figures in the British psychotherapeutic community. Following the Ferenczi discussions Jones then left London for Liverpool and on February 1, 1913 boarded the SS Mauretania and was already back in Toronto on February 17, 1913. In a letter, dated March 5, 1913, Freud made it clear how pleased he was that Jones was soon to be back in England.

> You can not easily imagine how much I rejoice in the satisfaction of your taking up an influential and highly respected position in London and nowhere else! But you must promise formally never to spoil it when you have got it at last, *by no private motive*. (Paskauskas 1993, p. 194)

This was clearly an *unambiguous* warning from Freud concerning what he knew, or thought he knew, about Jones's predilections for illicit relationships with his female patients (Kuhn 2015, pp. 49–51).[1] Jones then left Toronto for

Washington on 4 May and sailed to Europe, probably on the 10 May, because he planned to "reach Vienna around 27th [May]" (Paskauskas 1993, pp. 195 and 197). Even before leaving Toronto Jones was plotting the creation of what would become the LPAS because, as he told Freud, on April 25, 1913:

> My thoughts are occupied by the [Psycho-Analytic] movement, and I am full of schemes. It is a grand time to be alive, better than any other period in history because it is fuller of fighting on which much depends. (Paskauskas 1993, p. 199)

During his short analysis with Ferenczi in Budapest during July Jones was beginning to have second thoughts especially given the now anticipated fight with Jung.

> Eder is behaving more and more suspiciously in many ways, and I am now in doubt whether the time is ripe for a Verein [Association]. At all events we must put it off until after the Munich Congress [September 1913], when I shall know more of what is going on in England. (Paskauskas 1993, p. 212)

At the end of July Jones travelled to Vienna where he met up with Loe Kann and the two of them then returned to London in time for Jones to attend the PMS meeting on 5 August where he heard Jung (1913b, p. 229n) deliver a paper '[General Aspects of] Psycho-Analysis.' Jones told Freud he thought the meeting "went off smoothly, with a good discussion" (Paskauskas 1993, pp. 213 and 215). Then three days later, on Friday morning August 8, 1913, Jones attended the 'Psycho-Analysis' debate in the Psychiatry Section of the Seventeenth International Congress of Medicine [ICM][2] which was held in the Chemical Library of London's Imperial College, with Crichton-Browne (1840–1938) as President of the Section and Maurice Craig as its Acting Secretary (*BMJ* July 5, 1913, p. 29). This very public debate between Janet (1913; 1914), who read a long and critical report on psychoanalysis in French, and Jung (1913b) who defended it in English, was framed, both at the time and subsequently, as a gladiatorial contest concerning the 'truths' of psychoanalysis. Part of that subsequent framing can be traced back to the highly distorted report which Jones sent to Freud that same evening in which he claimed that Janet "exposed himself so naively to attack" because Janet was then forced to endure the rapier-like intellect of Jones, who opened the discussion, and was then "also battered by others." Freud was delighted "on your defeating Janet in the eyes of your countrymen. The interests of [psychoanalysis], and of your person in England is identical, now I trust you will ['strike while the iron is hot']." (Paskauskas 1993, pp. 215–17; *JMS*, 1913, Vol. 59, p. 659). This may well indicate Freud's impatience for Jones to establish a London Psycho-Analytic Society to secure the English ground as part of their wider strategy against Jung. Although Ellenberger (1994, pp. 344; 817–19) offers a corrective by re-focusing on Jung, he nonetheless still framed "that memorable session," in the shadows of the Jones Account.

Now Jones told Freud that the "onesided account . . . in *The Times* . . . was due to the fact that no reporters were present, so they wrote their account purely from the printed Rapporte of Janet and Jung." (Paskauskas 1993, p. 222). This, however, was not exactly the case. So far as the British were concerned the ICM being considered of national significance was covered in three separate accounts in *The Times*, which Ellenberger (1994, pp. 818–19, 878n), somewhat unusually, fails to cite. Those accounts help reveal the wider context for Jones's own bellicose framing. So for example *The Times* (August 9, 1913, p. 8) noted, with good justification that

> Janet, of Paris, one of the greatest psychologists living, made a very damaging attack on Dr. Freud's school of thought, in a discourse abounding in acute criticism and as full of wit as any novel by Bourget or Anatole France.

That same report also hinted at Freud's theory of "sexual causes" adding: "The subject of abnormal psychology does not lend itself to a full report in the public press." But beneath its stylized account there lay an ugly subtext of nationalism and jingoism in which Janet was said to have exposed "the rather unsavoury doctrines of the German and Austrian propagandists of 'psychoanalysis,'" while "Anglo-Saxon common sense" was "usefully imported by [T. A. Williams] an American Professor." In a second, somewhat fuller report, *The Times* (August 9, 1913, p. 3), noted that Janet first "criticised Freud for borrowing his terms and attaching new meanings to them" before criticizing Freud's sexual theory on the basis that psychoanalysis "spends all its time in discovering the [sexual] trauma and does not enquire if it had any bearing on the neurosis—an enquiry that [Janet] considers essential." In concluding his talk Janet "hoped he had not been led into being unfair to Dr Freud. He looked forward to good work being done by the supporters of psychoanalysis in spite of the criticisms he had made." Another report noted that: "The discussion which followed seemed likely, on one or two points, to take an acrimonious tinge": and, if somewhat belatedly, urged moderation on all sides (*The Times* August 11, 1913, p. 3). Ultimately however, the framing of this, at times, fiery debate in the Chemical Library, was bound to produce passions. That Jones, Eder and Forsyth, all took part in attacking Janet, rather than Jung, suggests Jones may well have organized an ambush on Janet with the help of Coriat, from Boston, who now believed in "the complete validity of the psycho-analytic theory, both from the psychological and the therapeutic standpoint." (ICM 1913, Pt. 2, p. 51).[3] But the Session also needs to be seen as a very public 'scientific' discussion held against the backdrop of mounting anti-German sentiment as well as the more 'local difficulties' concerning the imminent break with Jung, a point highlighed many years later when in his subsequent account of the Congress, Jones (1955, p. 112), somewhat bizarrely, transformed himself into Jung by describing the session as "a duel between Janet and myself."[4] But there is a further problem with Jones's subsequent account because he completely fails to mention that Eder (1913a; 1913b) also delivered a paper to the ICM. And as a result of this 'oversight' Eder's important contribution to the psychoanalytic treatment of stammering[5] has been, more or less, written out of the histories.

It is generally taken that the final break with Jung occurred during the Munich Congress which was held between September 7 and 8, 1913. A few days later, when he was back in London, Jones met with Eder to discuss the possibilities for founding "a London group" of psychoanalysts "next month." They identified "perhaps a dozen members" including British Imperial members of the American Association, such as "Berkeley-Hill &c."[6] Interestingly Jones (1959, p. 230), who clearly had imperial abitions, also believed "the Society in London should act as a mother to those elsewhere in the Empire." The timing of Jones's meeting with Eder is significant because, in the light of the problems with Jung, there was now one point on which Jones was absolutely clear; that *this* new group was to be tightly controlled or, in the words of Robinson (2012, p. 2), "unambiguously Freudian," because as Jones told Freud:

> In order not to leave the selection of new members to the society we will arrange that all names must first be passed by a committee consisting of the President [Jones], Secretary [Eder], and Vice President (who will probably be Bryan of Leicester).[7] We will be fairly strict, but at first shall have to pay as much attention to character and intentions as to 'orthodoxy', and thus include men like Eder and Hart. I am thinking of inviting also Havelock Ellis and McDougall . . . What would you say to this? (Paskauskas, 1993, p. 225)

By 14 October 1913 Jones had moved into his new flat at 69 Portland Court (Paskauskas 1993, p. 230) and, perhaps spurred by the favorable discussions on psychoanalysis in the PMS, and his imagined victories at the ICM, Jones clealy thought the time ripe to plant the psychoanalytic flag in "England" (Paskauskas 1993, pp. 215–16; 229, 233 &n). So, on Thursday 30 October 1913, a week later than originally planned, Jones chaired the inaugural meeting of the London Psycho-Analytic Society whereupon nine people joined with a further six joining shortly thereafter. But as Jones (1959, pp. 229–30) subsequently noted: "a third lived outside Great Britain." Later that same evening Jones, attended a "'Psycho-med. dinner'" (Robinson 2012) and then just six days later, on November 5, 1913, there was an inaugural meeting of experimental and medical psychologists, and psychotherapists in the Botanical Theatre of UCL and the London Medical-Psychological Clinic [MPC] was founded. All of a sudden practitioners of psychotherapy were spoilt for choice.

FOUNDING THE LONDON MEDICAL-PSYCHOLOGICAL CLINIC

Some time during Spring 1913 Jessie Murray (1867–1920),[8] a Consulting Physician at the Quinton Polyclinic, 57 Poland Street, Soho (Boll 1962, p. 311) who was also studying for a post-doctoral psychology degree at UCL (Raitt 2004, pp. 68–69), spoke with her supervisor Charles Spearman, about the possibilities of establishing a Clinic that would bring together the medical and experimental sides of psychology. Spearman (1913b) was enthusiastic. Although he had discussed the idea a few years earlier it had come to nothing because when he mentioned founding "a department for the study of psychotherapy [it] had been greeted with derision, but to-day the laughter had died down, and the knowledge that had been gained remained." Spearman continued to believe "there could be no doubt that science would gain from the foundation of the new clinic. There was a growing interest in, and demand for, psychotherapy which could not be disregarded." (*BMJ* November 15, 1913, p. 1312). So Spearman promised to lend his support to Murray if she would make the necessary practical arrangements. A medical committee was formed of Drs Hector Monro (1869–1949),[9] Jessie H Murray, John Spencer and Constance Long, with Miss Julia Turner (1863–1946), of 14 Endsleigh Street, as their Hon. Sec. A meeting was then arranged for July 10, 1913 to discuss the founding of a London Medico-Psychological Clinic [MPC]. Although Lord Sandwich[10] was originally invited to chair the meeting he was unable to attend, probably because he had only recently returned from a trip to India with 'Dr. Coulter,' (Mrs Herbine's 'control'). So the barrister Mr Stanley Bligh stood in his stead (*BMJ* July 19, 1913, p. 132). In outlining their plans Munro said,

> it was proposed to start a clinic where certain diseases might be treated by means of psycho-therapy, and where a practical alliance might be brought about between psycho-therapy and general psychology. The object of the clinic was three-fold—to provide a place where treatment by psycho-therapy might be carried out, to bring this method of treatment within the reach of the poorer classes, and to provide inquirers with opportunities for study and investigation.

Spearman said "psycho-therapy, which had been practised for the last two thousand years, had undergone certain changes in modern times, and was becoming more and more widely known and needed." He also said that "Psycho-analysis was, after all, nothing but an extension of the process followed in every psychological laboratory; and no one who knew anything of the subject could doubt that the foundation of the proposed clinic would be of very real and valuable service to science." Constance Long said

> the psychological moment for the foundation of the clinic had arrived, for the public were beginning to ask that psychic disorders should be treated in a psychic way. The readiness of the public for psychic medicine was shown by the rapid growth of Christian Science amongst educated people.

But then, perhaps catching herself, Long "hastened to explain that psychotherapy had no connexion with the doctrines of Christian Science, the present movement, indeed, being anathema to the professors of that creed." She also went on to say "that the supporters of the scheme did not propose to break new ground, but merely wished to follow the pioneers who had been working on these lines in London for the last thirty years." She also confirmed that the Clinic "proposed to use all forms of psychic treatment, such as persuasion, re-education, psycho-analysis, and even hypnotism," and that their plan was "to form a centre where psycho-therapy might not only be obtained, but studied." Tuckey, in seconding Long's contribution, said "One reason why the medical profession should give its support to the clinic was that if legitimate medicine did not give the public what it wanted, the public would go elsewhere." Maurice Wright said the new clinic would "support all doctors who employed psychic forms of treatment, as up to the present this sort of work had only been done by isolated units, and there was great need for co-ordination." He also hoped

> it would be of assistance to neurologists and alienists. Psycho-neurotics were to be found in every class, and such cases amongst the very poor were in urgent need of help. If the clinic only devoted itself to the treatment of alcoholism it would amply justify its existence.

Dr Wilkinson then spoke about the Liverpool Medico-Psychological Clinic [LPMC]

> which had only been in existence for nine months and started with twenty patients a week, now had on an average about sixty. Patients came to Liverpool from every part of the country, so that the Liverpool clinic really did work for the whole of England. He added that, though England was really the home of this treatment, it was practically the last country to adopt it.

Dr Wingfield said his interest lay more

> in the experimental than in the clinical side of the movement, because it was many years since hypnotic experiments had been carried out in this country, and the proposed clinic would offer an almost unique opportunity in this country for such experiments. As regards psycho-analysis, it was impossible in general practice and he doubted if it would ever come into general use in this country. But it was his firm belief that enormous good might be done by means of psycho-therapy in cases of alcoholism, and that chronic drunkards who had undergone a course of psycho-treatment might be so far cured as to regain sufficient self control to keep from drinking for several months at a time.

During the subsequent discussions Jessie Murray said they

> proposed to rent four rooms in some quiet place within easy reach of University College, where patients could come for treatment. The nominal charge for each visit was to be half a crown [2s 6d], but, as it was hoped that a large proportion of the patients would belong to the very poor, the smallest offerings would be received. It was hoped that in time the clinic would be self-supporting.

Although by invitation somebody "leaked" a report of the meeting to the *Observer* (July 13, 1913) along with an appeal for subscriptions. The Committee were appalled. Not only were details of the scheme not yet finalized but protocol required that medical statements should be given, "in the first instance" to the medical press and "not to any non-professional papers." (*The Lancet*, July 19, 1913, p. 175). But the Committee weathered this first storm. Then several weeks later the *BMJ* (August 23, 1913, pp. 521–22) published a letter from Middlemiss who, in mentioning the Liverpool clinic, said he wanted "to call the attention of the profession to the need for such institutions."

> It is known that psychotherapy has been and is daily practised by men all over the country, whether in the form of suggestion, hypnotism, persuasion (Dubois), education of the attentive control, or psycho-analysis. The increased interest shown by the medical profession and the public in general in mental therapy, and the undoubted stimulus derived from the brilliant achievements of the Vienna school in particular, make it imperative that the subject should be given a wider recognition. The establishment of clinics in the large industrial centres for the express purpose of carrying out the various forms of mental treatment are a need of the times, and but a reflection of the change of medical opinion in this direction. In addition to meeting an undoubted want on the part of suffering humanity, they would help to co-ordinate the efforts of those already working

on those lines, and serve as teaching centres and foci for the dissemination of knowledge on the subject. The establishment of such clinics would, moreover, help to popularize this form of treatment with the general public and divest it of any residual aroma of charlatanism which may remain from former days. Hypnotism, for instance, is still unfortunately associated in many people's minds (and those not the least cultivated) with a species of histrionics and showman claptrap which hardly conduces to its serious consideration as a therapeutic agent. Thanks to the courage and perseverance of pioneers in this treatment, much of the unfortunate prejudice has been lived down, and it remains for a later generation to consolidate the success so hardly won by its predecessors. It is time, too, one would imagine, that a therapeutic agency, which on the Continent and in America has long been regarded as a legitimate item in the physician's armamentarium, should be accorded such sanction and status as are enjoyed by any other form of treatment. Any one who is acquainted with the psychotherapeutic clinics on the Continent, private or public, cannot but feel a little ashamed and mortified to think that Great Britain should lag behind in a matter of such strong importance.

Perhaps it was these very public words of support which now prompted the Committee to arrange their inaugural meeting for the November 5, 1913. According to Jones it was "a large public meeting with most of the London neurologists and psychiatrists present" (Wittenberger & Tögel 1999, p. 141) although it is not clear if Jones actually attended and whether or not he saw it as a threat. Edward Montague [Lord Sandwich], who chaired the meeting said, in his introductory remarks, that he "expressed his belief in the immense power exercised by the mind over the human body. He said that, although he knew nothing of medical or surgical science, he had had great experience of healing." He then "went on to say that there were few serious maladies that he had not treated with success, and he believed he could say with truth that he had never failed to relieve people in agonies of pain." He could not explain "his powers" but "could only say what happened."

He was convinced, however, that many other people besides himself possessed it, if not to the same extent at least in a lesser degree, and in the proposed clinic there would be an opportunity for them to exercise it with great usefulness. (*BMJ* November 15, 1913, pp. 1311–12)

One can only imagine what went through the minds of those like Tuckey, Wright, and Spearman, who must have visibly shuddered at what Lord Sandwich had just said. For her part Long, who spoke next, appears to have continued as if nothing had happened because she said the aim of the clinic "was to provide and equip with suitable apparatus a small place where treatment by psychotherapy might be obtained by the poorer classes, and where inquirers would be provided with opportunities for study and investigation."

> It was particularly important for the public to understand that the clinic would not be in opposition to orthodox medicine, but supplementary and complementary to it, and that it was hoped to join forces with medical practitioners in a suitable building.

Although the project would, at first, cater for outpatients only she was confident "that before long it would be possible to consider the provision of a certain number of beds for the accommodation of the more serious cases." Maurice Craig said "there was no general hospital in the country where there were beds in which patients suffering from incipient mental disorder could be treated, and that it was left to private charity to lead the way." (*BMJ* November 22, 1913, p. 1410).[11]

THE SANDWICH AFFAIR

Following that 5 November meeting the committee met in emergency session to try and deal, as best they could, with what they must have considered to be Lord Sandwich's outrageous remarks which, just as they feared, were widely reported the following day (*Times* November 6, 1913, p. 4). The *BMJ* should have reported the meeting on Saturday 8 November but for some reason they remained silent until the 15th by which time the Committee had composed a statement announcing that Sandwich had apologized for the misunderstanding he had caused and had terminated "his association with the clinic and the committee."

> It is distressing to the committee to find that a great deal of misunderstanding has arisen, and we feel bound, in justice to ourselves, to the pioneers of psychotherapy, and to the supporters of our movement, to dissociate ourselves entirely and absolutely from the occult powers Lord Sandwich claims for himself. . . . We profess nothing but ordinary medical knowledge, acquired in the ordinary way—we have no gift or method not open to every practitioner. . . . The whole of the healing art was cradled in superstition. In the minds of many psychotherapy is still tinged with charlatanism, and from this the clinic will help to dissociate it. (*BMJ* November 15, 1913, p. 1312; *Lancet* November 15, 1913, p. 1432).[12]

With hindsight Sandwich's appointment, as chairman, was a monumental blunder. The members of the Committee should have known about Sandwich's reputation as "an independent spiritual healer" (*BMJ* June 18, 1910,

p. 1496) to say nothing about his evidence to the Ryle Committee (1914, pp. 46–48; Erskin 1919, pp. 274–75) in early 1913.

> That he recognised his power as a Divine gift. That he acted entirely on direction or intuition as to what cases he should treat. That the means he chiefly employed were the laying-on of hands and prayer. . . . He was unwilling to undertake to furnish the Committee with particulars of his cures. They were indisputable and could be supported by the evidence of very many people, including members of the medical and clerical professions.

And yet there were probably good reasons as to why the Committee approached him. His title would have invested credibility; as a visiting governor of both 'St. George's' and the 'Royal Free' Hospitals, he could justly claim to be "on the best of terms with the doctors." Sandwich was also known, along "with his good friend Colonel Philip Smith, to have done missionary work in the East End of London," and by 1913 his "healing powers" had become "widely known" and his "real, honest, sympathetic interest in the sick and the suffering" would have "made him an ideal healer" (Erskin 1914, pp. 273, 271). No doubt in their naivety the Committee saw him as an ideal figure-head who could attract money from the rich while at the same time enticing the poor into the clinic. Although Raitt (2004, p. 67) suggests this was a 'misunderstanding' because Sandwich thought "he had been invited 'to give the meeting a short account of [his] own experiences in Spiritual Healing,'" the débâcle may not have been quite as innocent as Rait suggests because Sandwich subsequently claimed, with some pride, that following the widespread Press reports he had been "inundated with appeals for spiritual assistance 'from all parts of the world.'"

The fall-out from Sandwich's remarks was serious. Tuckey withdrew saying he would "only support a movement conducted on strictly professional lines." Long, and probably Spencer, followed suit by withdrawing from the Committee: and when Wingfield and Wright also withdrew their support the whole scheme seemd to be thrown into doubt (*The Lancet* November 29, 1913, p. 1587; *BMJ* November 29, 1913, p. 1462).[13] But on 20 December *The Lancet* published a letter from Spearman re-affirming his support for the venture and arguing that Sandwich's words, as reported,

> cannot be taken as expressing the views of those really responsible for the project. It consisted chiefly in the description of cures which [Sandwich] claimed to have effected himself by the exercise of some, apparently, occult power.
>
> Now the declared object of the clinic was to 'bring about a practical alliance between general psychology and psychotherapy.' The medical staff have

> already . . . dissociated themselves from this speech. Having been invited to represent, the 'general psychology' of the clinic, I should like unreservedly to join in this dissociation.

The Sandwich Affair having eventually died down the MPC was installed at 30 Brunswick Square, near the London School of Medicine for Women and also the Royal Free Hospital, where Sandwich was still a governor and which was, at the time, also the clinical hospital for the School of Medicine (*BMJ,* December 26, 1914, p. 1118). It remains unclear, however, when the clinic first started operating because the *Journal* (December 1914, p. 310) seems to suggest that the clinic only opened its doors shortly after the outbreak of War when it was noted, alongside Lord Knutsford's scheme, as one of the "two organizations which aim at alleviating the mental strain and shock caused by the war." For her part Raitt (2004, p. 67) notes that although Sandwich was removed from the Board of Directors he "resurfaced barely eighteen months later as a Member of the Council of the psychotherapeutic training programme." And she also notes:

> The intensity and the swiftness with which the founder members of the Clinic repudiated both lay analysis and occultism show that, like many early analysts, they were struggling to establish the public legitimacy, in medical terms, of their methods. The assumption was that any serious doctor would be unlikely to support a therapeutic organization that included among its practitioners people, however central to the British establishment, who had no medical training and believed in the power of occult healing. But some, at least, of the denials framed by the directors of the Clinic were largely for show.

And to support this view, with which I mainly concur, Raitt (2004, p. 68) noted:

> It would be a mistake, then, to assume either that the Medico-Psychological Clinic was as purist in its methods as its founders wanted to make out; or that their beliefs and practices were as different from those of the mainstream as their disclaimers might suggest. In truth, in British psychotherapy in the years before the First World War there was no clear dividing line between the practice of qualified doctors and that of enterprising lay people such as Julia Turner, or even of the mesmerizing Earl of Sandwich.

Raitt, however, may not have sufficiently accounted for the vast changes brought about during the War. For example Mrs Herbine, who subsequently worked with W.B Yeats, was instrumental in helping found and part finance The Coulter Hospital (1915–1919), named after her 'control,' which was then accepted by the War Office for treating wounded soldiers. At the same time Herbine's close friend Sandwich, and financial contributor to the Coulter, was appointed its first President (Anon 2016a). Ultimately, however, as both Martindale (2004) and Raitt (2004, p. 82) have noted: "The history of the Clinic has become one of the most significant repressed narratives in the history of psychoanalysis in Britain."[14]

WHAT ELSE DIDN'T JONES SAY

Some of the distortions found in the Jones Account can be traced back to Jones's late 1913 letters to Freud where he singularly fails to record how he had returned to a very different medical culture from the one he left when he was forced into exile in September 1908. So, for example, Jones fails to make clear that the subject of psychoanalysis was now quite literally *everywhere*. In June his old friend David Forsyth (1913), who like Jones and Eder had originally specialized in children's medicine, lectured "On Psycho-Analysis" to the London Polyclinic and the substance of his two lectures were then published in early July in an unusually long article in the *BMJ*. This article, which as we have already seen was noticed almost immediately by Freud, prompted a response from Arthur J. Brock who was sympathetic to psychotherapy (*BMJ* July 16, 1910, p. 175). Brock believed Freud "has doubtless, in certain directions, rendered quite good service to psychology" but had failed to take account of other instincts and "under the term 'sexual,' he has over-reached himself; he has tried to make the part include the whole." (*BMJ* July 12, 1913, p. 102). It tended to be sentiments like these which were the norm rather than the uninformed, implacable and bigoted opposition recounted by Jones. Not long after it had published Forsyth's article the *BMJ* (July 19, 1913, p. 84) published the BMA's Programme for its Annual Meeting in Brighton. That year the President of the Section was to be James Taylor, the highly respected neurologist and subsequently editor of John Hughlings Jackson's writings.[15] But at least two of the vice presidents were already interested in psycho-therapy; W. H. B. Stoddart, another recent convert to 'Freudianism,' and Helen Boyle (1869–1957) director and founder, in 1905 of The Chichester, one of the first British hospitals to offer psychotherapy to outpatients,[16] and "in which every variety of known treatment is used, has been doing excellent work for over eight years, and has stood alone in its attempt to give a lead to the early treatment of mental disorder in hospital wards." (*BMJ* November 22, 1913, p. 1410). It was perhaps because Boyle was no friend of psychoanalysis that her "magnificent . . . important pioneer work" (*JMS* Vol. 55, p. 692) is also now largely forgotten.[17]

And yet despite Taylor and Boyle the subject of psychoanalysis was extensively discussed in the Section through Wingfield's 'Suggestion in the Treatment of Alcoholism;' William Brown's "A Case of Extensive Amnesia of Remote Date Cured by Psycho-analysis and Hypnosis";[18] and Eder's "The Present Position of Psycho-Analysis"; while T. A. Williams, from Washington, offered a paper on "the truths and fallacies connected with Mind Healing." Brown's (1913, p. 1218) paper is of particular interest because it reveals an eclectic mix of psychotherapeutic techniques in a case he had started treating in late April 1913. Brown began the treatment with "a preliminary psycho-analysis . . . in the form of word-association tests .." in order to try and identify the repressed complex: although time did not allow him to explore the possibility that the patient's problems may be due to a repressed sexual complex. Then Brown having put the patient into the hypnoidal state subsequently hypnotized him. He then

> psycho-analysed him with the same words that [he] had used previous to the hypnosis and now got very different replies. The hypnosis had evidently broken down much of the previous resistance, but an interesting point was that this second psycho-analysis succeeded now in overcoming still other resistances, thus seeming to conflict with Freud's view that hypnotism, while overcoming some resistances, increases the stubbornness of those which it does not succeed in subduing.

The *BMJ* (August 2, 1913, p. 252) subsequently noted: Friday's session (25 July) contained "with two exceptions [papers] related to questions of psychotherapeutics." Furthermore the papers by Eder (1913c) and Brown (1913) were then extensively abstracted. Then shortly afterward, at the start of the new academic year, a special course in psychology, for medical students, was inaugurated at KCL where William Brown delivered the opening lecture on the 'Problem of Mental Disease,' where he reviewed the theories of hysteria held by Janet, Prince, Freud and Jung.

> In particular he showed that Freud's theory of the activity of the repressed mental tendencies and of the distinction between the preconscious and the unconscious mind was an advance on earlier views in furnishing a plausible explanation of the dissociation of consciousness and disaggregation of personality. Dr Brown showed how a sensitive mirror-galvanometer would indicate the presence of unconscious emotional tendencies in a patient and also demonstrated other apparatus for measuring mental efficiency fatigue and powers of attention. (*The Times* 9 October, 1913, p. 10)

Then on 11 December the London Medical and Chirurgical Society, with Jones's old friend Dr T Wilson Parry in the chair, met to discuss

'Psycho-therapy,' with invitations having been extended "specifically to those who worked in the subject of psycho-therapy." That meeting which discussed Long's paper, "Complex Formation in Relation to Hysteria and the Psycho-neuroses,' was, in many ways, an extension of the recent BMA discussion. Following brief comments on the history of hysteria Long then discussed Jung's word-complex, which

> embraced the "dissociated state" of the French school and "the foreign body in the unconscious" of Freud. A complex was made up of normal experiences and emotions, but in the case of a morbid development the emotional tone or 'affect' has obtained an undue value because of its fixation to buried or forgotten experiences; it is thus thrown out of relation to the general stream of consciousness. This division of energy between the conscious and unconscious parts of the personality was the result of inhibitions and gaps in higher control, leading to a loss of will power, split-off states, &c. An example of dream analysis was given, and instances were offered of subconscious ways in which certain hysterical patients cherish their symptoms. This was not common to all hysterics, many of whom are most anxious to get well. It is the task of the analyst to disentangle the underlying nervous mechanism which conceals or distorts their unconscious wishes into symptoms. Dr. Long made a plea for a more rational understanding of the aims and methods of psychotherapy, since there are many cases in which it is the therapy of choice. It should not be left as a 'last resource' but be tried early in the treatment of a psychoneurotic. (*The Lancet* December 27, 1913, p. 1824)

Long's final remarks were, no doubt, a subtext to the recent furor over Sandwich's remarks at the inaugural MPC meeting. Tuckey praised Long's paper and "said that he was entirely in accord with the views she had brought forward." Wingfield "thought that psycho-analysis should only be tried as a last expedient owing to the long time and considerable expense incurred," while Helen Boyle "said that she preferred to call her treatment 'getting the run of people's minds' rather than psychotherapy. She expressed herself as entirely opposed to the sexual theory of hysteria and other neuroses" and spoke of "the value of treatment by suggestion in neuromimesis and early mental disorders." Eder said

> that in his experience psycho-analysis was not suitable for psychoses . . . but was eminently satisfactory in hysteria, neurasthenia, and the obsessions. Cases must, of course, be selected. It could not be regarded as an 'all-round' treatment for every case that came to the consulting-room. Psycho-analysis required as much care, attention, study, and practice as a major surgical operation. Cases took a long time, at least three or four months, giving from five to six sittings a week. He supported Freud's view of the sexual origin of neuroses, pointing out

> the wide view that Freud took of sex, including therein affection, friendship, and parental and fraternal love. (*The Lancet* December 27, 1913, p. 1824)

THE SILENCE THAT FOLLOWS

In his forward to Violet Firth's *The Machinery of the Mind* (1922, p. 6), A. G. Tansley claimed that in the period after the War "Psychoanalysis has indeed become a fashionable craze." If Tansley's comments are read purely from the vantage of the Jones Account then one would say with confidence, following Jones (1959, p. 230), that "British psychology was transformed by the Great War" (Forrester 2008, p. 39) and that psychoanalysis was the manifestation of that transformation following its successes in piecing together those traumatized minds shattered on the battlefields of the Somme. But once examined from the vantage of this book that postwar psychoanalytic craze now looks very different. The British hypnotism debates, waged during the early 1890s, were the catalyst first for the "Mind Healing" debates and then for the psychotherapeutic debates which ran through the first long decade of the twentieth-century thereby helping to shape the experimental and medical-sychological discourses. Arguably if it had not been for those hypnotism debates "the principles and practice of psychotherapeutics, in all its forms, would have been impossible" (Mitchell et al. 1919). But those debates did occur and had profound influences upon the early psychotherapeutic movement in all its vigorous and various guises: secular, medical, spiritual, psychical, psychological, psychiatrical, religious, even electrical. This was the soil into which British psychotherapeutics planted its roots, and it was from those roots that the swift growing tendrils of psychoanalysis emerged and spread. By 1910 most well informed medical and experimental psychologists would have heard of Freud and known something about his theories even if only second hand. By 1913 there would have been no excuse for ignorance. This re-orienting of the early history has now removed Jones from his self-proclaimed star attraction, occupying center stage, and relegated him, instead, to a cameo role of a restless man pacing the wings and watching as individuals, disparate groups and organizations circled Freud. And this closing of the old Jones Account now enables questions which the old Jones Accountants would previously have dismissed as irrelevant, even absurd.

So, for example, the widespread interest in Freud and psychoanalysis in the years leading up to the War, suggests that Jones's first attempts to establish a psychoanalytic society in London was a very paltry affair. Of the seventeen members who eventually joined, in late 1913, four lived abroad. Of the remaining thirteen, counting Jones himself, only six lived in London and four of them—Hart, Forsyth, and David and Edith Eder, were all old [medical] friends of Jones's. As Jones reported to Abraham, in early 1914, "Only eight come regularly to the meetings" (Wittenberger & Tögel 1999, p. 37). So why then did the LPAS attract so few members when there were already a substantial number of medical men and women interested in and even practicing psychoanalysis? One simple answer might well be Jones! Although Jones had, by 1913, established a reputation as the "Englishman" most knowledgeable about the works of Freud he was nonetheless already considered by many, with deep suspicion. Mitchell (1913, pp. 5–6) may well have had Jones in mind when he said, during the Ferenczi discussions:

> But I cannot, at present, follow Freud the whole way, and still less can I keep company with many of his followers. For even if all that they mean to imply in their writings should ultimately prove to be, in some sense, truth, there must surely be something wrong with an exposition of the truth that it leave such a bad taste in the mouth of almost everyone who tries to assimilate it.

Hart, another shrewd student of Freud, also had his reservations and ultimately kept his distance (Paskauskas 1993, p. 262). And so too did many others, wary of Jones's passion for absolutism and perhaps fearful lest Jones's dogmatic hand should hang like a shroud over the eclecticism of the psycho-therapeutic movement. The manner in which Jones 'negatived' and then 'purged' the LPAS rather than allow the Eders, Long, Nicol and the other handful of members to discuss, debate and explore Jung's work, was perhaps indicative of his dictatorial leanings to come (Paskauskas 1993, pp. 288, 302–3, 310, 331–2; Glover 1995, p. 537; Wittenberger & Tögel 1999, pp. 37 and 203–4; Jones 1959, p. 239). Or to put it more succinctly Jones, with Freud's active encouragement (Falzeder 2002, p. 202), was determined to create British psychoanalysis as his own personal fiefdom rather than as a potentially dynamic addition to that psychotherapeutic *armamenta medica* for the salving of the psyche or the spirit or the soul. Jones's politicking with psychoanalysis can also be found in the "crucial role" he played in the break with Jung; a rupture which had far profounder effects on British psychoanalysis than even Paskauskas (1988, p. 111) allowed. On the surface the Jung Affair appears to have been, more or less, resolved by the outbreak of War and yet the traumas it inflicted, especially on the early British Freudians, were never confessed, confronted, exorcized let alone psychoanalyzed. And yet such traumas repressed can often turn in their subterranean hauntings before finally manifesting themselves as imagined ghosts or ghouls or revenants. And so it is perhaps no wonder that the shade of Jung should have suddenly returned, on February 10, 1958, spooking Jones on his death-bed patiently reminding him that Jung was far too important for a footnote. An eloquent elegy for the silence that followed.

NOTES

1. These same *private motives* may have been one of the reasons Jones fought shy of seeking an official hospital appointment once back in London.

2. Jones, who was originally listed as part of the Canadian delegation, was to deliver a paper to the Section on Neuropathology, not Psychiatry. (Anon 1913c, p. 325).

3. Janet's powerful talk is well worth reading and offers not just an important commentary on his own practice and theories but also an astute critique of psychoanalysis—"this somewhat peculiar psychology"—which, Janet (1914, pp. 35, 157) says, rests on "a general principle which was fixed in the beginning as incontrovertible" and is now routinely applied "to the facts."

4. In his 'official' account for the *IZAP* Jones (1913b, p. 596) frames his own contribution in belecose terms—"scharf," "protestierte"—whereas the official account suggests he adopted a more conciliatory tone (ICM 1913, p. 51).

5. There is a short but useful synopsis in *The Advertiser* (September 20, 1913, p. 21).

6. The British Imperial members were: H. Watson Smith (Beirut), Davidson (Toronto), Col. Sutherland (d.1921) (Jubbalpore, India)—who visited Freud in 1911 (*IJPA* 1920, Vol. 1, p. 341)—and Sunderland's "younger friend" Berkeley-Hill (Bombay) (Paskauskas 1993, p. 105). However Berkeley-Hill (1939, p. 76) was also an old UCH medical friend of both Jones and Trotter. See also Berkeley-Hill (1913a and 1913b).

7. Ellis (1913, p. 240) says Bryan informed him that "in several cases he has succeeded in removing sexual coldness and physical aversion in the wife by hypnotic suggestion": while Long (1913, p. 376), who reproduces Bryan's "account of his practical experience of psycho-analysis," says: "As he is an enthusiastic hypnotist, his success in certain cases after hypnotism had been conscientiously tried, and had failed to relieve, is most convincing."

8. Murray, qualified MD from Durham in 1909, attended Pierre Janet's lectures, and was subsequently a member of the SPR.

9. Born in Glengarry, Inverness-shire, to Hector, a Civil Servant, Munro was educated at Aberdeen before joining the staff of the Bradford Infirmary and then becoming acting resident MO of the Anti-Vivisection Hospital, Battersea. (*LDN* December 29, 1909, p. 9). A widower living in Lower Seymour Street, Munro became "a figure in [London] society," known as "a socialist, vegetarian, suffragette and nudist." He was involved in the 'Ripsos Nature Cure Exhibition,' 15–17 July, 1913 (Anon 2016b; *HSLO* July 12, 1913, p. 8). When War broke out he visited various towns in Belgium which inspired him to set up a small motor ambulance corps, with the help of May Sinclair and he then took his motor ambulance and field kitchen to the front.

(*LSC* September 25, 1914, p. 4; *Times*, 29 November, 1914, p. 4; *Hull* December 15, 1914, p. 7). Although most biographies have him die in 1916 he survived the War and was known as a 'Harley Street Specialist' in psychotherapy who "has always shown immense enterprise in taking up curative ideas." (*Aberdeen Journal* November 26, 1934, p. 6; *The Scotsman* December 10, 1949, p. 6). Jones subsequently claimed Munro, "known to our friends in Wien & Budapest," had founded the clinic. (Wittenberger & Tögel 1999, p. 141).

10. Jones suggests that Munro was "well supported by high society, where he has much influence." Hector's father was in the ministry of War in 1914, while Sandwich's nephew, George Montague, would subsequently become interested in Psychoanalysis (Wittenberger & Tögel 1999, p. 141).

11. The original report said the MCP would offer a chance to treat patients with "incipient mental disorders" rather than leave them struggling on their own "until they were ready to be admitted into lunatic asylums." Often such people were not the "derelicts of society but were frequently very highly endowed and gifted persons, and for this reason he regarded this particular form of preventive medicine as being of the very highest importance to the race" (*BMJ* November 15, 1913, p. 1312; November 22, 1913, p. 1410).

12. Sandwich subsequently said: "My gift and knowledge, however revered by many are to a great extent ridiculed by some and disparaged by others through ignorance and the want of understanding." (*Times* February 28, 1914, p. 5).

13. The resignations by Long and Wright may also have been strategic as their prior membership of the LPA may have clashed with their involvement with the MPC.

14. "Ernest Jones, in his zeal to establish his own primacy as father of the British movement, even failed to mention [the MPC] in his published reminiscences . . ." (Raitt 2004, p. 63). See also Valentine (2009, pp. 158–59).

15. Jones had a serious run-in with Taylor in 1903 (Kuhn 2001).

16. Winslow's British Hospital for Mental Disorders & c., may have been an early model.

17. See however Westwood (2001) and also Boyle's (1909) own account.

18. Originally a Professor Brown was also announced to speak on "The Psycho-Analytical Method by Freud," but this was probably a mistake.

Bibliography

Abelson, A. R. 1911a, The Measurement of Mental Ability of 'Backward' Children, *BJP* 1911, Vol. 4, pp. 268–314.

———.1911b, The Measurement of Mental Ability of 'Backward' Children. *BJP* 1911, Vol. 4, 315–41.

Aberdeen Journal, *Aberdeen Journal*, Aberdeenshire, Scotland.

Advertiser, *The Advertiser*, Adelaide: Southern Australia.

AG, *Ashburton Guardian*. Canterbury: NZ.

AJP (1887–), *American Journal of Psychology*, ed. Stanley Hall.

AJS, *The American Journal of Sociology*.

Akavia, N. 2013, *Subjectivity in Motion: Life, Art, and Movement in the Work of Hermann Rorschach*. New York: Routledge.

Alderson, F. H. 1894, *The Origin, Aims, Object, and Usefulness of the Incorporated Medical Practitioners' Association* [Presidential Address delivered before the Medical Practitioners' Association], Leicester.

Alexander, F., Eisenstein, S., Grotjahn, M. 1995, *Psychoanalytic Pioneers*. New Brunswick: Transactions Publishers.

Alexander, S. 1911, Foundations and sketch-plan of a conational psychology. *BJP* 1912, Vol. 4, pp. 239–67.

Alienist (1880–), *The Alienist and Neurologist, A Journal of Scientific, Clinical and Forensic Neurology and Psychology, Psychiatry and Neuriatry*, ed. Charles H. Hughes. St. Louis: MO.

Allbutt, C. 1910, Reflections on Faith Healing. *BMJ* June 18, 1910, pp. 1453–57.

Allbutt, C., & Rolleston, H. D. eds. *A System of Medicine by Many Writers*. 1911, Vol. 8, London: Macmillan.

Alpheus, A. 1903, *Complete Hypnotism: Mesmerism, Mind-Reading and Spiritualism: How to Hypnotize, being an Exhaustive and Practical System of Method, Application and Use*. Chicago: MA Donohue & Co.

André, G. 1894, The Study of Hypnotism: 'A Parable' and Two 'Fables'. *Irish* Vol. 2, pp. 144–48.

Anon. 1895, Review of Karl Schaffer's 'Suggestion Und Reflex: Eine, Kritisch-Experimentelle Studie Ueber Die Reflexphaenomene Des Hypnotismus'. *BMJ* December 28, 1895, pp. 1619–20.

———. 1896, Psychological Medicine. *BMJ* September 5, 1896, pp. 589–60.

———. 1898, Hypnotism and Practice. *BMJ* 10 September. 1898, pp. 735–36.

———. 1903, Epileptic Colony, Ewell, Surrey. *BMJ* July 4, 1903, p. 43.

———. 1904, Review [The Psychopathology of Everyday Life]. *BMJ* September 17, 1904, pp. 691–92.

———. 1905, The Phenomena of Obsessions. *BMJ* March 25, 1905, p. 661.

———. 1906a, Expression of the Emotion in Disease, *BMJ* June 30, 1906, pp. 1531–32.

———. 1906b, Obituary: George Wyld. *PTJ* July 1906, p. 61.

———. 1906c, The Dissociation of a Personality. *BMJ* August 18, 1906, pp. 380–82.

———. 1907a, Hospital and Dispensary Management: A New London County Council Asylum. *BMJ* August 3, 1907, p. 276.

———. 1907b, General Meeting. *Journal* 1908, Vol. 13, pp. 83–87.

———. 1907c, The Galvanometer in the Study of Mental Diseases, *BMJ* 26 October 1907, pp. 1175–76.

———. 1908a, Professor Freud and Hysteria. *BMJ* January 11, 1908, pp. 103–4.

———. 1908b, Reviews: Hysteria and Dementia Praecox. *BMJ* February 8, 1908, pp. 325–26.

———. 1908c, *Conference of Bishops of the Anglican Communion: Holden at Lambeth Palace 6 July–5 August 1908. Encyclical Letter from the Bishops with the Resolutions and Reports*. London: SPCK.

———. 1908d, The Galvanometer and Subconscious Ideas. *BMJ* September 26, 1908, pp. 943–44.

———. 1909a, The Pathology of Insanity. *BMJ* April 24, 1909, pp. 1014–16.

———. 1909b, Experimental Psychology. *BMJ* 2 October 1909, pp. 989–90.

———. 1910a, Report of Mitchell's paper 'A Study in Hysteria and Double Personality, with Report of a Casc. *Journal* 1910, Vol. 14, pp. 263–65.

———. 1910b, Mental Healing. *BMJ* June 18, 1910, pp. 1483–97.

———. 1911a, Unqualified Practice in the Eye of the Law. *BMJ* May 27, 1911, pp. 1277–81.

———. 1911b, Report on the Subject of 'Spiritual Healing' submitted by the [BMA] Council. *BMJ* July 15, 1911 [Supplement] pp. 125–32.

———. 1911c, Puberty and the neuro-psychic system. *BMJ* June 3, 1911, pp. 1337–38.

———. 1912, Freud's Theory of Dreams, *UMR* 1912, Vol. 2, pp. 307–12.

———. 1913a, Psycho-analysis. *UMR* 1913, Vol. 3, pp. 37–39.

———. 1913b, London Medico-Psychological Clinic. *BMJ* 15 November. 1913, pp. 1311–12.

———. 1913c, Seventeenth International Medical Congress of Medicine, *CMAJ* 1913, Vol. 3, pp. 324–26.

———. 1914, *Report of the Eighty-Third Meeting of the British Association for the Advancement of Science* [Birmingham September 10–17, 1913]. London: John Murray.

———. 1920, *Conference of Bishops of the Anglican Communion: Holden at Lambeth Palace 5 July–7 August 1920. Encyclical Letter from the Bishops with the Resolutions and Reports*. London: SPCK.
———. 1932, Obituary: George M. Robertson. *BMJ* April 9, 1932, pp. 688–89.
———. 1940, Obituary: Henry Devine. *BMJ* May 11, 1940, p. 792.
———. 1941, Obituary: David Forsyth. *BMJ* April 26, 1941, pp. 652–53.
———. 1944, Obituary: Sir Humphrey Rolleston, *BMJ* September 30, 1944, pp. 452–54.
———. 1948, Obituary: Thomas Gwynne Maitland. *BJIM* 1948 October, Vol. 5, p. 236.
———. 1950, Obituary: W. H. Butter Stoddart. *BMJ* April 29, 1950, p. 1010.
———. 1951, *The Living Church. Index for January to June 1951*, Vol. 122. Milwaukee (Wisconsin): Morehouse-Gorham Co.
———. 1966, Obituary Notices: B. Hart, *BMJ* March 26, 1966, p. 806.
———. 2015, The Story of Crowhurst Christian Healing Centre, The Old Rectory, and The Divine Healing Mission: Beginnings. http://www.crowhursthealing.co.uk/ourhistory2.
———. 2016a, Lost Hospitals of London. *Lost Hospitals of London: Coulter Hospital*. http://ezitis.myzen.co.uk/coulter.html.
———. 2016b, The Eldwick Sanatorium – Postscript. *Eldwick, Village Society Newsletter*. Issue 447, February 2016, http://www.eldwickvillage.co.uk/.
APS (1905–), *The Annals of Psychical Science: A monthly journal devoted to critical and experimental research in the phenomena of Spiritism*, ed. Dr. Dariex & Professor C. Richet. London: APS.
Archives, *Archives of Neurology from the Pathological Laboratory of the LCC Asylums, Claybury*, ed. F. W. Mott. London: P. S. King & Son.
ARR, *Archives of The Roentgen Ray*.
AS, *Auckland Star*, New Zealand.
Ash, E. L. 1906a, Some Experiments in Hypnosis. *The Lancet* January 27, 1906, pp. 216–20.
———. 1906b, The Induction of Hypnosis. *The Lancet* August 25, 1906, pp. 501–4.
———. 1906c, Modern Hypnotism. A Lecture delivered before the PTS [November 5, 1906]. *PBH* December 29, 1906, p. 8; *PTS*, November 1906, pp. 93–94.
———. 1907a, *Hypnotism and Suggestion; A Practical Handbook*. London: J. Jacobs.
———. 1909, Nervous Breakdown: The Disease of the Age. *MTHG* Vol. 37, January 16, 1909, pp. 35–37, 54–56.
———. 1910a, *Mind and Health: the mental factor and suggestion in treatment, with special reference to neurasthenia and other common nervous disorders*. London: H. J. Glaisher.
———. 1911, Some Thoughts on Psychic Influence [Letter to Arthur Hallam]. *HR* November 1911, pp. 122–23.
———. 1912, *Faith and Suggestion* [with an account of the case of Dorothy Kerin]. London: Herbert & Daniel.
———. 1913, *The Nursing of Nervous Patients*. London: The Scientific Press.

———. 1914, *How to Treat by Suggestion with and without Hypnotism: A Notebook for Practitioners*. London: Mills & Boon.
———. 1919, *The Problem of Nervous Breakdown*. London: Mills & Boon.
———. 1920, *Mental Self-Help*. London: Mills & Boon.
———. 1922, *Middle Age Health and Fitness*. London: Mills & Boon.
Auckland, *Auckland Star*, New Zealand.
AWJ, *Aberdeen Weekly Journal*. Aberdeen: Scotland.
Bakman, N. 2013, Thirty Years On: K. R. Eissler's Interview with Joan Riviere (1953). *P&H* 2013, Vol. 15, pp. 91–104.
Bachner-Melman, R. & Lichtenberg, P. 2001, Freud's Relevance to Hypnosis: A Revaluation. *American Journal of Clinical Hypnosis*. 2001, Vol. 44, pp. 37–50.
BAFP, *Buckingham Advertiser and Free Press*. Buckingham.
Bampton, A. H. 1907, Scepticism in Therapeutics. [Abstract of Presidential Address to the Leeds and West Riding Medico-Chirurgical Society. *The Lancet* January 19, 1907, pp. 142–44.
Barham, G. F. 1907, Notes on the management and treatment of the epileptic insane, with a special reference to the NaCl-free (or 'hypo-chlorisation') diet. *JMS* 1907, Vol. 53, pp. 361–67.
———. 1911, Two Cases of 'Washing-Hand' Mania with Some Observations on their Etiology. *Archives* 1911, Vol. 5, pp. 101–19.
———. 1912, Insanity with Myxoedema, *JMS* 1912, Vol. 58 (April 1912), pp. 226–35.
———. 1913, Review of Brill's Psychoanalysis: its Theory and Practical Application. *JMS* (October 1913), Vol. 59, pp. 666–68.
Barrett, W. F. 1911, *Psychical Research*. London: Henry Holt and Co.
———. 1917, *On the Threshold of the Unseen; An examination of the phenomena of Spiritualism and of the evidence for Survival after Death*. New York: E. P. Dutton & Co.
Bartrip, P. W. J. 1990, *Mirror of Medicine: A History of the British Medical Journal*. Oxford: BMJ & Clarendon Press.
Bastian, H. C. 1893, *Various Forms of Hysterical or Functional Paralysis*. Philadelphia: J. B. Lippincott Co.
BC, *The Brisbane Courier*. Queensland.
Bellamy, R. 1915, An Act of Everyday Life Treated as a Pretended Dream and Interpreted by Psychoanalysis. *JAP*, 1915–1916, Vol. 10, pp. 32–45.
Benedikt, M. 1898, History, Uses, and Dangers of Hypnotism, *BMJ* September 10, 1898, p. 677.
Bennett, E. T. 1903, *The Society for Psychical Research: Its rise and progress and a sketch of its work*. London: R. Brimley Johnson.
Berkeley-Hill, O. A. R. 1913a, The Psychology of the Anus. *IMG* Vol. 48, pp. 301–3.
———. 1913b, A report of two cases successfully treated by psychoanalysis. *IMG* Vol. 48, pp. 97–99.
———. 1939, *All Too Human: An Unconventional Autobiography*. London: Peter Davies.
Bernard, L. L. 1923, Instincts and the Psychoanalysts. *JAP* 1923, Vol. 17, pp. 350–66.

Bernheim, H. 1890, *Suggestive Therapeutics: A Treatise on the Nature and Uses of Hypnotism* (2nd edition), trans. Christian A. Herter. Edinburgh: Young J. Pentland.

BET, *Boston Evening Transcript*. Boston.

Bewley, T., nd., Madness to Mental Illness. A History of the Royal College of Psychiatrists. Online archive 13, Edward Mapother (1881–1940), www.rcpsych.ac.uk.

BHR (1909–1910), *British Health Review*, ed. Lily Hodgkinson. London.

Bible. 2006, *The Bible: King James Version with The Apocrypha*. Edited by David Norton. London: Penguin Books.

BJI (1903–), *British Journal of Inebriety*, ed. T. N. Kelynack. London: Baillière, Tindall & Cox.

BJMP (1920–), *British Journal of Medical Psychology*, ed. T. W. Mitchell. Cambridge: Cambridge UP.

BJP (1904–), *The British Journal of Psychology*, ed. James Ward & W. H. R. Rivers. Cambridge: Cambridge UP.

Bloch, I. 1907, *Das Sexualleben unserer Zeit*. Berlin: Marcus.

———. 1908, *The Sexual Life of our Time in its Relation to Modern Civilization*, trans. M. EdenPaul. London: Rebman Ltd.

———. 1909, *The Sexual Life of our Time in its Relation to Modern Civilization*, trans. M. Eden Paul. London: Rebman Ltd. (Reprint).

Blumer, G. A. 1906, The coming of psychasthenia. *JNMD* Vol. 33. 1906, pp. 336–53.

BM, *Barrier Miner*. Broken Hill, NSW.

BMA 1909, *Secret Remedies, What they Cost and What they Contain*. London: BMA.

BMJ, *British Medical Journal*, ed. Dawson Williams. London.

BMSJ, *Boston Medical and Surgical Journal*, ed. George B. Shattuck. Boston.

Boll, T. E. M. 1962, May Sinclair and the Medico-Psychological Clinic of London. *Proc. of the American Philosophical Society* Vol. 106, pp. 310–26.

Bolus, P. R. 1903, Hypnotism: Its Therapeutic Value. *GHG* 1903, Vol. 17, September 12, 1903, pp. 375–79.

Borch-Jacobsen, M. 1996, *Remembering Anna O.: A Century of Mystification*, trans. by Kirby Olson, London: Routledge.

Borch-Jacobsen, M. & Shamdasani, S. 2008, Interprefactions: Freud's legendary science. *HHS* Vol. 21, pp. 1–25.

Borderland (1893–1897), *Borderland: A Quarterly Review and Index*, ed., W. T. Stead. London.

Botham, R. H. 1914, Psycho-analysis. *BMJ* January 24, 1914, p. 224.

Boyle, H. 1909, Account of an Attempt at the Early Treatment of Mental and Nervous Cases (With Special Reference to the Poor). *JMS* 1909, Vol. 55, pp. 683–92.

BPAS, Archives of the British Psychoanalytical Society, Institute of Psychoanalysis.

Brabant, E., Falzeder, E., Giampieri-Deutsch, P. 1993, *The Correspondence of Sigmund Freud and Sándor Ferenczi. Vol. 1, 1908–1914*, trans Peter T. Hoffer. Cambridge, MA: The Belknap Press.

Braid, J. 1853, Hypnotic Therapeutics: Illustrated by Cases with an Appendix on Table-Moving and Spirit-Rapping, ed. D. J. Robertson 2013, pp. 83–109.

Brain, (1878–), *Brain. A journal of Neurology*, ed. R. Percy Smith [then Henry Head]. London: Macmillan & Co.

Bramwell, J. M. 1897, Personally Observed Hypnotic Phenomena. *Proceedings* 1897, Vol. 12, pp. 176–203.

———. 1898, A Discussion on The Phenomena of Hypnotism, and the Theories as to its Nature [66th BMA Annual Meeting]. *BMJ* September 10, 1898, pp. 669–74.

———. 1900a, Hypnotism, ed. Watson. 1900, Vol. 5, pp. 88–109.

———. 1900b, Hypnotic and Post-Hypnotic Appreciation of Time; Secondary and Multiplex Personalities. *Brain* 1900, Vol. 23, pp. 161–238.

———. 1903, *Hypnotism: Its History, Practice and Theory.* Grant Richards, London.

———. 1908, Hypnotism, *PRSM* (Therapeutical and Pharmacological Section) March 24, 1908, pp. 49–64.

———. 1909, *Hypnotism and Treatment by Suggestion*, London: Cassell & Co.

———. 1910, Suggestion and its Role in the Treatment of Inebriety [Abstract of address to SSI, 12 October 1909]. *BJI.* 1910, Vol. 7 pp. 133–40.

———. 1921, *Hypnotism: Its History, Practice and Theory* (3rd edition). London: William Rider & Son.

Breuer, J. & Freud, S. 1893, On the Psychical Mechanism of Hysterical Phenomena: Preliminary Communication. Freud S. E. 2, pp. 1–17.

———. 1895, *Studies on Hysteria.* Freud S. E. 2.

Brill, A. A. 1913, *Psychanalysis: Its Theories and Practical Application.* Philadelphia: W. B. Saunders & Co.

———. 1939, The introduction and development of Freud's Work in the United States of America. *Journal of Sociology* 1939, Vol. 45, pp. 318–28.

Brome, V. 1983, *Ernest Jones: Freud's Alter Ego.* New York: W. W. Norton & Co.

Brown, H. 1921, *Advanced Suggestion (Neuroinduction)*, 2nd edition. London: Baillière: Tindall & Cox.

Brown, P. S. 1991, Medically Qualified Naturopaths and the General Medical Council. *Medical History* 1991, Vol. 35, pp. 50–77.

Brown, W. 1913a, Freud's Theory of Dreams. *Lancet* April 19, 1913, pp. 114–18; April 26, 1913, pp. 1182–84.

———. 1913b, A Case of Extensive Amnesia of Remote Date Cured by Psycho-Analysis and Hypnosis. [Paper read at BMA Annual Meeting]. *BMJ* November 8, 1913, pp. 1217–19.

———. 1921, Criticisms of Present-Day Psycho-Analysis. *JMS* 1921, Vol. 67, pp. 17–26.

———. 1924, Psychology and Medicine. In *Psychology and the Sciences*, ed. William Brown. London: A & C Black Ltd., pp. 141–57.

———. 1936, Psychology at Oxford. *BMJ* May 30, 1936, pp. 1121–22.

Brown, W., & Thomson, G. H. 1921, *The Essentials of Mental Measurement.* Cambridge: Cambridge UP.

Bryan, D. 1906, Notes on Two Hypnotic Cases. *GP*, December 15, 1906, p. 787.

———. 1907, Hypnotism and Treatment by Hypnotic Suggestion. *GHG* November 30, 1907, Vol. 21, pp. 490–94.

Bulletin (1920–), *Bulletin of the International Psycho-Analytic Association.*

Bunn, G. C., Lovie A. D., Richards G. D., eds. 2001, *Psychology in Britain. Historical Essays and Personal Reflections.* Leicester: BPS Books.

Burial (1905–), *Burial Reformer; a quarterly devoted to the scientific investigation of trance and the various forms of suspended animation, the necessity for a more efficient method of death verification and certification and the reform of the present burial system*. Ed. Arthur Hallam, London: Burial Reform Society.

Burt, C. 1909, Experimental Tests of General Intelligence. *BJP* 1909–1910, Vol. 3, pp. 94–177.

———. 1916, Psychology and the Emotions. *School Hygiene* 1916, Vol. 6, pp. 57–69.

Butlin, H. T. 1910, Remarks on Spiritual Healing. *BMJ* June 18, 1910, pp. 1466–70.

Buzzard, T. 1891, *On the Simulation of Hysteria by Organic Disease of the Nervous System*. London: J.&. A Churchill.

———. 1902, A Discussion on the Differential Diagnosis of Functional and Organic Paralysis. *BMJ* November 1, 1902, pp. 1401–5.

Cameron, L. & Forrester J. 1999, 'A Nice Type of the English Scientist': Tansley and Freud. *History Workshop Journal* 1999, 48, pp. 65–100.

———. 2000, Tansley's Psychoanalytic Network: An Episode out of the Early History of Psychoanalysis in England. *P&H* 2000, Vol. 2, pp. 189–256.

Campbell, C. M., et al. 1925, *Problems of Personality: Studies Presented to Dr MortonPrince Pioneer in American Psychopathology*. New York: Kegan Paul.

Cambria, *The Cambria Daily Leader*. Swansea.

Canney, M. 1921, *Encyclopedia of Religions*. London: G. Routledge & Sons.

Caplan, E. 1998, *Mind Games: American Culture and the Birth of Psychotherapy*. Berkeley: UCP.

CC, *Chelmsford Chronicle*. Chelmsford: Essex.

Cerullo, J. J. 1982, *The Secularization of the Soul: Psychical Research in Modern Britain*. Philadelphia: ISSHI.

Chertok, L. 1966, *Hypnosis*. Trans. D. Graham. Oxford: Pergamon Press.

———. 1984, Hypnosis and Suggestion in a Century of Psychotherapy: An Epistemological Assessment. *JAAPA* 1984, Vol. 12, pp. 211–32.

Chettiar, T. 2012, 'Looking as Little Like Patients as Persons Well Could': Hypnotism, Medicine and the Problem of the Suggestible Subject in Late Nineteenth-Century Britain. *Med. Hist.* 2012, Vol. 56, pp. 335–54.

Chronicle, *Chronicle*. Adelaide, S. Australia.

Clarke, J. M. 1896, Review [Studien über Hysterie]. *Brain* 1896 Vol. 19, pp. 401–14.

Clouston, T. S. 1897, *Clinical Lectures on Mental Diseases* (4th edition). Philadelphia: Lea Brothers & Co,.

CMAJ, Canadian Medical Association Journal.

Coates, J. 1906, *Seeing the Invisible. Practical Studies in Psychometry, Thought Transference, Telepathy, and Allied Phenomena*. London: L. N. Fowler & Co.

Cobb, W. F. 1914, *Spiritual Healing*. London: G. Bell & Sons Ltd.

Cocke, J. R. 1894, *Hypnotism: How it is Done; Its Uses and Dangers*. Boston: Arena Publishing Co.

Cole, R. H. 1913, *Mental Diseases. A Text-Book of Psychiatry for Medical Students and Practitioners*. London: University of London Press.

COMC, *County Observer and Monmouthshire Central*. Usk: Wales.

Commissioners. 1910, *64th Report of the Commissioners in Lunacy to the Lord Chancellor*. London: HC; Cmn 204.

———. 1911, *65th Report of the Commissioners in Lunacy to the Lord Chancellor*. London: HC; Cmn 207.

———. 1914, *68th Report of the Commissioners in Lunacy to the Lord Chancellor*, London HC; Cmn 264.

Coomaraswamy. 1911, The Work of the Psycho-Therapeutic Society, *Light* November 18, 1911, p. 547–49.

Cooper, J. W. A. 1910, The Treatment of Alcohol Inebriety by Psycho-Therapy. *BJI* 1911, Vol. 8, pp. 135–42.

Coriat, I. H. 1907, Abstract: The question of tactile aphasia. *JAP* 1907, Vol. 1, pp. 283–85.

———. 1910, *Abnormal Psychology*. New York: Moffat Yard & Co.

Crabtree, A. 1993, *From Mesmer to Freud: Magnetic Sleep and the Roots of Psychological Healing*. New Haven: Yale UP.

———. 2007, Automatism and Secondary Centres of Consciousness. Kelly *et al.* 2007, pp. 301–65.

———. 2008, The transition to Secular Psychotherapy: Hypnosis and the Alternate-Consciousness Paradigm. In *History of Psychiatry and Medical Psychology: With an Epilogue on Psychiatry and the Mind-Body Relation*. Edwin R. Wallace and John Gach (eds). New York: Springer. pp. 555–86.

Craig, M. 1905, *Psychological Medicine: A Manual on Mental Diseases for Practitioners and Students*. London: J. & A. Churchill.

———. 1910, Faith Healing, or the Mental Factor in Disease. [Meeting of the Physical Society] *GHG* November 12, 1910, Vol. 24, pp. 435–39.

———. 1912, *Psychological Medicine: A Manual on Mental Diseases for Practitioners andStudents*. London: J. & A. Churchill (2nd edition).

Crookes, W. 1898, The Wheat Supply of the World [Presidential Address to the British Association for the Advancement of Science]. *BMJ* September 10, 1898, pp. 730–33.

Cruise, F. R. 1907, Introductory Chapter. In Tuckey 1907, pp. xi–xxiv.

CT, *The Church Times*. London: Longman, Green & Co.

DC, *The Daily Chronicle*. London.

Daily Mail, *The Daily Mail*. London.

David 2012, Abdu'l-Baha in Britain, 1913. The Diary of Abd'l-Baha's Translator. http://www.paintdrawer.co.uk/david/folders/Spirituality/001=Bahai/sohrab-diary-uk-1913.pdf.

Davis, A. E. 1926, Psychic Traumas. *Lancet* July 17, 1926, pp. 117–20.

DC, *Dundee Courier*. Dundee.

DDT, *Derby Daily Telegraph*. Derby.

Dearmer, P. 1909, *Body and Soul: An Enquiry into the effect of Religion upon Health, with a description of Christian Works of Healing from the New Testament to the Present Day*. New York: E. P. Dutton & Co. 1923.

DEP, *Dundee Evening Post*. Dundee.

DET, *Dundee Evening Telegraph*. Dundee.

Devine, H. 1909, Some Observations on a Case with Impulsive Obsessions of Suicide and Auto-Mutilation, *Archives* 1909, Vol. 4, pp. 300–10.

———. 1910, An Account of Kraepelin's Clinic at Munich. *JMS*.

———. 1911a, Abnormal Mental States Associated with Malignant Disease. *JMS* 1911, Vol. 57, pp. 348–61.
———. 1911b, Pathogenesis of a Delusion [Paper delivered to the Northern & Midland Division of the Association, April 27, 1911], *BMJ* 20 May, p. 1180.
———. 1911c, The Pathogenesis of a Delusion. *JMS* 1911, Vol. 57, pp. 458–75.
———. 1911d, The Significance of Some Confusional States [Paper read at BMA Annual Meeting] *BMJ* 30 September, pp. 747–748.
———. 1914, The biological significance of delusions. *PRSM* (Psychiatry section), Vol. 7, pp. 89–103.
Dill, J. G. 1895, Dipsomania and Hypnotism. *Proceedings* 1895, Vol. 11, pp. 18–22.
DNL, *Daily News and Leader*. London.
Dominion, *The Dominion.* Wellington: New Zealand.
Dubois, P. 1909, *The Psychic Treatment of Nervous Disorders (The Psychoneuroses and their moral treatment*). Trans. Smith Ely Jelliffe & William White (7th ed). New York: Funk & Wagnalls Co.
Du Prel, C. 1889, *The Philosophy of Mysticism.* Vol. 1, trans. C. C. Massey. London: George Redway (1885 ed.).
Dundee Courier, *The Dundee Courier & Argus.* Dundee, Scotland.
Dupont, J. (ed). 1998, *The Clinical Diary of Sándor Ferenczi*, trans. Michael Balint & Nicola Zarday Jackson. Cambridge, MA: Harvard UP.
Eddy, Mrs, aka M. B. Glover. 1875, *Science and Health.* Boston: CSP Co.
Eder, M. D. 1907a, The Origin of 'Circumcision', *BMJ* July 13, 1907, p. 117.
———. 1907b, Industrial Outlook. *New Age* August 15, 1907, p. 243.
———. 1907c, International Congress on School Hygiene. *New Age* August 15, 1907, p. 244.
———. 1907d, Reviews: Sociological Papers. *New Age*, 17 October 1907, pp. 394–95.
———. 1908, *The Endowment of Motherhood.* London: New Age Press.
———. 1911, A Case of Obsession and Hysteria Treated by the Freud Psycho-Analytic Method [Paper read at the BMA Annual Meeting]. *BMJ* September 30, 1911, pp. 750–52.
———. 1912, Freud's Theory of Dreams. *Transactions* 1912, Vol. 3, pp. 1–20.
———. 1913a, Stammering as a psycho-neurosis and its treatment by psycho-analysis. ICM 1913 (Section 12, Psychiatry), pp. 187–92.
———. 1913b, Das Stottern, eine Psychoneurose, und seine Behandlung durch Psychoanalyse. [Paper read at the ICM, August 1913], *IZPA* 1913, pp. 547–55.
———. 1913c, The Present Position of Psycho-Analysis. [Paper read at the BMA Annual Meeting]. *BMJ* November 8, 1913, pp. 1213–15.
———. 1917, *War Shock, The Psycho-Neuroses in War Psychology and Treatment.* London: William Heinemann.
Edgell, B. 1947, The British Psychological Society. *BJP* [General Section] 1947, Vol. 37, pp. 113–32.
EE, 1849–1910, *Evening Express.* Cardiff.
EEN, *Edinburgh Evening News.* Edinburgh.
Einstein, A. et al. 1936, Memorial to Dr. David Eder. *BMJ* 24 October 1936, p. 846.
Ellenberger, H. F. 1994, *The Discovery of the Unconscious: The History and Evolution of Dynamic Psychiatry*, London: Fontana Press.

Ellis, H. 1898a, Auto-Erotism: A Psychological Study. *Alienist* 1898, Vol. 19, pp. 260–99.

———. 1898b, Hysteria in Relation to the Sexual Emotions: A Retrospect, *Alienist* 1898, Vol. 19, pp. 599–615.

———. 1898c, Review of Felix Gattel's 'Ueber die Sexuellen Ursachen der Neurasthenie und Angstneurose.' *JMS* 1898, Vol. 44, pp. 850–52.

———. 1900a, *Studies in the Psychology of Sex: Vol. 1 Sexual Inversion*. London: The University Press.

———. 1900b, *Studies in the Psychology of Sex: Vol. 2 The Evolution of Modesty, The Phenomena of Sexual Periodicity* and *Auto-Eroticism*. London: The University Press.

———. 1901a, Review of Freud's 'Ueber den Traum.' *JMS* 1901, Vol. 47, pp. 370–71.

———. 1901b, *Studies in the Psychology of Sex: The Evolution of Modesty, The Phenomena of Sexual Periodicity* and *Auto-Eroticism* Philadelphia: F. A. Davis Company.

———. 1905, *Studies in the Psychology of Sex: Vol. 2, The Evolution of Modesty, The Phenomena of Sexual Periodicity* and *Auto-Eroticism*. F. A. Davis Co., Philadelphia.

———. 1906, Review of 'Fragment of a Case History of Hysteria.' *JMS*. 1906, Vol. 52, pp. 406–7.

———. 1907a, Review of Freud's 'Sammlung Kleiner Schriften zur Neurosenlehre.' *JMS* 1907, Vol. 53, pp. 172–73.

———. 1907b, Review of Bloch's 'Das Sexualleben unserer Zeit. *JMS* 1907, Vol. 53, pp. 637–39.

———. 1907c, Review of Zur Psycho-pathologie des Alltagsleben. *JMS* 1907, Vol. 53, pp. 830–32.

———. 1907d, Review of Sadger's 'The Value of Freud's Psycho-analytic Method.' *JMS* 1907, Vol. 53, p. 834.

———. 1908a, Review of Friedländer's 'Freud's Doctrine of the Sexual Aetiology of Neuroses. *JMS* 1908, Vol. 54, p. 588.

———. 1908b, Review of Magnus Hirschfeld's Jahrbuch für Sexuelle Zwischenstufen. *JMS* 1908, Vol. 54, pp. 753–55.

———. 1913, *Studies in the Psychology of Sex: Vol. 3, Analysis of the Sexual Impulse: Love and Pain: The Sexual Impulse in Women*. Philadelphia: F. A. Davis & Co.

———. 1939, Freud's Influence on the Changing Attitude Towards Sex. *AJS* 1939, Vol. 45, pp. 309–17.

Engel, S. 1912, *The Elements of Child-Protection*. Trans. Eden Paul. New York: The Macmillan Co.

EP, *Evening Post*. Wellington: New Zealand.

EPG, *Exeter and Plymouth Gazette*. Exeter.

Era, *The Era*. London.

Ehrlich, P. & Hata, S. 1911, *The Experimental Chemotherapy of Spirilloses*, trans. A. Newbold; revised by Robert W. Felkin. London: Rebman.

Erős, F., Szekacs-Weisz, J., & Robinson, K. 2013, *Sándor Ferenczi - Ernest Jones, Letters 1911–1933*. London: Karnac.

Erskin, S. 1919, ed., *Memoirs of Edward Earl of Sandwich 1839–1916*. London. John Murray.

ES, *The Essex Standard, West Suffolk Gazette, and Eastern Counties' Advertiser*. Colchester.

Evans, R. I. 1964, *Conversations with Carl Jung and Reactions from Ernest Jones*. Toronto: D. van Nostrand Co.

Examiner, *Examiner*. Launceston: Tasmania.

Falzeder, E. 2002, *The Complete Correspondence of Sigmund Freud and Karl Abraham: 1907–1925*, trans. Caroline Schwarzacher. London. Karnac.

———. 2007, Is there still an unknown Freud? A note on the publications of Freud's texts and on unpublished documents. *P&H* 2007, Vol. 9, pp. 201–32.

———. 2015, *Psychoanalytic Filiations. Mapping the Psychoanalytic Movement*. London: Karnac.

FCP, *Fitzroy City Press*. Victoria: Australia.

Feilding, A. 1899, *Faith-Healing and Christian Science*. London: Duckworth & Co.

Féré, C. 1886, Sensation and Movement. *Brain* 1886, Vol. 8, pp. 210–29.

Ferenczi, S. 1910, The Psychological Analysis of Dreams. *AJP* (April 1910), Vol. 21, pp. 309–28.

———. 1912, The Psycho-Analysis of Suggestion and Hypnosis, trans. A. Newbold. *Transactions* 1913, Vol. 3 (4). Cockermouth: Brash Bros.

———. 1916, *Contributions to Psycho-Analysis*. Trans. Ernest Jones. Boston: Richard G. Badger.

Firth, V. M. 1922, *The Machinery of the Mind*. New York: Dodd, Mead & Co.

Fitzroy, A. 1910, *Report as to the Practice of Medicine and Surgery by Unqualified Persons in the United Kingdom*. London: HMSO [CD5422].

Fleury, M. de. 1900, *Medicine and the Mind*, Trans by Stacy B Collins. London: Downey & Co.

Flügel J. C. 1945, Book Reviews: Hobman etc., *IJPA* 1945, Vol. 26, pp. 77–78.

Forel, A. 1906, *Hypnotism or Suggestion and Psychotherapy. A Study of the Psychological, Psycho-Physiological and Therapeutic Aspects of Hypnotism*. Trans by H. W. Armit. London: Rebman.

Forrester, J. 2006, Remembering and Forgetting Freud in Early Twentieth Century Dreams. *Science in Context* 2006, Vol. 19, pp. 65–85.

———. 2008, 1919: Psychology and Psychoanalysis, Cambridge and London – Myers, Jones and Maccurdy. *PH* 2008, Vol. 10, pp. 37–94.

Forsyth, D. 1913, On Psycho-Analysis. *BMJ* July 5, 1913, pp. 13–17.

———. 1922, *The Technique of Psycho-Analysis*. London: Kegan Paul, Trench, Trübner & Co.

Fortune, C. 1993, The Case of 'RN'. In Aron, L. & Harris A. (eds), *The Legacy of Sándor Ferenczi*. Hilsdale, NY: The Analytic Press, pp. 101–20.

Fotherby, H. 1907, Emotion and Colour: The Influence of Environment on the Associated Evolution of certain Colours Perception with Certain Mental Faculties. *APS* 1907, Vol. 6, pp. 315–34.

Fowler, C. 2014, *Bryant & May the Bleeding Heart*. London: Bantam Books.

Fraser, D. 1920, The Mind Factor in Disease. *JNMD*. 1920, Vol. 52, p. 84.

Freud, E. L. 1970, *Letters of Sigmund Freud, 1873–1939,* trans. Tania and James Stern. London: Hogarth Press.

Freud S. 1892, *The Standard Edition of the Complete Psychological Works of Sigmund Freud*, trans. James Strachey, The Hogarth Press, London. [*Hereafter SE*]

———. 1892–1893, A Case of Successful Treatment by Hypnotism, with some remarks on the origin of hysterical symptoms through 'counter-will.' SE 1, pp. 115–28.

———. 1893, Some Points for a Comparative Study of Organic and Hysterical Motor Paralyses. SE 1, pp. 155–72.

———. 1894, The Neuro-Psychoses of Defence (An attempt at a psychological theory of acquired hysteria, of many phobias and obsessions and of certain hallucinatory psychoses). SE 3, pp. 41–61.

———. 1895a, Obsessions and Phobias: Their Psychical Mechanism and Their Aetiology. SE 3, pp. 69–82.

———. 1895b, On the Grounds for Detaching a Particular Syndrome from Neurasthenia under the Description 'Anxiety Neurosis.' SE 3, pp. 85–115.

———. 1895c, The Psychotherapy of Hysteria. SE 2, pp. 253–305.

———. 1896a, Heredity and the Aetiology of the Neuroses. SE 3, pp. 141–56.

———. 1896b, Further Remarks on the Neuro-Psychoses for Defence. SE 3, pp. 157–85.

———. 1896c, The Aetiology of Hysteria. SE 3., pp. 187–221.

———. 1900, *The Interpretation of Dreams*. SE 4–5.

———. 1904a, Freud's Psychoanalytic Procedure. SE 7, pp. 247–54.

———. 1904b, On Psychotherapy. SE 7, pp. 257–68.

———. 1904c, On Psychotherapy. [See also Freud 1909a, pp. 175–85].

———. 1905, *Three Essays on Sexuality*. SE 7, pp. 123–243.

———. 1909a, *Selected Papers on Hysteria, and Other Psychoneuroses*. Trans. A. A. Brill. New York: JNMD Publishing Co.

———. 1909b, Notes upon a Case of Obsessional Neuroses. SE 10, pp. 151–320.

———. 1910a, The Origin and Development of Psychoanalysis. *AJP* (April 1910), Vol. 21, pp. 181–218 [SE 11, pp. 7–55].

———. 1910b, *Three Contributions to the Sexual Theory*. Trans. A. A. Brill. New York: JNMD Publishing Co.

———. 1912a, A Note on the Unconscious in Psycho-Analysis. *Proceedings* 1912, Vol. 26, pp. 312–18.

———. 1912b, A Note on the Unconscious in Psycho-Analysis. SE 12, pp. 260–66.

———. 1912c, *Selected Papers on Hysteria and Other Psychoneuroses* (2nd edition). Trans. A. A. Brill. New York: JNMD Publishing Co.

———. 1913, *The Interpretation of Dreams* (3rd edition). Trans. A. A. Brill. New York: The Macmillan Co.

———. 1914a, On the History of the Psycho-Analytic Movement. SE14, pp. 1–66.

———. 1914b, *On Dreams*. Trans. M. D. Eder. New York: Rebman Co.

———. 1916–1917, Introductory Lectures on Psycho-Analysis. SE 15–16.

———. 1923, A Short Account of Psycho-Analysis. SE 19, pp. 189–209.
———. 1924a, Collected Papers, Vol. 1. Authorised English translation. London: The Hogarth Press.
———. 1924b, Collected Papers, Vols. 1–3, supervised by Joan Riviere. New York: International Psychoanalytic Library.
———. 1933, New Introductory Lectures on Psycho-Analysis. SE 22, pp. 1–182.
———. 1939, Moses and Monotheism: Three Essays. SE 23, pp. 1–137.
Fromm, E. 1959, *Sigmund Freud's Mission: An Analysis of His Personality and Influence*. New York: Harper & Brothers.
Gardner, T. F. 1910, 'Lest We Forget.' [Presidential Address to the Dorset and West Hants Branch of the BMA]. *BMJ* June 11, 1910, pp. 362–66.
Gartrell-Mills, C. F. 1991, *Christian Science: an American Religion in Britain, 1895–1940*. Phd Thesis, Wolfson College: Oxford University.
Gauld, A. 1992, *A History of Hypnotism*. Cambridge: Cambridge UP.
GE, *Gloucestershire Echo*. Cheltenham.
Genome 2016, BBC Genome Project. http://genome.ch.bbc.co.uk/.
Gerrish, F. H., ed. 1909, *Psychotherapeutics*. Boston: Richard G. Badger.
GHG, *Guy's Hospital Gazette. London; Guy's Hospital.* Liddell Hart Centre for Military Archives, King's College London.
Glover, E. 1995, Psychoanalysis in England. In Alexander et al. 1995, pp. 534–45.
Gleigg, A. 2012, The Return of the Repressed? Psychoanalysis as Spirituality. *Implicit Religion* 2012, Vol. 15, pp. 209–24.
Goodall, E. 1890a, Hypnotism of the Insane. *JMS* 1890, Vol. 36, pp. 157–58.
———. 1890b, Observations on the Treatment of the Insane. *Lancet* May 24, 1890, pp. 1119–20.
———. 1890c, Suggestion during hypnosis in the Insane. A Case with remarks by Edwin Goodall. *JMS* 1890, Vol. 36, pp. 367–71.
Goodrich-Freer, A. 1899, *Essays in Psychical Research*. London: George Redway.
Gowers, W. 1907, Sudden Cerebral Lesions. *BMJ* July 6, 1907, pp. 1–6.
———. 1909, Hospital Clinics: A demonstration of Medical Cases. *The Hospital*, 12 June1909, pp. 279–81.
GP., *The General Practitioner. The Official Journal of the Incorporated Practitioners' Association*. ed George Brown and A. Percy Allan. London.
Graham, W. 1911, Psycho-therapy [Paper delivered to the Annual Meeting of the Association]. *BMJ* August 19, 1911, pp. 396–97.
Grosskurth, P. 1985, *Havelock Ellis: A Biography*. New York: New York UP.
———. 1991, *The Secret Ring. Freud's inner circle and the politics of psychoanalysis*. London: Jonathan Cape.
Gurney E., Myers, F. W. H. & Podmore, F. 1886, *Phantasms of the Living*. London: SPR.
Guthrie, D. 1945, *A history of Medicine*. London: Thomas Nelson & Sons Ltd.
Gyimesi, J. 2012, Sándor Ferenczi and the problem of telepathy. *HHS*. 2012, pp. 131–48.
Hacking, I. 1995, *Rewriting the Soul: Multiple Personality and the Sciences of Memory*. Princeton: Princeton UP.

Hale, N. G. 1971, *James Jackson Putnam and Psychoanalysis: Letters between Putnam and Sigmund Freud, Ernest Jones, William James, Sandor Ferenczi, and Morton Prince, 1877–1917*. Cambridge, MA: Harvard UP.

Hallam, A. 1899a, [Review] 'Faith Healing and Christian Science.' *Humanitarian* 1899, Vol. 15, pp. 372–75.

———. 1899b, Two Aspects of Hypnotism. *Humanitarian* 1899, Vol. 15, pp. 419–24.

———. 1900, Mesmerism and Hypnotism. *Humanitarian* 1900, Vol. 16, pp. 424–29.

———. 1901a, The Higher Phenomena of Mesmerism. *Humanitarian* 1901, Vol. 18, pp. 43–50.

———. 1901b, The Educational Use of Hypnotism. *Humanitarian* 1901, Vol. 18, pp. 433–38.

———. 1910, Perfect Health. How to Acquire and Maintain it: with special reference to Psycho-Therapeutics. *HR* June 1910, pp. 62–66.

———. 1911a, Mental Therapeutics [Lecture delivered to PST, May 8, 1911]. *HR* May 1911, pp. 49–54.

———. 1911b, Suggestive Therapeutics and Hypnotism. [Lecture delivered to PST,December 4, 1911]. *HR* December 1911, pp. 134–37.

———. 1912a, Psycho-Therapeutics. [Lecture in the Theosophical Hall, Leeds August 18, 1912]. *HR*, September 1912, pp. 86–89.

———. 1912b, *The Key to Perfect Health and the Successful Application of Psycho-Therapeutics: A Practical Guide to both Operator and Patient* [Text-Book of the Psycho-Therapeutic Society]. London: St Clements Press Ltd.

———. 1914, The Psycho-Therapeutic Society: Its Origins and Principles. *HR* September 1914, pp. 63–64; October–November, p. 100.

Harbinger, *The Harbinger of Light: A Monthly Journal Devoted to Zoistic Science, Free Thought, Spiritualism and the Harmonial Philosophy*. Melbourne: Australia.

Hart, B. 1907, A Case of Severe Head Injury in a Psychasthenic, *BMJ* 17 August. 1907, pp. 389–90.

———. 1908a, A Philosophy of Psychiatry. *JMS* 1908, Vol. 54, pp. 473–90.

———. 1908b, [Review of Jung] The Psychology of Dementia Praecox [Über die Psychologie der Dementia Praecox, 1907]. *JMS* 1908, Vol. 54, pp. 584–85.

———. 1908c, [Review of Muthmann] Psycho-therapy [Zur Psychologie und Therapie Neurotischer Symptome, 1907). *JMS* 1908, Vol. 54, p. 753.

———. 1908d, [Review of Claparède] The Definition of Hysteria [Quelques Mots sur la Définition de l'Hystérie]. *JMS*. 1908, Vol. 54, pp. 757–58.

———. 1910a, The Conception of the Subconscious. *JAP* (March) 1910, Vol. 4. pp. 351–71.

———. 1910b, The Psychology of Freud and his School, *JMS* (July) 1910, Vol. 56, pp. 431–52.

———. 1910c, Freud's Conception of Hysteria. *Brain* 1911, Vol. 33, pp. 339–66.

———. 1911, The psychological conception of insanity. *Archives* 1911, Vol. 5, pp. 90–100.

———. 1912a, A Case of Double Personality. *JMS* 1912, Vol. 58, pp. 236–43.

———. 1912b, *The Psychology of Insanity*. Cambridge: Cambridge UP.

———. 1925, The Development of Psychopathology as a Branch of Science. In Campbell *et al.* 1925, pp. 229–41.

———. 1927, *Psychopathology: Its Development and Its Place in Medicine*. Cambridge: Cambridge UP.

———. 1940, Obituary Notice: Henry Devine, *British Journal of Psychiatry* 1940, Vol. 86, pp. 1153–54.

Hart, B., & Spearman, C. 1912, General Ability, its Existence and Nature. *BJP* (March) 1912, Vol. 5, pp. 51–84.

———. 1913, An experimental investigation into the general nature of dementia. ICM 1913, pp. 25–29.

———. 1915, Mental Tests of Dementia, *JAP* 1914–1915, Vol. 9, pp. 217–64.

Hart, E. 1896, *Hypnotism, Mesmerism and the New Witchcraft*. London: Smith Elder & Co.

Hayward, R. 2007, *Resisting History. Religious Transcendence and the Invention of the Unconscious*. Manchester: Manchester UP.

———. 2010, The Maudsley Hospital 1908–1939 in ed. V. Roelcke, P. Weindling & L. Westwood, *International Relations in Psychiatry: Britain, Germany, and the United States*. Rochester, NY: University of Rochester Press, pp. 67–90.

———. 2014, *The Transformation of the Psyche in British Primary Care, 1870–1970*. London: Bloomsbury.

HC (1881–), *The Homoeopathic Courier: A Monthly Journal Devoted to Homeopathic Medicine and Surgery*. ed. Wm. C. Richardson. Saint Louis: H. L. Verdier.

HDM, *Hull Daily Mail*. Hull.

Head, H. 1908, Opening comments to 'A discussion on "tics." *PRSM* (Neurological Section), January 30, 1908, Vol. 1, pp. 41–44.

Herald, *The Herald of the Golden Age. The Official Journal of The Order of the Golden Age: A Philanthropic Society founded to proclaim Hygienic Truth, to advocate the Humane Life and to promote Social Amelioration* [*a Message of Peace and Happiness, Health and Purity, Life and Power*], ed. Sidney Hartnoll Beard. Exeter, http://ordergoldenage.co.uk/page12.html.

Heuer, G.M. 2016, *Freud's 'Outstanding' Colleague/Jung's 'Twin Brother': The suppressed psychoanalytic and political significance of Otto Gross*. London: Routledge.

Hewlett, R. T. 1914, *A Manuel of Bacteriology, Clinical and Applied*. Saint Louis: C. V. Mosby Co.

HHS, *History of the Human Sciences*. New York: Sage Publications.

Hilger, W. 1912, *Hypnosis and Suggestion. Their Nature, Action, Importance and Position amongst Therapeutic Agents*, translated by R. W. Felkin, with an introduction by Dr. Van Renterghem, trans by A. Newbold. London: Rebman.

Hill, W. 1901, Occultism and Quackery: An Introductory Address. *Lancet* 12 October 1901, pp. 960–65.

Hinshelwood, R. D. 1995, Psychoanalysis In Britain: Points Of Cultural Access, 1893–1918. *IJPA* 1995, Vol. 76, pp. 135–51.

———. 1998, The Organizing of Psychoanalysis in Britain. *P&H* 1998, Vol. 1, pp. 87–102.

Hitschmann, E. 1913, *Freud's Theories of the Neuroses*. Trans. C. Payne. New York: JNMD Publishing Co.

Hobman, J. B., ed. 1945, *David Eder. Memoirs of a Modern Pioneer*. London: Victor Gollancz.

Hoch, [A.]. 1906, Review of three of Jung's studies on association. *JAP* 1906, Vol. 1, pp. 95–100.

Holland, H. 1852, *Chapters on Mental Physiology*. London: Longman, Brown, Green & Longmans.

Hollander, B. 1907, Unorthodox Methods of Investigation and Treatment of Disease. *HR* April 1907, pp. 38–40.

———. 1908, The Psycho-Therapeutics of Insanity. Can Insanity be treated by Suggestion? *HR* July 1908, pp. 83–84, August 1908, pp. 86–88.

———. 1910, *Hypnotism and Suggestion In Daily Life, Education, and Medical Practice*. London: Sir Isaac Pitman & Sons.

———. 1912, *The First Signs of Insanity, Their Prevention and Treatment*. London: Stanley Paul &Co.

———. 1920, *In Search of the Soul and the Mechanism of Thought, Emotion, and Conduct*. London: Kegan Paul, Trench, Trübner & Co.

———. 1932, Hypnosis and Anaesthetics. *PRSM* March 25, 1932, Vol. 5, pp. 597–610.

Horsley, V., 1909. The Linacre Lecture on the Function of the So-Called Motor Area of the Brain. *BMJ* July 17, 1909, pp. 121–32.

HR, 1907–1915, *The Health Record, Formerly the Psycho-Therapeutic Journal, Devoted to the Rational Consideration of Health Reform, Medical Hypnotism, Suggestive Therapeutics, Curative Human Radiations, Drugless Healing, And the treatment of Disease by Psychic and Mental Processes, with regard to Diet, Hygiene and the observance of Natural Laws of Health*, ed Arthur Hallam. London: PTS.

HS, *Hastings Standard*. Hawke's Bay: New Zealand.

HSLO, *Hastings and St Leonards Observer*. Hastings.

Hughes, A.1991, *The Inner World and Joan Riviere: Collected Papers 1920–1958*. London: Karnac Books.

HDM, *Hull Daily Mail*. Hull.

Humanitarian (1892–1901), *The Humanitarian: A Monthly Review of Sociological Science*, ed. Victorian Woodhull Martin & Zula Maud Woodhull. London & New York.

Hunt, K. 1996, *Equivocal Feminists: The Social Democratic Federation and the Woman Question 1884–1911*. Cambridge: Cambridge UP.

Hunter, R. A., & MacAlpine, I. 1953, Follow-Up Study of a Case treated in 1910 by 'The Freud Psycho-Analytic Method.' *BJMP* 1953, Vol 26, pp. 64–67.

Hutchinson, M., [nd], The Worcester Circle: An Anglo-Catholic attempt at Renewal in the1920s. Alphacrucis College. http://webjournals.ac.edu.au.

Hyslop, T. B. 1895, *Mental Physiology especially in its relation to Mental Disorders*. London: J. & A. Churchill.

———. 1899, On 'Double Consciousness.' *BMJ* September 23, 1899, pp. 782–86.

———. 1910, Faith and Mental Instability, in Rhodes 1910, pp. 101–13.

iapsop, *International Association for the Preservation of Spiritualist and Occult Periodicals*. www.iapsop.com/archive.

IJPA, (1920–), *International Journal of Psycho-Analysis.*

ICM. 1913, *17th International Congress of Medicine. Section XII, Psychiatry.* (Pt.1, pp. 13–71, Pt. 2, pp. 51–55). London: H. Frowde.

IMG, *Indian Medical Gazette; A Monthly Journal of Surgery, Public Health, and General Medical Intelligence Indian and European.* Calcutta: Thacker's Press.

Inglis, K. S. 1963, *Churches and the Working Classes in Victorian England.* Abingdon, Oxon: Routledge (2007).

Ion, R. M. & Beer, D. (2002) The British reaction to dementia praecox. *History of Psychiatry* 2002, Vol. 13, pp. 285–304; 419–31.

Irish (1892–1897), *The Irish Theosophist: A Monthly Magazine devoted to the Universal Brotherhood, the Study of Eastern Literature and Occult Sciences,* ed. D. N. Dunlop Dublin.

IZPA, (1913–), *International Zeitschrift für Psychoanalyse.* Leipzig / Wien: Hugo Heller.

JAAPA, *Journal of American Academy of Psychoanalysis.* New York.

Jackson, L. 2012, The Long Grove Psychiatrists of 1911, http://www.epsomandewell-historyexplorer.org.uk/LongGrovePsychiatrists.html.

James, H., ed. 1926, *The Letters of William James.* Boston: Little, Brown & Co.

James, W. 1890, *The Principles of Psychology.* New York: Henry Holt & Co. (1910).

———. 1902, *The Varieties of Religious Experience: A Study in Human Nature.* New York: Penguin Books (1985).

———. 1911, *Memories and Studies.* London: Longmans, Green.

Janet, P. 1894, État Mental des Hystériques: Les Accidents Mentaux. Paris: Rueff et Cie.

———. 1895, Review of H. C. Bastian; Various Forms of Hysterical, or Functional, Paralysis. *Brain* 1895, Vol. 18, pp. 585–97.

———. 1898, *Névroses et idées fixes, I: Etudes expérimentales sur les troubles de la volonté de l'attention, de la mémoire, sur les emotions, les idées obsédantes et leur traitement.* Paris: Félix Alcan.

———. 1901, *The Mental State of Hystericals: A study of Mental Stigmata and Mental Accidents*, trans. Caroline Corson. New York: G. P. Putnam.

———. 1903, *Les Obsessions et La Psychasthénie: Études Cliniques et Experimentales sur les Idées Obsédantes, Les Impulsions, Les Manies Mentales, La Folie du doute, Les Tics, Les Agitation, Les Phobies, Les Délires du Contact, Les Angoisses, Les Sentiments D'Incomplétude, La Neurasthénie, Les Modifications du Sentiment du Réel*, Vol. 1. Paris: Félix Alcan.

———. 1905a, The psycholeptic crises. *BMSJ*, 26 January. 1905, Vol. 162, pp. 93–100.

———. 1905b, Mental pathology. *PR* 1905, Vol. 12, pp. 98–117.

———. 1906a, The pathogenesis of some impulsions. *JAP* 1906, Vol. 1, pp. 1–17.

———. 1906b, The classical symptoms of hysteria. *BMSJ* 1906, Vol. 165 [15 lectures spread over issues 17–23], pp. 459ff.

———. 1907, *The Major Symptoms of Hysteria: Fifteen Lectures Given in the Medical School of Harvard University.* New York: The Macmillan Company.

———. 1913, Psycho-Analysis. Rapport par M. Le Dr. Pierre Janet. ICM 1913, pp. 13–64.

———. 1914, Psychoanalysis (Being a translation of Janet 1913 by Mrs W. G. Bean). *JAP* 1914, Vol. 9, pp. 1–35; 153–87.

Jastrow, J. 1906, *The Subconscious*. Boston: Houghton, Mifflin & Co.

Jelliffe, S. E. 1907, [Reviews of articles in Brain]. *JNMD* 1907, Vol. 34, pp. 213–16.

JHBS, *Journal of the History of the Behavioural Sciences*.

JMS, *Journal of Mental Science*. (see text).

JNMD, *The Journal of Nervous and Mental Diseases, Official Organ of the American Neurological Association, The New York Neurological Society, Boston Society of Psychiatry and Neurology, The Philadelphia Neurological Society and the Chicago Neurological Society*. ed. Smith Ely Jelliffe. New York: JNMD.

Johnson, G. M. 1990, *The Early Influence of Second Wave Psychology on British Prose Fiction* [Phd., McMaster University: Hamilton, Ontario].

Jones, A. E. 1901a, Calcification of the Pericardium, shown to the Pathological Society (21 May). *Transactions of the Pathological Society*. 1901, Vol. 52, pp. 181–93 & *BMJ* 25 May, p. 1269.

———. 1901b, A Case of Tumour Cerebri in which Rotation of the Tongue was present. *Lancet* 1901, Vol. 79(2), pp. 848–49.

———. 1906, The Onset of Hemiplegia in Vascular Lesions. *Brain* 1906, Vol. 28, pp. 527–55.

———. 1907a, La Vraie Aphasie Tactile. *RN* 1907, Vol. 15, pp. 3–7.

———. 1907b, Peripheral facial paralysis with instantaneous onset. Contribution to the Clinical Meeting of the Neurological Society of UK (21 March). *Brain* 1907, Vol. 30, p. 146.

———. 1907c, The Clinical significance of Allochiria [Amsterdam Paper (5 September).]. *Lancet* 1907, Vol. 85(2), pp. 830–32.

———. 1907d, A Simplified Technique for Accurate Cell Enumeration in Lumbar Puncture. *RNP* 1907, Vol. 5, pp. 539–50,

———. 1907e, Mechanism of Severe Briquet Attack as Contrasted with that of Psychasthenic Fits. *JAP* 1907, Vol. 2, pp. 218–27.

———. 1908a, The Precise Diagnostic Value of Allochiria. *Brain* Vol. 30, pp. 490–532 [reprinted: London: John Bale 1908].

———. 1908b, La Coté Affecté par L'Hemiplégie hystérique. *RN* 1908, Vol. 16, pp. 193–96.

———. 1908c, Case of Primary Spastic Paraplegia illustrating the nature of Schäfer's Reflex [contribution to the 12 March meeting of the RSM (Neurological Section)], in Nachbar 1907–1908, p. 59.

———. 1908d, The Clinical significance of Allochiria, in Wayenberg 1908, pp. 408–14.

———. 1908e, The Significance of Phrictopathic Sensation. *JNMD* 1908, Vol. 35, pp. 427–37.

———. 1909a, Psycho-analysis in Psychotherapy. *JAP* 1909, Vol. 4, pp. 140–50. (Jones 1913, pp. 182–92).

———. 1909b, The Pathology of Dyschiria. *RNP* 1909, Vol. 7, pp. 499–522 & pp. 559–87.

———. 1909c, The Dyschiric Syndrome. *JAP* 1909, Vol. 4, pp. 311–27.
———. 1910a, The Oedipus-Complex as an Explanation of Hamlet's Mystery: A Study in Motive. *AJP* (January 1910), Vol. 21, pp. 72–113.
———. 1910b, Freud's Theory of Dreams. *AJP* (April 1910), Vol. 21, pp. 283–308 (Jones 1913a, pp. 312–45).
———. 1910c, Freud's Psychology. *PB* 1910, Vol. 7, pp. 109–28.
———. 1910d, The Action of Suggestion in Psycho-Therapy. *JAP* 1910, Vol. 5, pp. 217–54 (Jones 1913a, pp. 241–82).
———. 1910e, The Practical Value of the Word Association Method in the Treatment of the Psycho-Neuroses, in Jones 1913a, pp. 206–40.
———. 1910f, A Modern Conception of the Psychoneuroses, in Jones 1913, pp. 122–33.
———. 1911a, Review of the Recent English and American literature on Clinical Psychology and Psychopathology. *Archives* 1911 [1909], Vol. 5, pp. 120–47.
———. 1911b, The Psychopathology of Everyday Life, in Jones 1913a, pp. 35–102.
———. 1913a, *Papers on Psycho-Analysis* (First edition). New York: William Wood.
———. 1913b, Internationaler Kongreß für Medizin. London, August 1913. *IZPA* 1913, pp. 592–97.
———. 1918, *Papers on Psycho-Analysis* (Second edition). London: Baillière, Tindall & Cox.
———. 1923, *Papers on Psycho-Analysis* (Third edition). London: Baillière, Tindall & Cox.
———. 1936a, Gedenkworte für M. D. Eder (1866–1936). *IZPA* 1936, Vol. 23, pp. 295–98.
———. 1936b, M. D. Eder 1866–1936, *IJPA* 1936, Vol. 17, pp. 143–46.
———. 1944a, 'Draft manuscript of Free Associations.' (Ernest Jones Collection, Archives of the BPAS, P04-A-F).
———. 1944b, Obituary: Owen Berkeley Hill 1874–1944. *IJPA* 1944, Vol. 25, p. 177.
———. 1945a, Letter from Ernest Jones to Anna Freud, April 28, 1945. (Ernest Jones Collection, Archives of the BPAS P04-C-C-06).
———. 1945b, Reminiscent Notes on the early History of Psycho-Analysis in English-Speaking Countries. *IJPA* 1945, Vol. 26, pp. 8–10.
———. 1954, The Early History of Psycho-Analysis [Paper read at the Association, July 31, 1953]. *JMS* 1954, Vol. 100, pp. 198–210.
———. 1955, *Sigmund Freud, Life and Work. Vol. 2, Years of Maturity 1901–1919*. London: The Hogarth Press.
———. 1959, *Free Associations; Memories of a Psycho-Analyst*. London: The Hogarth Press.
Jones, E., 2010 Shell Shock at Maghull and the Maudsley: Models of Psychological Medicine in the UK. *Journal of the History of Medicine and Allied Sciences*. 2010, Vol. 65, pp. 368–95.
———. 2014, 'An atmosphere of cure': Frederick Mott, shell shock and the Maudsley. *History of Psychiatry* 2014, Vol. 25, pp. 412–21.
Jones, M. 1987, *Chances: An Autobiography*. London: Verso.

Jones, R. 1897, The London County Council Asylum at Claybury and a Sketch of its first Working Year. *JMS* 1897, Vol. 43, pp. 47–58.

Journal (1884–), *Journal of the Society for Psychical Research*. London. SPR (Private Printing).

J. R. 1945, Obituary [Thomas Walker Mitchell 1869–1944]. *BJMP* 1946, Vol. 20, p. 204.

JRAI, *Journal of the Royal Anthropological Institute of Great Britain and Ireland*,.

Jung, C. G., *The Collected Works of C.G. Jung*. London: Routledge and Kegan [hereafter CW plus Volume].

———. 1902, A case of hysterical stupor in a prisoner in detention. CW Vol. 1, pp. 137–56.

———. 1905a, The reaction-time ratio in the association experiment. CW Vol. 2, pp. 221–71.

———. 1905b, The psychological diagnosis of evidence. CW Vol. 2, pp. 318–52.

———. 1906a, Psychoanalysis and association experiments. CW Vol. 2, pp. 288–317.

———. 1906b, *Diagnostische Assoziationsstudien: Beiträge zur Experimentellen Psychopathologie*, Vol. 1. Leipzig: Verlag Von Johann Ambrosius Barth.

———. 1907a, On Psychophysical Relations of the Associative Experiment. *JAP* (February 1907), Vol. 1, pp. 247–55.

———. 1907b, Über die Psychologie der Dementia praecox: Ein Versuch, Carl Marbold, Halle.

———. 1908a, 'Die Freud'sche Hysterietheorie' - Jung's 1907 Amsterdam Paper, in Wayenburg 1908, pp. 273–84.

———. 1908b, The Freudian theory of hysteria. CW Vol. 4, pp. 10–24.

———. 1909a, The Association Method. *AJP* (April 1910), Vol. 21, pp. 219–69 [CW Vol. 2, pp. 439–63.).

———. 1909b, *The Psychology of Dementia Praecox*, trans. Frederick Peterson & A. A. Brill. New York: JNMD Publishing Co.

———. 1910, The Association Method. *AJP* (April 1910), Vol. 21, pp. 119–269.

———. 1913a, On Psychoanalysis. Report by Dr. C. G. Jung. ICM 1913, pp. 65–71.

———. 1913b, General Aspects of Psycho-Analysis. [Paper read before the PMS, August 5, 1913] *Transactions* Vol. 4(2). Cockermouth 1913 [CW Vol. 4, pp. 229–42].

———. 1919, *Studies in Word Association: Experiments in the Diagnosis of Psychopathological conditions carried out at the Psychiatric Clinic of the University of Zurich*, trans. M. D. Eder. New York: Moffat, Yard & Co.

———. 1931, Problems of Modern Psychotherapy. CW (2014 ed.) Vol. 16, pp. 7339–58.

Jung, C. G. & Riklin, F. 1904, The associations of normal subjects. CW Vol. 2, pp. 3–196.

Keeley, J. P. 2001, Subliminal Promptings: Psychoanalytic Theory and the Society for Psychical Research. *American Imago* 2001, Vol. 58, pp. 767–91.

———. 2002, *'The Coping Stone on Psycho-Analysis': Freud, Psycho-Analysis and The Society for Psychical Research*. Columbia University phD.

Kelly, E. F., et al. 2007, *Irreducible Mind: Toward a Psychology for the 21st Century*. NewYork: Rowman & Littlefield Publishers, Inc.

Kelly, E. F. 2007, Toward a Psychology for the 21st Century, in Kelly, E. F. et al. 2007, pp. 577–643.

Kelly, E. F. & Grosso, M. 2007, Genius, in Kelly et al. 2007, pp. 423–93.

Kelly, E. W. 2007, F. W. H. Myers and the Empirical Study of the Mind-Body Problem, in Kelley et al. 2007, pp. 47–115.

Kerr J., & Wallis, E. W. (eds.), 1907. *Second International Congress on School Hygiene.* London: The Royal Sanitary Institute.

Kerr, J. A. 1994, *A Most Dangerous Method: The Story of Jung, Freud, & Sabina Spielrein*. London: Sinclair-Stevenson.

Kiell, N. 1988, *Freud Without Hindsight: Reviews of His Work (1893–1939).* Madison, CT: International UP.

Kim, H.-C. 1999, *Distinguished Asian Americans: A biographical dictionary.* Westport, Connecticut: Greenwood Press.

Kingsbury, G. C. 1891, *The Practice of Hypnotic Suggestion: Being an Elementary Handbook for the use of the Medical Profession.* Bristol: John Wright & Co.

Kline, M. V. 1953, Freud and Hypnosis: A Critical Evaluation. *British Journal of Medical Hypnotism.* 1953, Vol. 4, pp. 2–11.

———. 1955, Freud and Hypnosis II. Further Observations on Resistance and Acceptance, *Journal of Clinical and Experimental Hypnosis.* 1955, Vol. 3, pp. 124–29.

Knapp, P. C. 1907, Recent Progress in Neurology: Aphasia. *BMSJ.* 1907, Vol. 156, pp. 669–72.

Krafft-Ebing, R. von. 1893, *Psychopathia Sexualis, with special reference to Contrary Seuxal Instinct: A Medico-Legal Study*, trans Charles Gilbert Chaddock. Philadelphia: The F. A. Davis Co.

KSC, *Kent & Sussex Courier.* Tunbridge Wells, Kent.

Kuhn, P. 2000, A Scandal in Salzburg, Or Freud's Surreptitious role in the 1908 Abraham-Jung Dispute. *IJPA* 2000, Vol. 81, pp. 705–31.

———. 2002 "Romancing with a wealth of detail": Narratives of Ernest Jones's 1906 trial for indecent assault. *Studies in Gender and Sexuality* 2002, Vol. 3 pp. 344–79.

———. 2012, 'George Bedborough Traitor!' or The Bedborough Case revisited. (Unpublished).

———. 2014a, Footnotes in the History of British Psychoanalysis: Observing Ernest Jones discerning the works of Sigmund Freud, 1905–1908. *P&H* 2014, Vol. 16, pp. 5–54.

———. 2014b, Subterranean Histories: The dissemination of Freud's work into the British discourse on Psychological Medicine, 1904–1911. *P&H* 2014, Vol. 16, pp. 153–214.

———. 2015, In 'the dark regions of the mind': Readings for the Indecent Assault in Ernest Jones's 1908 dismissal from the West End Hospital for Nervous Diseases. *P&H* 2015, Vol. 17, pp. 7–57,

———. 2016, "Pleasurable, Laughable, Instructive," hypnotism and mesmerism in late 19th century Britain (Unpublished).

Kurella, H. 1911, *Cesare Lombroso: A Modern Man of Science.* Trans. M Eden Paul. London: Rebman Ltd.

Ladell, E. W. J. 1907, Hypnotism as a Therapeutic Agent. *BMJ*, 19 October 1907 p. 1106.

LAH, *Los Angeles Herald*. Los Angeles.

Lancet, *The Lancet. A Journal of British and Foreign Medicine, Surgery, Obstetrics, Physiology, Chemistry, Pharmacology, Public Health, and News*, ed. Thomas H. Wakley [then Samuel Squire Sprigge]. London.

Langdon-Brown, W. 1945, Obituary: T Wilson Parry, *BMJ* 13 October 1945, p. 515.

Laplanche, J. & Pontalis, J.-B. 1973, *The Language of Psycho-Analysis*, trans. Donald Nicholson-Smith. London: Karnac Books (1988).

LDN, *London Daily News*. London.

Lea, C. H. 1913, *A Plea for the Thorough and Unbiased Investigation of Christian Science: by an Enquirer*. London: J. M. Dent and Son.

Leeds Mercury, *Leeds Mercury*. Leeds.

LEP, *Lancashire Evening Post*. Lancashire.

LES, *London Evening Standard*, London.

Lewis, A. 1969, Edward Mapother and the Making of the Maudsley Hospital, *JMS* 1969, Vol. 115, pp. 1349–66.

Lewis, A. M. 1910, *Ten Blind Leaders of the Blind*. Chicago; Charles H. Kerr & Co.

LG, *London Gazette*. London.

LHSA, Lothian Health Services Archive, University of Edinburgh.

Liébeault, A. A. 1891, Hypnotism and Therapeutic Suggestion. *MA* 1891, pp. 273–77.

Light (1881–), *Light: A Journal of Psychical, Occult, and Mystical Research*, ed. W. Stainton-Moses ['M. A. (Oxon.)']. London: Eclectic Publishing Co.

LM, *Liverpool Mercury*. Liverpool.

Long, C. 1911, Psycho-Therapy [talk given to the Association of Registered Medical Women]. *BMJ* December 2, 1911, p. 1476.

———. 913, Introduction to the Study of Psycho-Analysis, in Tuckey 1913, pp. 353–77.

Long Grove. 1911, http://www.epsomandewellhistoryexplorer.org.uk/LongGrove-Psychiatrists.html.

Löwenfeld, L. 1894, *Pathologie Und Therapie der Neurasthenie und Hysterie*. Wiesbaden: J. F. Bergman.

———. 1904, *Die psychischen Zwangwserscheinungen: Auf klinischer Grundlage dargestellt*. Wiesbaden: J. F. Bergmann (Glasgow: F. Bauermeister).

LSC, *Leamington Spa Courier*. Leamington, Warwickshire.

LTA, *Luton Times and Advertiser*. Luton, Bedfordshire,.

MA (1882–), *The Medical Annual and Practitioner's Index, A Work of Reference for Practitioners*. Bristol: John Wright & Co.

Macdonald, A. 1892, The International Congress of Experimental Psychology (London, August 1892). *Science* 1892, Vol. 20, pp. 288–90.

Mackenzie, H. G. G. 1910a, Methods of the Psycho-Therapeutic Society, *BMJ* March 26, 1910, pp. 783–84.

———. 1910b, Medical Aspects of Mental Healing, in Rhodes ed. 1910, pp. 115–71.

Mackenzie, H. G. G. & Rhodes, G., [1921], *Health and the Mind*. London: Andrew Melrose Ltd.

Macmillan, M. 1997, *Freud Evaluated: The Completed Arc*. Cambridge, MA: The MIT Press.

Maddox, B. 2006, *Freud's Wizard: The Enigma of Ernest Jones*, John Murray, London.

Maehle, A.-H. 2014, The Powers of Suggestion: Albert Moll and the debate on hypnosis. *History of Psychiatry*. 2014, Vol. 25, pp. 3–19.

Makari, G. 2008, *Revolution in Mind. The Creation of Psychoanalysis*. New York; Harper Collins.

Mapother, E. 1925, [Review of Freud's Collected Papers Vol. 1]. *Eugenics Review* 1925, Vol. 17, pp. 181–83.

Martindale, P. 2003, '*The ceasing from the sorrow of divided life': May Sinclair's women, texts and contexts (1910–1923)*: Durham E-Theses, http://etheses.dur.ac.uk/3691/.

———. 2004, 'Against All Hushing Up and Stamping Down': The Medico-Psychological Clinic of London and the Novelist May Sinclair. *PH* 2004, Vol. 6, pp. 177–200.

Massicotte, C. 2014, Psychical Transmissions: Freud, Spiritualism, and the Occult. *Psychoanalytic Dialogues* 2014, Vol. 24, pp. 88–102.

Masson, J. M. 1984, (ed). *The Complete Letters of Sigmund Freud to Wilhelm Fliess,1887–1904,* Cambridge MA: Harvard U. P.

Maudsley, H. 1867, *The Physiology and Pathology of the Mind*. New York: D. Appleton & Co.

Mayer, A. 2006, Lost Objects: From the Laboratories of Hypnosis to the Psychoanalytic Setting. *Science in Context* 2006, Vol. 19, pp. 37–64.

———. 2013, *Sites of the Unconscious. Hypnosis and the Emergence of the Psychoanalytic Setting*. Chicago: University of Chicago Press.

McDonald, W. 1911, Progress of Psychiatry in 1910: America. *JMS* 1911, Vol. 57, pp. 517–20.

McDougall, W.,1903, Critical Notices [Review of Human Personality and Its Survival of Bodily Death]. *Mind* 1903, Vol. 12, pp. 513–26.

———. 1907a, [Review of Sidis & Goodhart's, Multiple Personality]. *Proceedings* 1907, Vol. 19, 345–53.

———. 1907b, The Case of Sally Beauchamp. *Proceedings* 1907, Vol. 19, pp. 410–31.

———. 1908, The State of the Brain during Hypnosis. *Brain* 1908, Vol. 31 pp. 242–58.

———. 1910, Instinct and Intelligence. *BJP* 1910, Vol. 3, pp. 250–66.

———. 1911, *Body and Mind: A History and a Defence of Animism*. New York: The Macmillan Company.

McGuire, W. 1974, *The Freud/Jung Letters: The Correspondence between Sigmund Freudand C. G. Jung,* trans. Ralph Manheim & R. F. C. Hull. London: Hogarth Press.

MCLGA, *Manchester Courier and Lancashire General Advertiser*. Manchester.

MD, *Medical Directory*. London: Lancet & BMA.

ME, *Mataura Ensign*. Otago: New Zealand.

Medical Act. 1858, *An act to regulate the Qualifications of Practitioners in Medicine and Surgery*. 21 & 22 Victoriae, Ch. 90.

Medical Record, *Medical Record, A Weekly Journal of Medicine and Surgery*, ed. Thomas L. Steadman. New York: William Wood & Co.

Medical Times (1873–), *The Medical Times*, [Official Organ of the Association of Physicians and Surgeons of the Society of Apothecaries], ed. George Brown. London.

Melland, C. H. 1908, Rôle of Suggestion in Treatment [paper given to the Clinical Society of Manchester, February 18, 1908]. *GP* March 7, 1908, p. 150.

Mercier, C. A. 1898, Suggestion and Crime. *BMJ* September 10, 1898, p. 678.

Meynell, G. G. 1981, Freud translated: an historical and bibliographical note. *JRSM* 1981, Vol. 74, pp. 306–9.

Micale, M. S. 1993, Henri F. Ellenberger and the origins of European psychiatric Historiography. In Mark Micale (ed.), *Beyond the Unconscious: Essays of Henri F. Ellenberger in the History of Psychiatry*, trans. Françoise Dubor & Mark S. Micale. Princeton: Princeton University Press.

Mickle, W. J. 1892, The Traumatic Factor in Mental Disease. *Brain* 1892, Vol. 15, pp. 76–102.

———. 1901, Mental wandering. *Brain* 1901, Vol. 24, pp. 1–26.

Middlemiss, J. E. 1904, [Review of] The Psychopathology of Every-Day Life. *RNP* 1904, Vol. 2, pp. 489–90.

———. 1912, "Answers," *BMJ* June 1, 1912, p. 1275.

———. 1914, Some cases of psychological interest from private practice. *JMS* 1914, Vol. 60, pp. 451–61.

———. 1942, Treatment by Hypnosis, *BMJ* November 14, 1942 pp. 558–59.

Miller, H. C. 1912, *Hypnotism and Disease: A Plea for Rational Therapy*. Boston: Richard G. Badger.

Mind, *Mind, A Quarterly Review of Psychology and Philosophy*, edited by G. F. Stout. London: Williams & Norgate.

Mitchell, T. W. 1907a, [Experiments on the Appreciation of Time by Somnambules], *Journal* June 1907, Vol. 13, pp. 83–87.

———. 1907b, Hypnotic and Post-Hypnotic Appreciation of Time [Abstract of 1908 SPR paper]*GP* August 3, 1907, pp. 483–86; August 10, 1907, pp. 508–9; August 17, 1907, pp. 516–19.

———. 1907c, A Curious Case of Deformity Treated by Hypnotic Suggestion. *GP* 14 September1907, p. 578.

———. 1907d, Hypnotic Suggestion as a Therapeutic Agent in General Practice. [Paper read before the BMA Seven oaks Branch]. *GP* November 30, 1907, pp. 754–57; December 7, 1907, pp. 771–74; December 14, 1907, pp. 786–89; December 28, 1907, pp. 819–20.

———. 1907e, The Appreciation of Time by Somnambules. *Proceedings* 1907, Vol. 21, pp. 2–59.

———. 1908, Hysteria and Hypnosis [paper read to the MSSST May 1, 1908]. *GP* May 9, 1908, pp. 290–94; May 16, 1908, pp. 306–10 [*ARR*. 1908, Vol. 13, pp. 57–58].

———. 1909a, Notes on Current Periodicals. *Journal* 1909, Vol. 14, p. 80.

———. 1909b, Review of Religion and Medicine by Worcester, M'Comb, & Coriat. *Journal* June 1909, Vol. 14, pp. 100–104.

———. 1909c, Modern Hypnotism. *The Quest*, October 1909, Vol. 1, pp. 44–60.
———. 1910a, 'A Study in Hysteria and Double Personality, with Report of a Case'. *Journal* 1910, Vol. 14, pp. 263–65.
———. 1910b, Notes on Current Periodicals. *Journal* 1909–1910, Vol. 14, pp. 353–56.
———. 1910c, Some Recent Developments in Psychotherapy. *Proceedings* 1910, Vol. 24, pp. 665–86.
———. 1911a, Notes on Current Periodicals. *Journal* 1912, Vol. 15, pp. 12–14.
———. 1911b, The Hypnoidal State of Sidis. [Presidential Address to the PMS, January 26, 1911 in *Transactions* 1911, Vol. 2(3)]. *Proceedings* June 1911, Vol. 25, pp. 338–52 (Sidis 1914, pp. 405–21).
———. 1911c, Dr. van Renterghem on the Family Physician. *Journal* 1912, Vol. 15, pp. 109–10.
———. 1912a, Some Types of Multiple Personality. *Proceedings* 1912, Vol. 26, pp. 257–85.
———. 1912b, A study in Hysteria and multiple personality with report of a case. *Proceedings* 1912, Vol. 26, pp. 286–311 [Mitchell 1922, pp. 69–102].
———. 1913, A discussion on the paper: The psycho-analysis of suggestion & hypnosis by S. Ferenczi. *Transactions* 1913, Vol. 4(1).
———. 1918, Psychology of the Unconscious and Psychoanalysis. *Proceedings* [Special Medical Part July 1918] 1920, Vol. 30, pp. 134–73.
———. 1919, Memorial on behalf of Dr. Lloyd Tuckey, signed by T. W. Mitchell et al. (PROT1/12460 C677293).
———. 1920, The Doris Fisher Case of Multiple Personality. *Proceedings* 1920, Vol. 31, pp. 30–74.
———. 1921, *The Psychology of Medicine*. London: Methuen & Co.
———. 1922, *Medical Psychology and Psychical Research*, Methuen & Co, London.
———. 1923, Presidential Address. *Proceedings* 1923, Vol. 33, pp. 1–22.
———. 1938, The Contributions of Psychical Research to Psychotherapeutics. *Proceedings* 1938–1939, Vol. 45, pp. 175–86.
Moll, A. 1902, *Christian Science, Medicine, and Occultism*, trans. F. J. Rebman. London: Rebman, Ltd.
———. 1912, *The Sexual Life of the Child*, trans. Eden Paul. New York: The Macmillan Company.
Morris, H. 1910, 'Suggestion' in the Treatment of Disease. *BMJ* June 18, 1910, pp. 1457–66.
Motherwell, *Motherwell Times*. Motherwell, Lanarkshire.
Mott, F. W. 1907, Preface, *Archives* 1907, Vol. 3.
———. 1908, Two Lectures on the Physiology of the Emotions. *BMJ* April 11, 1908 pp. 853–58.
———. 1911, The Relation of Head Injury to Nervous and Mental Disease. *BMJ* September 30, 1911, pp. 733–44.
———. 1918, Obituary: William Julius Mickle. *BMJ* January 19, 1918, pp. 102–3.
Moulton, T. G. 1906, *An Exposure of Christian Science*. London: James Nisbet & Co. Ltd.
MPC (1838–), *Medical Press & Circular. A Weekly Journal*. London.
MS (1862–), *Musical Standard*. London.

MT, *Manchester Times*. Manchester.

MTHG (1873–), *Medical Times & Hospital Gazette: A Weekly Review of Medicine and Surgery and Chronicles of Hospital and College News,* ed. George Brown [& Bedford Fenwick]. London.

Münsterberg, H., et al. 1910, *Subconscious Phenomena*. Boston: Richard G. Badger.

Murchison, C., ed. 1930, *A History of Psychology in Autobiography*. Vol. 1. Worcester, MA: Clark UP.

Murphy, J. K. 1912, *The Practitioner's Encyclopedia of Medicine and Surgery in All their Branches*. London: Henry Frowde, Hodder & Stoughton.

Muthmann, A. 1907, *Zur Psychologie und Therapie Neurotischer Symptome: Eine Studieauf Grund der Neurosenlehre Freuds*. Halle: Carl Marhold.

Muthu, C. 1913, A Short Review of the History of Ancient Hindu Medicine. *PRSM* (History of Medicine Section). 1913, Vol. 6, pp. 177–90.

Myers, C. S. 1909, *A Text-Book of Experimental Psychology*. New York: Longmans Green.

Myers, F. W. H. 1886a, On Telepathic Hypnotism, and its Relation to Other Forms of Hypnotic Suggestion. *Proceedings* July 1886, Vol. 4, pp. 127–88.

———. 1886b, Introduction, in Gurney, Myers, Podmore et al. 1886, Vol. 1, pp. xxxv–lxxi.

———. 1888a, The Work of Edmund Gurney in Experimental Psychology. *Proceedings* 1888, Vol. 5 (Supplement), pp. 359–73.

———. 1890a, Binet on the Consciousness of Hysterical Subjects. *Proceedings* July 1889, Vol. 6 (Supplement), pp. 200–206.

———. 1893a, Professor Wundt on Hypnotism and Suggestion. *Mind* January 1893, Vol. 2, pp. 95–101.

———. 1893b, The Subliminal Consciousness. *Proceedings* 1893–1894, Vol. 9, pp. 3–25, 26–128.

———. 1894, The Drift of Psychical Research. *The National Review* October 1894, Vol. 24, pp. 190–209.

———. 1897, Hysteria and Genius. *Journal* 1897–1898, Vol. 8, pp. 51–59; 69–70.

———. 1898, The Psychology of Hypnotism [Paper delivered to the BMA Annual Meeting July]. *BMJ* September 10, 1898, pp. 674–77; *Proceedings* 1899, Vol. 14, pp. 100–108.

———. 1901a, Pseudo-Possession [Reviews of Janet and Flournoy]. *Proceedings* 1901, Vol. 15, pp. 384–415.

———. 1901b, On the Trance Phenomena of Mrs Thompson. *Proceedings* 1903, Vol. 17, pp. 67–74.

———. 1903, *Human Personality and its Survival of Bodily Death*. London: Longman, Green & Co.

Nachbar J., (ed.), 1907–1908, *PRSM* (Neurological Section) 1, pt 2. London: Longmans.

Nandy, A. 1995, *The Savage Freud and Other Essays on Possible and Retrievable Selves*. Princeton: Princeton UP.

Negrine, A. 2008, *Medicine and Poverty: A Study of the Poor Law Medical Services of the Leicester Union, 1867–1914*. Phd Thesis Centre for English Local History. University of Leicester.

NEM, *Nelson Evening Mail*. Nelson: New Zealand.

NEP, *Nottingham Evening Post*. Nottingham.

New Age, (1907–1922), *The New Age*, ed. A. R. Orage. London: New Age Press.

Newton, A. [nd], *The Electric Wizard – The Amazing Story of Dr. Walford Bodie*. http://www.newtonhypnosis.com/electric-wizard-amazing-story-dr-walford-bodie/.

Noakes, R. 2004, The 'Bridge which is between Physical and Psychical Research': William Fletcher Barrett, Sensitive Flames, and Spiritualism. *History of Science* 2004, Vol. 42, pp. 419–64.

Nölleke, B. 2016, *Psychoanalytikerinnen. Biografisches Lexikon. Women Psychoanalysts in Great Britain*. http://www.psychoanalytikerinnen.de/greatbritain_biographies.html.

Northridge, W. L. 1924, *Modern Theories of the Unconscious*. London: Kegan Paul, Trench, Trübner & Co. Ltd.

NR, *The Nursing Record and Hospital World,* ed. Mrs Bedford Fenwick. London.

Nunberg, H. & Federn, E. 1962, *Minutes of the Vienna Psychoanalytic Society*. Vol. 1, New York: International Universities Press.

NZH, *New Zealand Herald*. Auckland: New Zealand.

Observer, *The Observer*. Adelaide: Southern Australia.

OM, *The Occult Magazine. A Monthly Journal of Psychical and Philosophical Research*. Glasgow.

Oppenheim, J. 1985, *The other world: Spiritualism and psychical research in England, 1850–1914*. Cambridge: Cambridge UP.

Ormerod, J. A. 1911a, Two Theories of Hysteria [Presidential Address to the RSM (Neurological Section), November 1910]. *PRSM* 1911, Vol. 4 (Neurol Sect) pp. 1–18.

———. 1911b, Hysteria, in Allbut & Rolleston. 1911, Vol. 8, pp. 687–726.

———. 1911c, Two theories of hysteria. *Brain* 1911, Vol. 33, pp. 269–87.

———. 1914, The Lumleian Lectures on Some Modern Theories Concerning Hysteria (Lecture 3). *Lancet* May 9, 1914, pp. 1299–305.

OW, *Otago Witness*. Otago: New Zealand.

Owen, A. 2004, *The Place of Enchantment: British Occultism and the Culture of the Modern*. Chicago: University of Chicago Press.

Paget, S. 1909, *The Faith and Works of Christian Science*. New York: The Macmillan Company.

Pall Mall (1865–), *Pall Mall Gazette*. London.

Parker, G. M. 1902, Mental dissociation in functional motor disturbance, in Sidis 1902, pp. 255–319.

Parry, T. W. 1905, Ménière's Complex of Symptoms: With a criticism on Quincke's lumbar puncture treatment and an account of the first recorded case treated successfully by hypnotic suggestion. *MPC* 3 & May 10, 1905, pp. 445–48 & 476–78.

———. 1907a, Inveterate Cases of Ménière's Complex of Symptoms by Hypnotic Suggestion, with Remarks on the Necessity of Including Hypnotism among our Scientific Remedial Agents. *MPC* 1907, Vol. 134, pp. 336–37.

———. 1907b, On the Differential Diagnosis between Ménière's Disease and other cases exhibiting Ménière's Complex of Symptoms: With remarks on the practical value of the seton in obstinate cases of both conditions, together with case illustrating the excellent results obtained by seton in the latter condition. *BMJ* May 11, 1907, pp. 1107–10.

Paskauskas, R. A. 1985, *Ernest Jones: A critical study of his scientific development 1896–1913*. Unpublished doctoral dissertation, Toronto Institute for the History and Philosophy of Science and Technology.

———. 1988, The Jones-Freud Era, 1908–1939, in Timms & Segal 1988, pp. 109–23.

———. 1993. ed, *The Complete Correspondence of Sigmund Freud and Ernest Jones 1908–1939*. Cambridge: Belknap Press,.

Paton, S. 1905, *Psychiatry, A Text-Book for Students and Physicians*. Philadelphia: J. B. Lippincott Co.

Payne, S. 1946, An Address on the Occasion of Presenting his Portrait to Ernest Jones. *IJPA* 1946, Vol. 27, p. 6.

PB (1904–), *Psychological Bulletin*. ed. by J. Mark Baldwin, Howard C. Warren and Charles H. Judd.

PBH, *Poverty Bay Herald*. Gisborne: New Zealand.

Pear, T. H. 1914a, The Analysis of Some Personal Dreams, with Reference to Freud's Theory of Dream Interpretation. *BJP* 1914, Vol. 6, pp. 281–303.

———. 1914b, The Rôle of Repression in Forgetting. *BJP* 1914, Vol. 7, pp. 139–46.

———. 1921, Critical Notice [Review of W. H. Rivers Instinct and Unconscious]. *BJP* 1921, Vol. 11, pp. 349–57.

———. 1941, Psychoanalysis and Normal Psychology. [*Bulletin of the John Rylands Library* Reprint. 1941, Vol. 26]. Manchester: Manchester UP.

———. 1960, Some Early Relations Between English Ethnologists and Psychologists. *JRAI* 1960, Vol. 90 (July–Dec. 1960), pp. 227–37.

———. 1962, Personalities in the early days of the British Psychological Society. *BJP* 1962, Vol. 53, pp. 223–28.

Peterson, F. W. 1907a, The Galvanometer as a Measurer of Emotions [Paper read at BMA Annual Meeting]. *Lancet* August 17, 1907, p. 449.

———. 1907b, The Galvanometer as a Measurer of Emotions. *BMJ* September 28, 1907, pp. 804–6.

Peterson F. W. & Jung C. G. 1907, Psychophysical Investigations with the Galvanometer and Pneumograph in Normal and Insane Individuals [*Brain* July 1907 Vol. 30, pp. 153–218], CW. 2, pp. 492–553.

P&H, *Psychoanalysis and History*. Edinburgh: Edinburgh UP.

Pierce, B. 1910, Diagnosis in States of Depression [Read before the LWR Society]. *BMJ* June 4, 1910, pp. 1333–38.

———. 1912a, On Psycho-analysis [Read before the LWR Society]. *BMJ*, 30 November, p. 1551.

———. 1912b, Psycho-Analysis. *MA* 1912, pp. 457–63.

———. 1914, Psycho-Analysis. *MA* 1914, pp. 466–67.

Pierce, B. & Kemp, N. 1910, Mental Diseases. *MA* 1910, pp. 438–55.

———. 1911, Psycho-Neuroses. *MA* 1911, pp. 533–36.

Pierri, M. 2010, Coincidence in Analysis: Sigmund Freud and the Strange Case of Dr Forsyth and Herr von Vorsicht. *IJPA* 2010, Vol. 91, pp. 745–72.

Podmore, F. 1910, *Mesmerism and Christian Science. A Short History of Mental Healing*. Philadelphia: George W. Jacobs & Co.

———. 1911, *The Newer Spiritualism.* New York: Henry Holt & Co.
PR, *Psychological Review*, ed. by J. Mark Baldwin, Howard C. Warren and Charles H. Judd. New York: Macmillan Company.
Practitioner, *The Practitioner: A Journal of Practical Medicine*, ed. Malcolm Morris, [then W. Cecil Bosanquet]. London: Cassell & Co.
PRSM, *Proceedings of the Royal Society of Medicine.* London: Longmans, Green & Co.
Prince, M. 1906a, *The Dissociation of a Personality: A Biographical Study in Abnormal Psychology.* New York: Longmans, Green & Co.
———. 1906b, Hysteria from the point of view of dissociated personality. *JAP* 1906 Vol. 1, pp. 170–87.
———. 1908a, *The Dissociation of a Personality: A Biographical Study in Abnormal Psychology* (2nd edition). New York: Longmans, Green & Co.
———. 1908b, Critical reviews: motor aphasia and its cortical localization. *JAP* 1908 Vol. 2, pp. 227–35.
———. 1908–1909, The Unconscious. *JAP* 1909, Vols. 3–4, pp. 261–97, 36–56.
Prince, M., & Peterson, F. 1908, Experiments in Psycho-Galvanic Reaction from Co-Conscious (sub-conscious) Ideas in a Case of Multiple Personality. *JAP* 1908, Vol. 3, pp. 114–31.
PRO, Public Records Office, Kew.
Proceedings 1883–, *Proceedings of the Society for Psychical Research.* London: Trübner &Co.
PTJ, 1901–1906, *The Psycho-Therapeutic Journal: A Journal of the Proceedings of the[London] Psycho-Therapeutic Society.* London: Arthur Hallam.
Puller, F. W. 1904, *The Anointing of the Sick in Scripture and Tradition, with some considerations on the Numbering of the Sacraments.* London: SPCK.
Putnam, J. J. 1906, Recent experiences in the study and treatment of hysteria at the Massachusetts General Hospital: with remarks on Freud's method of treatment by 'psycho-analysis.' *JAP* 1906, Vol. 1, pp. 26–41.
Putnam, J. J. & Waterman, G. A. 1905, Certain aspects of the differential diagnosis between epilepsy and hysteria. *BMSJ* 1905, Vol. 152, pp. 509–16.
Quest, *The Quest: A Quarterly Review*, ed. G. R. S. Mead. London: J M Watkins.
Rachford, B. K. 1905, *Neurotic Disorders of Childhood.* New York: E. B. Treat & Co.
Raitt, S. 2004, Early British Psychoanalysis and the Medico-Psychological Clinic. *History Workshop Journal.* 2004, Vol. 58, pp. 63–85.
Randi, J. [nd], 'James Randi Debunks Peter Popoff Faith Healer'. https://www.youtube.com/watch?v=q7BQKu0YP8Y.
Rankin, G. 1903, Neurasthenia: The Wear and Tear of Life. *BMJ* May 2, 1903, pp. 1017–20.
———. 1909, A Clinical Lecture on the Neurotic Element in Disease. *BMJ* June 5, 1909, pp. 1337–34.
Ranschburg, P. & Hajós, L. 1897, *Neue Beiträge zur Psychologie des hysterischen Geisteszustandes. Kritisch-experimentelle Studien.* Leipzig: Deuticke.
Rapp, D. 1990, The Early Discovery of Freud by the British General Educated Public. *Social History of Medicine* 1990, Vol. 3, pp. 217–43.
Read, C. 1911, The function of relations in thought. *BJP* 1912, Vol. 4, pp. 342–85.

Renterghem, A. W. van. 1910, The Rehabilitation of the Family Physician [Paper read before the PMS, January 28, 1910 [Reprinted from *ARR,* March–May 1910]. *Transactions* 1910, Vol. 2(1).

Rhodes, G. 1910a, Health Values. *BMJ* June 4, 1910, pp. 1497–98.

———. 1910b, ed., *Medicine and the Church: Being a series of studies on the relationship between the practice of medicine and the church's ministry to the sick.* London: Kegan Paul, Trench, Trübner & Co.

Richards, G. 2001, Edward Cox, the Psychological Society of Great Britain (1875–1879) and the meanings of an institutional failure, in Bunn et al. 2001, pp. 33–53.

Richardson, S. 2014, Transforming the Body Politic: Food Reform and Feminism in Nineteenth-Century Britain, in Scott et. al. 2014, pp. 45–58.

Rickman, J. 1928, *Index Psychoanalyticus 1893–1926*. London: The Hogarth Press.

Rivers, W. H. R. 1920, *Instinct and the Unconscious*, Cambridge: Cambridge UP.

RN (1893–), *Revue Neurologique*, ed. Edouard Brissaud and Pierre Marie. Paris.

RNP (1903–), *Review of Neurology and Psychiatry*, ed. Alexander Bruce (Edwin Bramwell). Edinburgh: Otto Schultze & Co.

Roazen, P. 1992, *Freud and His Followers*. New York: Da Capo Press.

———. 2006, The Creation and Social transmission of Psychoanalytic Knowledge: Commentary on Richards. *Journal of the American Psychoanalytic Association.* 2006, Vol. 54, pp. 389–95.

Roberts, E. 1910, The Church and Mental Healing, in ed. Rhodes 1910, pp. 227–41.

Robertson, D., 2000–2005, Special Report: The Medical & Scientific Status of Hypnotherapy. www.rebhp.org/articles/Special.pdf.

Robertson, D. J. 2013, *The Discovery of Hypnosis. The Complete Writings of James Braid, The Father of Hypnotherapy* (2nd revised edition). No designation: Lulu.

Robertson, G. M. 1892a, Psycho-Therapeutics: Another Fragment. *Lancet* September 17, 1892, pp. 657–58.

———. 1892b, Hypnotism at Paris and Nancy. Notes of a Visit. *JMS* 1892, Vol. 38, pp. 494–531.

———. 1893, The Use of Hypnotism among the Insane. *JMS* 1893, Vol. 39, pp. 1–12.

Robertson, J. 1908, *Spiritualism: The Open Door to the Unseen Universe. Being Thirty Years Personal Observation and Experience concerning Intercourse between the Material and Spiritual Worlds.* London: L N Fowler & Co.

Robinson, J. 2014, *Divine Healing: The Years of Expansion, 1906–1930: Theological Variations in the Transatlantic World.* Eugene, Oregon: Pickwick publications;.

Robinson K. 2012, A Brief History of the British Psychoanalytical Society. www.psychoanalysis.org.uk.

Robinson, S. C. 2010, Victoria Woodhull-Martin and the Humanitarian (1892–1901): Feminism and Eugenics at the Fin de Siècle. *Nineteenth Century Gender Studies* 2010, Vol. 6, http://www.ncgsjournal.com/issue62/issue62.htm.

Rolleston, H. 1928, Obituary: [Dawson Williams]. *BMJ* March 10, 1928, p. 417.

Root, S. 2005, *The Healing Touch: Spiritual Healing in England, c. 1870–1955*. PhD thesis: University of Warwick.

Rush, B. 1789, Duties of a Physician: Closing Lecture to Medical Students. In *The Selected Writings of Benjamin Rush*, ed. Dagobert D. Runes. New York: Philosophical Library (1947), pp. 308–21.

Ryan, M. B. 2010, The Resurrection of Frederick Myers. *The Journal of Transpersonal Psychology* 2010, Vol. 42, pp. 149–70.

Ryle, H. E. 1914, *Spiritual Healing: Report of a Clerical and Medical Committee of Inquiry into Spiritual, Faith and Mental Healing*. London: Macmillan & Co.

Sage, M. 1904, *Mrs. Piper & the Society for Psychical Research*, trans. Noralie Robertson. New York: Scott-Thaw Co.

Savi, J. nd., 'Abdu'l-Bahá in Egypt Early September 1910 – 5 December 1913. http://irfancolloquia.org/, pp. 321–65.

Savill, A. 1916, Psychoanalysis. *MPC* May 17, 1916, pp. 446–48.

Schaffer, K. 1895, *Suggestion Und Reflex: Eine, Kritisch-experimentelle Studie über Die Reflexhaenomene des Hypnotismus* [Suggestion And Reflex: A Critical And Experimental Study of The Reflex Phenomena of Hypnotism]. Jena: Gustav Fischer.

Schmideberg, M. 1971, A Contribution to the History of the Psycho-Analytic Movement in Britain. *British Journal of Psychiatry* 1971, Vol. 118, pp. 61–68.

Schofield, A. T. 1894, On Mental Therapeutics. *Lancet*, February 3, 1894, pp. 262–63.

———. 1896, Mental Therapeutics [An Address delivered before the Harveian Society]. *Lancet* August 29, 1896, pp. 585–89.

———. 1904, *Unconscious Therapeutics, or, the Personality of the Physician*. London: J. & A. Churchill.

School Hygiene (1910–), *School Hygiene: A Monthly Review for Educationalists and Doctors*, eds. M. D. Eder & R. C. Elmslie. Letchworth (Herts): Garden City Press.

Schröter, M. 1996, The Beginnings of a Troubled Friendship: Freud and Ferenczi 1908–1914. *International Forum of Psychoanalysis* 1996, Vol. 5, pp. 133–50.

Schwartz, J. 1999, *Casandra's Daughter: A History of Psychoanalysis*. London: Penguin Books.

SCKA, *Sevenoaks Chronicle & Kentish Advertiser*. Sevenoaks.

Scott, F., Scarth, K., Chung, J. W., (eds) 2014, *Picturing Women's Health*. Pickering & Chatto.

Scott, W. D. 1909, An Interpretation of the Psycho-Analytic Method in Psychotherapy with a Report of a Case so Treated. *JAP* 1908–1909, Vol. 3, pp. 371–77.

SDESG, Sunderland Daily Echo and Shipping Gazette. Sunderland.

Selby, J. 2008, *Dion Fortune and her Inner Plane Contacts: Intermediaries in the Western Esoteric Tradition*. Vol. 1. Exeter: Unpublished Phd.

SET, *Sheffield Evening Telegraph*. Sheffield.

Severn, E. 1913, *Psycho-Therapy: It doctrine and Practice*. London: William Rider & Son (1914 reprint).

SFC, *San Francisco Call*. San Francisco.

Shamdasani, S. 2003, *Jung and the Making of Modern Psychology: The Dream of a Science*. Cambridge: Cambridge UP.

———. 2005, 'Psychotherapy': the invention of a word. *HHS* 2005, Vol. 18, pp. 1–18.

Shaw, J. 1902, Insanity. *MA* 1902, pp. 351–61.

Shaw, T. C. 1907a, Progress in the Treatment of Mental Disease [President's Introductory Remarks BMA Annual Meeting]. *BMJ* September 28, 1907, pp. 795–97.

———. 1907b, A Contribution to the Analysis of the Mental Process in Criminal Acts [Paper delivered at the 1907 Amsterdam Congress]. *Lancet* November 9, 1907, pp. 1306–9.

———. 1909, The Influence of Mind as a Therapeutic Agent. *Lancet* November 6, 1909, pp. 1369–73; *BMJ* November 6, 1909, pp. 1352–56.

———. 1911, An Address on the Clinical Aspects of Emotion and Action [to the North-London Medico-Chirurgical Society]. *The Lancet* February 11, 1911, pp. 353–57.

Shepherd, M. 1986, Psychological medicine *redivivus*: concept and communication. *JRSM* 1986, Vol. 79, pp. 639–45.

Shettle, R. C. 1890, *Hypnotism, Its Nature & Its Cause* [Address Delivered at the Annual Meeting of the Reading Pathological Society]. Reading: Reading Pathological Society.

Sidis, B. 1898, *The Psychology of Suggestion: A Research into the Subconscious Nature of Man and Society*, New York: D. Appleton & Co.

———. 1902, *Psychopathological Researches: Studies in Mental Dissociation*. London: G. E. Stechert.

———. 1906, Review of Freud's Psychopathology of Everyday Life. *JAP* 1906, Vol. 1, pp. 101–3.

———. 1912, The Theory of the Subconscious. *Proceedings* 1912, Vol. 26, pp. 319–43.

Sidis, B., & Goodhart, S. P. 1905, *Multiple Personality: An Experimental Investigation in the Nature of Human Individuality*. New York: D. Appleton & Co.

Sidis, B., & Prince, M. 1904, A Contribution to the Pathology of Hysteria based upon an Experimental Study of a Case of Hemianesthesia with Clonic Convulsive Attacks Simulating Jacksonian Epilepsy. *BMSJ* 1904, Vol. 60, pp. 674–78.

Simkin, J. 2013, Margaret MacMillan, *Spartacus Educational*. http://www.spartacus.school.co.uk (consl. February 21, 2014).

Sinnett, A. P. 1892, *The Rationale of Mesmerism*. Boston: Houghton, Mifflin & Co.

SMH, *The Sydney Morning Herald*. Sydney.

Smith, R. 1992, *Inhibition, History and Meaning in the Sciences of Mind and Brain*. Berkeley: University of California Press.

Smith, R. P. & Myers, A. T. 1890, On the Treatment of Insanity by Hypnotism. *JMS* 1890, Vol. 36, pp. 191–213.

Sommer A. 2013a, Normalizing the Supernormal: The formation of the 'Gesellschaft für Psychologische Forschunung.' ('Society for Psychological Research') c.1886–1890. *JHBS* Vol. 49, pp. 18–44.

———. 2013b, *Crossing the Boundaries of Mind and Body: Psychical Research and the Origins of Modern Psychology*. Unpublished PhD. London UCL.

Southland, *Southland Times*. Otago: New Zealand.

Spearman, C. 1904a, The Proof and Measurement of Association between Two Things. *AJP* 1904, Vol. 15, pp. 72–101.

———. 1904b, 'General Intelligence', Objectively Determined and Measured. *AJP* 1904, Vol. 15, pp. 201–92.

———. 1905, Analysis of 'Localisation', illustrated by a Brown-Séquard Case. *BJP* 1905, Vol. 1, pp. 286–314.

———. 1913a, London Medico-Psychological Clinic. *BMJ* December 13, 1913, p. 1564.

———. 1913b, The Medico-Psychological Clinic. *Lancet* December 20, 1913, p. 1803.

———. 1929, Psychiatric Use of the Methods and Results of Experimental Psychology [The Maudsley Lecture]. *Lancet* June 1, 1929.

———. 1930, 'C. Spearman,' in Murchison 1930, pp. 299–333.

Spiller, W. G. 1907, Psychasthenic attacks simulating epilepsy. *JAP* 1907, Vol. 1, pp. 256–68.

Spiritual Healing. 1914, *Spiritual Healing: Report of a Clerical and Medical Committee of Inquiry into Spiritual, Faith, and Mental Healing*. London: Macmillan & Co.

SR (1908–), *Sociological Review*, ed. L. T. Hobhouse. Manchester: MUP.

SSI (1903–), *British Journal of Inebriety* published under the direction of the Society for the Study of Inebriety, ed. T. N. Kelynack. London: Baillière, Tindall & Cox.

ST, *The Straits Times*. Singapore.

Stannard, J. 1900a, The Theory of a Universal Fluid: Its Relation to Magnetic Healing. *Light* June 30, 1900, pp. 307–10.

———. 1900b, The Psychological Congress in Paris. *Light* September 8, 1900, pp. 431–33.

———. 1900c, The Spiritualistic Congress in Paris. *Light* September 15, 1900, pp. 443–44.

———. 1900d, The International Congress of Spiritualists in Paris. *Light* 13, 20, 27 October; 3, November 10, 1900, pp. 486–88, 503–5, 510–11, 527–29, 540–42.

Stanton, M., *Sándor Ferenczi: Reconsidering Active Intervention*. New Jersey: Jason Aronson Inc.

Steiner, R. 1987, A World Wide International Trade Mark of Genuineness? Some Observations on the History of the English Translation of the Work of Sigmund Freud, Focusing Mainly on his Technical Terms. *IJPA* 1987, Vol. 4, pp. 33–102.

Stern W. 1910, Abstracts of Lectures on the Psychology of Testimony and on the Study of Individuality. *AJP* 1910, Vol. 21, pp. 270–82.

Stewart, P. 1909, Hysteria. *MA* 1909, pp. 376–79.

Stoddart, W. H. B. 1908, *Mind and Its Disorders: A Text-Book for Students and Practitioners*. London: HK Lewis.

———. 1912, *Mind and Its Disorders: A Text-Book for Students and Practitioners* (2nd edition). London: HK Lewis.

———. 1914, Case of (?) anxiety hysteria. *PRSM* (Psychiatric Section) 1914, Vol. 7, pp. 16–17.

———. 1933, T. B. Hyslop M. D. *BMJ* February 25, 1933, p. 347.

Strachey, J. 1955, Editor's Introduction [to Studies on Hysteria]. SE 2, pp. ix–xxviii.

———. 1963, Joan Riviere. *IJPA* 1963, Vol. 44, pp. 228–35.

———. 1966, Editor's Introduction [to Papers on Hypnotism and Suggestion] *SE* 1, pp. 61–69.

Sumner, A. 1915, Appendix – Dramatis Personae, in *Ordo R-R et AC – Arthur Edward Waite*. pp. 44–46. The Esoteric Library, www.sacred-magic.com.

Sydney, *The Sydney Stock and Station Journal*. New South Wales: Australia.

Taplin, A. B. 1907, Notes of a Few Cases Treated by Hypnotic Suggestion. *GP* August 31, 1907, pp. 546–48; September 7, 1907, pp. 562–66.

Taylor, J. H. 1911, The Practice of Medicine and Surgery by Unqualified Persons. *BMJ* May 27, 1911, pp. 1243–46.

Thomas, J. J. 1908, Review of M. Friedman's 'Brief Narcoleptic Attacks not due to Epilepsy'. *JAP* 1908, Vol. 2, pp. 131–34.

Thompson, E. R. 1914, An Inquiry into some questions connected with imagery in Dreams. *BJP* 1914, Vol. 7, pp. 300–18.

Thomson, H. C. 1903, The Treatment of Epilepsy by Psychical Methods. *Lancet* April 18, 1903, pp. 1092–95.

———. 1910, Mental therapeutics, with special reference to Freud's and other methods of treatment. *BMJ* November 19, 1910, pp. 1628–30.

Thomson, M. 2001, The popular, the practical and professional: psychological identities in Britain 1901–1950, in Bunn *et al.* 2001, pp. 115–32.

———. 2011, 'The Solution to his Own Enigma': Connecting the Life of Montague David Eder (1865–1936), Socialist, Psychoanalyst, Zionist, Modern Saint, *Medical History* 2011, Vol. 55, pp. 61–84.

Timms, E., & Segal, N., eds. 1988, *Freud in Exile: Psychoanalysis and its Vicissitudes*. New Haven: Yale UP.

Timms, J. 2012, Phantasm or Freud: Nandor Fodor and the Psychoanalytic Approach to the Supernatural in Interwar Britain. *P&H* 2012, Vol. 14, pp. 5–27.

Transactions, *Transactions of the Psycho-Medical Society*. Cockermouth: Brash Bros.

Trevelyan, G. M. 1913, *Clio, A Muse and other Essays Literary and Pedestrian*. London: Longmans Green & Co.

Trotter, W. 1908, Herd Instinct and its Bearing on the Psychology of Civilized Man, *SR* July 1908, Vol. 1, pp. 227–48.

———. 1909, Sociological Applications of the Psychology of Herd Instinct. *SR* 1909 Vol. 2, pp. 36–54.

———. 1916, *Instincts of the Herd in Peace and War*. London: Fisher Unwin Ltd.

Tuckett, I. L. 1911, *The Evidence for the Supernatural: A Critical Study made with 'Uncommon Sense.'* London: Kegan Paul, Trench, Trübner & Co. Ltd.

Tuckey, C. L. 1888, Faith-Healing as a Medical Treatment. *Nineteenth Century* 1888, Vol. 24, pp. 839–50.

———. 1889a, *Psycho-Therapeutics, or Treatment by Sleep and Suggestion*. London: Baillière, Tindall & Cox.

———. 1891a, *Psycho-Therapeutics; or Treatment by Hypnotism and Suggestion*. London, Baillière, Tindall & Cox (3rd edition).

———. 1891b, Note on [Hypnotism and Therapeutic Suggestion by A. A. Liébeault]. *MA* 1891, pp. 277–79.

———. 1898, Hypnotism and Suggestion. *MA* 1898, pp. 77–85.

———. 1900, *Treatment by Hypnotism and Suggestion: Or, Psycho-Therapeutics* (4th edition). London: Baillière, Tindall & Cox.

———. 1903a, Some Notes on Hypnotic Suggestion. *GP* June 6, 1904, pp. 350–51; June 13, 1904, pp. 367–68; June 20, 1907, pp. 382–84.

———. 1903b, Notes on Some Cases of Obsession. *GP* September 26, 1903, pp. 607–8.

———. 1903c, Notes on Sexual Perversion. *GP* November 7, 1903, pp. 703–4.
———. 1907a, The Utility of the Study of Suggestion to the Student and Practitioner. *GP* April 6, 1907, pp. 210–13.
———. 1907b, *Treatment by Hypnotism and Suggestion; or Psycho-Therapeutics* (5th edition). New York: G P Putnam's Sons.
———. 1907c, [Discussion], in Wayenberg 1908, p. 869.
———. 1913, *Treatment by Hypnotism and Suggestion; or Psycho-Therapeutics* (6th edition). London: Baillière, Tindall & Cox.
Tuke, D. H. 1873, *Illustrations of the Influence of the Mind upon the Body in Health and Disease. Designed to Elucidate the Action of the Imagination*. Philadelphia: Henry C. Lea.
———. 1884a, *Sleep-Walking and Hypnotism*. London: J. & A. Churchill.
———. 1884b, *Illustrations of the Influence of the Mind upon the Body in Health and Disease, Designed to Elucidate the Action of the Imagination* (2nd edition). Philadelphia: Henry C. Lea.
———. 1892, ed., *A Dictionary of Psychological Medicine: Giving the definition, Etymology and Synonyms of the Terms Used in Medical Psychology with the Symptoms, Treatment, and Pathology of Insanity and the Law of Lunacy in Great Britain*. Philadelphia: P. Blakiston, Son.
Tuke, J. B. 1898, Address in Psychology: Modern Conceptions of the aetiology of the insanities. *BMJ* August 6, 1898, pp. 341–44.
Tuke, T. H. 1873, An Address Delivered at the BMA Annual Meeting. *BMJ* August 16, 1873, pp. 188–89.
Turner, J. 1995, David Eder: between Freud and Jung. *D. H. Lawrence Review* 1995, Vol. 27, pp. 289–309.
Turner W. A. 1911, Neurasthenia, Hysteria and Allied Neuroses. *BMJ* November 11, 1911, p. 1289.
———. 1920, The influence of psychogenic factors in nervous disorders. *PRSM (Neur.* Sec) 1920, Vol. 13, pp. 1–16.
TW nd, *The 'Two Worlds' Portrait Album of Spiritual Mediums, Workers and Celebrities with Brief Biographical Sketches*. Manchester: Two Worlds Publishing Co. (1897?).
Tweedy, J. 1919, Obituary: Alfred George Bateman. *BMJ* April 19, 1919, p. 504.
UMR (1912–), *The Universal Medical Record*. London: 36 Whitefriars Street.
UP 1912, University of Pennsylvania: Contributions from the Department of Neurology and the Laboratory of Neuropathology, for the years 1911–1912. (reprints). 1912, Vol. 4, Philadelphia: University of Pennsylvania.
Valentine, E. R. 2009, 'A Brilliant and Many-Sided Personality': Jessie Margaret Murray, Founder of the Medico-Psychological Clinic. *JHBS* 2009, Vol. 45, pp. 145–61.
Verrall, A. W. 1906, On a Series of Automatic Writings. *Proceedings* 1906, Vol. 20, pp. 1–432.
Walsh, J. J. 1912, *Psychotherapy: including the history of the use of mental influence, directly and indirectly in the healing and the principles for the application of energies derived from the mind to the treatment of disease*. New York: D. Appleton & Co.

Ward, L. F. 1911, *Pure Sociology: A Treatise on the Origin and Spontaneous Development of Society* (2nd edition). New York: Macmillan & Co.

Watson, C., ed. 1900, *Encyclopaedia Medica*. 1900, Vol. 5. Edinburgh: William Green & Sons.

Wayenberg, G. A. M. van. 1908, *Compte rendu des travaux du (Premier) Congrès international de psychiatrie, de neurologie, de psychologie et de l'assistance des Aliénés* (Amsterdam September 2–7, 1907). Amsterdam: J. H. Bussy.

Wells, *Wells Journal*. Wells: Somerset.

WC, *Worcestershire Chronicle*. Worcester.

WDN, *Western Daily News*. Cardiff.

WDP, *Western Daily Press*. Bristol.

Webb, S., & Webb, B. 1919, *The History of Trade Unionism, 1666–1920*. London: Webb &Webb.

Westwood, L. 2001, A quiet revolution in Brighton: Dr Helen Boyle's pioneering approach to mental health care, 1899–1939. *Social History of Medicine*, Vol. 14. pp. 439–57.

Wetterstrand, O. G. 1897, *Hypnotism and its application to practical medicine*, trans. Henrik G. Petersen. New York: G. P. Putnam's Sons.

WG, *Western Gazette*. Yeovil: Somerset.

White, E. W. 1907, The Treatment of Incipient and Borderland Cases of Insanity in General Practice. *BMJ* March 9, 1907, pp. 546–49.

———. 1918, Observations on Shell Shock and Neurasthenia in the Hospitals in the Western Command. *BMJ* April 13, 1918, pp. 421–22.

White, W. A. 1902, Mental dissociation in psychic epilepsy, in Sidis. 1902, pp. 123–58.

Whyte, J. M. 1910, The Study of Psychiatry in Munich. *Edinburgh Medical Journal* 1910, Vol. 4, pp. 7–17 (LHSA, GD17/8/2/56).

Wilson, J. M. 2009, *Isaac Rosenberg: The Making of a Great War Poet. A New Life*. London: Phoenix.

Wilson, S. A. K. 1907a, True Tactile Aphasia: Abstract of Jones (1907a), *RNP* 1907, Vol. 5, pp. 229–30.

———. 1907b, Apropos of Tactile Agnosia. *RNP* 1907, Vol. 5, p. 800.

———. 1911, Some modern French conceptions of hysteria. *Brain* 1911, Vol. 33, pp. 293–338.

Wingfield, H. E. 1910, *An Introduction to the Study of Hypnotism Experimental and Therapeutic*. New York: William Wood & Co.

———. 1911, Four Cases Illustrative of Certain Points in Psycho-Analysis. *BMJ* 5 August. 1911, pp. 256–57.

Winnicott, D. W. 1958, Ernest Jones. *IJPA* 1958, Vol. 39, pp. 298–304.

Winslow, L. F. 1910, The Suggestive Power of Hypnotism. *HR*, March 1910, pp. 25–28.

Winter, A. 1998, *Mesmerized: Powers of Mind in Victorian Britain*. Chicago: The University of Chicago Press.

Winton, H. E. 1908, Report of the Committee Appointed to Consider and Report upon the Subject of Ministries of Healing; (a) The Unction of the Sick; (b) Faith Healing and 'Christian Science.' pp. 133–38, in Anon 1908c.

Wittenberger, G., & Tögel, C. 1999, *Die Rundbriefe des 'Geheimen Komitees.' Band 1:1913–1920*. Tübingen; edition diskord.

WN, *World's News*. Sydney: Australia.

WO, *Watford Observer*. Watford.

Wolfstein, D. I. 1905, Periscope. *JNMD* 1905, Vol. 32, pp. 139–41.

Woodcock, J. L. 2003, James Allen, An Illustrated Biography. http://jamesalleninstitute.org/about-james-allen (accessed January 24, 2016).

Woods, J. F. 1898, Hypnotism in Organic Disease. *BMJ* September 10, 1898 pp. 677–78.

———. 1904, The Psychic Side of Therapeutics. *The Lancet* February 20, 1904, pp. 489–92.

———. 1907, A Discussion on Hypnotism – Opening paper BMA Annual Meeting. *BMJ* September 28, 1907, pp. 809–12.

Woolley, V. J. 1912, Review of Bleuler's 'Die Psychanalyses Freud's Verteidigung undkritische Bemerkungen.' *Proceedings* 1913, Vol. 26, pp. 367–69.

Worcester, E., McComb, S., Coriat, I. H. 1908, *Religion and Medicine: The Moral Control of Nervous Disorders*. New York: Moffat, Yard & Co.

Wright, M. B. 1945, Obituary: Thomas Walker Mitchell, 1869–1944. *BJMP* Vol. 20. 1946, p. 203.

Wyld, G. 1880, *Theosophy and the Higher Life, or Spiritual Dynamics and the Divine and Miraculous Man*. London: Trübner & Co.

Yellowlees, D. 1898, The Uses and Dangers of Hypnotism. *BMJ* September 10, 1898, p. 677.

Young, M. 2016, *"Don't Laugh At Me. Just Try It For Yourself And See What Happens" Trying Psychoanalysis: Treating Distressed Imperial Minds In 1920s And 1930s Colonial India*. University of Huddersfield Repository. http://eprints.hud.ac.uk/28120/.

YPLI, *Yorkshire Post and Leeds Intelligencer*. Leeds: West Yorkshire.

YH, *The Yorkshire Herald, and The York Herald*. York: North Yorkshire.

Index

About the Author

Philip Kuhn was born in London where he studied History, first at King's College and then at Birkbeck College as a postgraduate student of Eric Hobsbawm's. Having resolved not to pursue an academic career he chose, instead, to work in his parents' business as a way of funding his interests, passions and obsessions. Despite the delightful disruptions after the birth of his son, Philip has continued to follow his parallel careers as poet, historian, independent scholar, researcher and writer. For the last twenty years he has lived and worked on Dartmoor with his partner, the sculptor, Rosie Musgrave.

Lightning Source UK Ltd.
Milton Keynes UK
UKHW010039180719
346380UK00006B/241/P